J. Howard Beales III

BUSINESS & GOVERNMENT RELATIONS

An Economic Perspective

Second Edition

Kendall Hunt
publishing company

Cover images © Shutterstock, Inc.

Kendall Hunt
publishing company

www.kendallhunt.com
Send all inquiries to:
4050 Westmark Drive
Dubuque, IA 52004-1840

Copyright © 2009, 2012 by Kendall Hunt Publishing Company

ISBN 978-1-4652-0395-3

Printed in the United States of America
10 9 8 7 6 5 4 3 2 1

Contents

WELFARE ECONOMICS AND THE MARKET ECONOMY

Chapter 1

In analyzing business-government relations, a crucial question is whether a particular public policy serves the public interest. Although there are many possible ways to approach what constitutes the public interest, the economic approach is known as welfare economics. That is, how well does an economic system, a company, or a public policy serve the goal of enhancing our collective welfare? This chapter discusses the operation of a competitive market economy and the conclusion that competitive markets achieve the best possible outcome for consumers.

I. THE NATURE OF WEALTH

Welfare economics has its roots in the work of Adam Smith. His seminal work, *The Wealth of Nations*, begins with an examination of the nature of wealth. Like many others, Smith believed that the goal of the economy is the creation and accumulation of wealth. Thus, to evaluate an economic system or a particular economic policy, we need to ask whether it facilitates or impedes the creation of wealth.

Before Smith, there were competing views of just what constituted a nation's wealth. Some argued that wealth is measured by the accumulation of gold or other precious commodities. Others believed that wealth consists of production in general, or agricultural production in particular. Smith, however, rejected these notions. Gold may be useful as a medium of exchange or a store of value, but its value depends crucially on the ability to use it for some other purpose. A nation with plenty of gold and no food is not "wealthy" in any meaningful sense. Similarly, production of commodities that no one wants has no intrinsic value, whether it is agricultural production or manufacturing.

Instead, Smith argued, wealth consists of the goods and services that all of the people in the society *consume*. That is, it is consumption that constitutes wealth. Gold may enable purchase of other goods for consumption, and production of goods is obviously necessary before they can be consumed. But either gold or production is a means to an end, and the relevant end is consumption.

Thus, for Smith, consumer satisfaction is the object of the economic system. At one point, he wrote, "we should not attend to the interests of the producer except insofar as they serve the interests of consumers." We should evaluate an economic system against the standard of consumer satisfaction. Similarly, we can evaluate public policies based on whether they increase or decrease consumer satisfaction. This is the fundamental economic concept of the public interest: the goal is to maximize consumer welfare as judged by consumers.

Consumer satisfaction as the measure of well-being takes consumer preferences as given. Different consumers will attach different values to the various goods and services available for consumption, and it is their preferences that determine value. Of course, there are policies that deviate from this respect for consumer preferences, such as prohibitions on certain recreational drugs. But in general, consumer preferences are treated as given, and respected. Any other approach would require choosing whose preferences should be used as a standard of value, and there is no objective basis for making such a choice.

For the same reason, the economic measure of consumer welfare also ignores distributional issues. Without some external or absolute standard of value, there is no economic basis for choosing one distribution over another. The economic approach focuses on maximizing the size of the pie, not on how it should be divided up.

In the economic conception of the public interest, the guide is self-interest. Self-interested consumers pursue their own welfare, as do self-interested firms. It is their collective choices that determine how much of which goods and services are produced. Competition governs the system and prevents the pursuit of self-interest from degenerating into exploitation. With competition, self-interest will lead someone else to offer a better deal than the would-be exploiter.

II. INDIVIDUAL DEMAND

If consumer satisfaction is the object of the economic system, the logical place to begin exploring how the system operates is with consumer demand. Whether individually or in the aggregate, the fundamental precept of demand analysis is the Law of Demand: at higher prices, consumers will buy less. By the same token, the only way to sell more of a good is to reduce the price. The law of demand is summarized in the downward-sloping individual demand curve for a particular good, as shown in Figure 1-1.

The traditional argument for the law of demand is the notion of diminishing marginal utility. The demand curve reveals how much a consumer will purchase at any given price, and it also reveals how much a consumer is willing to pay for any given quantity. That willingness to pay should be related to the utility that the consumer derives from the product. Diminishing marginal utility argues that each additional unit of the product is less valuable than the one before, and consumers will therefore purchase another unit only at a lower price.

Consider, for example, bottled water. For a thirsty consumer, a bottle of water is valuable, and he or she is willing to pay for it. A second bottle of water would likely still be valuable, but it is also likely less valuable than the first. Therefore, the consumer would be willing to pay less for the second bottle than for the first. Similarly, a third bottle is still less valuable, particularly if it must be consumed at the same time—and at some point, the consumer is not likely to be willing to pay anything at all for yet another bottle of water for immediate consumption.

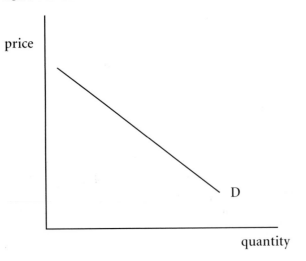

Figure 1-1. The Law of Demand.

price

D

quantity

A deeper argument for the law of demand is the notion of scarcity. Consumers are constrained by a budget, and they cannot have everything they want. Because of the budget constraint, consumers *must* purchase less of something if the price of one good is increased, and one of the things they will purchase less of is the good that increased in price. Indeed, even if consumers choose their consumption randomly, on average the law of demand will hold: at higher prices, consumers will purchase less.

Economists interested in the law of demand have done experiments with rats to determine demand curves. The rat can press a lever to receive a reward of food, or another lever to receive water. The "price" of food and water is the number of times the lever must be pressed to receive the reward, and it can be varied. The rats are given a budget constraint, because only the first hundred presses of the lever count. Under these conditions, rats have downward-sloping demand curves. Perhaps rats are really rational utility maximizers who exhibit diminishing marginal utility, but it seems more likely that rat demand is governed by scarcity.

Figure 1-2. Consumer surplus.

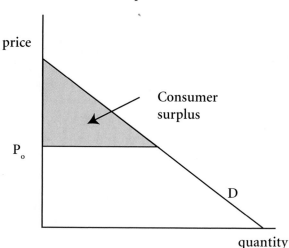

The demand curve provides a measure of the value of a particular market to the consumer, known as consumer surplus. Suppose consumers can purchase as much of the good as they want at a specified market price. We know they will continue to purchase until the value of another unit is just equal to the price. That is, consumers will purchase the quantity given by the individual demand curve. The first unit purchased, however, is worth more to the consumer than the price. The gain is consumer surplus. Similarly, the next unit, and the next, are also worth more than the price, and each generates additional consumer surplus. In general, the shaded triangle in Figure 1-2 represents consumer surplus.

Consumer surplus represents the net gain to the consumer from being able to purchase goods at a fixed price in the marketplace, after taking into account the price of the purchase. Thus, the goal of maximizing consumer welfare as judged by consumers is equivalent to maximizing consumer surplus.

The law of demand holds that, at higher prices, consumers will purchase less, but it says nothing about how much less. A key characteristic of demand is the elasticity of demand, which measures how much quantity responds to a change in price. Technically, elasticity is the percentage change in quantity for a 1 percent change in price. Demand is said to be elastic if the elasticity is greater than 1; it is inelastic if the elasticity is less than 1. The distinction is based on what happens to total revenue (or expenditures) if price changes. If demand is inelastic, an increase in price will increase total spending on the good, because the reduction in quantity is not enough to offset the increase in price. If demand is elastic, however, the quantity change is larger than the price change (in percentage terms), and total spending will decline when price increases.

Figure 1-3. Polar cases of demand elasticity.

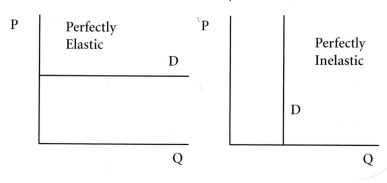

There are two limiting cases of demand elasticity, depicted in Figure 1-3: perfectly elastic demand and perfectly inelastic demand. If demand is perfectly elastic, the demand curve is a horizontal line. A trivial change in price results in an infinitely large change in quantity. Thus, the elasticity is infinite. A perfectly competitive firm faces a perfectly elastic demand—it can sell as much as it wants at the market price. The wheat farmer in the middle of Kansas, for example, likely faces a perfectly elastic demand.

If demand is perfectly inelastic, the demand curve is a vertical line, which says that consumers will purchase a fixed quantity of the product no matter what (elasticity is zero). Although theoretically interesting, perfectly inelastic demand is not particularly relevant in the real world. Taken literally, perfect inelasticity claims that consumers will devote literally all of their resources to a single good. Although demand may be very inelastic for some goods, such as life-saving prescription drugs, demand likely responds to price even for such products. Consumers may, for example, take a smaller dose than they are supposed to, or they may skip some days. At some point, demand must become less than perfectly in elastic, or the consumer would starve to death!

Even with inelastic demand, the law of demand holds: at a higher price, consumers will purchase less. The reduction in quantity, however, is smaller than it would be if demand were more elastic.

There are two key determinants of the elasticity of demand. First, demand will be more elastic when more and better substitutes are available. For example, the demand for a particular brand of a product will be more elastic than the demand for the product category as a whole. If Coke raises its price but other soft drink prices remain unchanged, many consumers are likely to switch to a different brand. Pepsi, after all, is a pretty close substitute for Coke. The demand for Coke is therefore likely to be fairly elastic. If the prices of all soft drinks go up, however, the substitutes are not as close, and consumers are likely to reduce quantity by less. Water, milk, and other beverages are not as close substitutes as are competing brands of soft drinks.

Second, elasticity depends on the time available to adjust to the change in price. With more time available, demand is more elastic. Time available to adjust is related to the availability of substitutes, because there are usually additional alternatives that are possible with more time to adjust to a persistent change in price.

Gasoline prices provide a good example of the importance of time to the elasticity of demand. When the price of gasoline goes up, in the short run there is little that consumers can do to reduce their use of gasoline other than to drive less. If the price increase is expected to persist, however, there are other alternatives. Consumers can purchase a more fuel-efficient car and drive the same number of miles with less gasoline. Or they can relocate to live closer to where they work (or closer to convenient mass transit), reducing the number of miles they need to drive. Thus, demand for gasoline is more elastic in the long run than it is in the short run.

For any commodity, demand in the long run is more elastic than short-run demand. The magnitude of the difference varies from product to product, but long-run demand is always more responsive to changes in price. Thus, long-run demand is flatter than short-run demand, as shown in Figure 1-4.

Figure 1-4. Long-run and short-run demand.

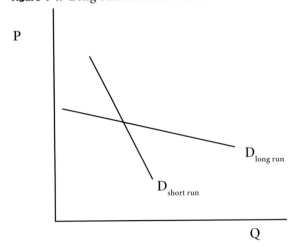

Unfortunately, public policy decisions often neglect the law of demand. Consider, for example, the market for electricians. There is a demand for services of electricians, and a supply of people who are willing to offer their services as an electrician. Incompetent electricians, however, can cause problems. If wiring is not done properly, the result may be a short circuit and an electrical fire. To reduce the number of bad electricians, many states impose licensing requirements. Before offering themselves as electricians, individuals must meet certain educational, testing, or experience requirements. As shown in Figure 1-5, the effect of such licensing requirements is to reduce the supply of electricians and consequently increase the price of electrical services.

The law of demand says that consumers will purchase fewer electrical services in response to this increase in price. Instead, they will use available substitutes for the services of an electrician. Unfortunately, one such substitute is doing it yourself, and many consumers are not very good electricians. The critical policy question is how much will the quantity demanded change in response to the price increase. If the reduction is large, licensing may make the quality problem worse, as consumers do it themselves. Empirically, states with stricter standards for licensing electricians have more

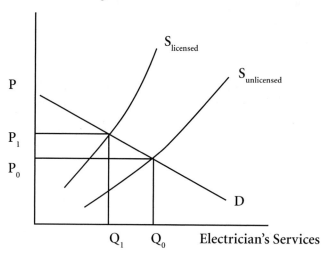

Figure 1-5. Licensing electricians.

accidental deaths from electric shock. This finding suggests that the substitution is important, at least in this case.

Another example is the Corporate Average Fuel Economy standards, known as CAFÉ. Under these requirements, the average car in each manufacturer's fleet of vehicles must achieve a specified gas mileage standard, 30.2 miles per gallon in 2011 and scheduled to increase to 54.5 miles per gallon in 2005. The rules are intended to reduce gasoline consumption, for reasons that have varied over time between reducing dependence on foreign oil and reducing carbon dioxide emissions. The rules are relevant in two markets, one for miles driven and one for new cars.

In the market for miles driven, demand for miles driven depends on the price of driving a mile. The effect of CAFÉ in this market is to reduce the price of driving a mile, because at any given price of gasoline, it will take less gasoline to drive a mile in a more efficient car. This reduction in price will lead consumers to drive more, which will tend to offset the gasoline savings the policy seeks to produce. How much driving will change is an empirical question, but it is important in assessing the efficacy of the policy.

In the market for new cars, the rules will likely increase the price of new cars (at least adjusted for quality characteristics that matter to drivers). This increase in price will encourage consumers to look for substitutes for new cars—such as buying a used car or keeping an old car longer. Because gasoline prices have risen over time, however, new cars even without CAFÉ get better gas mileage than older cars. Thus, without the rule, substituting new cars for older cars would tend to reduce the demand for gasoline. Higher prices for new cars will slow this process, increasing the average age of the fleet of cars. Again, tighter standards have a counterproductive effect, because of the law of demand. Holding older cars longer is potentially quite important, because new cars account for approximately 2 percent of U.S. energy use. Old cars, however, account for 23 percent of energy use.

III. INDIVIDUAL FIRMS

For individual firms, self-interest implies profit maximization. To make profits as large as possible, a firm must compare the incremental, or marginal, revenue from producing another unit with the marginal cost of producing that unit. If the marginal revenue exceeds the marginal cost, the firm should increase its output. If marginal revenue is less than marginal cost, the firm should reduce its output. Thus, for profit maximization, the firm should operate at the output level where marginal revenue equals marginal cost, if it produces at all.

The short-run cost structure of a typical firm is depicted in Figure 1-6. Some costs are fixed, such as rent and the cost of capital equipment, and do not vary with output. Average fixed costs therefore decline smoothly as output increases. Other costs, such as labor and raw materials, are variable, depending on the level of output. Typically, average variable costs decline for some range of output, but then they

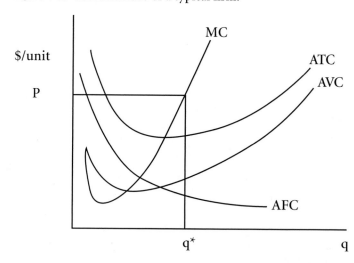

Figure 1-6. Cost structure of a typical firm.

begin to increase as diminishing returns set in. Adding average fixed costs and average variable costs gives average total costs.

The most important cost for determining output is marginal cost, the cost of producing one more unit of output. For the first unit, marginal cost is essentially the same as average variable cost. Marginal costs typically decline at first (which is why average variable costs are declining), but then begin to increase. Marginal cost will pass through the minimum point on the average variable cost curve, and through the minimum point on the average total cost curve.

A perfectly competitive firm is one that can sell all it wants at the market price. For such a firm, the marginal revenue from selling one more unit is just the price—it can, after all, sell all it wants at the market price. That is, the demand facing the firm is perfectly elastic. (This is true only for the perfectly competitive firm, however.) Thus, for a perfectly competitive firm, the condition for profit maximization is that price (which equals marginal revenue) must equal marginal cost. At any given market price, the firm will produce the amount corresponding to that price on its marginal cost curve. Thus, the firm's marginal cost curve is also the firm's supply curve, which tells how much it will supply at any given price.

If there is a change in cost conditions, a firm's output will change. In particular, suppose that there is an increase in variable costs, perhaps because raw material prices increase or because of a new labor agreement that increases labor costs. Average total costs and marginal costs will shift upward, as shown in Figure 1-7. Given the market price, the firm will find that a smaller output will now maximize profit, and output will fall from q_0 to q_1. Increases in costs will reduce output; decreases in cost will increase output.

Operating where price equals marginal cost will produce the best possible result if the firm operates at all, but whether the firm is profitable or not depends on the relationship between price and average total cost. If the price is above average total cost at the profit-maximizing output, the firm will make a profit, as depicted in the first panel of Figure 1-8. The difference between price and the corresponding average total cost at

Figure 1-7. Cost changes and firm output.

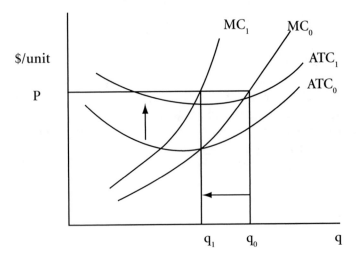

Figure 1-8.

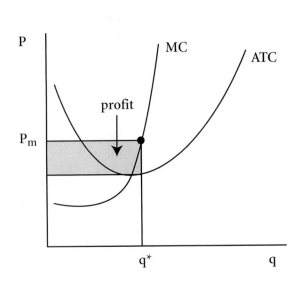

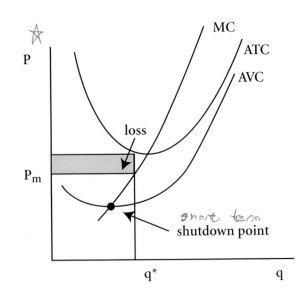

the profit-maximizing output of q^* is unit profit. Unit profit times output is total profit—the area of the shaded rectangle in Figure 1-8. If price is below average total cost, however, the firm will suffer a loss, as shown in the second panel of Figure 1-8. The difference between price and average total cost is now the unit loss, and the shaded rectangle in the second panel represents total losses.

It may seem as though the firm should stop producing if price is below average total cost, but that is not necessarily the case in the short run. Some costs are fixed, and the firm must pay those costs whether it produces or not in the short run. As long as prices are higher than average variable costs, continuing to operate will produce at least some revenue to contribute to paying fixed costs, and the firm should do so. If price falls below average variable cost, however, producing would only increase total losses, because revenue is not sufficient to cover even variable costs. Thus, the short-run shutdown point is where the marginal cost curve meets the average variable cost curve, as shown in Figure 1-8. If price is lower than the minimum of average variable cost, the firm should shut down in the short run; at any higher price, it should produce where price equals marginal cost.

Of course, in the long run, the firm must cover all of its costs, both fixed and variable, or look for a new line of business. Thus, the long-run shutdown point corresponds to the minimum of the average total cost curve. If price is below average total cost and likely to persist at that level, the firm should eventually shut down.

IV. INDIVIDUAL INDUSTRIES

With self-interest as the guide, competition acts as a governor in determining the equilibrium in a particular industry. Market demand is just the sum of the individual demands, discussed above. Market supply is the sum of the individual firm supply curves; that is, it is the sum of the firms' marginal cost curves. Equilibrium, as shown in Figure 1-9, occurs where supply equals demand, and it determines the price in the competitive market.

Figure 1-9. Competitive market equilibrium.

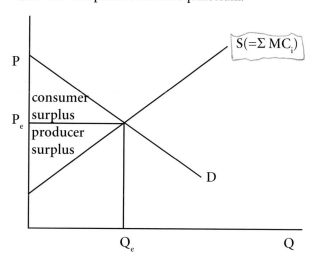

Analogous to consumer surplus, we can define the benefit of the market to producers as producer surplus. Producers sell each unit at the market price, but they pay only the marginal cost to produce that product. The gain on each unit is producer surplus. In the market diagram in Figure 1-9, producer surplus is the triangle below the price line and above the supply curve. Producer surplus must cover the firm's fixed costs and any profits in the industry.

The diagram in Figure 1-9 is relevant only with a fixed number of firms. In the long run, there will be entry or exit, depending on whether firms are earning profits or losses. Figure 1-10 depicts the situation facing the firm and the industry when there are short-run profits for producers.

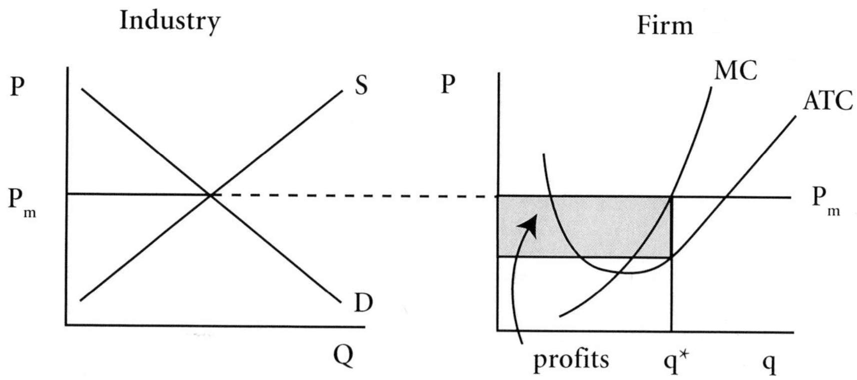

Profits induce entry. As entry occurs, the supply curve shifts to the right and gets flatter, because there are more firms whose marginal cost curve

Figure 1-10. Profits and entry.

Figure 1-11. Long-run equilibrium.

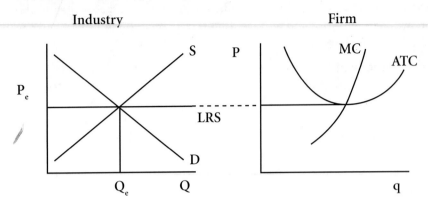

The market supply curve shown in Figure 1-11 is actually a short-run supply curve, with a fixed number of firms. If demand were to increase, creating new profit opportunities in the industry, the number of firms would increase. In the long run, price would return to the original level, corresponding to the minimum point of the average total cost curve. All that would change is the number of firms in the industry. Thus, the long-run supply curve is flat. If policy increases costs, this long-run supply curve shifts upward, and the increase in cost is passed on to consumers. In the long run, consumers pay all costs, although some costs may be borne by producers in the short run.

must be added in to determine the industry supply. The increase in supply reduces the price, which reduces profits for each individual firm in the industry. As long as profit remains, however, entry will continue. The long-run equilibrium is shown in Figure 1-11. All profits have been competed away, so each firm is operating at the minimum of its average total cost curve.

V. RESOURCE ALLOCATION ACROSS INDUSTRIES

The analysis so far has considered a particular product. Markets, however, also allocate resources across different products. We consider a simplified example in Figure 1-12.

Figure 1-12. Resource allocation across industries.

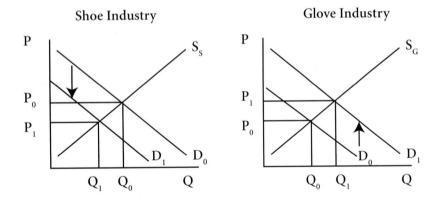

Suppose there are two markets, one for shoes and one for gloves. Current fashion dictates that consumers generally want multiple pairs of shoes to go with particular outfits, but most consumers probably have only a single pair of gloves. The supply and demand curves with the "0" subscript in Figure 1-12 depict this initial equilibrium.

Now suppose that fashion changes, and that consumers want just a single pair of shoes but a pair of gloves for every occasion. The demand for shoes will decrease, and the demand for gloves will increase. Sellers in the shoe market will find that they cannot sell all their shoes, and the price of shoes will therefore fall. Facing a lower price, shoe producers will reduce their output of shoes, and, if the change persists, some will eventually go out of business. In the shoe market, price and quantity both fall as the industry contracts. In the glove market, on the other hand, sellers will experience excess demand for gloves, and consumers anxious for a pair will bid up the price. In response, glove manufacturers will expand output. Thus, the price and quantity of gloves both increase as the industry expands.

The adjustment in the shoe and glove industry unfolds as a result of the operation of the market mechanism. No one needs to conduct a demand study to find out that demand has shifted, and that gloves are now in greater demand. Choices of individual consumers and firms reveal this information in changing prices. Price is a source of information for market participants: it tells them that shoes are now less valuable compared to the cost of producing them, and that gloves are more valuable. Price is also an incentive to act on that information—it is in the self-interest of both firms and consumers to respond to the change in relative values.

The shift in demand also has consequences in the labor market. In the shoe industry, there will be layoffs and wage reductions for workers. Demand for glove workers, however, will increase, bidding up wages. The wage reductions for cobblers and wage increases for glove makers will induce some cobblers to become glove makers, shifting resources from one industry to the other.

The situation is not fundamentally different if the shoe and glove industries happen to be located in different places. If gloves are produced in California, for example, and shoes in Massachusetts, the same fundamental process unfolds. Because reallocating labor requires either moving glove firms to Massachusetts to take advantage of lower wages, or moving shoe workers to California to work in the glove industry, the process is likely to take longer, but it is not fundamentally different. Costs to firms and workers of having chosen a particular location under the original demand structure are sunk costs—they cannot be recovered. In markets, sunk costs will not influence the adjustment process or the new equilibrium. Sunk costs are sunk, and they have no continuing influence on the market.

If we consider the response to the change in demand in the political process, however, the result is likely to be very different. In response to the decline in shoe production, the political representatives from Massachusetts are likely to argue for some form of intervention to assist ailing shoe manufacturers. That intervention may take many forms, including subsidies for shoe producers, relocation assistance to help glove producers move, or many other forms of creative intervention. Political representatives are highly unlikely, however, to urge their constituents to move to California. Rather than ignoring sunk costs, the political process often seeks to protect such investments long after they have lost their economic relevance.

VI. Market Outcomes Are Efficient

Consider again the competitive market equilibrium depicted in Figure 1-9. This equilibrium is the best possible outcome, given the standard for the public interest. That is, the competitive equilibrium will maximize consumer welfare as judged by consumers. As discussed above, demand reflects the marginal benefit of another unit of the product to consumers. Supply reflects the marginal cost of producing that unit. To maximize consumer welfare, we should increase output if the marginal benefit of another unit exceeds the cost. We should reduce output if the marginal benefit is less than marginal cost. Thus, at the welfare-maximizing output, marginal benefit is just equal to marginal cost. That, of course, is the competitive outcome, where supply equals demand.

There are two other ways to think about the welfare properties of the competitive equilibrium. First, the competitive outcome maximizes consumer surplus plus producer surplus. Consumer plus producer surplus is simply the area between demand and supply at any given output. It is clear from Figure 1-9 that this area is as large as possible at the competitive equilibrium.

Another way to describe the competitive outcome is that it exploits all possible gains from trade. Producers value goods at the marginal cost of producing another unit; consumers value them at the marginal benefit given by the demand curve. At the competitive equilibrium, all possible gains from trade have been exploited; there is no other transaction that can make both parties to the transaction better off.

This inability to improve outcomes for anyone without hurting someone else is the economic criterion for optimality known as Pareto optimality, named for the Italian economist who developed the concept. An outcome is Pareto optimal if it is not possible to make anyone better off without making someone worse off. Thus, at a Pareto optimal outcome, we cannot improve the outcome without specifying that some people are more important than others. The competitive equilibrium outcome satisfies the Pareto criterion because all possible gains from trade have been exhausted. We cannot make consumers, or any individual consumer, better off without harming producers or some other consumer.

In one sense, the Pareto criterion is a weak criterion for welfare. Many possible allocations or outcomes are Pareto optimal, and the criterion offers no basis for choosing between one Pareto optimal outcome and another. In another sense, the criterion is quite powerful. After all, if there is some policy that would improve welfare for even one person, and no one would be harmed by the implementation of that policy, it seems obvious that the policy should be adopted. Such a policy is said to be a Pareto improvement, even if it does not achieve a Pareto optimal outcome. As we shall see, however, in many circumstances public policies do not satisfy the Pareto criterion.

An important concept in welfare economics is the distinction between transfers and so-called deadweight losses. A transfer is simply a reallocation of some benefit from one person to another. Evaluated against the standard of consumer welfare as judged by consumers, a transfer produces no net benefit or cost. A benefit to the recipient is precisely offset by the cost to whoever pays the transfer, unless we specify that one person is more important or more worthy than another. Thus, from an economic perspective, the transfer is a wash.

In contrast, a deadweight loss is a net loss to the economy. It results from a failure to achieve a Pareto optimal outcome. A deadweight loss simply vanishes; no offsetting gain to anyone results from the deadweight loss.

Producing either too much output or too little output (compared to the competitive equilibrium) will result in a deadweight loss. These deadweight losses are depicted in Figure 1-13. If we choose to produce some output lower than the competitive equilibrium Q_e, such as Q_L, the deadweight loss is triangle A. Additional units of output up to the competitive equilibrium would be worth more to consumers than the cost of providing them. We could make consumers better off without making anyone worse off, but the output restriction prevents the achievement of this objective. Triangle A is an opportunity loss; the value to consumers could have been greater than it is, but we gave up the opportunity to increase value because of the restriction on output.

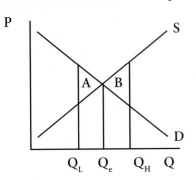

Figure 1-13. Deadweight losses from too much or too little output.

There is also a deadweight loss if output exceeds the competitive equilibrium, such as Q_H. Output above the competitive equilibrium is worth something, as indicated by the demand curve, but unfortunately the cost of producing those additional units is higher than the value of the goods to consumers. Thus, triangle B is also a deadweight loss. It represents the net loss to the economy from producing more of the good than the competitive equilibrium quantity.

VII. Summary

From an economic perspective, the standard that defines the public interest is to maximize consumer welfare as judged by consumers. Individual demand guides the economic system. At higher prices, consumers will purchase less of a product, even if demand is inelastic. Quantity is more responsive to changes in price when there are more and better substitutes available, and in the long run. Consumer surplus measures the value of a market to consumers.

Profit-maximizing firms will produce at a level where marginal revenue is equal to marginal cost. For a perfectly competitive firm, which can sell all it wants at the market price, marginal revenue is equal to the price. Thus, the firm's supply curve is its marginal cost curve. If price falls below the minimum point of average variable cost, the firm should shut down in the short run. In the long run, the firm must cover its average total costs to survive.

With a given number of firms, the competitive market equilibrium occurs where supply equals demand. Profits to individual firms will create incentives for entry into the industry; losses will lead some in the industry to exit. Entry will continue until each firm is operating at the minimum point of average total cost. When changes in demand can be met entirely by changes in the number of firms in the industry, the long-run supply curve for the industry is flat.

Shifts in demand across industries lead to expansions where demand increases and contractions in industries with declining demand. Price provides information about the shift in demand to market participants, and it also provides an incentive for those participants to act on that information. Competitive market outcomes are efficient, and they maximize consumer plus producer surplus. Higher or lower levels of output would create deadweight losses for the economy.

RATIONALES FOR GOVERNMENT INTERVENTION

An Introduction to Market Failures

Chapter 2

If competitive markets are efficient, why is government intervention in the market economy necessary? From an economic perspective, the rationale for intervention must stem from some market failure. With a market failure, something in the structure of the market, or in the incentives the market creates, prevents the market from achieving the best possible outcome for consumers. If that is the case, it is at least possible that government intervention can improve consumer welfare. In the absence of a market failure, however, intervention will inevitably reduce consumer welfare, not enhance it.

This chapter introduces the market failures that are the most common rationales for regulatory intervention. They include monopoly, externalities, public goods, and imperfect information. The chapter discusses each failure, and provides some examples of where that particular market failure is offered as a justification for intervention. Later chapters will explore the market failure responsible for certain policies in more detail. The purpose here is to introduce the market failures, the problems they create, and the types of solutions frequently adopted based on each market failure.

There are two basic approaches that can be taken to address problems that arise from market failures. One approach, generally favored by economists, is known as incentive-compatiblity solutions. The basic idea of an incentive-compatible solution is to correct the underlying problem that is preventing efficient market outcomes, but leave to market participants as many decisions as possible about what to produce, how to produce it, and how much to produce. If, for example, the market failure problem is that consumers lack information, a disclosure requirement that provides the information can correct the problem but still leave it to the market to determine how much of what products to produce.

The other major approach to correcting market failures is command and control. With command and control, the government requires particular conduct that it believes will correct the problem. Basically, it tells people what to do about the problem that is the basis for intervention. A common form of command and control regulation is technology requirements. Firms are often required to utilize a particular technology to address, for example, many pollution problems.

Both command and control and incentive-compatible approaches to addressing market failures are frequently imposed through statute or regulation. The distinction is not between regulatory and non-regulatory approaches; rather, the difference is in the approach to regulation. Command and control regulation attempts to discover and then impose the outcome that should have occurred in the market. Incentive-compatible approaches try to determine what caused the problem initially, and how it can be corrected with minimal intervention.

In some circumstances, however, incentive-compatible approaches are not regulatory at all (although they are still interventions in the market). Better definition of property rights, for example, may address some market failures without requiring much, if any, regulation. Similarly, taxing emissions is an incentive-compatible approach to addressing pollution problems, but it is implemented through the tax system rather than through regulation.

I. MONOPOLY

One of the first market failures widely recognized was monopoly. The problem actually occurs whenever a firm possesses market power (in the sense that the demand facing the firm is less than perfectly elastic), but the logic of the problem is clearest in the case of a monopoly—a market in which there is one and only one seller.

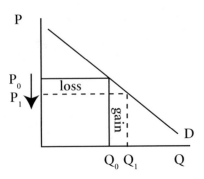

Figure 2-1. Revenue change from a price reduction.

A competitive firm takes price as given by the market. A monopolist, in contrast, faces the market demand curve. It understands that the only way to sell more to consumers is to reduce the price, and it understands that by selling less, it can charge more for its product. If a monopolist faces the demand curve shown in Figure 2-1, and is currently charging price P_0, it understands that reducing the price to P_1 will have two, offsetting effects on its revenue. If it cuts price just enough to sell one more unit, revenue will increase by P_1 from the sale of that unit, as shown in Figure 2-1. To sell that unit, however, the monopolist will have to reduce the price on the Q_0 units it could have sold at the higher price of P_0. Thus, the top rectangle in the figure is the loss of revenue on these units that could still have been sold at a higher price.

Because the monopolist will always lose revenue on units it could have sold at a higher price if it wishes to sell one more unit of output, the marginal revenue for the monopolist will always lie below price. The marginal revenue curve facing the monopolist is shown in Figure 2-2. The logic of profit maximization is the same for the monopolist as for any other firm: it wants to operate where marginal revenue equals marginal cost. Because marginal revenue is less than price, however, the monopolist will choose to produce a smaller output: Q_M in the figure, rather than the competitive output of Q_C.

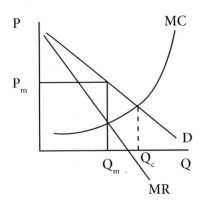

Figure 2-2. The monopolist's output choice.

Given the monopoly output, a monopolist will of course sell that output for as much as possible. Even a monopolist is limited by demand, however. The most the monopolist can charge is given by the demand curve at the monopoly output, or P_M in Figure 2-2.

As shown in Figure 2-3, a monopoly reduces consumer surplus. There are two components of the reduction in surplus, however, with different

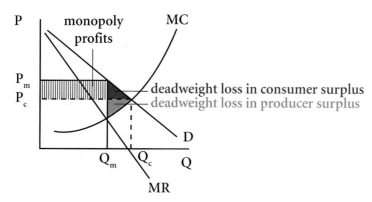

Figure 2-3. Welfare losses from monopoly.

implications. First, because the monopolist charges more than the competitive price, it realizes monopoly profits: the shaded rectangle in the figure. These monopoly profits are a transfer, from consumers to the monopolist. From a welfare perspective, the transfer is a matter of indifference. We cannot say whether it is good or bad without saying whether consumers or the shareholders of the monopolist are more important. If we think of the classic monopolist of an electric utility, shareholders may be widows and orphans, because utility shares are relatively stable in price and a reliable source of dividend income.

The shaded triangles in Figure 2-3, however, are deadweight losses, stemming from the fact that the monopolist does not produce enough output to maximize consumer welfare. Additional output would be worth more to consumers than it costs to produce it, but the monopolist will not provide that output on its own. To do so, it would have to give up the monopoly profits. Consumers, however, would be better off if output were expanded. Producer surplus would be larger as well.

Unlike the competitive equilibrium, the monopoly outcome is not Pareto optimal. It would be possible to improve the welfare of consumers without making anyone, even the monopolist, worse off. If we could let the monopolist keep the monopoly profits, but condition those profits on producing the competitive output, consumers would be better off and the monopolist would be no worse off.

A special case of the monopoly problem is the so-called natural monopoly. With a natural monopoly, there are such significant economies of scale in producing output in a single firm that there is only room for one firm in the market. A classic example is a retail natural gas distribution company. It would be quite costly to create another natural gas pipeline system, which may be necessary to have effective competition in retail gas distribution. If production costs are sufficiently lower with one firm than with two, it is possible that the net effect of a natural monopoly is beneficial for consumers, even if it is allowed to set the monopoly price.

Many firms have some degree of market power, in the sense that they will not lose all of their customers if they increase their price. Such deviations from the perfectly competitive ideal, however, are rarely of policy concern unless the firm has a substantial share of the market. Examples of firms where monopoly is a concern include utilities such as natural gas and electricity, as well as the conduct of large firms that dominate their markets, such as Microsoft or Google.

One incentive-compatible way to address the monopoly problem is the antitrust laws. Restrictions on mergers are a particularly good example, because they seek to preserve the conditions for competition by preventing the emergence of monopolies. Antitrust laws also restrict combinations of firms or agreements among firms that might restrict competition. Again, the goal is to preserve competition without otherwise intervening in the market.

The typical command and control solution to monopoly is rate regulation. If the problem is that monopolies set prices that are too high, specifying that the firm must charge the competitive price is a way to attempt to address the problem. Rate regulation, however, often creates incentives for firms to increase their costs in ways that allow them to capture some of the available monopoly profits. Studies of utility regulation have not found much evidence of success in keeping rates below the monopoly price.

II. EXTERNALITIES

Externalities occur when one person's actions create either costs or benefits for another person, where there is no compensation for those effects. Of course, most actions have consequences for others. The critical feature of externalities is that those who create costs for others do not have to pay them, or those who create benefits for others are not compensated for them. We consider three kinds of externalities: common property resources, external benefits, and external costs.

A. Common Property Resources

Common property has no owner, but anyone who wants to use the property can do so. Thus, the property can produce benefits for users. Consider, for example, a lake that is common property. Anyone can use the lake, and, if they catch a fish, it is theirs to keep. Everyone with access to the lake has an incentive to catch as many fish as possible. As more fish are taken, however, the likelihood of catching a fish declines, because there are no longer as many fish in the lake. Thus, each person who fishes reduces the productivity of others who fish, which is the externality.

Common property resources will certainly be overused.[1] In the lake example, the fish may or may not be exterminated entirely, depending on how good the technology is for finding fish and whether there are enough hiding places in the lake for some fish to survive. But the stock of fish will certainly be smaller than it should be to maximize the value of the fishery. Because there is no owner, no one has an incentive to worry about preserving the resource to harvest fish next year.

Although the common property analysis has obvious relevance to the problem of endangered species, it is worth emphasizing that the problem is one of property rights, not demand. Demand is far higher for beef cattle than for any endangered species, but there is no risk of extinction because cattle have owners who worry about preserving the value of the herd.

Common property is relevant to a number of other policy issues as well. Radio spectrum is one example. If two people try to use the same frequency for different messages, both will likely get static. Some system of allocating rights is necessary to maximize the value of the resource. Other examples are less obvious. Airport "slots," the right to land or take off at a particular time, are a common property resource. Airlines have private incentives to schedule their flights to leave at the most popular time (e.g., 5 p.m.), without regard to the fact that only one flight at a time can use the runway. The result is delays as aircraft line up to wait their turn. A system that allocated runway use more precisely would space out schedules and likely reduce delays.

Since the root of the common property problem is the lack of property rights, incentive-compatible solutions focus on better definition of property rights. Licenses have long been assigned for particular uses of the radio spectrum. Increasingly, such licenses are auctioned to the highest bidder, who can then use the spectrum for any desired use. However they are distributed, such licenses define property rights in a particular part of the spectrum.

Licenses based on aggregate quantity limits are also increasingly used to regulate fisheries. The details of the structure, however, can greatly affect incentives. If a season opens on a specified day and then closes whenever the aggregate limit is reached, the regulatory structure creates incentives for a race. Each boat has an incentive to catch as many fish as possible, as quickly as possible. Aggregate quantity limits are more likely to maximize welfare if they do not limit the time of the catch and can be reallocated among boats.

Command and control approaches to address common property problems are often technology limits. Some species of fish, for example, can only be taken with hook and line. Seasons, size limits, and similar approaches are also forms of command and control regulation.

---

[1] Each person who uses the resource will receive the average product of an hour spent fishing. It will be worthwhile to fish as long as the average product exceeds the cost of fishing. If costs are constant, fishing will continue until the average productivity equals the average cost. Thus, there is no net gain from the resource at all. Optimal use of the resource would require the marginal product of an hour spent fishing to equal the constant cost of fishing, which would maximize the net gain from the lake.

Figure 2-4. External benefits.

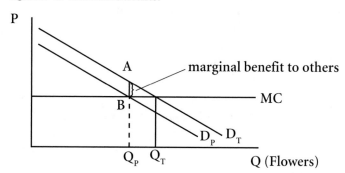

B. External Benefits

A second type of externality is external benefits, where one person's actions create benefits for others that are not fully captured. A clear example is planting flowers. One homeowner may enjoy flowers, and is therefore willing to plant flowers in his or her yard. The homeowner's private willings to pay for flowers is given by D_P in Figure 2-4. Doing so has a cost, however, particularly in the time and effort it takes to plant and maintain the garden. Based on his or her own private benefits, a homeowner would choose to plant the number of flowers given by Q_P.

Planting flowers, however, also generates benefits for the neighbors, who can usually enjoy them without charge or obligation. Including these additional benefits, the total demand (and the marginal total benefit) for flowers is D_T in Figure 2-4. Thus, the optimal quantity of flowers is Q_T, where marginal total benefit equals the marginal cost of planting more flowers. With beneficial externalities, the person making the decision will choose to produce too little of the good.

Flowers are not a particularly important policy issue in most circumstances. Amsterdam, however, is known for its window boxes of flowers over its picturesque canals, and those with apartments along the canals are required to maintain flowers in their window boxes (a command and control solution). A more significant external benefit from a policy perspective is research and development, particularly basic research. The transistor, for example, made possible virtually all of modern electronic technology, from personal computers to high-definition televisions. Although John Bardeen, Walter Brattain, and William Shockley received a Nobel Prize for their discovery of the transistor, and patented the device itself, it seems unlikely that they captured more than a small fraction of the benefits their invention made possible.

Like common property, incentive-compatible solutions are built around better definitions of property rights. Patents, copyrights, and trademarks are all definitions of intellectual property rights that seek to enable the creator of the invention or product to capture more of the returns.

Subsidies can also provide an incentive-compatible approach to external benefit problems. If the government provides a subsidy to the activity that is just equal to the marginal benefit to other parties, then private actors will face exactly the right incentives in choosing how much to produce. The private benefit plus the subsidy will equal the total social benefit. In Figure 2-4, for example, a subsidy equal to the vertical distance AB will give homeowners the right incentives to plant flowers.

Despite the presence of external benefits, markets may function quite well. For years, the classic example of external benefits was bees and blossoms. Honeybees produce external benefits, because their activities gathering nectar and pollen are essential to pollinating many crops. Indeed, the United States has a long-standing honey subsidy program, based on the notion that without a subsidy, the presence of external benefits will lead to too few honeybees.

Then someone studied the market for bees. It turns out there is a two-sided market, depending on the nature of the crop. Some crops, such as clover, produce a large amount of nectar and therefore a large amount of honey. For such crops, beekeepers pay farmers for the right to place their hives in the clover field. Other crops, such as apples, produce relatively little nectar. For these crops, growers pay beekeepers, essentially renting the beehives to provide pollination services in the spring. In the end, there is little reason to believe we have too little of either bees or pollination.

C. External Costs

With external costs, one person's choices impose costs on others that the person who made the choice does not have to pay. The classic example is pollution. A steel mill, for example, minimizes its costs by using the air and

Figure 2-5. External costs.

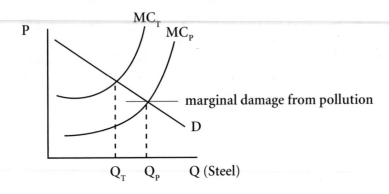

water to dispose of numerous waste products. Unfortunately, that practice generates costs, frequently in the form of adverse health effects, for those who are downwind and downstream. As shown in Figure 2-5, the steel mill will consider the private marginal cost, MC_P, of its decisions, and choose to produce Q_P quantity of steel. To maximize the benefits of this market, however, we should consider all of the costs, including those borne by the downstream neighbors. These costs, too, are part of the cost of producing steel. Adding these external costs to the private marginal costs yields the total marginal cost of producing steel. Considering all costs, the optimal output of steel is Q_T. Because the steel producer ignores the external costs of its activities, we end up with too much output of steel.

As will be discussed in more detail in a later chapter, incentive-compatible schemes based on property rights are beginning to come into more widespread use. Known as "cap and trade," these approaches limit the total emissions of regulated pollutants, and leave it to firms and the market to decide how and where to make the necessary reductions. Another incentive-compatible approach is based on taxing emissions, also known as effluent fees. If the tax rate in the steel example is set equal to the external damages to others, the steel producer has exactly the right incentives to choose how much steel to produce.

More common in the environmental area are command and control regulatory approaches. Such approaches might, for example, require firms to employ a particular technology to reduce emissions. Other command and control approaches require all firms to make an equal percentage reduction in emissions, or set specific emission quantities that each firm must meet.

III. PUBLIC GOODS

Most goods in the marketplace are private goods. If one person consumes the good, it is not available for others to consume. Public goods are different, because they do not exhibit rivalry in consumption. That is, one person's consumption does not reduce the amount available for others to consume. With public art, for example, everyone can enjoy it and, putting crowding aside, there is still just as much available for consumption. Other examples are a lighthouse or an uncrowded highway.

It is the lack of rivalry in consumption that defines a public good, but many public goods share another characteristic: it is difficult to exclude those who do not pay. National defense is a classic example; there is no feasible way to not defend those who do not wish to participate. Sometimes exclusion is possible. We can, for example, charge tolls for the uncrowded highway or admission to an art museum. Even where exclusion is possible, however, it is not necessarily efficient. If it is possible for everyone to consume the good, leaving some people out would reduce welfare.

Provision of public goods is subject to the free rider problem, particularly when exclusion is difficult. Because each person will be able to consume the public good whether they contribute to its provision or not, there is a private incentive to let others pay. The benefits will be the same, and the private costs will be lower. Thus, individually, consumers can try to take a free ride on the contributions of others. As long as some people reason this way, the public good will be underprovided.

Sometimes, public goods are provided in the market, particularly when they can be tied to the provision of some private good. Television broadcasting, or numerous Web site content providers, are good examples. From the point of view of the consumer, a television program or an entertaining Web site is a public good. However, the provision of the program also attracts an audience to watch advertising, and the advertising is a private good for the advertiser. Subsidies to public television aside, there is little reason to think the market produces too little of such public goods.

A common solution to public good problems is direct provision of the good by the government. Because participation in the tax system is mandatory, the government can overcome the free rider problem.

IV. IMPERFECT INFORMATION

The assumption in the standard model of perfect competition is that all market participants have complete information. Consumers, for example, are assumed to know the prices of all providers, and know everything there is to know (or at least everything that might matter) about the characteristics of the goods that are offered. If consumers lack certain information, we may not achieve the optimal outcome.

If consumers lack information about product prices, then each seller has some degree of market power. A seller who raises prices will not lose all of its customers, because at least some consumers do not know that a better price is available elsewhere. The price increase will, however, reduce consumption, and lead to the same kind of restriction on output that characterizes monopoly.

Imperfect information about price, however, tends to be self-limiting. The more the price goes up, the more incentive there is for the consumer to look for a better price. Thus, there is little reason to think that imperfect price information would lead to significant or persistent distortions in the competitive economy.

Interventions based on imperfect information about price are most often based on the notion that, because prices are complex in some industries, consumers need assistance in comparing prices. Comparing credit terms, for example, can be difficult, because both the interest rate and up-front payments may vary from one seller (or competing product) to another. The Truth in Lending Act adopts a standardized measure of the cost of credit, the annual percentage rate (or APR), designed to facilitate such comparisons. The calculation, however, makes assumptions about how long the credit will remain outstanding (usually until maturity for closed ended credit like mortgages) that are not correct for many consumers.

A more serious source of potential concern is missing information about product characteristics. If consumers are not adequately informed about the benefits and costs of a particular product, their choices will not properly guide competitive markets.

The impact of missing information about product characteristics depends on the nature of the missing information. Consumers may be missing positive information about a product. Consider, for example, the market for cereals high in fiber. Given the information they have about high-fiber cereals, consumer demand is shown as D_U in Figure 2-6 (the uninformed demand). Assuming the marginal cost of producing high-fiber cereals is constant, consumers will choose to purchase Q_U units of high-fiber cereal.

Some consumers, however, may not know that diets high in fiber reduce the risk of some kinds of cancer. If they had this information, the value they assign to a given amount of high-fiber cereal would presumably increase, to D_I in Figure 2-6 (the informed demand). Their consumption of high-fiber cereal would therefore increase. If consumers are missing positive information about a product, they will consume too little of that product, resulting in too little output. (We will examine the actual market response to the provision of information about fiber and cancer risk in more detail in a later chapter.)

Figure 2-6. Missing positive information.

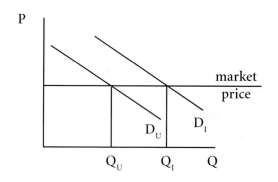

Consumers may also lack negative information about a product. Again, in the absence of information, demand will be D_U in Figure 2-7. To continue with the cereals market as an example, suppose it is discovered that the food coloring used to color red fruit loops causes cancer. That information would reduce the demand for fruit loops to D_I if it became known. Demand would not necessarily disappear entirely, because

Figure 2-7. Missing negative information.

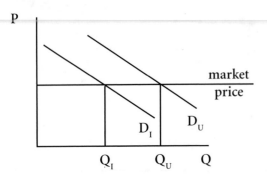

some may be willing to take the risk and others may be willing to eat around red fruit loops, but it will surely decline. Given the informed demand, quantity will decline as well. With missing negative information, the market outcome will result in too much output of the product.

The fruit loops example is entirely hypothetical, but a similar incident affected M&M candies. In the late 1970s, concern about the possibility that Red Dye No. 2 caused cancer led many consumers to avoid red foods, including red M&Ms. In response, Mars eliminated red M&Ms from 1976 until 1987, even though they had never used the suspect food coloring. As a result of imperfect information, a decade of children grew up without red M&Ms!

One obvious incentive-compatible solution to imperfect information problems is to remove barriers to the provision of truthful and accurate information. Many barriers, such as prohibitions on advertising by various professionals or advertising of prescription drug prices, have been removed over the last 30 years or so, but others remain. Pharmaceutical manufacturers, for example, cannot promote their products for uses that have not received FDA approval, even if the product is the treatment of choice of most physicians who treat the condition. Regulatory requirements continue to make it more difficult for food manufacturers to talk about the health effects of their products as well. In addition to removing barriers, truth in advertising requirements are an incentive-compatible way to address imperfect information problems. These issues are explored in more detail in a subsequent chapter.

Another common incentive-compatible regulatory strategy is disclosure requirements. Nutrition labels, ingredient labels, warnings about the health effects of alcoholic beverages, warnings about the health effects of workplace chemicals, and similar kinds of requirements are all attempts to provide information but leave it to consumers to make their own choices about how much or how little of the product to consume.

Command and control approaches to imperfect information problems generally involve regulation of the product itself. The economic rationale for auto safety regulation, for example, is imperfect information. If consumers had complete information, there is little reason to think that they would make inappropriate safety choices. Although there are some disclosure elements in auto safety regulation, such as the crash rating program, the primary tool is direct regulation of the product. Cars cannot be sold without numerous federally required safety devices. Similarly, regulation of food additives relies on direct regulation of acceptable additives, rather than providing information to let consumers choose. Essentially, the command and control approaches make the information irrelevant. Consumers do not need to concern themselves about whether cars meet minimum safety standards (although they may well be interested in more safety than the government requires), nor do they need to inquire about the safety of specific food additives (though some may not trust the government's determination that an additive is safe).

V. Non-economic Rationales for Intervention

In the absence of a market failure, there is no economic rationale for regulatory intervention. If the goal is to maximize consumer welfare as judged by consumers, intervention in the absence of a market failure can only make things worse. There are, however, non-economic rationales for intervention in the economy that are frequently invoked, although not always explicitly.

First, equity is a rationale for many types of intervention in the economy. In the market outcome, distribution is irrelevant. Moreover, with consumer preferences taken as given, there is no direct way to value a different income distribution. Like other transfer payments, changing the income distribution produces gains to some consumers offset by losses to others. Nonetheless, many individual consumers would be willing to give something up for a more equitable outcome, and society might collectively determine that it would prefer to alter the distribution.

Perhaps the most obvious equity-based interventions are laws against discrimination. Although some business owners may have a "taste" for discriminating against certain groups in deciding whom they hire or whom they serve, indulging that taste is generally prohibited. Moreover, numerous tax and spending programs are designed explicitly to alter the distribution of income, by giving more money to those who have less at the expense of those who are relatively well off. Although we can ask about the costs and benefits of different ways to redistribute income, there is no economic basis for evaluating alternative distributions themselves.

Perhaps more common as a rationale for intervention, but far less frequently articulated than equity, is paternalism. Paternalism is simply substituting some other set of preferences for those of the consumer. Policies such as prohibitions on certain recreational drugs are much more difficult to justify if the consumer's preferences are taken as given, but it is straightforward to argue that they serve the consumer's best interests by some other standard.

Less dramatic deviations from respect for consumer preferences include policies such as requirements to use seat belts or wear a motorcycle (or bicycle) helmet. These policies put aside the consumer's own judgment about the risks and benefits of using these devices, essentially arguing that consumers "should" use them, and therefore must do so. Applied to children, many such policies can be defended as ways to protect children from the poor judgment of their parents, but this rationale does not extend to adults.

Motorcycle helmet laws are particularly interesting, because they have gone through cycles as the relative importance of respecting individual preferences and protecting public safety has changed. In 1967, Congress required states to either adopt motorcycle helmet laws or risk the loss of some federal highway funding (the same device was later used to require states to adopt seat belt laws). By the early 1970s, most states had helmet laws covering all riders. But some states, beginning with Michigan in 1968, repealed their laws. In 1976, Congress prevented the Department of Transportation from imposing monetary penalties on states without laws, and by 1980, most states had either repealed their laws entirely or limited them to riders under 18 years of age. Today, 20 states have laws that require all motorcycle riders to wear a helmet.[2]

VI. SUMMARY

The economic rationales for intervention in the economy are based on market failures. In the absence of a market failure, intervention can only make things worse, if the goal is to maximize consumer welfare as judged by consumers. Market failures can be addressed by incentive-compatible remedies, which seek ideally to correct the underlying market failure and leave everything else to the market. They are also addressed by command and control regulations, which tell firms precisely what they must do. Non-economic rationales for intervention include equity and paternalism.

The market failure of monopoly results in too little output to maximize consumer welfare. Antitrust policy is an incentive-compatible approach to address monopoly; price controls are a command and control approach.

Externalities stem from poorly defined property rights. Common property, which has no owner, results in overuse of the resource and may destroy it entirely. External benefits result in too little output of the product that produces the externality; external costs lead to excessive output. In some circumstances markets may address externalities well, but often they do not. Incentive-compatible approaches seek to better define property rights. Command and control approaches are frequently based on requiring the use of particular technologies.

---

[2] Insurance Institute for Highway Safety. Helmet Use Laws, January 2009. http://www.iihs.org/laws/HelmetUseOverview.aspx (January 26, 2009).

Public goods do not exhibit rivalry in consumption; all can consume the good without reducing the amount available for others. Because it is often difficult to exclude consumers from using public goods, they are subject to the free rider problem, and may be underprovided. Sometimes, public goods are adequately provided through the market, such as with broadcast television or Internet content, by using the public good to generate the private good of advertising. Often, government provides public goods directly.

Imperfect information about price may occur, but is a self-limiting problem. Imperfect information about product characteristics is potentially more significant. If consumers are missing positive information about the product, they will consume too little of it. If they are missing negative information, they will consume too much. Disclosure requirements and truth in advertising laws are examples of incentive-compatible approaches to imperfect information. Direct product regulation is the most common command and control approach.

MARKET DYNAMICS

Chapter 3

In Chapters 1 and 2, we considered the operation of a market economy at a particular point in time. This chapter considers two different views of changes in the market over time. One view, that of Thomas Malthus, is remarkably pessimistic but remains highly influential. Malthus argued that population growth would eventually overwhelm available resources, leading to war, famine, and doom. Although more than 200 years have elapsed since his prediction was first made, there is little evidence to support it. Nonetheless, Malthus's view is the root of concerns we hear with considerable frequency that resources are running out.

Another view, that of Joseph Schumpeter, is a much more optimistic view of the development of a market economy. He saw the market economy as an engine for continuous progress, leading to growth and improvement over time. In a sense, Schumpeter explains the mechanism that has prevented the Malthusian prophecy from coming true.

1. THOMAS MALTHUS AND THE ECONOMICS OF DOOM

A. The problem of population growth

Central to the Malthusian analysis of market dynamics is the analysis of population growth. Population growth, Malthus argued, was a geometric process. That is, population grows at a more or less constant percentage rate. As a result, the absolute number of new mouths to feed in each succeeding generation gets larger and larger.

To see the power of the geometric progression, consider two flies in a room that is $10' \times 12' \times 10'$, or just over 2,000,000 cubic inches of volume. Assume the flies have everything they need; the only limited resource is the space available. Moreover, assume that each pair of flies will produce 1,000 offspring.

In the first generation, there are 2 flies. In the second generation, there are 1,000 flies. In the third generation, there are 500 pairs of flies, each producing 1,000 offspring, for a total population of 500,000 flies. In the fourth generation, there are 250,000 pairs, each producing 1,000 offspring, so the population is 250,000,000—about 125 flies per cubic inch. In the fifth generation, the population would be 125,000,000,000, but there clearly is not enough space in the room to accommodate them all.

People, of course, do not breed like flies, but the world's population, now about 6.8 billion, continues to grow.[1] Although the population growth rate is lower than in the past, and has been declining, a growing population will inevitably put increasing pressure on any fixed resource.

The resource that particularly concerned Malthus was food. Population growth puts increasing pressure on the food supply. We can, of course, expand the food supply by bringing more land into production and using more labor and capital to produce crops. Indeed, a growing population means that there will be more laborers available to help produce additional food. To Malthus, however, growth in food production was essentially a linear process. We can only add so many additional acres of farmland per year, and each additional acre of land is likely to be less productive as well. Inexorably, Malthus contended, population growth will outstrip the possible expansions in agricultural production, and we will not have enough to eat.

Figure 3-1. Malthusian dynamics.

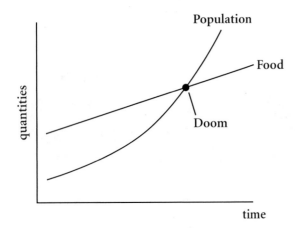

The situation according to Malthus is depicted in Figure 3-1. Over time, population is growing at a geometric rate, and food production is increasing at a linear rate. Even if we start out with plenty of food, at some point, population growth will overwhelm the available supply, and we will run out of food. When that happens—the point of Doom—we will experience famine, war, pestilence, and disease, reducing the population to a level that can survive on the available resources.

B. Malthus and the market

In competitive markets, the Malthusian scenario will show up as an increase in prices for key resources. Consider first the case of a resource with literally fixed supply, as shown in Figure 3-2. With the initial population, demand for this resource is at D_0, and the market clearing price is P_0. Over time, population grows, and demand therefore increases to D_1. Because supply is fixed, price increases to P_1. Population growth continues, however, and as a result demand increases to D_2, pushing the price to P_2. Thus, over time, we should see a steady increase in the price of this resource as population growth pushes up demand.

Figure 3-2. Population growth with fixed supply.

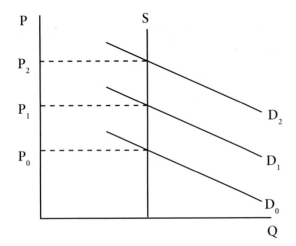

---

[1] You can watch both world and U.S. population growth at the U.S. Census Bureau's population clock, at http://www.census.gov/main/www/popclock.html.

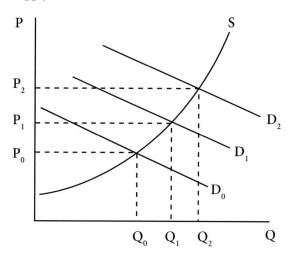

Figure 3-3. Population growth with increasing supply.

Figure 3-4. Population growth with exhaustible resources.

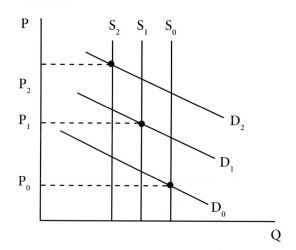

It is not clear that there is a resource in literally fixed supply. Perhaps land in Manhattan is an example, but from an economic perspective, a skyscraper is just another way to produce more land in Manhattan. Even an upward-sloping supply curve will not change the fundamental prediction, however, as shown in Figure 3-3.

The increase in demand from D_1 to D_2 calls forth an increase in the quantity supplied (from Q_1 to Q_2). The price increase provides an incentive to expand output, although it is costly to do so. Clearly, however, the price will still increase with successive increases in demand. Compared to the fixed supply cases, prices will not rise as rapidly, but they will nonetheless increase over time.

Modern Malthusians often add an additional wrinkle to this picture: the notion of an exhaustible resource. With an exhaustible resource, supply is greater initially, and declines over time as the resource is used up. A simplified exhaustible resource scenario is shown in Figure 3-4.

Initially, demand is D_0 and supply is S_0. As population grows, demand increases to D_1. Because some of the exhaustible resource has been used up, however, supply has shifted back to S_1. Price increases by more than it would in either the fixed supply case we considered initially or in the upward-sloping supply curve case. In the next generation, further population growth will increase demand to D_2, but supply has shifted back to S_2. Again, the reduction in the availability of the resource amplifies the increase in price.

Still, the Malthusian prediction of doom has obviously not come to pass, and there is little evidence to suggest that it is just around the corner. Have we just been lucky, or is there some more fundamental flaw in the Malthusian analysis?

C. Simon's answer: population as a resource

Economist Julian Simon argues that, indeed, the Malthusian argument is fundamentally flawed, because it does not properly consider the nature of economic resources. Resources, Simon argues, are the product of human intellect. Nature gives us various raw materials, but until some clever human figures out that a particular raw material can become a resource, it has no economic significance. Iron ore is a raw material that has always been with us, but until the beginning of the Iron Age in 450 B.C., it was not an economic resource. Uranium, the foundation of nuclear electricity generation, was not even discovered until 1789; it was only 70 years ago that it was discovered that uranium is fissionable, and today it supplies roughly 19 percent of U.S. electricity. And who knew until very recently that sand on the beach, which has many obvious and longstanding uses, could also form the basis for an electronics revolution based on silicon? All of these resources, and many others, are the product of clever people figuring out how available raw materials can be used to serve human ends.

Human intellect, however, grows at least as fast as the human population. More people means more clever people who might discover new ways to conserve on existing resources, or utilize things that were not previously regarded as resources. There is a certain power in billions of people that Malthus simply did not appreciate. According to one Internet factoid, for example, there are more honors students in China than there are students in the United States. Many of them are, or soon will be, looking for ways to make the raw materials of planet Earth go farther than they do today.

Moreover, there is reason to believe that the power of human intelligence grows qualitatively, as well as quantitatively. It is not just that there are more people, but they are also much better educated than people have been in any prior generation. They do not need to start over from scratch; they start from a base of knowledge that has been painstakingly assembled over hundreds of years. Thus, to Simon, human intellect—the basis of all economic resources—is likely to grow *faster* than population. We will not "run out" of resources, because we will invent more resources as we need them.

One outstanding example of this phenomenon is the first energy crisis—the charcoal crisis in England. At the beginning of the Industrial Revolution, the primary fuel on which the English relied for heating, cooking, and essentially all other energy uses was charcoal. Charcoal, of course, comes from wood that is partially combusted to leave behind charcoal. England, however, is located on a relatively small island. Just as Malthus might have expected, the demand for charcoal was depleting English forests (other than the game reserves that were preserved for hunting by royalty) and leading to a potential crisis.

Then someone noticed that there were strange black rocks that would burn if they get hot enough—what we know today as coal. Human intellect discovered a new resource to supplement and indeed largely replace the traditional energy source, and it was coal that powered the industrial revolution. Had charcoal remained plentiful and cheap, there would have been no reason to experiment with coal. But increases in the price of charcoal set in motion incentives to use less charcoal, and to find ways to avoid the need for charcoal entirely. The result was coal, and the industrial revolution.

Oil, the quintessential exhaustible resource, offers a similar tale of the role of human innovation in identifying and exploiting raw materials to bend nature to human objectives. We first became seriously concerned about oil supplies in the 1970s as a result of the Arab oil embargo that led to sharply increased oil prices around the world. As an exhaustible resource, one would expect that the available reserves of oil have decreased since that time. In fact, however, they have not. The relevant statistics are summarized in Figure 3-5.

Since 1971, countries outside of OPEC have produced well over twice as much oil as they thought they *had* in 1971—and they ended up in 2004 with reserves that were *larger* than what they started with! For OPEC, the figures are even more dramatic. Production was about three-quarters of proven reserves that were available in 1971—and proven reserves in 2004 were more than double what the OPEC nations started with. Collectively, the world produced 25 percent more oil between 1971 and 2004 than what it started with, and ended up with two-thirds more oil. So much for exhaustible resources!

Figure 3-5. "Exhaustible" oil reserves over time.

Oil Reserves and Production, 1971–2004 (billions of barrels)			
	Non-OPEC nations	OPEC Nations	Total
Proven reserves, 1971	200	412	612
Production, 1971–2004	460	307	767
Proven reserves, 2004	209	819	1028

Of course, some of the expansion in both production and proven reserves was the result of major new oil discoveries, such as the North Slope of Alaska and the North Sea oil fields. Presumably, such large-scale discoveries cannot be repeated indefinitely. But a large part of the increase in proven reserves after 30 years of record levels of production was also due to technological progress. Oil that could not be economically extracted in 1971 was available for human use in 2004, and was therefore part of "proven reserves." Heavier oil could be economically exploited, for example, as well as oil in deeper waters offshore. Thus, a substantial proportion of the increase in "proven reserves" was because we learned how to economically extract oil that we had known for some time was there, but extraction was not feasible.

Technological improvements have continued to expand available resources of fossil fuels. In the last few years, for example, the development of hydraulic fracturing (commonly known as "fracking") has greatly expanded exploitable oil and gas reserves in the United States, leading to drilling booms in states such as Pennsylvania, where oil and gas production virtually disappeared many years ago.

Simon was so convinced that human intellect would overcome the limitations on the availability of key resources that he offered a bet to the leading neo-Malthusian of his day, Paul Ehrlich, who wrote a book titled *The Population Bomb* in 1968. As we have seen, the Malthusian theory implies rising prices of critical resources over time. Simon, in contrast, predicted that such prices would either remain flat or decline as human intellect figured out new ways to both economize on scarce resources and develop better (or alternative) ways to obtain them. The bet was a hypothetical investment in resources over a decade, from 1980 to 1990. Ehrlich, the Malthusian, picked the resources and specified the allocation of a $1,000 portfolio. He chose five key metals that he was convinced would increase in price because of growing scarcity. If prices rose, as the Malthusian argument predicted, Simon would pay Ehrlich the increase in the value of the portfolio. If prices fell, as Simon believed they would, Ehrlich would pay Simon the reduction in value. Simon won. In fact, on the $1,000 investment that Ehrlich specified, he won $567—not a bad return at all! Simon offered to renew the bet for another decade, but Ehrlich declined.

When the price of any commodity rises, it sets in motion important economic forces. On the demand side, there is an incentive to use less of that commodity. The market will divert the commodity from its least valued to its most valued uses. It will also create incentives to find ways to avoid using the expensive commodity in some or all of its uses. On the supply side, there is an incentive to find new ways to supply the commodity. That may include finding new sources (e.g., new oil fields), but it also includes finding new ways to produce the commodity from existing sources. The greater the pressure on the resource is, the greater the increase in its price—and the greater the incentives to find more and to do without it wherever possible. Simon bet on that process, and won.

D. The limits of long-term predictions

By its nature, the Malthusian prediction is long term. Perhaps the 200 years since Malthus wrote is not actually long enough to see the consequences of population growth. There are certainly those who believe that Malthusian doom is (at least figuratively) just around the corner. Or perhaps the increase in world population from about 900 million when Malthus wrote to over 6.7 billion today is not enough to induce the consequences he saw as inevitable. If we add another billion people (2 billion? 6 billion?), however, the consequences might be far more serious than what we have seen so far. Or perhaps Simon was right—human beings are good at solving actual and potential problems.

More fundamentally, any long term-prediction is subject to substantial error, because long-term forecasts inherently cannot anticipate the nature of the technological changes that unfolding events will set in motion. As economist Herb Stein once noted, "That which cannot go on forever won't." Thus, unsustainable trends will not continue. Almost by definition, trends that will produce disaster if they continue into the indefinite future are not sustainable, and they will not continue. The end of the trend might produce serious consequences, but the only safe prediction is that such trends will set in motion incentives to invest in methods and technologies to avoid the problem. Predicting how the trend will change, or what technology may emerge to avoid the need to sustain the trend, is exceedingly difficult.

To help appreciate the problems, it is useful to consider previous long-term predictions that went astray. First, in his 1968 book, Paul Ehrlich predicted that by the year 2000 (only 30 years distant at the time), the pressures of expanding population would mean that 65 million people would starve to death—in the United States! It didn't happen, in part because Ehrlich did not anticipate the technological changes in food production that were already underway, both in the United States and in the rest of the world. Another such forecast was prepared for New York City in 1870, attempting to predict what the city would be like in 1900, 30 years down the road. Its central prediction was that the city would be buried in horse manure, because the increasing population traveling by the only known means of practical personal transportation would require far too many horses producing far too much manure. New York has many problems, but they do not appear to include mountains of horse manure.

The obvious inadequacies in these particular forecasts are not necessarily because of the limitations of the forecasters. They are instead the result of the inherent difficulties of predicting what technologies will emerge to address trends that would otherwise be unsustainable. We can safely predict that unsustainable trends will not continue, but it is vastly more difficult to predict how they will change.

Consider another long-term forecast, this one from the Club of Rome, an anti-growth group that predicted in 1990 that the point of Malthusian Doom would arrive in 2050. To appreciate the difficulties of this 60-year forecast, it is worth looking back 60 years, to 1930, and considering how the world has changed since then. In 1930, there were no antibiotics, no computers, and no satellites. The far-reaching implications of those technologies obviously could not have been anticipated. Technology has progressed in more mundane areas as well. Compared to 1930, the United States in 1990 produced three times the amount of food, on one-third of the acreage, using one-third of the manpower that was required in 1930.

No forecast on this timescale can be expected to anticipate correctly the technological changes that will inevitably occur. We can know with a very high degree of confidence that the forecast has omitted significant technological changes that will surely occur. Moreover, the underlying economics of change imply that these technological changes will likely be concentrated on precisely the problems that the forecast identifies as the most likely problems. There is, however, no reliable way to identify precisely what will change, nor how it will change. Any long-term forecast should therefore be taken with at least a grain, and probably a shaker, of salt.

II. JOSEPH SCHUMPETER AND THE ECONOMICS OF GROWTH

It is all very well to say, as Simon did, that the market creates incentives for the human intellect to develop solutions to resource scarcity. But it would be useful to have a more complete view of exactly how such changes might actually play out in the market. Joseph Schumpeter provided such a vision. He saw the market economy as an evolutionary process, constantly developing new ways of doing business, and in the process improving well-being.

A. The nature of profit

Schumpeter's starting point was the nature of profit. Profit is a central feature of a market economy. It is the motivation for business decisions about what to produce, how much to produce, and how to organize the production process. Yet, in a long-run competitive equilibrium, there is no profit—it is all competed away. As shown in Figure 3-6, profit will attract entry until, in the long-run equilibrium, each firm is operating at the minimum point of its long-run average total cost curve, with price equal to marginal cost, and no profit. In fact, the existence of profits serves as a signal to allocate more resources to this industry, and entry by additional firms is a means of doing so. However, the response to the signal will inevitably eliminate the profits that were the signal initially.

In the competitive equilibrium, owners of resources, whether labor, raw materials, or capital, are paid the value of their contribution to the output, but there is no residual for the firm's owners to claim. There is, of course, a cost of capital, which is included in average total costs, and some of what is usually measured as accounting profits is in fact returns to capital. But if returns exceed the cost of capital, more capital will enter and profits will erode. Profit drives the market economy, but in equilibrium, profit disappears.

Figure 3-6. Long-run competitive equilibrium.

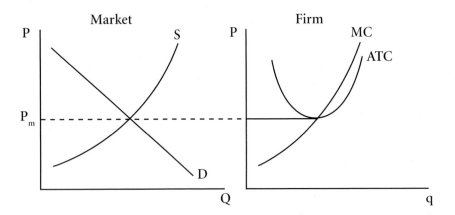

Schumpeter argued that profits arise from change. Profits only exist when the market has not achieved equilibrium. They are the signal that something new needs to be done, to take advantage of the profit opportunity. It may be new markets, new technologies, or new business arrangements, but something changes that disrupts the competitive equilibrium. Profits will exist until, and only until, the market reaches the new competitive equilibrium.

The easiest way to see how change generates profits is to consider a cost-reducing technical change in a competitive market. Suppose the market is in a long-run competitive equilibrium, as shown in Figure 3-7. Each firm has costs shown by ATC_0 and MC_0 in the figure. Then one firm develops a new technology that reduces its costs to ATC_1 and MC_1. Because the firm is small relative to the market, the new technology does not immediately change the market price. The firm's profit maximizing choice is still to operate where price equals marginal cost, so given the market price and its new cost structure, the innovator finds it profitable to expand its output, from Q_0 to Q_1. The market price is now above the innovator's average total costs, and the innovator therefore earns profits

Figure 3-7. Cost-reducing technical change.

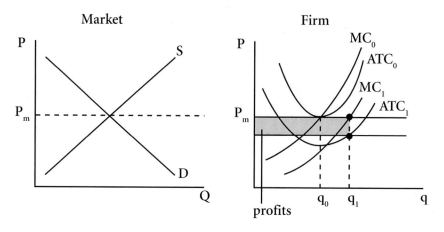

given by the shaded rectangle in Figure 3-7.

The profits resulting from this or any other innovation, however, are *transient*. The existence of profits indicates to others that something has changed, and a swarm of imitators will borrow money to make the investments necessary to copy the new idea. As they do, competition will begin to force the market price down. Eventually the market will reach a new equilibrium, one where the market price has fallen to the minimum point of the new average total cost curve, and no firm is earning profits.

Profits from innovation are the reward for successful innovation, the payment to the entrepreneur who puts the idea into practice. To Schumpeter, entrepreneurs are key figures in the market economy. They are the people who implement new ideas, even if someone else invented the technology. It takes a special ability, Schumpeter argued, to recognize the potential in a new idea and overcome the obstacles to putting the idea into practice. Profit is the reward for success in this endeavor.

We often think of the modern economy as one that is dominated by larger firms. A majority of all jobs, however, are in firms with fewer than 500 employees. Moreover, in 2006, firms with fewer than 10 employees accounted for just over 10 percent of total employment. Thus, small businesses and the entrepreneurs who run them remain a critical component of the economy. Moreover, even large firms can be entrepreneurial. Microsoft and Google, for example, are hardly small, but they have certainly been entrepreneurial.

Profit flows to the owners of the firm that implements the innovation, because they are the risk takers. The risks are substantial, because many innovations simply do not succeed in the market. Most new product introductions are failures, with estimates of the failure rate ranging as high as 95 percent. The money invested in launching these products is simply lost in most instances. Risks are also large because the market is a moving target. An idea that might be extremely promising at one point in time may be far less appealing to consumers when it actually reaches the market, simply because market conditions have changed.

Consider, for example, the Laserdisc, an optical storage device developed by Phillips Electronics that allowed consumers to play back video content. The discs themselves looked like modern compact discs, but they were

12 inches in diameter. Phillips thought there would be a significant market among consumers who wanted to watch movies in their home, and the Laserdisc would be the way to deliver those movies. The product was first demonstrated in 1972, and introduced into the commercial marketplace in 1978. Unfortunately for Phillips, that introduction was three years after the introduction of the Betamax VCR, and two years after the introduction of VHS format VCRs. There certainly was a market for movies at home, but it was a market that was satisfied by movies on tape, rather than movies on disc. Moreover, tape could record programs from television and play them back whenever the consumer chose. Laserdisc could only play, not record. The market had moved before the product was ready.

The entrepreneur may or may not be the inventor of the underlying technology. Often the successful implementer is someone other than the inventor. Consider, for example, the development of xerography. The basic process was first patented by Chester Carlson in 1937. He tried for years to interest companies in investing in the idea, but was turned down by at least twenty companies, including IBM. It was not until 1944 that he found a nonprofit research institute to help develop the process, and in 1947, the company that eventually became Xerox bought the rights to develop a copier. The first convenient copier was introduced in 1959. The inventor certainly profited, but there is little doubt that Xerox, which successfully implemented the technology and created an industry that it is hard to imagine doing without, earned far more.

To summarize, profit provides a *signal* to rearrange resource allocation. It is the *incentive* to find better ways to do things, and the *reward* for successful implementation of new ideas. Profit is *transient*, and goes to whoever takes the risk that is inherent in innovation.

B. The process of creative destruction

Schumpeter saw the market economy as an evolutionary process. It was set in motion by change, driven by the pursuit of profits. Change might come in the form of new goods, new methods of production, or new markets, but change was the one constant. These changes, or "industrial mutations" as Schumpeter termed them, were constantly revolutionizing the economic system. They are the drivers of creative destruction—the process of destroying the old way of doing business and replacing it with something new. Indeed, Schumpeter argued, implementing a new idea will inevitably lead to the destruction of the old way of doing things.

Judged in the context of an evolutionary system, Schumpeter argued, the usual economic analysis of the competitive equilibrium asks the wrong question. Our consideration of the market failure of monopoly in Chapter 2 considered a static question: How well does monopoly administer the available resources, compared to competition? As we saw, the competitive outcome is better than monopoly. But the entire analysis was static. Demand was constant and unchanging, as were production costs and technologies. To Schumpeter, the important question is how well an economic system can administer the process of change. In other words, how effective are markets in destroying old ways of doing business and replacing them with something new and better?

From this perspective, the important competition is not price competition. Instead, the important competition over time is competition from new ideas and new technologies. Successful new ideas and technologies are improvements over what was available before, as judged by consumers; otherwise they will not succeed in the market. Because the new approaches are better for consumers, they are more profitable than the alternatives. The lack of price competition produces the static welfare loss from monopoly, but there is far more at stake if we interfere with the competition of ideas. Here, Schumpeter thought, monopoly may actually facilitate the process of creative destruction, an idea we consider in more detail in the next section.

To Schumpeter, the economic attraction of a market economy is this dynamism. In the decade between 1996 and 2006, the U.S. economy lost 16 million jobs. That is the destructive part of creative destruction. But it also created 17 million new jobs, often in businesses that had not existed at the beginning of the decade. The market encourages and facilitates change, leading to continuous improvements over time. Over the long haul, it has clearly brought almost unthinkable improvements in standards of living.

Creative destruction is all around us. Consider, for example, Sears and Wal-Mart. For decades, Sears was the giant of American retailing, selling every imaginable item in its department stores and through its catalog. Then came Wal-Mart, with a new business model characterized by low prices for a wide range of items, but with a smaller number of choices within each category. It relied on low-cost imported goods, tight management of its suppliers, and sophisticated information technology to make sure it had the goods customers wanted when they wanted them—and it has come to dominate retailing. Many of the old department stores are gone. Sears still survives, but is a shadow of its former self. Moreover, the Wal-Mart model has spread to "big box" retailers in numerous other product categories. Wal-Mart created a new way of doing business that destroyed the old model, and replaced it with something better for consumers.

Similarly, consider the American automobile industry. General Motors's share of the domestic auto market hovered around 50 percent for years. The business was built on numerous model lines, catering to differences in consumer demographics and preferences, with products ranging from Chevys to Cadillacs. Then came the Japanese manufacturers, particularly Nissan and Toyota (and later Honda). In part, they offered a somewhat different product, with smaller, more economical cars. But they also produced them differently. They offered fewer options, reducing the number of distinct automobiles that must be produced, distributed, held in inventory, and eventually sold. Different models shared parts to the maximum possible extent, simplifying the production process and reducing costs. With fewer parts and the introduction of just-in-time inventory management, Japanese manufacturers had significantly lower costs. General Motors survived its recent brush with bankruptcy, but it is unlikely to regain its former glory.

Or consider the computer industry. Almost from its inception, the mainframe computer industry was dominated by IBM. A generation of programmers learned their craft using IBM's software on IBM's hardware. Antitrust authorities alleged that the company had monopolized the industry in a 1969 complaint, and litigation continued until the case was ultimately dismissed in 1982. But IBM was skeptical of the personal computer revolution, initially leaving the field to Apple and a host of even smaller companies. Why would anyone want a computer on their desk, after all? It was influential enough to set the standard for personal computers when it finally introduced its own product in 1981 (and partnered with Microsoft to develop operating system software for the new machine), but personal computing quickly passed it by. Again, a wave of change destroyed the old mainframe-based way of doing business and replaced it with something new.

Although creative destruction is economically attractive, it is more problematic from a political perspective.[2] We will explore the political process in more detail in subsequent chapters, but three aspects of the political implications of creative destruction foreshadow that discussion.

First, there is likely to be political discontent with destruction. The consequences of destroying an old way of doing business tend to be highly visible, and concentrated on a relatively small group that is intensely affected. We all see automobile factories closing, and storefronts that used to house some now defunct retailer. The workers in the affected companies can be expected to object and seek help in the political process. Many communities have had lengthy political fights when Wal-Mart seeks to open a new store, as existing merchants try to use the political process to stop a powerful new competitor. As we will explore in more detail when we consider the theory of public choice, such relatively small, concentrated groups are often highly influential in the political process.

---

[2] Schumpeter was exceedingly optimistic about the economic prospects for capitalism and the market economy, but much more pessimistic about its political future. Indeed, he thought that, essentially for political reasons, socialism would replace capitalism. Rational arguments, he thought, could not effectively answer political criticism. Most people would not be able to understand the critical role of market institutions, and would therefore be receptive to political changes that undermined those institutions. At one point, he wrote, "Why, practically every nonsense that has ever been said about capitalism has been championed by some professed economist."

Second, the benefits associated with the creation of a new way of doing business tend to be more diffuse. They are spread out over a large number of consumers who each realize a relatively small benefit. Many may not even be aware that there will be a benefit. If Wal-Mart is entering a new market, for example, many consumers in that market may not have shopped at a Wal-Mart, and therefore may not appreciate the benefits that Wal-Mart will offer. Diffuse groups with relatively little at stake are less likely to participate in the political process. As a result, there may not be enough defenders of the benefits of creating a new way of doing business to carry the day.

Third, the costs of destruction tend to be short term and immediate. The benefits of the new way of doing business will be realized over a much longer period of time. Lower prices from Wal-Mart, for example, will persist for many years. The political process often worries more about short-term consequences, with less attention to the longer run. Indeed, in politics, the key time horizon is often the next election. Thus, the political process may weigh the short-term costs of destruction too heavily, and discount the future benefits of a new way of doing business.

C. Monopoly may facilitate creative destruction

As we noted, Schumpeter believed that the usual market failure analysis of monopoly asked the wrong question. Instead, he argued, we should think about monopoly and competition in the context of the competition of ideas, rather than price competition. In that arena, he argued, monopoly may facilitate the process of creative destruction.

First, monopoly provides an incentive. New products, new ideas, and new processes compete with the established way of doing things in an effort to become the next monopolist. For example, surely part of what has motivated Google's competitive efforts is the desire to do what Microsoft did so successfully: build a dominating market position in an important, growing, and highly profitable market.

At one level, some monopoly power is essential if innovation is to occur. In a world where competitors could instantly imitate every successful move that any other company made, there would be little reason to undertake the risks inherent in trying something new. Instant imitation would mean instant equilibrium for successful ideas, and the immediate disappearance of profits.

Because public policy generally recognizes the need for some degree of monopoly, government creates intellectual property rights. Patents, for example, give the inventor exclusive use of the invention for a fixed period of time. The patent holder can choose whatever strategy to exploit the invention that will maximize the returns, without the need to worry about competitors. In exchange, details of the patent must be made public, allowing others to attempt to build on the invention or improve on it, all in the hopes of developing their own intellectual property and achieving some protection from competition. Similarly, copyright laws protect the expression of ideas, although not the ideas themselves. Music, novels, textbooks, and movies are all reserved for the original author to exploit as he or she sees fit. Others can use the idea, but they cannot copy the material.

The tension between preserving competition and exploiting intellectual property rights has been a longstanding one in antitrust policy. In the 1970s, the Federal Trade Commission settled an antitrust complaint against Xerox with an agreement that required Xerox to license all of its patents, and also supply its unpatented "know-how" in applying the patents to its competitors. Arguably, the result was a more competitive industry in photocopying equipment, bringing the benefits of competition to consumers.

More recently, the FTC has filed a series of cases involving drug manufacturers' efforts to protect their patents. When a prescription drug's patent expiration approaches, other manufacturers have an incentive to try to be first to market with their own generic versions of the drug. One way to do that is to file for generic approval before the patent actually expires, and in the process challenge the validity of the patent itself. In some instances, the patent litigation has settled with an agreement by the original manufacturer to make "reverse payments" to the potential entrant to stay out of the market for some specified period of time. The FTC alleges that these reverse payments are anticompetitive, and violations of the antitrust laws. The drug companies, of course, contend that they are simply defending their intellectual property rights.

The Schumpeterian perspective argues that we should worry more about the incentives for innovation (and hence about preserving intellectual property rights) than about getting the static benefits of competition to consumers a little more rapidly. To be sure, there are benefits of competition, and preserving intellectual property rights reduces those benefits. Schumpeter, however, would argue that those costs are small compared to the costs of undue reductions in the incentive to innovate.

Second, some arguably monopolistic practices may operate as insurance by reducing the risk of imitation. Of course, insurance against the risk that someone will imitate your idea is not available. Schumpeter contends, however, that some practices that seem to impair competition are actually insurance—a legitimate attempt to reduce the risk of imitation.

Perhaps the clearest example of "monopoly as insurance" is the practice known as building ahead of demand. For a typical new product, demand starts out low and grows slowly for a while after the product is first introduced, and then grows more sharply and eventually levels out. This pattern is shown in Figure 3-8. Initially a company must build production capacity that will almost certainly exceed demand. Over time, however, if the product is successful, demand will grow and approach capacity.

Figure 3-8. Capacity choices and demand growth.

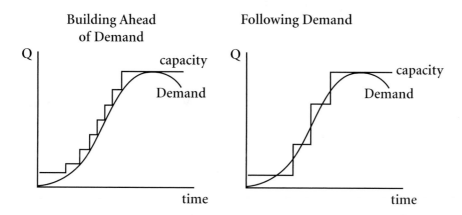

Now the company faces a choice. It can expand its capacity in anticipation of further demand increases, before its capacity is fully utilized. This pattern of capacity is shown in the first panel of Figure 3-8. Alternatively, the company might choose to follow demand—to wait for additional demand to materialize, and then expand its capacity. This pattern of capacity is shown in the second panel of Figure 3-8.

Arguably, building ahead of demand is an anticompetitive practice. If the innovator follows this strategy, there will always be excess capacity in the industry, which reduces the likelihood that another firm will enter the market. After all, a market with excess capacity is not an obvious candidate for new entry. Thus, the innovator will have the market to itself, or at least it can hope to have the market to itself for a little longer. In Schumpeter's terms, the practice reduces the risk of competitive imitation. In the following demand strategy, entry is more likely. Particularly during periods when demand exceeds capacity, other firms can see, and take advantage of, the opportunity to get into the market.

A challenge to the practice of building ahead of demand was part of the FTC's case against DuPont, alleging monopolization of the market for titanium dioxide (the pigment used to make white paint). Eventually, the FTC dismissed the charges.

Third, Schumpeter argued that monopoly gives "greater scope to the better brains." For Schumpeter, entrepreneurial ability was critical to the operation of creative destruction. That talent, however, is scarce. If we assume that entrepreneurial ability is normally distributed, most people have some ability, but only a few are truly good at entrepreneurship. These are the individuals in the upper tail of the distribution of ability, who earn outsized rewards in the marketplace. We could make a similar argument about musical ability. Nearly everyone can sing a little, but only a few have enough musical ability to become an opera star or a rock star.

When we find someone with extraordinary levels of entrepreneurial ability, we would like them to exercise that ability as broadly as possible. To Schumpeter, this meant running a large enterprise, one that could implement innovations—and make profits—in numerous areas.

There is another way to think about this argument as well, which is essentially an evolutionary argument. Successful firms grow and get bigger. Moreover, they keep growing as long as they are successful. Thus, firms that are successful become larger firms. When we observe (as we do) that large firms in more concentrated markets earn higher returns than firms in less concentrated markets, it may be because those firms found some advantage that made them more successful. Once they found an advantage, they grew more rapidly than their competitors and became larger both in absolute terms and relative to the market. Even if the discovery of a successful innovation is random, it may produce a correlation between size and profitability, because "lucky" firms will be more profitable and will grow larger. Indeed, simulation studies of random discoveries that lead to growth produce a size distribution of firms that is remarkably similar to what we actually see.

The evolutionary perspective is not an argument that large firms are better innovators than smaller ones. Rather, the causation is in the other direction. Better innovators become larger firms precisely because of their successful innovation. This is not an argument that monopoly (as reflected in market power) is necessarily better; rather, it is an argument that some degree of monopoly is an inevitable consequence of the process of creative destruction.

III. Summary

Thomas Malthus was concerned about the problem of population growth. He believed that population would grow at a geometric rate, but that key resources such as food could only grow at a linear rate. Eventually population growth would overwhelm the available resources, and we would reach the point of doom, with war, famine, and pestilence reducing the population to more manageable levels. If the Malthusian argument is correct, we should see rising prices of key resources over time as the increasing population increases demand for these materials.

In contrast, Julian Simon argued that resources depend on human intellect, which grows at least as fast as population, and probably faster. A raw material is not a resource until someone recognizes that it can be used to help solve an economic problem. As population increases, more clever people will find ways to use less of scarce materials for their current uses, find alternative ways to produce those materials, or find alternative materials to solve the same economic problem. Prices for key materials should therefore remain stable or decline over time, despite increasing demand.

Long-term forecasts such as the Malthusian forecast of doom are inherently unreliable. They cannot anticipate technological changes that will almost certainly affect what happens over time, often in dramatic ways.

Joseph Schumpeter considered the process of change in the market economy. He argued that all profits arise from change—from the invention of new methods, the discovery of new products, or the emergence of new markets. Profit provides a *signal* to rearrange resource allocation. It is the *incentive* to find better ways to do things, and the *reward* for successful implementation of new ideas. Profit is *transient*, and goes to whoever takes the risk that is inherent in innovation.

Change drives the process of creative destruction. "Industrial mutations" set the system in motion, creating a new way of doing business and ultimately destroying the old way of doing things. This continual process of change makes possible increasing standards of living over time. To assess an economic system, we must consider how well it administers the process of change. To Schumpeter, the critical competition is competition from new ideas, not competition over prices. The usual market failure analysis of monopoly assumes a static world with constant demand, technology, and prices. The more important question is whether monopoly or competition better facilitates change.

Schumpeter argued that monopoly could facilitate the process of creative destruction. Monopoly is an incentive for change, as companies compete to be the next monopolist. Some monopoly is essential, because instant imitation would destroy the incentive to take risks to implement change. Monopolistic practices may also serve as insurance by reducing the risk of imitation and increasing the rewards to developing a new approach. Finally, monopoly serves to give greater scope to the better brains. Market power may be the result of successful innovation, even if it does not create more innovation.

ANTITRUST ISSUES

Chapter 4

Contrary to the assumption of the perfectly competitive marketplace, we do not live in a world of atomistic firms. Instead, many industries are dominated by a small number of key players that collectively control a large fraction of the marketplace. A commonly used measure of concentration is the four firm concentration ratio, CR_4. This measure is simply the sum of the market shares of the four largest firms in the industry (the Census Bureau also reports concentration ratios for the largest 8, 20, and 50 companies). For example, the four largest companies in the dog and cat food industry accounted for 64 percent of the market in 2002. For breakfast cereal manufacturing CR_4 was 78 percent, for breweries it was 91 percent, for petrochemical manufacturing it was 85 percent, and for light truck and utility vehicle manufacturing it was 86 percent.

Concentrated industries such as these are oligopolies. Unlike competitive firms, oligopolists cannot ignore the effect of their choices on the choices of other important firms. Instead, they must take into account how rivals will respond to price and output decisions.

Across industries, many studies have found that profit rates, whether measured as return on equity or price cost margin,[1] are positively correlated with concentration ratios, particularly in industries where there are significant barriers to entry. Although dispute remains, most industrial organization economists probably agree that more concentrated industries are more profitable. There is substantially more disagreement, however, about the meaning of this finding.

This chapter begins with a brief discussion of oligopoly theory. It then turns to antitrust policy and the principal antitrust statutes. Section III discusses the merger guidelines, which indicate which mergers the government is likely to challenge. Section IV considers single firm conduct and, in particular, the antitrust case against Microsoft.

---

[1]Price cost margin is defined as $(P - MC)/P$, where P is price and MC is marginal cost.

I. Concentration and Profitability

A. Oligopoly Theory

We begin with the Cournot model of oligopoly, which was the first economic theory of oligopoly. Consider an industry with two identical firms, each with constant marginal cost equal to MC and facing industry demand as shown in Figure 4-1. Each firm has to choose how much to produce. Each firm also assumes that its rival will maintain its chosen output, so the problem for each firm is to choose its own profit maximizing output, given the output of the other firm. We saw in Chapter 1 that a profit maximizing firm will choose to operate where marginal revenue is equal to marginal cost, and our duopolists are no different.

We can see the logic of the Cournot theory most clearly if we think about the problem sequentially. Suppose firm 1 has to choose its output first. It assumes that firm 2 will maintain its output, which is zero initially, so firm 1 essentially faces the market demand and the corresponding marginal revenue, MR_1. It will choose to produce where $MC = MR_1$, and produce Q_m, the monopoly quantity. With a linear demand curve and constant marginal costs, this is exactly half the competitive quantity, Q_c.

Figure 4-1. Cournot Duopoly.

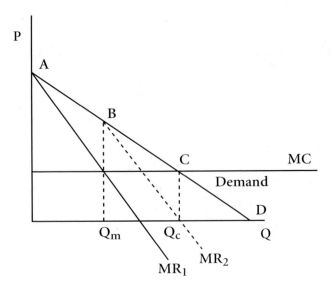

Now firm 2 has to decide how much to produce. Firm 1 is already producing Q_m, and firm 2 assumes that it will maintain this output. Thus, the demand curve facing firm 2 is the industry demand curve, but only the portion to the right of Q_m (the segment BCD in Figure 4-1). In essence, we are just shifting the price axis to pass through Q_m. Firm 2 will choose to operate where MR_2, the marginal revenue curve associated with the remaining portion of the industry demand, is equal to MC, and will supply half of the remaining demand, or one fourth of the competitive output.

This is not an equilibrium, because firm 1 assumed that firm 2 would produce nothing, which is obviously no longer correct. So firm 1 has to reconsider its profit maximizing choice, and will reduce its output. In turn, firm 1's new choice will lead firm 2 to reconsider its decision, and increase its output (because firm 1 is no longer supplying as much). The market reaches equilibrium when each firm determines its profit maximizing output on the assumption that its rival will not change output, and that assumption is correct. This occurs when each firm produces one third of the competitive output, so total output is two thirds of what a competitive industry would produce.[2] Because output that falls short of the competitive output represents a deadweight loss to the economy, the Cournot duopoly result is better than the monopoly outcome (half the competitive output), but worse than the perfectly competitive outcome.

---

[2]It is much easier to find the equilibrium algebraically. Suppose $P = 100 - Q$, and $MC = 40$. Substituting $Q = Q_1 + Q_2$, firm 1 wants to maximize its profits, $PQ_1 = (100 - Q_1 - Q_2)Q_1$. It does so by setting marginal revenue equal to marginal cost, or $100 - 2Q_1 - Q_2 = 40$. The profit maximizing choice for firm 1 obviously depends on Q_2. Rearranging, we have $2Q_1 = 60 - Q_2$, or $Q_1 = 30 - .5Q_2$. This is firm 1's reaction function, which specifies its profit maximizing output choice for any output firm 2 chooses. Because the firms are identical, firm 2's reaction function is $Q_2 = 30 - .5Q_1$. Also because the firms are identical, in equilibrium, $Q_1 = Q_2$. Using firm 1's reaction function, this means that in equilibrium, $Q_1 = 30 - .5Q_1$, or $1.5Q_1 = 30$, or $Q_1 = 20$. The competitive output would occur where $P = MC$, which means $100 - Q = 40$, which in turn means $Q = 60$. Thus, each firm produces one third of the competitive output, and total output is two thirds of what perfect competition would produce. With constant marginal costs, we would obtain the same result − each firm produces one third of the competitive output − for any linear demand function.

The results for two firms can be extended to any number of firms. If there are N firms in the industry with linear market demand and constant marginal costs, in equilibrium each firm will produce $1/(N + 1)$ of the competitive output, and total output will be $N/(N + 1)$ times the competitive output. The more firms there are in the industry, the closer we will get to the perfectly competitive ideal, but we will never get there exactly. Price will remain above the competitive price, and firms in the industry will earn positive profits. Moreover, profits will be higher if there are fewer firms in the industry.

Figure 4-2. Bertrand duopoly.

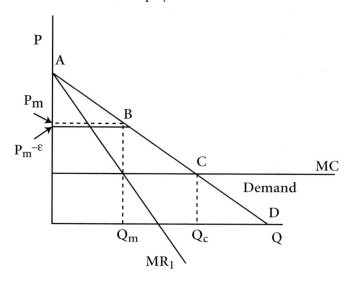

A radically different picture of equilibrium in oligopolistic markets emerges from the Bertrand model of oligopoly behavior. In this model, each firm assumes that its rival will maintain its *price*, rather than its quantity. As in the Cournot model, we assume that the firms are identical and face the industry demand. The situation is depicted in Figure 4-2.

As with the Cournot model, we can see the logic of the Bertrand model most clearly if we imagine sequential decisions by the firms. Firm 1 chooses first, and again chooses the monopoly price and quantity. Firm 2 now believes that firm 1 will maintain its price; if so, firm 2 can reduce its price by a small amount and take over the entire market. Firm 1 will be left with no sales at all. Given firm 2's price, firm 1 will reason that a small reduction in price will allow it to recapture the entire market, and it will therefore cut its price to undercut firm 2. It is easy to see that this competitive interaction will continue until no firm has anything to gain by reducing the price—that is, until price equals marginal cost, the competitive equilibrium. At that point, price reductions by either firm would result in losses. Even with only two firms in the market, neither firm will earn profits in equilibrium.

Given that oligopoly theory may, or may not, imply a relationship between concentration and profitability, what are we to make of the observed correlation between highly concentrated industries and higher profitability? There are at least two possible explanations, with very different implications.

B. Concentration and Collusion

One possibility is **collusion**. In highly concentrated industries, with a small number of large players, it may be easier for the leading companies to agree what price to charge, either explicitly or implicitly. As discussed in the next section, explicit agreements to set price are illegal under the antitrust laws, but firms may be able to coordinate their actions informally to maintain higher prices. With a smaller number of firms, reaching any agreement is easier, and a price fixing agreement is no different. Of course, if the firms do collude, they will behave as a single firm and will therefore restrict output enough to set the monopoly price.

There are, however, important constraints on the possibility of collusion in the marketplace, particularly in a world where such agreements are illegal under the antitrust laws. First, each participant privately has a short run incentive to cheat. From each firm's perspective, it will always be more profitable in the short run to let other firms restrict their output to maintain a supra-competitive price, but expand its own output to take advantage of the higher price.

Consider our duopoly example, with two identical firms and marginal cost of zero. At the industry profit maximizing price and quantity, we know that the extra revenue from a small price reduction will just equal the loss in revenue on the units that could have been sold at a higher price. The situation is shown in Figure 4-3.

Figure 4-3. The gain from cheating in a duopoly.

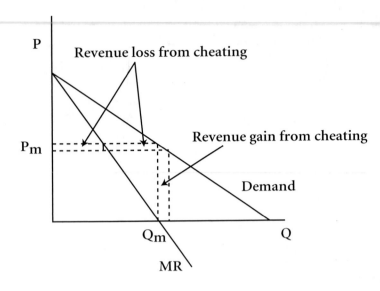

Each firm individually, however, will only bear half of the revenue loss from a small price reduction if its rival maintains its own output, but it will receive all of the revenue gains. Thus, each firm has a private incentive to expand its output.

Of course, if all participants decide to cheat, a price fixing agreement will quickly dissolve, and firms will lose the long term benefits of maintaining the agreement. If the agreement is expected to last long enough, these long term benefits may outweigh the short term gains from cheating.

Collusion becomes even more difficult when firms are not identical. Firms with lower costs will want a lower price and a larger output than firms with higher costs, for example, a difference that can greatly complicate agreement on a price.

A second constraint on the possibility of collusion is the threat of **entry**. If collusion produces higher profits, those profits will attract other firms to try to enter the industry. Unless there is some barrier to entry, an industry cannot sustain supra-competitive prices for long. Barriers to entry might include government licensing requirements, patents, or the high capital costs of entry. If entry is easy, however, there is little reason for policy to be concerned about concentration.

Actual entry will reduce prices because it will expand total output in the industry. But the potential for entry may constrain prices as well, even if no entry actually occurs. Because higher prices would make entry more attractive, firms already in the industry may find it more profitable in the long run to keep prices lower than they would otherwise, thereby reducing the risk of entry. Thus, either actual entry or the potential for entry can limit collusive behavior.

C. Concentration and Efficiencies

Another interpretation of the relationship between concentration and profitability is also possible. In this view, the positive relationship exists because of **dynamic efficiencies** that lead to both higher levels of concentration and higher levels of profitability.

Suppose that a particular firm develops a competitive advantage. Perhaps it has developed a new and more efficient process, or figured out a way to use less of critical raw materials. This cost advantage will make the firm more profitable. Whatever the source of its advantage, the firm is also likely to grow, and increase its share of the market. As its market share increases, however, concentration in the industry is also likely to increase. Even if the firm was small initially, if its advantage persists it will eventually become large enough that its continued growth increases industry concentration. Thus, the initial innovation creates both higher levels of profit, and a more concentrated industry. Empirical studies suggest that somewhere between half and two thirds of the profit advantage of more concentrated industries is due to such cost reductions, rather than price increases.

Even with some efficiency loss from supra-competitive prices, we may still be better off with more concentrated industries than with the alternatives. One primary reason is the existence of economies of scale. If average total costs are declining throughout a significant portion of the total industry output, the market may not be large enough to support very many firms operating at the minimum of average total cost. If we insist on more firms, average total costs will be higher, because firms cannot achieve all of the available economies of scale. We may have fewer losses due to output restrictions, but we will also have more losses because we are not producing at minimum average cost.

The extreme form of economies of scale is the natural monopoly problem. If average costs are continuously declining at all quantities, it will be cheaper to produce in a single firm. A common example is retail distribution of electricity or natural gas. It would make no sense to build another network of power lines or natural gas pipelines to facilitate competition; it is cheaper to distribute the product through a single firm. The result, however, may be some losses due to monopoly pricing.

II. ANTITRUST POLICY

A. Goals and Objectives

There are two primary goals of the antitrust laws. One goal is to improve economic efficiency: to advance the goal of maximizing consumer welfare as judged by consumers. From the perspective of the efficiency goal, practices should be permitted if they enhance consumer welfare, and restricted otherwise. Most economists would agree that this is the most important goal of antitrust.

A second goal is to preserve a competitive market structure. Seen from the perspective of this goal, antitrust is an incentive compatible approach that simply seeks to assure enough firms so that normal market forces can work to achieve the best outcome for consumers.

In many cases, these goals are entirely consistent. Preserving a competitive market structure will, in general, improve economic efficiency, and enhancing efficiency will usually mean we want to restrict consolidations that would seriously threaten a competitive market. In other cases, however, these goals are in tension. If there are significant cost reductions from a merger, for example, the efficiency goal may argue that the merger should be approved. If the merger involves two large firms in an industry with few other large players, however, its approval may undermine the competitive market structure. One goal or the other must take precedence.

The merger between AT&T and T-Mobile that the Justice Department blocked in 2011 may be an example of the tension between goals. AT&T was the number two firm in the cell phone industry, and T-Mobile was number four. If combined, the merged entity would have replaced Verizon as number one. Thus, the Justice Department argued, the merger threatened the existence of the competitive market structure and should be stopped. On the other hand, the merger arguably would use the scarce spectrum available for broadband services more efficiently, particularly in markets like New York where high levels of demand mean that service is sometimes degraded. Thus, the merger might have increased consumer welfare.

Antitrust law is primarily concerned with agreements and combinations in any form between otherwise independent firms. If a firm becomes large because of internal growth, we can have considerable confidence that the growth occurred because the firm had some competitive advantage over its rivals. Thus, internal growth is presumptively efficient. If a firm grows through mergers and acquisitions, however, it may reflect efficiency improvements that benefit consumers, but it may also reflect the desire to acquire a large enough share of the market to effectively control it, which would reduce consumer welfare.

B. The Principal Antitrust Statutes

Although there are a number of laws that can be considered as part of the antitrust laws, there are two primary statutes that are the focus of most cases and investigations: the Sherman Act and the Clayton Act. They are enforced by both the Department of Justice and the Federal Trade Commission. Both agencies can bring civil enforcement actions, but only the Department of Justice can bring criminal actions. There are also private rights of action under the principal antitrust statutes, and successful plaintiffs can collect three times their actual damages.

1. The Sherman Act

The Sherman Act, passed in 1890, is the original antitrust law and one of the earliest federal attempts to regulate the national economy. Section 1 of the Act prohibits contracts, combinations, and conspiracies "in restraint of trade." This language gave early courts some difficulties. After all, any contract between a buyer and a seller, particularly a long term contract, restrains trade in some sense, because it means that whatever quantity the buyer agreed to take will not be available to other sellers in the market. Surely, however, Congress did not intend to ban all contracts. Thus, the courts created a distinction under Section 1 between so-called per se violations and cases that are judged under the rule of reason.

Per se violations are those where the government need only prove that the firms engaged in certain conduct. Naked price fixing, for example, is a per se violation. If the government can show that the firms agreed on a price, that is the end of the inquiry. There is no need to assess whether the agreed price was "good" or "bad;" the mere fact that it was agreed upon establishes a violation. Top officials of companies found guilty of price fixing are frequently prosecuted criminally, and frequently sent to prison.

The rule of reason requires a broader inquiry into the competitive effects of the conduct or practice at issue. In these cases, the court must evaluate the costs and benefits of the practice to consumers. If, on balance, a practice improves consumer welfare, it is permissible under Section 1, even if it is a contract or agreement that otherwise restrains trade.

For example, there are thousands of private "consensus" standards in use throughout the American economy. These standards govern a wide range of product characteristics. Standards specify the sizes of nuts and bolts, for example, along with the thread counts. The result is that a nut from one manufacturer will fit on the bolt made by another. There are also product safety standards, standards for the physical and chemical properties of motor oils, standards to ensure that different components of a complex system are compatible, and a host of others.

As agreements among competitive firms, product standards are subject to suspicion under the antitrust laws. One way to raise price, for example, might be to agree not to produce a low cost version of a particular product. A standard that the low cost version could not meet might be a way to implement this agreement. On the other hand, many standards clearly increase competition, as in the case of the standardized sizes of nuts and bolts. Thus, attempts to attack private standards must be judged under the rule of reason to determine whether, on balance, they advance competition or impede it.

Per se rules can be thought of as proxies for efficiency. If a per se rule identifies a practice that is almost always inefficient, it can enable courts to avoid the costs of a detailed inquiry into the competitive consequences. It is enough that the practice occurred. Again, price fixing is a good example. Indeed, price fixing is one of the relatively few practices where per se rules are still important. Over time, courts have tended to evaluate more and more cases under the rule of reason.

Section 2 of the Sherman Act prohibits "monopolization" or "attempts to monopolize." Note that what is prohibited is an action, not the state of being a monopoly. A monopoly achieved by a successful invention or a superior product or a cost advantage does not violate the Sherman Act. Monopolization requires some action to preserve or obtain a monopoly. Usually this is some action that is itself thought bad, such as selling a product below cost, but in the case of a firm that already has monopoly power in a market, even actions that other firms might be allowed to take may constitute monopolization if they have the effect of preserving the monopoly. For example, one part of the government's 1998 monopolization case against Microsoft challenged restrictive licensing provisions, such as not allowing computer manufacturers to change the look of the Windows desktop. Such a licensing provision would be of no concern, however, if Microsoft did not already have market power.

2. The Clayton Act

Before the Sherman Act was passed, the most common way for firms to combine was through trusts, which are essentially contractual agreements between firms that remain nominally independent. When the Sherman Act made this approach illegal, firms tried a new approach—they merged, becoming a single entity. Since there was only one firm, the courts ruled, there could be no combination or conspiracy, and hence no violation of the Sherman Act.

Congress did not like this result, and in response passed the Clayton Act in 1914. Although the Clayton Act has a number of different provisions, our focus will be on Section 7, which prohibits any merger that "substantially decreases competition or tends to create a monopoly." The same prohibition applies regardless of how the transaction is structured. A complete merger, a purchase of assets, or acquisition of another company's stock are all subject to the same standard.

Merger reviews are governed by the Hart-Scott-Rodino Antitrust Improvements Act ("HSR"), originally enacted in 1976. Before then, the government found that even if it won a challenge to a merger, by the time the case was resolved the companies had long since consummated the merger. Breaking up the company to restore an effective competitor often proved extremely difficult—a problem that was referred to as "unscrambling the eggs."

Under HSR, companies must notify the government prior to the consummation of a transaction, and provide basic information about the competitive overlap of the parties to the deal. Either the Antitrust Division of the Department of Justice or the Federal Trade Commission a specified amount of time (usually 30 days) to review the deal. If the government has questions about the transaction, it can make a "second request" for additional information, and can take additional time (again, usually 30 days but frequently extended by mutual agreement) to further consider the transaction. Typically, fewer than five percent of transactions are subject to a second request.

If the government believes the merger would violate the Clayton Act, it can then go to court to seek a preliminary injunction to block the merger pending a judicial determination of whether the merger violates the law. The court will grant the injunction if it finds that the government is likely to prevail on the merits. Usually, the court's decision about the preliminary injunction is the end of the matter. If the government wins, the parties usually decide that the deal is not worth the costs of litigation to defend it. If the government loses, it generally either abandons its challenge or agrees to a consent agreement that allows most of the transaction to proceed.

III.   THE MERGER GUIDELINES

The Department of Justice first adopted merger guidelines in 1968 to offer more guidance to businesses about which mergers were likely to be subject to challenge. The premise of the original guidelines was that nearly any appreciable increase in concentration as a result of a merger was likely to result in a challenge. Nonetheless, they were a first, tentative step to import more careful economic analysis into merger policy. The guidelines have been revised several times since, most recently in 2010, with each successive revision increasing the emphasis on economic analysis. The guidelines have been influential in the courts as well, and judicial decisions have increasingly recognized economic efficiency in antitrust analysis.

Each revision of the merger guidelines has reduced the emphasis on the presumption that any increases in concentration are bad. The 2010 revisions emphasize that the objective is to assess the "competitive effects" of a proposed merger, using multiple sources of evidence and a variety of analytical tools. Nonetheless, an examination of the structural effects of a merger remains at the heart of the guidelines.

The goal of merger analysis is to determine whether the resulting new firm will have the ability to restrict output and raise prices for consumers. Merger review is conducted product by product, and market by market. Often, merger partners overlap in some products and in some geographic areas, but not in others. Conceptually at least, significant adverse effects in any product in any market are enough to block the merger. In practice, however, the anticompetitive effects of limited overlap are usually resolved by an agreement to divest certain assets to another firm, thereby avoiding the problem.

The primary measure of market structure used in antitrust analysis is a concentration measure known as the Herfindahl Hirschman Index, or the HHI. The index is defined as the sum of the squares of the market shares (in percentage points) of all of the firms in the market. If the market is monopolized, one firm has 100 percent of the market, and the HHI is 10,000. If there are five equal sized firms, each with 20 percent of the market, the HHI is 2,000.

The HHI has its roots in the Cournot oligopoly theory discussed above. It is attractive because it gives greater weight to a firm with a larger market share, compared to the standard four firm concentration ratio. It is also a "numbers equivalent" index, because 10,000 divided by the HHI gives the number of equal sized firms that would produce the same value of the index.

Before we can calculate the HHI, however, we need to define the product market. The "market" should include all of the products that are substitutes on the demand side. That is, the market should include the product of interest, along with any other products that customers are willing to substitute for that product in response to a price increase. If, for example, the merger partners both sell the same product, but perfect substitutes for that product are readily available, the combined firm will have little ability to raise price. If it does so, consumers will simply switch to the substitute product. The 2010 revisions to the merger guidelines placed less emphasis on the definition of the market than earlier versions, although it remains a key issue if a merger challenge (or other antitrust action) goes to court.

The government prefers a narrow definition of the market, which tends to produce higher market shares for the combined firms; firms usually argue that the market is actually broader. Some "markets" are quite narrowly defined. In the 1998 monopolization case against Microsoft, for example, the market was defined as operating systems for Intel-compatible personal computers. Defined this way, Microsoft's market share was 95 percent. Adding in Apple's operating system would reduce Microsoft's share to 80 percent. Adding in operating systems for non-PC devices such as games and phones would have reduced its share still further.

A key concept in identifying an appropriate market definition is the "hypothetical monopolist" test. This test asks whether a single firm that controlled all of the production in the market as defined would find it profitable to impose a "small but significant non-transitory increase in price," known as a "SSNIP." In practice, a SSNIP is usually a price increase of five percent. If a monopolist would find such a price increase was unprofitable, the market is too narrow, and additional products need to be added. But if a monopolist could profitably raise the price, then changes in the structure of the market as a result of the merger could potentially reduce competition and result in price increases for consumers. Essentially, the hypothetical monopolist test adds products, one at a time, to obtain the smallest group of products where a monopolist could profitably raise price.

Once the product market is defined, the analysis considers the appropriate geographic market. Many markets are national, but others are more limited in scope. Geographic markets are usually based on the location of suppliers, and are largely determined by transportation costs for the good in question. Geographic markets can also be defined based on the location of customers, when goods are sold on a delivered basis. As with product markets, the same incremental approach to determining which areas are part of the market is used, to identify the smallest geographic area in which a monopolist could profitably raise the price.

Once the relevant markets are defined, it is possible to calculate the HHI for the market, and the change in the HHI that would result from the merger. Both the HHI after the merger and the increase in HHI that results from the merger are relevant to the decision about whether to try to block the merger.[3] The possibilities are indicated in Figure 4-4.

Under the guidelines, any merger is likely to be approved if the post-merger market is unconcentrated. Similarly, mergers that increase HHI by less than 100 points face little risk regardless of the level of concentration. In a moderately concentrated market, mergers that increase the HHI by more than 100 points face a significant risk of challenge, as do mergers that raise HHI by 100 to 200 points in a highly concentrated market. If the merger increases HHI by more than 200 points in a highly concentrated market, it is presumed

[3]The increase in the HHI can be calculated by subtracting the HHI before the merger from the HHI after. An easier solution, however, is that the increase in the HHI is equal to twice the *product* of the market shares of the merging firms. Thus, if a firm with 5 percent of the market merges with a firm with a 10 percent share, the increase in the HHI is $2 \times 5 \times 10 = 100$ points.

Figure 4-4. The likelihood of challenging mergers based on structural characteristics.

	Post Merger HHI	Increase in HHI	Likelihood of challenge under Merger Guidelines
Unconcentrated	HHI < 1500	—	Unlikely to raise concerns
Moderately Concentrated	1500 < HHI < 2500	< 100	Unlikely to raise concerns
		> 100	"potentially raise significant competitive concerns and often warrant scrutiny."
Highly Concentrated	HHI > 2500	< 100	Unlikely to raise concerns
		100 to 200	"potentially raise significant competitive concerns and often warrant scrutiny."
		>200	"presumed likely to enhance market power"

to have anticompetitive effects. These thresholds are slightly relaxed from previous versions of the guidelines, expanding the number of mergers that are unlikely to raise concerns and reducing the cases in which anticompetitive effects are presumed likely.

When the structural changes due to the merger indicate that there may be a problem, a key consideration is entry. If an increase in price as a result of a merger would result in rapid entry, there is little risk of adverse effects on competition or of price increases to consumers regardless of the level of concentration. The antitrust agencies consider firms that would enter rapidly and easily in response to a SSNIP to be market participants, and assign them a market share (based on their potential sales) in calculating the HHI. Other firms, however, may also enter, and if doing so is sufficiently easy, the prospect of entry may alleviate concerns about anticompetitive effects. To do so, entry must be timely (rapid enough to make a course of action that would attract entry unprofitable in the long run), likely (profitable, even after accounting for costs that the entrant could not recover if it later exits), and sufficient to counteract the anticompetitive effects of the merger. Entry that would lead to a new competitor at least as large as one of the merger partners would be sufficient, but entry by several smaller competitors is also sufficient if they would not face any significant competitive disadvantage. The assessment of the timeliness, likelihood, and sufficiency of entry is based largely on the actual history on entry in the market.

Apart from structural considerations, merger analysis is also concerned with the possibility of "unilateral effects" that may reduce competition, even in a market that appears to be structurally competitive. Concern about unilateral effects has increased considerably over the years, and is a frequent focus of merger challenges.

Unilateral effects arise when an important pricing constraint on one product involved in the merger is that sales would be diverted to a product made by the other merger partner. Suppose, for example, that Firm A sells product X. If Firm A tries to raise the price of X, significant sales would be diverted to product Y, made by firm B, but diversion to other products in the market would be smaller. From Firm A's point of view, the diversion of sales to product Y may make a price increase unprofitable. If A and B merge, however, the diversion of sales to product Y is a less effective constraint on the price of X, because the merged firm will earn more as a result of the increased sales of product Y. Thus, the merged firm may find it profitable to raise the price of X where a separate firm would not.

Even if a merger increases market power and leads to a price increase in the relevant market, it may still be beneficial to society as a whole if it creates efficiencies. Suppose, for example, that without a merger, two firms have the same average total costs of AC_0, and that there is enough competition in the market to force the price down to AC_0. After the merger, costs fall to AC_1, but because competition is reduced, the merged firm is able to increase price from P_0 to P_1. The reduction in output creates a deadweight loss for consumers, equal to the shaded triangle in Figure 4-5. The reduction in average costs, however, creates an efficiency benefit given by the shaded rectangle in the figure. It is easy to see that even with an adverse effect on competition the merger may increase economic efficiency if there is a large enough decline in costs.

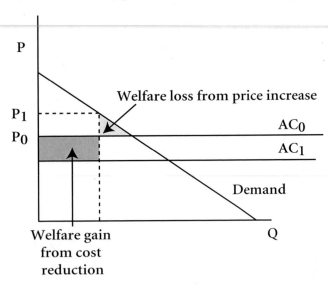

Figure 4-5. Efficiency gains and welfare loss from merger.

Antitrust policy recognizes the possibility that mergers may create net economic benefits, but it has generally been skeptical about claims that such efficiencies exist. Under the merger guidelines, efficiencies must be "merger specific" before they will be considered—that is, the claimed efficiency must be likely to result from the merger, and unlikely to occur except through the merger or some other mechanism with comparable anticompetitive effects. Moreover, the merger partners must document the gains in a way that the antitrust agencies can verify the likelihood and magnitude of the efficiency, how and when it would be achieved, and why it is merger specific. Doing so is not an easy task. The agencies have most often recognized efficiencies that result from shifting output among different production facilities in a way that reduces the marginal cost of production; they have generally been skeptical of efficiencies resulting from procurement, management changes, or capital costs.

If there are efficiencies, they may be enough to eliminate any anticompetitive effects. In the case of unilateral effects, the fact that sales diverted to another product of the merger partners will not constrain price increases is an upward pressure on price. Any efficiencies that result, however, are a downward pressure on price. If the downward pressure is great enough, the net effect may be lower prices for consumers.

The merger guidelines indicate that the agencies are most likely to recognize efficiencies in cases where the anticompetitive consequences of the merger are relatively small. When the adverse effect on competition is greater, efficiencies must be significantly greater as well to allow the merger to go forward.

However strong the business case for a merger or acquisition, it may be thwarted by antitrust concerns. Firms contemplating a transaction need to be aware of the potential antitrust implications, because the costs of a failed merger effort can be substantial.

IV. Single Firm Conduct—Monopolization and the Microsoft Case

Many recent antitrust controversies involve conduct by a single company with significant market power. The government, urged on by competitors, has been particularly vigilant about conduct in technology industries. Attention first focused on Microsoft, which led the Department of Justice to file its first monopolization case in many years. More recently, attention has shifted to Google, which has been the subject of numerous complaints by competitors and is currently subject to a Federal Trade Commission investigation.

A. The Politics of Antitrust

In its early history, Microsoft believed that its fate would be determined by the market, not the government. Based on this belief, it largely avoided the political process. Indeed, it did not even have a government affairs office in Washington until 1995. Competitors, however, notably Sun and Novell, were urging the government to investigate Microsoft, and investing in legal and economic consultants to develop a theory of an antitrust violation that the government might be willing to pursue. In 1991, the FTC launched an antitrust investigation of the company.

In 1993, the staff's recommendation for an antitrust complaint came to the Commission, but the Commission deadlocked 2-2 about whether to proceed. In an ordinary case, that would have been the end of the matter.

Given the visibility of the matter, however, the Commission referred the investigation to the Department of Justice, something it has never done before or since. The Department negotiated a narrow agreement with Microsoft, which primarily restricted the use of blanket licenses for original equipment manufacturers ("OEMs"). Under these licenses, computer manufacturers paid for a license based on the total number of computers they sold, rather than on the number of computers that actually had a Microsoft operating system installed. The government argued the practice was anticompetitive, because it forced manufacturers to pay Microsoft for an operating system license even if it actually installed a different system. In 1997, DoJ sued Microsoft alleging violations of the consent agreement, but it lost a key appeals court ruling.

In 1998, DoJ filed a new, broader antitrust case, alleging violations of Sections 1 and 2 of the Sherman Act. The government's central charge was that Microsoft was tying the sale of its Internet Explorer web browser to the sale of its operating system. It also engaged in a variety of practices to protect its operating system monopoly from potential competition, and attempted to monopolize the browser market. A group of 19 state Attorneys General filed a companion suit, but they also alleged that Microsoft was attempting to monopolize the applications market with programs such as Microsoft Office. At trial, the DoJ largely prevailed, and the judge proposed to break up Microsoft into an operating system company and a separate applications company. On appeal, however, the appeals court reversed on key elements of the decision, and remanded the case to a different district court judge. Rather than re-try the case, in 2002 the government negotiated a relatively narrow consent agreement that addressed specific practices it had challenged. The states continued to litigate, but ultimately lost their case.

B. Network Externalities

A key issue in challenges involving technology companies is network externalities. Network externalities occur when additional users of the product increase the value of the product for others. That is, the more consumers who use the product, the more valuable the product is to each consumer. The clearest example is the telephone. One telephone is not particularly useful, but a telephone connected to a network with many users is considerably more valuable. Moreover, the more extensive the network, the more each consumer is willing to pay for access to the network.

Another example of network externalities involved the format used to record information on video tape when home VCRs arrived on the market. Sony first introduced the VCR with the beta format for recording information. About a year later, the VHS format entered the market from several different manufacturers. The VHS format arguably produced inferior picture quality, but it allowed for longer recording time on a given cassette. If the only use of a VCR was to play back programming the consumer recorded from the television, choice of format would make little difference to anyone other than the individual consumer. If consumers want to exchange tapes, however, network externalities arise. More importantly, if consumers want to buy or rent tapes, they need a format that is sufficiently widespread to encourage movie studios to produce programs in that format. The more consumers use a particular format, the more attractive it is for producers to make products in that format. This is a "virtuous cycle," because the more programming available in a particular format, the more attractive is that format to the consumer. Eventually, the VHS format came to dominate the market, with the beta format largely gone even before VCRs began to be replaced by DVDs.

When network externalities are present, consumers may not switch to a competing product even if it offers better features or a lower price. If they switch to a smaller network, they will lose some of the benefits that network externalities create. Thus, there are "switching costs" for consumers who adopt a competing product that can act as a barrier to entry into the market.

There is an argument in the economics literature about whether markets will make the optimal choice of technologies when network externalities are present. If switching costs are high enough, we may find ourselves "locked in" to an inferior technology simply because it was the first technology that was successful in the marketplace.

One alleged example of the market locking in an inferior technology is the layout of the alphabetic keys on the familiar keyboard. The standard layout, called "qwerty" because those are the first letters on the first row of the keyboard, was originally developed for manual typewriters where the typist's fingers drove a lever to strike a ribbon and print the letter. If two keys on the same side of the keyboard are struck in rapid succession, the levers could get jammed. The qwerty layout reduces the risk of this problem by putting the letters in frequently used combinations on opposite sides of the keyboard. An alternative keyboard layout, called the Dvorak keyboard after its inventor, was designed to optimize typing efficiency and was introduced in the 1930s. Nonetheless, the qwerty keyboard has persisted. Most people who learn typing learn on the qwerty keyboard, because that is what they are most likely to encounter, and most keyboards are qwerty because that is the keyboard most typists learned on. Some have argued that the market has locked in an inefficient choice.

The only problem with the keyboard layout as an example of the market locking in an inferior choice is that it does not appear to be true. There is no good evidence the Dvorak keyboard is actually better. Early studies, some sponsored by Dvorak, were biased in favor of his keyboard, and some argue that some of the studies were perhaps rigged. Later, more carefully controlled studies found no advantage for the Dvorak layout. Thus, generations of typists apparently made the efficient choice.

Switching costs are real, and unless they perceive an advantage large enough to justify the costs, consumers are likely to stay with what they have. Nonetheless, the progression of changes in the software industry makes clear that if they perceive a sufficient advantage, they will make the switch. Wordstar was the original personal computer word processing program, but it was displaced by WordPerfect, and later by Microsoft Word. The initially dominant spreadsheet program, Visicalc, was displaced by Lotus 1-2-3, which was in turn displaced by Microsoft Excel. This progression of predominant programs in a relatively short period of time hardly seems like strong evidence of lock in effects.

Network externalities were a central element of the government's antitrust case against Microsoft. The government argued that there was an applications barrier to entry in the operating system market that effectively prevented the emergence of competing operating systems. Consumers preferred an operating system that could run numerous software applications, because it was the applications that ultimately made the computer useful. Software developers preferred to write their programs for the most popular operating system, at least initially, because that was the largest market. At the time of the case, there were 70,000 different applications programs that would run on a Windows machine. At its peak, there were only about 2,500 applications that would run on IBM's OS/2, the only other significant offering in the market for Intel-compatible personal computer operating systems (the relevant market as the government defined it).

C. The Government's Theories

The government's case against Microsoft involved four major allegations. One allegation was exclusive dealing, in violation of Section 1 of the Sherman Act, based on Microsoft's practice of offering contract terms to OEMs who agreed to provide Internet Explorer as the only browser on their machines. The district court found insufficient evidence to support this theory. Another allegation was that Microsoft was attempting to monopolize the market for Internet browsers, in violation of Section 2. The government prevailed on this theory at trial, but the appeals court reversed. It found that the government had not shown a "dangerous probability" of successful monopolization, an essential element of the offence. This was so because the government had not offered a definition of the browser market, and, in the appeals court's view, had not shown that the network externalities in the browser market were sufficiently important to constitute a significant barrier to entry. The government also alleged that Microsoft engaged in monopolization of the market for operating systems, a Section 2 violation, and that it engaged in "tying" by requiring purchasers of the operating system to also purchase the Internet Explorer browser. These theories are discussed in more detail below.

1. Monopolization

In the district court and on appeal, the government prevailed on its central charge that Microsoft was engaging in monopolization of the market for Intel-compatible personal computer operating systems. Microsoft possessed significant market power; its share of the market was 95 percent. There were significant barriers to entry, because of the applications barrier to entry. Moreover, Microsoft engaged in a number of restrictive practices, directed against competing Internet browsers in general and Netscape in particular, that the government saw as attempts to preserve its monopoly power.

The heart of the monopolization case was the idea that Netscape posed a potential threat to the applications barrier to entry that protected the operating system monopoly. Netscape itself ran on 17 different operating systems. Moreover, it offered what are knows as "application programming interfaces" ("APIs") that enable software developers to instruct the browser to perform various functions in much the same way that the operating system itself makes APIs available to applications developers. Although the operating system itself offered vastly more APIs than a browser, future development of browsers could make more interfaces available. In essence, the government believed, applications programmers could develop applications that would run in the browser, independently of the operating system. If it could cut off this potential development of browsers, Microsoft could preserve the applications barrier to entry, and thereby preserve its monopoly power in the operating system market.

The monopolization allegation was based on a number of specific practices, which the government argued would let Microsoft retain power over the price of operating systems. More importantly, and more controversial, the government also alleged that these practices were a threat to independent innovation. They were thus a threat to independent innovators who might challenge Microsoft in various ways. Two types of practices are illustrative of the charges.

Microsoft's licenses for Windows included a number of restrictive provisions that allegedly protected its market power. OEMs could not delete folders or icons from the desktop. Thus, a manufacturer who offered the Netscape browser would have to leave the Internet Explorer icon as well, leading to potential consumer confusion about why there were two browser folders. OEMs also could not alter the initial boot sequence (the set of programs that runs when the machine is first turned on). This provision prevented OEMs from offering Internet service providers who used Netscape, because Microsoft would not include them in the initial boot sequence. Moreover, OEMs could not otherwise alter the appearance of the Windows desktop, by, for example, providing a larger icon for a service they wished to promote. The appeals court agreed these provisions were unduly restrictive, although they would be harmless in a company with no market power that was simply trying to protect the image of its product. The appeals court, however, allowed Microsoft to retain a license provision that prohibited OEMs from replacing the Windows desktop with a different interface.

The case also challenged Microsoft's integration of Windows and Internet Explorer. In particular, it challenged Microsoft's failure to include Internet Explorer in the list of add/remove programs. Thus, consumers could not delete Internet Explorer. This was a concern to large buyers in particular, who wanted to make sure that all machines in a company had the same configuration to simplify training and help desk management. There was no plausible efficiency explanation for the practice. Similarly, Microsoft included code specific to browsing in files that also contained code for operating system functions. This practice made it virtually impossible to remove Internet Explorer without impairing the functioning of the operating system itself. Because the code was specific to browsing, there was no plausible efficiency justification for including it in the operating system files. Microsoft's practice of overriding the consumer's default browser choice in certain circumstances, however, was permitted. Because Netscape did not support some features that were essential to operating system functions, such as the Windows 98 help function, there was an efficiency justification for using Internet Explorer in such circumstances.

As noted above, the same kinds of arguments are being made today about Google. Practices that would not be considered anticompetitive if employed by any other search provider are the basis of competitor complaints that the government should pursue an antitrust case against Google, because of its alleged market power in the search market. Even if Google has market power in the search market, however, which is by no means clear, there is no clear link between its alleged practices and the preservation of that market power.

2. Tying

The government also alleged that Microsoft was engaged in tying, or conditioning the sale of one product on the customer's agreement to purchase a different product. Microsoft was charged with tying the operating system to Internet Explorer, because it would not sell the operating system unless the customer also purchased Internet Explorer.

The legal theory of tying is that a company with monopoly power in one market might use that power to extend its monopoly into an otherwise competitive market. Because Microsoft had market power in the operating system market, it could, according to the government, use tying to extend its monopoly into the browser market.

From an economic perspective, the "extension of monopoly" theory of tying is not plausible in the vast majority of cases. A firm with a monopoly in one market can charge the monopoly price in that market, but if it requires consumers to pay a higher than competitive price for another product, it will reduce consumers' willingness to pay for the monopolized product. A monopolist can collect one monopoly price, but it cannot collect more than the monopoly price by tying an otherwise competitive product. The extension of monopoly theory is even more problematic when, as in the Microsoft case, the tied product—Internet Explorer—is provided at no additional charge.

A firm can use tying to increase its profits through price discrimination. If different users attach different values to the monopolized product, the monopolist may be able to use tying to charge a higher price to the users who most value the product. The classic case involved IBM, in the days of mainframe computers. IBM tied sale of its mainframe computers to the customer's agreement to purchase punch cards from IBM. At the time, punch cards were the primary means of inputting data into the computer. It is easy to see that the extension of monopoly theory cannot explain this behavior. What buyers value is the services of the computer; those services also depend on the punch cards used to communicate data to the computer. If IBM sells cards at more than the competitive price, it will reduce what consumers are willing to pay for the mainframe computer component of the package by however much it increases the price of punch cards above the competitive level. What tying accomplishes is charging a higher price to users who value the mainframe computer most highly. Because high value users are likely to use the machine more, they will need more punch cards. Charging a lower price for the machine and a higher price for punch cards enabled IBM to charge a higher price to the high-value users.

From an efficiency perspective, this form of price discrimination is likely an efficiency enhancement. A single price monopolist will restrict output to obtain the monopoly price from all users. Users who value the product less than the monopoly price are priced out of the market. Charging a lower price for the computer reduces the number of users who are priced out of the market, thereby increasing output and enhancing welfare. Price discrimination is not always welfare enhancing, but in many instances it reduces the losses that would otherwise result from monopoly power.

The Microsoft case was tried as a violation of the per se rule against tying. To establish a per se tying violation, the government must show that there are two separate products, with market power in the tying product, that consumers have no choice but to purchase the tied product, and that the requirement forecloses a substantial volume of commerce.

The rub in the Microsoft case was the separate product requirement. Nearly any "product" is a bundle of characteristics that could be regarded as separate products. An automobile, for example, commonly bundles an engine, transmission, seats, body, and tires with a sound system, seat warmers, and a GPS navigation system. A computer bundles a display, hard drive, and various other drives such as DVD and CD drives, video chips, memory, and a sound card. Bundling related products offers enormous savings in transactions costs for consumers, who would otherwise have to assemble complex products on their own.

The issue in tying cases is whether the bundle has become so commonplace that it constitutes a single product, or whether it is in fact separate products that are tied. The usual test is whether there is a separate demand for the tied product. One source of information is the behavior of the competitive fringe companies in the industry. If everyone bundles, there is no separate demand for the tied product, and the bundle is most likely efficient.

In the Microsoft case, there was a separate demand for browsers. Some corporate users wanted to standardize their browser across different platforms, which required a browser other than Internet Explorer if their platforms included non-Windows machines. Other operating system producers included browsers with their products, but they allowed purchasers to uninstall the browser components. It was unclear from the trial record whether fringe operating systems offered a different price for the operating system without a browser. Thus, the district court concluded that there was a separate demand for browsers; therefore, browsers and operating systems were separate products. It concluded that Microsoft was guilty of a per se tying violation.

The appeals court disagreed, and sent the case back to the district court for further proceedings. It held that the separate demand test was unfair if there really were benefits of integrating the browser with the operating system, as Microsoft claimed. Unlike Microsoft, other operating system providers had not (yet) invested in integrating the products, and were therefore offering separate products. They were, in essence, still producing operating systems using the old approach, rather than implementing the new integrated approach that Microsoft had pioneered.

Moreover, the appeals court noted, there is a risk in software platform markets like the operating system market that is not present in the typical tying case. The whole point of a software platform is to make useful APIs available to programmers. Programmers, in turn, need to know what APIs are available, and that the APIs they use will in fact be available on a particular user's machine. If they are not, because consumers in effect customized their operating system, applications software may not work as well, if it works at all.

Because the separate demand test was inappropriate, and because of the risks unique to software platforms, the appeals court ruled that the tying allegations should have been tried under a rule of reason approach, rather than as a per se violation. The rule of reason approach would require full exploration of the potential benefits of integration and the potential risks to software developers. The court therefore returned the case to the district court for further proceedings on the tying issue.

Tying has been a central element of the European Union's proceedings against Microsoft. Among other things, the E.U. has required Microsoft to offer Windows with, and without, Windows Media Player. As noted earlier, tying was also a central element of the state actions against Microsoft. Although they did not prevail, the states argued that Microsoft was tying Windows and Microsoft Office, even though it also offered separate prices on both products.

3. A Schumpeterian Perspective

Throughout its early history, Microsoft seems to have been a classic Schumpeterian entrepreneur. It was not particularly an inventor; rather, its key strategy was to license or clone (and later buy) competing or complementary products, make relatively small improvements both initially and over time, and market the improved product to consumers. During the course of that improvement, operating systems came to encompass numerous functions that were originally sold as separate products. Memory management software, SCSI disk drivers, file compression, disk defragmentation and scanning, and fax utilities, to name a few, all started out as separate products that ran on the Microsoft operating system. Today, all are part of that operating system.

Predicting the evolution of a rapidly changing technology is difficult. Browsers are certainly a useful tool, but contrary to the government's theory, they hardly seem likely to threaten operating systems. Cloud computing may be a greater threat, and certainly the Internet will continue to change the competitive landscape. It is difficult to see any real impact of the Microsoft case on the state of competition in those markets, for better or for worse.

V. Summary

In the Cournot model of duopoly, each firm assumes that its rivals will maintain their output and makes its own profit maximizing output choice given that assumption. In equilibrium, that assumption is correct, and each firm produces one third of the competitive output. Industry output is therefore two thirds of the competitive output. The outcome is better than monopoly, but worse than perfect competition. The model can be extended to more firms, but it predicts there will always be some output restriction compared to perfect competition. In contrast, in the Bertrand theory of oligopoly, each firm assumes that its rivals will maintain their price, rather than quantity. The result is the perfectly competitive outcome, even with only two firms.

Empirically, there is a relationship between industry concentration and profitability, with more concentrated industries earning higher profits. One possible reason for this result is collusion: with fewer firms in concentrated industries, it is easier for firms to agree, explicitly or implicitly, on the price. Such agreements are illegal under the antitrust laws. Moreover, each participant privately has a short run incentive to cheat—to expand its output to take advantage of the supra-competitive price, while its rivals maintain that price by restricting their own output. Collusion is more difficult if firms have different cost structures. Finally, collusion is constrained by the possibility of entry, which would compete away any gains from prices above the competitive level.

The relationship between concentration and profitability may also reflect dynamic efficiencies that lead to both more concentration and greater profitability. Firms with a cost advantage are likely to be more profitable, but they are also likely to grow relative to the market. As they do, concentration increases, generating a relationship between concentration and profitability. Concentrated industries may also result from economies of scale, and the cost savings from those scale economies may outweigh any losses that result from higher concentration.

Antitrust policy has two primary goals: to improve economic efficiency, and to preserve a competitive market structure. Although these goals are consistent in many cases, in some cases they are in tension. If significant cost reductions would result from a merger, for example, the goals may be in conflict. Antitrust is primarily concerned with agreements and combinations between otherwise independent firms.

The Sherman Act restricts contracts, combinations, and conspiracies in restraint of trade. Per se violations are those where the plaintiff only needs to prove that firms engaged in certain conduct. Naked price fixing is an example of a per se violation. Per se rules can be thought of as proxies for efficiency, if they apply only to conduct (like price fixing) that virtually always reduces consumer welfare. Other cases are judged under the rule of reason, which essentially requires an analysis of the competitive costs and benefits of the challenged practice. If, on balance, a practice improves consumer welfare, it is permissible, even if it might be considered a restraint of trade. Over time, courts have tended to evaluate more and more cases under the rule of reason. The Sherman Act also prohibits monopolization (not monopoly), which occurs when firms engage in some "bad" act to preserve or obtain a monopoly.

The Clayton Act prohibits mergers that substantially decrease competition or tend to create a monopoly. Firms proposing a merger must notify the government before the transaction is consummated and provide information about the competitive overlap of the parties. The Department of Justice or the Federal Trade Commission has a specified amount of time, usually 30 days, to review the transaction. The government can also extend the time and request additional information. If the government believes the merger will impair competition, it can seek a preliminary injunction to block the deal.

The substantive antitrust analysis of a proposed merger is set forth in the merger guidelines, most recently revised in 2010. The guidelines emphasize that the objective is to assess the competitive effects of a merger. Market structure is measured using the Herfindahl Hirschman Index, defined as the sum of the squares of the market shares of each firm. The product market includes all of the products that are close substitutes on the demand side. The government uses the hypothetical monopolist test to identify the smallest group of products for which a monopolist would find it profitable to make a small but significant non-transitory increase in price, usually five percent. Geographic markets are defined by transportation costs, and again identify the smallest geographic area in which a monopolist could profitably raise the price.

Any merger is likely to be approved in an unconcentrated market, as are mergers that increase the HHI by less than 100 points. There is a significant risk of challenge if the HHI is raised by more than 100 points in a moderately or highly concentrated market. A merger that raises HHI by more than 200 points in a highly concentrated market is presumed to have anticompetitive effects. If a price increase would attract timely, likely, and sufficient entry, the merger may be approved even if the HHI calculations indicate a significant risk of challenge.

Merger analysis is also concerned with the possibility of unilateral effects—i.e., that the merging firms are a significant constraint on each other's pricing decisions because substantial sales would be diverted from one merger partner to the other. A merger would remove this competitive constraint.

Even a merger with anticompetitive effects may enhance consumer welfare if it creates sufficient efficiencies, through cost reductions or otherwise. The government recognizes that efficiencies are possible, but tends to be skeptical of them. The merging parties must show that the efficiencies are merger specific, and document them in a way the antitrust authorities can verify. Efficiencies are most likely to be considered in cases where the potential anticompetitive impact of the merger is relatively small.

Some current antitrust controversies concern monopolization, and particularly the conduct of a single firm with significant market power. Attention first focused on Microsoft, and is currently focused on Google. Microsoft initially ignored the political process, but key competitors consistently urged the government to take action. In 1998, the government filed a broad monopolization case, which eventually led to a settlement in 2002.

A key issue in the Microsoft case and other cases involving technology industries is network externalities, where additional users of a product increase the value of that product to existing users. When network externalities are significant, consumers may not switch to another product even if it offers better features or a lower price. Some argue that markets may lock in an inferior technology when network externalities are present, but the evidence for this proposition is scant. Nonetheless, switching costs can constitute a barrier to entry. In the Microsoft case, the government argued that network externalities created the applications barrier to entry, protecting Microsoft's operating system monopoly.

One key allegation in the government's case was monopolization: the government charged that Microsoft engaged in conduct intended to protect its monopoly from the threat that browsers could reduce the applications barrier to entry. Microsoft's conduct included restrictive license provisions that would have posed no problem if the firm had not been a monopoly. The government also challenged Microsoft's integration of Windows and Internet Explorer.

A second key theory was tying. Tying can be a per se violation of the antitrust laws, because of the fear that a firm can use its monopoly in one product to extent that monopoly to an otherwise competitive product. In most cases there is little economic basis for this fear, because the monopolist can only charge the monopoly price once—a higher price on an otherwise competitive product will reduce consumers' willingness to pay for the monopolized product. Tying is better understood as a form of price discrimination, charging a higher price to users who value the monopolized product most highly. Such price discrimination frequently is welfare enhancing, however.

The tying case against Microsoft was tried as a per se violation. A key hurdle in the tying case is the requirement that there be two separate products. The usual test is whether there is a separate demand for the tied product, and in the case of Internet browsers, there was. On appeal, however, the appeals court ruled that the separate demand test was unfair if there really were efficiencies from integrating the operating system and the browser, as Microsoft contended. Moreover, it was concerned about possible risks because of the operating system's role as a software platform for developers. It therefore held that the case should have been evaluated under the rule of reason.

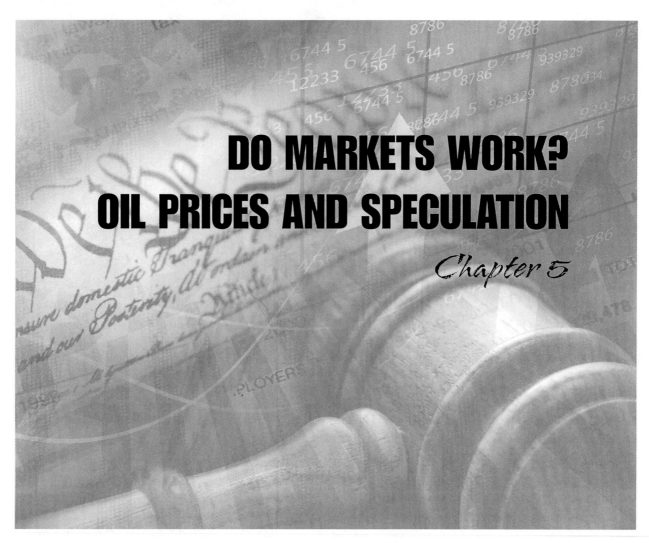

DO MARKETS WORK?
OIL PRICES AND SPECULATION

Chapter 5

In the spring and summer of 2008, crude oil prices rose sharply, followed in short order by gasoline prices. In July 2008, crude oil reached a peak of $147 per barrel on the New York market; gasoline prices peaked at over $4.00 per gallon for regular gasoline. The escalation of oil prices, and their subsequent decline as a recession reduced worldwide demand, is shown in Figure 5-1.

Although prices rose far more sharply in early 2008, the increase was actually the culmination of a long upward trend in prices that began in 2004.

Gasoline prices are politically sensitive. Everyone pays them regularly, and notices when they increase—particularly when the increases are substantial. The media amplifies that attention, often chronicling increases in prices on a day-to-day basis. Moreover, there are no good substitutes for gasoline in the short run, so consumers facing higher prices have no good alternatives other than to pay the price. The only thing to do is to complain, and when constituents complain, politicians listen.

Politically, elected representatives have every incentive to respond to the pain their constituents feel. There is a tremendous desire to "do something." Ideally, doing something would actually reduce the problem and the pain it causes, but even if there are no effective or short-term solutions, there is a political need to respond. That often leads politicians to seek a scapegoat for the increase in prices. There may be nothing of substance that they can do to bring about a short-term reduction in prices, but they can seek to point the finger at some imagined culprit who is responsible for the increases.

Frequently, the culprit is the oil companies. Every significant increase in oil prices has been accompanied by calls for an antitrust investigation to hold oil companies accountable. None of these investigations have ever

Figure 5-1. Oil price trends.

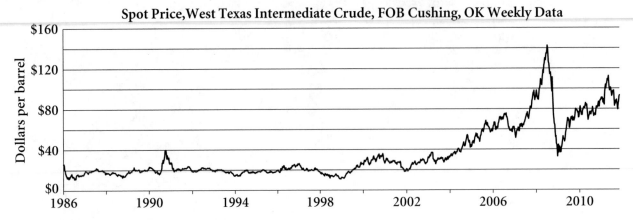

Source: U.S. Energy Information Administration

found evidence of either price manipulation or antitrust violations. When oil prices again rose sharply in late 2010 and early 2011, the Obama administration formed a task force to investigate possible fraud and market manipulation, including Departments of Justice, Energy, Agriculture, and Treasury, along with the Federal Trade Commission, the Commodity Futures Trading Commission, and the Securities and Exchange Commission. It is a safe bet that the next significant increase in oil prices will lead to yet another call for an investigation.

Because the increase in oil prices in 2008 had begun much earlier, Congress had already called for investigations. Indeed, the 2004 nomination of Deborah Majoras to be Chairman of the FTC was put on hold by senators upset about high oil prices. By 2008, the FTC had already reported, indicating that it could find no evidence of market manipulation or antitrust violations.

Still, a culprit was politically necessary, and in 2008 that culprit was "speculation." Numerous politicians attacked speculation and called for various policies to make speculation more costly for its practitioners. These proposals ranged from higher margin requirements for trading to taxes on all commodity market transactions. As oil prices again rose sharply in 2012, politicians again pointed to the role of speculators.

This chapter examines oil markets and the role of speculation and manipulation. It begins with a discussion of oil market fundamentals. Section II discusses futures markets, which are the primary focus of concerns about speculation and manipulation. Finally, Section III considers the relationship between speculation and market performance.

I. OIL MARKET FUNDAMENTALS

Supply and demand are fundamental in any market. The critical characteristic of demand in oil markets, and in the market for gasoline in particular, is that demand is extremely inelastic. The FTC reports that the estimated short-run elasticity of demand for gasoline is somewhere between −.05 and −.1. Thus, a 10 percent increase in price will reduce the quantity demanded by somewhere between 1 percent and only half of a percent. Looking at the market from the perspective of quantity, a 1 percent reduction in quantity will lead to a price increase of 10 to 20 percent. As shown in Figure 5-2, because short-run demand is very inelastic, even small reductions in supply will lead to substantial increases in price.

The short-run inelasticity of demand contributes to the political sensitivity of oil prices. Even small disruptions in supply require large price changes to clear markets. It is easy to see that the price response is out of all proportion to the reduction in supply. It is more difficult to see that the reason for the disproportionate response is the inelasticity of demand. Sharp price increases may be efficient and therefore produce the best possible outcome for consumers, but that doesn't make it any more pleasant to pay those prices.

Figure 5-2. Extremely inelastic demand.

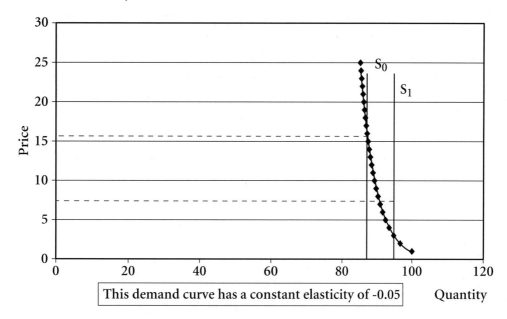

This demand curve has a constant elasticity of -0.05

Even in the long run, oil demand is relatively inelastic. Estimates of the long-run elasticity of demand for gasoline are around –.6. Thus, even in the long run, a 10 percent increase in price will only reduce quantity by 6 percent. Moreover, a 1 percent reduction in quantity will lead to a 1.67 percent increase in price, even in the long run. Because demand is inelastic, quantity reductions require disproportionate price increases to clear the market.

Oil markets are basically competitive,[1] but there is one very large player—OPEC, the Organization of Petroleum Exporting Countries. OPEC sets production quotas for its members, with an eye toward maintaining prices above the competitive level. Its success has been mixed, because (as with any cartel) each country has an incentive to increase its own output beyond its quota. Thus, the restrictions on output and the consequent increases in price are usually less than what the members agreed. Nonetheless, OPEC remains an important factor in determining the market equilibrium.

OPEC is also the world market's primary source of excess production capacity to expand output rapidly. Until relatively recently, there was significant capacity for expansion. In 2002, OPEC had an estimated 6 million barrels per day of excess production capacity. Changes in OPEC output could therefore cushion disruptions in supply or changes in the demand for oil. Over time, however, tightening markets have absorbed much, if not all, of that capacity. By 2008, OPEC's estimated excess reserves were less than 2 million barrels per day, and not all of that may have been available in fact.

Although there is room for doubt about the reliability of the OPEC excess capacity statistics, such measures do not exist for other production areas. In early 2008, however, it is unlikely that excess capacity existed anywhere else in the world. As prices increased to extraordinary levels, the incentive for anyone with oil production facilities was to pump and sell oil as rapidly as possible.

Excess production capacity can cushion supply shocks or supply disruptions directly by replacing the missing supply. Without excess capacity, however, it is consumers who must adjust to changes in supply. Because demand is inelastic, the necessary price changes can be quite large, particularly in the short run.

The rising market price in 2008 also reflected growing world demand, particularly in China and India. Over the period of 2006 to 2008, demand growth in both countries was greater than oil markets had anticipated. In part, increased oil demand reflected the resources needed to power continuing industrial expansions. It also

---

[1]The fact that long-run demand is inelastic is itself evidence that the oil market is not monopolized. A monopolist facing inelastic demand would increase the price. Doing so would increase revenue, and, because output is lower, reduce costs. Thus, the monopolist would continue to increase price until demand becomes elastic. Note that the converse is not true—elastic demand is not necessarily evidence of monopoly.

reflected the growing consumer wealth in those rapidly developing countries. Among other things, that increased wealth led to increased demand for automobiles—and the gasoline needed to power them.

Supply decisions in oil markets are generally characterized by significant lead times. One factor contributing to price increases in 2008 was delays in several major new projects that meant supply was not available when expected. It takes time to drill a new well even in an existing oil field, and it obviously takes even longer to bring a new field on-line. Companies must drill wells, arrange for transportation capacity to bring the oil to market, and locate refinery capacity that can process the oil.[2] Decisions made today may not affect the actual supply available until years in the future.

Supply in 2008 was also reduced because production from several older fields declined more rapidly than expected. In addition, there were supply disruptions in central Asia and the Gulf of Mexico. Moreover, geopolitical uncertainties contributed to uncertainty about future supply. Rebels in Nigeria attacked a key pipeline, for example. Venezuela's future production became more uncertain as Chavez continued to rant against the United States.

Supply decisions, of course, are based in significant part on expectations of future demand and other sources of supply that may be coming to the market. When demand growth is faster than expected, supply decisions based on those predictions will turn out to be inadequate—and prices will inevitably rise. That appears to be exactly what happened in early 2008. With demand rising faster than expected and no substantial excess production capacity, prices had nowhere to go but up.

When crude oil prices go up, of course gasoline prices must rise. Frequently, however, retail prices seem to rise quite rapidly as crude oil prices go up, but then fall more slowly when prices decline. This phenomenon is sometimes called "rockets and feathers": gasoline prices rise like a rocket, but fall like a feather.

The best supported explanation for the rockets and feathers behavior of prices is the nature of competition in retail gasoline markets. Particularly when prices are rising rapidly, a price increase in a highly competitive retail market is likely to lead many consumers to look for a better price. To avoid losing their own customers (and to attract other consumers who are searching for a lower price), retailers have a profit incentive to reduce their margin, thereby keeping the retail price lower than it otherwise would be, even though it is rising rapidly. Falling prices are less likely to prompt consumers to search for a better deal, however, and retailers can and do rebuild their margins to more normal levels. Thus, cost pressures when crude oil prices are rising push retail prices up rapidly, but with some reduction in the retail margin because of retail competition. When crude prices fall, less intensive consumer search behavior reduces competitive pressures and leads prices to decline more slowly.[3]

One other market fundamental relevant to gasoline price increases, especially in response to supply disruptions due to hurricanes or pipeline problems, is that gasoline in one location is not necessarily a perfect substitute for gasoline in another location. The reason is the special fuels required under environmental regulations in certain markets. One major federal program requires oxygenated gasoline in certain markets at certain times. This gasoline burns more cleanly than ordinary gasoline. The other federal requirement is for lower-volatility gasoline in polluted markets in the summertime. This gasoline evaporates more slowly, reducing pollution that stems from evaporation during refueling. In addition, a number of states have their own special gasoline requirements. Although we are familiar with three varieties of gasoline at the local station, there are about 45 varieties of gasoline in the U.S. market. Special fuel requirements apply in 32 designated areas, accounting for 29 percent of total demand. Because fuels in nearby locations are not always substitutable, supply disruptions can have substantial effects on local prices. The normal market response—move gasoline from nearby areas that are not affected—is not always available.

A change in the additive used to produce oxygenated gasoline also had a significant impact on gasoline markets. Until 2006, refiners had been using an additive called MTBE to meet the requirements. There was

---

[2]Differences in the physical and chemical characteristics of different crude oils mean that the characteristics of the refinery must be matched to the characteristics of the crude oil it processes. Adjustments are possible to allow a refinery to handle crude oil with different characteristics, but they too take time.
[3]Gasoline Price Changes and the Petroleum Industry: An Update, Federal Trade Commission, Bureau of Economics Staff Report, September 2011 (available at http://www.ftc.gov/os/2011/09/110901gasolinepricereport.pdf).

concern, however, that MTBE could contaminate groundwater supplies. Faced with significant potential liability, refiners asked for protection from liability for contamination. When Congress said no, refiners substituted ethanol to meet the requirements. Unlike gasoline, however, ethanol cannot be transported by pipeline because it is too corrosive and because it combines readily with water. Instead, ethanol must be trucked to the local market and blended at the last minute. Thus transportation logistics became more complicated, further increasing potential sensitivity to supply disruptions.

II. FUTURES MARKETS

A key factor in production decisions for crude oil (and many other commodities) is the expected price in the future. If the expected future price is higher than the current price, it makes sense to hold inventories, either in tanks or in the ground, to sell at the higher future price. Holding inventories in these circumstances is efficient because it smoothes out the price path over time. Prices are higher today than they would be in the absence of increased inventories, but they are lower in the future than they would be otherwise.

Expected prices at future dates are determined in futures markets. These markets trade standardized contracts for future delivery of a specified good at a specified location. For example, the standard NYMEX contract for crude oil futures specifies delivery of 1,000 barrels of West Texas Intermediate crude oil at Cushing, Oklahoma. There are futures markets for other energy products, many agricultural commodities, and numerous financial products. As the contract delivery date approaches, the price of the futures contract converges to the current spot price for the commodity itself.

For exchange-traded contracts, the exchange clearinghouse is the counterparty to every transaction. Thus, if a person purchases a contract to buy 1,000 barrels of oil in December, it is actually the exchange that is obligated to deliver the oil. Similarly, someone who sells a contract to deliver 1,000 barrels is obligated to deliver the oil to the exchange. The exchange takes no net position in the commodity itself. It will only sell a contract to buy if there is a corresponding contract to sell from another trader. Because of the clearinghouse, however, buyers and sellers do not have to worry about whether the counterparty to the contract will honor it. The clearinghouse takes that risk, which it manages by imposing margin requirements to protect against the possibility of large losses by a trader. The margin requirements are generally based on the trader's net position, which determines the risk that adverse price movements will create losses. The exchange controls the risk that a trader will go bankrupt and default on its position for reasons unrelated to the position itself by controlling who can become a member of the exchange.

Futures contracts are a form of derivative, and are essentially financial instruments. Like other financial instruments, they are typically settled by an offsetting transaction, rather than actual physical delivery of the commodity. Thus, a trader who purchased a contract to buy 1,000 barrels of oil in December will eventually offset that obligation by selling a contract to deliver the same amount at the same time. What remains is a financial gain or loss, but there is no longer an obligation to deliver the commodity. The vast majority of trades are settled by such offsetting transactions. Physical delivery of the commodity, as specified by the contract, is rare.[4]

In addition to organized futures markets, which are regulated by the Commodities Futures Trading Commission (CFTC), similar contracts trade in unregulated forward markets. Forward contacts are customized contracts between identified parties. They allow parties to arrange future terms for commodities that differ from the standardized contracts on futures exchanges in various ways. For example, a trader seeking delivery at a different location than the exchange-traded contract, or for a different grade of the commodity, could only arrange that transaction as a private contract. Like any other private contract, there is always some risk that the other party to the contract will default. Thus, forward contracts allow customization, but they do so at the cost of imposing more risk on the parties than the exchange-traded instruments. In recent years, forward contracts for commodities and "swaps" for various financial transactions have grown substantially.

---

[4]One reason that physical delivery is rare is that those obligated to deliver have an obvious incentive to deliver the cheapest commodity that meets the terms of the contract, which is usually the lowest quality available.

Futures markets enable buyers and sellers in the market for the commodity to transfer the risk of price changes to others. These markets enable traders to "hedge" against the possibility of adverse price changes. By taking offsetting positions in the cash and futures markets, traders can essentially lock in the price for a transaction that will occur on some future date.

Consider, for example, a farmer with a crop expected in the fall. Although the farmer knows the current market price of his crop, he does not know what price it will command when it is actually harvested and delivered to market. The farmer can, of course, take the risk of price changes, hoping that prices will be higher when the crop is harvested. Alternatively, the farmer can use futures markets to lock in the price for his crop today, transferring the risk of price changes to whoever takes the other side of his contract. The farmer would sell a futures contract to deliver his crop at some future date, say, in September. The price received for this contract "locks in" the price he will receive for the crop. If the price increases (compared to the futures contract price), the farmer will suffer a loss when he buys back the contract to settle his position, but he will realize an offsetting gain because of the increase in the price of his crop. Similarly, if the price falls, the farmer will suffer a loss on his crop, but realize an offsetting gain on the futures contract. Thus, profits in the futures market offset losses in the physical commodity market, or vice versa. Either way, the hedging farmer knows today the effective price he will receive for his crop at harvest.[5]

For buyers, hedging can also lock in the cost of key inputs in production. During the oil price run-up, for example, as crude oil hit $140 per barrel, Southwest Airlines was widely reported to have used hedges that enabled it to pay the equivalent of $80 per barrel for jet fuel. As other airlines saw fuel costs soar, Southwest had yet another source of significant cost advantages over other carriers.

As oil prices increased significantly, the hedges paid off for Southwest. Presumably, however, continuation of the same strategy meant that Southwest had effectively locked in higher prices than the current market price when oil fell back to the $40 to $50 per barrel range.

Risk transfer is a private benefit of futures markets, because parties who wish to avoid risk can do so. The total risk, however, does not change. For society as a whole, the risk of price change remains—it is just borne by someone who is more willing to take the risk.

A key function of any market is price discovery, or the process of finding the price that will clear the market. In futures markets, price discovery determines the best estimate of the market clearing price that will prevail at some future date. Futures markets are very effective institutions for aggregating information from numerous private parties to determine the best estimate of the future balance between supply and demand, and hence the price that will clear the market at that future date.

Many traders in futures markets have private information about future supply and demand conditions. Crude oil producers, for example, have private information about likely changes in the condition of their oil fields that is relevant to assessing future supply conditions. Similarly, they know about production and exploration projects that are ahead of schedule or behind schedule, again affecting future supply. Oil refiners have private information about the status of capacity expansions, the need for maintenance, and similar matters likely to affect future supply. Both producers and refiners have their own assessments of future demand, which they use in making investment decisions. Oil users have information about their current needs and how those needs are likely to change over time; pipeline and shipping companies have information about the likely cost and availability of transportation arrangements in the future. All of this information is relevant to assessing the likely future balance of supply and demand, and hence the likely future market clearing price of the commodity.

The private information available to actual and potential traders will influence the positions they take in futures markets. As in any market, those with better information can profit by trading based on that information.

---

[5]The effectiveness of using futures markets to hedge depends in significant part on the correlation between price changes on the standardized contract that trades on the exchange and the actual commodity that matters to a particular buyer or seller. If the prices of the commodity someone wishes to hedge and the exchange-traded contract do not track one another closely, the hedge is less effective, and can result in gains or losses due to changes in the relative prices of the commodity and the contract. Part of the attraction of private forward markets is that, assuming a trader can find an appropriate counterparty, it is possible to write a contract to hedge or transfer the precise risk the trader wants to shift.

A crude oil producer who knows that capacity expansions are behind schedule, for example, knows that future supply will be lower and future prices therefore higher. Buying contracts for future delivery of crude oil will allow the producer to profit from that knowledge, because the contracts can be sold in the future at a higher price. Bringing that information to the market changes the balance between potential buyers and sellers, and increases the price of the futures contract. Thus, the producer's private information is impounded in the current market price of the contract. The current price of the futures contract for delivery on a future date is the best available estimate of the market clearing price on that date.

Price discovery operates more efficiently in more liquid markets. A larger volume of transactions reduces the variability of prices. This is the advantage of standardized contracts on organized exchanges over the private forward market. The larger volume of trade increases liquidity, leading to more efficient price discovery.

III. SPECULATION AND MANIPULATION

A. Speculation

The sharp increase in oil prices in early 2008 provoked concern that somehow the reason for the price increase was speculation. Historically, the most common source of concern about speculation in futures markets has come from farmers, who have frequently complained that speculation was driving crop prices down. Concern about speculation has at times been great enough to provoke legislative restrictions. In 1958, for example, Congress prohibited futures contracts for onions, a prohibition that remains in place today.

The concern in early 2008 focused on financial investors in futures markets, such as pension funds and hedge funds. These investors have no particular stake in the oil market themselves; they are simply making an investment in oil futures. In particular, they were taking long positions in oil, which would profit if the price of oil increased. One popular strategy was investments that mirrored an index of commodities including oil, intended to track the overall movement of commodity prices. Indeed, the prices of numerous commodities rose significantly throughout the first half of 2008.

The argument that speculation was responsible for these increases was essentially an argument that there was a bubble in commodities markets, fed by increased demand from financial investors. According to this story, the influx of demand led inexorably to an increase in price. This is indeed what would have happened if financial investors were buying oil. Instead, however, they were buying oil futures contracts. Unlike oil, futures contracts can be created at will.

Figure 5-3. Perfectly elastic supply.

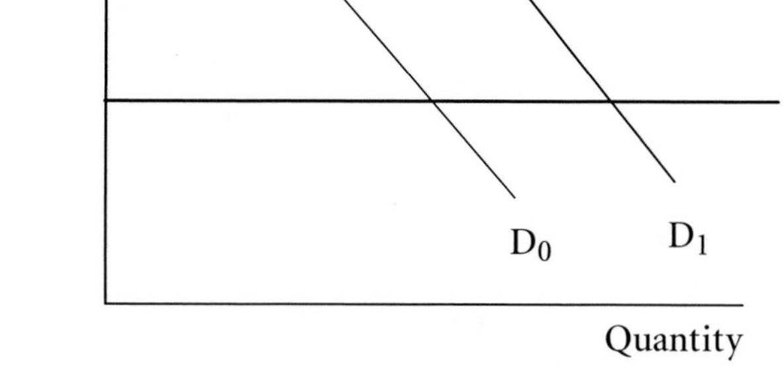

A common economic intuition is that an increase in demand will lead to an increase in price. Although that intuition is correct if the supply curve is upward sloping, it is not correct if the supply curve is flat, as shown in Figure 5-3. If supply is perfectly elastic, the increase in demand will not change the price at all; it will simply increase the quantity traded. Moreover, if the information about future conditions of supply and demand is unchanged, there is every reason to think that supply in futures markets is perfectly elastic. After all, anyone who thinks that the current contract price is too high can sell a contract to deliver oil on the contract date. If they are correct, and the price as the contract expiration date approaches is below the current price, they will profit when they buy back their contract at the lower price. Thus there is no reason to think that more demand for commodity futures from financial investors will increase the price. Of course, if the financial investors have information about future supply and demand conditions indicating that the market clearing price will be higher, the price will rise. That, however, is the normal process of price discovery in futures markets, and there is no reason to think that restricting or discouraging such investments would be useful.

In any event, increased demand in futures market will not necessarily increase the price in cash markets, which depend on the actual quantities demanded and supplied. Futures contracts are financial instruments, linked to the cash markets by the possibility that the contract holder can settle the contract via physical delivery. In the long run, cash prices will only go up if there is a reduced supply or an increased demand for the physical commodity. If it was speculation that drove cash prices to record heights in 2008, someone must have been accumulating significant inventories of actual oil. In fact, however, inventories declined from the middle of 2007, and were at the low end of historical norms by the middle of 2008.[6]

Other facts about the behavior of commodity prices are also inconsistent with the speculation story. If financial investors trying to track commodity price indexes were the driving factor, prices should have increased for all of the commodities in the indexes. Instead, however, prices actually declined or increased only slightly for some futures that were included in popular indexes. Moreover, some commodities not included in futures market indices also experienced substantial price increases, along with commodities for which there was no futures market at all.[7]

In some sense, of course, everyone involved in futures markets is speculating. The future, after all, is not known, and all market participants other than pure hedgers are therefore "speculating" about what the future will bring. That, however, is a useful process, because it allows market participants and other observers to determine the best estimate of future conditions and make their investments accordingly. The concept of a "speculator" who somehow interferes with this process has never been well defined. Even financial investors, with no long-term stake in the commodity itself, may be hedging against the risk of inflation. If inflation increases, commodity prices will likely increase as well. Investors who hold bonds, for example, will see the value of those investments decline as inflation increases, but the loss will be offset by the increase in the value of their commodity holdings.

Most importantly, all *successful* speculation is stabilizing, because it smoothes out the price adjustment path over time. If speculators are correct in believing that prices will increase in the future, prices of futures contracts will tend to increase. If futures prices exceed current prices, there is an incentive to hold on to the commodity today to sell it at the higher future price. That process will raise current prices, but it also means that prices in the future will be lower than they would have been otherwise. We will have more of the commodity in the future than we would have otherwise, when it will be scarcer and therefore more valuable. Thus, successful speculation helps to stabilize prices over time.

Unsuccessful speculation, where the speculator is wrong about the direction of price changes, might be destabilizing. It is also, however, its own punishment—the unsuccessful speculator loses money.

Despite the lack of evidence that speculation causes commodity price increases, as part of the Dodd-Frank Financial Reform legislation, Congress required the Commodity Futures Trading Commission (CFTC) to set limits on the positions that traders can maintain in futures and swaps markets. In October 2011, the Commission adopted its final rule. The rule sets separate limits on positions in the "spot month," the period of time close to the contract expiration date, when physical delivery would have to occur if the contract remains open, and all other contracts. In the spot month, positions are limited to 25 percent of the estimated physically deliverable supplies at the contract settlement point. In other months, a trader's cumulative position is limited to 10 percent of the open interest for the first 25,000 contracts, and 2.5 percent of the open interest for any additional contracts. Although as discussed below the spot month position limit may help to

---

[6]Interim Report on Crude Oil, Interagency Task Force on Commodity Markets, July 2008 (available at http://www.cftc.gov/ucm/groups/public/@newsroom/documents/file/itfinterimreportoncrudeoil0708.pdf).

[7]Scott H. Irwin, Dwight R. Sanders, and Robert P. Merrin, Devil or Angel? The Role of Speculation in the Recent Commodity Price Boom (and Bust), *Journal of Agricultural and Applied Economics*, vol. 41, pp. 377–391 (August 2009).

reduce the risk of market manipulation, there is little reason to believe that the limits will have an appreciable impact on commodity price trends. Their most likely impact will be to reduce market liquidity, and thereby increase price volatility.

B. Market Manipulation

Although there is little reason to believe that speculation impacts commodity prices in any significant way, there are possibilities for traders to manipulate commodity markets in ways that distort prices and create inefficiencies. There is no reliable evidence about the actual incidence of successful manipulations, or of attempts to manipulate commodity markets.

On possible form of manipulation, based on fraud, is straightforward. A trader, who reports false information about commodity supplies, for example, or oil refining capacity, or output, may be able to influence the market price. If a trader falsely reports information that would, if true, mean higher (or lower) future prices, that trader can profit as the market reflects the inaccurate information in the price. These forms of manipulation are prohibited under the Commodity Exchange Act (enforced by the CFTC), and similar provisions allow the Federal Energy Regulatory Commission and the Federal Trade Commission to proceed against fraud-based market manipulation in energy futures markets.

An entirely different form of market manipulation arises from the fact that futures contracts can be settled by delivering (or taking delivery of) the physical commodity at a specified location. If a trader has market power, resulting from a position that is large relative to the amount of the commodity available at competitive prices at the settlement location, he or she may be able to force a higher (or lower) price, and profit as a result.

It is easiest to see the impact of manipulation based on market power in the commonly described strategy of "cornering" the market. In a corner, a trader takes a long position (i.e., they are entitled to physical delivery of the commodity) that is large compared to the supply of the commodity that is available for delivery. This may be done entirely in the futures market, but it may also be combined with a strategy of buying up the available supplies at the delivery location. Rather than liquidating its position as the settlement date approaches, the trader trying to corner the market insists on physical delivery. The result is that the price for the commodity at the delivery location rises, and more of the commodity flows to the delivery location. Traders on the other side of the transaction face a dilemma: they can incur extra costs for transportation of the commodity from somewhere else to the delivery location to satisfy the contract, or they can pay the long trader a premium to liquidate their position. As long as the premium is below the added costs of physical delivery, these traders would prefer to pay the trader who has cornered the market a premium to get out of their contract.

In the aftermath of a corner, there are excess supplies of the commodity at the delivery location. Thus, the price falls, returning to its normal competitive level, and commodities flow out of the delivery market and to other places where they are valued more highly. This fall in price is known as "burying the corpse." If the trader actually had to take delivery on all of his or her contracts, the corner would not be profitable because of this subsequent fall in price. But if the manipulator takes enough delivery to push the cash price up, it can then collect a premium price on the remainder of its futures market position without actually taking delivery.

Thus, a corner leaves clear market evidence. The price rises at the delivery location as the contract settlement date approaches, relative to the normal price relationships between different markets, and relative to the price at different points in time. More of the commodity is moved to the delivery location, resulting in an increase in inventories in that market. After the settlement date, prices in the delivery market fall below normal levels, creating the incentive to move the commodity back to where it was most valuable.

It is also possible to pursue a similar market power manipulation with a short position. A large short can make excess deliveries into the market, driving down the cash price (and therefore the futures price), enabling him to profit on his short futures market position.

The Commodity Exchange Act specifically prohibits attempts to corner the market, but the CFTC's regulatory decisions have made it very difficult to prosecute such attempts. The Commission has rejected the use of the straightforward price comparisons that are the essence of the "corner" strategy, in favor of a far reaching exploration of all possible supply and demand anomalies that may explain the price. Markets, the Commission, has said, are not limited by their historical norms. Moreover, the Commission has given accused manipulators considerable leeway to argue that they did not intend to manipulate the market, and intent is an essential element of the offense. The recently adopted spot month position limits may help to reduce the risk of manipulation, but they are a far more blunt instrument than prosecution of manipulations when they occur, based on the kinds of economic evidence that can relatively easily identify the manipulation.

Although manipulation can be profitable in the short run, it is unlikely to persist, even without regulatory intervention. Anyone who repeatedly tried to corner the same market would find that few traders would be willing to take the other side of their contract. Instead, they would use other markets, or forego the use of futures markets entirely.

IV. Summary

Oil prices are highly visible in the U.S. economy. When they increase sharply, there is considerable political pressure to do something to address the problem—even if there are no effective short-term solutions.

Oil prices rise sharply in response to relatively small reductions in supply because demand, particularly in the short run, is extremely inelastic. A small quantity change requires a large price change to clear the market. Oil markets are basically competitive, although OPEC is a large player. Markets tightened in 2008 because of the fundamentals of supply and demand. Demand growth, particularly in developing countries, was greater than had been anticipated. Supplies were tighter than had been expected, because excess production capacity in the OPEC nations had been largely exhausted, major new projects to produce oil suffered unexpected delays, and some major producing fields declined more rapidly than had been expected. The result was significant increases in price.

Gasoline markets have become more sensitive to disruptions because of environmental regulations requiring special "boutique" fuels to meet clean air standards. Because different fuels are not always substitutable, disruptions in local markets can have greater and longer lasting effects.

The expected price in the future is a key factor in current production decisions. If prices are expected to rise, it makes economic sense to hold on to oil (or any other commodity) today, in order to sell it at the higher future price. Futures markets trade standardized contracts for future delivery. They are basically financial markets, with the vast majority of trades settled by offsetting financial transactions, rather than by physical delivery of the commodity. Futures markets enable market participants to transfer the risk of price change to others who are willing to take that risk. They aggregate the information available to all market participants to form the best estimate of the likely market clearing price at a future date. More liquid markets are more efficient, with less variability in prices.

The political issue surrounding price increases in 2008 centered on speculation by financial investors such as pension funds and hedge funds. These investors were taking "long" positions in oil and other commodities, investments that would be profitable if prices increased. There is little reason to believe that such investments would drive up futures prices, however. Because anyone can sell a contract to supply oil at a future date, if financial investors are betting on a price that is too high, the supply of contracts will simply expand, pushing the price back down. Moreover, all successful speculation is stabilizing, because it smoothes the adjustment of prices over time. Unsuccessful speculation loses money, which is its own punishment.

It is possible to manipulate commodity markets, although there is no reliable evidence of how frequently such attempts occur. One form of manipulation is based on fraud. A trader who disseminates false information relevant to assessing the future state of supply and demand can influence the price, and thereby profit from the deception.

Another form of manipulation arises from market power that results when a trader's market position is large relative to the amount of the commodity that is available for physical delivery at the location specified in the contract. In a market corner, a manipulator with a large long position demands excessive deliveries, pushing up the price of the commodity at the settlement location as the settlement date approaches. Traders on the other side of the transaction must either pay a premium to obtain additional quantities of the commodity to make delivery, or pay a premium to liquidate their futures market position. The manipulator can profit when other traders pay a premium to liquidate, rather than make physical delivery. The cash price temporarily rises at the delivery location, the commodity flows to the delivery location from other places, and the cash price falls after the contract expiration date as the manipulator "buries the corpse" by disposing of the physical commodity.

Both forms of market manipulation are illegal, but the CFTC's approach to manipulation has made it difficult to successfully prosecute attempts to corner the market. Although manipulation can affect short run price relationships, it is unlikely to have a long term impact on the level of commodity prices.

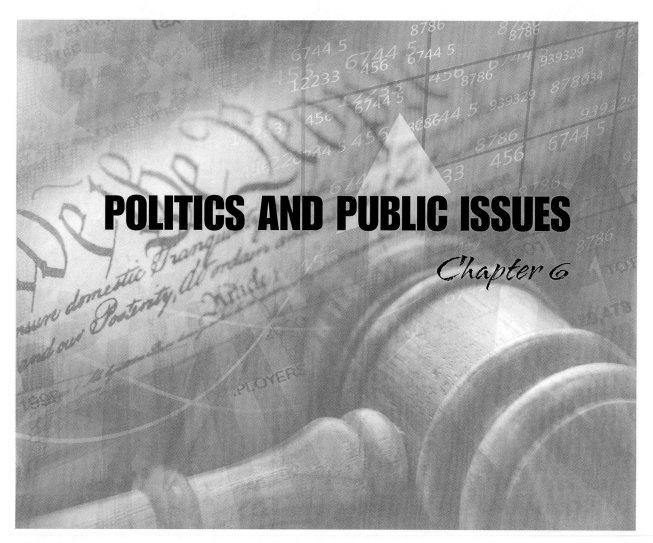

POLITICS AND PUBLIC ISSUES

Chapter 6

All public policy decisions are political. They are not necessarily partisan in the sense of Democrats versus Republicans, or even liberals versus conservatives. However, they are political in the sense that the identity of the winners and losers is critical in determining the outcome. Political considerations are frequently explicit in legislative decisions, and often in presidential or high-level executive branch decisions as well. Even seemingly technical administrative decisions, however, are also heavily influenced by political considerations.

Just as politicians have constituencies that they seek to serve, regulatory agencies have constituencies as well. These constituencies are key sources of political support, and the agency considers their interests in deciding how to proceed. For OSHA, for example, labor unions are an important constituency. The agency is likely to consider union priorities in deciding what issues to pursue. Indeed, OSHA regulations are more likely to affect unionized industries than nonunion industries. Important constituencies for the SEC include the financial community on Wall Street and the top managers of publicly traded companies that are subject to SEC oversight. The SEC takes into account the interests of these constituencies, as discussed in more detail in a later chapter. For the FDA, the public health community is an important constituency.

This chapter considers how a public issue unfolds, and contrasts political decisions with the exchange process of the market economy.

I. THE PUBLIC POLICY PROCESS

Public policy issues develop in a series of stages that are often useful in thinking about how to influence an issue and which issues are worthy of attention. There are no clear divisions between stages, and for some issues two or more stages may occur essentially simultaneously. Nevertheless, the stages are a useful way to think about the issues that a company might confront. Different strategies are appropriate at different stages, and there are different opportunities to participate in the political process at different stages. Usually it is easier to influence an issue early in the process, when opinion is still developing. Even late in the process, however, there are important, frequently utilized opportunities to influence policies.

A. Development: identifying the problem

The first stage of the public policy process is development, or identifying a particular problem as a potential issue for the public. Problems are identified in three different ways.

Probably the most common way that a problem is identified is as a result of some dramatic crisis or event that brings the problem to widespread public attention. The terrorist attack on September 11, 2001, for example, immediately launched a new problem on the public policy agenda. Similarly, the financial crisis in 2008–2009 was a problem that demanded attention. Extreme events such as these are likely to provoke immediate attention and rapid policy change.

Many other public issues and public policies are launched by less catastrophic events that nonetheless bring public attention to a problem. The Enron and Worldcom bankruptcies in 2001 and 2002 as a result of fraudulent financial statements brought corporate governance and accounting issues to the public's attention. The recall of the prescription drug Vioxx when it became known that the drug increases the risk of heart attacks provoked renewed attention to drug safety issues. Contaminated spinach in 2006, jalapeno peppers in the summer of 2008, and peanuts discovered in 2009 provoked considerably more attention to how we regulate food safety and the need for regulatory change. Many current regulatory programs and policies can be traced to dramatic events such as these, which attracted public attention and prompted a demand to "do something."

When dramatic incidents occur, an important analytical question is what systemic failure, if any, provoked the particular incident. In many cases, the problem is actually the result of a bad actor—someone who engaged in conduct that clearly violated existing rules. Enron was clearly such a case. Cooking the books is a well-recognized offense, and Enron's principals were convicted of fraud. Similarly, it seems clear that the peanut company that shipped products despite test results indicating they were contaminated with salmonella was violating clear legal standards.

If a problem results from a bad actor, additional regulatory change may not be necessary or desirable. After all, adding yet another prohibition on conduct that is already illegal is not likely to improve compliance by bad actors. Enforcement against bad actors, however, may not be sufficient to satisfy the political desire to "do something."

A dramatic incident may also stem from problems in the regulatory structure. The financial collapse of 2008 certainly pointed to the need for regulatory changes to try to reduce the risk that such events will happen again. The food safety incidents over the last few years highlighted the limitations of a regulatory system that relied on infrequent inspections. If the problem stemmed from bad rules, as opposed to bad actors, regulatory or policy change is more likely to be appropriate.

On occasion, a dramatic event may trigger a regulatory process that becomes essentially self-perpetuating, leading to a policy change long after the event itself. For example, in December 1977, five explosions in grain elevators caused 59 deaths. At the time, the underlying causes of grain elevator explosions were poorly understood. The 1977 events provoked a study by the National Academy of Sciences that led to the conclusion that better control of grain dust was the key to preventing explosions. In turn, that finding led to a reduction in the incidence of explosions. It also led to the initiation of a rulemaking at the Occupational Safety and Health Administration to set standards for grain elevators. In 1987, 10 years after the dramatic event that triggered the rulemaking, OSHA issued a final rule requiring elevators to control dust.

Absent a dramatic event, an issue may emerge from persistent frictions among different groups in society. If those frictions are significant, they may give rise to the perception that there is a problem that needs attention—that is, a policy issue may be identified. Labor and management have different interests, for example, and frictions between them can lead to identifying a problem that needs attention. Of course, friction and tension between different groups are common and do not necessarily lead to the perception of a problem. But when the frictions are persistent, and the potential consequences important, the source of those frictions may be identified as a problem.

A good example of an issue that emerges from persistent frictions is entitlement programs like Social Security. Social Security has always been a pay-as-you-go system, with taxes levied on current workers providing the money to pay current retirees. When the system was established, and the retirement age set at 65, life expectancy at birth was 62, and about half of those who lived to adulthood died before they reached 65. Moreover, there were 42 workers paying taxes for every retiree, so the pay-as-you-go system was workable. Today, however, life expectancy for a 65-year-old is almost 20 years, and there are only 3.3 workers per beneficiary. Benefit levels have increased substantially as well. Expenses now exceed tax revenues, and will continue to do so indefinitely As baby boomers age, the tension between workers and retirees has led to the identification of a problem—something needs to be done to address the system.

Finally, problems are sometimes identified by policy entrepreneurs. These entrepreneurs may be academics studying a particular issue, interest groups with a stake in the issue, or politicians seeking a politically attractive issue to gain public support. Deregulation of airlines and freight transportation by truck and rail, for example, began with a series of academic studies indicating that regulation significantly increased prices for consumers. Interest groups are in the business of seeking public support for their issues; they can and do make efforts to bring particular problems to the public's attention. Problems such as excessive regulatory burdens or restrictions on foreign trade may arguably emerge from frictions among different interest groups, but they have been pushed by politicians acting as policy entrepreneurs.

B. Politicization: the problem becomes a political issue

Many dramatic events never become political issues. They may matter a great deal to isolated groups, but they never attract sufficient public attention to make the problem an issue in the political process. The politicization stage of the public policy process determines whether an identified problem will disappear (perhaps to reappear later), or become an issue that commands political attention and demands a political response. If an issue becomes politicized, it gets more widespread attention and becomes known to more people. Individuals start to form opinions about the problem and what might be done about it.

A key feature of the politicization stage of the process is competition for media attention. There is competition for attention between groups with different views about an issue, as well as competition between different issues. The media does not pay the same amount of attention to all issues, and a particular issue may get limited attention simply because it arises at a time when there are more pressing or more dramatic events demanding media attention. On occasion it has even been alleged that presidents have launched military missions to distract attention from some domestic political issue.

To attract media attention, interest groups often stage protests or demonstrations. Although the number of people attending may be a crude indication of interest in the issue, the real point of many such events is media coverage. In explaining why the demonstrators are there, the media will also explain the issue—and bring it to the attention of more members of the public.

Interest groups are also an important source of information for the media. Reporters often turn to interested groups as they cover a story, particularly "public interest" groups. Often they seek to find out whether a particular incident or issue is important, and whether it deserves more attention. Groups with an interest in the issue use these opportunities to try to encourage more attention to it. Groups may also seek out reporters to push a particular story.

The interplay between the media and interest groups is particularly important when there is a dramatic event. Groups interested in a policy issue, for whatever reason, will frequently attempt to link their issue to current events. Current events, such as an ongoing outbreak of salmonella poisonings, will attract coverage and attention in any event. Anyone interested in food safety policies has a natural incentive to try to piggyback on that coverage to gain more attention for their issue. Sometimes, as in the salmonella example, the linkage is quite natural, but groups will often attempt to link their issue to events that are much less connected to it. Interest groups follow the adage of Rahm Emanuel (Obama's first chief of staff) that "you never want a serious crisis to go to waste."

In addition to competing for attention with other issues, competition to define the issue also characterizes the politicization stage. Ultimately, issue definition is likely to result in a label for the problem: fair housing, global warming, or energy independence, for example. Each group with an interest in the issue will seek to define the issue in the way that is most favorable to their position, and develop a label that conveys that position.

The label an issue acquires can be important in how the public thinks about the problem. If the problem label is, for example, "predatory lending," many people may find it difficult to say they are in favor of predatory lending. If the label is more neutral, such as "subprime lending," it is possible to imagine that the issue has two sides and that reasonable people might be in favor of facilitating subprime lending. However, no one will favor more predation. In a similar vein, downloaded software, often without express consent or clear disclosure, came to be known as "spyware." Again, it is difficult to imagine favoring spyware. But what many such programs actually do is simply serve different (and sometimes more) advertisements than an Internet surfer might otherwise see, often in exchange for free software. If the label is "adware," it is again possible to imagine an issue that has two reasonable sides.

How an issue is defined may determine how much traction the issue has in the political arena. A good example is the legislative debates about peer-to-peer file-sharing networks, widely used to share music and other material. Such networks also allow computer owners to donate their unused computation time to projects such as the search for extraterrestrial intelligence. When the issue first emerged, the Recording Industry Association of America (RIAA) saw it as an intellectual property problem: users were sharing music over Napster, for example, without paying and without permission from the copyright owner. For many members of Congress, the intellectual property definition of the issue was unattractive because it required them to tell their constituents they were engaged in illegal behavior and needed to pay up. Then RIAA made a shocking discovery: there is pornography on the Internet, and some of it was being shared through file-sharing software! That characterization of the issue had much more resonance with members of Congress. Opposing pornography, especially pornography available to children, was a much more attractive issue, and led to many congressional hearings on the topic.

C. Legislative stage: developing a preferred solution

In the legislative stage of a policy issue, the focal point becomes the Congress and the staff on Capitol Hill. In this stage, there is an attempt to build consensus around a preferred solution to the problem. If there is sufficient consensus, the result will be legislation that eventually passes. If consensus cannot be reached, the issue may end as a political issue, or, more often, it may return at some future date with another effort to build consensus. Thus the central feature of the legislative stage is compromise among competing interests in a search for sufficient political support to enact legislation.

Figure 6-1. The Iron Triangle.

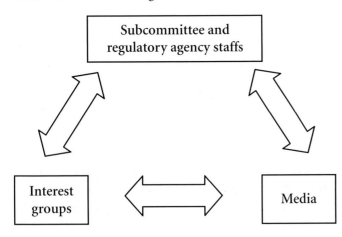

At the center of the consensus-building process are subcommittee staffs in Congress.[1] This is where the legislative process begins. There are three key players in what is known as the Iron Triangle: subcommittee staffers, often in consultation with regulatory agency staffers; interest groups with a stake in the issue; and the media. The Iron Triangle is depicted in Figure 6-1.

Subcommittee staffers are in regular contact with the members they work for. Some staffers work for the subcommittee or the committee; others work for individual members with an interest in the issue. They are sensitive to the politics of the issue and how it might affect their boss's interests. Although there are exceptions, at the beginning of

---

[1]Each house of Congress is organized into committees, each with jurisdiction over a particular area of policy. In turn, committees are organized into subcommittees. When legislation is introduced, it is referred first to the relevant committee and subcommittee. The House and Senate each have separate appropriations committees that handle funding for the entire government.

the process the staffers often know relatively little about the substance of the issue. Frequently, subcommittee staffers will consult with the staff at the relevant regulatory agencies. The agency staff is likely to have far more detailed knowledge of the issue, about the potential impact of various approaches to solving the problem, and about what solutions are most likely to work. They are consulted as a source of relatively disinterested expertise, unlike the interest groups who are clamoring for attention. Perhaps not surprisingly, agency staffers frequently believe that the answer should more authority (and more budget dollars) for their agency.

Subcommittee staffers will reach out to key interest groups to determine what they are willing to support. Staffers may seek to broker compromises among competing interests to gain additional support. Interest groups also try to influence the shape of the developing legislation independently, seeking to lobby staffers about their preferred alternative. They talk to staffers about what they think will work to address the problem, about its costs and benefits, and about what kinds of changes they would be willing to support. Frequently, interest groups (particularly those with a common interest in the issue) are talking to one another as well, attempting to develop a consensus about a possible solution. The currency in these discussions is political support. Subcommittee staffers are searching for a consensus that will command enough support from interest groups to pass, and will bring political benefits to the members they work for. Often, however, they have their own ideas about the best solution, and may resist suggestions from interest groups that are inconsistent with their views.

Of course, groups opposed to addressing the problem, or opposed to a particular solution, are also participants in the process. They attempt to persuade staffers that the possible solutions will not work, or will cost more than they are worth. In addition, opponents may attempt to convince staffers that the issue will not bring political benefits for their principal.

The process of building consensus is usually quite unstructured. Subcommittee staffers will reach out to politically important groups that they know have an interest in the issue, but many groups with an important stake may not be obvious to the staffers. Moreover, interested parties may not know which staffers are relevant to the issue or which members are key to the fate of a particular piece of legislation. Lobbyists are frequently the intermediaries, either learning and presenting the interests of the party they represent, or putting their principals in contact with the right players.

The media are the third leg of the Iron Triangle. In part the media are covering the process of developing legislation, but more often they are covering the problem or issue itself—and the legislative process is only a part of the story. The media contact interest groups for information, and interest groups seek to influence how the story is covered. Subcommittee staffers watch the media coverage with professional interest, because the media coverage will have a lot to do with whether the issue remains a politically attractive one for their principals.

In the legislative stage, groups with an interest in the issue face a strategic choice: should they try to negotiate, to influence the shape of possible legislation, or should they try to resist any legislation? It is very difficult to do both, because the primary source of leverage in negotiation is the ability to promise support for an acceptable solution. If a group has said that it is unalterably opposed to any legislative solution, it cannot credibly offer support. Often, opponents of legislation will resist initially, but, as it becomes more likely that some legislation will pass, they will shift to a strategy of negotiation. The decision to switch strategies depends on an accurate reading of the likely outcome of the legislative process. Timing can also be critical. Waiting too long may mean that a compromise has already been reached that cannot be reopened. Negotiating too quickly may give up an opportunity to prevent undesirable legislation entirely.

D. Policy implementation

Once legislation passes, it must be implemented. Although some legislation directly requires action by private parties subject to the new requirements, implementation usually requires the relevant regulatory agency to write new rules specifying private sector obligations in more detail. Once promulgated, agency rules have the force of law, and there are penalties for violations of the rules.

Some statutes establish an agency and give it a broad statutory mandate. The Occupational Safety and Health Act, for example, requires employers to provide a workplace "free of recognized hazards that are likely to cause death or serious injury." Details are left to the implementing regulations of the Occupational Safety and Health Agency (OSHA). Some regulations might be adopted shortly after the statute is enacted, but agencies have the authority to revisit their regulations and add other requirements at a later date. Other statutes pose specific questions for the regulatory agency to answer. The Nutrition Labeling and Education Act of 1990, for example, required the Food and Drug Administration (FDA) to define certain terms used on food labels, such as "light" or "low," as well as "more" or "less."[2] Companies could not fully comply with the statute until those rules were written.

Regulatory agencies write rules through the process of notice and comment rulemaking.[3] In a series of steps, agencies provide information to the public about the rules they are considering and ask for comment. The same process is used to amend existing rules. Anyone can comment, and based on the comments and other information, the agency decides whether to adopt the rule, revise the rule, or abandon the rule altogether. Throught the formal process, interested parties frequently talk to the agency staff about now they believe a rule should be written.

The first step in the rulemaking process is an Advance Notice of Proposed Rulemaking (ANPRM). Because this stage is optional, not every rule starts with an ANPRM. Like all rulemaking documents, the ANPRM is published in the *Federal Register*, the official compendium of all regulatory notices and proposals. It will explain the problem the agency is interested in addressing, what it knows about the problem, and possible approaches to addressing the problem that the agency is considering. Usually, an ANPRM will pose a number of specific questions about which the agency is soliciting information. Anyone can file comments with the agency, and typically interest groups, individual companies, and individual members of the public do so. Members of Congress with a particular interest in the issue often file comments as well. The agency then analyzes the comments and decides whether to proceed.

If the agency proceeds, it publishes a Notice of Proposed Rulemaking (NPRM) in the *Federal Register*. The NPRM will explain the problem, what the agency knows about it, and why the agency thinks a regulation is necessary. If the process started with an ANPRM, the agency will also address the issues raised in the comments. It will either explain any changes it made in response to the comments, or explain why it disagrees with the comments and is not making changes. In addition, the NPRM generally includes the text of a proposed rule to address the problem. Again, the document is subject to public comment, typically for 60 days. The agency then analyzes the comments and decides whether to proceed, and if so, how the rule should be revised.

The last agency step in the process is to publish a final rule in the *Federal Register*. The final rule includes a "preamble" or "statement of basis and purpose" that explains why the agency believes the rule is necessary, and sets out in detail the agency's rationale for its specific requirements and the evidence supporting its decision. This explanation will include a response to public comments received during the proceeding. The document also includes the text of the final rule the agency is adopting, and specifies an effective date, which is when enforcement of the rule will begin. The effective date is usually set taking into account how long it is likely to take the private sector to come into compliance with the new requirements, and may be a year or more in the future.

Rules are codified in the *Code of Federal Regulations* (the CFR). The CFR includes only the text of the final rules adopted by agencies; it does not include the detailed explanations that accompany the final rule. The CFR is divided into numerous parts, published in separate volumes, each approximately 9 inches by 6 inches. Together, the CFR occupies about 32 linear feet of bookshelf space, and has more than 1,000 pages of indexes. Each business, of course, is familiar with every word and in compliance with every requirement!

The public comment process is an important opportunity to influence public policy. Agencies take public comments seriously, particularly if they are well reasoned and well supported. Regulators understand that they do not know everything they might like to know about how a particular requirement will impact those who must comply with it, or how well it will work. Public comments are an opportunity to acquire more

---

[2] Because they were written with different nutrients in mind, the definitions of "more" and "less" are not symmetric. Brand A may be allowed to say it has "more" of a particular nutrient than Brand B, but Brand B cannot say it has "less" than Brand A!

[3] Agency rulemaking is subject to oversight by the Office of Information and Regulatory Affairs, which is part of the Office of Management and Budget in the Executive Office of the President. Presidential oversight of the regulatory process is discussed in Chapter 10.

information and write a better rule. Many rules are changed significantly from the initial proposal because of information that comes to the agency's attention through the public comment process.

Groups or individuals affected by a final rule who do not like the result can appeal the agency's decision to the federal courts. Courts, however, generally give considerable deference to agency decisions, and will overrule the agency only if its decisions are "arbitrary and capricious." This is another reason that agencies take public comments seriously: it is very easy for a reviewing court to conclude that an agency was arbitrary and capricious if it ignores well-reasoned public comments. Agencies do not always make the changes that commenters want, but they are usually careful to explain why they disagree with significant comments. Courts are more willing to overturn agency rules if they believe the rule exceeds the agency's statutory authority or is unconstitutional. Even here, however, courts tend to defer to agency expertise in interpreting their own statutes.

Once the rules are written, it is up to the private sector to come into compliance with the new requirements. When the rules become effective, agency enforcement actions can begin. The enforcement process, and the consequences of violations, differs considerably from agency to agency. Some agencies (like the Federal Trade Commission) rely on law enforcement actions to impose civil penalties for rule violations to achieve compliance. Others (like the Food and Drug Administration) may rely primarily on inspections of plants and other facilities to achieve compliance, backed up by the threat of more formal enforcement actions.

E. Policy evaluation

The final stage of the public policy process is policy evaluation. Not all policies succeed, and some policies may end up costing substantially more than originally expected and/or producing considerably smaller benefits than anticipated. Evaluation asks whether the policy worked as expected, and whether the benefits of the policy were worth the cost.

Unfortunately, policy evaluation is very infrequent in any formal way. A few agencies periodically request public comment on existing rules to conduct an evaluation, but most do not. Even the request for public comment is a very limited evaluation; it relies on the public to provide the evidence rather than conducting an empirical study to assess the rule. Moreover, even that limited evaluation is the exception, not the rule. In practice, evaluation depends on studies by academics and others, and the experiences of those who have to live with the rule.

Even if the evaluation is negative, there is no formal process to implement revisions. Instead, the issue must go back to the beginning of the public policy process. At most, evaluation can identify a problem, but to effect change, the problem must be politicized, it must go through the legislative stage (or a similar stage in persuading a regulatory agency to revise its rules), and the revised policy must be implemented. Like any other issue, a failed regulatory policy must compete with many other issues to gain public attention and policy action.

One recent example of policy evaluation concerns the Sarbanes-Oxley Act of 2002, enacted in response to the Enron scandal. Stock exchanges argue that the costs of complying with the act are driving securities issuers to overseas financial markets, particularly London, where the requirements of Sarbanes-Oxley do not apply. In support of that argument, the City of New York commissioned a study released in January 2007, which concluded that indeed some issuers were moving overseas. The attempt was to identify a new problem in the public policy process to persuade Congress to make changes. It remains to be seen whether the interest in reform generated by this and other studies will survive the reaction to the panic of 2008.

F. Corporate political strategies

Companies pursue three major strategies for influencing the public policy process: communication strategies, participation strategies, and compliance strategies. Different strategies are most appropriate at different stages of the policy process.

Communication strategies aim to provide information to the public. They are most appropriate for the development and politicization stages of the process, when influencing public opinion is easier because many people have not yet formed an opinion. Companies use vehicles such as speeches addressing relevant issues by the CEO or other top executives. Many companies, especially larger ones, also use their annual reports to communicate their views on the impact of potential public policies. Companies also employ advocacy advertising to speak directly to the public without the filter of the media. Such advertising might be narrow, issue-specific advertising, or it might stress broader policy themes.

Companies using communication strategies must think carefully about the credibility and consistency of their messages. Companies speaking on public issues often have an obvious stake in the issue, which can lead the media and the public to discount their views. It is therefore vital that the company's expressed views be consistent with its actions, and that its positions on different issues are consistent as well. Inconsistencies, even seemingly minor ones, are often reasons for discounting the message entirely.

In *participation strategies*, the focus shifts to office holders and public officials, including congressional and regulatory agency staff members. These strategies are most appropriate in the politicization and legislative stages of the policy process.

Lobbying is a key tool in participation strategies. Effective lobbying depends on providing accurate information to officials, who are frequently not well informed on the details of a particular issue. Lobbying may be conducted through general business organizations such as the Chamber of Commerce, the National Association of Manufacturers, the Business Roundtable (200 large companies), or the National Federation of Independent Businesses. Lobbying is also conducted through industry-specific trade associations, ranging from the American Chain Association to the Vinegar Institute, and by individual companies on their own behalf.

Another tool used in participation strategies is constituency building, or attempting to build a grassroots constituency on the issue. Often, constituencies are built through "independent" groups, formed as special organizations to address a particular issue. In many respects, the most valuable constituencies are local ones, because they are present in every congressional district. Automobile dealer networks, for example, are a natural local constituency, as are insurance agents. Constituency building seeks to make sure these potential networks are aware of the issue and will express their opinion to their elected representatives.

Perhaps the most controversial tool in participation strategies is campaign contributions. Although corporations cannot directly contribute to campaigns, their managers and employees can contribute to political action committees, or PACs. There are also PACs for labor unions, for particular causes, and "independent" PACs not tied to a particular issue. PAC contributions, which totaled $372 million in 2006, have tended to go primarily to incumbents. Since 2010, corporations have also been able to contribute to "independent" super PACs that are not coordinated with any candidate's campaign.

Compliance strategies are appropriate for the implementation stage. One important compliance strategy is communication with regulatory agency staff to influence the implementing rules. Typically many key issues remain unresolved as an agency begins to write rules, and involvement can lead to significant policy changes. For example, the first emissions trading mechanisms developed as an administrative adjustment by EPA, suggested by companies that were willing to push the benefits of the idea. Compliance strategies may also include judicial challenges to a law or its implementing regulations. Finally, compliance strategies may include an attempt to create a new issue to revise existing requirements. In the late 1970s, for example, businesses supported a number of studies detailing the impact of growing levels of regulation on the economy.

II. POLITICAL DECISIONS VERSUS MARKET EXCHANGE

Political decisions differ from the kinds of decisions that result from the exchange process in the marketplace. There are three notable contrasts between the two systems of making decisions.

First, political decisions tend to focus on distribution. The political process is often a zero-sum game, concerned with how to divide up what is available. In contrast, the market process focuses on wealth creation. In fact, wealth creation is inherent in the voluntary market exchange process, because an exchange will only occur if it benefits both parties. That is, trades only occur if there is a gain from trade. Thus the exchange necessarily increases value.

Of course, the political process can create value. There are many useful things that government does. However, there is nothing inherent in the process that assures that there are gains. Moreover, in many instances policies that seek to enhance outcomes for one group at the expense of another, such as agricultural price supports or trade restrictions, actually reduce wealth. As noted in Chapter 1, the distributional consequences of decisions are ignored in the market, but they are central in political decisions.

Second, political decisions are coercive. Everyone is bound by the result, like it or not. In contrast, market transactions are voluntary. Consumers who do not like particular features in a product are free to purchase something else. If those features are specified through the political process, however, there is no choice. Everyone who wants the product must purchase the required features.

Because political decisions are coercive, choices in the political process need to be made simultaneously. In the market, different buyers may make choices at different times without affecting the eventual result. If safety features of automobiles such as anti-lock brakes are determined in the market, for example, each consumer will make a decision about the feature when they purchase a new car. For some, that may be almost immediate, but for others it may be years away. If we are making a political decision about whether to require anti-lock brakes, however, we must all decide now, because if we decide to require the feature there will be no option for future buyers to decline it.

Similarly, because political decisions are coercive, they require universal participation (or at least the universal option of participation). There is simply no acceptable basis for leaving some people out of the decision. In markets, people with more information and more concern about the issue are likely to have a greater influence on the outcome, but even the uninformed and unconcerned must be able to participate in the political process.

The need for simultaneous decisions with universal participation gives rise to representative institutions to determine our collective preferences. We cannot all make simultaneous decisions about any significant number of issues. We can, however, elect representatives who can all participate and decide simultaneously.

Third, political and market decisions differ in accountability. Because markets are governed by the invisible hand, there is no individual to point to as the person responsible for the market outcome. Who is to blame (or who should get the credit), for example, for the market decision to replace long-playing vinyl records with compact discs as the principal medium for distributing music? Or who is responsible for the decision to replace videotape with DVDs? Although politicians will frequently search for a responsible party, as they do when oil prices rise, such decisions are outcomes of the market process, with contributions from everyone involved in the market.

Political decisions are more accountable. Elected representatives cast votes, and if we do not like the policies they voted for, we can in turn vote them out of office. Executive branch officials are not directly elected, but the president is accountable for their decisions. We know who was responsible for a political decision in a way that we cannot know with a market outcome.

Because accountability is a two-edged sword, however, there are a number of common mechanisms that serve to diffuse responsibility for political decisions. One such device is the enactment of a broad statutory framework. Such statutes set a general structure for public policy in a particular area, but leave critical details to the implementing agency. This approach lets politicians take credit for the goals of the policy and the broad structure but shift blame for the details to the implementing agency.

A second mechanism for diffusing responsibility is fuzzy statutory language that leaves critical questions to agency or judicial interpretation of the law. In fact, the legislative process creates incentives to obscure meaning, because ambiguous language can often attract more political support, at least initially. For example, when Congress created OSHA in 1970, a central element of the legislative debate was how the agency should consider costs. Some argued that costs should be irrelevant: employers should provide a safe workplace no matter what it cost. Others argued that considering costs was essential, because we cannot eliminate all risks in the workplace or elsewhere and must set sensible priorities. The legislative compromise required OSHA to regulate "to the extent feasible." Those who thought costs should be irrelevant accepted this language. They recognized that eliminating some risks might be impossible, and were certainly not asking business to do the impossible. Those who thought considering costs was important believed that "feasibility" included economic feasibility, which would necessarily include consideration of regulatory costs. So how exactly did Congress want OSHA to consider costs? Subsequent court decisions have held that OSHA is not required to consider costs, but have left open the question of whether it can do so if it chooses.

A similar example involved the 1990 Civil Rights Act. There was widespread agreement to reverse a series of Supreme Court decisions about what was necessary to prove job discrimination, but no agreement over whether the revised standard should be retroactive, covering cases that had already been filed. Congress spent six months developing compromise language that could be read either way. In essence, it punted on the question of retroactivity, leaving the final decision up to the courts. Eventually, the Supreme Court said that if Congress wanted statutes to apply retroactively, it had to say so clearly and unambiguously. The new standard therefore was applied only to cases filed after the statute passed.

A third mechanism to diffuse responsibility is broad, omnibus legislation that must pass. The economic stimulus bill of 2009 is a good example. Other examples include budget reconciliation bills that essentially fund the entire government; if they do not pass, the government will have to shut down. For such broad enactments, there are almost inevitably provisions that would not have survived the legislative process if they had been subject to a separate vote. Individual politicians can tell their constituents that they only voted for the package because it had to pass, while maintaining that they did not support any individual item that a constituent complains about.

III. SUMMARY

Public policy issues are inherently political. They unfold in a series of stages, beginning with development, in which a problem is identified. Problems emerge from persistent frictions among different groups, as a result of dramatic events, or from the efforts of policy entrepreneurs. In the politicization stage, the problem becomes a political issue. There is competition for media attention, as well as competition to define the issue and give it a label. The legislative stage is characterized by a search for compromise and consensus around a preferred solution to the problem. The key players in the legislative stage form the Iron Triangle of congressional subcommittee and regulatory agency staffs, interest groups, and the media. In the implementation stage, notice and comment rulemaking develops detailed rules to implement the new policy, followed by private sector compliance and enforcement actions if necessary. Policy evaluation asks whether the policy worked and was worth the costs. Formal evaluations are rare, and negative results from an evaluation simply start the policy process over again, seeking to develop a new issue.

Companies pursue communications strategies during the development and politicization stages, using speeches by top managers, statements in annual reports, or direct advocacy advertising to provide information to the public. They pursue participation strategies, focused on office holders, during the politicization and legislative stages. These strategies employ lobbying, constituency building, and campaign contributions. Compliance strategies are appropriate in the implementation stage. They focus on influencing regulatory agencies, judicial challenge, or developing a new issue to reform the policy.

Political decisions are different from the market exchange process. Political decisions focus on distribution, whereas the market exchange process focuses on creating value. Political decisions are coercive; market exchange is based on voluntary transactions. Political decisions are made by theoretically accountable politicians, whereas markets are guided by the invisible hand.

THE THEORY OF PUBLIC CHOICE

Chapter 7

Economists' early thinking about the role of government in the economy was built around the notion of market failures, discussed in Chapter 1. If some failure prevented the market from achieving the outcome that would maximize consumer welfare as judged by consumers, it fell to government to try to correct the problem. Government might make mistakes, of course, but economists tended to assume that it would systematically pursue the public interest as they understood it.

As economists studied public policies in more detail, however, it became apparent that many policies could not be understood as government attempts to achieve the best outcome for consumers. Instead, policies in numerous areas systematically reduced consumer welfare. Agricultural price supports, for example, or barriers to trade, may benefit farmers or domestic manufacturers, respectively, but there is no respectable case to be made that they bring us closer to the perfectly competitive ideal. Indeed, in many cases they are designed to prevent competitive market outcomes.

In an effort to understand why public policies might systematically deviate from the pursuit of the public interest, economists turned the tools of economic analysis on the political process itself. Spearheaded by the work of Nobel laureate James Buchanan and Gordon Tullock, these efforts led to what has come to be known as the theory of public choice.

This chapter begins with an analysis of majority rule as a system for making collective decisions. It considers the outcomes that will result under majority rule, and the problems that majority rule can pose. Section II considers voter decisions about whether to participate in a particular policy issue in light of rational ignorance, a central principal of the theory of public choice. The costs of individual participation in the political process create a role for interest groups, addressed in Section III. These interest groups engage in what public choice theorists call rent-seeking behavior, considered in Section IV. Politicians and other institutional participants in the public policy process are incorporated in Section V. Finally, Section VI will assemble the pieces into a general model of political decision making.

I. Majority Rule

Because policy decisions are coercive, some mechanism is necessary to determine a group's collective preferences about what policy should prevail. Majority rule is the primary tool used in democratic societies for this purpose. We first consider what outcome will prevail under majority rule, and then consider some theoretical problems with majority rule.

A. Operation

Suppose that voters have preferences regarding some policy dimension, such as how much education the government should provide. Each individual voter has a most-preferred level of education, and a lower preference for education levels that are farther away from that ideal level. Thus, in any choice between two different levels of education, each voter will vote for the level closest to his or her most preferred level. Figure 7-1 depicts three such voters, A, B, and C, and their most preferred levels of education, E_A, E_B, and E_C.

Under majority rule, it is easy to see that neither A nor C can achieve their most-preferred outcome. Voters A and B will vote down C's preferred alternative, and B and C will defeat A's first choice. In fact, the only option that can command a majority is voter B's preferred outcome. A will vote for that choice over any higher amount that C might propose, and C will vote for it over any lower amount that A would prefer. This is the median voter theorem: under majority rule, the most-preferred outcome of the median voter will prevail. In fact, it is the only outcome that can command a majority.

The crucial role of the median voter arises simply because he or she is in the middle, not because the voters with more extreme preferences compromise and end up with B's preferred choice. In Figure 7-1, it would not matter how far to the right we moved voter C's preferred outcome; B's preferred outcome would still prevail. Without the voter in the middle, there can be no majority.

The median voter outcome is not optimal as judged by the Pareto Optimality criterion. In the market, each voter will choose a different level of education. If the choice is made collectively, however, all must consume the same level—and it is only optimal for the median voter. Other voters realize less consumer surplus than they would otherwise. Even if the choice concerns a public good, where all must consume the same level of the good in any event, majority decisions will likely impose costs on the minority, which are not taken into account in choosing the level of the good. Thus, there are likely gains from trade that are not captured in a majority rule decision.

Every four years, presidential politics provides a demonstration of the relevance of the median voter theorem. Republicans tend to run toward the right in the primaries, because the median Republican voter is more conservative than the population as a whole. Democrats, in contrast, tend to run toward the left during primary season, competing for the left-wing groups that are a crucial part of the party's constituency. Once the nomination is secured, both candidates tend to moderate their positions—they head for the policy preferences of the median voter.

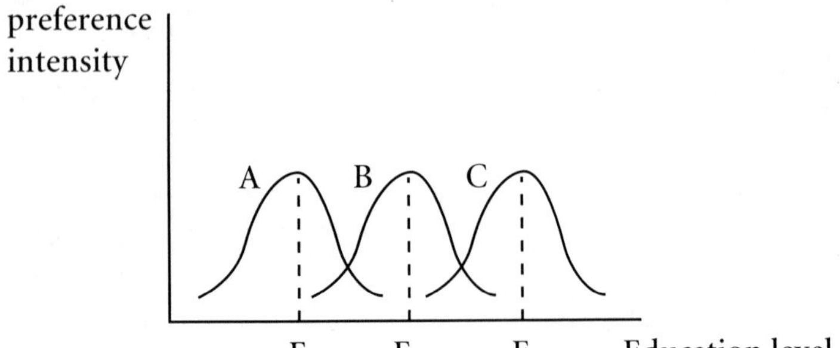

The critical importance of the median voter implies that we should tend to see policies that favor the interests of the middle class. The middle class is a large portion of the American electorate, and surely includes the median voter. Social Security and Medicare are perhaps the most outstanding examples of such policies. Because the programs are

Figure 7-1. The median voter theorem.

not means tested, the vast majority of beneficiaries are neither rich nor poor—they are the middle class. The median voter theorem helps to explain why these programs have been described as the third rail of American politics—touch them and you die.

Of course, redistribution toward the middle is not complete. In addition to seeking programs that benefit their interests, many voters also have preferences for a more equitable distribution of income. Those preferences lead them to support policies such as progressive taxation, under which the wealthy pay a disproportionate share of taxes. In 2009, the top one percent of income tax returns reported 16.9 percent of all income, and paid 36.7 percent of total income taxes. Similarly, numerous programs such as food stamps, Medicaid, and housing support programs distribute money to those with lower incomes. Nonetheless, a large fraction of government programs are designed to provide benefits to the middle class.

B. Theoretical problems of majority rule

Although democratic societies depend on majority rule to make political decisions, there are difficulties with how well majority rule serves the public interest. According to Winston Churchill, "It has been said that democracy is the worst form of government, except all the others that have been tried."

1. Tyranny of the Majority
One problem of majority rule is known as the tyranny of the majority. In a strict majority rule system, the majority can do whatever it wants. Unfortunately, however, at many times and in many places, majorities have wanted some very ugly things that few would defend today. Perhaps the most outstanding example is the persistence of legally enforced segregation in the American south from the end of the Civil War until the 1960s. No doubt there was majority support for these policies, perhaps even a substantial majority. That hardly means that segregation served any useful role in protecting the public interest, however.

To limit the potential for the tyranny of the majority, the U.S. system relies on constitutional safeguards. There are some things that government is not allowed to do under the Constitution, whether they have majority support or not. For example, a majority cannot prohibit unpopular speech under the First Amendment, and it cannot send people to jail without due process of law. Moreover, these constraints are very difficult to change. Amending the Constitution requires a two-thirds vote in the House and Senate, and the proposed amendment must then be ratified by three-fourths of the states. Overcoming these hurdles requires a substantial and persistent majority, not simply bare majority support.

Supermajority requirements are used in other contexts as well as a protection against tyranny of the majority. Many state budget or tax statutes require supermajorities, such as 60 percent, to approve certain policies such as tax increases or budget deficits.

One of the most commonly invoked protections against majority rule in politics today is the filibuster in the Senate. Cutting off debate in the Senate requires 60 votes under Senate rules. As a practical matter, any matter that is even moderately controversial requires 60 votes to pass, because otherwise the minority will filibuster to prevent consideration of the matter.

Originally, conducting a filibuster required opponents of the proposed legislation to conduct debate. The result was some dramatic occasions of considerably less than relevant speeches on the Senate floor. Senator Strom Thurmond, for example, holds the record for a one-person filibuster, established when he held the Senate floor for 24 hours and 18 minutes during consideration of a Civil Rights bill in 1957. Such tactics, however, disrupt the conduct of other business. To avoid those consequences, Senate majority leaders have taken to pulling proposals that are subject to a filibuster from the agenda until there are 60 votes to end debate. The result is that any senator can conduct a filibuster simply by declaring the intention to do so. If the matter is brought up at all, an early vote will establish whether there are enough votes to end a filibuster. If not, the leadership will pull the matter and move on to other business. No one actually ever has to conduct the filibuster. Not surprisingly, as filibusters became less costly for participants, they became more common as well. Even Senators have downward sloping demand curves!

Figure 7-2. Intensity of preferences.

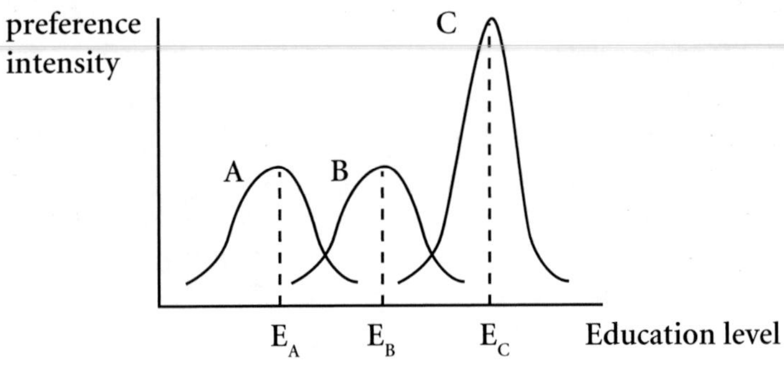

preference intensity

C
A   B

E_A E_B E_C Education level

2. Intensity of Preferences

A second problem with majority rule is that it does not reflect the intensity of preferences very well. Indeed, in a simple majority rule system, intensity of preferences about a choice is not reflected at all. Because each person has only one vote, there is no way to give greater weight to the person who cares most about the outcome. Consider, for example, Figure 7-2, which is a slight modification of Figure 7-1.

Voters A and B do not care very much about the level of education provided, but voter C cares a great deal. Nonetheless, each person has only one vote. As long as A and B care enough to vote, they will outvote C, and the median voter's preferred outcome will still prevail. There is no formal way to reflect the intensity of C's preferences in the outcome. Again, this outcome is not Pareto optimal. Because C cares more, he or she is presumably willing to offer some compensation to A and B in return for a higher level of education. Under majority rule, however, there is no way to achieve such an outcome.

Typically, small groups of individuals will consider the intensity of preferences. If three friends are considering where to go for dinner, for example, and one person in the group has a strong objection to, say, Chinese food, the group is likely to end up somewhere else. They will take into account the intensity of preferences. A formal majority rule voting mechanism, however, does not.

One method that allows some reflection of intensity of preferences is vote trading, better known as logrolling. If voter C cares intensely about education and voter A cares intensely about health care, they may agree to trade their votes. A will vote for C's preferred level of education, and in exchange C will vote for A's preferred level of health care. Thus, each voter's intensely preferred outcome will prevail over the median voter.

There is, unfortunately, no assurance that this outcome is better for voters as a whole, and it may be worse. Vote trading based on intensity of preferences is the basis of pork barrel politics. The one thing that each politician cares strongly about is the welfare of his or her own constituents. Projects that are good for their constituents are important to members, even if they are not necessarily good for the country as a whole. Thus, vote trading may produce a lot of bad projects—one in each congressional district.

Projects driven by pork barrel politics are not hard to find. Richmond, Virginia, and Morgantown, West Virginia, are not exactly the most obvious places to put the National White Collar Crime Center—but that is where they are located. It is hard to see the national benefits of the $320 million "bridge to nowhere" connecting Ketchican, Alaska, (population 8,900) to its airport on the island of Gravinia (population 50), or federal support for the National Wild Turkey Federation in South Carolina. Contractors and others who do business with the federal government are well aware of the need to deliver benefits in key congressional districts, and structure their operations accordingly. The F-22 Raptor program to build a next-generation air superiority fighter plane, for example, has contractors and suppliers in 44 states. Intensity of congressional preferences will make cutting the program far more difficult.

3. Instability of Outcomes

A third problem with majority rule is that in certain circumstances, there may be no stable equilibrium outcome. That is, voters may not have consistent "collective preferences" among policy options. This result is known as the Arrow Impossibility Theorem, after Kenneth Arrow, the Nobel prize–winning economist who developed it. The problem is easiest to see through an example, which is summarized in Figure 7-3.

Figure 7-3. The Arrow Impossibility Theorem.

Voter	Policy Options (Preference Ranking)		
	A	B	C
X	3	2	1
Y	1	3	2
Z	2	1	3

Suppose there are three mutually exclusive policy options, A, B, and C, and three voters, X, Y, and Z. Elections are between pairs of options. Each voter can rank the three options from first to last, and will vote for whichever choice he ranks highest.

Consider first the election between options A and B. Voters X and Z will vote for B, which they both rank more highly than A. B wins, 2 votes to 1. In the election between B and C, C wins, because voters X and Y prefer it to B. So C beats B, and B beats A. If there is a stable outcome, C should beat A. However, it does not. If the choice is between options C and A, A wins, because it is voter Y's first choice and voter Z's second choice. We are back where we started, at option A. In essence, the example has no median voter. As a result, there is no stable outcome.

Of course, the example is a constructed one. Is the Arrow Impossibility Theorem really relevant in practice? There are some notable examples that suggest it is, at least in some cases. In 1988, for example, campaign finance reform was a hot topic in California. That year, an initiative was placed on the ballot to replace the existing system of campaign finance with a system of public financing of political campaigns. Another group opposed this proposal, and introduced a competing initiative to prohibit public financing of political campaigns. The debate went to the voters, with one initiative positioned and defended as pro public financing of campaigns, and the other initiative positioned as anti public financing. Both initiatives won a majority, with 52.8 percent supporting the pro public financing initiative and 58 percent supporting the anti public financing initiative. A few years later, a similar pair of initiatives supporting and opposing term limits for city council members in Cincinnati, Ohio, both passed.

These are exactly the kind of outcomes that the Arrow Impossibility Theorem anticipates. Either alternative can command a majority, compared to the status quo. There is no stable outcome.

Better evidence for the practical significance of the Arrow Impossibility Theorem comes from observing the political process. The theorem implies that control of the agenda is critical in determining the outcome. Indeed, in the example in Figure 7-3, whoever controls the agenda—the order in which options are presented for a decision—can determine the final outcome completely. In contrast, if there is a stable majority vote outcome, there is little reason to believe that agenda control makes any difference. The outcome would be the same regardless of the order of voting. Politicians in general, and legislators in particular, spend considerable time and effort struggling over control of the agenda. These efforts imply that they believe the agenda matters—just as Arrow says it does.

Similarly, a common legislative strategy to defeat legislation is known as the "killer amendment." The idea of the strategy is to enact an amendment that will itself pass, but, once passed, it will make the legislation to which it is attached unattractive, killing both the legislation and the amendment. One of the clearest examples of the strategy concerned a legislative proposal for the U.S. government to notify individuals that the government knew might have been exposed to toxic chemicals. Most of those who would have received notification would not have been at any meaningful risk as a result of their exposure, but the idea of telling them was politically attractive to many. The bill provided only notification; it would be up to individual consumers to talk to their doctor and decide what if any action was appropriate. The killer amendment added cigarette smoke to the list of toxic substances that was part of the legislation. When the amendment passed, the revised bill said in essence that the government should write a letter to everyone in the country telling them that they might have been exposed to toxic chemicals. On its face, that was pointless, and the legislation died.

The killer amendment strategy was used more recently by Democrats in Congress to delay proposals for bankruptcy reform for several years. The proposals were strongly supported by Republicans, and opposed by many Democrats. The killer amendment provided that anti-abortion protesters could not use bankruptcy to avoid court judgments resulting from their protests. The amendment passed, but was unpalatable to Republicans. The result was, in two consecutive Congresses, bankruptcy reform failed (although it was eventually passed in 2005).

Killer amendments are a strategy based on agenda control. If there is a stable majority, the order should be irrelevant—the outcome will be same regardless of the order of voting. With killer amendments, order matters, just as Arrow says it can.

II. Rational Ignorance and Voter Participation

One of the primary ways that intensity of preferences gets reflected in the American political system is in decisions about whether to participate in the process at all, whether in general (as in presidential elections) or on a particular issue. A central idea of the theory of public choice is that participation decisions are driven by the benefits and costs of obtaining information about policy issues.

From an economic perspective, information is a commodity like any other good or service. Obtaining information has costs, whether in the time and effort to find and utilize information or in direct payments for a magazine or newspaper subscription. Depending on the nature of the information, it also offers benefits, in the form of improved consumption decisions or policies that more closely conform to an individual's preferences.

Because information is costly, it will not pay for anyone to be perfectly informed. Instead, individuals will balance the marginal benefits of better information against the marginal costs. As a result, they will not obtain complete information about public policy issues, or anything else for that matter. They will instead choose, quite rationally, to remain ignorant. This is the idea of rational ignorance, which is central to the theory of public choice.

The intuition behind rational ignorance is straightforward if we think in terms of finding information about the lowest price for a commodity. Obtaining information has a cost, usually in the form of time spent searching. It offers a benefit, in the form of a lower price for the product. If the product is chewing gum, the benefits of searching for a lower price are quite small. As a result, most consumers will purchase from a convenient retailer without much thought about the price, and without much search for a better deal. In contrast, in searching for a new car the benefits of finding a better price are far more substantial, and consumers are more likely to shop around for the best possible deal. It is rational to remain ignorant about the price of gum at competing retailers; it is probably not rational to remain ignorant about the price of cars.

Information about policy issues is no different. Critical to decisions about who will choose to be informed, and to participate in the process, are the benefits and costs of information about policy options.

Consider first the benefits of being informed about a policy issue. As with price search, the benefits depend critically on the consumer's stake in the issue. If the consumer has a small stake in the issue, that is, if it is relatively insignificant to that consumer, it will be rational to remain ignorant. If the stake is large, the benefits of paying attention to the issue are more substantial, and consumers are more likely to be informed and to participate in the decision.

Many government programs impose relatively small per capita costs on consumers, who therefore have a small stake in the issue. The aggregate amount of money, however, can be quite substantial, and is frequently provided to some much smaller group as a government benefit of one sort or another. The consumers who pay the costs have a relatively small stake in the issue, and choose to remain rationally ignorant. The program beneficiaries, however, have a larger stake—sometimes much larger—and are therefore more likely to participate. The result is a bias in who participates in the decision. The median voter theorem may still hold, but the median voter whose preferences prevail is the median of those who choose to participate. Participants, however, may be dominated by beneficiaries, not those who pay the costs.

Consider, for example, the U.S. sugar price support program. Like many agricultural price support programs, this one maintains the domestic price of sugar above the world market price. Currently, the domestic sugar price is about two-and-one-half times the world price. For the average sugar user, the annual cost of the program is about $6.50. Even for someone with a serious sweet tooth, the benefits of paying attention to the latest developments in the sugar price support program are small. It is rational to remain ignorant. The aggregate costs, however, are far more substantial: about $1.9 billion in 1998.[1]

---

[1]The total cost to consumers, i.e., the loss in consumer surplus, is $1.9 billion. The deadweight losses from the program are estimated at $532 million. That is the net cost to the economy of the sugar price support program. The remaining $1.4 billion is a transfer from sugar consumers to producers.

In contrast, sugar growers have a much larger stake in the issue. There is $1.9 billion available, and a far smaller number of growers. Thus each grower has vastly more at stake, and much more incentive to be informed about the program. Benefits for the average sugar grower are approximately $50,000 per year. That is an amount worth paying attention to. For the largest producers, the disparity is even greater. The largest two sugar producers received $156 million in benefits. That is not only worth the costs of paying attention, it is also worth paying some serious money for lobbyists to try to influence the political process.

The result of rational ignorance is that when the sugar price support program is up for renewal or discussion, growers pay attention but users do not. Participation in the political process is skewed in a way that favors the interests of the relatively compact group of beneficiaries, at the expense of the public at large. The consensus that forms in the legislative stage of the public policy process includes the beneficiaries, but not those who pay the costs.

Costs of information in the political process can also be quite significant. There are at least four reasons why policy information is often hard to come by.

First, information relevant to policy choices is sometimes deliberately hidden. It may be very hard to learn about a new product, not yet on the market, that is awaiting regulatory approval. Indeed, the regulatory process often treats the fact that a product has been submitted for approval as a trade secret which the government cannot reveal. Even consumers with a large stake in the outcome—for example, someone with an incurable disease that a new drug might treat—may not know that the decision is pending, and may not pay attention to the issue.

Second, information is often costly because of the complexity of many governmental programs. For many reasons, programs often have many interrelated components that fit together in ways that are not necessarily obvious. Changes in one part of the program may have consequences in far different parts of the program that undermine the objective of the original change, and may even defeat the purpose of the change entirely. Because understanding the entire program is necessary to assess the impact of particular changes, information about the benefits and costs of changes can be costly to obtain.

There is no better example of program complexity thwarting seemingly straightforward policy changes than the honey subsidy program. Based on the argument that honeybees produce external benefits through pollinating crops and are therefore underprovided, beekeepers have succeeded in obtaining a government subsidy. Since early in the Reagan administration, the program has been a target for elimination. Early in the 1990s, a group of congressmen decided that they would simply kill the annual appropriation for the program, and thereby, they thought, effectively kill the honey subsidy.

In fact, the effect of this seemingly straightforward solution was to *increase* the cost of the program. The reason is hidden in the structure of the program. The subsidy is actually in the form of a nonrecourse loan, secured by the beekeeper's honey at the target price for honey. If the market price is above the target price, the beekeeper will pay off the loan, redeem his honey, and sell it at the market price. If the market price is below the target, however, the beekeeper defaults on the loan, keeping the loan proceeds (at the target price) and leaving the government with the honey. There is no other consequence for the beekeeper. The federal budget process accounts for loan losses separately and does not treat them as "expenditures" for purposes of the annual budget process. Moreover, the government does not want the honey. The reason there were "expenditures" in the honey subsidy program is that the government was essentially bribing beekeepers to take their honey back. In the absence of expenditures, beekeepers would simply default on the loans, leaving the government with the same loan losses, plus the costs of storing and disposing of the honey. Zero expenditures actually increased program costs! The congressmen backed off their plan, and the honey subsidy program lived on for another year or two.[2]

A third factor contributing to the costs of information about public policy is the lack of a common denominator for comparing outcomes. Markets value everything in dollar terms, making it straightforward to compare the value of apples and oranges. In government, however, there is no simple way to compare the value of national defense outcomes to health outcomes or education outcomes. Because comparing outputs is difficult,

---

[2]The honey subsidy program was briefly killed in 1993. It was revived in 2000, and it remains with us today.

there is a tendency to compare programs based on the one input they have in common: tax dollars. Thus the policy argument tends to be how much should we spend, rather than how can we get better outcomes. Inputs, however, are the wrong measure. There are many ways to increase costs, and hence expenditures, without increasing the value of the outcome.

Finally, costs of obtaining information can be relatively high because of the monopoly status of government. There is no standard of comparison, at least at the federal level. In the private sector, companies facing a difficult problem can benchmark themselves against other companies with similar problems. This approach may provide ideas about how to address the problem, and provides a basis for assessing how well a particular company is doing. Although state and local governments can benchmark their performance compared to other governments, no such standard is available for benchmarking many federal programs.

Because information is costly, and many voters have a small stake in the outcome, many voters choose to remain rationally ignorant about policy issues. The result is skewed participation in the political process, and numerous programs that deliver benefits to a relatively small group with a large stake in the outcome at the expense of the general public.

III. THE ROLE OF INTEREST GROUPS

The costs of information in the policy process create an advantage for organized groups. Groups can spread the costs of obtaining information across their membership. Whereas individuals may not find it worthwhile to follow a particular issue, if they can share the costs with similarly inclined voters, they may be able to participate at lower cost.

Groups have at least four advantages over individuals in participating in the policy process. First, they have a greater ability to **communicate**. A group knows who its members are, and can communicate with them relatively easily. Groups use a variety of communication techniques, from regular letters (often asking for money!) to newsletters to e-mail blasts. More importantly, the group leader can communicate more easily with politicians and other participants in the process on behalf of group members. In turn, politicians or policymakers can communicate with the group leadership, who in turn communicate with the members. For politicians, a group is a source of a mailing list of people known to be interested in whatever issues are important to the group.

Groups also have a greater ability to **negotiate** on behalf of their members. Discussions to build consensus around a policy proposal are time consuming and involve considerable transaction costs. Groups can share those costs among their members, negotiating on their behalf. The process of building consensus at the subcommittee level would be completely unwieldy if it were necessary to deal with any significant fraction of affected individuals, but it is much more manageable when dealing with the much smaller number of interest groups with a stake in the issue.

Third, groups have an advantage in **monitoring** politicians. Occasionally, politicians have been known to say one thing and do another. Groups allow their members to share to cost of monitoring whether the politician actually follows through on the deal.

Finally, groups have a greater ability to **sanction** politicians who do not agree with their position or do not follow through on their promises. If an individual tells his or her senator or representative that he or she is withdrawing support because of the politician's position on a critical issue, the most likely response is "I'm sorry to hear that." If the leader of a significant group withdraws support, however, the politician is far more likely to try to find another issue where he agrees with the group, or a modification of his position that will enable the group to support him once again. The larger the group is, the greater the ability to sanction politicians.

Groups are often willing to use the ability to sanction politicians, even those who are ordinarily their allies. A good example occurred when Congress ratified the Central American Free Trade Agreement (CAFTA) in the summer of 2005. The agreement was controversial and passed the House by only one vote, in part because the United States agreed to a very small relaxation of its restrictions on sugar imports from the CAFTA countries. Groups that had opposed CAFTA, including labor unions and some environmental groups, decided to retaliate against representatives who had supported the agreement. They targeted 30 congressmen, 15 Democrats and 15 Republicans, for opposition in the 2006 elections, including in primary campaigns in some cases. Four of the CAFTA 30 were defeated in 2006; eight more lost in 2008.

The advantages of groups work both ways. It is easier for groups to deal with politicians than would be the case for unorganized individuals, but it is also easier for politicians to deal with the group. Group leaders can serve as a sounding board for politicians to assess how a policy position will be received, and as a vehicle for communicating with voters likely to be receptive to a particular policy.

Because politicians find dealing with groups advantageous, they have an incentive to encourage groups to organize. With a group organized around a particular issue, politicians can take advantage of the lower costs of dealing with a group, if only they can get the group to organize. One example of a program designed in part to encourage more groups to organize is the Superfund program, which provided federal money to clean up abandoned toxic waste sites. When Congress passed the program, it specified that funding priority should go to the 100 worst dumps, as determined by EPA.

There is, of course, some incentive for those who live near a dump to organize, to argue that their dump should be on the list. Arguing that a particular dump is one of the 100 worst, however, may be difficult, which reduces the incentive to organize in the first place. To encourage more groups to form, Congress specified that the list must include at least one site in each state. Now the task is simply to argue that your neighborhood dump is the worst in the state, and far more people have an incentive to organize groups.

Interest groups also have incentives to try to build themselves into the institutional process of policy making. Doing so enables them to assure their continued influence, even after Congress passes a policy and entrusts some regulatory agency to administer it. Environmental groups have been some of the most successful at institutionalizing their role in the process. Many environmental statutes allow interest groups to sue to enforce the law, and require that if the government loses, it must pay the winning party's legal expenses. Cases frequently settle, but part of the settlement is likely to be a payment to the group for its legal expenses. Environmental groups use lawsuits to influence policy, but they also use them to fund their operations. Some significant environmental groups derive a substantial share of their revenues from legal fees paid by the government.

Given the advantages of groups, it is important to ask, why doesn't everyone organize? Why isn't there an organized interest group of sugar users, for example, that will participate in the policy process and offset the influence of the sugar growers?

The key factor determining who is successful in organizing is the free rider problem. Because public policy is coercive, it is usually difficult to exclude anyone from the benefits of that policy, whatever it might be.[3] As a result, everyone will benefit from any policy that a group gets enacted, whether they participate in the group or not. Privately, each potential member has an incentive to take a free ride, allowing others to bear the cost of group participation but receiving all of the benefits. Of course, if everyone reasons this way, there will be no group. The theory of who organizes is built around the factors that make it easier or harder to overcome the free rider problem.

One factor that facilitates organization is small numbers. With a small number of potential members, the free rider problem is more apparent to each one. If the group only has a dozen potential members, each is likely to see that his or her contribution to the group will be important in determining its success. If there are tens of thousands of potential members, each person's contribution is far less critical. Moreover, with small numbers it is easier to negotiate mutually agreeable arrangements to overcome free riding.

The small numbers case describes many industry groups. In many industries, there are a relatively small number of key players. Thus, the organizational task is easier than it is for larger groups. Partly as a result, nearly every industry has its trade association.

---

[3]In some cases, policies can be structured to narrow their impact somewhat. Subsidy programs, for example, may establish eligibility criteria that effectively exclude some people. Matching such criteria to the characteristics of members of a group, however, is often difficult. Tailoring regulatory policies to apply only to members of a group is far more difficult.

A second factor facilitating organization is a strong parallel purpose for the group. If there is some other reason for the group to exist, one that provides private benefits to those who join, the free rider problem is easier to overcome. Once the group is organized, adding public policy objectives to its activities is a simpler task. Much of the overhead of maintaining an office and staff is already covered by the parallel purpose for the group.

Again, the strong parallel purpose describes many industry trade associations. Trade associations provide a way for members to share information about the state of their markets. Many associations compile statistical data that is useful to member companies in assessing demand and capacity in the industry, and useful in considering their own strategic and investment decisions. Once the association is organized to share information, adding public policy objectives is relatively easy.

One group that has been highly successful in exploiting the parallel purpose is the American Association of Retired Persons, now AARP, the leading group representing senior citizens. AARP offers discounts for seniors on many products and services, including insurance. People join for the discounts, but AARP also maintains a formidable public policy presence on any issue related to senior citizens.

A few groups are organized by statute or regulations. For these groups, the government helps in overcoming the free rider problem by requiring membership or allowing the group to collect dues from non-members who benefit from the group's activities. The primary example is labor unions, which in many cases can collect dues from employees who choose not to join the union. Indeed, the term "free rider" comes from the early days of labor organizing, when unions argued that workers who did not join were taking a free ride on the efforts of union members.

Recently, there has been considerable litigation over the use of union dues for political purposes. Individual workers have successfully argued that requiring them to fund political views they disagree with violates the First Amendment's prohibition on restricting free speech. The Supreme Court has held that union members are entitled to a refund of the portion of their dues used for political purposes, and has allowed states to prohibit unions from collecting that portion of dues in the first place unless the worker explicitly agrees to help fund political activities.

One type of group is something of a puzzle from the perspective of the free rider problem. There are a number of groups that have broad-based membership, where members have a relatively small stake in the issue. Such groups should be difficult to organize, but they nonetheless exist. Examples include the National Rifle Association, numerous environmental groups such as the National Wildlife Federation or the Sierra Club, and health and safety groups such as the Center for Science in the Public Interest.

Although many such groups are either self-proclaimed or media-labeled as "public interest" groups, there is no particular relationship between such groups and the public interest as economists understand it. Most people would recognize the National Rifle Association as a special interest group, but it is not qualitatively different from the Sierra Club. What differs is the group's issue, not its approach to the issue or whether its position is in the "public interest." From an economic perspective, all such groups are trying to achieve a policy result that they have been unable to achieve in the market—not a hallmark of pursuing the public interest in the economic sense. Like any other label, the "public interest" label can color how voters react to the message, but it has no substantive significance.

Those who join broad-based interest groups are likely to be those who care most about the issue. They are not representative of the public at large, and almost certainly prefer more of their cause—whether it is environmental protection or freedom for gun owners—than the average voter. That was why they joined the group in the first place. At best, the leaders of the group will represent the interests of the group's members—and the members are those who care most about the issue, not the general public.

Broad-based interest groups often face an issue in fundraising. To sustain themselves, they depend on a continual flow of memberships and/or contributions from sympathetic members of the public. Raising money, however, is likely to be more successful if the group can point to a problem that only the group can help to solve. Environmental groups do not seek to raise money based on their track record of securing environmental improvements, for example. Instead, they seek money to address the next environmental crisis. Other groups are similar; they look for a dramatic problem to use as a "hook" for raising money. However much progress is made, there is always a need for another "problem" to use as a basis for an appeal for contributions.

IV. RENT-SEEKING BEHAVIOR

However they get organized, interest groups engage in what public choice theorists call rent-seeking behavior. Basically, they try to use the advantages that organized groups enjoy in the political process to persuade the government to provide essentially private benefits for the group and its members.

Figure 7-4. Rents in the short run.

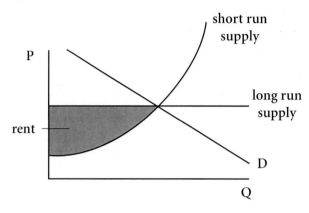

Technically, a rent is a payment that does not affect the availability of a resource. The term originates with land rents. Obviously, the same amount of land will be available regardless of the rent; the amount of the rent does not affect the quantity of the resource that is available. Rents can also be thought of as consumer or producer surplus. They are the result of the market, but do not directly affect ongoing resource availability. Rents also arise from the difference between short-run and long-run equilibrium. Consider, for example, a perfectly competitive industry with a horizontal long-run supply curve, as shown in Figure 7-4.

In the short run, with some fixed number of firms in the industry, the supply curve is upward sloping. There is producer surplus, the area between the long-run supply curve and the short-run supply curve, which covers fixed costs. If they lose some of this surplus, however, firms will not exit the industry. They will be better off continuing to produce and covering some of their fixed costs, even though they will suffer losses. Again, the surplus is a rent.

Groups use a number of common techniques to create and extract rents. One common approach is to limit competition to create monopoly rents. Numerous industries have at various times obtained entry controls to make new competition more difficult, or protection from imports in the form of tariffs or quotas, both of which create monopoly rents for incumbent firms. Other industries have sought to limit competitive products, thereby assuring increased demand for their own product.

In 2007, for example, Congress passed an energy bill that, among other things, bans incandescent light bulbs. Manufacturers of energy-efficient compact fluorescent bulbs had tried for years to interest the public in their product, but at $12 to $15 per bulb, demand was relatively limited. Banning the low-cost competitive product will virtually assure a substantial increase in demand, to the benefit of existing producers of compact fluorescents.

Another technique for creating and extracting rents is to seek policies that raise rivals' costs. Rather than limit competition directly, this approach seeks to create an artificial competitive advantage by making competitive products more expensive. For example, some firms may support increases in the minimum wage because it raises rivals' costs. A large capital-intensive firm may see little adverse impact from an increase in the minimum wage because it uses relatively little unskilled labor where the minimum wage is most relevant. Its competitors, however, may be much more labor intensive, and may therefore experience a more significant increase in costs. The policy raises rivals' costs, and creates an artificial advantage for the more capital-intensive firm.

One colorful example of a policy to raise rivals' costs involved dairy farmers and the introduction of margarine as a cheap substitute for butter. Dairy farmers were not happy about the low-cost new product, and in many states they persuaded the legislature to ban the use of food coloring in margarine. In its natural, uncolored state, margarine is a somewhat translucent white blob of fat, not nearly as appetizing as farm-fresh butter. As long as this policy was in place, margarine was sold with a separate packet of food coloring. The first thing consumers had to do was to knead in the food coloring to make the product look like butter. Wisconsin, a major dairy producing state, was one of the last states to abandon this policy, but not until the late 1960s.

Groups can also extract rents in the details of the structure of a policy. These details may assure that compliance with the requirement benefits certain groups, or they may offset adverse effects of a different compliance strategy that firms would otherwise choose. Either way, the policy details may create benefits for particular groups.

One good example of rent creation in the policy details concerns sulfur dioxide emissions and West Virginia coal. When the federal government first started regulating sulfur dioxide emissions from coal-fired power plants, they set a permissible level of emissions and left it up to firms to decide how to comply. There were two primary compliance strategies. One involved the use of lower-sulfur coal. With less sulfur in the coal to begin with, sulfur dioxide emissions were lower. The other involved the use of a device called a scrubber, which processes the exhaust gasses and removes sulfur dioxide, leaving behind a sludge that must be disposed of. Either strategy could achieve compliance, but with different consequences for West Virginia coal. Coal from Appalachia is relatively high in sulfur content. Low-sulfur coal is found in the Midwest and in the west. Thus, complying with the requirement by switching to low-sulfur coal reduced the demand for West Virginia coal. Senator Byrd from West Virginia was at the time the Senate Majority Leader, and succeeded in enacting a requirement that new power plants must use scrubbers. The requirement offered no real environmental benefits, because firms had the same compliance obligations in any event. However, it increased the demand for West Virginia coal, because once a scrubber was installed, there was no reason for firms to pay the higher costs (including transportation costs) of low-sulfur coal. The policy details created a particular benefit for West Virginia coal and West Virginia coal miners.

Another example of rent creation in the policy details involved the Federal Communication Commission's initial allocation of television licenses. The Commission could have chosen to allocate spectrum and licenses to maximize the number of viewing options that consumers would have. Under this approach, it would have authorized fewer stations operating at higher power and reaching more consumers. Instead, it allocated licenses to maximize the number of local television stations. Thus, it decided to give licenses to as many different people as possible, even though the effect was to reduce the number of stations most viewers could actually receive.

V. POLITICIANS

The theory of public choice views politicians, bureaucrats, and other institutional participants in the political process from an economic perspective. In the public choice view, these participants are not pursuing some abstract notion of the public interest, whether it is the economist's definition or some other. Rather, politicians and other participants are self-interested, with private motivations for the policy and political choices they make. This is the self-interest axiom: politicians and other participants in the political process will pursue their own self-interest.

The usual private motivations for politicians are political power and the perquisites of office. Political power is simply the ability of a politician to implement his or her policy choices. Political power in the hands of a politician whose positions agree with your own is a fine thing, but power in the hands of someone who will make different choices is more problematic. Politicians seek to maximize political power or political support in order to implement their own choices.

The perquisites of office are also privately attractive. Senators have their own special dining room, for example, heavily subsidized and offering far better fare than what is available to mere tourists. High government officials have nice offices, often in historic buildings. Their views and opinions are in demand. Cabinet secretaries have a car and driver who picks them up to take them to work every morning, and brings them home at the end of the day. Many other officials have cars available to ferry them around town as needed. These fringe benefits are attractive, and self-interest in protecting or acquiring them is a motivator for many.

Self-interest also motivates other participants in the policy process, such as interest group leaders. They too are interested in achieving political power. Many have their own ideas of what public policy should be, and seek the ability to turn those preferences into policy. In some cases, this leads group leaders to advocate policies well beyond what their members are willing to support.

One of the clearest examples of this problem was catastrophic health insurance, the shortest-lived government benefit program ever. The program was passed in 1989, and repealed in 1990, without ever really going into effect.

Catastrophic health insurance was intended to cover the relatively small number of elderly individuals who exceed the lifetime benefits cap under the Medicare program. When that happens, individuals can either pay for their own medical care, or spend down their remaining assets until they qualify for the Medicaid program, which covers low-income individuals. Interest groups representing the elderly were sure their members would highly value a catastrophic health insurance policy to avoid this dilemma. Because budget times were tight, the political compromise was that any program would have to be financed by its beneficiaries. That is, Medicare recipients would have to pay higher insurance premiums to cover the added costs of catastrophic health insurance. Interest group leaders were convinced the elderly would support this deal, and it was enacted in 1989.

Then the elderly found out about the program, and discovered their insurance premiums would rise. Many already had catastrophic health insurance under a previous employer's retirement plan, and were not interested in paying for something they were already getting for free. Others had considered catastrophic insurance in the private market, and decided it was not worth the costs. In any event, tens of thousands of intended beneficiaries wrote to their elected representatives, leading to the repeal of the program in 1990. It was a clear case of interest group leaders out ahead of what their constituents were willing to support.

The theory of public choice views politicians as political firms. These firms seek to maximize political support, rather than maximizing profits, in the pursuit of the self-interest of their members. To produce support, political firms need two crucial inputs: votes and money.

Votes are obviously critical in a democratic system. A political firm in an election with two choices needs at least 50 percent of the vote plus one. There is, however, more political influence from a landslide, so more votes are always better. Interest group support is a key source of votes, because individual voter support is skewed by rational ignorance.

Political firms also need resources. Political campaigns require money for advertising, polling, political consultants, communications, and a host of related services. A political campaign is an exercise in marketing a candidate, and like any other large-scale marketing campaign, it is expensive to do it right. Because any political firm must expect to lose on occasion, the firm needs employment opportunities for its supporters that will leave them free to assist the campaign when needed, enter the government if they so desire, and return to the private sector if and when political defeat ends the opportunity for public service. Law firms or political consulting firms frequently offer just these kinds of employment opportunities.

Just as capital and labor are substitutes in producing goods, votes and resources are substitutes in producing political support. The tradeoff is shown in Figure 7-5. A political firm can obtain a given level of support with a large number of votes and not very many other resources, or it can achieve the same level of support with far more resources and a lot fewer votes. More of both is of course better, so with more votes and more resources the political firm can achieve higher levels of political support.

To obtain support, political firms seek support from interest groups. The most obvious way of seeking support is to promise benefits (i.e., rents) to interest groups. This is the familiar world of campaign promises ("If I am elected . . ."). Sincere or not, the promise is an offer of benefits in exchange for support.

Figure 7-5. Constant levels of political support.

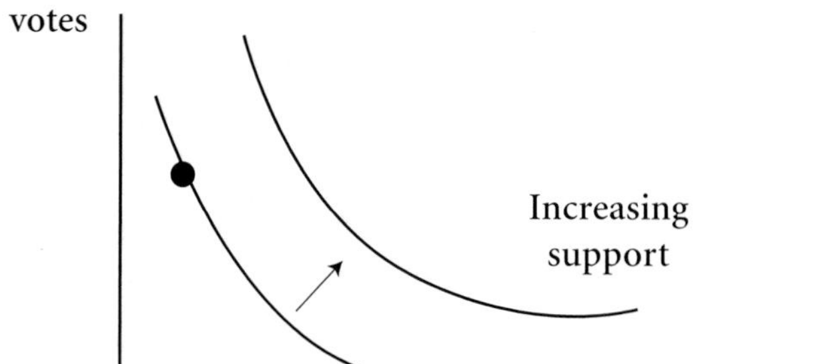

One of the clearest examples of offering rents in exchange for support occurs every four years in Iowa. Potential presidential candidates trek to Iowa to take the ethanol pledge. Seeking support in the Iowa presidential caucuses, they promise to support programs to encourage ethanol production and protect it from foreign competition. Whether using corn to produce ethanol to fuel cars is good for the country or not, there is no doubt that it offers substantial benefits to Iowa corn farmers. Since at least

1988, every presidential candidate save one has gone to Iowa to take the ethanol pledge. The one exception was John McCain in 2000, who refused to take the pledge—and lost. In 2008, he took the pledge.

A less savory means of seeking political support from interest groups is by threatening rent extraction. Politicians may threaten to remove or reduce benefits that an interest group is already receiving—unless, of course, the politician receives sufficient support from the group to change his mind. In its most blatant forms, such as former Illinois Governor Blagojevich's alleged attempt to sell off President Obama's vacant Senate seat or his alleged threat to withhold aid from a children's hospital unless he received campaign contributions, such threats are illegal.

More subtle forms of rent extraction threats occur with some frequency, however. A politician may introduce a legislative proposal not because he expects it to be enacted, but because it stakes out a position that threatens rents of important interest groups, in the hopes that those groups will offer political support to help avoid the damage. At the state level, these legislative proposals often have very colorful names. In some states, they are "milker" bills, to milk groups for campaign cash. In others, they are known as "cash cows," or "fetcher" bills, to fetch campaign contributions.

An interesting feature of proposals designed to elicit contributions is that there is an incentive to delay resolution of the issue. The incentive to contribute results from the fact that the issue is pending. If it is resolved, the incentive disappears.

Consider two examples of long-standing issues that generate substantial amounts of campaign contributions. One example is product liability reform, which has been an issue at the federal level since at least 1984. There are well-funded interest groups on both sides of the issue. Some will offer support, and contributions, to protect the benefits that the current system offers for them; others will make contributions to try to reshape the system to their benefit. Ralph Nader described product liability reform as "a PAC annuity for members of Congress. It's like rubbing the golden lamp." If the issue were resolved, the need for contributions would disappear, but as long as it is pending, many groups have incentives to offer support.

Another example is legislation to reform the structure of the financial services industry, removing many structural restrictions that date from the Great Depression. Administrative efforts to reduce or remove restrictions, mostly by the Federal Reserve Board, began in the late 1970s. It was not until 1999, however, that Congress passed the Gramm Leach Bliley Act, removing the artificial barriers that prevented financial institutions from poaching on one another's turf. In the meantime, many industry groups, including commercial banks, investment banks, insurance companies, brokerage firms, and others all had incentives to make contributions to help produce a result that was to their liking.

In the theory of public choice, politicians and other institutional participants in the political process are seen as self-interested political firms seeking to maximize political support. To gain support, they need both votes and resources. They seek support from interest groups, by promising rents and by threatening rent extraction.

VI. A GENERAL MODEL OF REGULATORY AGENCY BEHAVIOR[4]

We can assemble the pieces of the theory of public choice into a general model of how regulatory agencies or other decision makers will make policy choices. The model was developed to address regulatory agencies, but its central implications are equally applicable to any political decision-making institution, whether it is Congress or the executive branch.

Any agency has a set of authorities and constraints that define the range of policies it can pursue. For a regulatory agency, the key constraints are usually statutory. Congress has authorized the agency to do some things but not others, and it can only pursue policy choices that are within its authority. For Congress or the executive branch, the key constraints are constitutional. But all political decision makers face constraints that limit the policies they can pursue.

---

[4]This model is largely taken from Haddock and Macey, "Regulation on Demand: A Private Interest Model, with an Application to Insider Trading Regulation," *Journal of Law and Economics* 30(1): 311–339 (October 1987).

Figure 7-6. Support for policies in the agency's choice set.

Policy	Interest Group Support Group 1	Group 2	Total Support
A	S_{A1}	S_{A2}	S_A
B	S_{B1}	S_{B2}	S_B
...			
Z	S_{Z1}	S_{Z2}	S_Z
AA	S_{AA1}	S_{AA2}	S_{AA}
...			
ZZ	S_{ZZ1}	S_{ZZ2}	S_{ZZ}

The agency is interested in pursuing policy choices that will maximize its political support. That support will come from interest groups potentially affected by its decisions. We can consider a relatively simple case in which there are only two interest groups that matter, group 1 and group 2. For any given policy, each group will deliver some amount of support. Policy choice A, for example, might generate an amount of support given by S_{A1} from group 1, and an amount given by S_{A2} from group 2. Of course, a group may oppose a particular policy, but we can think of opposition as negative support and retain the same basic notion. Because the agency is concerned about maximizing total support, it does not care how the support is divided between the groups. That is, it only cares about the total amount of political support that policy choice A will generate, given by $S_A = S_{A1} + S_{A2}$. A similar calculation can be applied to any other possible policy choices the agency might make from the policies within its choice set. A few such possibilities are listed in Figure 7-6.

Figure 7-7. Policy options and interest group support.

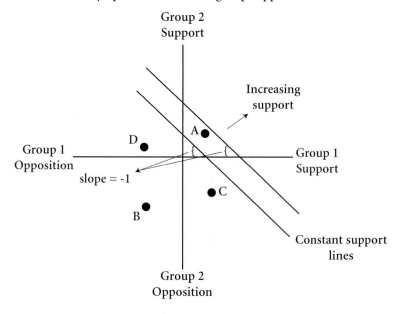

Moreover, we can depict the support that the agency receives from any policy choice graphically. A few such choices are shown in Figure 7-7; there will be many points, one corresponding to each policy choice the agency might make.

Policies in the upper right quadrant of the graph, such as A, receive support from both groups. Both groups oppose policies in the lower left quadrant (e.g., B), and one group supports but the other opposes policies in the remaining two quadrants (e.g., C or D).

Figure 7-7 also includes straight lines that indicate all the points with the same amount of total support from the two groups combined. These lines are simply the points where S1 + S2 is a constant; the lines farther up to the right are higher levels of total support. The slope of each of these lines is –1, because along a line loss of support from one group is precisely offset by an increase in support from the other.

Groups may differ in their ability to produce political support. One key factor influencing how much support a group will provide is its stake in the issue. If the group has a small stake in the issue, it will generate little support for a policy decision addressing that issue, even if it would like the choice. Instead, the group and its members will remain rationally ignorant about the policy. On the other hand, a group with a large stake in an issue will generate much more support. Groups may generate support in the form of either money or votes, or, of course, a combination of the two.

Consider first the case where the two groups are equally able to produce support. There will be some frontier of the amount of support the agency can achieve from each of the policy options open to it, as shown in Figure 7-8. This frontier is just the outer edge of the set of points indicating support from each group that

Figure 7-8. The support-maximizing decision.

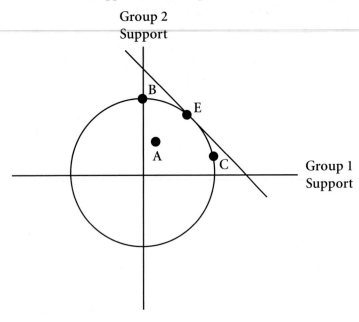

A support-maximizing agency will never choose a policy like A in Figure 7-8 that lies inside the frontier of choices it could make. It can gain more support from both groups by moving outward toward the frontier, and will continue to do so until it can go no further. Similarly, it will not choose policy B, which is group 2's most preferred policy. It can change the policy in a way that will cost it a little support from group 2, but gain considerably more support from group 1. Instead, it will move around the circle to the right as long as it can continue to increase total support. For the same reason, it will not choose policy C, which is group 1's preferred choice. It can sacrifice a little support from group 1 to gain considerably more support from group 2.

In fact, the support-maximizing agency will continue to trade off support from the two groups until it cannot achieve a higher level of total support. That is, it will choose the point where the frontier of choices it can make reaches the highest level of total support possible. At this point, the choice frontier will be just tangent to one of the constant support lines. This equilibrium policy is point E in Figure 7-8. Because the slope of the constant support lines is -1, at this point the slope of the policy frontier is also -1. That is, if the agency changes its policy in a way that generates a little more support from one group, it will lose the same amount of support from the other group. Small changes in policy cannot increase total support from the equilibrium policy E.

The same basic model applies if one group is more able to produce political support than the other, but the shape of the frontier is different. If, for example, Group 1 is more able to produce political support, the agency will receive more support from that group for policies it prefers. Given the amount of support from Group 2, the additional support from group 1 stretches the circle into an ellipse, as shown in Figure 7-9.

Figure 7-9. Unequal ability to produce support.

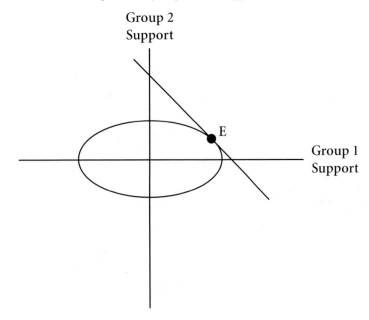

Even though Group 1 is more able to produce support, it will not get the policy it likes most. The agency will still trade off a small loss in support from Group 1 for a larger gain in support from Group 2. As in the case of equal abilities to produce support, the agency will choose the support-maximizing decision (policy E in the figure) where the frontier is just tangent to the highest possible support line.

The model can also be used to address policy choices that involve inconsistent objectives. For such choices, policies that one group favors will generate opposition from the

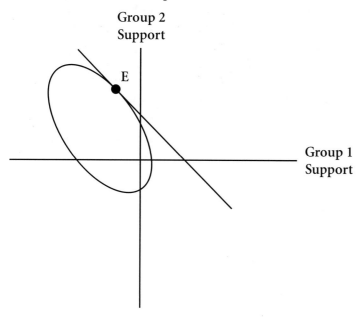

Figure 7-10. Redistributional policies.

other group. Redistribution policies are one example: gaining more support from the recipients will mean higher costs, and more opposition, from those who must pay the costs. The choice frontier for such policy choices is shown in Figure 7-10. Still, the condition for the support-maximizing choice is the same, and the agency will again choose the equilibrium policy E in the figure.

One immediate implication of the general model of regulatory agency behavior is that the political process will inevitably compromise. A support-maximizing political agency will give up support from one group to get a greater amount of support (or a greater reduction in opposition) from another. Even if one group is significantly more able to produce support than another, it will not get everything it wants. The agency will still compromise, as we saw in Figure 7-9.

Another implication is more interesting. We can think of the public interest in the economic sense of maximizing consumer welfare as judged by consumers as a group. Even if it were a powerful group, the political process would compromise the public interest. Politicians can increase total support by giving up a little of the public interest in order to gain more support from other groups. Unfortunately, however, the public interest is likely to be a very weak group. For a great many policy decisions, the public at large has a very small individual stake in the issue, and therefore remains rationally ignorant. Thus, the public interest "group" is likely to be relatively weak at generating political support. Public policies adopted through the political process are particularly likely to favor other interest groups, at the expense of the broader public interest.

This, of course, is exactly what the public choice theorists set out to understand. Deviations from pursuing the public interest are not accidents or aberrations; rather, they are the systematic result of the forces at work in the political system. In the interests of maximizing political support, the public interest will be compromised.

VII. SUMMARY

Under majority rule, the preferred outcome of the median voter will prevail. This is the only policy that can command a majority. Majority rule decisions tend to be centrist, and to redistribute income toward the middle class. Without constraints, however, majority rule can result in the tyranny of the majority. Simple majority rule does not reflect the intensity of voter preferences about a particular issue, and mechanisms that allow some reflection of preference intensity (such as vote trading) may make things worse. As the Arrow Impossibility Theorem shows, there may be no stable outcome under majority rule. Instead, the outcome may be determined entirely by the order in which we vote on the alternatives.

Voter participation in the policy process on a particular issue depends on balancing the benefits and costs of obtaining information about the issue. Because information is costly, it is rational for voters to remain ignorant about many issues. When individual voters have a small stake in the issue, the benefits of participation are low, and rational ignorance is likely. Those with a large stake, however, are more likely to find that participation is worthwhile. Moreover, information about policy choices can be costly to obtain. Some information is hidden, as with many new product approval decisions. Program complexity increases the costs of obtaining information. The lack of a common denominator for outcomes makes comparisons across programs difficult, and there is no external standard of comparison to facilitate evaluation.

Interest groups have advantages over individuals in the political process. Because they can share the costs of information, they are better able to communicate, to negotiate, and to monitor and sanction politicians. Groups must overcome the free rider problem to get organized initially. The task is easier if the number of potential group members is small, if there is a strong parallel purpose for the group to exist, or if statutory or regulatory requirements facilitate organization. There is no good theory to explain broad-based groups with a relatively small stake in the issue. However they identify themselves, they are not "public interest" groups in the economic sense. At best, such groups will pursue the interests of their members. Group members are likely to be those who care most about an issue. Broad-based interest groups frequently depend on using the existence of a perceived problem to raise money.

Once organized, interest groups engage in rent-seeking behavior: they seek private benefits from the government. Techniques for obtaining rents include limiting competition, raising rivals' costs, and creating rents in the policy details.

The theory of public choice sees politicians and other institutional participants in the policy process as self-interested, seeking to maximize political support. On occasion, self-interested group leaders may not represent their members very well. To maximize political support, politicians need votes and money. They seek support from interest groups by offering rents, and by threatening rent extraction.

Regulatory agencies will choose policies to maximize political support. They will compromise between the interests of different groups, as long as giving up a little support from one group will result in gaining even more support from another group. Even powerful groups will not get everything they want. If we see the public interest (in the sense of maximizing consumer welfare as judged by consumers) as a group, it too inevitably will be compromised. Moreover, because of rational ignorance, the public interest is likely to be a relatively weak group with limited ability to deliver political support. Policies will therefore favor other interest groups at the expense of the broader public interest.

APPLYING THE THEORY OF PUBLIC CHOICE: INSIDER TRADING REGULATIONS

Chapter 8

The theory of public choice holds that economic considerations are critical to understanding most regulatory decisions. Interest groups offer political support for policies that favor their interests, and to understand the choices regulators make, understanding the interests at stake is essential. In this chapter, we use the general model developed in the last chapter to consider the SEC's decisions about insider trading regulations. Although insider trading is more often thought of as an ethical issue, the economic interests of the key groups provide critical insights into regulatory decisions.

The story concerns the SEC's original regulations regarding insider trading, and the political equilibrium that produced them. It then considers the changes that resulted when the Supreme Court ruled in the *Chiarella* case in 1980 that the SEC did not have the authority to regulate as broadly as it had claimed. The result was a significant change in the regulatory regime. The changes that resulted from the court decision can also be understood through the lens of the theory of public choice.

Section I considers the different types of insider trading and the regulations that restrict it. In Section II, we consider the effects of insider trading, which forms the basis for Section III's identification of the interest groups and the political equilibrium that prevailed before the *Chiarella* decision. Section IV considers how the initial impact of the regulatory changes resulting from *Chiarella* changed in the long run as the financial services industry expanded, and generalizes the notion of policy irreversibility: that policies frequently generate an interest group with a stake in the continuation of that policy, even if the policy no longer offers benefits.

I. Types of Insider Trading and Regulatory Restrictions

Insider trading occurs when an insider, such as the manager of a corporation, buys or sells the securities of his or her firm in anticipation of a firm-specific change in price, when that anticipation is based on material, nonpublic information. Insider trading can occur whether the transaction is a purchase or a sale of securities. The expected price change must be firm-specific, as opposed to an expected increase (or decrease) in the market in general or in the fortunes of a particular industry. Finally, the expectation of a price change must be based on information that is likely to affect the stock price, but is not publicly available.

Insider trading can be classified based on the effects on the costs of the firm whose shares are traded. One type of insider trading is theft insider trading, which raises the costs of the firm whose shares are traded. In theft insider trading, managers essentially use information against the shareholders. A hypothetical example of the nature of the problem is Walt Disney's 1993 plan to build a Civil War theme park in northern Virginia. Before it announced its plans, the company acquired options on the land it would need to build the park because it knew that once the plans were announced, land values would increase. An employee who used knowledge of the plan to acquire some of the necessary land on his or her own would essentially be bidding against the shareholders, raising the cost for the company to accomplish its objective.

The most common type of insider trading is ordinary insider trading. In ordinary insider trading, an employee with knowledge of, for example, a forthcoming earnings report that is better than expected, buys shares based on the information. When the earnings report comes out, the share price will rise, and the insider will profit. However, there is no effect on the company's costs at all. The information would have been released in any event, and the impact on stock prices and the company would have been precisely the same.

A third type of insider trading, known as arbitrage insider trading, occurs in connection with takeover transactions. Arbitrage insider trading makes it easier for a company to achieve its objectives, and thus effectively lowers the company's costs. In fact, the acquiring company is most often the source of the information, which it provides to selected traders.

The idea behind arbitrage insider trading is this. A company planning to launch a hostile takeover knows that the management of the target company is likely to resist the takeover because their jobs are at stake. To complete the takeover, the acquiring company would like as many shares as possible in the hands of investors who are willing to sell to the highest bidder, with no particular interest in the company or the merits of the strategy its managers are currently pursuing or the changes in strategy that the potential acquirer would adopt.[1] If the potential acquirer tells selected traders about the planned transaction, they can make purchases before the proposal is announced. As a result, more shares will be in the hands of investors with no ties to the existing management. The takeover offer is therefore more likely to succeed.

There are three separate legal restrictions on insider trading. One restriction is statutory: insiders must disgorge profits from any purchase and sale (or sale and subsequent purchase) completed within six months. Thus, insiders cannot profit from short-term trading in their employer's securities. An insider who buys, holds the shares for less than six months, and then sells must give up any profits on the transaction. If the insider holds the shares for just over six months, however, the statutory restriction does not apply.

A second restriction on insider trading is the SEC's rule 10(b)5, the primary tool to address ordinary insider trading. Under this rule, as the SEC originally interpreted it, anyone in possession of material, nonpublic information must either disclose the information or refrain from trading. The focus is on nonpublic information rather than the identity of the party who trades. On its face, it would apply to market professionals, such as analysts who follow the company, who may have nonpublic information as a result of their research with customers, suppliers, or others. In the *Chiarella* case in 1980, the Supreme Court narrowed this rule to those with a fiduciary duty to the company's shareholders. That decision effectively excluded most market

---

[1] The acquiring company can acquire some shares on its own before it makes an announcement, but once it has acquired five percent of the shares, it must announce its investment. If it is known as a company inclined to make acquisitions, that announcement is likely to lead the target company's management to initiate steps to resist a takeover, and to an increase in the price of the target company's shares.

professionals from the rule's prohibitions, because they generally have no fiduciary duty to the company or its shareholders.

The third restriction is SEC rule 14(e)3, which was adopted shortly after the *Chiarella* decision was announced. Under this rule, anyone who obtains nonpublic information about an impending tender offer from either the offeror or the target of the offer must either disclose the information or refrain from trading. Again, the focus is on the information, but the rule is narrowed to a particular type of information, namely, information about takeover offers. On its face, the rule also applies to anyone, regardless of their relationship to the company.

II. THE EFFECTS OF INSIDER TRADING

The effects of insider trading depend to some extent on the type of insider trading that is involved. Theft insider trading is unambiguously bad. Insiders win at the expense of the shareholders they are supposed to serve. Like any other form of theft, there is no reason to think it serves any useful purpose.

Ordinary insider trading is more complicated. Consider the impact of new information, such as an earnings report, in a market with no insider trading at all. Before the earnings report is released, the stock is trading at a particular price level, as shown in Figure 8-1.

When the earnings report is released, the price will change, based on the information in the report. If the report is better than expected, the share price will increase; if the report is worse than expected, the price will decrease.[2] The change in price upon release of the information creates a trading gain: an opportunity to buy low, before the price has adjusted to the new information, and sell high, after the information is incorporated into the market price.

Figure 8-1. Stock price adjustment to new information.

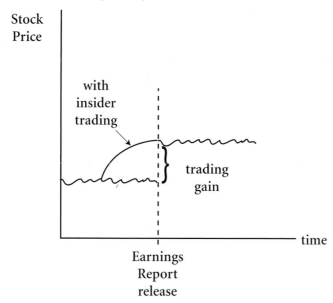

If insiders can trade, they will know the content of the earnings report before it is released, and they will capture the trading gain. Before the release, they will have the opportunity to purchase at the low price, and sell later when the price increases. Clearly, then, insiders will profit from insider trading. But who loses?

There are no meaningful losses to ordinary investors in the company who choose to sell before the release of the earnings report. For whatever reason, those investors were willing sellers. They went to the market before the report to sell at the then-prevailing market price. It makes no difference to them whether the other party to the trade was an insider or not; they had decided to sell in any event.

It is true, of course, that if the investors who sell just before the earnings report is released had known what was in the report, they might have made a different decision. That is simply the return on having information in the market.

Given the information they had, these investors believed the best choice was to sell. The buyer in that transaction believed the best choice was to buy. Whether that belief was based on different information, or a different judgment about the same information, the effect is the same—the seller at the low price would have been

---

[2]For simplicity, both the figure and the discussion in the text consider only unexpectedly good news. The situation is not fundamentally different for unexpectedly bad news. The fall in price creates an opportunity to sell short at the high price and cover at the new, lower price.

better off if he or she had made a different choice. If there is any injury to non-insider investors, it is from the lack of information, not from the identity of the other party in their transaction. Parties who have information profit from that information, at the expense of other investors who do not have the same information. That is the economic incentive to generate relevant information and bring it to the market.

The real losers from insider trading are the people who would otherwise capture the trading gains that are possible when new information arrives in the market. Absent insider trading, the competition for trading gains is essentially a race to buy shares at the pre-report price. That process bids up the price, which creates the opportunity to sell and realize a gain. Overwhelmingly, the winners of this race will be market professionals: brokers, dealers, analysts who follow the company, and similar participants in financial services markets. An analyst who follows the company, for example, knows that the earnings report is coming, and knows what the market expects from the report. If the report is unexpectedly good news, it will be immediately apparent to the analyst. Moreover, the analyst has immediate access to the trading floor to begin purchasing shares before the information is incorporated into the price. In all likelihood, by the time ordinary investors even find out about the earnings report, the opportunity for trading gains is already gone. Anyone who depends on the *Wall Street Journal* to find about the new information is far too late, because the information will already be reflected in the market price.

In short, insider trading will change who gets the trading gains. With insider trading, it is insiders who will win the race and capture the trading gains. Without insider trading, these gains will go to market professionals.

Insider trading also affects the informational content of the stock price. If the insiders can trade, the process of trading will incorporate the information that insiders have into the stock price. Almost whatever the information might be, insiders are likely to know before others. If they can trade, that information will be reflected in stock prices more rapidly. With insider trading, the market price prevailing at any point in time will be a better reflection of all available information. Without insider trading, the information that only insiders have cannot be reflected in share prices.

Insider trading will also smooth the adjustment of stock prices over time. Because the insiders know what is in the earnings report before it is released, the price will increase before the release date. Even before the earnings report is prepared, the insiders are likely to have information that others do not about how the current quarter is looking and what the earnings report is likely to show. As they trade on this information, it too is built into stock prices. With insiders trading on what they know, stock prices will adjust more gradually over time. As shown in Figure 8-1, instead of a sharp increase in price on the date of the report, we will see a gradual increase in price to the post-report equilibrium price.

Finally, insider trading will lead to higher transactions costs in the market. Market professionals are in the business of providing trading services, but they also trade for their own accounts. If they cannot earn as much from trading because insiders capture the trading gains, that effectively increases the costs of providing trading services. Thus, transactions costs increase, typically widening the spread between bid and asked prices that prevails in the market.

Both ordinary and arbitrage insider trading will change the distribution of trading gains from market professionals to insiders, result in smoother stock price adjustments, better reflection of all available information in prices, and higher transactions costs. There is one additional effect of arbitrage insider trading: arbitrage insider trading facilitates takeovers. Because more shares will be in the hands of investors who are willing to sell to the highest bidder, with no commitment to existing management or its strategies, it will be more difficult for incumbent managers to resist. That, of course, is why the acquiring firm shares the information with selected traders in the first place: it is seeking assistance in accomplishing its objective.

III. INTEREST GROUPS AND THEIR STAKES IN INSIDER TRADING REGULATION

We can use the general model of agency decisions developed at the end of the last chapter to consider the regulatory decisions about insider trading regulation. There are two key groups with an interest in insider trading regulation: the insiders themselves, and market professionals. The groups, however, have different concerns about different types of insider trading. Their interests are summarized in Figure 8-2.

Figure 8-2. Interest groups and their stakes.

Interest Group	Type of Trading	
	Ordinary Insider Trading	Arbitrage Insider Trading
Insiders	Support trading: realize trading gains Small Stake: gains small part of income	Oppose trading: facilitates takeovers Large Stake: jobs at risk
Market Professionals	Oppose trading: lose trading gains Large Stake: substantial fraction of income from trading	Divided Interest: recipients of tips benefit, others lose Small Stake: not very important to them collectively

Consider first the insiders. There are more insiders than market professionals, but they are a more diffuse group. They would like to engage in ordinary insider trading because they would realize additional income from trading gains. Ordinary insider trading, however, would likely constitute a relatively small fraction of their income. The insider's salary and bonus package is likely to be far more significant. Moreover, if insider trading were legal, one would expect that compensation packages would be reduced by the amount of the expected trading gains for the insider. Thus, insiders have a relatively small stake in ordinary insider trading. If this were the only issue, insiders would likely be less effective than professionals in delivering political support.

Arbitrage insider trading, however, is different. Insiders are likely to oppose arbitrage insider trading because it makes takeovers easier and thereby threatens their jobs. Because their jobs are at risk, insiders have a relatively large stake in seeing restrictions on arbitrage insider trading. On this part of the issue, they will be more willing to deliver political support than market professionals.

For market professionals, it is ordinary insider trading that is most important. If ordinary insider trading is allowed, market professionals will lose the race for trading gains. Income from trading is likely to be a large share of income for many market professionals. Thus, they have a large stake in seeking restrictions on ordinary insider trading, and they will be willing to deliver political support for restrictions.

Figure 8-3. Political equilibrium before *Chiarella*.

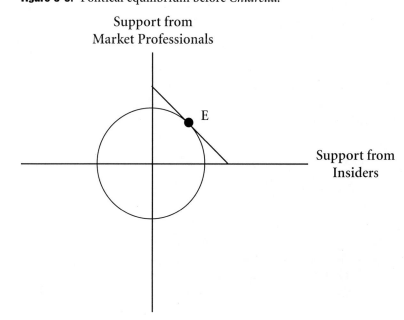

Market professionals are somewhat divided about arbitrage insider trading. The professionals who receive information from potential acquirers would like to be permitted to trade based on that information. Most professionals, however, do not receive such information, and therefore do not benefit. Because their interests are divided, market professionals collectively have a relatively small stake in seeking or opposing restrictions on arbitrage insider trading.

Because each group has a large stake in one portion of the insider trading issue, it seems most reasonable to regard the two groups as more or less equally able to deliver support. The situation confronting the SEC is depicted in Figure 8-3.

For different reasons, each group is willing to strongly support restrictions on one type of insider trading. Before the *Chiarella* decision, the result was rule 10(b)5: insider trading on any kind of information was illegal for anyone, whether a market professional or an insider. Those with material nonpublic information had to either disclose the information or refrain from trading. That is the equilibrium point E in Figure 8-3.

With insider trading illegal for everyone, there is relatively little incentive for market professionals to cooperate in facilitating enforcement. Their cooperation is vital to identifying potential cases, however, because they are in a position to watch for the kinds of trading patterns that indicate insider trading may be occurring. A suspicious trading pattern occurs when new information arrives, such as the release of an earnings report, which should have caused a jump in the stock price but did not. When the trading pattern is the smooth price adjustment path depicted in Figure 8-1, rather than the expected discrete jump, it may be the result of insiders trading. It may also, however, be the result of diligent market analysts who have ferreted out nonpublic information based on their own research and correctly anticipated the earnings report. There is little incentive for organized groups of market professionals, such as the exchanges, to identify such patterns for the SEC when they may be turning in their own members.

The result was relatively few cases. In the 12 years before the *Chiarella* decision, there were a total of 37 SEC cases alleging violations of rule 10(b)5, or an average of about three cases per year. There were prosecutions in blatant cases, but significant amounts of insider trading in violation of the rule were almost certainly occurring but not being prosecuted.

Then came the *Chiarella* decision in 1980. When the Supreme Court held that the SEC could prohibit insider trading only by those with a fiduciary duty to the company, it effectively eliminated market professionals from the coverage of the rule. In effect, the Court ruled that part of what the SEC had thought was included in its choice set was not. The result was the policy that market professionals would most prefer: trading on nonpublic information was illegal for insiders, but not for market professionals.

One result of the changed legal environment was that there was now a greater incentive for market professionals to cooperate in enforcing the rule. Because the rule did not apply to them, any cases would be addressing exactly what the market professionals care most about, which is ordinary insider trading by insiders. After *Chiarella*, with more cooperation, the SEC brought substantially more enforcement actions under the rule. In the first four-and-one-half years after the decision, the agency brought 79 rule 10(b)5 cases, an average of just over 17 per year.

The *Chiarella* decision cost the SEC considerable political support from insiders. The rule no longer restricted the arbitrage insider trading they cared most about, because the arbitrageurs had no fiduciary duty to the company. To gain back some of the support from insiders, the agency adopted rule 14(e)3, which narrowly targeted arbitrage insider trading. Although that effort eventually failed when the courts limited the rule to those with a fiduciary duty in 1991, it regained political support from insiders for a considerable period of time.

Finally, there was a greater willingness on the part of both insiders and professionals to support increased sanctions for insider trading. Together, the rules targeted the type of insider trading that each group cared most strongly about. Higher penalties would increase deterrence, leading to less of the trading that most concerned each group. The result was the 1984 Insider Traders Sanctions Act. The law was narrowly tailored to avoid disturbing any of the SEC's rules, but gave the SEC the authority to seek treble damages in any case of insider trading.

The theory of public choice enables us to understand more clearly the forces at play in producing the insider trading regulations. Although often thought of as an ethical issue (and for theft insider trading it is), in fact the rules can be better understood by considering the economic interests of the groups with the most at stake. The theory helps to understand both the initial result, and the changes that resulted from the Supreme Court's 1980 decision.

In the wake of the financial crisis, the SEC launched a new wave of prosecutions against insider trading. The cases challenged practices of hedge funds, which the SEC alleges are sometimes trading based on tips from corporate insiders. Many of the cases have involved arbitrage insider trading, with the fund trading ahead of announcements about merger and acquisition activities. The Commission has also challenged trading based on "expert networks," which put companies in contact with potential experts in a particular field. Often, these experts are insiders at some other company, and may end up providing material, nonpublic information to the client of the network for a price. Some analysts have expressed fears that these cases could discourage hedge funds, and other analysts, from careful research, because of the increased risk of prosecution.

IV. RENT SEEKING AND THE EFFECTS OF ENTRY

The changes in enforcement of insider trading regulations that followed the *Chiarella* decision created gains for market professionals who were in the market at the time. Market professionals provide trading services for investors. One factor in the cost of providing those services is the amount of income professionals can expect to generate from trading. The increase in enforcement against insiders effectively reduced the cost of providing trading services. Thus the short-run supply curve for trading services shifts downward to S_1, as shown in Figure 8-4.

Figure 8-4. Rents to existing traders.

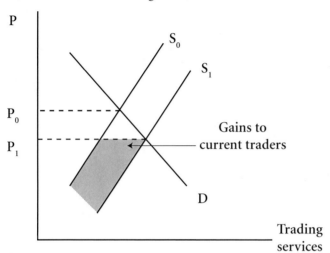

Part, but not all, of the reduction in cost is shared with consumers as the price of trading services falls from P_0 before the decision to P_1 after. The area between the original supply curve and the new supply curve, however, represents short-run gains to existing market professionals when the policy change takes place.

Over time, the increased profitability of providing trading services will attract entry. As entry occurs, the supply curve will shift to the right, and become flatter as well. Because the reduction in costs lasts as long as insider trading is effectively prohibited, the long-run supply curve shifts downward by the same amount as the short-run supply curve. Eventually, all of the cost reduction will be passed on to consumers, as shown in Figure 8-5. There will no longer be abnormal returns to market professionals; all such gains will have been competed away.

Thus, in the short run, professionals who are in the market when the policy change occurs will realize extra profits as their costs fall. Over time, entry will erode those extra profits as more resources enter the business of providing trading services. In the new equilibrium, there will no longer be excess profits.

Today, market professionals are unlikely to realize any excess profits, because entry has long since competed away the gains. Nonetheless, even though they do not profit from the current policy, they have a stake in its continuation. If the SEC were to reverse itself and allow insider trading, the immediate effect would be precisely that shown in Figure 8-4, but with the supply curve shifted up

Figure 8-5. The effects of entry.

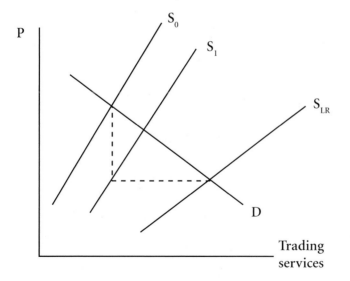

instead of down. As insiders capture the trading gains, costs of providing trading services would increase. The price would increase, but not by the full amount of the increase in costs, thereby imposing losses on all those in the market at the time of the policy reversal. Thus, even though it does not generate current profits, the existing policy has created a group with a stake in its continuation. Changing policies would create real losses for those presently in the market.

Many public policies create groups with a stake in the continuation of the policy, even though they do not create current profits for that group. Consider, for example, New York City taxicabs. In the 1930s, the city attempted to deal with growing traffic problems by restricting the number of taxicabs. Taxi drivers at the time were "grandfathered" into the new system, and were given a medallion that authorized them to drive a cab. When they wanted to retire, they could sell their medallion to someone else who would then be authorized to drive a cab. Over time, the demand for taxis in New York has grown, but the supply of medallions has not. The result has been increasing taxi fares, and increasing prices for taxi medallions. Recently, the price of a taxi medallion reached $600,000.

Although taxi fares are obviously higher than they would be in the absence of the medallion system, there are no gains to current drivers. After all, they had to pay for a medallion to enter the industry, and the higher fares are just enough to cover the cost of the required investment. If the system changed, however, to eliminate the need for a medallion, existing drivers would suffer a real loss. Their $600,000 investment would become worthless. Thus, taxi drivers have a stake in seeing the current system continue.

A similar situation occurs with agricultural price supports, which keep commodity prices higher than they would be otherwise. Over time, the value of price supports gets bid into land values. In the first half of 2008, as corn prices soared, for example, the prices of prime Iowa farmland rose as well. Current farmers do not receive excess profits, because they have to pay more for farmland than they would otherwise. But they would suffer real losses if price supports ended, as the value of their investment in land fell. As many policies do, this policy creates a group with a stake in making sure the policy continues.

V. Summary

Insider trading occurs when insiders, such as a firm's managers, buy or sell securities of their firm in anticipation of future firm-specific price changes, when that anticipation is based on material, nonpublic information. Theft insider trading raises costs to the firm. Ordinary insider trading, such as trading in anticipation of a better than expected earnings report, has no effect on the firm's costs. Arbitrage insider trading facilitates takeovers and makes it easier for the acquiring firm to accomplish its objectives, thereby reducing costs.

The statutory restriction on insider trading requires insiders to disgorge the profits on any purchase and subsequent sale (or sale and subsequent purchase) completed within six months. Rule 10(b)5 requires anyone in possession of material nonpublic information either to refrain from trading or to disclose the information. It was narrowed to those with a fiduciary duty to the firm in the 1980 *Chiarella* case. Rule 14(e)3 prohibits arbitrage insider trading. Although the rule by its terms applies to anyone, it has also been narrowed by the courts to those with a fiduciary duty to the company.

Insider trading changes the distribution of trading gains. With insider trading, the insiders will capture trading gains because they have the information first. Without insider trading, market professionals are most likely to capture the trading gains when new information arrives. Insider trading smoothes stock price adjustments over time and results in prices that better reflect all available information about the company. Insider trading also increases transactions costs. In addition, arbitrage insider trading facilitates takeovers.

The primary interest groups with a stake in insider trading regulation are insiders and market professionals. Market professionals have a large stake in prohibiting ordinary insider trading, because trading gains are an important component of their income. Insiders have a small stake in allowing it, because their compensation packages from their company are a far larger fraction of their income. Insiders, however, have a large stake in restricting arbitrage insider trading, because their jobs are at stake. Because market professionals are divided on this issue, they have a small stake collectively. The two groups are more or less equally able to produce political support for their position, because they each have a large stake in part of the issue.

Before *Chiarella,* the political equilibrium was a regulation that prohibited all insider trading by anyone, but was rarely enforced, in part because market professionals had little incentive to cooperate with the SEC. Insider trading was almost certainly occurring.

When the Supreme Court narrowed rule 10(b)5 to apply to insiders only, the political situation changed. Because professionals now had an incentive to cooperate (the rule did not apply to them), enforcement increased substantially. To gain back support from insiders, the SEC adopted rule 14(e)3. With the kind of trading that each group cared most about prohibited, both groups were willing to support stronger penalties for insider trading violations.

The change in insider trading regulations created gains for market professionals who were in the market at the time of the change. Over time, however, entry competed those gains away. Although there are no current excess profits for market professionals, they have a stake in the continuation of the current policy. Changes would impose real losses on professionals currently in the market.

Many policies generate a group with a stake in seeing the policy continue. They may not derive excess profits from the policy, but they would suffer real losses if the policy were revised.

IDEAS MATTER: PRIVACY AND THE DO NOT CALL REGISTRY

Chapter 9

The theory of public choice, with its emphasis on the economic interests at stake in policy decisions, offers valuable insights into the operation of the political process. But ideas also matter in developing and implementing public policy. Changes in the Federal Trade Commission's approach to privacy and the introduction of the Do Not Call Registry in 2003 provide a good case study of the importance of ideas.

Information exchange has long been common in the world of commerce. Database companies compile information from a wide variety of sources. Some comes from public records, such as land records, voter registration lists, or driver's licenses, or from other public information such as telephone books, professional directories, or the Internet. Other information is nonpublic. Financial institutions routinely share data about payment history and obligations with credit reporting agencies. Catalog companies exchange data to offer more items similar to what the consumer has purchased in the past. Magazine publishers rent out their subscriber lists. Surveys, warranty registration cards, and other such sources of information may also be included. Often individual-level data are augmented with demographic information from the census, based on the average for small geographical areas such as zip code plus four or a census tract.

Shared information is used for numerous purposes. Companies use information about a consumer for fraud control. Information is used to locate an individual, for example, to collect a debt. Public records searches are a common part of background checks, and are also used to identify bankruptcies or liens that have been filed against a consumer's assets. And of course information is used for marketing. A thriving industry of list brokers offers lists of people with particular interests or demographics.

The growth of commerce on the Internet provoked new concerns about information sharing, which became an important issue at the FTC. When I arrived as the Director of the Commission's Bureau of Consumer

Protection in 2001, privacy was a new issue to the chairman and me. We set about assessing the commission's approach to privacy to determine what kind of a privacy agenda we should pursue. This chapter discusses that analysis, approach, and agenda.

Section I discusses the traditional approach to privacy issues that the FTC had taken, the problems with that approach, and the alternative approach we developed. Section II discusses the Do Not Call Registry, which became the centerpiece of the Commission's privacy agenda. Section III considers another element of that agenda, information security.

I. ANALYZING PRIVACY ISSUES

A. Fair information practices

The traditional approach to analyzing privacy issues is based on the so-called fair information practices, or FIPs. At their core, the fair information practices are built around the notion that personal information is personal property. That is, information about an individual is regarded as the property of that individual, who can then control the uses of the information. Although this notion has never been incorporated in U.S. law, it was the basis of several FTC reports in the late 1990s and remains influential.

The FIPs identify a number of basic principles for collecting and utilizing information. The starting point is **notice**: consumers should be given notice of what information is being collected about them and how the information will be used. Financial institutions, for example, are required to provide detailed privacy notices annually to each person who has an account. Health care providers must give each patient an even more detailed disclosure of what information they collect and how they use it. Internet sites provide notice in their (largely voluntary) privacy policies.

A second FIP is **choice**: consumers should be able to choose how their information is used. That is, they should be able to block whoever collects the information from using "their" information in certain ways. In the financial sector, for example, consumers can "opt out" of some sharing of information (mostly for marketing purposes), but they cannot prevent other instances of information sharing such as the sharing that is necessary to complete a transaction or for purposes of credit reporting.

FIPs also specify that consumers should have **access** to the information that is collected about them, and that they should be able to correct that information if it is erroneous. Whoever holds the information must provide **security** for it, to protect it from loss or theft. Finally, FIPs include the principle of **onward transfer**, which states that restrictions on the use of the information must go with the information if it is shared. That is, information collected for one purpose as specified in the notice remains subject to the same restrictions, even if it is shared with someone else. Thus, information cannot be used for a different purpose from what was contemplated in the original collection of information. There are other FIPs, but these are the most important ones.

B. Problems with FIPs

Using FIPs as a basis for privacy protection poses some serious problems. The difficulties start with the seemingly unobjectionable principle of notice, which is fundamental to the way FIPs are supposed to work. Everyone who has an account with a financial institution receives at least one privacy notice every year. Few people seem to have realized they received one, and even fewer have read the notice. Those who do read them have found them complicated, full of legal jargon, and something less than easy to understand. Similarly, few consumers read online privacy policies. Indeed, one study estimated that the opportunity cost of actually taking the time to read online privacy policies is $781 billion.[1] The premise of FIPs, however, is that consumers will not only read the notices they receive, but if they do not like the privacy policies of a particular financial institution, they will seek out privacy notices from other institutions, read and compare, and choose the

---

[1] McDonald, A. and Cranor, L. The Cost of Reading Privacy Policies. I/S: A Journal of Law and Policy for the Information Society. 2008 Privacy Year in Review issue.

institution that best meets their privacy preferences. Judging from marketplace behavior, most people have better things to do with their time than read privacy notices. Reading a notice is not a particularly costly activity, but it does not appear to be worth the benefits to the vast majority of consumers. Of course, some who care more intensely about privacy issues may do so, but such consumers appear to be few and far between.

The FIPs principle of choice fares no better. For consumers, the costs of exercising choice regarding information sharing involve more than the small investment of time to read the notice and implement the choice. To exercise choice, a consumer first must *decide* to do so. Because consumers literally have (at least) hundreds of ways that they can use their time, they must overcome both the costs of decision making and the opportunity cost of not using their time elsewhere even to care about choices regarding their information.[2] The costs involved in deciding to choose may pose a more fundamental barrier to FIPs than the mere time costs involved.

A more fundamental problem with choice is that there are vital uses of information sharing that work only because consumers cannot choose whether to participate. One such example is credit reporting, which depends on the absence of consumer choice. Creditors report, on a voluntary basis, consumers' payment histories. If consumers could choose not to have some of their information reported, the credit reporting system likely would experience significant adverse selection. Consumers with poor payment histories would simply choose not to have that information reported. Such information loss, however, would significantly compromise the value of the system to identify consumers who are poor risks, leading to some combination of increased defaults and reduced credit availability.

The system for recording property is another example in which giving consumers choice about use of their information would seriously undermine an important information system. Although the laws governing property recordation vary from state to state, they share two separate but interdependent purposes. The first is to protect purchasers who acquire interests in real property. The second purpose, critical to achievement of the first, is enabling prospective purchasers—and lenders—to determine the existence of prior claims that might affect their interests. Thus, claims against property are a matter of public record, accessible to all. If consumers could choose not to have liens against their property included, or if they could limit access to the records, these important purposes would be thwarted.

The core difficulty with the FIPs approach to privacy is its approach to information as property. Information about a consumer is seen as "belonging" to the consumer, who therefore is entitled to control how and where that information is disseminated. In fact, however, the consumer and the other party to a transaction generally jointly produce commercial information. Information about a consumer transaction is both information about the consumer and part of the business records of the seller. There is no obvious way to assign property rights, particularly exclusive property rights, to either party. In a real estate transaction, for example, or an auction on eBay, both the buyer and seller know all of the pertinent details of the transaction, and may benefit from using that information for other purposes. Which party should be given control? Thus, U.S. law does not treat commercial information in the possession of sellers as something over which consumers can exercise exclusive control—it is not the consumer's property.

Moreover, if personal information is personal property, it is a very peculiar form of ownership. It may be "my" zip code, but it has 29,454 other owners. "My" city and state have far more owners; even "my" street has a substantial number of owners. Attempting to approach personal information as personal property leaves us with a quandary about who has control.

Finally, it is difficult to square FIPs with the First Amendment's guarantee of freedom of speech. It may be "my" reputation, but other people are free to say what they want about me. Squaring the notion that an individual can prevent others from using information about him with the recipient's right to say what he pleases is difficult at best. Subject to the bounds of libel, we are all free to use whatever information we have about anyone else.

---

[2]The tendency of consumers to choose not to decide has been observed in other contexts as well. European countries have different default rules for organ donation, for example. In countries where the default rule is that organs are available for donation, more than 60 percentage points more consumers make their organs available than in countries where the default rule is that organs are not available. Consumers simply do not exercise the choice, so whatever rule is the default ends up prevailing.

C. Privacy regulation based on consequences

Rather than continuing to approach privacy based on FIPs, the FTC in 2001 decided to focus on the consequences of information use and misuse in approaching privacy questions. There is little reason for concern about information sharing as such; rather the basis for concern is that sharing of information might lead to adverse consequences. The fact that information is shared among several different parties to complete an ATM transaction or a credit card transaction hardly matters. What is crucial is that the information is not used in ways that create avoidable adverse consequences for consumers.

Adverse consequences include physical harm. That is the heart of parents' concern about their children giving out information online; the information may be used by a child predator to cause physical harm. It is also the concern about stalking: information may be used to find or follow someone, and in some cases, do them harm. Consequences may also be economic. One example is identity theft, in which the thief uses information about a consumer to borrow money in the consumer's name. Economic harm can also occur when erroneous information in a credit report is used as the basis for denying credit or extending credit on less favorable terms. Consequences can also be intrusion or annoyance. Telemarketing calls during the dinner hour or unwanted spam in an e-mail inbox are commonplace examples.

Analyzing privacy issues based on consequences points immediately to the need to think about the benefits and costs to consumers of information uses. In the summer of 2001, however, much of the discussion about privacy presumed that privacy was an absolute right, and could not be balanced against anything. A privacy agenda based on balancing benefits and costs was potentially quite controversial.

Then came the events of September 11, 2001. Suddenly it was clear that there were other values besides privacy, and that we might want to consider steps that improved security with minimal intrusions on privacy. The idea of balancing competing considerations became much more acceptable than it had been before, which simplified the FTC's shift to a new, consequences-based approach to privacy.

A new approach required a new agenda to demonstrate that the approach was a productive approach to addressing privacy issues. The agenda focused on controlling adverse consequences of information use and misuse. Its centerpiece was the Do Not Call Registry, discussed in detail in the next section. The agenda also included a series of law enforcement actions to address information security, discussed in Section III. Other elements of the agenda, not discussed here, included cases to pursue deceptive spam, efforts to improve credit reporting, and steps to educate consumers about identity theft and assist those who were victims.

II. The Do Not Call Registry

Throughout the 1990s, the incidence of telemarketing calls had been increasing. Falling prices of telecommunications meant that the communications component of the call was cheaper than it had ever been before, and marketers took advantage of that fact. Perhaps more important in spurring the growth of telemarketing was the development of predictive dialers, which made possible an enormous increase in productivity. Before predictive dialers, a sales agent spent a significant amount of time dialing a number and waiting for an answer. Predictive dialers automated that task, and "predicted" when the next agent would be available. Ideally, as soon as an agent completes one call, there is another call waiting for the agent to make the pitch again. If no agent is available, the dialer "drops" or abandons the call, leaving the consumer with an open line with no one on the other end. Thus, sales agents' time is used far more efficiently, with more pitches and less dead time. Together, predictive dialers and falling telecommunications prices reduced the cost per sale of telemarketing, and telemarketers responded with more calls.

From the telemarketers' perspective, consumers are a common property resource. Like the fish in the lake, consumers are not owned, but if a seller can "hook" one, he or she can profit from the sale. Like any other common property resource, market incentives will result in overuse of the resource. From the consumers' perspective, there were too many calls. As calls increased, so did the annoyance factor—exactly the kind of consequence of information use that many consumers wanted to avoid.

The Do Not Call Registry sought to address these consequences by better defining property rights. Consumers can prevent unwanted door-to-door sales solicitations with a no trespassing sign, but before Do Not Call there was no effective way to post the equivalent of a no trespassing sign on a telephone line. The list gave consumers the opportunity to avoid the unwanted intrusion of telemarketing calls, with government enforcement to ensure that the consumer's wishes were respected.

Although Do Not Call gives consumers a choice, it is a choice about the consequences, not about the information sharing. Under the rule, consumers cannot prevent telemarketers from sharing information about their telephone number, or their purchasing habits. They can, however, prevent telemarketers from using that information to make another call. The FIPs approach to unwanted telemarketing calls is far more obtuse and far less effective, because it depends on the consumer keeping their telephone number secret. Once the consumer has given permission to even one seller to share their number or published it in a public directory, there is no further way to avoid use of the information for unwanted calls. Moreover, the FIPs approach cannot help consumers at all if the telemarketer uses random-digit dialing to reach potential customers without even knowing who they are. Letting consumers address the consequences directly is a far more effective way to avoid unwanted calls.

A. Statutory authority

Two statutes are relevant to the Do Not Call Registry. The Telephone Consumer Protection Act, passed in 1991, required the Federal Communications Commission to consider a national do not call list. The FCC did, but rejected a national list as too costly. It recognized that the only practical way to manage a national list would be to computerize it. At the time, however, many small businesses that would have had to comply with the list did not even own computers. Thus, a significant part of the cost estimate was the cost of purchasing computers.

Instead, the FCC adopted restrictions on the hours during which telemarketing calls were permitted, and a company-specific do not call list. Under the company-specific approach, if a consumer asks a particular company not to call again, the consumer must be placed on the company's list and not called again. Thus, each company gets one free call to each consumer, but if the consumer so requests, they cannot call again.

The Telemarketing and Consumer Fraud and Abuse Prevention Act of 1994 gave the FTC similar authority. It allowed the agency to prohibit telemarketing calls that a reasonable consumer would consider abusive or an invasion of privacy. Under this authority, the FTC adopted rules that mirrored the FCC approach, restricting calls to certain hours and establishing a company-specific do not call requirement. The FTC had launched a review of this rule in 2000, and had held a workshop on the possibility of establishing a national do not call requirement. Thus, the stage was set to move forward with a proposed rule to establish the Registry.

B. Initial concerns about do not call

In considering whether proposing a national do not call list was wise, there were four initial concerns. First, it was not clear whether an FTC rule would cover enough telemarketing calls to make a meaningful difference to consumers who signed up. If the rule had too little coverage, benefits would be lower, but consumers might be frustrated and angry as well. Although the FTC has broad jurisdiction, there are gaps in its authority that would limit the applicability of an FTC rule to some important telemarketers. In particular, the FTC does not have jurisdiction over banks, which are regulated by their functional regulators. Nor does it have jurisdiction over common carriers regulated by the FCC, in particular, telephone companies. Both groups were significant telemarketers. Moreover, the FTC lacks jurisdiction over nonprofit organizations, so charitable solicitations by such organizations could not be covered either.

We decided to proceed with a rule, despite the jurisdictional gaps that would limit coverage. In part, we believed that even an FTC-only rule would make a meaningful difference to consumers. More importantly, we believed that if we proceeded, the FCC would see the political attractiveness of the proposal, and could be persuaded to adopt comparable rules. Together, FTC and FCC rules would reach all telemarketers except nonprofit organizations.

A second concern was whether the FTC had the institutional capability to manage a do not call list. Although the agency has an extremely talented staff of lawyers and economists, it is basically a law enforcement agency. Law enforcement does not demand a great deal of customer service. Managing a do not call list, however, would require considerable customer service expertise. The list would have to make it easy for consumers to sign up. More importantly, strong customer service would be necessary to get the list to telemarketers who would have to comply with the requirements. Breakdowns in customer service on either front would frustrate consumers, either because they could not sign up or because telemarketers could not comply.

We decided that, rather than try to build in-house expertise, we would contract with a private company to build and manage the database. Somewhat ironically, the initial contractor was AT&T, one of the largest telemarketers at the time.

A third concern was constitutionality. Truthful telemarketing calls are commercial speech, protected under the First Amendment to the Constitution. To restrict truthful commercial speech, the government must show a substantial interest, a remedy that directly advances that interest, and that the remedy is no more intrusive than necessary to achieve the objective. We believed the rule could meet this test, particularly given that it was consumers who would choose not to receive calls, rather than government prohibiting calls that some consumers might want to receive. Concerns about constitutionality, however, argued that the rule should make as few distinctions as possible among different types of calls. Courts are especially likely to see First Amendment problems if the rules are content-based, prohibiting certain calls based on what the government thinks consumers should hear. A rule that applied to all calls, regardless of content, would be more likely to withstand scrutiny.

A final concern was funding. Although the contract for building the system and the necessary resources for enforcement, consumer education, and other related tasks were not expected to be a large amount, the FTC is a small agency, and the necessary funds would have been a significant fraction of its consumer protection budget. We planned to raise the money from user fees on telemarketers, charging them for access to the information they would need to comply. Doing so, however, required congressional action. As with the approach to the FCC, we believed that once the rule was in place, Congress would see the political merits of authorizing the user fees necessary to put the system into operation. The need for funding, however, made Congress a necessary participant as the rule moved forward.

C. The rulemaking proceeding

The FTC published the proposed national Do Not Call Registry on January 30, 2002. As proposed, the rule covered all calls subject to the FTC's jurisdiction, with no exemptions of any sort. Moreover, the proposal would have covered calls made by for-profit telemarketers, even if the call was on behalf of someone not subject to the FTC's jurisdiction (such as a charitable organization).

More than 65,000 comments were filed during the public comment period, far more than in any prior FTC rulemaking proceeding. (The previous record had been about 46,000 comments in a rulemaking involving warnings on smokeless tobacco, when companies passed out postcards at NASCAR events.) Many were from individuals, often with colorful things to say about the evils of telemarketing.

The comments led to changes in two aspects of the final rule, which was published on January 29, 2003. The final rule exempted calls to consumers on the Do Not Call list with whom the seller has an established business relationship. It also exempted charitable solicitations using paid telemarketers, requiring instead a company-specific do not call list for such solicitations.

The comments made a convincing case that consumers want and expect certain calls. One obvious example is when the consumer calls to inquire about a product or service and the seller needs to call back. Another is a brokerage account, where the consumer may rely on the broker to call and advise about either profitable opportunities or the advisability of an immediate sale of some security. A third example is an expiring magazine subscription, where publishers reported a very high incidence of renewals when they called consumers whose subscription was about to expire. Apparently many such consumers had simply neglected to renew, but wanted to continue getting the publication.

Under the proposal, if consumers who signed up for the Do Not Call list wanted to receive such calls, they would have had to give express permission to the seller to call them. Starting from a clean slate, express authorization would be a workable approach to the problem. Consumers setting up a brokerage account, for example, could authorize the broker to call; consumers subscribing to a magazine could authorize reminders at renewal time. Tens of millions of consumers, however, already had brokerage accounts and magazine subscriptions. Without an exemption, they would have to provide express authorization to sellers with whom they already had a relationship. Logistically, that would be quite difficult, and almost inevitably, a significant number of consumers would neglect to do so even if they wanted the calls.

Evidence that consumers do not find all calls equally intrusive also came from the experience of state do not call lists, most of which exempted existing business relationships. Although there were numerous complaints about violations of state requirements, there was no evidence of significant numbers of complaints about sellers with whom the consumer had a business relationship. Nor was there evidence that sellers who did not have a legitimate relationship had managed to use the exemption as a loophole to make calls to people on the list. Thus, the state experience indicated that consumers did not find calls from businesses they dealt with equally intrusive, and that an exemption for such calls was a workable solution.

Based on these comments, the final rule allowed calls to consumers on the Do Not Call Registry if the seller had an established business relationship with the consumer.[3] Such calls, however, are subject to the company-specific do not call list requirement. Thus, if a consumer does not wish to receive more calls from someone with whom they have an established relationship, they can ask to be added to the company-specific list. Moreover, we expected the exemption would significantly reduce the rule's impact on telemarketers, and thus help reduce potential congressional opposition.

The final rule also exempted calls for charitable solicitations that were made using a for-profit telemarketer. As with the established business relationship exemption, such calls remained subject to the company-specific do not call list requirement. As originally proposed, the rule would have allowed calls seeking charitable solicitations if they were made by the nonprofit organization on its own behalf, because nonprofit organizations are not subject to FTC jurisdiction. For-profit telemarketing firms were covered, however, no matter who they were calling for—including charities.

The comments made a convincing case that many charities, especially smaller ones, depend on telemarketing for a significant fraction of their fundraising. Large charities could move their telemarketing in-house and thus avoid the rule. Small charities, however, could not afford to bring telemarketing in-house, and needed the expertise that paid telemarketers provided them. Thus, the effect of the rule as proposed was to create an artificial disadvantage for small charities compared to larger ones.

A charitable solicitations exemption was also politically attractive. Charities have always received a sympathetic hearing in Congress, and their arguments about the impact of Do Not Call found a receptive audience. The Bush Administration was also concerned about the potential impact. The president was promoting faith-based initiatives, and the last thing the Administration wanted was new impediments to charitable solicitations. Exempting charitable solicitations was a way to increase the likelihood of congressional support for the rule.

D. The role of telemarketers

At the beginning of the rulemaking process, there had been hope that some telemarketers would offer some support for the rule. An FTC rule would provide a uniform national standard and, for national telemarketers, would likely simplify the task of complying with the growing number of state do not call lists. Such lists were often quite cumbersome, including, for example, one state that maintained its list on index cards, and another that indicated those on the list with a black dot next to their name in the telephone book. Telemarketers, however, were not interested in offering support.

---

[3]A seller has an "established business relationship" for 18 months after the conclusion of a transaction or for 3 months after an inquiry by the consumer.

Instead, telemarketers argued (mostly through two trade associations) that the rule would destroy a billion-dollar industry. Although telemarketing was at the time a billion-dollar industry, the rule did not affect a sizable fraction of the industry at all. About half of telemarketing is inbound telemarketing, where a consumer calls to place an order in response to an advertisement or a catalog. The Do Not Call Registry would not affect inbound telemarketing at all. Moreover, about half of outbound telemarketing was business-to-business marketing, which is also not subject to the rule. Businesses, after all, pay someone to answer the phone; calls are not the annoyance they are for individual consumers. The exemptions in the final rule for established business relationships and charitable solicitations further reduced the likely impact.

To date, there do not appear to be reliable studies of the rule's actual impact on telemarketing. Anecdotal evidence in the first two years after it was adopted indicates that call service centers were less likely to specialize in outbound telemarketing, and that predictive dialers limited to handling outbound calls were no longer offered. Both telemarketing firms and providers of predictive dialers apparently found it more attractive to provide services more broadly, rather than limiting their service to outbound calls. Systematic evidence of the impact on the industry, however, has not yet emerged.

When the telemarketers failed to stop the rule at the FTC, they turned to Congress. Funding for the rule had already been included in the budget and approved by Congress. Budget issues, however, are handled by the Appropriations Committee rather than the Energy and Commerce Committee, the substantive authorizing committee with jurisdiction over the FTC. Telemarketers approached the FTC's authorizing committee, and the chairman and ranking member wrote a letter to the Commission objecting that the Commission could not go ahead with the Do Not Call Registry without the authorizing committee's approval.

The committee held a hearing in January 2003. It began with skeptical statements from the chairman and the ranking minority member about how the committee's approval was essential before Do Not Call went forward. The next member to speak was Congressman Markey, who was a strong supporter of the rule. As he began his statement, his cell phone rang. He answered it, pretending that it was a telemarketing call, and explained that he was signing up for the Do Not Call Registry as soon as he could. Everyone laughed, and from then on, the tone of the hearing was, what can we do to help? Within weeks after the hearing, the committee and Congress passed legislation authorizing the FTC to proceed, and directing the FCC to adopt a substantially similar rule promptly (the FCC had already started the rulemaking process).

Having failed to block the rule in Congress, telemarketers turned to the courts. Two separate groups filed legal challenges, one in Oklahoma and one in Denver, both part of the Tenth Circuit. In August 2003, the district court judge in Oklahoma ruled that the FTC did not have statutory authority to enact a Do Not Call Registry. Within 24 hours, Congress had passed new legislation essentially overruling the district court, specifying that the Commission did have the authority to adopt the rule it had already promulgated.

In a demonstration of what gets the attention of Congress and the public, there are two prior occasions when Congress has acted within 24 hours after the triggering event. The first was after the Japanese attack on Pearl Harbor, when Congress declared war within 24 hours. The only other occasion was when the National Football League attempted to enforce a new rule blacking out home market broadcasts of sold-out football games.

Before the new legislation was signed, however, a federal district court judge in Denver ruled that the registry was an unconstitutional restriction on truthful commercial speech. Although signups were briefly suspended, the Tenth Circuit Court of Appeals stayed the ruling pending appeal, consolidated the challenge to the FTC rule with a challenge to the FCC rule that was already before the court, and expedited the schedule for resolving the matter. In the end, the court upheld the rule's constitutionality. Although the telemarketers appealed to the Supreme Court, the Court declined to hear the case. The Do Not Call Registry was fully established.

E. Results

Signups for the National Do Not Call Registry began the first week of June 2003. In the first week, 10 million numbers were added to the list. The online signup site was the fastest-growing Internet site in history to that point. By September 2004, the registry had grown to 64 million numbers; four years later it had reached

172 million numbers. Nearly any publicity increases registrations. For example, a common and recurring spam claims that telemarketers are about to begin marketing to cell phones unless the owner signs up for the Do Not Call Registry. Although the claim is not true (a separate statute restricts marketing calls to cell phones), when the spam first appeared in the summer of 2005, roughly 20 million more numbers were added to the registry.

A Harris Interactive Poll in February 2004 assessed consumers' knowledge and experience with the registry. Of those surveyed, 91 percent knew about the registry, a remarkably high level of awareness. Of those who knew, 57 percent had signed up for the registry, a number that was roughly consistent with actual registrations at the time. Among those who had signed up, 92 percent reported that they were receiving fewer calls. Among everyone on the list, 25 percent reported that they had received no telemarketing calls since the rule took effect in September 2003. Fifty-three percent reported receiving far fewer calls.[4]

The National Do Not Call Registry is probably the most popular federal consumer protection program in history. One commentator even called FTC Chairman Timothy J. Muris "the savior of the American dinner hour." For many consumers, the rule removed an increasingly annoying and intrusive invasion of their privacy. Focusing on the consequences of information use rather than the sharing of information per se proved a productive way to address privacy issues.

III. INFORMATION SECURITY

Willie Sutton, a famed bank robber of the 1930s, once reportedly said that he robbed banks because that was where the money was. In today's information economy, sensitive information is increasingly the target of thieves for the same reason. Compromised information, particularly social security numbers, can create serious adverse consequences for consumers via identity theft. Indeed, for many consumers, concerns over privacy are primarily about keeping their information secure from theft. Thus, information security is a natural component of an approach to privacy based on the consequences of information use and misuse. This section considers first the nature and extent of the identity theft problem, and then the approach that the Federal Trade Commission has developed to try to reduce data breaches.

A. The problem

Virtually all businesses have at least some sensitive information that can lead to significant consequences for consumers if it falls into the wrong hands. All businesses have Social Security numbers for their employees, for example, and a great many businesses have credit card numbers from numerous consumer transactions. If this information is compromised, it can cause significant economic losses.

Unfortunately, sensitive information is compromised in many ways. It may be deliberately stolen by hackers, for example, or sold by company insiders to thieves. Computer hardware with sensitive information stored on it may be stolen. Moreover, sensitive information may simply be lost. That is what occurred when Citibank shipped credit reporting information to a credit reporting agency, and one tape containing some 3.9 million records was lost in transit.

In 2008, the Identity Theft Resource Center estimated that a total of 656 data breaches were reported, involving the compromise of more than 35 million records.[5] There is a great deal of uncertainty in these estimates, because some breaches may not come to public attention despite state laws requiring notice to consumers whose records were compromised. Moreover, in many instances it is known that some records were accessed, but the actual number of records compromised is not known. Nonetheless, it is clear that breaches occur with disturbing frequency.

When a breach occurs, the risk to consumers (and the financial system) is that the compromised information will be used for identity theft. Intuitively, the risk of identity theft is greatest when information is deliberately stolen,

---

[4]Available at http://www.harrisinteractive.com/harris_poll/index.asp?PID=439.

[5]http://www.idtheftcenter.org/artman2/uploads/1/ITRC_Breach_Report_2008_final_1.pdf.

Figure 9-1. The costs of identity theft, 2006.

| | New Account Fraud | Existing Account Fraud | | All Forms, Combined |
		Non-Credit Card Account	Credit Card Account Only	
Number of Victims, Millions	1.8	3.3	3.2	8.3
Amount Thief Obtained, dollars				
Median	$1,350	$457	$350	$500
90th percentile	$15,000	$3,800	$4,000	$6,000
Victim's out of pocket expenses, dollars				
Median	$40	0	0	0
90th percentile	$3,000	$900	$132	$1,200
Hours spent resolving problem				
Median	10	4	2	4
90th percentile	100	44	25	55

for example, by a hacker. Risk is likely somewhat lower when computer hardware such as a laptop computer is stolen, because such items are frequently stolen for their own sake rather than for the information they may contain. Similarly, the risk is likely lower when information is simply lost. Although limited data are consistent with this intuition, there is no definitive evidence about how often breaches actually result in identity theft.

As revealed in Figure 9-1, the costs of identity theft can be substantial.[6] By far the most serious form of identity theft is new account fraud, in which the thief uses information about the victim to open a new account in the victim's name. There were 1.8 million victims of this form of identity theft in 2006, with the thief obtaining a median of $1,350 per victim. In 10 percent of the cases, however, the thief obtained $15,000 or more. Most of what the thief obtains comes from creditors, rather than the consumer victim. The median victim spent $40 out of pocket and 10 hours resolving the matter. For ten percent of victims, however, out-of-pocket costs for legal fees, notary fees, or payments to creditors exceeded $3,000. Moreover, 10 percent of victims spent more than 100 hours—two-and-a-half weeks of full-time work—to resolve the problem. Despite these efforts, 37 percent of victims were still experiencing problems at the time of the survey.

Less serious, but still significant, is identity theft that involves only the compromise of an existing account. For example, a credit card number or bank account number might be compromised. There were 3.3 million victims who had a non-credit card account compromised, and 3.2 million more who had only a credit card account compromised.

When only a credit card number is compromised, the identity theft problem is much easier for the consumer victim to address. From the beginning, credit card issuers have recognized that cards can be stolen, and have sophisticated fraud monitoring systems to detect suspicious activity quickly. The median victim has no out-of-pocket costs and spends only two hours resolving the problem. Ninety percent of victims lose less than $132 out of pocket, and spend less than 25 hours addressing the problem. For the median case, the thief gets $350. Ten percent of thieves, however, realize $4,000 or more. Compromise of an existing account other than a credit card account is slightly more serious, but costs and losses are much closer to the credit card results than to new account fraud.

Identity theft is an information-based crime. It is therefore somewhat ironic that one promising approach to reducing identity theft problems involves more information sharing. The central idea of all these information sharing tools is that an identity thief cannot just use your information—he or she has to change something. Otherwise, when the thief goes online to order a high-end flat screen TV in your name, you will get the merchandise.

---

[6]The data in Figure 9-1 are from Federal Trade Commission, 2006 Identity Theft Survey Report, November, 2007 (available at http://www.ftc.gov/os/2007/11/SynovateFinalReportIDTheft2006.pdf).

The simplest information tools to combat fraud are fraud databases. These databases include, for example, identities that have been compromised in previous incidents, or addresses that have been used in prior cases of mail fraud. In the same vein are databases of campground addresses or prison telephone numbers. A business might want to seek more information before engaging in a transaction with someone flagged by such a database.

Somewhat more sophisticated are identity verification tools. These tools look for inconsistencies between the information provided in a particular transaction and information that the real person has provided on other occasions. Has this name been associated with this address in previous transactions? Has it been associated with this Social Security number or another one? Such inconsistencies are a trigger to look further, to be sure that the individual seeking to enter the transaction is really who they say they are. And, typically, that is all that happens. A real person provides further information to resolve the inconsistency. A thief walks away, in search of an easier target.

Still more elaborate are probability models, which seek to quantify the likelihood that a particular transaction is fraudulent. Much like credit scoring models, these models use past cases of fraud to identify patterns that may indicate problems. For example, they seek to quantify the risk that a particular inconsistency in the way an identity is used indicates that a transaction is fraudulent.

Finally, the identity element approach to fraud detection pools application and other data from as many users as possible. Rather than predicting the likelihood of fraud directly, they consider the different elements of identity, such as name, address, social security number, phone number, and the like. Looking across applications, and considering also the data that users provide about account performance, new users on an account, address changes, and the like, the models seek to detect anomalous elements of identity in a new application. Suspicious patterns frequently involve linkages across applications to different businesses made at a similar point in time. For example, one fraud ring was detected when numerous individuals, all using the same business telephone number, applied for credit or other transactions within a relatively short period of time. These approaches are extensions of the analytical tools that have been used to reduce credit card fraud significantly.

Information tools to reduce fraud risk are used in numerous transactions. They are of course used in decisions about extending credit, but they are also used in many other remote transactions. Transactions over the Internet or by telephone, for example, are frequently screened using these systems. In 2004, my own survey of 10 large providers of such tools found they were used in almost 2.7 billion transactions.

B. FTC law enforcement principles

Because data breaches can create significant costs, the FTC has used its law enforcement authority to improve the security precautions that businesses take. The most comprehensive statement of the Commission's view of security is its Safeguards Rule, which applies to financial institutions like mortgage brokers that are subject to FTC jurisdiction. The rule views security as a process. Companies must develop a security plan identifying the security risks that the company faces, implement reasonable steps to address these risks, and provide for reassessment and revision as the risks change. There is no specific requirement for particular security measures or technologies. Rather, each company's security plan must be appropriate for its own situation. FTC orders addressing particular security violations impose a very similar set of requirements.

Although the Commission has brought several cases enforcing the Safeguards Rule, most of its information security cases have been based on the prohibition on "unfair or deceptive acts or practices" in Section 5 of the FTC Act. The Commission's first information security cases were based on deception: a company had promised to keep sensitive information secure and failed to honor that promise. Recognizing that perfect security is impossible, the Commission's complaints construe a promise to protect sensitive information as one to take steps that are "reasonable and appropriate under the circumstances." In turn, what is reasonable and appropriate depends on the sensitivity of the information. Thus, the cases establish a sliding scale, with more sensitive information requiring more elaborate security precautions to protect it.

The Commission has avoided a standard of strict liability for any breach. Clever thieves can defeat virtually any security system on at least some occasions. Commission statements about information security have repeatedly said that not all breaches are actionable. Instead, the issue is whether the company was employing reasonable and appropriate security measures.

The first information security case, in 2002, involved an inadvertent breach. Eli Lilly sent a daily reminder to Prozac users (a medication used to treat depression) to take their medicine. Messages were sent blind, so that each subscriber received an e-mail with a blank "to" line, thus preserving the subscriber's confidentiality. When Lilly decided to terminate the service, however, it sent the announcement using a newly-created program that listed each subscriber's e-mail address on the "to" line, thus revealing the addresses of all subscribers to the service. The complaint alleged that the company had not taken steps appropriate under the circumstances because it failed to provide adequate training and oversight, and failed to implement appropriate checks and controls on the process.[7]

Although not all breaches are violations, the Commission has also brought cases where it could not prove that a breach of security had occurred. In the Microsoft case, the FTC complaint alleged that the Passport system did not employ "sufficient measures reasonable and appropriate under the circumstances" to keep its promise to protect the information, including credit card numbers that were stored in Passport Wallet. Although there was no known actual breach, the complaint alleged that the company failed to implement procedures to prevent and detect unauthorized access, or to retain sufficient information to conduct security audits. Thus, even if breaches had occurred, they could not reliably be detected.[8]

Because the Commission views security as a process, an important component of information security is adapting to new and emerging threats. In *Guess.com*, the complaint alleges that the company's Web site was vulnerable to a well-known and easily prevented vulnerability known as an "SQL injection" attack. Through this attack, a hacker could gain access to customer information, including credit card numbers and expiration dates. Even if the security system were state-of-the-art when first installed, the failure to adjust to avoid a new and widely known vulnerability was alleged as a violation.[9]

More recently, the Commission has applied the same general principles even in the absence of a security promise. These cases have alleged that the failure to maintain reasonable security policies and practices is unfair. *BJs Wholesale Club* was the first unfairness case.[10] Like many retailers, BJs collected credit card information to obtain authorization for transactions in its stores, and transmitted and stored the information over its computer network without encryption. The network also included wireless access points that supported hand-held barcode readers used to help manage inventory. Unfortunately, these access points allegedly did not employ "readily available security measures to limit access," which allowed unauthorized users with a wireless connection to enter BJs computer network. Once in the network, hackers found credit card information stored in files that could be accessed anonymously, using default user names and passwords supplied with the software. The complaint also alleged that measures to detect and investigate unauthorized access were inadequate, and that BJs unnecessarily increased the risk by retaining information for which it no longer had a business need. Many cards used at BJs were counterfeited, and used to make "several million dollars in fraudulent purchases." The complaint alleged these problems constituted a failure to employ reasonable and appropriate security measures in violation of the FTC Act.[11]

Unfairness was also the basis for prosecuting CardSystem Solutions,[12] a credit card processor responsible for a breach that compromised an estimated 40,000,000 credit card numbers. CardSystem Solutions retained full data from the magnetic stripe on the back of the cards, including the security code used to verify that the card

---

[7]*In the Matter of Eli Lilly and Company*, File No. 012 3214 (May 10, 2002).

[8]*In the Matter of Microsoft Corporation*, File No. 012 3240 (Dec. 24, 2002).

[9]*In the Matter of Guess?, Inc., and Guess.com, Inc.*, File No. 022 3260 (Aug. 5, 2003). The same issue, and the same vulnerability, was involved in the case against Petco. *In the Matter of Petco Animal Supplies, Inc.*, File No. 032 3221 (Mar. 5, 2005).

[10]*In the Matter of BJs Wholesale Club, Inc.*, File No. 042 3160 (Jun. 16, 2005).

[11]The Commission also brought a substantially similar case against DSW. *In the Matter of DSW, Inc.*, File No. 052 3096 (Mar. 13, 2006). There, the wireless vulnerability was the access points used to transmit requests for authorization of a transaction from the cash register to the store network. Like BJs, once in through the wireless access point, a hacker could access files anywhere in the store or corporate network. The result was the theft of information on more than 1.4 million credit and debit cards. Again, the Commission alleged that failure to take reasonable and appropriate security measures was an unfair practice.

[12]*In the Matter of CardSystems Solutions, Inc.*, File No. 052 3148 (Feb. 23, 2006).

is genuine. Thus, thieves could produce counterfeit cards that were indistinguishable from the genuine card in the approval process. As in other cases, the complaint alleged a series of poor security practices that, taken together, constituted a failure to maintain reasonable and appropriate security measures, and was therefore an unfair practice.

The Commission also used an unfairness theory to prosecute ChoicePoint for a breach that compromised records of more than 163,000 consumers.[13] ChoicePoint supplies sensitive identifying information, as well as credit reports, to some 50,000 business clients, who use the information for a wide variety of purposes, including fraud control. What ChoicePoint sells is exactly the kind of identifying information that an identity thief needs, because it is the information that many businesses use to verify that an applicant is who he or she claims to be. Indeed, ChoicePoint offers information products for that precise purpose. The core problem was that ChoicePoint signed up putative business clients without adequate verification—including its failure to use the identity verification tools that it sells to its customers. As a result, fraudulent businesses signed up as legitimate ChoicePoint customers, often using public fax machines to send in their applications, and reporting conflicting or incomplete information about their business need for the information.

Any business with sensitive information, which is to say virtually any business, should take steps to prevent compromises of that information. If security measures are not reasonable and appropriate in the circumstances, the business may face enforcement action by the FTC.

IV. Summary

Information in a modern economy is widely shared, for purposes that most people consider useful, and sometimes vital. The growth of electronic commerce on the Internet provoked new attention to what measures might be appropriate to protect that information, and to protect consumers' interest in their privacy.

The original approach to privacy at the FTC was based on the Fair Information Practices, or FIPs. These principles include notice, choice, access, security, and onward transfer. They are based on an approach that treats personal information as personal property. There are, however, serious problems in basing privacy protection on FIPs. Notices do not seem to be worth reading for the vast majority of consumers, and few if any read and compare privacy notices to find the seller that best fits their privacy preferences. Critical information systems, such as credit reporting or property recordation, will not work if consumers are given a choice about whether information about them can be included. Consumers with a poor credit history, for example, would simply choose not to have the information reported, and the system would lose its ability to identify risks. Information about transactions is jointly produced by the parties to the transaction, and not "owned" by either of them in any meaningful sense. If information is property, it is a peculiar form of property in which many people share "ownership" of items of information such as a zip code. Granting individuals control over information about them is difficult to square with the First Amendment's protection of freedom of speech. U.S law has never treated personal information as personal property.

In 2001, the FTC developed an approach to privacy based on the consequences of information use and misuse. Consequences may be physical or economic consequences. Intrusion and annoyance are also consequences that concern many consumers. Concern about preventing adverse consequences for consumers led to a privacy agenda that included the Do Not Call Registry and information security.

Falling telecommunications prices and increased productivity in telemarketing led to an increasing number of calls to consumers. Both the FCC and the FTC had authority to consider a do not call list under separate statutes. In considering whether to propose a do not call list, the FTC was concerned about whether it would reach enough calls to make a meaningful difference to consumers, but decided that it could persuade the FCC to adopt a companion rule to expand coverage. It was also concerned about whether the agency could provide the necessary customer service, but decided it could contract with the private sector to manage a list. It was concerned about constitutionality, but believed the rule would be upheld. The list would require additional

---

[13] *United States v. ChoicePoint, Inc.*, Complaint, No. 106-CV-0198 (N.D. Ga. Feb. 15, 2006).

funding, but the FTC believed that Congress would see how popular the list was and be willing to provide the authority to charge user fees to telemarketers to provide the necessary funds.

As proposed, the Do Not Call Registry would have covered everyone subject to FTC jurisdiction. The rulemaking process led to two significant exemptions. Companies are allowed to call consumers on the list if they have an established business relationship with the consumer. Consumers find such calls less intrusive, and there were few complaints about them in states with do not call lists. Requiring consumers to give express permission for such calls would have been very difficult logistically. The final rule also exempted charitable solicitations. Under the proposal, large charities would have been able to make calls on their own, because they are nonprofits and not subject to FTC jurisdiction. Smaller charities, however, depend on paid telemarketers, and would not be able to do so. The exemption removed what would have been an artificial advantage for larger charities.

Telemarketers were unwilling to support the Do Not Call Registry. When they failed to convince the FTC to reject the rule, they turned to the FTC's authorizing committee in the House. The committee held a hearing about the rule, but members were very supportive and Congress quickly passed authorizing legislation. Telemarketers challenged the rule in court, but it was ultimately upheld against challenges based on both lack of statutory authority and constitutionality. The rule was immensely popular, with millions signing up. The vast majority of consumers reported receiving fewer calls, with most receiving far fewer calls or none at all.

Businesses have sensitive information about consumers that, if compromised, can lead to identity theft. The costs of identity theft to consumers can be substantial, particularly when identity theft involves the creation of new accounts in the consumer's name. Identity theft involving existing accounts is more common, but easier for consumers to fix.

FTC law enforcement actions challenging failure to maintain adequate security were originally based on breaches of security promises. The FTC believed that a promise of security was a promise to take measures to protect information that were reasonable and appropriate in the circumstances, including the sensitivity of the information. Information security is viewed as a process of identifying risks and taking reasonable steps to reduce those risks. Companies are liable if they do not take such steps, but not all breaches are law violations. Breach is not necessary to establish a violation if the FTC can show that the company failed to take reasonable steps to protect information. More recent cases have been based on unfairness, even if there was no security promise to consumers. The basic principles of when inadequate security is a violation are the same under either legal theory.

FEDERAL RISK REGULATION

Chapter 10

We often think of Congress as the primary body that establishes federal requirements for the private sector. In fact, however, far more of those requirements result from regulations adopted by administrative agencies, rather than directly from congressional enactments. Congress gives regulatory agencies authority to regulate, and they do. In 2011, Congress passed 101 laws—and regulatory agencies promulgated 3,780 final rules.

Regulation is one of the primary tools government uses to implement social choices. Since the 1960s, federal regulation has grown substantially and at times quite rapidly. Most of this growth has been in regulation related to risks of various sorts, whether to health, safety, or the environment. This chapter begins with an overview of the costs of regulation. Section II examines the nature and measurement of risk. Section III considers how consumers make choices involving risk. Section IV discusses approaches to valuing risks to human life.

I. THE COSTS OF REGULATION AND ATTEMPTS TO CONTROL IT

A. *The costs of regulation*

Accounting for regulatory costs is notoriously incomplete, but it is clear that costs are substantial. There are costs of regulatory agencies, which are reconsidered and adjusted annually as part of the federal budget process. Regulations also impose private sector compliance costs, including costs of required paperwork, which are far larger and far less precisely measured. In addition, there are indirect costs of regulation, which are measured only occasionally and inconsistently.

The most accurately measured cost of regulation is the cost of running the regulatory state. Regulatory agencies require staff to write rules, as well as inspectors, new product reviewers, and enforcement officials—over

270,000 of them in 2010. The Obama administration's budget for fiscal year 2012 requested $57.3 billion to fund regulatory agencies, up from $48 billion in 2008. Figure 10-1 shows the real costs of regulatory agencies since 1960.

Growth has been substantial, driven by expanding social regulations such as those addressing health, safety, or the environment. There is considerable accountability for these costs, because they are approved annually as part of the federal budget. Each year the administration and Congress consider needed adjustments, either up or down, in each agency's budget. As conditions and priorities change, budgets are adjusted to reflect current needs.

Most of the costs of regulation, however, are the compliance costs imposed on the private sector. Measurement of these costs depends primarily on efforts of academics to assess the burdens regulation imposes. The most comprehensive estimates of costs include paperwork costs and the costs of compliance with the tax system. They indicate that federal regulation imposed costs on the private sector that totaled about $1.75 trillion in 2008.[1] That was 12 percent of gross domestic product, or almost $15,000 per American household. It is substantially larger than the government's total revenue from the individual income tax.

The Office of Management and Budget (OMB) produces a much narrower estimate of the costs of regulation. As discussed below, certain rules are subject to review by OMB before they are adopted. As part of that review, the regulatory agency must conduct a cost-benefit analysis of the requirement. OMB reports on the total costs of regulations it has reviewed over the previous 10 years. Combining data from various reports, the "major" regulations (those with an impact of $100 million or more) adopted from April 1, 1995, through

Figure 10-1. Budgetary costs of federal regulation, adjusted for inflation.

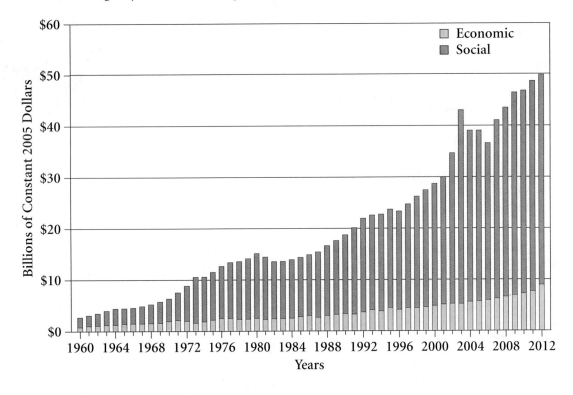

Susan Dudley and Melinda Warren, "Fiscal Stalemate Reflected in Regulators' Budget: An Analysis of the U.S. Budget for Fiscal Years 2011 and 2012," Regulators' Budget Report 33, Weidenbaum Center on the Economy, Government, and Public Policy and Regulatory Studies Center, George Washington University (May, 2011).

---

[1]Nicole V. Crain and W. Mark Crain, "The Impact of Regulatory Costs on Small Firms," Report prepared under contract to Small Business Administration Office of Advocacy, September 2010 (available at http://archive.sba.gov/advo/research/rs371tot.pdf)

September 30, 2011, imposed annual total costs of $117 billion to $152 billion in current (2011) dollars. There was much more uncertainty about the annual benefits, which were estimated to range from $236 billion to just over $1 trillion. These estimates, however, cover only the major rules where agencies monetized both costs and benefits, exclude the substantially larger number of smaller rules, and exclude the rules written by independent regulatory agencies (including, for example, most financial regulation).

There is far less political accountability for compliance costs the government imposes on the private sector. Regulatory agencies usually consider compliance costs when they decide to adopt a rule, but they often do not measure those costs with any real precision. There is inevitably uncertainty in estimating the costs of a requirement that is not yet in place, for example. Unfortunately, however, there is no ongoing mechanism for monitoring costs. If compliance costs turn out to be substantially different than the agency predicted, there is no systematic way for the agency to learn that fact. Moreover, regulations are rarely revisited. Rules typically create ongoing costs of compliance each year, but unless a particular rule becomes a political issue, agencies do not reconsider whether those costs are necessary or appropriate.

The costs that regulation imposes on the private sector are not subject to congressional approval. Congress, of course, must authorize the regulatory agencies to act, and controls their budgets. But when an agency adopts a rule, there is no congressional review of whether the costs are worthwhile, and no vote on whether requirements should be adjusted to raise or lower costs. The decision is up to the regulatory agency, without specific congressional review.

The difference in the way costs are accounted for creates a political incentive to shift costs to the private sector. If the federal government performs some function or provides some service, the costs show up as part of the federal budget, and Congress must approve those costs and raise the money to pay for them through taxes or borrowing. If the federal government requires the private sector to provide precisely the same function or service, the costs just disappear from public view, shifted to businesses and ultimately consumers through the regulatory process.

One example of this process, although in reverse, is apparent in Figure 10-1. The sharp spike in regulatory spending in 2003 is the result of the attacks of September 11, 2001. Part of the reason for the spike is growth in some regulatory functions, such as customs and border patrol, which seemed more important. But the primary reason is a shift in responsibility for airport security. Before 9/11, airport security screening was a regulatory requirement imposed on the airlines. Thus, the costs were not part of the budget process. After 9/11, the federal government took responsibility for airport security, resulting in a sharp increase in regulatory expenditures by the government, but a far smaller change in regulatory expenditures for the economy.

In part because of the lack of accountability for compliance costs, regulation has grown significantly over time. The growth in agency budgets is apparent in Figure 10-1. A crude measure of the amount of regulatory activity is the number of pages that appear each year in the Federal Register, where all proposed and final rules must be published. In the 1970s, the Federal Register averaged 45,000 pages per year. That figure grew to 53,000 pages a year in the 1980s, 62,000 pages in the 1990s, and 73,000 pages in the 2000s. The Code of Federal Regulation, which includes the text of all federal rules, grew from 71,000 pages in 1975 to 169,000 pages in 2011.

Federal regulation also imposes a variety of indirect costs. Many times these costs are idiosyncratic, and depend on the structure of particular programs. Most often, if they are measured at all, they are measured by academics well after the policy is put in place. We will consider four types of indirect costs.

First, regulation results in a loss of consumer surplus. If we ban a product, it might be argued that there are no compliance costs because consumers will just substitute some other product. At best, the cost of compliance might be estimated as any increase in price for the substitute product. In fact, the cost to consumers is greater, because they lose the consumer surplus the product would have created had it been available. In Figure 10-2, for example, the shaded triangle is the loss in consumer surplus from the ban.

Any regulation that increases costs will create some loss in consumer surplus, as shown in Figure 10-3. The increase in cost means that consumers will purchase less of the product, and will therefore lose some of the surplus they could otherwise have realized.

Figure 10-2. Lost consumer surplus from banning a product.

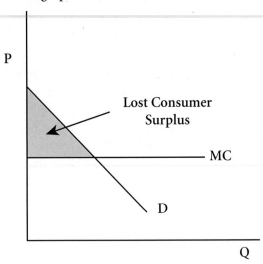

A second indirect cost of regulation is delay. When regulations require approval of a new product before it can be sold, there will be some period of time while the product is under review that it will not be available. Regulation of prescription drugs and food additives are examples of this kind of regulatory structure. The products that are eventually approved are not available until later, often much later, than they otherwise would have been. The artificial sweetener aspartame, for example, better known by its brand name NutraSweet, spent 15 years in the regulatory approval process.

A third indirect cost of regulation is reduced innovation. A business deciding whether to make an investment in developing a new product or technology must consider the pattern of cash flows over time. Typically, cash flows will be negative in the early years as the business is developing the technology, with a large expenditure when it is necessary to build a plant to manufacture the product. Eventually, if the product is successful, it generates positive cash flows. A typical pattern of cash flows for investing in a new product is shown in Figure 10-4.

Figure 10-3. Lost surplus from cost-increasing regulation.

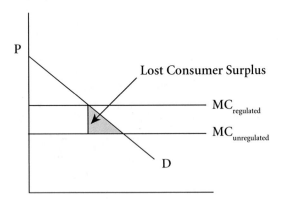

In deciding at time zero whether to invest in developing this product, a business must consider the discounted present value of the cash flow. If this net present value is positive, the investment is profitable and should be pursued. If it is negative, however, the business should not pursue this particular project.

Regulatory delay can have a considerable impact on the net present value of the project, because it pushes positive cash flows farther into the future. Discounted at 10 percent, the present value of a dollar in 5 years is 62 cents. Delaying that dollar another year reduces its present value to 56 cents; delaying it two years reduces its present value to 51 cents. In addition, the company must be able to cover the capital costs of its initial investment, which will mean some period of extra costs while the product is under review.

Figure 10-4. Cash flow for an investment in innovation.

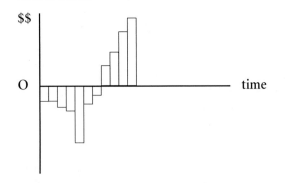

One study of the impact of delay examined new prescription drugs introduced between 1980 and 1984. Using the actual cash flows of the investments and the eventual returns in the market, it found that the average net present value of the investment was $23.4 million. Cutting one year off of the regulatory review time for these products would have increased the net present value to $40.7 million, an increase of 73 percent.

Defenders of regulatory delay often argue that a company with, say, a cure for cancer (or perhaps even better, the common cold) would not be deterred by the need to wait an additional year for product approval. The product would be so profitable that it would still be worthwhile to produce it. This, however, is an ex-post view of the investment. It is likely true, *if* it is known for certain that the product will be successful, that it would still be worth pursuing. But the decision to develop the product must be made ex ante—before the results are known, back at time zero on the timeline. Examined from the point in time when the investment decision must be made, the costs of delay are far more substantial—as the study of prescription drug regulation makes clear.

A final indirect cost of regulation is unintended side effects. Sometimes the way in which companies choose to comply with regulatory requirements generates other consequences that are in fact costs of the regulation. By their nature, anticipating unintended side effects is quite difficult. Like other indirect costs, they are usually only recognized after the regulation has been in place for some time.

A good example of unintended side effects is CAFE, the corporate average fuel economy requirements. A critical compliance strategy for improving gas mileage is to reduce the weight of the vehicle. That is why, for example, most new cars come with a reduced size spare tire designed only to get the car to a place where the tire can be fixed or replaced. The smaller tire is lighter, and carrying it around will not use as much gas.[2]

Unfortunately, a lighter car is a riskier car. Anyone contemplating a big truck bearing down on them on the highway would surely rather be in a Ford Expedition or some similar vehicle than a Smart car. Statistical analysis confirms that intuition. On average, a one percent reduction in the weight of the vehicle increases the chance of dying in an accident by two percent. Over the first 10 years that cars of a new model year are in use, the better fuel economy required by the CAFE standard resulted in an estimated 2,200 to 3,900 additional fatalities.[3]

B. Controlling the costs of regulation

As discussed above, Congress is not directly accountable for the costs of regulations. Even members who voted for a regulatory statute can truthfully say that they were not responsible for the specific requirements in the rule, and are therefore not responsible for the fact that compliance costs are as high as they are. Nor are the civil servants who actually make regulatory decisions accountable. They are not elected, and we cannot vote them out of office if we do not like their decisions. The one elected official we can hold accountable is the president. He, after all, appoints the heads of the regulatory agencies, and can determine their approach to regulatory issues.

As regulation grew, and political controversy about its impact grew as well, presidents tried to gain more influence and control over regulatory decisions. The efforts began during the Nixon administration, and have been consistently strengthened and focused on the most important decisions since then. The central features of presidential oversight as it is practiced today were put in place through an Executive Order at the beginning of the Reagan administration. With relatively minor changes, these features are still in place today.

There are two key mechanisms that facilitate presidential oversight of the regulatory process. First, regulatory agencies are required to conduct a formal cost-benefit analysis of "major" rules. A major rule is one that has an impact of $100 million or more, or has a substantial impact on a smaller industry. Since the beginning of the regulatory review process in 1981, the number of major new rules has generally ranged from 50 to 60. From 2008 through 2010 major final rules averaged just over 90 per year. The spring 2011 edition of the Unified Agenda (which lists essentially all federal rulemaking activity) included a total of 4,257 rules, of which 219 were "economically significant" (a designation that corresponds closely to "major" rules). Whether or not a formal cost-benefit analysis is required, agencies are supposed to adopt rules only if the benefits reasonably justify the costs. A few statutes, however, preclude agencies from considering costs.

Second, regulatory agencies must obtain approval from the Office of Management and Budget[4] before publishing a "significant" proposed or final rule in the Federal Register. Because publication is an essential step in the rulemaking process, OMB can block regulatory proposals if it disagrees with them. Major rules are significant, but other rules can be designated as significant by the agency or at OMB's discretion. The Office of Information and Regulatory Affairs (OIRA), the office in OMB responsible for rulemaking matters, conducts roughly 600 to 700 rule reviews per year.

---

[2]Indeed, one study estimated that if Americans weighed today what they did in 1960, before the obesity epidemic, we would use 938 million fewer gallons of gasoline than we do. That is the average annual gasoline consumption of 2 million cars. Lindsey Tanner, Associated Press, "Americans' obesity adds to gasoline consumption, study says." *USA Today*, October 25, 2006.

[3]Robert W. Crandall and John D. Graham, "The Effect of Fuel Economy Standards on Automobile Safety," *Journal of Law and Economics* 32(1):97–118 (April 1989).

[4]The Office of Management and Budget is part of the Executive Office of the President. Its best known task is the preparation of the president's budget.

Although OIRA can reject rules, it rarely does so. In 2011, for example, only three rules were "returned for reconsideration." By far the most common result of review, in 77 percent of cases, is that the rule is found "consistent with change," meaning that after some changes, usually negotiated between OIRA and the agency, the rule is consistent with cost-benefit principles. Only 12 percent were found "consistent without change," and six percent were withdrawn by the agency.

OIRA's oversight of the regulatory process is a tool to enable greater presidential control. Both the head of OIRA and the head of a regulatory agency are presidential appointees; if they cannot reach agreement about a regulatory decision, the disagreement is resolved in the White House. Thus, oversight is in essence a way to bring key regulatory choices to the attention of the president or his top advisers.

II. THE NATURE OF RISK

Numerous regulatory regimes, from food safety to product safety to many environmental regulations, are justified by the need to "save lives." In fact what these regulations do, at least if they are successful, is reduce risks. With a lower risk of bad outcomes, applied to a population experiencing the risk, fewer people will die. The risk, however, will remain—it will just be smaller than it was before.

Figure 10-5. Activities creating a one in 1 million risk of death.

Activity	Risk
6 minutes in a canoe	Accident
Traveling 150 miles by car	Accident
Traveling 1,000 miles by jet	Accident
3 hours in a coal mine	Accident
Eating 40 tablespoons of peanut butter	Cancer from aflatoxin
2 months in average stone or brick building	Cancer from radon gas
Drinking Miami tap water for 1 year	Cancer from chloroform
Living 2 months in Denver	Cancer from cosmic radiation
1 chest X-ray	Cancer from radiation

Adapted from Paul Slovic, Baruch Fischhoff, and Sarah Lichtenstein, "Informing People about Risk," in Louis A. Morris, Michael B. Mazis, Ivan Baroftsky, eds., *Product Labeling and Health Risks*, Banbury Report 6, Cold Spring Harbor Laboratory, 1980.

A commonly used threshold for risks worthy of regulatory concern is a risk that is greater than a 1 in 1 million chance of dying. The FDA, for example, in considering general safety issues, considers a risk below that level as "safe."[5] Figure 10-5 considers a number of everyday activities that give rise to a risk of death that reaches one in 1 million.

Some of these risks are relatively well known, although it is perhaps surprising how quickly they exceed the one in a million threshold.

Others are more obscure, but nonetheless real. The risk from peanut butter is the result of a potent carcinogen, aflatoxin, produced by a mold that grows on peanuts. Natural stone and the clay used to make bricks contain small amounts of the radioactive element radium, which produces radon gas as a decay product. The EPA estimates that radon is the number two cause of lung cancer deaths, after cigarettes. Denver, the mile high city, is above much of the dense lower atmosphere that offers more protection from cosmic rays to those at lower altitudes.

The examples make clear that risk is everywhere. Choices about risk are not typically binary choices of risk or no risk. Rather, they are choices about how much risk to take, because some risk is inevitable. Although many risks can be reduced, we cannot achieve zero risk, either individually or collectively. Moreover, consumers are clearly willing to take small risks in return for benefits. There is no better evidence of this than the incidence of jaywalking on an urban campus. It really would be safer to cross at the

---

[5]Cancer risks are treated differently, however, because of a legislative provision known as the Delaney clause. This provision prohibits approving any food additive that has been shown to cause cancer in animals. In one case, the FDA had to ban a color additive even though it estimated the human cancer risk was about one in 19 *trillion*.

corner and wait for the light, but it is a little more convenient to just cross where you are when the way seems reasonably clear. The question is one of degree: how much risk are we willing to take, and in exchange for what?

Some risks, such as accident risks, are readily identifiable and easy to measure. It is straightforward, for example, to determine how many people die each year in canoeing accidents and develop an estimate of how much time people spend in canoes. Such risks are easy to see and easy to measure. Measuring cancer risks, however, particularly human cancer risk, is far more difficult. Often there is no reliable evidence of the effects of relatively low-level exposure in human populations. Instead, estimates must be derived from animal studies, often at much higher levels of exposure than those that are relevant to human populations.

Unfortunately, many cancer risk assessments build in extremely conservative assumptions, "just to be careful." Because cancer risks are particularly frightening to many, risk assessors want to avoid underestimating the risk—and as a result, they frequently overestimate the risk, sometimes substantially. Although considering the uncertainty inherent in any risk assessment is surely appropriate, overestimating the risk does not make the uncertainties go away, it simply hides them from the ultimate decision maker. Older risk assessments are particularly prone to these problems.

There are numerous examples of overcautious practices in cancer risk assessments. First, animal studies are frequently conducted using the maximum tolerated dose. This dosage is the maximum daily dose that does not cause acute toxicity. Physiological changes in how the chemical is metabolized at high doses, however, may greatly reduce the relevance of these doses to what actually happens at doses that are more relevant to the risk that people may face.

Another common practice is to use the most sensitive animal species as the basis of the risk assessment, rather than considering which species is likely to best predict the impact on humans. If a chemical causes cancer in rats but not mice, for example, the risk assessment may be based on the rat results, ignoring the mice. In some instances, however, the mechanisms that lead to cancer in laboratory animals may simply not be relevant to humans. Saccharin, for example, causes bladder cancer, but only at high doses and only in rats, apparently because of characteristics of the rat urinary system that are not relevant to humans.[6]

Because animal studies are conducted at high doses, it is necessary to extrapolate the results to the lower doses relevant to humans. Cancer risk assessments often assume that the risk is linear at low doses—that is, that there is no safe dose. Typical dose response curves, however, are not linear. As shown in Figure 10-6, dose response curves typically start out with a small percentage of a population responding at very low doses. At higher doses, the curve gets much steeper, with an increase in dose leading to a more substantial increase in the percent of the population responding. Eventually the curve levels out at very high doses, when the vast majority of those who will ever respond have already done so. If this typical dose-response relationship prevails, the assumption that the effect is linear at low doses will overstate the risk.

The linearity assumption is problematic for other reasons as well. For some chemicals, there may be thresholds of exposure, with no response at all for doses below the threshold. Such a dose-response

Figure 10-6. A typical dose-response curve.

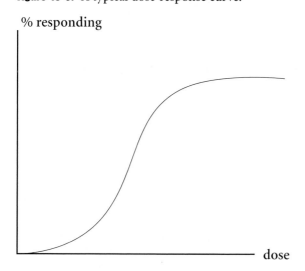

% responding

dose

---

[6]Lois Swirsky Gold, Bruce N. Ames, and Thomas H. Slone. Animal Cancer Tests and Human Cancer Risk: A Broad Perspective. http://potency.berkeley.edu/MOE.html, September 2008.

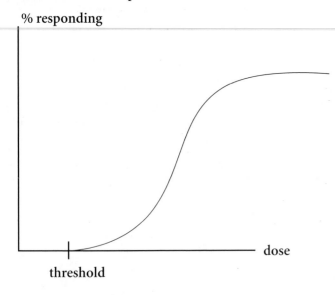

Figure 10-7. Dose-response curve with a threshold.

% responding

dose

threshold

curve is shown in Figure 10-7. The linearity assumption ignores the possibility that a threshold exists, and therefore overestimates risk if there is a threshold. In essence, the linearity assumption says that because stepping off the roof of a 30 foot tall building causes significant damage, stepping off of a one foot curb will cause 1/30 of the damage. In fact, you probably won't notice it at all.

An additional difficulty with the linearity assumption is the phenomenon of hormesis. For some chemicals, a low dose may actually be beneficial. Selenium, for example, is an essential nutrient at low doses, but toxic at high doses. If low doses of a potential carcinogen are actually beneficial, the linearity assumption will result in further overestimation of the cancer risk.

A fourth practice that tends to overstate risk is that risks are often calculated for the maximum exposed individual. This is the hypothetical individual in the population who experiences the highest level of exposure to the chemical. For an airborne pollutant, for example, the maximum exposed individual spends 70 years outdoors, at the point downwind of the emissions source where the concentration of the chemical is highest. By definition, such an individual will experience higher exposure, and hence a higher risk, than anyone else in the population.

Finally, risk assessments sometimes use the upper bound of the 95 percent confidence interval for the risk estimate, rather than using the estimate itself. Since there is a 95 percent chance that the true value lies in the confidence interval, there is a 97.5 percent chance that the true value is lower than the upper bound of the confidence interval. Again, the result is an overestimate of the likely risk.

If a cancer risk assessment depends on five multiplicative factors, and we double each one just to be sure we do not underestimate, the final estimate will be 2^5 times the most likely estimate, or 32 times larger. In some cases, the overstatement can be even greater. One study, for example, found that the most widely used estimate for the cancer risk from dioxin[7] was about 5,000 times higher than the most likely estimate of the risk.

There are, of course, uncertainties in any estimate of cancer risk, and the risk that an estimate is too low should be considered in deciding whether, and how, to regulate that risk. But systematically overestimating the risk is difficult to defend. It hides uncertainties rather than bringing them to the forefront. Moreover, there may well be situations where the relevant policy choice is between a cancer risk and a non-cancer risk. If we systematically overstate the cancer risk, that choice will almost inevitably be distorted.

III. CHOICES INVOLVING RISK

As discussed above, ordinary consumers are willing to take risks in exchange for some benefits. However, ordinary consumers are also willing to pay for risk reductions, as the market for safety devices of all sorts makes clear. From an economic perspective, consumers make choices about risk and safety in the same way they make any other kind of consumption decision: they balance the marginal benefits and the marginal costs of a little more risk to find the level of safety that maximizes their satisfaction. An individual consumer's choices about safety are depicted in Figure 10-8.

---

[7]Dioxin was originally identified as a contaminant in the Agent Orange defoliant used in the Vietnam War. As detection technologies have improved, it appears that trace amounts of dioxin are widespread, and the chemical is present wherever chlorine is present.

Figure 10-8. Optimal safety choices.

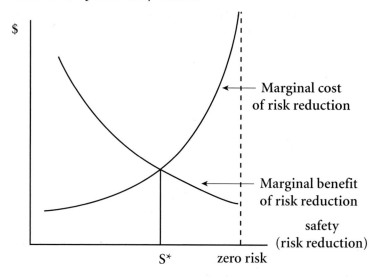

We can think of safety as a reduction in risk. The theoretical maximum level of safety is therefore zero risk, identified by the dotted line in Figure 10-8. If the level of risk is high, the consumer is presumably willing to pay a sizable amount to reduce the risk, so the marginal benefit of more safety (or more risk reduction) is relatively high when the level of risk is high. Moreover, there would presumably be some benefit in eliminating even the last unit of risk, so the marginal benefit of safety remains positive even at the zero risk point. When the level of risk is high, relatively cheap steps to reduce risk are likely available. Thus, the marginal cost of risk reduction presumably starts out low. Costs may be direct monetary costs, or they may be the loss of benefits that taking the risk entails. For example, the cost of risk reduction by giving up jaywalking is the extra time and effort necessary to cross at the light. Marginal cost increases, however, as the cheap steps are taken. Moreover, marginal cost is likely to explode as we approach the zero risk frontier. Thus, each additional reduction in risk is more costly. Consumers will choose the level of safety where the marginal benefits of risk reduction are equal to the marginal cost, S^* in Figure 10-8.

Figure 10-9. Effects of an income increase on safety choices.

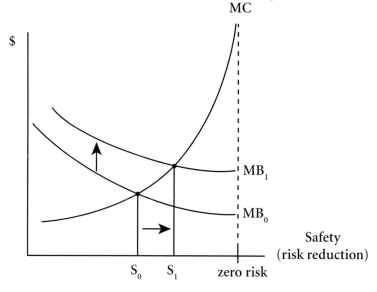

One important factor likely to influence safety choices over time is income. If safety is a "normal" good, and the evidence indicates that it is, increases in income will increase consumers' willingness to pay for safety improvements. Thus, the marginal benefit curve will shift up as income increases, as shown in Figure 10-9. Empirical studies indicate that a 10 percent increase in income leads to an increased demand for safety of 5 to 6 percent.

Because safety is a normal good, we should expect to see safety improvements over time, as incomes have increased. Moreover, we should expect to see more risk-reducing choices among higher-income consumers than among those with lower income.

Given the amount of safety they desire, consumers must also decide how to produce safety. In most cases, there are at least two important ways to reduce risk. Consumers can purchase products with additional safety features, or they can use products with fewer features more carefully. In the market for automobiles, for example, consumers can reduce risk by purchasing a car with side airbags, anti-lock brakes, and other safety features. But they can also reduce risk by driving more carefully, giving up texting while driving, and obeying the speed limit.

The trade-off between product features and the degree of care in producing a given level of safety is shown in Figure 10-10. To produce a given level of safety, consumers can purchase a product with many safety features

Figure 10-10. Producing safety.

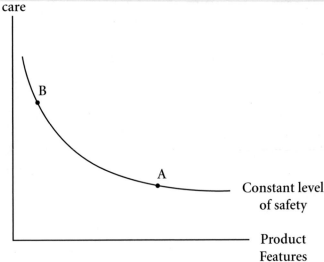

and not use very much care, as in point A in the figure. Alternatively, they can purchase a product with fewer features and use more care, as in point B in the figure. Of course, consumers can choose to do both, buying more features and using more care, which will produce a higher level of safety. However, for a given level of safety, care and product features are likely to be substitutes: they are alternative ways of accomplishing the same objective.

Given the trade-off between using care and product safety features, regulations that seek to require product safety improvements may not produce the benefits we might expect. Consider, for example, a consumer who has decided on safety level S_0 in Figure 10-11, and has chosen to produce that level of safety with some care and some product features, at point A. Suppose the government decides to require additional product safety features, to the level F_r in Figure 10-11. What the government clearly hopes is that the consumer will maintain his or her level of care, and therefore end up at point B, with a higher level of safety. The consumer, however, may decide that if he or she must purchase additional safety features, there is less reason to maintain the same level of care. Consumers may therefore reduce care, and move toward point C. By relying more on product features and using less care, consumer safety may not improve at all. This is the phenomenon of offsetting behavior. When regulators require changes in products, consumers may change their behavior in ways that reduce or, in the extreme, completely offset the impact of the product changes.

Figure 10-11. Offsetting behavior.

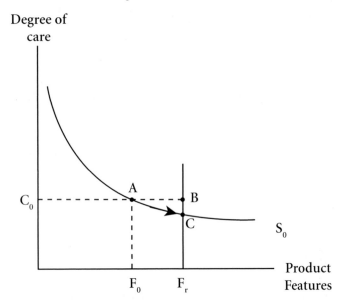

There is considerable evidence that offsetting behavior occurs, both in general and in specific instances. Viscusi, for example, studied the effects of the Consumer Product Safety Commission (CPSC), which was formed in 1972.[8] He found that although accident rates declined after the CPSC was formed, they continued to decline at the same rate they had declined for the previous 30 years. Existing trends continued, driven largely by increasing income and improving technology, but there was no statistically significant effect of the CPSC on the home accident death rate, the death rate from fires, or the incidence of poisonings.

Viscusi also considered the impact of particular CPSC regulations. He found no significant effect of regulations intended to reduce the risk from mattress fires, matchbooks, carpets and rugs (a flammability standard), cribs, or bicycles. Nor were there significant effects on the death rates of young children, a population groups that has been a frequent focus of CPSC concern. Death rates among children under 5 from poisonings, burns,

---

[8]The discussion in the next few paragraphs is based on W. Kip Viscusi, "Consumer Behavior and the Safety Effects of Product Safety Regulation," *Journal of Law and Economics*, 28(3): 527–553 (October 1985).

and swallowing small objects were not significantly different from the trends that prevailed before the CPSC was formed.

To understand why regulations did not appear to have the expected effect of reducing risk, Viscusi studied the requirement for childproof caps on medicines in more detail. Initially, the regulation applied only to aspirin, which was the primary cause of poisonings in young children. There were three possible reasons for the failure of the regulation. One reason is the lulling effect. Although the caps are frequently called childproof, they are really only child-resistant. If people use less care in keeping medicine away from children because they believe the caps are childproof, some children will get them open. In fact, the regulatory standard allows a certain number of children to succeed in opening the cap, because a truly childproof cap is not possible.

Another possibility is the avoidance effect. Child-resistant caps are also often harder for adults to open as well. It is therefore tempting for adults to simply leave the bottle open, avoiding both the difficulty of opening the bottle and whatever protective effect the cap might have. Consistent with the avoidance effect, the fraction of poisonings from open bottles increased after the regulation.

A third possibility is the spillover effect. Consumers are likely to develop habits about how they store and use their medicines, rather than differentiating among medicines with different packaging. If they are less careful with aspirin because of the child-resistant cap, those habits may spill over to other medicines that, at least initially, did not have child-resistant caps. The fact that poisonings from non-aspirin products increased after the rule is consistent with spillover. With more poisonings from other medications, the regulation was broadened to require child-resistant caps for most medicines.

Offsetting behavior has also been found in studies of automobile safety requirements. In an early study of automobile safety regulations, Peltzman found that the death rate among people in the vehicle declined significantly. Although engineering estimates of how much the newly required safety features would reduce risk predicted a 20 percent reduction in the death rate, the actual reduction was only 7 percent for those in the vehicle. Apparently drivers changed how they drove in cars with more safety features, thereby offsetting the effect of the devices themselves. Moreover, Peltzman found a significant increase in the pedestrian death rate, as might be expected if drivers use less care.[9]

A study of the introduction of airbags when they were still optional equipment also found evidence that drivers changed their behavior in ways that offset the risk reduction from the airbags themselves. For both drivers and passengers, deaths were significantly higher than would have been expected based on the fraction of cars equipped with airbags and the estimated effectiveness of airbags in saving lives.[10]

Thus, requiring safety features will likely lead to changes in behavior. Those changes may not eliminate the effect of the new features entirely, but they will surely reduce it below what we might have expected. Consumers choose both the level of safety they desire, and the combination of care and product features that is the best way for them to achieve the desired level. We cannot simply assume that consumers will always exercise the same level of caution. In general, they will not.

IV. VALUING RISKS TO LIFE

A. The willingness to pay approach

To use cost-benefit analysis as a basis for making regulatory choices, we need a way to value reductions in risk. In common parlance, this is often thought of as the value of saving lives, or the value of a statistical life saved. In valuing market resources, a cost-benefit analysis ordinarily uses the market price, which reflects consumers' willingness to pay for the good. It is not a meaningful question to ask consumers what they are willing to pay

---

[9]Sam Peltzman, "The Effects of Automobile Safety Regulation," *The Journal of Political Economy*, 83(4): 677–726 (August 1975).
[10]Steven Peterson, George Hoffer, and Edward Millner, "Are Drivers of Air-Bag-Equipped Cars More Aggressive? A Test of the Offsetting Behavior Hypothesis," *Journal of Law and Economics*, 38(2): 251–264 (October 1995).

to save their lives, however. Presumably, they are willing to pay whatever they have, and the answers tell us more about the distribution of income than about the value of life-saving regulations.

There is another, more meaningful way to address the issue. In the aggregate, risk reduction translates into some number of lives saved, but the regulation operates by reducing risk. As discussed above, it is perfectly reasonable to ask what consumers are willing to pay for a small reduction in risk. Consumers make that choice on numerous occasions throughout their daily lives, and we can examine market evidence of what they are actually willing to pay for small reductions in risk, or what they must be paid to accept small risks.

Figure 10-12. Compensating differential in the product market.

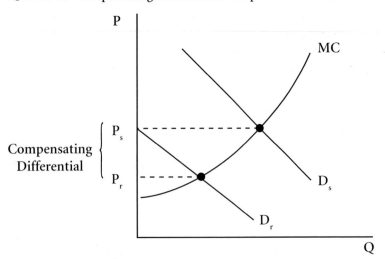

Consider first the demand for risky products. We can consider the market for a "safe" version of some product, such as an automobile equipped with side airbags, antilock brakes, and any other safety features we might imagine. The demand for the safe version, D_s, is downward sloping, and the marginal cost of producing a safer product is upward sloping, as shown in Figure 10-12. The market-clearing price is P_s.

Now consider the demand for a riskier version of the product. This demand, D_r, starts at P_s, because if the price were the same, presumably everyone would prefer the safer version of the product. Consumers must be compensated, in the form of a lower price, for purchasing the riskier version. The market price of the risky product, P_r, is where demand intersects the marginal cost.

Figure 10-13. Compensating differential in the labor market.

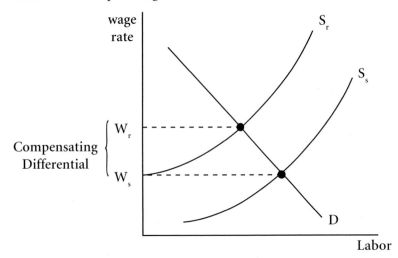

The difference between P_s and P_r is a compensating differential. It is what consumers must receive in the form of a lower price to induce them to accept the higher level of risk in the riskier version of the product. We can observe this compensating differential in the market, as long as we control for the other characteristics of the product that are likely to affect the price. Moreover, we can observe the difference in risk between the two versions of the product, and can therefore observe what consumers are willing to pay for the reduction in risk from the safer version of the product.

A similar analysis can be conducted in labor markets, where jobs differ considerably in the risk they pose for workers. Being a librarian is very low risk, for example, but there is considerably more risk in being a coal miner. We consider first the supply of workers to a "safe" job, S_s in Figure 10-13. The market-clearing wage rate for the safe job is W_s, where supply of workers to safe jobs intersects the demand for labor.

Some workers are willing to accept a riskier job, however, if they are paid enough to make the risk worthwhile. The supply of workers to a risky job, S_r, begins at the market-clearing wage for the safe job, because if the wage is the same, all workers would prefer the safer job. The market wage for the riskier job, W_r, is determined where

S_r meets the demand for labor. Again, the difference in wages is a compensating differential. Controlling for other job characteristics that influence wages, we can observe this differential in labor markets. It is the added compensation workers require to accept the higher risk of a more dangerous job.

We can use compensating differentials, which reflect consumers' willingness to pay for small differences in risk, to estimate the value of the statistical lives saved as a result of this reduction in risk. As discussed in Section III, consumers will equate the marginal benefit of a little less risk to the marginal cost. In turn, the marginal benefit of a risk reduction is the risk reduction itself times some value—the value consumers attach to the "lives saved" as a result of the reduction. We need only equate this marginal benefit to the marginal cost of the risk reduction and solve for the value.

It is perhaps easiest to follow the logic in a concrete example. One everyday risk we all face is the risk of dying in a household fire. In the United States, the annual risk of death is approximately 1 death for every 100,000 homes. One way to reduce that risk is to purchase a smoke detector. Assume that the smoke detector cuts the risk in half, so the risk reduction is 1 in 200,000. The marginal cost is just the price of the smoke detector, which we assume is \$25. Then we have

$$\text{Marginal benefit} = \text{Marginal cost}$$
$$(\text{Risk reduction})(\text{Value}) = \text{Price}$$
$$(1/200,000)(\text{Value}) = \$25$$
$$\text{Value} = \$5 \text{ million}$$

This is the willingness-to-pay value of a statistical life saved. It is based on observed consumer behavior, usually in product markets or labor markets, and the compensating differentials for differences in risk across products or jobs. Those compensating differentials correspond to the price in the smoke detector example. Once we determine the risk difference, we can use the compensating differential to determine the value of a statistical life saved.

Numerous studies have estimated the value of a statistical life saved. Good studies using market data produce estimates that range from \$4 million to \$9 million per statistical life saved. Results are similar whether the analysis is based on wage differences in labor markets or price differences in product markets. The midpoint of the "best" studies is about \$7 million per statistical life saved. In valuing environmental risk reductions, the EPA uses a value of \$6.2 million.

B. Why value lives?

Employing a value-of-life estimate to value reductions in risk is one of the most controversial issues in cost-benefit analysis of regulatory decisions. Nonetheless, it reflects the need to think systematically about the choices we confront. Removing a ton of some pollutant to benefit 1,000 asthmatics at a cost of \$1 million is not the same as removing the same amount to benefit 1 asthmatic at a cost of \$1 billion. Considering the value of risk reductions, as reflected in actual market choices of consumers, is a systematic way to compare such choices.

Any decision to undertake a risk reducing intervention, or not to undertake some other intervention, implicitly places a value on life. In deciding to proceed in one case, we are saying implicitly that the lives saved are worth at least that much. In deciding not to proceed with some other intervention, we are similarly concluding that the lives at stake are not worth the cost—that other priorities (including other ways to save lives) are more important.

Failure to think systematically about the choices can lead us astray. Before economists started to think seriously about the value of life, the approach that was widely used was the human capital approach. This approach, which is still used in wrongful death actions in the courts, argues that we can value lives the way we value a machine. The value of a machine is the net present value of the income stream it produces. Thus, the human capital approach argues that the value of a life is the net present value of the person's income stream. This approach yields values that are considerably lower than the willingness-to-pay estimates of the value of life. In one application, for example, a human capital-based valuation of saving 50-year-old workers was only 15 percent of the valuation based on willingness to pay.[11]

[11]Donald Kenkel, "Using Estimates of the Value of a Statistical Life in Evaluating Regulatory Effects," in Fred Kuchler, Valuing the Health Benefits of Food Safety: A Proceedings, USDA, Economic Research Service, MP No. (MP1570), April 2001.

Moreover, the human capital approach to valuing lives has some unfortunate implications. Most people, for example, regard a newborn baby as quite precious. From the human capital perspective, however, the infant represents 20 or more years of substantial expenditures, with the first dollar of income at an age of, say, 20, worth only 14 cents in present value terms, discounted at 10 percent. A child isn't worth much! Retirees and the disabled are positively worthless; they have only expenditures, not income. It is difficult to square these results with any reasonable concept of the value of life.

Because any decision implicitly assigns a value to saving lives, thinking systematically about what value to use is important. Willingness to pay is one of the best approaches available.

Consideration of the costs of saving lives is also important because these costs represent resources used that could have been used elsewhere, and therefore represent reductions in incomes for those who must pay them. Earlier we noted the fact that increases in incomes lead to increased expenditures on safety. Across countries, over time within a country, or across different demographic groups, increases in income are associated with increased life expectancy. By the same token, reductions in income will lead to reduced expenditures on risk reduction in numerous other areas. Empirical estimates indicate that $21 million in costs will "cost" one statistical life. We may not be able to identify the precise risks that change, because consumers make expenditures to reduce risk in numerous areas. In the aggregate, however, reductions in income will "cost" statistical lives, in the same way that risk-reducing regulations "save" statistical lives.

The effects of income reductions on the net benefits of regulatory changes are important. One study of 21 rules that were primarily intended to reduce mortality risk found that, taking into account the mortality effects of costs, 13 of the rules (62 percent) actually *increased* fatalities. Seven rules reduce net mortality by fewer than 100 lives per year; the remaining four resulted in larger estimated reductions in net mortality.[12]

Figure 10-14. Cost of federal regulations per life saved.

Regulation	Annual Lives Saved	Cost per Life Saved (thousands of dollars)
NHTSA Steering Column	1,300	$100
NHTSA Passive Restraints	1,850	$300
FRA Alcohol and Drug Testing	4.2	$500
Children's Sleepwear	106	$1,300
Hazard Communication	200	$1,800
Arsenic/Glass Plant	0.1	$19,200
Asbestos	74.7	$89,300
DES in Cattle feed	68	$132,000

Adapted from John F. Morall, "A Review of the Record," *Regulation,* Vol. 10, No. 6, November/December 1986.

An alternative to assigning a specific value to a statistical life saved is cost-effectiveness analysis. This approach considers the cost per life saved for different interventions. As shown in Figure 10-14, these differences can be quite dramatic.

Some interventions, such as the rule requiring steering columns in automobiles to collapse on impact, are quite cheap, with a cost per life saved of around $100,000. At the other extreme, OSHA's asbestos rule cost more than $89 million per life saved, and the ban on the drug DES in cattle feed cost $132 million per life saved.

The idea of cost-effectiveness analysis is that we should look for regulatory interventions at the low end of the cost per life saved. Only when there are no more low-cost changes should we consider interventions that are more costly per life saved. One study found that if we allocated regulatory resources this way, we could double the number of lives saved for the same total cost.[13] However much we are willing to spend on regulatory requirements, we would presumably all like to save as many lives as possible for those expenditures. Cost-effectiveness analysis is a way to achieve that objective.

---

[12]Robert W. Hahn, Randall W. Lutter, and W. Kip Viscusi, "Do Federal Regulations Reduce Mortality?" AEI Brookings Joint Center for Regulatory Studies, Washington, DC (2000).

[13]Tammy O. Tengs and John D. Graham, "The Opportunity Costs of Haphazard Social Investments in Life-Saving," in Robert W. Hahn, editor, *Risks, Costs, and Lives Saved: Getting Better Results from Regulation.* New York and Oxford: Oxford University Press; Washington, DC: The AEI Press, 1996.

V. SUMMARY

Costs of regulatory agencies have grown substantially, driven largely by increased regulation to address health and safety risks. Running the regulatory agencies themselves costs over $50 billion per year. Private sector compliance costs are far larger, roughly $1.75 trillion. Although the costs of regulatory agencies are part of the federal budget and subject to congressional approval each year, private sector compliance costs are not. Congress authorizes the agencies to write rules, but it does not approve the costs of the regulations they adopt or review them on a regular basis. Regulation also creates indirect costs, including a loss of consumer surplus, delay in the availability of new products, reduced innovation, and unintended side effects.

To help control the costs of regulation, agencies are required to conduct a cost-benefit analysis of "major" rules. These rules and other "significant" rules are subject to review by the Office of Management and Budget before they are published in the Federal Register. This process gives the president more control over the regulatory agencies.

Choices about risk are a question of degree. There is always risk; the issue is how much risk, and in exchange for what benefits. Measuring some risks is straightforward, but other risks are difficult to measure precisely. Cancer risks in particular are hard to measure with confidence. Cancer risk assessments often make assumptions that overestimate the risk. Animal studies are based on the maximum tolerated dose, and often use the most sensitive species rather than the species most relevant to human risk. Risk assessments often assume that the risk is linear at low doses, and use the risk for the maximum exposed individual. The result is risk assessments that may dramatically overstate the best estimate of the risk.

Consumers make choices about risk by balancing the benefits and costs of risky activities. They are frequently willing to take small risks in exchange for small benefits. Higher incomes tend to increase the demand for risk reductions. Consumers must also decide how to reduce the risks they face. One way to reduce risk is to purchase products with more safety features. Alternatively, consumers can reduce risk by exercising more care in their use of the product.

Because consumers can substitute between product features and using more care, requirements for additional product safety features do not necessarily reduce risk. Consumers may instead reduce the amount of care they exercise, a phenomenon known as offsetting behavior. The failure to find significant effects of CPSC regulations on overall accident death rates, on death rates from product risks that have been the subject of specific regulations, or on death rates of young children who have been a frequent focus of regulatory concern is consistent with offsetting behavior. Auto safety regulations also produce offsetting behavior, leading to increases in the pedestrian death rate and smaller reductions in accident deaths than would have been expected.

The willingness-to-pay approach to valuing lives relies on market evidence of consumers' willingness to pay for small changes in risks. Compensating differentials, the difference in prices between riskier and less risky versions of a product, or between riskier and safer jobs, provide such evidence. Because consumers equate the marginal benefit of risk reduction to the marginal cost, compensating differentials can be used to estimate the value of a statistical life saved through risk reductions.

Any policy decision implicitly places a value on life, so thinking about a reasonable way to value lives is important. For example, the human capital approach uses the net present value of earnings as the value of life. This approach implies lower values for the lives of children and the elderly or disabled. Neglecting the costs of regulatory interventions can lead to increases in mortality, because at higher incomes consumers choose more risk-reducing activities. Cost-effectiveness analysis focuses on the cost per life saved. Reallocating resources to more cost-effective regulations could double the number of lives saved for the same total cost.

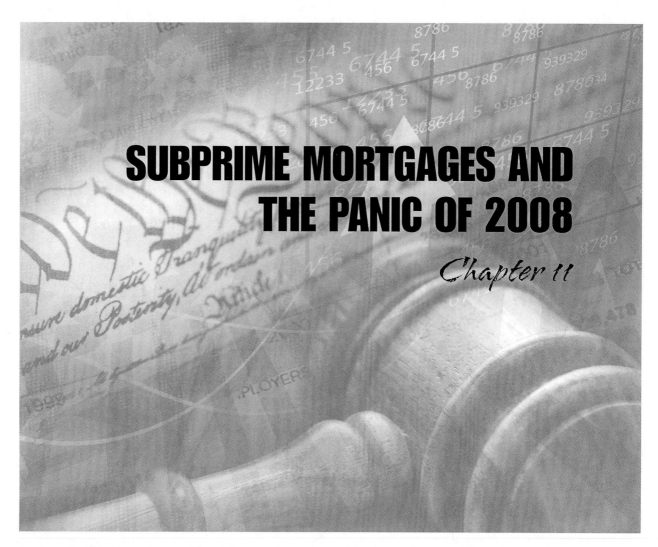

SUBPRIME MORTGAGES AND THE PANIC OF 2008

Chapter 11

In the fall of 2008, as the presidential campaign was reaching its peak, financial markets in the United States and around the world faced the very real prospect of collapse. Stock markets gyrated wildly, and credit markets threatened to freeze up entirely. In the 50 trading days after September 15, the market moved by more than 4 percent (up or down) 25 times—the same number of 4 percent moves that occurred in the previous 25 *years*.

As dramatic events often do, the Panic of 2008 provoked substantial changes in the relationship between government and the private sector. The Federal Reserve Board made unprecedented use of its emergency authority to prevent the collapse of some major financial services firms, and Congress authorized a $700 billion program to provide additional capital to ailing financial institutions. The government became a majority shareholder of one automobile company and a significant minority shareholder in another.

The Panic provided the impetus for a major reform of the structure of financial regulation to try to prevent such a calamity from ever occurring again. The Dodd Frank Act, passed in 2010, extended federal regulation to numerous previously unregulated firms, and substantially altered the regulatory structure that dates from statutes enacted in the wake of the Great Depression. Many issues remain to be resolved in the more than 300 rulemakings that the law requires.

We begin by describing the changes in the mortgage market that are in many respects the roots of the crisis. Section II turns to the growth of subprime lending, where problems began, and the housing bubble that caused huge losses when it deflated. The section also considers the role of securities rating agencies and derivatives in the crisis. Section III describes the unfolding crisis and the bailout legislation that resulted. Section IV considers the regulatory changes in the Dodd Frank Act to reduce the risk of a repetition of the crisis.

I. The Roots of the Crisis: Changes in the Mortgage Market

In the traditional mortgage market, origination, servicing the loan, and holding the investment until it was paid off were all combined in a single entity. Typically a bank or a savings and loan, the institution had a clear incentive to exercise care about the creditworthiness of the borrower and the adequacy of the property as security for the loan, because if things went bad, it was the institution that would suffer the loss.

In the 1970s, Fannie Mae and Freddie Mac began to issue mortgage-backed securities. The company purchased mortgages from banks, guaranteed the stream of payments from borrowers, and issued securities to investors backed by the stream of payments on the underlying mortgages.

Fannie Mae was originally a government agency, created in the 1930s to support the housing market. It was privatized in 1968, in part because the revenue from selling the company enabled Lyndon Johnson to balance his last budget before leaving office. The original model was that Fannie Mae would issue securities to raise money, and use the proceeds to purchase mortgages from banks and savings and loans, thus freeing up the banks' capital to make additional mortgage loans. Once Fannie Mae was privatized, there was no reason for it to have a monopoly on the business, so Congress charted Freddie Mac as a competitor. It was widely believed, however, that although Fannie and Freddie were private companies, the federal government implicitly stood behind their debt, and the companies collectively were known as "government sponsored entities" (GSEs). Because of this implicit guarantee, the companies could obtain capital at a lower cost than the private investment banks that entered the market in the 1980s.

Securitization grew rapidly, particularly after the investment banks entered, and as it grew, it also became more complex. Investment banks divided mortgage-backed securities into different tranches, with differing levels of risk. As money came in from the borrowers' mortgage payments, it went first to pay holders of the first tranche of the securities, then to the second tranche, and so on. The lowest tranches were the riskiest securities, because if there were too many defaults or delinquencies on the mortgages, there would not be enough to cover the payments to investors in the lower-rated securities. Complex issues might have a dozen different tranches, each with its own unique level of risk.

The core idea behind securitization is the benefits of diversification. As long as the risks of default on the underlying mortgages are uncorrelated, a broader pool of mortgages reduces the risk, compared to the risk of a single mortgage. The key assumption is that the risk that a homebuyer in Miami will default is independent of the risk that a borrower in Phoenix will default, so a security backed by the mortgages is less risky than the individual mortgages themselves. If risks are correlated, however, then there is less reduction in risk from pooling. If, for example, housing markets collapse around the country, then homebuyers around the country are all more likely to default.

Issuers of mortgage-backed securities also offered various credit enhancements to reduce the risk that investors in some of the securities would lose money. These enhancements included approaches such as purchasing insurance from companies such as municipal bond insurers, or using letters of credit from a bank to back the securities. Another approach was overcollateralization, in which the interest rate on the securities is lower than the average interest rate on the mortgages, thus reducing the risk of a cash shortfall.

Because securitization was so successful, it spread to numerous other areas of the economy. Auto loans, student loans, credit card receivables, and commercial real estate loans were all assembled in pools and used to back what came to be known as "asset-backed securities."

Typically, the investment bank that assembled the pool of assets and issued the securities did not want to carry the underlying assets on its own books. They therefore created "special purpose vehicles" to hold the assets. As long as there was enough outside participation in the special purpose vehicle, the issuer did not need to consolidate the vehicle into its own financial statements. Thus the risk of losses on the pool of underlying assets did not show up on the books of the issuer of the asset-backed securities. As the crisis unfolded, the use of special purpose vehicles meant that it was very difficult to determine any individual financial institution's true exposure to the risks of mortgage defaults.

Because mortgages were increasingly held in pools owned by a special purpose vehicle, there was a need for a servicer: someone to collect the payments, manage late payments, make sure the borrower is complying with the terms of the mortgage such as insuring the property, and initiate collection actions in the event of late payments or default. Thus a market developed for the servicing rights for pools of mortgages. Typically the servicer is paid through fees, but at least initially, the servicer must cover any shortfalls due to late payments from the borrower. Compensation arrangements try to give the servicer an incentive to keep borrowers current, to avoid default and foreclosure.

The servicer is the borrower's only contact point. Borrowers do not know who actually owns their mortgage, or whether or how it is securitized. The contracts between the owner and the servicer, however, sometimes prohibit any modification in the terms of the loan. As foreclosures increased in 2008, the difficulties of trying to modify the terms of many loans became apparent.

The last part of the traditional mortgage business to split off from the banks and savings and loans was loan origination, the process of taking an application, obtaining approval of the borrower to get a loan, issuing the loan, and handling the closing. Over time, origination was increasingly done by mortgage brokers, who might originate loans for many different lenders. By 2004, brokers accounted for about two-thirds of all subprime loan originations. In part, the shift to mortgage brokers was cost driven. Brokers typically had lower overhead than a bank, and could therefore originate a loan for less.

Brokers, however, are typically small and often independent entities. Because they may originate for several different lenders, they are more difficult for any one lender to monitor and control. They are also harder to regulate, particularly at the federal level, because of their small size.

Mortgage brokers are compensated with a fee for their service in originating the loan. Because they do not plan to hold the loan, they have relatively little incentive to worry about the quality of the loan. Thus the broker is not at risk if the loan goes bad. If the lender is willing to fund the loan, the broker will profit from writing it.

Thus, by the early 2000s, the traditional mortgage industry had been replaced by four separate actors: originators, servicers, securitizers, and investors. Banks and other financial institutions served as intermediaries to fund the loans in the first instance, but they did not plan to hold the loans themselves. Instead they would sell the loans to an investment bank that would assemble a pool used to back mortgage-backed securities.

There were serious incentive problems in the new arrangements. In the unified process, the bank cared about the borrower's creditworthiness because they were at risk. In the new arrangement, there is less incentive for everyone in the chain to assess credit risk, because that risk is being passed on to investors at the end of the chain. Originators, servicers, and securitizers were all compensated by fees, so what mattered to them was the volume of loans they could process, more than the credit quality of the paper they wrote.

To protect the buyer of a loan, contracts commonly included a clause requiring the originator to buy back the loan if it went bad within a relatively short period of time (often the first six months). This clause provided some incentive for the originator to be concerned about risk, because they might have to buy back bad loans. Unfortunately, however, many originators were thinly capitalized. As defaults began to rise, the first companies to fail were subprime originators who could not cover their repurchase obligations.

II. Subprime Lending and the Housing Bubble

A. The growth of subprime lending.

The 1990s saw the growth of subprime lending, a new form of lending to borrowers with poor credit histories. Initially, subprime lenders were relatively small, but the industry was growing rapidly by the mid-1990s and attracting entry from much larger financial services companies. Subprime lending began with mortgages, but it soon spread to other credit markets, such as credit cards.

Before subprime lending, loan terms were generally standardized across borrowers and the lender's decision was only whether to accept or reject a particular borrower. The key difference in subprime lending was the introduction of risk-based pricing. Under this approach, lenders adjusted their terms to reflect the credit risk of different borrowers. In particular, subprime borrowers generally paid higher interest rates and perhaps more points than prime borrowers. The end of regulation of mortgage interest rates in 1980 was also a key enabling factor; without charging higher interest rates to cover the risks that subprime borrowers pose to the lender, subprime lending would not have been possible.

Subprime lending was always recognized as a riskier proposition than prime lending. In mid-2004, while subprime lending and housing prices were still rising briskly, 4.6 percent of subprime loans were in foreclosure, compared to only 0.49 percent of prime loans.

As subprime lending began, there were numerous concerns about "predatory lending" to borrowers who, some felt, could not afford the loans. The Federal Trade Commission and several states brought a number of enforcement actions against various subprime lending practices in the late 1990s and early 2000s. These cases involved practices such as "packing," or packaging optional services such as credit life insurance with the loan but not giving the consumer a chance to decline the option, and "flipping," repeated refinancing to collect fees on each transaction while stripping the equity out of the property. Other actions involved legitimate lending products, such as mortgages with balloon payments, where the originator did not adequately disclose the characteristics of the product to the consumer. From the consumer's perspective, the problem was one of missing information. Despite these difficulties, however, subprime lending enabled the first substantial expansion in home ownership in some time, from 65 percent of households owning their own home in 1995 to 69 percent in 2006. The home ownership rate declined to 66 percent in the third quarter of 2011.

Because subprime lending proved profitable initially, it expanded, and a number of larger lenders entered the market. Many of these entrants thought they had a comparative advantage in risk assessment and risk modeling, and could make money by more finely differentiating risks that other lenders lumped together. Improvements in credit reporting and credit scoring facilitated this trend. There was rapid consolidation in the industry, with the top 25 originators increasing their share of the market from under 40 percent in 1995 to over 90 percent in 2003.[1]

As competition increased, spreads between subprime and prime mortgages also narrowed. In the late 1990s, the spread was typically around 3.5 percentage points, and sometimes considerably more. By the middle of the 2000s, spreads had narrowed to 2.5 percentage points. Underwriting standards also declined. From 2001 through 2007, each vintage of subprime mortgage originations had a greater risk of default than the one before.[2]

Initially, subprime loans were not widely securitized. Loans were often somewhat customized, and particularly at the beginning, the risks were difficult to evaluate. Lenders believed they would earn enough in higher interest charges to cover the additional risk, but whether that would actually prove to be the case remained uncertain. Both factors made it more difficult to pool mortgages to use as backing for securities. But as the industry grew, and larger players entered, securitization grew as well. In 1995, $11 billion in subprime mortgages were securitized, 28 percent of subprime originations. By 2003, securitization had grown to $200 billion, 59 percent of all subprime originations.[3]

B. Fannie Mae and Freddie Mac

The role of the GSEs in creating the panic of 2008 is murky and controversial. The initial wave of securitization of subprime loans was virtually all handled by private investment banks. Fannie Mae and Freddie Mac,

---

[1]Souphala Chomsisengphet and Anthony Pennington-Cross, "The Evolution of the Subprime Mortgage Market," *Federal Reserve Bank of St. Louis Review*, 88(1): 31–56 January/February 2006.
[2]Yulia Demyanyk and Otto Van Hemert, "Understanding the Subprime Mortgage Crisis," Review of Financial Studies, 24:1848–1880, 2011.
[3]Ibid.

however, were substantial buyers of these securities. Moreover, as the subprime market expanded, the GSEs became increasingly significant players.

In 1992, Congress established affordable housing goals for the GSEs, requiring that a certain percentage of their mortgage purchases must be loans to low and moderate income individuals. Initially, the goal was 30 percent of purchases, roughly equal to what the GSEs were actually purchasing. Over time, however, the Department of Housing and Urban Development increased the goal: to 42 percent in 1995, 50 percent in 2000, and 56 percent in 2008. In 1995, the GSEs were allowed to count subprime mortgage backed securities toward the affordable housing goals. The only other way to meet the increasingly aggressive goals was to reduce underwriting standards—to buy and guarantee lower quality, riskier mortgages.

In 2000, the GSEs expanded their mortgage purchases to include so-called "Alt-A" loans (loans with little or no documentation, pejoratively called "liars loans"), "A minus" loans (borrowers with credit records between subprime and prime borrowers), and subprime loans. To accommodate these purchases, they began using risk based pricing to lenders from whom they purchased loans, and changed their underwriting standards to purchase loans they had previously refused to buy. Beginning in 2003, they invested heavily in private mortgage backed securities, most backed by subprime mortgages. These holding reached a peak of $240 billion in 2006. Many of these securities lost 90 percent of their value. According to the Government Accountability Office, these losses precipitated the takeover of the GSEs.[4]

Risk managers at Freddie Mac objected to the company's increasing exposure to "no documentation" loans in 2004, arguing for a cap on total exposure to such loans. Freddie Mac had tried purchasing no-doc loans in the 1990s, experienced significant losses, and stopped making such purchases. Nonetheless, it decided not to impose a cap on its purchases, which it feared would be seen as a sign that it was not committed to meeting affordable housing goals.[5]

Total subprime originations increased substantially as the GSEs increased their purchases. In 2003, total subprime and Alt-A originations were $395 billion; they rose to over $1 trillion in 2006. By one estimate, in the middle of 2007, half of all mortgages outstanding, with an aggregate value of $4.5 trillion, were subprime or Alt-A mortgages.[6]

The GSEs maintained that their exposure to the risks of subprime mortgages was limited. In early 2007, for example, Fannie Mae, in its first public disclosure of its subprime exposure, estimated that at the end of 2006, 2 percent of its book was privately issued securities backed by subprime mortgages. An additional 0.2 percent of its single family housing book of business ($4.8 billion) was subprime mortgages or its own mortgage backed securities backed by subprime loans. This figure was based on a list of subprime lenders, rather than any objective definition of what constituted a subprime loan. It excluded $43.3 billion in loans that Fannie Mae had purchased under its expanded approval program to allow purchases of mortgages to borrowers with weaker credit histories. At the end of 2006, this portfolio had a serious delinquency rate that was *higher* than the rate for the mortgages Fannie Mae had identified as subprime. In addition, Fannie Mae reported, 11 percent of its book of business consisted of Alt-A loans, but this figure excluded certain low-documentation loans identified by lenders. In fact, 28 percent of its 2006 acquisitions were reduced documentation loans.[7]

These facts led the Securities and Exchange Commission to file suit in December 2011 against three former Fannie Mae executives for misleading statements, along with a companion suit against three former Freddie

[4]Theresa R. DiVenti, "Fannie Mae and Freddie Mac: Past, Present, and Future," Cityscape: A Journal of Policy Development and Research, HUD, Office of Policy Development and Research, Vol. 11, No. 3, 231–242.

[5]Charles W. Calomiris, "The Mortgage Crisis: Some Inside Views," The Wall Street Journal, October 27, 2011.

[6]Peter J. Wallison, Dissent from the Majority Report of the Financial Crisis Inquiry Commission, January 14, 2011 (available at http://www.aei.org/files/2011/01/26/Wallisondissent.pdf).

[7]Non-prosecution Agreement between Fannie Mae and the Securities and Exchange Commission, December 13, 2011 (available at http://www.sec.gov/news/press/2011/npa-pr2011-267-fanniemae.pdf).

Mac executives. It agreed not to prosecute the companies themselves. In exchange, the companies agreed that the basic facts were correct, and to cooperate in the SEC's prosecution.

C. Monetary policy and the housing bubble

The bubble in housing prices began in 1997. Incomes had been increasing, and in 1997 the capital gains tax on the first $500,000 of profits from the sale of a principal residence was eliminated. Housing prices began a climb that lasted for most of a decade. Between 1997 and 2006, home prices rose 124 percent, a tremendous increase in a relatively short period of time. Prices peaked in 2006, were relatively flat for most of that year, and in late 2006 began to decline significantly. Consistent with the influx of home buyers that subprime lending made possible, price decreases when the bubble burst were greatest in the lowest tier of housing prices.[8] The bubble was more inflated in some markets than in others. For example, Los Angeles, Phoenix, and Miami were particularly hard hit as prices began to decline.

Throughout most of this period, short-term interest rates were at extremely low levels by historical standards. In response to the collapse of the dot-com bubble in the stock market in 2000, the Federal Reserve lowered the federal funds rate, the short-term rate it controls most directly. In 2003 and 2004, the federal funds rate was at the lowest levels it had ever been since the rate series began in 1955. Long-term interest rates, however, which are primarily determined by market forces rather than the Federal Reserve, fell far less.

The result was that adjustable-rate mortgages, which are tied to short-term interest rates, became more attractive relative to the traditional 30 year fixed-rate mortgage. In both the prime and subprime markets, the share of mortgage originations that were adjustable rates climbed, reaching two thirds of the nonprime and almost 40 percent of the prime market.

Competition in the mortgage markets also spurred product innovations to make loans more affordable. Mortgages were marketed with "teaser" rates that would increase after a relatively short period of time. The most common products were so-called "2/28" and "3/27" mortgages, where the interest rate was fixed for the first two or three years, and adjustable for the remaining life of the 30 year mortgage. Although some loans had shorter fixed rate provisions, with some resetting in as little as 6 months, they were less than one percent of subprime loans. Originators also introduced optional payment rates. Under this arrangement, interest accrues at one interest rate, but payments are based on a lower interest rate (or consumers are permitted to make only a portion of their payment for some period of time). The difference is added to the outstanding loan balance, resulting in negative amortization. In another common arrangement, payments were interest only for the first few years of the loan, after which payments reset to amortize the loan over its remaining life.

Although these arrangements were common in both prime and subprime markets, they were probably more common in the subprime market, where an affordable monthly payment was often the key to closing the deal. Teasers and optional payment rates began to appear in 2004, and were quite common in loans originated in 2005. If subprime borrowers paid regularly during the period of relatively low rates, they could improve their credit score and hopefully qualify for better terms. Moreover, as long as housing prices were rising rapidly, they could always refinance.

Traditional mortgages require a 20 percent down payment. The source of this requirement is Fannie Mae and Freddie Mac, which are not permitted to purchase loans with a loan-to-value ratio of more than 80 percent unless there is some credit enhancement (such as private mortgage insurance). Many potential home buyers, however, do not have sufficient capital to make a significant down payment. To help these borrowers, there were a variety of different options available. One was private mortgage insurance, which would pay the loan holder a significant fraction of the outstanding balance if the buyer defaulted. Another was so-called piggy-back loans, in which a buyer takes out an 80 percent mortgage, combined with one or two second mortgages to cover the remaining 20 percent. These types of arrangements made it possible for many consumers to purchase a house with little or no money down. Indeed, the median loan to value ratio for subprime loans originated from 2005 through mid 2007 was 100 percent.

---

[8] Steven Gjerstad and Vernon L. Smith, "From Bubble to Depression?" *The Wall Street Journal*, April 6, 2009, p. A15.

A down payment serves two functions. One is to provide a cushion in the event of default, so that the lender can dispose of the property without losing money on the deal. The second is to give the borrower a stake in the transaction. With little or nothing invested in the deal, it is easier for the borrower to walk away if the deal goes bad. Moreover, for a borrower in trouble, there is less reason to sacrifice other things to keep the house when there is little or nothing at stake. Transactions with little or no money down were therefore more likely to result in default and less likely to generate enough money to cover the losses if default did occur.

By 2007, the consequences of the housing bubble were becoming apparent as prices fell sharply. Many borrowers with little or no money invested in the property were facing escalating payments as a result of planned resets of the interest rate, the end of a teaser rate period, or the general increase in short-term interest rates. Although escalating monthly payments are frequently blamed for the rise in mortgage defaults and the subsequent wave of foreclosures, most defaults on subprime mortgages occurred before the interest rate reset; this is further evidence of the low initial quality of many of these loans. Because housing prices were now declining, many borrowers were under water—the house was worth less than the outstanding balance on their loan. Refinancing was therefore not a possibility. Defaults, followed by foreclosures, began to skyrocket. Losses on these transactions began to spread through the financial system, around the country and around the world.

D. Managing risk: ratings agencies, capital requirements, and derivatives

1. Securities Rating Agencies

One factor that has been widely discussed as a possible contributing factor in the financial meltdown is the role of the securities rating agencies, such as Standard and Poor's, Moody's, and Fitch. These companies, which have been features of the market for bonds for decades, assess the risks inherent in any financial offering and give it a rating. Investors frequently lack direct information about the risk of a security, and therefore often rely on these ratings to determine how much risk they are taking, and whether the returns are sufficient to justify the risk.

When new asset-backed securities were introduced, it was natural for market participants to turn to the ratings agencies. Originally, securities rating agencies were purely private companies selling information to investors in the form of a manual of ratings of various securities. Their opinions were enshrined into the regulatory structure beginning in 1936, when the Comptroller of the Currency prohibited banks from investing in securities that were below investment grade in one of the recognized manuals. Other regulators followed, using the ratings to restrict permissible investments by insurance companies and pension funds. In 1975, the SEC issued rules that determined the capital requirements for regulated broker-dealers based in part on the securities ratings of their bond portfolio. Also in the early 1970s, the ratings agencies switched to an "issuer pays" model for ratings. Under this approach, an investment bank or other securities issuer would pay one or more ratings agencies to evaluate the securities and issue a rating.[9] The issuer would then provide the rating to potential buyers, who decide whether to invest based in part on the rating. The shift to the "issuer pays" model was likely facilitated by the fact that issuers could hardly refuse to pay for a rating—the role of ratings in regulatory requirements meant that many potential investors could not purchase the securities unless they were rated.

There is an obvious potential for a conflict of interest in this arrangement. The rating agency, after all, is being paid by the issuer, and the issuer clearly wants a good rating to make the securities more marketable. The check on this conflict is the rating agency's reputation. If good ratings are for sale for the right price the ratings lose credibility with buyers, and sellers will no longer be willing to use that rating agency because buyers will not believe its ratings. Moreover, there is no other obvious way to fund the process of assessing a security and giving it a rating. The beneficiaries of the rating are the potential buyers, but many of them will decide, based in part on the rating, not to buy. It is therefore difficult to arrange for buyers to pay for the rating. Sellers are

---

[9]Lawrence J. White, "A Brief History of Credit Rating Agencies," Mercatus Center, George Mason University, October, 2009 (available at http://mercatus.org/sites/default/files/publication/59_CRA_history_(web).pdf).

the obvious solution: they have an incentive to provide information to buyers (discussed in more detail in Chapter 14), and are therefore willing to pay the cost of the rating.

There have been a significant number of downgrades of mortgage-backed securities, however, as the crisis unfolded. Of the mortgage-backed securities issued between 2005 and 2007 and rated by S&P, 56 percent were downgraded by late 2008. Most of the downgrades were concentrated in the securities that were lower rated to begin with. Among securities initially rated AAA, for example, 15 percent were downgraded by late 2008. Among securities initially rated BBB, the lowest "investment grade," 76 percent were downgraded, as were nearly 87 percent of securities initially rated BB or below.[10] By September of 2009, two thirds of the securities originally rated AAA had been downgraded.

The seller-paid model of paying for securities ratings has worked well in other portions of the securities market. There is no apparent reason why the conflict of interest is any more acute in rating mortgage-backed securities or other such instruments than it is in rating municipal or corporate bonds, for example. The payment arrangement is the same, and there is no evidence of systematic overrating of these types of securities.

It seems far more likely that mortgage-backed securities were overrated because the rating agencies shared the same assumption that all of the other participants in the housing bubble shared. Although real estate prices might fall in some markets for some period of time, the widespread belief was that there would not be a nationwide decline in housing prices that was both widespread and substantial. Under that assumption, the risks of mortgage-backed securities looked much lower than actually turned out to be the case. Some of the risk assessments were apparently based on only 20 years of historical data, a span that did not include any significant reductions in real estate values. Moreover, Moody's reportedly did not update its model of the mortgage market after 2002, relatively early in the housing boom.[11]

Another factor contributing to overly optimistic ratings of asset backed securities may be the interplay between the models used by the ratings agencies and the choices made by the investment banks structuring the securities that will be rated. In rating municipal and corporate securities, the primary issue is likely to be the creditworthiness of the issuer. For asset backed securities, however, the structure of the security is more likely to be a critical issue. Indeed, at least some ratings agencies never looked at loan-level data on the mortgages in a pool. Instead, they relied on information about the average characteristics of the loans. If, for example, ratings agencies looked only at the average credit scores of borrowers in a pool of loans, or at only the average loan to value ratio, investment bankers could improve the statistics by including a relatively small number of loans to borrowers with high credit scores or low loan to value ratios. The pool might look significantly better, but most of the included loans might still be very high risk. That is, the pool of loans could be designed to maximize the rating, given the model the rating agency was using to evaluate it.

2. Capital Requirements

One of the fundamental protections against the risk of losses is capital requirements. Capital provides a cushion to cover losses that may occur in other investments, thereby reducing the risks of insolvency and protecting creditors. One factor contributing to the financial crisis was high levels of leverage in the financial system, resulting in capital cushions that were inadequate to cover the losses that materialized.

Banks in particular have long been subject to capital requirements. The basic capital rules for both US and international banks were established by the Basel accords in 1988, which were adopted to standardize capital requirements across countries as international competition in financial markets increased.

The Basel accords specified that capital requirements vary depending on the risk levels of a firm's investments. No capital is required for government bonds, cash, or gold—these are regarded as essentially risk free investments. Investments in mortgages require a capital cushion of 4 percent; investments in commercial loans and

---

[10]James R. Barth, Tong Li, Wenling Lu, Triphon Phumiwasana, and Glenn Yago, "The Rise and Fall of the U.S. Mortgage and Credit Markets: A Comprehensive Analysis of the Meltdown," The Milken Institute, 2009.
[11]Jeffrey Friedman, "A Perfect Storm of Ignorance," Cato Policy Report, January/February 2010.

corporate bonds are subject to an 8 percent capital requirement. In 2001, the Accords were amended to reduce the capital requirement on asset backed securities issued by a GSE, or privately issued asset backed securities rated AA or AAA to 1.6 percent.

The interplay between risk-based capital requirements and the SROs is an interesting and potentially perverse aspect of capital requirements. The risk weights tend to channel investments toward investments that the regulators regard as low risk. If the regulators are wrong, or if the situation changes in a way that increases risk, the impact of the regulation may be to increase risk, not control it. The fact that no capital is required for government bonds, for example, is part of why European banks invested heavily in sovereign debt, including debt of countries such as Greece that in 2011 faced significant risk of default. As the risk of some sovereign debt became undeniable, it also became apparent that many European banks were in need of additional capital. Similarly, the reduction in the risk weight for asset backed securities in 2001 created an obvious incentive for banks to sell their mortgages and purchase mortgage backed securities. Doing so allowed them to achieve essentially the same returns, but with less capital required to support the investment.

3. Derivatives

One factor in the spread of the financial crisis beyond the mortgage market was derivatives. Derivatives are financial instruments whose value is derived from the value of some other instrument or asset. Commodity futures, for example, are derivatives, but there are numerous other derivatives in widespread use.

Beginning in the late 1980s, private swap markets began to emerge. These were contracts, typically between large and sophisticated companies, that were customized to the needs of the particular parties to enable them to manage various risks. A party receiving a stream of payments at a fixed interest rate, for example, might "swap" with a counterparty to obtain a similar stream of payments with a variable interest rate. Such contracts allow parties to transfer certain risks to others who are more willing to take the risk, or to match the interest rate structure of their receipts with their payment obligations.

The regulatory question that emerged was whether these private swap contracts could be required to trade on an organized exchange, as commodity and other futures contracts are traded. The answer was no. By their nature, exchange-traded contracts must be standardized, and much of the benefit of the swap market was the ability to customize the transaction. Thus derivative contracts, other than those traded on exchanges, were essentially unregulated. As discussed below, the Dodd Frank Act imposes new regulatory, requirements.

One form of derivative contract that grew in popularity was the credit default swap. Essentially, these contracts were insurance against the possibility that some other security issuer would default on their obligation. A prescient holder of General Motors bonds, for example, might have offered to pay someone else to take the risk that GM would default on its obligations. The price of the insurance obviously depends on the risk of default on the underlying instrument. As the depth of GM's problems became clear, the price of its credit default swaps soared. Credit default swaps can be issued by anyone, although buyers will clearly be concerned about the financial stability of the issuer. Similarly, anyone can purchase a swap, even if they do not actually own the underlying security. Thus market participants can place bets on the likelihood that an issuer will default. As doubts began to increase about the subprime market, credit default swaps were widely used to hedge against the risk of default on mortgage backed securities. One of the largest issuers of these swaps was AIG.

Another common form of derivative is the collateralized debt obligation, or CDO. A CDO is a debt obligation backed by other asset-backed securities, most commonly mortgage-backed securities. The pool of assets that backs the obligation is thus mortgage-backed securities, rather than the mortgages themselves. There are also CDOs squared, which are CDOs backed by other CDOs. As complexity increases, assessing the creditworthiness of the underlying assets becomes increasingly difficult, because more and more individual assets are part of the pool. As a result, investors are likely to become increasingly dependent on the rating agencies to assess the risk.

The derivatives market grew substantially from its inception. In June, 2007, the notional amount of outstanding contracts was estimated at $516 trillion with a gross market value of $11 trillion. Many of these contracts were offsetting, but there was no easy way to tell exactly who was exposed to what risks, nor who would be able to meet their obligations under these contracts.

III. THE UNFOLDING CRISIS

A. *The building crisis*

The timeline of the unfolding financial crisis is depicted in Figure 11-1, against the backdrop of changes in the "ted spread." The ted spread is the difference between the three month London Interbank Offering Rate (LIBOR) and the rate on three month treasury bills. It is a measure of the risk premium for lending to banks as opposed to risk free loans to the US government. In normal times, the ted spread is around 40 basis points. At its peak during the crisis, the ted spread reached 576 basis points.

The first failures among financial institutions were subprime originators. In April 2007, New Century failed when it could not cover its obligations to repurchase newly originated loans that had gone bad in a short period of time. New Century had been a large originator of subprime loans, but the largest by far was Countrywide. Countrywide negotiated an emergency loan in August 2007, and in January 2008 it was acquired by Bank of America.

The losses, of course, spread beyond originators. Investment bank Bear Stearns had been a major securitizer of subprime loans. In July 2007, two Bear Stearns hedge funds that had made heavy bets on subprime markets failed. Bear Stearns was also heavily involved in credit default swaps. As uncertainty about Bear Stearns's true exposure to both subprime and credit default swap losses grew, the company faced essentially a run on the bank. Because it was heavily leveraged and dependent on short term financing, it needed a constant influx of new cash to roll over maturing debt, and lenders were no longer willing to provide the necessary funds. Regulators feared

Figure 11-1. Ted Spreads Through the Crisis

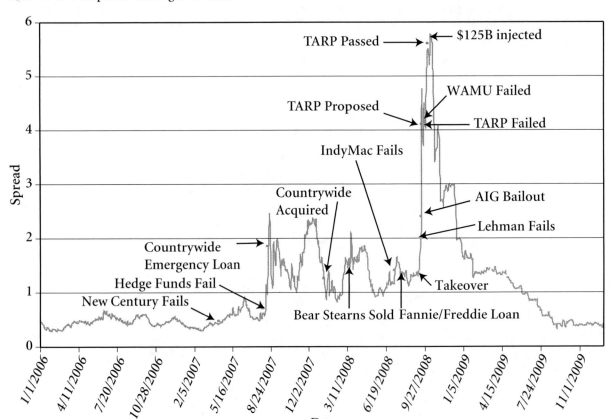

that a failure of Bear Stearns would create chaos in the credit default swap market, because it was a counterparty in a substantial volume of transactions. In March 2008, the Federal Reserve and the Treasury Department brokered a deal in which J.P. Morgan Chase acquired Bear Stearns, with the Federal Reserve agreeing to bear the losses (after the first $1 billion) on a $30 billion portfolio of Bear Stearns's riskiest assets. Initially the price was $2 per share, reportedly less than the value of the Bear Stearns headquarters building. Later the price was raised to $10 per share, still far below recent share prices for the company.

The Bear Stearns deal may have created a moral hazard problem. If the government was unwilling to let the company fail, market participants may have believed that it would not let other larger firms fail—especially if they were significantly larger firms than Bear Stearns. Other firms may have believed that at the end of the day, the government would step in with sufficient guarantees to close a deal. Thus, firms that desperately needed to seek new sources of capital may have felt the pressure was off, or at least significantly reduced.

Fannie Mae and Freddie Mac were the next dominoes to fall. In July 2008, the Treasury extended a $200 billion line of credit to the companies and made explicit the previously implicit guarantee of their debt. Reportedly the Treasury was urged to take this step by China, which was a major investor in bonds issued by the two companies. The companies were essentially taken over in September 2008. IndyMac, a savings and loan association that originated many subprime loans, also failed in July 2008, in the third largest bank failure in history. It was taken over by the Federal Deposit Insurance Corporation, which insures bank deposits.

The potential for problems at the GSEs had been recognized for a number of years, but there was no political willingness to address the problem. The companies have always been very thinly capitalized, and a significant threat to real estate values would leave them unable to meet their obligations. Proposals for reform ranged from privatizing the companies entirely and ending the implicit government guarantee, to stronger capital requirements that would increase their ability to withstand losses. Rather than addressing the problem, as noted above, the political pressure was for the companies to make even larger investments in subprime markets.

The takeover of Fannie and Freddie had a significant unintended consequence. Under the rules governing investments that banks can make, preferred shares of the GSEs had been regarded as safe investments, subject to the lowest level of capital requirements. With the takeover, these preferred shares became worthless—and a substantial amount of bank assets disappeared overnight.

The crisis reached a peak in the middle of September 2008. On September 15, after a failed weekend of efforts to make a takeover deal, Lehman Brothers filed for bankruptcy. The same weekend of negotiations produced a deal for Bank of America to acquire Merrill Lynch, another threatened investment bank. Originally proposed as a purely private transaction, Bank of America required substantial federal assistance to close the deal when Merrill Lynch's losses turned out to be significantly greater than expected. Unlike the Bear Stearns transaction, the federal government refused to participate financially in an effort to rescue Lehman, and no one was willing to take the risk on their own. Moreover, the federal government announced that it would not rescue other threatened institutions either; it was time for market discipline to decide which firms would survive and which would fail.

The reaction was swift and dramatic. Stock markets plunged, and credit markets threatened to freeze. Banks refused to make overnight loans to other banks, fearing the potential losses from even seemingly sound counterparties. This was in essence a run on the banks, not to withdraw deposits, but rather to avoid exposure to the risk of losses in the commercial paper market. Lacking information about the true condition of the borrower, and lacking confidence that the borrower would survive, lenders were simply unwilling to make loans. One money market fund, with heavy investments in Lehman commercial paper, suffered significant losses, and "broke the buck," meaning that investors in what had been regarded as a "safe" investment vehicle would not get all of their money back. Withdrawals from money market funds increased significantly, and the government began to fear a classic run on the funds. To stem the run, it announced a temporary program to guarantee deposits in money market funds.

The Lehman failure created huge market turmoil. Over the course of the week, the ted spread doubled, to more than 4 percentage points. At the time, the stated reason for allowing the failure was the desire to rely on market discipline. Subsequently, Federal Reserve officials have said that Lehman was not just illiquid, it was in fact insolvent—it did not have sufficient assets to cover its liabilities. In contrast, Bear Stearns and other firms that received federal assistance were by and large sound, but illiquid. They simply could not cover short term funding needs.

Whatever the motivations, they were short lived. On September 16, 2008, the government announced the first round of bailouts of AIG, committing $85 billion in loans in exchange for a 79.9 percent equity stake in the company.[12] AIG was a major player in credit default swaps, particularly on mortgage backed securities. When its rating was downgraded in early September, it was obligated under the terms of its contracts to post an additional $14.5 billion in collateral, and could not raise the money. Because purchasers of a credit default swap are justifiably concerned about the financial health of their counterparty, contracts commonly allow them to demand additional collateral if certain events, such as a ratings downgrade, occur. That was what happened to AIG. The government concluded that AIG was too integrated in the markets, with too much credit insurance issued to too many different parties, to let it fail.

The initial rescue strategy for AIG was unsuccessful. The strategy had been to give the company time to sell off pieces of itself to raise money, but to do so over time rather than at fire sale prices. The turmoil in financial markets, however, made that strategy essentially impossible. Even had there been a willing buyer offering a reasonable price, it is difficult to see how the buyer could have raised the money to complete the deal. Moreover, the rescue led to an additional downgrade of AIG, and additional collateral calls under its credit default swap contracts. The result was a series of additional government commitments that eventually totaled $182 billion. Much of the money was essentially passed through to AIG counterparties as additional collateral under the terms of their original contracts with the company.

As financial markets returned to more normal conditions, AIG was able to execute the original strategy of selling off other assets to repay its obligation to the government. Late in 2011, the government's remaining investment in the company was approximately $50 billion.

Also in late September 2008, the remaining investment banks became commercial banks. The long-standing separation between investment banking and commercial banking, a uniquely American reaction to the Great Depression, was over. Investment banking remained, but it was now an operation conducted within a commercial bank, as had always been the case in the rest of the world. The statutory separation of investment and commercial banking in the United States ended in 1999 with the passage of the Gramm-Leach-Bliley Act. Although, in the heat of the campaign, some tried to blame this legislation for the unfolding financial disaster, the legal ability to combine investment and commercial banking was essential to rescuing the investment banks.

September 2008 saw one other dramatic event, the takeover of another large subprime originator. Washington Mutual (WAMU), based in Seattle, had made heavy commitments to subprime mortgages in hard-hit markets, particularly California. When depositors began to flee, the FDIC seized the company on September 26, and sold the bulk of its operations to J.P. Morgan for $1.9 billion. Ironically, J.P. Morgan had offered to buy WAMU for $7 billion in March, but the offer was spurned.

B. The bailout

On September 19, 2008, the Bush administration proposed legislation to authorize the federal government to purchase up to $700 billion in "toxic" assets from banks and other financial institutions. As originally proposed the bill was only three pages long, but by the time it passed, it had grown to 451 pages.

As proposed, the program would only have authorized the purchase of assets from financial institutions. Congress added authority to inject capital into banks, and to use some of the money to help prevent foreclosures. On September 29, the House of Representatives rejected the legislation, leading to a huge adverse market reaction. Staring financial catastrophe in the face, the legislation was sweetened with mostly cosmetic additions to attract more votes, and passed on October 3.

---

[12]The stake was 79.9 percent because, if the federal government owned 80 percent of the company, it would have to consolidate the company's books with its own under standard accounting rules. To avoid having to do so, it took only 79.9 percent of the company.

The idea of the program was for the federal government to purchase the bad assets, particularly mortgage-backed securities, which were weighing down the balance sheets of banks and other financial institutions. With the bad assets off their books, the thinking was, financial institutions could resume lending and the financial crisis would end. This was the core notion of the Troubled Asset Relief Program, which became known as TARP.

There were three possible strategies for addressing the losses that financial institutions were facing. One was to inject additional capital into banks. Treasury Secretary Paulsen initially rejected this strategy, because he feared that with federal capital would come considerable temptation for political meddling in the day-to-day decisions of institutions in which the government had made an investment. Indeed, events have made clear that this concern is a real one, with politicians attempting to regulate the details of executive compensation decisions and to intervene on behalf of politically important constituencies to secure favorable lending decisions.

A second strategy was to address the underlying cause of the losses on mortgage-backed securities by reducing foreclosures. By bailing out overextended borrowers, the government could have cut the losses on mortgage loans, and subprime loans in particular. This strategy, however, would have rewarded many consumers who made unwise, and indeed highly speculative, financial decisions, at the expense of those who did the right thing. It would also create a potentially serious moral hazard problem. If the government will bail consumers out of bad financial decisions, why shouldn't those consumers take more financial risk in the future? That reaction, however, would only create additional problems.

The third strategy, incorporated in the administration's proposal, was to buy the bad assets. From the beginning, however, this strategy had two serious problems. One problem was determining the price for the assets. If the price were too low, it would do little to relieve the financial pressure on the institutions. If the price were too high, it would create a huge windfall to the asset owners, at the taxpayers' expense. Moreover, there was real uncertainty about the true value of many of these assets. Banks might legitimately believe that they would be better off holding the investments in the hopes that enough borrowers on the underlying mortgages would pay their obligations, thereby alleviating losses.

The second problem was adverse selection. It would be up to financial institutions to decide which paper they were willing to sell to the government, and their obvious incentive would be to sell the worst paper at the highest price.

Because the Bush administration never developed a reasonable way to address these problems, particularly in a short time frame, it shifted to the strategy of capital injection. The Obama administration developed a plan for buying bad assets, involving public-private partnerships with federal funding and some loan guarantees to invest in these assets. These partnerships have purchased just under $30 billion of mortgage backed securities, and hope to profit from future appreciation in the value of the securities.

Once it shifted to a strategy of injecting capital, the Bush administration provided $125 billion to 9 of the nation's largest banks on October 13, 2008. One fear about capital injections was that the market would see them as a sign of weakness. If a bank needed government money, the reasoning went, it must be in more trouble than was apparent, and therefore investors and lenders might flee. If that happened, capital injections could doom banks that received them. To avoid the stigma, the Treasury essentially insisted that banks it selected accept the money. It was not necessarily because they all needed the money, although some clearly did, but rather because the administration wanted to make clear than receiving or accepting money was not a sign of imminent failure.

The TARP program was debated, and continues to be discussed, as a $700 billion program. In reality, the actual cost will be far lower, because much of the money was effectively loans to financial institutions that eventually were repaid. Moreover, there is a profit opportunity for the government and the taxpayers. In return for its capital contributions, the government received warrants to purchase shares. As institutions and the economy recover, these warrants could produce significant gains for the government.

The TARP program eventually disbursed $428 billion of the $700 billion that was authorized. The 17 largest recipients received 80 percent of the money, and by mid 2011, all had exited the program after repaying the government in full. Approximately 400 smaller and mid sized banks were still in TARP at that time, and nearly half of them were not paying their required dividends to the government. Of the funds disbursed to banks,

$17 billion remains outstanding. In addition, $50 billion of aid to AIG remains outstanding. In December 2011, the Congressional Budget Office estimated that the net subsidy over the life of the capital injection program would be only $1 billion, with government gains on investments in banks roughly offsetting the estimated net cost of the AIG bailout. The government retains a substantial stake in AIG, and the eventual cost will depend on what the government realizes when it sells its stock in the company.

TARP funds were also used to bail out Chrysler and General Motors. The companies and their financing arms received a total of $79 billion. The government acquired a 10 percent stake in Chrysler, which it subsequently sold, and a 60 percent stake in General Motors. Although the government sold some of its GM stock, it still owns roughly 33 percent of the company. CBO estimates that the total subsidy cost of the bailout will be $20 billion. As with the cost of AIG, the eventual cost depends on what the government gets for its GM shares.

Finally, TARP funds have been used to help refinance mortgages to reduce the number of consumers who lose their homes. At the end of 2011, these programs were ongoing, and their eventual cost depends on how many homeowners actually participate. To date, participation has been rather low. Because it expects relatively low participation, CBO estimates the net cost of this portion of TARP will be $13 billion. The Office of Management and Budget is more optimistic about participation, and estimates that the cost will be $46 billion.

The CBO's overall estimate of the net cost of the TARP program is $34 billion, as of November 2011. In addition, the government has spent $130 billion on Fannie Mae and Freddie Mac as of mid-2011, and will likely spend more over time. The CBO estimates that as of March 2011 the liabilities of the GSEs, which the government will eventually have to cover, exceed their assets by $187 billion. Recognizing the cost increases the total cost of the GSE bailout to $317 billion, far larger than the cost of TARP.

However necessary it was, the bailout legislation, as TARP came to be known, was wildly unpopular politically. A well functioning financial system is obviously essential to economic activity in the rest of the economy, but to many voters the legislation looked like a government decision to bail out Wall Street fat cats whose bad decisions had created the mess in the first place. To be sure, there is some truth in that allegation, because bad decisions in Wall Street firms were significant contributors to the crisis. Nonetheless, an economy without a functioning financial sector cannot function, and there was a very real prospect that we were facing precisely that scenario. However distasteful, government action to preserve a functioning financial sector was probably essential.

C. The role of the Federal Reserve

The Federal Reserve was designed in large part to serve as a lender of last resort to the banking system. As the crisis unfolded, the Fed filled this role aggressively, extending credit to the banks that traditionally borrow from the Fed, using its emergency powers (some of which were repealed in the Dodd Frank Act), and creating a variety of specialized lending programs to serve the needs of particular segments of the financial services industry. In addition, it aggressively eased monetary policy in an effort to reduce the impact of the crisis on the economy.

As a result of these activities, the Fed's balance sheet expanded enormously. Total assets went from around $900 billion before the crisis to almost $3 trillion at the end of 2011. Figure 11-2 shows the history of the Fed's total assets and selected asset categories over the course of the financial crisis.

The core difficulty confronting the Fed as the crisis unfolded was the substantial growth in non-bank financial intermediaries that has occurred over the past decades. The Fed was created when commercial banks were the key engines of credit in the economy, but financial market evolution has moved large volumes of lending out of the commercial banking sector. Money market funds, commercial paper markets, investment banks, hedge funds, and others have assumed increasingly important roles in finance. Nonetheless, in a crisis, all of these institutions potentially face the same liquidity constraints that have long been recognized as potential problems for commercial banks. The Fed is the lender of last resort for commercial banks, but in ordinary times it cannot lend to non-bank financial institutions, including investment banks.

Banks borrow from the Fed at what is known as the discount window. In normal times, use of the discount window is discouraged; banks are supposed to rely on market sources for their funding needs, but the Fed is

Figure 11-2. The Fed's Balance Sheet

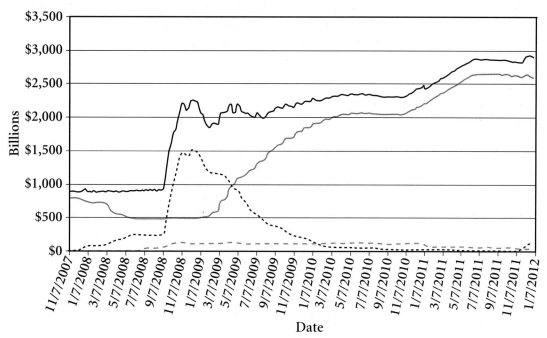

Total Assets ——— Securities Held Outright ---- All Liquidity Facilities* - - - Support for Specific Firms**

Source: Federal Reserve Board

available as a backstop. Loans are usually overnight, and the borrower must put up good collateral (and itself be in sound financial condition). The amount of the collateral must exceed the amount of the loan (a "haircut" for the collateral). Under normal conditions, such primary borrowing by financial institutions amounts to less than $50 *million* per day. At the peak of the crisis, in October 2008, depository institution borrowing was more than $100 *billion* per day. Daily borrowing remained over $4 billion through May 2010.

At least initially, investment banks could not borrow from the Fed's discount window, although they faced essentially the same liquidity problems that commercial banks faced. In mid-September 2008, separate investment banking ended in the United States. Merrill Lynch was acquired by Bank of America, Goldman Sachs and Morgan Stanley received emergency permission to become bank holding companies regulated by the Fed (and therefore eligible to borrow at the discount window), and Lehman filed for bankruptcy.

The Fed also created a number of special purpose lending facilities to expand the range of institutions that could borrow, the length of time they could borrow, and the types of assets acceptable as collateral. From March 2008 through February 2010 the Fed extended overnight loans of cash and securities to its primary dealers, who serve as counterparties in the Fed's implementation of monetary policy. Early in 2008, this facility provided access to Federal Reserve credit to investment banks who were primary dealers. Borrowing reached $147 billion in October 2008. As with lending to depository institutions, the value of the collateral exceeded the value of the loan.

The Term Asset-Backed Securities Loan Facility, opened in November 2008, extended the term of available credit considerably. The facility made loans of up to 5 years to holders of asset backed securities. Borrowing peaked at just under $50 billion per day in the first quarter of 2009; outstanding balances reached almost $500 billion in March. The facility closed in June 2010, but about $9 billion in loans remained outstanding at the end of 2011. The Asset-Backed Commercial Paper Money Market Mutual Fund Liquidity Facility financed depository institutions' purchases of asset backed securities from money market funds experiencing significant withdrawals between September 2008 and February 2010. In October 2008, borrowing reached $145 billion, but fell to less that $20 billion by January 2009. The Fed also purchased 3 month commercial paper directly from eligible issuers to facilitate liquidity in that market; it held $300 billion in commercial paper in early December 2008.

The Fed's aggressive lending likely significantly reduced the severity and duration of the financial crisis. Its most controversial lending decisions concerned the assistance to particular institutions, such as the Fed lending that made possible the Bear Stearns and AIG deals. Lending to support particular institutions peaked at $120 billion in April 2010 and declined to $34 billion by the end of 2011.

More controversial was the Fed's monetary policy decisions. Early in the crisis, it pushed its interest rate target for the federal funds rate to essentially zero, where it still remained in early 2012. To drive down mortgage interest rates directly, the Fed made substantial purchases of GSE securities, as well as GSE mortgage backed securities. Purchases of mortgage backed securities totaled $850 billion; purchases of GSE debt totaled $150 billion.

With no further leverage over short term interest rates, the Fed sought to influence long term rates more directly, engaging in "quantitative easing" or the direct purchase of federal government securities to push down particular interest rates. The effect of quantitative easing, which was unprecedented in the Fed's history, is to directly inject money into the economy, as the Fed pays for its purchases. Late in 2009, the Fed purchased $300 billion in treasury securities. In 2011, it purchased another $600 billion.

The difficult task of unwinding the Fed's balance sheet remains ahead. As economic recovery progresses, the Fed will need to contract its balance sheet to avoid significant risks of inflationary pressure. It must do so, however, in a way that allows recovery to continue.

IV. Regulatory Change: The Dodd Frank Act

No one wants to see the panic of 2008 repeated, and there was considerable political pressure to make changes in regulatory institutions to make sure it never happens again. There was, however, no very clear regulatory villain responsible for the crisis, and therefore no obvious change that would prevent a repetition. Despite the uncertainties about precisely what should be done, the crisis was also a political opportunity that many seized to advance their policy proposals.

There was also reason for caution about regulatory changes, despite the obvious need to avoid repeating the crisis. Financial market participants have learned valuable lessons from the experience, and have adjusted their strategies and behavior far more rapidly than any regulatory agency could have required. Institutions that have lost billions have strong incentives to figure out what went wrong and how to keep it from happening again. They have far more information, and a far deeper understanding of the environment in which they operate, than any regulatory agency is likely to possess. Ill-advised regulatory requirements may in the end prevent adjustments that would reduce the risk of another crisis, rather than requiring them.

In July 2010, Congress enacted the Dodd Frank Wall Street Reform and Consumer Protection Act. The most far reaching reform of financial services regulation since the 1930s, the act will have a significant impact on virtually every participant in financial services markets. Although Congress has acted, much uncertainty remains, because many crucial details were left to the rulemaking process. By one count, the law requires 385 separate rulemakings and 87 studies by more than 20 agencies. Statutory deadlines for required rules stretch through 2013, but of the 200 deadlines that had already passes at the end of 2011, only 51 rules had been finalized.

Although it comprehensively addressed financial regulation, Dodd Frank did not address the most costly pillar of the financial crisis, the role of Fannie Mae and Freddie Mac. Although there is widespread agreement that the federal role in housing needs to change, there is little agreement on how to change it.

A. Systemic risk oversight

Before the financial crisis, no agency was charged with considering systemic risk. In its purest form, systemic risk arises when a practice that works well if a small number of companies or traders are pursuing it creates serious adverse consequences if everyone follows the same strategy. One example is portfolio insurance, a strategy using program trading to hedge against the risk of adverse movements in the stock market. The strategy worked well when only a few traders were using it, but when a substantial number of market participants pursued the strategy all at once, it led to the stock market crash of 1987. Some people also conceive of systemic risk as the firm that is "too big to fail," such as AIG or, as it turned out, Lehman Brothers, where failure would spread adverse consequences so widely that it is not an acceptable outcome.

To address systemic risk, Dodd Frank establishes the Financial Stability Oversight Council, composed primarily of the heads of the various financial regulatory agencies and the Treasury Secretary. The Council is charged with identifying risks to financial stability, and with identifying systemically important nonbank financial companies. Banks holding companies with more than $50 billion in assets are presumed systemically important. Once designated, these systemically important financial institutions will be subject to regulation by the Federal Reserve, which must adopt more stringent prudential standards (such as capital requirements) than the standards applicable to other firms. For these firms, off balance sheet activities must be considered for purposes of meeting capital requirements, and they must limit their credit exposure to any individual counterparty. They must also prepare and maintain a "living will," a plan for rapid and orderly resolution if the firm encounters financial problems, and are subject to annual stress tests by the Federal Reserve. The Council must also study the possibility of other restrictions on systemically important companies, such as limitations on their size or activities, and report to Congress.

To be sure, there are new powers and new regulatory authority under Dodd Frank. Fundamentally, however, we are asking the same regulators we have always had to identify potential risks and prevent them. It is not clear they will be any more successful.

B. Too big to fail

As noted above, the vote on TARP was a very difficult vote for many members of Congress, and a number of those who voted for the bailout lost their seats in the elections of 2008 and 2010. One of the key goals of Dodd Frank was to end the "too big to fail" problem.

If markets believe that the government will not let a firm fail, capital market discipline on the firm may break down because of moral hazard. If potential investors believe that the government will limit their losses, they have less incentive to worry about the risk of loss in making the investment in the first place. Shareholders are unlikely to be protected against loss under any circumstances, but creditors, and especially senior creditors, may well face little risk of loss. They will therefore be more willing to lend money to a company taking inappropriate risks, because if the gamble fails, the government will make them whole. The result is a perverse incentive for firms to take more risk, not less, if they are too big to fail. As noted above, during the crisis there may have been precisely this reaction to the Bear Stearns bailout, which may in turn have contributed to the Lehman bankruptcy.

To address the too big to fail problem, the law provides a new resolution authority to unwind failing financial firms. Part of what makes a firm too big to fail is that unwinding its obligations through the bankruptcy courts can be a long and difficult process. In the meantime, counterparties may be unable to unwind positions with the failed firm and may suffer losses as a result. If there were a quicker process to take over a failing firm and sort out its obligations, then regulators can let even very large firms fail.

Under certain conditions, which are more likely to arise during a panic than at other times, the Treasury Secretary can appoint the FDIC as receiver of any financial company. The FDIC has considerable experience taking over and resolving failed banks, so it can presumably resolve other financial firms as well. Because government liquidation of a financial firm would be a drastic step, there are significant procedural safeguards. The Treasury Secretary makes the decision, but only upon the recommendation of two-thirds of the Federal Reserve Board, two-thirds of the board of directors of the FDIC, and in consultation with the President. If the Secretary determines that the firm is in default or in danger of default, that resolution through bankruptcy would have serious adverse effects, and no viable private sector alternative to prevent default is available, he can appoint the FDIC as receiver. Presumably the FDIC would be guided by the living will in the case of a systemically important firm, but it would not be bound by it.

As a receiver, the FDIC would stand in the shoes of the company. It could transfer any assets it chooses to a third party for fair value, and it could establish a temporary bridge company to hold all or part of the failed company until it can be liquidated or sold. It would not need the consent of creditors or court approval.

Creditors, however, have a right to receive at least as much as it would have received under bankruptcy law. If needed, the FDIC can borrow money from the Treasury to finance the resolution. Any funds that cannot be repaid from the failed company's assets would be made up by a special assessment on all surviving systemically important financial institutions.

We will not know whether, or how well, this resolution process will work until the next financial crisis. There are at least three potential problems, however. First, most large and complex financial institutions have significant foreign operations. The resolution, however, can only deal with the company's domestic operations and obligations.

Second, it is unclear whether the government would have the political will to use resolution authority preemptively, before losses have grown so great that they threaten the financial system. Would, for example, the government actually have used this power before Lehman filed for bankruptcy in 2008? The answer is not at all clear.

Third, someone will lose money in any potential liquidation, and it is not clear who would lose how much. Because losses are uncertain, the appointment of a receiver could create the same kinds of uncertainties that occurred after the Lehman bankruptcy, with creditors unwilling to lend to other larger financial institutions because of the risk of loss.

C. Securities rating organizations

The Dodd Frank legislation included three key provisions to address SROs. First, the legislation instructed the financial regulators to remove reliance on the ratings from their regulations. The bank regulators responded by proposing to rely instead on the risk categorizations of the Organization for Economic Cooperation and Development, a governmental organization of the United States and other developed countries. The OECD, however, considers most sovereign debt to be risk free—including, for example, the debt of Greece, Portugal, and other European states facing severe financial difficulties. At best, this approach simply substitutes one official source of risk determination for another—and one that is probably inferior at that.

Second, Dodd Frank attempted to increase accountability for SROs by making them liable for their opinions as "experts" under the securities laws. It did so by removing the regulatory exemption for including ratings in registrations and other filings even without the consent of the rating organization. If the rating organization agreed, the issuer could include the rating, but the organization would be potentially liable for the accuracy of its conclusion as an expert. Perhaps predictably, the SROs refused to give consent and accept the liability that went with it. Because SEC rules require the inclusion of ratings information in the registration statements for asset-backed securities, no new securities could have been issued. Rather than effectively prohibit asset backed securities, the SEC stated that it would not recommend enforcement actions under the provision until further notice.

Third, Dodd Frank created a new Office of Credit Ratings within the SEC, and authorized further regulation of the operation of SROs. The Office is supposed to conduct annual examinations of each recognized SRO to determine whether any enforcement action is appropriate. In May 2011, the SEC issued a 500 page proposal for tighter regulation. The proposed rules would require tighter internal controls of the review process. They would also require reviews of any rating issued by an employee who later goes to work for an issuer whose securities that individual rated, along with periodic testing of the competence of SRO employees. Another SEC proposal would require SROs to disclose how well their ratings have performed in the past.

D. Capital requirements

In the aftermath of the financial crisis, a new set of revisions to the Basel accords was adopted in 2011, known as Basel III. (An intermediate Basel II accord had not yet been implemented in the United States when the financial crisis hit.) Under these accords, banks must increase their so-called Tier 1 capital to 7 percent of their assets, compared to roughly 3 percent for the typical US bank. The accords also include a new, separate liquidity coverage ratio that requires banks to maintain enough high quality liquid assets to cover their total net cash flows over 30 days. Basel III is continuing to study countercyclical capital requirements, which would increase capital requirements in good times to "lean against" the tendency to take more risk when things are going well.

It is also exploring proposals that would increase the capital requirements for systemically important financial institutions.

The Dodd Frank law requires regulators to establish capital requirements for bank holding companies (in addition to those for the banks themselves) and for systemically important financial institutions. It also tightens the definition of what constitutes "tier 1" capital, which in effect raises capital requirements. For institutions with over $50 billion in assets (some 30 banks, plus systemically important financial institutions), the Federal Reserve has proposed to increase capital requirements to 5 percent. In addition, these large institutions are subject to separate liquidity requirements, requiring them to conduct internal liquidity stress tests and set their own quantitative limits to manage liquidity risks. They will also be subject to annual stress tests by the Fed.

US regulators are also likely to implement the Basel III requirements, but there are some inconsistencies between the accords and Dodd Frank. For example, the accords rely heavily on outside ratings agencies to assess risk and adjust capital requirements; Dodd Frank prohibits this approach. Subsequent rulemakings will be necessary to adopt Basel III requirements.

E. Previously unregulated financial market participants

Dodd Frank includes provisions to regulate market participants and financial instruments that were previously lightly regulated or not regulated at all. The primary unregulated participants are hedge funds; the principal unregulated financial instruments are derivatives.

Hedge funds are private investment vehicles, in essence private pools of capital, that pursue a tremendous variety of investment strategies. They are not publicly traded, and participation is limited to "sophisticated" investors whom the SEC deems able to protect their own interests. Before the crisis, virtually no regulations governed hedge funds. They made their deals with their investors, pursued their trading strategies, and either made money or went out of business.

There is little apparent connection between hedge funds and the panic of 2008. Hedge funds failed, as did other financial institutions, but no hedge fund was rescued or required governmental assistance. During the crisis, the average hedge fund fell in value by 20 percent, roughly half of the decline in equity markets. In 1998 the Federal Reserve negotiated a rescue for one large hedge fund (Long Term Capital Management), but there have not been other such incidents. Indeed, the structure for purchasing toxic assets from financial institutions is essentially a hedge fund, with a government capital contribution and government loan guarantees to help finance it. Nonetheless, some have long believed that hedge funds "should" be regulated (although the alleged problems have never been clear), and saw the financial crisis as an opportunity to achieve their objective.

Dodd Frank requires all hedge funds to register with the SEC. They must maintain records of assets under management, leverage, counterparty exposure, valuation practices, types of assets held, and other information the SEC specifies by rule. These records must be available to the SEC, but there is no reporting requirement. Thus, the primary goal of the regulatory approach is to enable regulators to gain more information about what hedge funds are doing, to determine whether they are creating systemic risks. Apart from the added compliance costs, these provisions seem unlikely to have much effect on hedge fund operations.

The principal previously unregulated financial instruments are derivatives, and Dodd Frank imposes significant new regulations on these instruments. Its central feature is a requirement for clearinghouses for derivative contracts, modeled on the clearinghouse in futures markets. Under this approach, a clearinghouse would act as the counterparty for all transactions, monitor the positions of individual traders, impose additional collateral requirements if the risks were too great, and determine the net position in swaps involving a particular issuer. Under Dodd Frank, if the CFTC or the SEC determines that clearing is appropriate, then all swaps of that type must be cleared. There is, however, an exception to this requirement for end users: non-financial firms that use swaps to hedge commercial risk are not subject to the clearing requirement.

It remains unclear whether the futures market approach can be effectively applied to other derivatives. In any derivative contract, whether it is a futures contract or some more exotic financial instrument, there are two distinct sources of risk. One risk is position risk: the possibility that some trader has taken a position that, if price moves against him, he will not be able to cover. Futures market clearinghouses are good at assessing position risk, and at imposing appropriate countermeasures when position risk is too large (such as increasing collateral requirements or limiting trading).

The other source of risk, central in credit default swaps and many other financial derivatives, is balance sheet risk. This is the risk that the counterparty in a particular transaction will not be able to cover their obligations because of other financial problems they may confront, regardless of the risk their position may entail. For example, if an insurance company trading credit default swaps faces substantial losses because of a bad hurricane season, this is a balance sheet risk, which may mean the company cannot honor its commitments regardless of the size of its positions in the swap markets. Although there are financial requirements for membership in a futures market such as the Chicago Board of Trade, there is no other effort to price balance sheet risk. Mispricing balance sheet risk, however, can lead to serious problems. That, after all, seems to be the core cause of the problems involving AIG. Its counterparties did not correctly assess the balance sheet risk facing the company.

As the regulatory agencies struggle to implement the clearinghouse requirements, a tension has emerged about clearinghouse membership. Should we pursue open access to clearinghouse membership, or should the primary goal be the financial stability of the clearinghouse? Under the CFTC's rule, a clearinghouse cannot set a minimum capital requirement for membership of more than $50 million. The requirement is designed to make sure that small traders can participate, as they have in the unregulated private swaps market. The result, however, is that the clearinghouse may not be very well capitalized. If a counterparty defaults, the clearinghouse is responsible in the first instance, and if it does not have adequate capital, it will not be able to cover its obligations. The $50 million maximum capital requirement led one of the two companies that had applied to be recognized as clearinghouses to withdraw its proposal.

We don't know what will happen if a clearinghouse fails. Moreover, we appear to be moving to a system of numerous relatively small clearinghouses, specializing in particular geographic markets or particular asset classes. If trades between two large financial institutions as counterparties in different derivatives trade through different clearinghouses, the counterparty risk that was confined to the institutions themselves is now filtered through the clearinghouses. The actual counterparty risk to the traders if one of them fails may become even more opaque, and may be increased by the risk that the clearinghouse fails, even though the trading partners do not.

F. The consumer financial protection bureau

The Dodd Frank Act established a new Consumer Financial Protection Bureau ("CFPB") with comprehensive authority over consumer financial services. Previously, each bank regulator exercised consumer protection oversight for the institutions subject to its jurisdiction. Although all enforced the same basic rules, usually written by the Federal Reserve, each regulatory agency dealt with its own institutions. For the regulator, the most important function was their safety and soundness oversight of the institutions they supervised. Consumer protection tended to be a much lower priority. The CFPB's sole mission is to protect consumers; it has no other statutory mandates that might compete for attention.

By design, the CFPB is an agency uniquely insulated from political oversight. Organizationally, it is part of the Federal Reserve System, but the Federal Reserve Board cannot oversee or supervise its decisions. The Director is appointed by the President and confirmed by the Senate for a fixed, 5 year term, and can only be removed for cause. The Director is therefore protected from political oversight by the President. The agency's budget is not subject to the appropriations process. Instead, the agency receives a specified percentage of the Fed's operating budget, protecting it from the political tug and pull that is ordinarily part of the appropriations process. Its decisions can only be overturned by a two thirds vote of the Financial Stability Oversight Council—and the CFPB director is one of the ten votes.

The CFPB's jurisdiction includes virtually all financial services firms, except those regulated by the CFTC, the SEC, or state insurance regulators. It will oversee consumer credit reporting agencies, debt collectors, lenders, mortgage brokers, payday lenders, and others. The agency can write rules to prohibit "unfair, deceptive, or abusive" practices, and it can bring enforcement actions against companies for engaging in such practices. The authority to prohibit "unfair or deceptive" practices is a transfer of authority from the banking regulatory agencies, but the prohibition on "abusive" practices is new.

Traditionally, consumer protection in the lending industry has relied primarily on disclosure. Regulators seek to assure that consumers are provided with the information they need, but it is up to consumers to make their own choices that they regard as in their best interest. The new CFPB is likely to rely more heavily on regulating the terms of financial contracts directly, by, for example, prohibiting terms in loan contracts or other financial service contracts that the agency regards as problematic.

In addition, and perhaps most important, the CFPB has the authority to "supervise" institutions subject to its jurisdiction. Although banks have long been subject to examination and supervision, other institutions have not. Under this authority, an examiner from the CFPB would go to, say, a debt collector, to examine its processes and procedures for ensuring compliance with the relevant legal standards. The examiner can, and likely will, ask for changes to improve compliance, backed up by the threat of enforcement action if the company does not comply.

Congress directed numerous specific rulemakings for the CFPB, including rewriting the disclosure requirements for mortgage lending transactions to make them more consumer friendly. How the agency will utilize its authority beyond these specific tasks remains to be seen.

V. Summary

Changes in the mortgage market were at the root of the panic of 2008. Functions that had traditionally been performed by a single entity became separated, with different parties performing different tasks. Securitization, using pools of mortgages as backing for securities that were sold to investors, began in the 1970s, and grew rapidly after private investment banks entered the market in the 1980s. Securities were divided into different tranches, which differed in the priority of their claim on the stream of payments from borrowers, and therefore differed in risk. Issuers also used various credit enhancements such as third-party insurance. Mortgage pools were held in special purpose vehicles that did not show up on the balance sheet of the investment bank that issued the securities.

The existence of pools of mortgages gave rise to servicers, who collected the payments, managed late payments, and if necessary engaged in collection activities when a borrower was late. Origination of the loan was also separated, with loans increasingly originated by mortgage brokers who might originate loans for several different lenders.

The disintegration of the mortgage business created serious incentive problems. Originators, securitizers, and servicers were all compensated through fees, and had little interest in the creditworthiness of the borrower as long as the loan could be approved. Although contracts required originators to repurchase loans that went bad in a short period of time, many lacked adequate capital to do so when the need arose.

Subprime lending began in the 1990s and grew rapidly. Although there were concerns and enforcement actions addressing "predatory lending," subprime lending enabled a significant increase in home ownership.

As larger players entered the subprime market, the industry consolidated. Securitization of subprime loans grew significantly, with private investment banks assembling pools of mortgages and issuing securities. Fannie Mae and Freddie Mac were significant purchasers of subprime mortgage-backed securities, because such investments counted toward their "affordable housing" goals. As the affordable housing goals grew more stringent over time, the GSEs weakened their underwriting standards to accept loans from less creditworthy borrowers, purchased low or no documentation loans, and increased their purchases of subprime mortgage backed securities.

The housing bubble began in 1997, with prices rising 124 percent by 2006. Low short-term interest rates in response to the end of the dot-com bubble in the stock market made adjustable-rate mortgages attractive compared to traditional fixed-rate products. Competition in the mortgage market spurred product innovations such as "teaser" rates, low initial rates, and optional payment rates. Moreover, mortgage arrangements such as piggyback loans enabled consumers to purchase a house with little or no money down. They therefore had little equity at stake, increasing the risk of default when prices began to fall.

Mortgage-backed securities are usually rated by securities rating agencies. Ratings agencies are paid by the issuer of the securities, creating the potential for conflict of interest. The seller-paid model, however, has worked well in other markets, such as corporate and municipal bonds, and there is little reason to think the conflict problems are significantly different in the mortgage-backed securities market. Although many such securities were downgraded, there were substantially more early downgrades among the securities with lower ratings initially. It seems more likely that downgrades occurred because the ratings agencies shared the common assumption that a significant, widespread decline in housing prices was extremely unlikely, and therefore discounted the risk of widespread borrower defaults. Issuers may also have gamed the ratings by manipulating the average charateristics of the pool of mortgages gain the best possible rating.

Inadequate capital in the financial system was a contributing factor to the panic. Bank capital requirements are set based on the amount of risk in the bank's investment portfolio, usually assessed by relying on ratings from the securities rating organizations. Differences in capital requirements between asset classes can potentially channel bank investments in a particular direction, such as to invest more in government debt or substitute mortgage backed securities for mortgages. These effects can be perverse. Derivatives emerged in the 1980s as customized private swap contracts. A common derivative contract that grew in popularity was the credit default swap, which essentially offers insurance against the possibility that the issuer of some other security (such as a corporate bond or a mortgage-backed security) will default. Derivative transactions were essentially unregulated.

The panic of 2008 actually began in 2007, as subprime originators began to fail when they were unable to honor their commitments to repurchase loans that went bad in a short period of time. Losses and failures quickly spread to investment banks involved with securitizing subprime loans. The government brokered a transaction to sell Bear Stearns in March 2008. In July 2008, it extended a $200 billion line of credit to Fannie Mae and Freddie Mac, and made explicit the government's backing of their debt securities. In September, it took over the companies.

The peak of the crisis was in September 2008. Lehman Brothers filed for bankruptcy on September 15. The stock market plunged, and credit markets threatened to freeze. The government decided to rescue AIG and committed $85 billion in loans in exchange for a 79.9 percent stake in the company. The original strategy of selling pieces of the company was not initially successful, and the government's commitment grew to a peak of $182 billion. Also in September, Bank of America agreed to acquire Merrill Lynch, the remaining investment banks converted to commercial banks, and another large bank with heavy subprime lending exposure failed.

The bailout legislation was introduced on September 19, and after a false start was passed on October 3. The Troubled Asset Relief Program committed up to $700 billion, originally to purchase toxic assets from banks. Serious difficulties with how such a program might be implemented, however, led the government to shift to a strategy of injecting capital into threatened institutions. The first $125 billion was committed to 9 large banks on October 13. To avoid stigmatizing institutions that received federal money, the Treasury insisted that the 9 banks accept the money whether they needed it or not. Most of the TARP money was repaid. At the end of 2011, the CBO estimated the net cost of the program would be $34 billion, mostly attributable to bailing out the automobile companies and foreclosure relief programs. In contrast, it estimated the cost of the Fannie Mae and Freddie Mac bailouts at $317 billion.

Throughout the crisis, the Federal Reserve acted as a lender of last resort to supply liquidity to the financial system. The size of its balance sheet tripled. It used its emergency authority to create special lending programs for non-bank financial intermediaries such as primary security dealers, money market funds, and the commercial paper market. It also engaged in quantitative easing of monetary policy, with direct purchases of federal government securities to inject more cash into the financial system.

The Dodd Frank Act made substantial changes in the financial regulatory structure, more significant than any since the post-Depression reforms of the 1930s. It created the Financial Stability Oversight Council, composed of the heads of other regulatory agencies, to oversee systemic risk. Systemically important firms and large banks and bank holding companies will be regulated by the Federal Reserve.

Firms that are "too big to fail" can create a moral hazard problem: investors may realize that the government will save the firm and therefore pay less attention to risks the firm takes. Dodd Frank attempts to address this problem by allowing the Treasury Secretary to place failing financial companies into FDIC receivership. The resolution, however, cannot resolve foreign operations. The government may not have the political will to liquidate a large firm that has not yet failed. And investors may fear the uncertain losses that would result from receivership, leading to the same kind of panic that occurred after the Lehman Brothers bankruptcy.

To address securities ratings organizations, Dodd Frank requires financial regulators to remove reliance on the ratings from their regulations. It attempted to make them liable as experts under the securities laws, but the ratings organizations refused to consent to the use of ratings in registration statements that would have triggered liability, and the SEC suspended the requirement. The Act also created a new office to regulate securities rating organizations and provided for annual audits of their rating process.

Dodd Frank requires regulators to establish new and stricter capital requirements for banks and other financial institutions. Large banks and systemically important firms will be subject to annual stress tests. There are inconsistencies between the Dodd Frank approach and the Basel III international agreement on bank capital standards that have not yet been resolved.

Dodd Frank also extended regulation to previously unregulated firms, primarily hedge funds, and previously unregulated financial instruments, primarily derivatives. Hedge funds must register with and provide information to the SEC. The Act requires most derivatives to trade through clearinghouses, patterned on commodity futures markets. Clearinghouses in commodities markets are good at addressing position risk, but they do not manage balance sheet risk of counterparties. Such risks are important in derivative markets, however, and it is not clear how well clearinghouses will work. It appears likely that there will be numerous relatively small clearinghouses, with relatively small capitalization.

Dodd Frank also established a new Consumer Financial Protection Bureau, carefully insulated from political influences. Its sole mission is consumer protection, at virtually all financial firms. It can write rules, engage in enforcement actions, and examine financial firms. It may rely more heavily on prohibiting "bad" contract terms in financial agreements, rather than the traditional approach of relying on disclosures.

PERSPECTIVES ON MACROECONOMICS

Chapter 12

The Great Recession of 2007–2009 brought the question of the government's role in the aggregate economy into sharp focus. By historical standards, the recession was extraordinary, as shown in Figure 12-1. Output fell 7.2 percent, compared to an average of 4.4 percent in post World War II recessions. Consumption fell 5.4 percent, more than double the postwar average of 2.1 percent. Investment fell 33.5 percent, compared to 17.8 percent in the average recession. The most politically sensitive component of a recession is the decline in employment: 6.7 percent in the Great Recession, compared to an average of 3.8 percent. Hours worked fell even more sharply, 8.7 percent, compared to 3.2 percent on average. Why employment fell so much more sharply than usual remains unclear.

The political response to the recession was a massive stimulus package enacted early in 2009, totaling $787 billion, or 5.9 percent of the previous year's GDP. Roughly two thirds of the package was spending increases, with the remainder a variety of tax reductions. Further stimulus programs followed. As detailed below, the stimulus was based on the Keynesian approach to macroeconomic analysis.

Microeconomics takes as its starting point the behavior of individual households and firms. Economic decisions are analyzed on the assumption that firms make choices to maximize profits and households maximize utility. In contrast, traditional macroeconomics started with assumptions about how economic aggregates—e.g., national income, unemployment, prices—behave in response to certain changes. These assumptions determine the kind of results that macroeconomists deduce, and the kinds of policy implications that follow from the analysis.

Unlike microeconomics, where there is widespread agreement among economists of all persuasions about the basic principles, macroeconomics is characterized by intense debate among competing schools of thought.

Figure 12-1. The great recession.

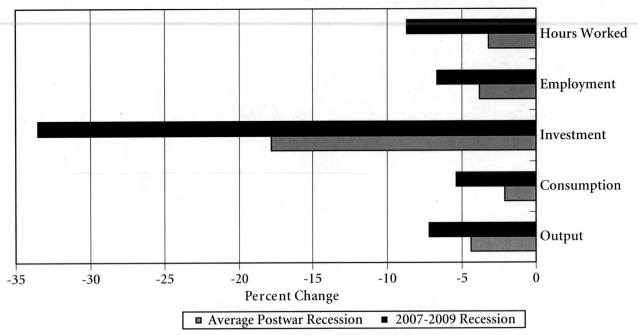

Data from Lee E Ohanian, "The Economic Crisis from a
Neoclassical Perspective, " *Journal of Economic Perspectives*,
Fall, 2010

Unfortunately, the policy implications of each approach to macroeconomics often differ substantially, and one's conclusion about appropriate policy will depend on the approach one takes.

We will consider two approaches to macroeconomics, the Keynesian and the Monetarist approaches, which follow this traditional methodology. We will also consider a third approach, Rational Expectations or real business cycle theory (also sometimes known as the neoclassical approach), which seeks to analyze the macro economy based on traditional micro economic analysis of individual households and firms.

I. THE KEYNESIAN THEORY

John Maynard Keynes, who was probably the first true macroeconomist, sought to develop a theory to explain the Great Depression, which was then an ongoing economic event. In 1929, the stock market crashed, in an episode that, at least until it happened again in 1987 and 1989, economists thought was unique. What followed was an economic contraction of unprecedented severity and persistence. National income had reached $87 billion in 1929; three years later, it has fallen by $50 billion. Unemployment reached levels never seen before (or since), averaging nearly 25 percent of the labor force in some years. Although there were brief and partial recoveries, the Depression did not really end until World War II, which provided plenty of work for everyone.

The prevalent economic theories at the time of the Depression maintained that no intervention was necessary or appropriate. Instead, the classical economists argued, the market, if left alone, would correct itself and restore high levels of economic activity. In essence, the conventional economic wisdom of the time maintained, the Depression would end of its own accord. It did not, however, seem to do so, and Keynes set out to try to understand why. The result was his General Theory of Income, Employment, and the Price Level.

The starting point for Keynes was the role of savings in the circular flow of income. In the economy as a whole, each person's expenditures represent income for someone else. In turn, the recipients of those expenditures buy goods and services from others, generating income for still more people. Thus, expenditures by one person provide income for others, and thereby support additional expenditures and additional income elsewhere in the economy.

Savings, however, represent "leakage" from the circular flow of income. Consider a person who saves a portion of his or her income by stashing money in a mattress. Because expenditures are reduced, incomes of others in the economy are reduced. These people in turn must reduce their spending, reducing income for still others. Thus, the withdrawal of money from the flow of income for the purpose of savings can lead to a contraction in the level of activity throughout the economy.

Of course, few people save by stashing cash in a mattress. Instead, they are likely to loan their money to someone who will pay interest. Such financial investments, however, do not solve the underlying problem.[1] Instead, they merely transfer the surplus cash to someone else. Unless the money is spent through investments in real goods and services, thereby generating income for the providers of those goods and services, savings will still require a contraction of economic activity. Indeed, the economy must contract until the level of investments (in the sense of real investments in plant, equipment, and the like) is equal to the level of savings in the community as a whole. Thus, a critical issue in macroeconomic performance is the matching of savings and investment flows.

Keynes argued there are likely to be times when desired savings and desired investment differ substantially. The desire to save, he argued, is constant. People save to provide for retirement, to cover the costs of education, to have a resource to cover unexpected contingencies, and the like. These desires are not likely to change significantly or rapidly. Investment, however, is different. Businesses will seek to make investments if they believe that the return on the investment will cover the cost of capital—i.e., if the investment will be profitable. If the economy is growing, investment looks attractive. If the economy is stagnant, however, or an individual firm's business is not growing, there is little reason to invest. Moreover, what matters is future profitability of an investment. Expectations of future profit, however, may be subject to much greater and more rapid change. If expectations change, the desire to invest may change significantly, and quite rapidly. Somehow, the economy must match the relatively constant desired savings with the variable and uncertain demand for investments.

The classical economists argued that the interest rate solves the problem of matching desired savings and investments. As depicted in Figure 12-2, savings (S) represent a supply of loanable funds. Since part of the motive for saving is the interest earned on those savings, an increase in the interest rate should increase

Figure 12-2. The market for loanable funds.

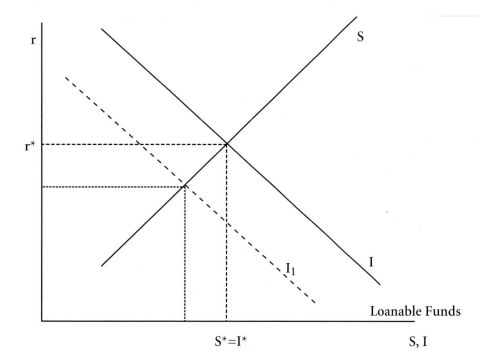

---

[1]In the macroeconomic sense, financial investments are not "investments" at all. Only those investments that represent a purchase of goods and services are investments in an economic sense, because they represent an increase in the capital stock of the economy.

savings. Investment (I) represents the demand for loanable funds. If the interest rate declines, investments that would not have been profitable at the old interest rate now look more attractive, and can cover the cost of capital. Thus, a decline in the interest rate will stimulate increases in investment. The supply of savings and the demand for investment determine the interest rate (r*) that will clear the market for loanable funds. If desired investment shifts downward to I_1, the interest rate will fall. With lower interest rates, additional investments will appear attractive. Thus, investment will increase (compared to what it would have been at the old interest rate) to restore equilibrium. In any event, savings and investment flows will be matched. The system should restore equilibrium, without the need for intervention, even if investment demand shifts considerably.

Figure 12-3. Savings may fall faster than investment.

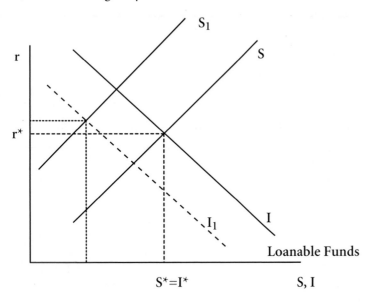

Keynes argued, however, this automatic adjustment mechanism would not work reliably. Restoring equilibrium depends on a reduction in the interest rate to stimulate investment. However, Keynes argued, desired savings depends on income. If investment declines, the initial effect will be a reduction in income. That reduction in income will reduce both willingness and ability to save. If desired savings falls far enough, there may even be upward pressure on interest rates, as shown in Figure 12-3. Thus, investment may contract further, resulting in further declines in income. As the cycle continues, savings and investment may be equal, but both may be equal to zero! There is, in short, no automatic adjustment mechanism to restore reasonable economic performance.

Keynes' General Theory of the economy can be summarized in three propositions. First, an economy in a depression could stay there. There is no automatic correction mechanism to restore growth. Equilibrium is therefore possible even with massive unemployment. Second, prosperity depends on investment. Reduced investment starts a spiral of contraction, and increased investment is necessary to restart a cycle of expansion. Third, investment is an undependable drive. There just might not be opportunities when they are needed.

The Keynesian prescription for the Depression (and any other recession) was to replace the missing investment. If business did not wish to soak up the pool of savings in productive investments, then government should pick up the slack. Through deficit spending—borrowing the excess savings from the private sector—the government could provide sufficient additional demand to restore prosperity.

According to Keynes, government intervention would have a multiplier effect on the level of economic activity. The source of a recession was seen as a reduction in investment demand. Demand was therefore too low to permit full employment of resources. Eventually, however, the level of demand would have to equal the level of actual output. Thus, if demand could be increased, output would be increased. As consumers spent their additional incomes, the additional increase in demand would induce still more increases in output. Thus, an additional dollar of government spending would induce more than an additional dollar of economic activity.

The situation as Keynes saw it is depicted in Figure 12-4, a diagram known as the Keynesian Cross. The vertical axis, Y^d, represents total demand for output; the horizontal axis labeled Y represents actual output. Along the line labeled $Y = Y^d$, the two are equal, as they must be in equilibrium. The Y^d curve represents total demand for output in the economy. The curve is upward sloping, because if income increases, demand will increase as well.

If the government increases spending by an amount A, the total demand for output shifts up, to the curve labeled $Y^d + A$. As a result, output expands. However, along the $Y = Y^d$ line, the change in output is exactly the

Figure 12-4. The keynesian cross.

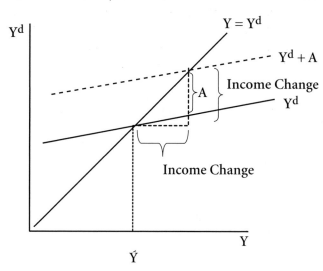

same whether measured horizontally or vertically. Thus, total output must expand by more than the increase in government spending. There is a multiplier effect, in which additional government spending stimulates additional private spending, and both increase the level of economic activity.

The Keynesian approach is the intellectual justification for the stimulus package, adopted early in 2009. Congress approved a package of mostly spending and some tax cuts originally estimated to cost $787 billion, and now estimated to cost $825 billion. The Congressional Budget Office estimates that the peak impact of the stimulus package was in 2010. In that year, it estimated the stimulus increased real GDP by 0.7 to 4.1 percent, reduced the unemployment rate by 0.4 to 1.8 percentage points, and increased employment by 0.7 to 3.3 million people. These estimates are controversial; as we will see when we consider the real business cycle perspective, other economists believe the stimulus had net negative effects. A generation of Ph.D. candidates will likely explore the impact of the stimulus in their dissertations.

Although it was developed to account for the Great Depression, the Keynesian theory was also applied to the much more common postwar economic problem of inflation. In the Keynesian view, recessions result from inadequate demand, with excess savings siphoning off incomes and requiring contraction. Inflation was seen as simply the same problem in reverse. Rather than deficient demand, the problem of inflation is one of excess demand. With excess demand, prices are bid up as consumers bid more for goods and firms bid more for resources. The solution, again, is government. By running a budget surplus, the government can force additional savings for the economy as a whole, thus restoring the balance between productive capacity and aggregate demand. Though often preached, this advice has rarely been practiced.

Figure 12-5. The phillips curve.

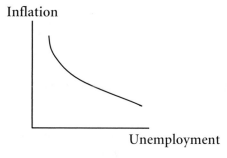

The Keynesian view that inflation is caused by excess demand implies that a relationship exists between the inflation rate and the level of unemployment. With too little demand, unemployment rates increase. Moreover, because demand is low, indeed inadequate, there is little upward pressure on prices, and inflation is low. With higher levels of demand, there is more demand for workers, and unemployment falls. Because demand is high, however, there is also upward pressure on prices, or inflation. The relationship between inflation and unemployment depicted in Figure 12-5 is known as the Phillips Curve, named for the British economist who first discovered it as an empirical regularity in data on the British economy.

The Phillips Curve depicts what is, in Keynesian models, an unavoidable tradeoff between inflation and unemployment. If we want less unemployment, we must be prepared to accept higher levels of inflation. Similarly, we can reduce inflation only by tolerating increased levels of unemployment.

Throughout much of the 1960s and 1970s, government policy makers saw the problem they faced as choosing where on the Phillips curve we should be. They debated the optimal tradeoff between inflation and unemployment, and how concerned we should be about each of these evils. Once we have chosen the amount of inflation and unemployment we want, simple manipulation of federal tax and spending policy could get us to that optimal point, and, by suitable adjustments, "fine tune" the economy to maintain the desired combination of inflation and unemployment.

It didn't work out quite that way. In the 1970s in particular, the US economy experience rising levels of both unemployment and inflation. At first, policy makers reasoned that the Phillips curve had simply shifted, for unknown reasons. Given the new Phillips curve, we could proceed as before: find the ideal combination of inflation and unemployment, and adjust policy to get there. The Monetarists, however, had a very different perspective. They argued there is no tradeoff between inflation and unemployment in the long run, and that policy would therefore have no effect.

II. THE MONETARISTS

Until the 1970s, the Keynesian approach to macroeconomics was the conventional wisdom. It was challenged, with an increasing impact over time, by the Monetarists, who argued that the critical economic policy was not the budget surplus or deficit, but rather the supply of money.

The basis of monetarism was the quantity theory of money. This theory starts with a simple accounting identity. We can measure the value of all the transactions that occur in the economy by counting the number of transactions, T, and multiplying by the average price per transaction, P. Alternatively, we can focus on the money used to conduct those transactions. From this perspective, the value of all transactions is equal to M, the supply of money, times V, the velocity of money, or the number of times each dollar bill is used in transactions. Obviously, the total value of transactions must be the same measured either way. Hence, $MV = PT$, the central equation of the quantity theory.

The quantity theory converts this accounting identity into a theory by making a variety of arguments about its component parts. The volume of transactions (T), they argue, is determined in the real economy. It reflects the willingness of workers to work, and firms to employ them, at a given wage, but it is determined by real economic factors independent of government policy. If, for example, the government announced that starting tomorrow, every dollar would be worth $10, clearly prices would change, but there would be no change at all in the number of transactions that occur. Thus, T is given, and cannot be changed. Velocity, the monetarists argue, is stable.[2] Policy changes will affect velocity little, if at all. The supply of money, M, is determined by the Federal Reserve. It is a policy variable, and can be anything the Fed wants it to be.

What is left is P, the price level. Since velocity and the number of transactions are independent of policy, changes in the supply of money must affect the price level—i.e., the rate of inflation. Moreover, that is all that monetary policy can affect, at least in the long run. By choosing the rate of growth of the money supply, the Federal Reserve can choose the rate of inflation, but it cannot choose anything else once the economy is given time to adjust.

In the short run, the Monetarists see business cycle developments as dominated by monetary policy. If the Fed increases the amount of money available, people find they have more money than they want to hold. The easiest way to get rid of extra money is to spend it. The recipients of the money, however, also find they have more money than they wish to hold, and therefore spend it. Initially, spending the extra money looks to businesses like an increase in demand, and they therefore seek to increase output. Thus, expanding the amount of money initially stimulates economic activity. Eventually, however, the continuing demand leads to increases in prices.[3] Indeed, the only way to get rid of money that consumers and businesses do not wish to hold is to reduce its value by increasing prices. As prices rise, however, the quantity of goods demanded falls back to what it was. The end result is a brief burst of economic stimulus, followed by higher prices and a return to the previous level of economic activity. The unemployment rate may decline initially, but it will return to its original level, determined by the number of transactions in the economy. In the long run, only the price level is different.

While Keynes focused on federal spending and borrowing, the monetarists focused on monetary policy. In their view, the actual impact of government deficits depends entirely on how the deficit is financed. One way to finance a deficit is to borrow the money from the public. If this route is chosen, argue the monetarists, the

---

[2]In simple versions, monetarists argued that velocity is constant, but more complex versions allow velocity to depend on such factors as interest rates.
[3]Modern Keynesians also believe that monetary policy has an influence, but they maintain it operates through interest rates. By making more credit available, monetary policy reduces interest rates, thereby increasing investment demand. The result is only inflationary if there is excess demand.

result is an increase in the demand for loanable funds equal to the amount of the deficit. In turn, the interest rate must increase, to balance the supply of savings available with the total demand for funds. That increase in interest rates, however, will "crowd out" private investment, with no change in total investment. Thus, if deficits are financed by borrowing from the public, they do not stimulate economic activity; they simply replace private investment with federal spending. Unemployment is unchanged.

The other way to finance a deficit—used repeatedly by governments around the world and throughout history—it to simply print more money. In that case, the monetarists argue, the only effects are those attributable to monetary policy. In the long run, the inflation rate increases, and nothing else happens. Again, deficit spending does not stimulate economic activity.

Thus, argue the strong monetarists, Only Money Matters. They point to historical US evidence suggesting that monetary changes are much more significant than changes in the federal budget deficit in explaining business cycles. And, they point to substantial international evidence making clear that money growth rates determine the inflation rate.

Rather than attempting to fine tune the economy, the monetarists argued, the government should simply adopt a stable monetary policy and do nothing else. Although monetary policy could potentially offset disturbances in the short run, they maintained that the precise effects were impossible to predict, and could not effectively guide policy. Instead, they contended, the Federal Reserve should simply set, and maintain, a target growth rate for the money supply, and let the economy adjust.

III. THE RATIONAL EXPECTATIONS / REAL BUSINESS CYCLE APPROACH

Unlike the Keynesians and the Monetarists, rational expectations theorists take a fundamentally different approach. Rather than starting with assumptions about how economic aggregates behave (i.e., the relationship between savings and investment for Keynesians, or between money and prices for monetarists), these economists seek to build up theories of macroeconomic activity by examining rational individual behavior. It is, therefore, micro based macroeconomics. Central to this approach are the notions of real business cycles and rational expectations.

Real business cycle economists maintain that fluctuations in economic activity are driven by real economic disturbances. They imagine an aggregate supply curve depicting total output of the economy, and attribute disturbances to shifts in the aggregate supply curve (or the aggregate production function). In part because this approach developed during the 1970s, and in part because they have been empirically significant, the classic examples of real disturbances giving rise to a business cycle are oil price shocks in 1970s. The Arab oil embargo in 1972–73, and the Iranian revolution in 1979, meant that less oil was available, and, given the other inputs available, they meant that the economy could produce less output. Recessions resulted, not because of some demand problem or a failure of monetary policy, but rather because, with less oil available, we simply could not produce as much. Contraction was inevitable, and unavoidable, until the flow of oil resumed. Similarly, changes in technology or productivity or financial shocks such as the Panic of 2008 can change the conditions of production in ways that produce a boom or a bust.

A second critical idea of this approach to macroeconomics is the notion of rational expectations. Basically, the notion of rational expectations maintains that individual consumers and firms who are part of the economic system understand the system and its responses at least as well as do academic economists. When the government changes policy, individuals have an obvious incentive to take into account the likely effects of that policy, and act accordingly. The result, in many instances, is that in a world of rational expectations, policy has no effect.

Consider the effects of monetary policy. In the view of the monetarists (which the rational expectations economists share), the long run effect of an increase in money growth is simply an increase in inflation. Because of rational expectations, when the Fed begins to expand the money supply, everyone understands that the result will be simply an increase in inflation. Therefore, they alter their plans to take into account the expected future inflation. Rather than a short run stimulus to economic activity as people try to spend excess cash, the price increase is immediate, with no effect at all on the level of employment or economic activity.

The effect is easiest to see in capital markets. Suppose people try to get rid of excess cash by investing in bonds. If so, the interest rate would fall, and investment would increase. If inflation will be higher in the future, however, lenders will demand a higher interest rate measured in current dollars to compensate for the fact that they will be repaid in dollars that are worth less. In fact, they will demand an interest rate equal to the current real interest rate (i.e., the interest rate adjusted for inflation) plus the expected future inflation. Similarly, borrowers will be willing to pay this higher interest rate, because they too understand that they will repay the loan in dollars that will buy less. Thus, the real interest rate does not change at all. Instead, the nominal interest rate increases, by the amount of expected inflation. Because the real interest rate is unchanged, investment is unchanged. Thus, because financial market participants understand that the long term effect of monetary growth is more inflation, that is the only effect.

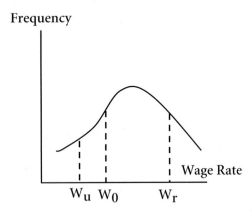

Figure 12-6. Searching for a wage rate.

Frequency

Wage Rate

W_u W_0 W_r

In short, the notion of rational expectations maintains that policy can only work if it fools people. Unexpected policies have an effect, because people cannot anticipate their impact and adjust accordingly. Because it is impossible to fool all of the people all of the time, however, policy of any sort will have little influence. People will figure it out and adjust.

The emphasis of analysis of individual behavior also leads to a very different view of unemployment. Indeed, real business cycle theorists argue that unemployment, to a large extent, exists because rational workers choose to remain unemployed.

Consider a worker who is looking for a job. A variety of jobs exist, and the worker is assumed to know the kinds of jobs and the wages they pay that are available in the economy as a whole. The distribution of potential wages might look something like the distribution in Figure 12-6.

Suppose our hypothetical worker receives an offer of a job at wage w_0. Should he take it? The answer depends on the benefits and costs of remaining unemployed. If the worker rejects the offer, obviously he loses w_0. However, in most instances unemployment compensation or other forms of financial support are available, at rate w_u, the wage while unemployed. Thus, the cost of rejecting the current offer is $w_0 - w_u$. On the other hand, the benefit of rejecting the offer depends on the likelihood of receiving a better offer. If w_0 is relatively low, as shown, there is clearly a substantial likelihood that the next job offer will be better. Thus, rather than take this job, a rational worker will choose to remain unemployed, waiting for a better offer. In fact, the worker's best strategy is to choose a reservation wage, w_r. If an offer is below the reservation wage, the worker should reject it, and wait for a better offer. If the offer is above the reservation wage, the worker should take it.[4]

In this theory, the reservation wage has an important influence on the unemployment rate. The higher the reservation wage, the longer the worker will remain unemployed on the average, because an offer above the reservation wage is less likely. Thus, higher reservation wages imply higher unemployment rates. Given worker search decisions, unemployment is determined only by the rate at which workers that have jobs quit or are laid off and the rate at which firms hire workers. The equilibrium unemployment rate that results is the "natural" rate of unemployment. Because it reflects decisions that are in the best interests of the workers and firms who make the choices, it can only be altered by policies that influence worker search decisions.

---

[4]We can imagine an essentially identical problem from the perspective of the employer, who must find a worker who is a good fit for the job at the lowest possible wage.

One factor determining reservation wages is the wage while unemployed, or unemployment compensation. Increases in unemployment compensation reduce the cost of rejecting the current job offer. They therefore tend to increase the reservation wage—and lengthen unemployment. Differences in skill levels among different workers also influence reservation wages. In particular, less skilled workers are likely to face a distribution of offers that is more spread out, and are therefore likely to choose a higher reservation wage. They will therefore experience higher average unemployment rates. Similarly, younger workers, who are less likely to know what kind of job they want, are likely to have higher quit rates, because the job they take is less likely to meet their expectations. Thus, young people too will have higher unemployment rates on average.

The notion of rational expectations is also relevant in labor markets. The wage rate that matters to workers in making job search decisions is the real wage rate, that is, the wage rate adjusted for changes in the level of prices. Because workers too recognize that printing more money will simply increase the inflation rate, they will demand higher nominal (i.e., dollar) wage rates to achieve the same real wage rate. If, however, workers do not realize that the Federal Reserve is busy printing more money, then the increase in demand will result in an increase in nominal wages. Because workers do not realize the money supply is growing, the increased nominal wage looks like a higher real wage. Workers therefore take job offers more quickly than they would otherwise. Because they do not realize that inflation is occurring, unemployment falls. Once workers learn that inflation is rising, however, they adjust their (nominal) reservation wage to maintain the same real wage they wanted, and the unemployment rate returns to its original level. As in financial market, policies that surprise people or fool them can have an effect, but policies that people expect have no effect.

The rational expectations focus on individual behavior also leads to a very different analysis of tax rates. Real business cycle theorists tend to stress the relationship between tax rates and incentives to work or earn income. If the marginal tax rate (i.e., the tax rate on an additional dollar of income) increases, it reduces the return to working harder, since the worker (or investor) gets to keep less of the return. Vacations, less demanding jobs, and investments that require less attention therefore look more attractive. Such choices, however, reduce income. Thus, real business cycle theorists argue, increases in tax rates tend to reduce the amount of income subject to tax. In essence, people attempt to convert taxable income into nontaxable income as tax rates increase. Because leisure is not taxed, one form of this substitution is to take more leisure, and work less. Because the choices households and firms made before the tax increase were the ones that would maximize aggregate economic activity, increases in tax rates tend to reduce the level of economic activity. Figure 12-7 displays the average marginal tax rates in the United States over the last century.

One of the most striking differences between the rational expectations and other approaches to macroeconomic analysis is in their treatment of federal budget deficits. Keynesians argue that deficits stimulate the economy. Monetarists argue that the effects of deficits depend on their financing, either crowding out private investments or resulting in inflation. Rational expectations theorists argue that deficits are simply irrelevant—they have no effects at all.

To focus on the pure effects of the deficit, imagine that the government cuts taxes by $1 this year, and borrows the money to pay for it. Next year, the government must repay the loan, with interest, which will require it to increase taxes by $1 + R$ (where R is the nominal interest rate).

The typical household's response to this arrangement will be nil. The household has an extra dollar now, and an extra future tax obligation of $1 + R$. The present value of that future obligation, discounted at an interest rate of R, is precisely $1. Its real opportunities are unchanged, and its real behavior should be unchanged as well. In essence, the current tax cut provides precisely the amount of money needed to finance the future tax obligation. This result, which is clearly controversial, is known as the Ricardian Equivalence Theorem, after the economist who first discovered it but did not necessarily believe it.

The restriction to a one year deficit is artificial, but not essential. However long the obligation is deferred, it is still there, and its present value is still $1. The only circumstance in which deferring the debt matters is if it is possible to pass it on to the next generation. If a household is willing to die in debt, in essence, leaving its tax liability to the next generation to worry about, then it is wealthier as a result of the deficit financed tax cut, and will behave accordingly.

Figure 12-7. Average marginal tax rates in the U.S., 1912–2006.

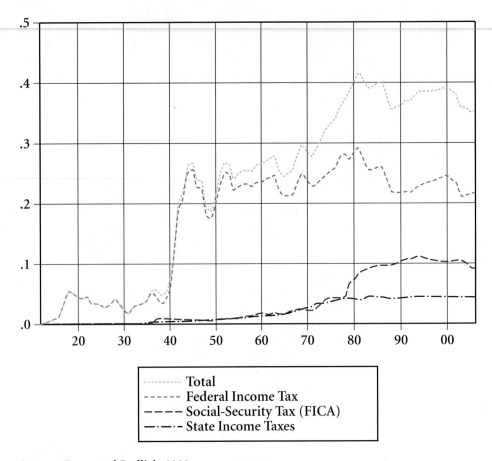

Source: Barro and Redlick, 2009

Presumably, however, most people care about their kids and try to leave an inheritance. If government deficits stick them with a bigger tax liability, parents should just increase their bequest. On the other hand, if the bequest motive is to control the kids (they'll cooperate or they won't inherit), there is no reason to increase the bequest to offset future tax liabilities. Ricardian equivalence then would not hold.

The implications of Ricardian Equivalence are striking. If it is valid, government deficits change nothing. There is no possibility for fiscal policy to do anything, and the only question remaining is exactly how large we would like the government to be. However the government finances its expenditures, each dollar of government spending will crowd out a dollar of private consumption spending in the long run.

In contrast, Monetarists argue that government borrowing will crowd out an identical amount of private borrowing, resulting in no net investment increase. Keynesians agree that there will be some crowding out, but argue that the reduction in private investment will not completely offset the increase in government investment. Demand therefore increases, and with it, interest rates. The empirical difficulty with either view is that there is no clear evidence that larger deficits lead to higher expected real interest rates. The empirical results are mixed, however, and remain controversial.

The real business cycle approach to macroeconomics takes a very different view of the 2009 stimulus package. Harvard economist Robert Barro argues that based on historical evidence, the multiplier for government spending is 0.4, implying that more government spending displaces some private spending, but does not do so completely. Therefore, if the stimulus spent an additional $300 billion each in 2009 and 2010, GDP would be higher by $120 billion in 2009 (0.8 percent of GDP), and higher by 180 billion in 2010 (1.2 percent). The borrowing that financed the stimulus must be repaid, however. The tax multiplier, Barro estimates, is −1.1. That is, an extra dollar of tax revenue reduces GDP by $1.10 in the following year, because it displaces private consumption and discourages productive activity. If we repay the stimulus spending with higher taxes in 2011 and 2012, he estimates, GDP falls by $330 billion in each of those years. Evaluating a five year plan from 2009 to 2013, he argues GDP will be +$120 billion, +$180 billion, +60 billion, –$330 billion, –$330 billion. The total is minus $300 billion. Moreover, private expenditures fall, both because of displaced spending and because of the tax increases, by a total of $900 billion over the five years. So, he concludes, we get an extra $600 billion of public expenditures in exchange for a $900 billion reduction in private expenditures.[5]

IV. How Much Government? Budget Deficits and the National Debt

In 2009, the Federal government ran a budget deficit of $1.4 trillion, or 10 percent of GDP. A record in dollar terms, the deficit was only larger relative to GDP during World War II. Long term historical trends for federal revenues and expenditures as a percentage of GDP are shown in Figure 12-8. Between 1980 and 2007 (before the great recession, which significantly reduced tax revenues), receipts averaged 18.3 percent of GDP. Outlays, however, averaged 20.8 percent of GDP, leaving an average deficit of 2.5 percent of GDP. A continuing flow of deficits of course implies a continuing increase in the national debt, which reached roughly 60 percent of GDP in 2011.[6]

To understand the debate about debt and deficits, it is important to understand two key features of how the government keeps its books. First, budgeting uses a concept of "baseline accounting," where expenditures

Figure 12-8. Federal Receipts and Outlays as a Percentage of GDP.

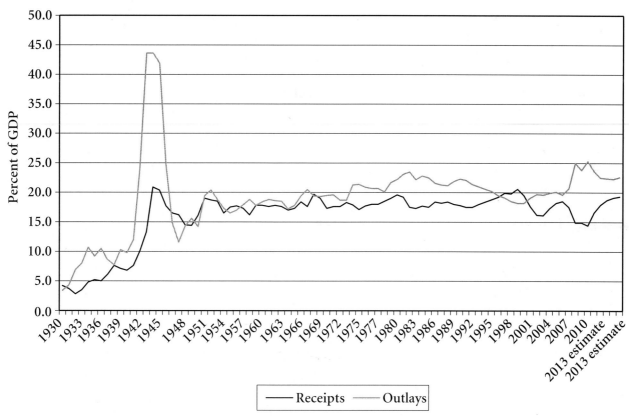

Source: Office of Management and Budget

---

[5]Robert J. Barro, "The Stimulus Evidence One Year On," *The Wall Street Journal*, February 23, 2010.
[6]From an economic perspective, what matters is debt held by the public, rather than gross federal debt. The difference between debt held by the public and gross debt is debt held in other federal accounts, primarily the trust funds for Social Security and Medicare.

and receipts are projected assuming current law is unchanged. Increases or cuts in taxes or expenditures are measured relative to this baseline, not relative to the previous year's expenditures. Thus, if current law promises an increase in benefits next year, and we decide to forego that increase, that is counted as cut in spending – even though next year's spending is exactly the same as this year's spending, and no beneficiary experiences an actual reduction in what they receive. The difference is particularly important when temporary programs expire. The tax cuts enacted during the Bush Administration, for example, were originally scheduled to expire at the end of 2010, later extended through 2012. Thus, the budget baseline for 2013 assumes the expiration of the tax cuts on schedule. Extending the tax rates further in time will be counted, for budget purposes, as a tax cut—even though everyone's taxes would stay the same as they have been for the last decade.

The other place where baseline accounting is particularly important is Social Security. Social Security benefits for future retirees are indexed to wages that prevail in the private sector. The original rationale for this arrangement was to keep the relative incomes of people who are in the labor force and retirees more or less the same. Nevertheless, because wages grow faster than prices, the current system implies increasing benefits in real terms for future retirees, compared to current retirees. If we changed the indexing system to base benefit changes on price changes, we could preserve the purchasing power of the current level of benefits that retirees actually receive. Every future retiree would receive more dollars, and the same purchasing power, as current retirees—but for budget purposes, this would be a massive cut in Social Security benefits.

Second, the usual budget is calculated on a cash basis. Thus, it does not take into account all of the future implications of today's decisions. Under current rules, the budget impact of program changes is assessed over a 10 year horizon, but impacts farther in the future are ignored. For example, the health care reforms enacted early in 2010 were scored for budget purposes as reducing the deficit. That result was possible because many of the new taxes and fees begin within the 10 year budget window, but many of the benefits do not kick in until late in the decade, or even after the 10 year horizon.

The Government Accountability Office publishes financial statements for the federal government that are calculated on an accrual basis, which recognizes the net present value of current obligations. In fiscal year 2011, GAO reported that the net present value of promised benefits under Social Security and Medicare reached $33.8 trillion dollars, up from $30.9 trillion in 2010. Roughly half of the increase is due to the aging of the population—one year later, the obligations to pay are closer to the present, and more expensive in present value terms. To put the number in some perspective, the total value of equity in companies in the Wilshire 5000 index of stock prices is $13.1 trillion, and Freddie Mac estimates that homeowner's equity totals $6.2 trillion.[7]

The long term prospects for federal receipts and expenditures are shown in Figure 12-9 under two different scenarios.[8] The extended baseline scenario follows the general approach to baseline budgeting described above, assuming that current law remains in place and is followed. Under this scenario, federal revenue rises to 23 percent of GDP in 2035, considerably higher than its previous peak of 20.9 percent during World War II. With continued growth, current law implies continued increases in federal revenue, which would reach 30 percent of GDP in 2080. Even so, the government would run a persistent deficit, and the debt held by the public would reach 79 percent of GDP in 2035. Moreover, both scenarios consider only "primary" spending— that is, spending other than net interest on the debt. The more the debt grows, however, the greater the increase in debt service costs, even if there is no impact on interest rates the government must pay.

The primary reason for significant revenue increases in the extended baseline scenario is the little know alternative minimum tax ("AMT"), designed to limit the tax benefits of various tax deductions to high income individuals. In its present form, it was enacted in 1982. Unlike virtually everything else in the tax code, however, the dollar amounts that trigger applicability of the AMT were not indexed for inflation. The result is that every year, the tax would reach deeper and deeper into the middle class, with more and more people subject to the AMT. In 2011, the tax affected 2.6 percent of all filers; had Congress not acted, that would have risen to 19 percent in 2012. Under current law, however, AMT coverage would continue to grow, reaching an estimated half of all

---

[7]Bryan R. Lawrence, "The Bad News Before Christmas," The Washington Post, December 28, 2011.
[8]Neither scenario reflects the deficit reduction deal reached in the summer of 2011. That agreement is unlikely to change the long run outlook substantially, however.

Figure 12-9. Revenues and Primary Spending, by category, under CBO's long-term budget scenarios.

(percentage of gross domestic product)

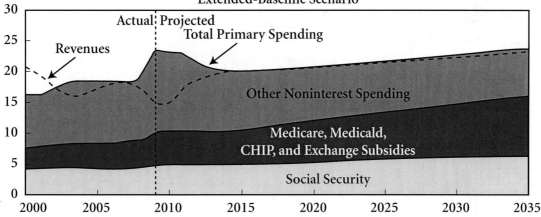

Extended-Baseline Scenario

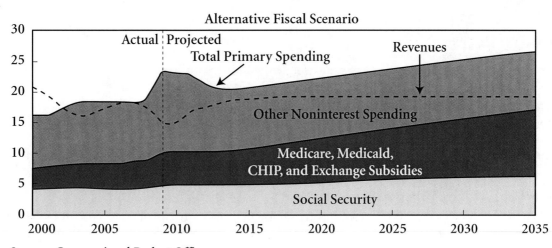

Alternative Fiscal Scenario

Source: Congressional Budget Office

households in 2035. It is exceedingly unlikely that these increases will actually occur. Rather, Congress will likely adjust the tax to prevent substantial expansion, as it has done repeatedly over the past decade.

More controversially, the extended baseline scenario includes expiration of the reductions in tax rates and expansions in various tax credits enacted in 2001 and 2003. It also includes a substantial reduction in payments to physicians under Medicare, currently about 27 percent, that Congress has repeatedly deferred.

The CBO's alternative scenario assumes that AMT coverage will remain at roughly current levels, that the 2001 and 2003 tax cuts will expire for those with incomes over $250,000, and that Medicare payments to physicians will grow with an index of Medicare costs, not the unrealistic formula in current law. The primary difference in the alternative scenario, shown in the bottom portion of Figure 12-9, is on the revenue side. Maximum revenue would increase to just over 19 percent of GDP, a value that exceeds the average of the last 30 years but within the historic range of tax revenues. With less revenue and some increase in expenditures, deficits would be larger, reaching 16 percent of GDP in 2035.

The key factor driving rising expenditures as a percentage of GDP is the aging of the population. Figure 12-10 shows the increase in the total costs of Social Security and Medicare, the two primary programs that benefit the elderly. Although the continued increase in medical costs is an important factor in rising total expenditures, the inevitable demographic consequences of an aging population account for 63 percent of the increase in the cost of these programs in 2035—roughly 2 percent of GDP. Over a longer time horizon, the effects of excess cost increases become more significant.

Figure 12-10. Sources of growth in federal spending on major mandatory health care programs and social security, 2010 to 2035.

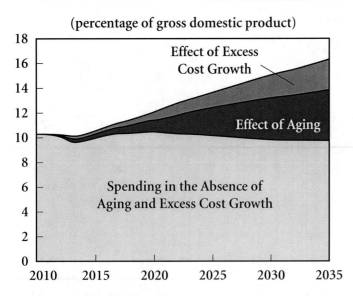

(percentage of gross domestic product)

Continuing deficits imply continuing increases in the debt held by the public, as displayed in Figure 12-11. Historically, debt peaked at just over 100 percent of GDP during World War II and fell rapidly in the postwar years until it began to grow again in the mid 1970s. Under the extended baseline scenario, debt would rise to 79 percent of GDP in 2035; it would be roughly 175 percent of GDP under the alternative scenario.

These rather gloomy projections all assume that the levels of spending and borrowing they consider have no other impact on the level of economic activity. The rational expectations/real business cycle theorists, however, stress the importance of considering changes in private sector behavior in response to policy changes.

The CBO considered only one such effect, crowding out. This is the monetarist (and Keynesian) implication that increasing government borrowing will increase interest rates as government competes for the available pool of savings, thereby crowding out private investment. In turn, reduced private investment means that GDP will grow more slowly than it would otherwise. The estimated effects of crowding out on per capita GDP are shown in Figure 12-12. Although GDP continues to grow even with the assumed degree of crowding out, it is significantly smaller than it would have been in the absence of crowding out. In 2035, per capita GDP would be an estimated 15 percent lower than it would have been in the absence of crowding out. Effects are smaller in the extended baseline scenario, because debt grows more slowly. That scenario, however, assumes significant increases in tax rates compared to current levels, and makes no allowance for the effect of those higher rates on incentives.

If GDP grows more slowly because of crowding out, debt will grow more rapidly. The effects on debt held by the public are shown in Figure 12-13.

Figure 12-11. Federal debt held by the public under CBO's long-term budget scenarios.

(percentage of gross domestic product)

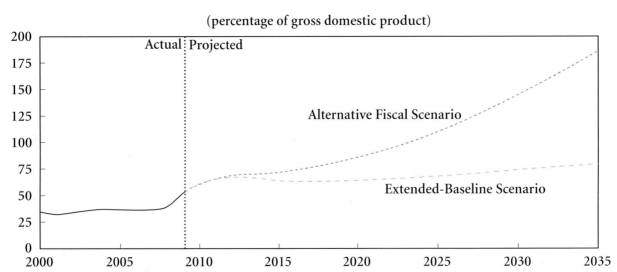

Source: Congressional Budget Office

Figure 12-12. The effects of crowding out on real GDP and GNP per person under CBO's alternative fiscal scenario.

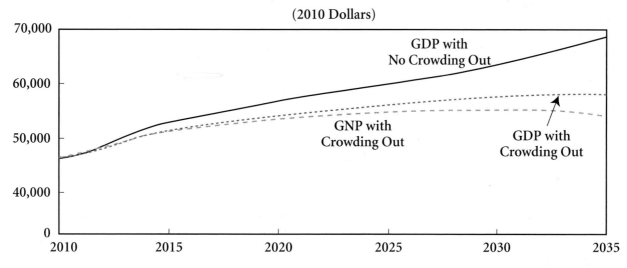

(2010 Dollars)

Source: Congressional Budget Office

Figure 12-13. The effects of crowding out on federal debt held by the public under CBO's alternative fiscal scenario.

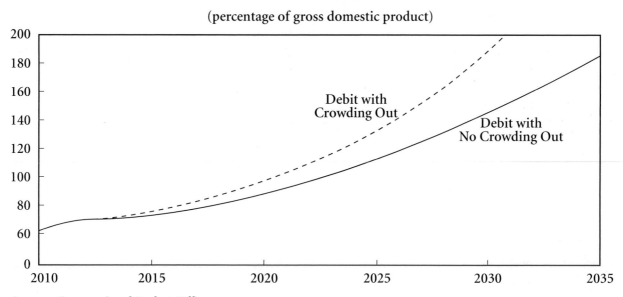

(percentage of gross domestic product)

Source: Congressional Budget Office

Whatever one thinks of the merits of deficit finance, we are clearly headed for territory with which we have little or no historical experience, particularly under the alternative scenario. In all probability, this is an unsustainable trend, and like other unsustainable trends, it will not continue. The question is how it will end.

There are at least three possibilities. Default in the sense of the federal government not paying off its debt in dollars seems unlikely, if only because we always have the option of printing more dollars. That, however, implies increasing inflation over time, and rising interest rates to compensate investors for the expected reduction in their purchasing power. One possibility is gradually increasing problems, as investors come to recognize that they are less likely to be repaid in dollars that will have the purchasing power they expected. At any point, this gradual increase could become the second possibility: a new financial crisis, with credit markets deciding that they are no longer willing to take the risk of repayment in a badly depreciated currency. The third possibility is a political decision to put revenues and expenditures on a more sustainable path.

Delay in reaching a decision increases the magnitude of the changes that will be necessary considerably, as debt continues to increase in the interim. The longer we take to reach a decision, the greater will be the necessary adjustments in spending or tax increases to achieve a sustainable path. CBO's 2010 estimate was that under the alternative scenario, starting changes in 2011 would require adjustments to revenue and/or outlays totaling 4.8 percent of GDP. That is, we would either need to cut spending or increase taxes (or some combination) by that amount to avoid increasing the outstanding debt beyond its current level of some 60 percent of GDP. Delaying action until 2025 would require adjustments totaling 12.3 percent of GDP to achieve the same objective.

V. SUMMARY

The Great Recession brought macroeconomic issues to the fore. Different schools of thought have very different views about what the government can, or should, do to facilitate economic recovery. The lack of agreement among macroeconomic analysts makes the policy makers' life difficult. Academically respectable, and widely held, schools of analysis have radically different implications for what the government can and should do.

The Keynesian approach to macroeconomics emphasizes aggregate demand. Savings represent leakage from the circular flow of income, and unless they are matched with investments in plant, equipment and the like, will require the economy to contract. Keynes argued that the desire to save was constant, but that the desire to invest was not. If investment demand was inadequate, the economy could go into a recession. Classical economists argued that the interest rate would match savings and investment flows, and restore equilibrium. Keynes argued the initial reduction in income might reduce desired savings so much that that there was actually upward pressure on interest rated, preventing the needed increase in investment. Government should step in to increase demand to replace the missing investment. Government spending is though to have a multiplier effect, leading to increases in income greater than the initial increase in spending. This theory was the justification for the stimulus package approved early in 2009.

The Keynesian theory sees inflation as a problem of excess demand. It implies there is a relationship between the unemployment rate and inflation, the Phillips curve, with high levels of demand leading to low unemployment but high rates of inflation. In the 1970s, however, both unemployment and inflation were rising.

The monetarists argue that the money supply is the key to understanding the economy. The supply of money, they argue, determines the price level, and growth in the supply of money will lead to inflation. If the Fed increases the amount of money, people find they have more money than they want to hold, which leads them to spend the extra money. Initially, this appears to be an increase in demand, but in time, prices rise, reducing the real value of the money supply to the amount that people want to hold.

To monetarists, the impact of deficit spending depends on how it is financed. If it is financed through borrowing, deficit spending crowds out private investment spending. If it is financed by printing more money, it simply results in more inflation. Although monetary policy might offset short term disturbances, monetarists generally argue the government should simply maintain a target growth rate for the money supply and let the economy adjust.

The rational expectations / real business cycle approach to macroeconomics is founded on analyzing rational individual behavior by firms and households. Real business cycle theory maintains that fluctuations in economic activity are driven by changes in the conditions of production, such as disruptions in oil markets.

Rational expectations is the notion that participants in the economic system understand the implications of government policy change, and take those effects into account in making their economic choices. When the Fed increases the money supply, participants understand that prices will increase. In financial markets, investors demand a premium to compensate them for expected inflation, so the real interest rate does not change. Thus, rational expectations holds that policy can only have an effect if it is unexpected.

Real business cycle theorists argue that unemployment is the result of rational worker choices in searching for a job. Workers will balance the gains from waiting for a better offer against the lost income from remaining unemployed. The higher a worker's reservation wage, the longer the worker is likely to remain unemployed. Unemployment compensation, because it increases incomes while unemployed, therefore tends to prolong unemployment. Younger workers are likely to have higher unemployment rates, because they are not as well matched with the jobs that best suit their preferences. Rational expectations in labor markets implies that workers also recognize the impact of monetary changes, and demand a higher nominal wage to compensate them for expected inflation. As in financial markets, there is no effect on unemployment unless the policy is unexpected.

Real business cycle theorists also stress the disincentive effects of tax rates. Higher marginal tax rates, they argue, will reduce incentives to work. Because leisure is not taxed, workers will reduce the amount they work if tax rates are increased.

Rational expectations / real business cycle theorists argue that deficits and taxes have the same effects on the economy. Households understand that deficit spending will require higher future taxes to repay the debt, and they take that future cost into account. The result is that deficit spending does not stimulate economic activity, according to this approach. Because government spending must be paid for, it displaces private consumption expenditures that would otherwise occur. This approach to macroeconomic analysis argues that the stimulus package was, in the long run, a bad deal.

Keynesians argue that activist government (particularly fiscal policy) is desirable, indeed essential, to preserving macroeconomic stability. Monetarists concede that government (or at least monetary policy) can work, but argue that the difficulties of stabilization with monetary policy mean that the best policy is to maintain stable monetary growth, ignoring any business cycles along the way. In essence, they agree that conceptually government policy could succeed, but argue that attempts to correct business cycles are more likely to create new problems than solve old ones.

Rational expectations economists, however, argue that, apart from the tendency of high tax rates to depress economic activity, there is little the government can do, even if it made perfect choices every time. Tax policies can depress economic activity, or channel it to tax-favored investments and activities. Monetary policy can provide a stable price environment to avoid the adjustment costs of high and, especially, fluctuating inflation. Government can, if it is successful, offset the disruptive effects of occasional panics, easing adjustment. But government cannot fine tune economic activity to maintain any particular level of employment.

Government budgeting uses the concept of baseline accounting, where revenues and expenditures are projected assuming current law is unchanged. Increases or decreases in taxes or spending are measured compared to the baseline, not compared to the prior year's level. In the Social Security program, for example, even if benefit levels increase every year, the government accounts for program changes as a cut if they reduce benefits below what has been promised.

Budgeting is usually on a cash basis, rather than an accrual basis. The budget impact of policy choices is assessed over a ten year horizon, but impacts farther in the future are not accounted for. On an accrual basis, the net present value of benefits promised under Social Security and Medicare is $33.8 trillion.

The government's current debt is roughly 60 percent of GDP. Long term budget projections show increasing expenditures over time, largely driven by the aging of the population. Even with the extended baseline, deficit spending will continue, and the national debt will continue to grow relative to GDP. The extended baseline, however, assumed continuous tax increases, primarily due to the effects of the Alternative Minimum Tax. Federal revenue would rise to a higher fraction of GDP than it has ever reached, even during World War II. An alternative scenario assumes these tax increases do not occur, and implies much more rapid growth in debt.

Federal spending is likely to crowd out some private spending. Taking crowding out into account, per capita GDP will be significantly lower than it would be otherwise. Because GDP is lower and tax revenues are lower as well, debt relative to GDP rises even more rapidly.

Current fiscal policy trends do not appear to be sustainable, but it is not clear how they will change.

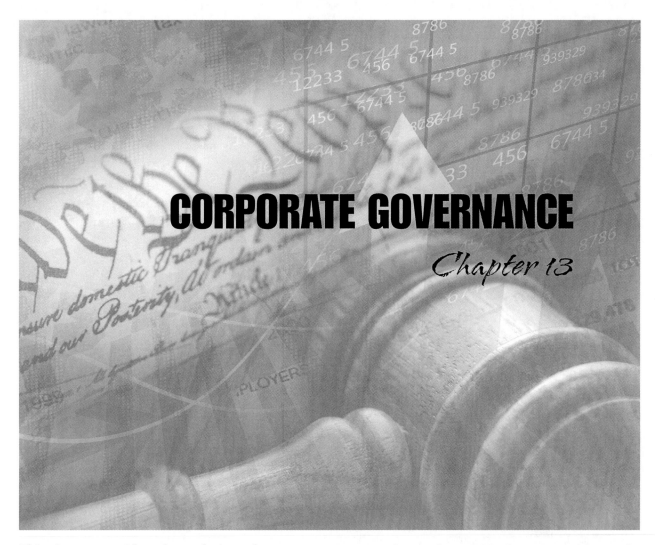

CORPORATE GOVERNANCE

Chapter 13

This chapter considers the evolution of corporate governance issues since 1980. Governance issues arise because of the inherently conflicting interests of managers and shareholders in a modern corporation. Governance institutions and policies are efforts to manage and align those interests as much as possible.

As we will see, there is no one right answer on governance issues. Every industry, and indeed every company, faces its own unique set of potential conflicts, and may find different governance arrangements most appropriate. Moreover, new arrangements to address newly recognized problems may create different, unanticipated problems when circumstances change.

We begin by examining the basic structure and theory of corporate governance, along with allegations that it is really the managers who are in control. We will examine the allegation in light of the agency problem, which exists whenever one person (the principal) hires someone else to perform a task. We will then consider the specific differences in incentives that can arise in the corporate governance context.

Section II considers the takeover boom of the 1980s. Driven by conflicts over free cash flows, and enabled by financing innovations, control of many large corporations changed hands. In many cases, the change in control occurred through a leveraged buyout, which significantly alters the incentives facing managers. Section III considers the lasting effects of the takeover boom, on executive compensation, in the growing role of institutional investors, and in changes in boards of directors. Section IV considers governance issues in the 21st century, beginning with the Enron scandal, which in turn led to the Sarbanes-Oxley Act of 2002. The financial panic of 2008 led to additional governance changes.

I. THE EVOLUTION OF CORPORATE GOVERNANCE

A. Structure and theory

There are three key groups in the corporate governance drama: shareholders, the board of directors, and managers. The shareholders are the owners of the company. Their property rights form the basis for corporate governance, and everything that happens is supposed to serve the best interests of the shareholders. Just as in government, however, shareholders obviously cannot run the company on their own, so they need representative institutions to deal with most matters. Thus shareholders elect a board of directors.

The board of directors, as the elected representatives of the shareholders, is legally responsible for the affairs of the corporation. The board has a fiduciary responsibility to the shareholder, that is, board members are supposed to put the interests of the shareholders ahead of their own personal interests. The board develops the objectives the corporation should pursue and sets its broad policies. They establish the organization's mission and vision, and exercise oversight to assure that the company's actions are consistent with that mission. Perhaps their most important responsibility is to hire and oversee the top managers of the corporation.

Top managers have day-to-day responsibility for corporate affairs. They are selected by the board, report to the board, and are responsible to the board. Because they must make the detailed decisions, they have access to and control over the detailed information that goes into those decisions. Top managers hire and supervise other managers and workers who actually make the products or perform the services the company sells.

Thus the theory of corporate governance argues that everything flows from the shareholders and serves their interests. Shareholders control the board through the election process, the board controls the managers through oversight and review, and the managers do the best they possibly can to advance the shareholders' interests.

There is a common allegation, however, that this simple picture is wrong. In fact, the allegation says, it is the managers who are in control. Advocates point to the fact that the Chairman of the Board is often the Chief Executive Officer, reducing the likelihood of effective board oversight. Other top corporate officials may also be board members. Moreover, when there are vacancies on the board, the board frequently turns to management for suggested replacements. Those suggestions are usually taken. Thus managers are in effect choosing the group that will then oversee management's performance. Finally, matters before the board are generally too complex for more than a cursory discussion. That discussion will be based on the information that managers choose to provide, because managers have control over the detailed information necessary for decisions. The result is that the management's position will usually prevail. Thus, the allegation goes, managers in effect select and control the board, and the shareholders are left out of the picture.

B. The agency problem

A useful way to understand the relationship between managers and shareholders, as well as the pure theory of governance and the allegation that managers are in control, is from the perspective of the agency problem. The shareholders obviously need someone to manage the business on a day-to-day basis, so they hire managers to do so. The shareholders are the principal, and the managers are their agents in accomplishing the tasks necessary to build and run a successful business.

The agency problem arises whenever one person hires another to perform some task. After the contract is set, the agent will have incentives that differ from those of the principal. Because their incentives differ, the principal and agent will sometimes prefer different choices, because different choices would advance their own interests. The potential for conflict arises whenever a principal and agent are involved.

Consider, for example, a typical real estate transaction. Someone wants to sell their house, and hires a real estate agent to assist in the task. The principal (the seller) clearly wants to get the best possible price for the property. That may mean waiting a little longer for a better offer, but the wait may be worthwhile to realize a somewhat higher price. The real estate agent is typically paid on commission (usually 6 or 7 percent of the sale price split between the listing agent and the agent who finds the buyer). Although a higher price will produce a larger commission, the agent realizes only a small fraction of the gain to the seller. Moreover, the agent can close this transaction and move on to sell another house. Real estate agents have a portfolio of properties they are trying to sell, and time and effort spent trying to get a better price for this property cannot be spent on trying to find a reasonable offer for other properties. Thus the agent's incentive is to close the deal. Closing the deal means that the agent collects his or her share of commission on the bulk of the price, even if it means giving up the incremental commission from a slightly better price. The principal has an incentive to wait longer than the agent, because the potential gain from waiting is larger.

A study of 100,000 real estate transactions in Chicago indicates the extent of the agency problem in this particular context. Some of the transactions involved properties that were owned by real estate agents as investment properties. In these transactions, the real estate agent is acting as his or her own agent—that is, the principal and the agent are the same person, so there is no difference in incentives. Agent-owned homes stayed on the market an average of 9.5 days longer, and realized a 3.7 percent higher price. Although the difference is not enormous, when acting for themselves, agents did a better job than when they were acting for a principal.

Consider another example, in which a consumer needs to hire an attorney to recover damages in a traffic accident. The principal—the consumer who is the accident victim—presumably wants their damages covered and as large a recovery as possible. The attorney's incentives depend significantly on how he or she is paid.

Many times, attorneys are paid by the hour. In this situation, the attorney's incentive is to do a very thorough job. That might involve interviewing numerous witnesses, conducting a thorough investigation in other respects, and researching every relevant legal precedent. Because the attorney is paid by the hour, the incentive is to leave no legal stone unturned. Of course, much of this work may be needed in any event, but the principal would want the attorney to stop investigating when the expected increase in the award from further investigation is no longer sufficient to cover the attorney's hourly rate. The attorney's incentive is to keep working.

In other circumstances, attorneys are paid a contingent fee. Under this arrangement, the attorney's compensation is a portion of the client's recovery. Contingent fees usually vary depending on when in the process the client receives their award. If a case settles before trial, the attorney may get 20 or 25 percent of the award. If there is a trial, the attorney gets one-third of the award, and if the case requires an appeal, the attorney gets half the award. With contingent fees, the attorney has an incentive to settle sooner than the client might prefer. As with the real estate agent, the attorney can move on to another matter. The contingent fee on the settlement at hand may be more attractive than the marginally larger fee on a somewhat better settlement.

As a third example, consider a doctor and patient facing an uncertain diagnosis. Suppose the diagnosis does not affect the next steps in the treatment; the treatment will be the same whichever diagnosis is correct. There is a test that will determine the correct diagnosis, but the test itself is painful, time consuming, and costly. However the patient chooses, he or she will be concerned about the pain and expense of the test. The doctor will be less concerned. The doctor will be paid for the test, and does not suffer the pain. Thus the doctor may have an incentive to encourage testing that the patient would not choose. Doctors regularly recommend that their patients should conduct regular self-examinations for breast cancer or testicular cancer. Reportedly, however, they do not usually follow that advice themselves. Again, the incentives of the agent and the principal are different.

There are a number of partial solutions to the agency problem, but none that can eliminate it entirely. One common approach is to develop a contract that better aligns incentives. In the attorney example, the contingency contract probably aligns the incentives of the principal and the agent more closely and therefore reduces the agency problem. Contracts that align incentives generally involve sharing some of the returns with the agent. The principal gets less, but the agent's incentives match those of the principal a little better. Incentives, however, cannot be perfectly aligned unless the agent receives all of the returns from additional effort, leaving nothing for the principal.

A second partial solution to the agency problem is bonding. With bonding, the agent has something to lose from performing poorly as an agent. Bonding is common in construction or home improvement contracts. The contractor puts up a bond, which is forfeit if the work is poor or not up to specifications. A claim on future returns can also serve as a bond. If the agent will lose a future income stream from poor performance, the incentives to be a good agent are reinforced. In the corporate governance context, the bonding that is most relevant is a manager's reputation in the labor market. A manager who is a poor agent for shareholders in one company may find it more difficult to find employment at another.

Bonding, however, generally has a cost. In the construction example, posting the bond itself is costly. The contractor either gives up the use of some of his capital, or pays someone else to post the bond.

A third partial solution to the agency problem is monitoring. The principal can simply watch closely what the agent is doing. The real estate seller, or the client in the attorney example, can monitor how much effort the agent is making, and can ask questions about the likelihood of a better offer and how much longer it might take. In the governance context, outside audits are a form of monitoring. They allow shareholders to obtain an independent look at what is really going on.

Some monitoring is probably essential in any principal-agent relationship. More monitoring can reduce the risk that the agent makes choices the principal would not have made, but more monitoring has a cost. Beyond some point, the gains from additional monitoring are not worth the costs.

The total costs of the partial solutions to the agency problem discussed above are the out-of-pocket costs—the direct costs of aligning contracts, bonding, and monitoring. The cost of the agency problem that remains is the residual loss. Total agency cost is residual loss plus out of pocket costs. These costs are summarized in Figure 13-1.

Figure 13-1. Agency costs.

	Costs of contract aligning incentives
+	Costs of bonding
+	Costs of monitoring
=	Out-of-pocket costs
+	Residual loss from remaining agency problems
=	Total Agency Cost

Corporate governance issues are about how to minimize total agency costs that arise from the shareholder-manager relationship. There are no perfect solutions, because the agency problem is inherent. Governance institutions and arrangements have evolved over time to address new problems, and have sometimes created additional problems of their own, leading to further evolution. In Schumpeter's terms, governance is a continual search for new and better ways of solving the agency problem.

C. Agency problems and managerial incentives

To understand agency problems that arise in the context of governance issues, we need to consider the incentives of the principals, the shareholders, and the managers who are their agents. The shareholders' interests are clear: they would like the maximum possible stock price. That represents the net present value of their interest, and they would like it to be as large as possible. Earnings, growth, and any other information that might interest shareholders are summarized in the stock price.

The precise goals of managers are likely to differ from one manager to another, and will depend on the details of their contract with the firm. Managers will be interested in maximizing their compensation, but how to do that will depend on the structure of the contract. A contract that ties bonuses to quarter over quarter growth in revenue, for example, will give managers an incentive to focus on quarter over quarter growth—regardless of what that might mean for share prices. Generally, however, there are several dimensions in which managers are likely to have different goals than shareholders.

First, managers are likely to have different attitudes than shareholders regarding **risk taking**. In particular, managers are likely to be risk averse, but shareholders are risk neutral. Managers are likely to care about job security, and that means an incentive to avoid choices where there may be a risk of failure. Moreover, managers are inherently more tied to the firm than are shareholders, because their human capital (their knowledge and skills) is specialized to the firm: it is more valuable in the firm than elsewhere. Thus a manager's capital is concentrated in the firm. Managers can diversify their financial portfolio, but they cannot diversify their human capital. Shareholders, on the other hand, can diversify their portfolios. Because diversification improves the risk-return relationship for shareholders, they are more willing to take risk. Shareholders should be risk neutral—that is, they are willing to take a fair gamble for an appropriate return.

Managers and shareholders are likely to differ in their **time horizons**. Because stock prices reflect the net present value of *all* future returns, shareholders care about the long run. Managers have a more limited time frame. They will certainly retire at some point, and they may not expect to remain with the same firm indefinitely. They will therefore care more about returns before their expected termination date than about returns in the more distant future. Shareholders will discount returns that are farther in the future more heavily, but they have no time horizon beyond which returns no longer matter. Managers do.

Managers and shareholders may also have divergent interests concerning **growth**. For managers, growth of the firm increases their power and prestige. It is more prestigious, and usually more rewarding to be the chief executive of a larger company than of a smaller one. Moreover, managers would like to reward lower level managers with promotions, because that is one way to keep promising younger managers in the firm. Promotions, however, require vacancies, which mean someone else has to go. Growth creates the need for more managers, and the potential for more promotions without needing to push someone else out. Although growth *may* be good for shareholders, they are only interested in *profitable* growth. Any company can expand its sales by lowering its price, for example, but that is not necessarily the profit-maximizing choice.

Managers also have an interest in **perquisites** that shareholders do not necessarily share. Spacious, well-decorated offices, with luxurious carpeting and fine art on the walls, are pleasant to work in. An executive dining room, or even an executive chef, is a wonderful benefit to have. Traveling by corporate jet is far more pleasant, and far less time consuming, than dealing with the routine hassles of commercial aviation. Any of these perquisites may also be good for the firm, because they increase managerial productivity. But they can also be taken to excess, because managers receive the benefits, but shareholders must pay the costs.

One instance in which managerial pursuit of perquisites got out of hand involved Adelphia Cable. The company was originally a family-owned business. Because the managers were the shareholders, the distinction did not really matter, and the top executives grew accustomed to paying for essentially personal expenses out of corporate funds. Then the company went public. Although the managers were now supposed to be protecting the best interests of the new shareholders, they continued their old ways. The result was criminal indictments and extensive jail time for the managers.

Finally, managers and shareholders may differ over choice of **effort**. Managers suffer the costs of working harder, but shareholders get the rewards. Thus managers may have an incentive to choose less effort than the shareholders would prefer, and less than managers would choose if they owned the company themselves.

II. THE 1980S: THE TAKEOVER BOOM

A. *The boom*

When managers are not acting as good agents for the shareholders, the price of the company's stock is lower than it could be. That creates a profit opportunity. If someone can buy the company and change the practices that are reducing shareholder value, stock prices will increase. The larger the agency problem, the larger the potential profit from a takeover. When it functions well, this market for corporate control is the ultimate market check on agency problems. Managers who are poor agents for the shareholders get replaced, and the firm may be restructured in ways that reduce the residual losses from agency problems that would otherwise occur.

In the 1980s, this market for corporate control boomed. Over the course of the decade, nearly half of major corporations received a takeover offer. Some outside investor saw a better way for the company to conduct its business and sought to take advantage of it. In competitive markets, investors will bid for the profit opportunity that a successful takeover provides, resulting in substantial gains to the original shareholders. On average, the 1980s takeovers that were accomplished through tender offers yielded a price premium of 30 percent. That is, the price the acquiring company offered was 30 percent higher than the stock price of the target company before the offer was announced.

One factor facilitating an active takeover market was a financing innovation: the development of "junk" bonds to finance takeovers. Before junk bonds, a potential acquiring company would have to raise the money to finance a takeover based essentially on its own creditworthiness. Because few firms could raise sizeable sums on this basis, only very large companies were potential buyers. Moreover, many firms were simply too big to take over, because there was essentially no company or individual who could raise the money to finance the transaction.

Junk bonds changed that. These high-risk debt securities greatly facilitated financing the transaction. The essential innovation was that a potential acquirer would offer the target company as collateral to back up the junk bonds. If bond buyers could be convinced that there was indeed a profit opportunity in the takeover transaction, they would be willing to finance the transaction. The result was that far smaller companies could be potential acquirers, because it was the target company that provided the collateral for the loan. Moreover, few, if any, firms were too big to acquire. Larger targets had more assets to serve as collateral and were therefore vulnerable as well.

As takeovers unfolded, managers resisted through the political process. There was little success at the federal level, although numerous ideas to restrict takeovers were debated. States, however, enacted more restrictive legislation. Often the state statutes allowed managers to consider interests other than those of the shareholders in deciding whether to accept a bid for the company. Thus managers could reject bids that were clearly better for the shareholders on the theory that the offer was worse for some other stakeholder. Judicial decisions also gave managers wide discretion to accept something other than the best offer. In the Time Warner merger, for example, Time Inc. and Warner Communications had been discussing a merger that would have required approval from Time's shareholders, in a stock-for-stock deal valued at $125 per share. Then Paramount offered $175 in cash per share for Time, and later raised the offer to $200. Time and Warner restructured the original deal so that it would no longer require shareholder approval, and Time rejected the Paramount offer without a shareholder vote. In 1990, the Delaware court allowed the restructured transaction to proceed without shareholder approval, and Time Warner was born.

The result of the legislative and judicial restrictions was that by the end of the 1980s, takeovers were far more difficult, and far less frequent, than they had been earlier in the decade. When an insider trading scandal disrupted the junk bond market, hostile takeover activity collapsed.

B. Conflicts over free cash flows

Probably the most common conflict between managers and shareholders that was behind many of the 1980s takeovers was disagreement about what to do with free cash flows. Free cash flow is cash in excess of what the company needs for ongoing operations and profitable investment opportunities in its core business. When there is extra cash, shareholders would like the money. They can invest it elsewhere on their own, and the appropriate investment will depend on the other holdings in their portfolio—something that will be different for each shareholder.

Managers, however, have an interest in retaining free cash flows. They have control over the resources, and do not necessarily want to give up that control. If there is no free cash available and a profitable investment opportunity comes along, managers will have to turn to the capital markets to fund the project. Bankers or other potential investors will scrutinize and question the project, its business plan, and its expected returns. In short, someone will be looking over the manager's shoulder and evaluating his or her recommendation. If free cash is available, however, there is little or no outside scrutiny. Managers can do what they think is best. Moreover, as discussed above, managers have a general interest in growth that shareholders do not necessarily share. Free cash can enable growth that may not be in the shareholders' best interests.

One solution to ongoing conflicts over free cash flows is a change in the capital structure of the firm to increase the amount of debt. Essentially, the company (or an outside investor in the case of takeovers) borrows the discounted present value of the free cash flow and gives the entire amount to the shareholders (in a stock buyback or a premium for their shares, for example). The cash flow that was formerly free cash is now needed to cover debt service obligations. Managers no longer have discretion over whether to keep the cash or pay it out, because the debt instrument is a legally binding obligation to make payments over time.

Most of the 1980s takeovers involved increases in the debt of the target firm, often substantial increases in debt. From an agency perspective, this debt increase was a way to remove an ongoing conflict over how to use free cash flows. In the post-takeover structure, managers no longer have a choice. They must make the debt service payments.

A. *The leveraged buyout solution*

One common solution to conflicts over free cash flows in 1980s takeovers was the leveraged buyout. In a leveraged buyout (LBO), a small group of investors buys the company and takes it private. In the classic LBO, it is the managers who purchase the company from the shareholders. In many instances in the 1980s, managers made an offer but were eventually outbid by an outside group. LBOs accounted for 30 to 40 percent of takeover transactions in the mid-1980s. They also commanded larger premiums than other transactions, averaging 56 percent over the share price before the bidding started.

An LBO results in a closer alignment of the interests of managers and shareholders, because managers are substantial shareholders. Managers have a large equity stake, typically 25 to 50 percent of the manager's net worth. They are therefore more committed to increasing the value of their stake in the company. In the mid-1980s, the median chief executive officer of a publicly traded company owned 0.25 percent of the equity in the company. In contrast, the typical head of an LBO unit owned 6.4 percent of the company. Because the company is not publicly traded, the manager's stake is relatively illiquid. There is no easy way to sell out or hedge the risk that value declines. With no easy exit, managers have a strong incentive to increase share value.

Compensation in an LBO was also much more closely tied to shareholder value. For the median CEO of a publicly traded company in the mid-1980s, creating $1,000 in shareholder value increased the CEO's compensation by $3.25. For an LBO chief, that same increase in shareholder value would increase compensation by $64. Thus the compensation structure helps to align the interests of managers and shareholders as well.

The other key difference in an LBO is the composition of the board of directors. In publicly traded companies, board members are frequently outsiders. They may be selected for their knowledge or expertise in a particular part of the business, but they typically do not have a personal stake in the company. Rather, they are acting as fiduciaries to protect the interests of shareholders. In an LBO, the board is usually composed of the outside capital providers who own the rest of the equity in the company. In seeking to do what is best for the shareholders, they are also seeking to increase the value of their own investments. Boards are usually smaller than comparable publicly traded companies, and they meet more frequently (often monthly). Again, incentives are more closely aligned than in a publicly traded company.

The effects of LBOs were quite consistent with the notion that better aligning incentives will result in better performance. One study examined a sample of early 1980s LBOs three years later. It found that earnings had increased an average of 42 percent. Cash flow increased 96 percent. This increase is particularly striking, because LBOs were more likely to occur in companies that had significant free cash flows to begin with. The LBOs were also much flatter organizations. They reduced the number of central office jobs per 1,000 production workers by 7.2. The typical LBO has fewer layers, and relies on line managers to make more decisions without extensive review or analysis from headquarters.

One particularly interesting finding concerns productivity before and after the LBO. Before the LBO, these companies had productivity that was 2 percentage points higher than the average company in their industry. After the LBO, productivity was 8.3 percentage points higher. Because these were more productive companies to begin with, it may have been harder for shareholders and directors to see how much better they could have been doing. That is, monitoring may have been less effective. After all, a common way to assess performance is to compare a company to other companies in the same industry. At least in terms of productivity these companies looked fine, but they clearly could have done much better.

III. THE 1990S: LASTING EFFECTS OF THE TAKEOVER BOOM

A. Changes in executive compensation

The success of the LBO model in the 1980s appears to have spurred changes in executive compensation that continued throughout the 1990s. Over the decade, total compensation of CEOs increased dramatically. In 1992, the average CEO in the S&P 500 received $2.7 million in total compensation. By 2000, that had risen to $14 million. All components of compensation increased significantly. Salary rose from $1 million to $2.4 million; bonuses rose from just under $600,000 to $2.4 million. But by far the most dramatic increase in compensation was options grants. In 1992, options grants were worth an average of $652,000 for a CEO of an S&P 500 company. In 2000, options grants were worth almost $6.9 million, more than 10 times as much. The result was a sharp increase in options grants as a fraction of total compensation, from 17 percent in 1992 to 49 percent in 2000. Total compensation declined somewhat in 2001 and 2002 when the dot-com stock market bubble burst, but options remained around half of the total.[1]

The result was a substantial increase in sensitivity of CEO pay to performance. Compared to the 1980s, the CEO's wealth was about three times more sensitive to either changes in shareholder value or changes in the return on equity in the 1990s. In the 1980s, an executive who could move his or her firm from the median market value to the 70th percentile in market value could increase personal wealth by about $250,000. In the 1990s, that same change was worth $1.4 million to the executive.[2]

Although other factors were undoubtedly at work, part of the growth of equity-based compensation was an attempt to emulate the success of the LBO model in the 1980s. There are, however, limits to pay for performance. In particular, pay for performance increases risk to managers, because stock prices change for reasons that have nothing to do with their contribution to firm performance. Because managers typically do not like risk, they must be compensated to accept a riskier pay package. That may account for some of the increase in salary over the period.

Another factor that contributed to the escalation in pay, and particularly the growth in options grants, was a legislative change. Faced with a populist outcry about executive compensation, Congress in 1994 limited the tax deductibility of executive compensation. Only $1 million in salary could be treated as an expense for corporate tax purposes, but the legislation did not limit "performance-based" compensation. The result was that many companies increased base compensation to the $1 million level that Congress had blessed, and added more performance-based compensation as well.

There are also important differences between the option-based pay for performance schemes of the 1990s and the LBO model. In the LBO model, the manager's investment in the company was relatively illiquid, both because it was in the form of stock rather than options and because the company was not publicly traded. Options are far more liquid, making it much easier for a manager to limit his or her losses.

Options may also create an incentive for managers to manipulate earnings, to maintain the short-term market value of their options. Some studies have found that firms with more options granted to executives were more likely to restate earnings at a later date. "Managed" earnings to meet market expectations were a key contributor to the Enron scandal, discussed later in this chapter.

Finally, options may create perverse incentives when a company's stock is overvalued. In the tech bubble that ended in 2000, many companies had market valuations that were considerably higher than their true value. When a company's shares are overvalued, it is not possible to increase share prices. Actions that seek to justify short-term stock prices that are too high may reduce long-run value.

---

[1]Jensen and Murphy. Remuneration: Where We've Been, How We Got to Here, What Are the Problems, and How to Fix Them. http://ssrn.com/abstract=561305 (July 2004).

[2]Carola Frydman and Raven E. Saks. Historical Trends in Executive Compensation, 1936–2005. http://www.vanderbilt.edu/econ/sempapers/Frydman1.pdf. January 18, 2007.

B. The growth of institutional investors

The 1990s also saw continued growth in the role of institutional investors. Institutional investors include mutual funds, insurance companies, banks, foundations, and pension funds. Often they are investing on behalf of others (e.g., mutual funds or pension funds). In 1980, institutions owned 37 percent of total U.S. equity. By 2000, their ownership share had risen to 51.4 percent. Among larger companies, the institutional ownership share is even higher. In 2000, institutional investors owned 61.4 percent of the 1,000 largest U.S companies. Institutional ownership has continued to grow, reaching $24 trillion in assets, amounting to 61 percent of all U.S. equity in 2005.[3]

Institutional investors are more able to monitor and attempt to influence corporate management than are individual investors. They clearly have a larger stake than do individual investors. They are professional investors, with the knowledge and expertise to understand how well managers are performing as agents for the shareholders. Individual investors who do not like management decisions have little choice but to sell. Institutions, however, because they often own large amounts of stock, find it difficult to sell without significantly influencing the market price and reducing the value of their remaining holdings.

State and local government retirement plans were early leaders of activism among institutional investors, and remain among the most active. These plans owned 2.75 percent of all U.S. equity in 1980, and 6.85 percent in 2005. One of the early activist institutional investors was CalPERS, the California Public Employees Retirement System, which began addressing governance issues with management in 1987. In 1992, it began publishing a list of companies that would be the focus of its attention. Usually CalPERS has pressed corporate governance issues, rather than specific management decisions. For example, it has frequently argued for independent board committees of outside directors to address various issues such as nominations or audits.

Activism by institutional shareholders was facilitated by an SEC rule change in 1992. The rule allowed shareholders whose only stake in the company was as an investor to talk to other shareholders without filing a proxy statement with the SEC. Before the change, an investor who wanted to talk to more than 10 shareholders had to file a proxy statement that was subject to review by the SEC staff, and could only say what was in the proxy statement. If management responded, any further response also required a new proxy statement, subject to the same review. With the elimination of the proxy statement requirement, communications among shareholders became easier, reducing the costs of coordinating group action.

It is clear that over the course of the 1990s, institutional investors became more active. The impact of that activism, however, is less clear. A review of 20 empirical studies of specific attempts to influence governance or management decisions concluded that "most evidence indicates that shareholder activism can prompt small changes in target firms' governance structures, but has negligible impact on share values and earnings."[4] A study of the short-run impact of a firm being added to the CalPERS focus list found a small positive impact on share value at the time of the announcement, indicating the market's assessment that targeting the firm will improve shareholder value. It could not find statistically significant evidence of a longer-run effect, however.[5] Other studies, however, have found that stock returns over the period from 1980 to 1996 were higher for companies that have more institutional ownership, suggesting that there may be a positive effect.

C. Changes in boards of directors

The decade of the 1990s also saw changes in corporate boards. Three trends were noteworthy.

First, there was increased use of nominating committees by boards of directors. As noted earlier in this chapter, when new board members are needed, boards have frequently turned to management for suggestions.

---

[3]The Conference Board. U.S. Institutional Investors Continue to Boost Ownership of U.S. Corporations. http://www.conference-board.org/utilities/pressDetail.cfm?press_ID=3046 (Jan. 22, 2007).

[4]J. M. Karpoff. "The Impact of Shareholder Activism on Target Companies: A Survey of Empirical Findings". Mimeo, University of Washington, September 2001.

[5]Brad M. Barber. Monitoring the Monitor: Evaluating CalPERS' Activism. http://papers.ssrn.com/sol3/papers.cfm?abstract_id=890321 (November 2006).

That approach can weaken the board's independence from management, and thus weaken its ability to oversee the managers to make sure they are operating in the shareholders' best interests. Nominating committees are a way to reduce that dependence on management. They allow the board to develop its own list of potential new members. Stock exchange rules adopted in 2003 now require all listed companies to have a nominating committee composed of outside directors.

Second, there was a trend toward smaller boards of directors. With a large board, directors may be tempted to rely on others rather than do the work necessary to evaluate matters that come before the board. This kind of free riding can undercut the board's effectiveness. With a smaller board, free riding is more visible to other board members, and is therefore less likely to occur. This trend has been reversed since the Sarbanes-Oxley Act, discussed in the next section, which significantly increased the workload on boards of directors.

Third, compensation for board members during the 1990s followed the trend of executive compensation toward equity-based compensation. As with executives, the idea is to better align the interests of shareholders and board members by giving board members a bigger stake in the success of the enterprise. Equity-based compensation for board members grew from 25 percent of compensation in 1992 to 39 percent in 1995. This trend has continued, with equity-based compensation now accounting for a majority of the compensation of board members.

VI. THE 21ST CENTURY: ENRON AND BEYOND

A. The Enron scandal

The 21st century opened with the collapse of a major American corporation due to accounting fraud. Enron began as a natural gas pipeline company. When natural gas was deregulated in the 1980s, Enron began transforming itself into a trading company. Initially it traded natural gas, but the business thrived and the company branched out into other areas. It became a trader and a market maker in electric power, coal, steel, paper and pulp, water, and broadband fiber optic cable capacity. By 2001, it operated in all of these physical markets, and engaged in extensive trading of the same products in financial markets as well. Although the company appeared to be extremely profitable, those profits were based on essentially fraudulent accounting for complex transactions with a number of "independent" partnerships that were in fact controlled by Enron insiders.

The collapse was rapid. In October 2001, the company disclosed $1 billion in losses, the chief financial officer was ousted, and the SEC launched a formal investigation. In November, the company revised its financial statements to reduce earnings over the previous four years by almost $600 million, and Standard and Poor downgraded its debt to "junk" status. In December 2001 the company filed for bankruptcy. Eventually, the former CEO and former chief financial officer were convicted of fraud.

From a governance perspective, key elements of Enron's structure looked fine. The board was mostly outside directors; only two of the 17 board members were insiders. The board had a separate audit committee, composed entirely of outsiders, with more expertise than was typical for many audit committees. The company had a well respected outside auditor in Arthur Andersen. But everything failed at once, leading to the rapid collapse.

Two problems were at the heart of the failure. One was the company's use of "mark to market" accounting. Under Enron's approach, when it signed a long-term deal, it would recognize the present value of the revenue and expenses from the entire time period of the contract immediately. Mark to market is a reasonable accounting approach if there is in fact a market for the asset, but in most cases there was not. Instead, the valuation depended on projections of future prices and interest rates over a period as long as 20 years, with very little objective basis for the projections. Changes in assumptions about future trends would change reported current earnings. For example, in 1999, Enron booked $65 million in profit from a South American natural gas deal based on a pipeline that had not yet been built.

A second problem was the use of off-balance-sheet "special purpose vehicles." These entities were carefully structured to avoid having to consolidate their financial statements with Enron's statements. Many of these special purpose vehicles were in fact funded with Enron stock, and were used to hedge risks of the company's other transactions. Because the only backing for the vehicles was company stock, the company was in effect insuring itself, but reporting the transaction as if the risk were hedged by a transaction with a third party. Moreover, a number of the special purpose vehicles were controlled by Enron insiders. What appeared on their face to be arms' length transactions were in fact self-dealing by the company's top officers.

Much of what Enron was trading was intrinsically difficult to value. For example, the company was trading futures in "dark fiber," which is installed fiber optic cable that has not yet been activated. Because the expensive part of installing cable is digging up the streets or stringing the wire, it is routine to install excess capacity, with the necessary electronics added later to activate that capacity as needed. Enron reasoned that such excess capacity would have value in the future, but it is very difficult to assess its current value.

Enron is also an example of the difficult incentives created when stock prices are too high and managers have a large stake in options in the company. At its peak, Enron's stock was over $90, a price that could only be justified by wildly unrealistic estimates of future growth. Rather than attempt to deflate expectations, Enron's managers launched projects that tried to justify the expectations, and used creative accounting to paint a rosy picture. These efforts ended up destroying shareholder value entirely.

Enron is perhaps also an illustration of the perils of success. Investors are likely to look much harder at a company that has problems to determine what it is really worth. But for a company that has been very successful over a long period of time, there appears to be less reason for scrutiny. Certainly Enron's principal investors could have looked harder, but they did not.

One factor contributing to limited scrutiny may have been the agency problems of portfolio managers. In early 2001, 60 percent of Enron's shares were held by institutional investors. Fund managers for institutions are frequently evaluated on how well they do compared to a benchmark such as the S&P 500. If Enron continued to do well, a fund manager who left it out of his or her portfolio would tend to underperform compared to the benchmark. If the stock is included, however, then even if it falls substantially, the manager will likely match the benchmark, simply because everyone else is also following the same strategy.

B. The Sarbanes-Oxley Act of 2002

Enron's failure was the dramatic event that provoked a political response. That response was the Sarbanes-Oxley Act of 2002. The law passed six months after Enron's bankruptcy filing, and, perhaps more importantly, three months before the midterm elections. As happens in many instances, Congress enacted legislation that had been pending without serious consideration for some time, and did so very quickly. Faced with a significant scandal, representatives were unwilling to tell the voters that they had not yet addressed the problem. The act, which applies to all publicly traded companies, required changes in three areas: the responsibility of top management, corporate governance, and the regulation of accountants and auditing.

Regarding top management responsibility, the act specified that the CEO and the CFO must personally certify the company's financial reports. If there are "knowing" misstatements in the financials, they are personally liable for a fine of $1 million and up to 10 years in jail. If financial statements are revised due to "misconduct," top officials must disgorge profits from any bonuses or stock sales during the year after the revised report. The effect of this requirement is to increase the risk of large stock sales, because there is some risk the gains will have to be returned, thereby making holdings less liquid.

Probably the most costly and controversial part of Sarbanes-Oxley is Section 404, which requires management to assess the adequacy of internal controls for financial statements. Auditors must also approve the adequacy of internal controls. The requirement has been very broadly interpreted as to where controls are necessary. Essentially anything that could affect the financial statements must be subject to adequate internal controls. Of course, anything that could affect either costs or revenues could affect the financial statements, giving the provision its breadth. For example, companies have found it necessary to assess the adequacy of internal controls to prevent the loss or theft of laptop computers and other hardware. Audits of these controls have significantly increased the demand for accountants, and are a significant component of the cost of compliance with the act.

From an agency perspective, the act generates an incentive to invest too much in controls. Managers realize major benefits from better controls, because controls reduce the risk in certifying the financial statements. Shareholders, however, pay the costs.

The act also required several governance reforms. A majority of the board must consist of outside directors. Companies must have an audit committee, composed entirely of outside directors. The audit committee must hire the auditor directly, rather than going through management. Auditors must report to the committee any alternative treatments of transactions that they discussed with management. The report must include the impact of alternative treatments and the treatment that the auditor prefers. Following passage of the act, other governance requirements were adopted as conditions for listing on the stock exchanges. Companies must have nominating committees composed of outside directors. Exchange rules also require shareholder approval of equity compensation plans.

Sarbanes-Oxley makes two major changes regarding accounting. First, auditors are prohibited from providing certain other services to their audit clients. These services include, for example, bookkeeping services, information systems, or certain kinds of consulting. Enron's auditor, Arthur Andersen, actually earned more in fees consulting for Enron than it earned from auditing the company. Concerned that auditors would give management favorable treatment to protect their consulting business, Congress prohibited many such services. Accounting firms can still provide the services, but only to companies that are not audit clients.

The act also established a Public Company Accounting Oversight Board (PCAOB, or "peekaboo") to make rules for the conduct of audits and rules governing how accounting firms are run. It can, for example, modify the list of services that accounting firms can or cannot provide for audit clients. Reflecting the distrust of accountants that characterized the debate over Sarbanes-Oxley, only two of the five members of the board can have an accounting background.

C. The impact of Sarbanes-Oxley

Sarbanes-Oxley was the first federal statute addressing U.S. corporate law in a substantive way. Previously, corporate law was exclusively a matter of state law, with a wide variety of approaches in different states.

The costs of complying with Sarbanes-Oxley proved considerable for many companies. One study estimated that first year compliance costs averaged $7.3 million for companies with market capitalizations over $700 million, and $1.5 million for companies with market capitalization between $75 and $700 million, a sharp contrast to the SEC's initial estimate that compliance would cost $91,000.[6] The costs have been disproportionately large for smaller firms. An SEC Advisory Committee charged with assessing the impact on small business estimated that in 2004, firms with revenues over $5 billion spent 0.06 percent of revenue on compliance, while companies with less than $100 million spent 2.55 percent of revenue.[7] The SEC repeatedly extended the compliance deadline for small firms for auditor assessment of Section 404 compliance. In the Dodd Frank Act, congress exempted firms with market capitalizations under $75 million permanently.

There is evidence that the act has led to some reduction in access to public capital markets. Because the act only applies to publicly traded companies, one way to avoid compliance costs is to go private, or stay private longer. In the 18 months after enactment, 146 companies delisted, roughly 60 percent more than the 94 companies that delisted in the 19 months before enactment. Firms going private were generally smaller firms, with less liquid markets and more management ownership compared to companies that remained publicly traded.

Sarbanes Oxley may also be responsible for a renewed surge in leveraged buyout transactions, although the evidence is far from clear. As noted above, going private transactions declined significantly after the 1980s takeover boom, particularly in the value of the companies taken private, with less dramatic declines in the number of transactions. Going private transactions increased substantially in the late 1990s, but there was a new surge of

---

[6] Joseph A. Grundfest and Steven E. Bochner, "Fixing 404," Michigan Law Review, Vol. 105, pp. 1643–1676 (June 2007).
[7] Final Report of the Advisory Committee on Smaller Public Companies to the SEC. http://www.sec.gov/info/smallbus/acspc/acspc-finalreport.pdf (April 23, 2006).

transactions in the 2000s, particularly from 2005 to the beginning of the financial collapse in mid 2007. In the last half of the 1980s, leveraged buyout transactions totaled $256 billion (in 2007 dollars); they reached $1 trillion in the period from 2000 to 2004. From 2005 to mid 2007, deals totaled almost $1.6 trillion. Although trends in the relative costs of debt and equity financing surely contributed to this surge, Sarbanes Oxley provided another reason for firms to consider going private.[8]

Several studies have indicated that the act has led some companies to conduct public offerings on foreign exchanges, particularly in London, rather than in the United States. Three different groups reviewed the evidence and came to the conclusion that Sarbanes-Oxley was a significant part of the reason. In 2006, the Committee on Capital Markets Regulation found a decline in foreign company IPOs in U.S. markets, an increase in domestic going private transactions, and venture capitalists exiting new companies through private sales rather than through IPOs. A study by McKinsey and Co., commissioned by the mayor of New York City and a senator from New York, reached similar conclusions in 2007, as did a commission created by the U.S. Chamber of Commerce.[9]

Sarbanes-Oxley has also led to changes in boards of directors. Boards have more meetings, particularly board members involved in audit and nominating committees. The increased workload for boards has led to some increase in board size, effectively reversing the reductions that occurred during the 1990s. It has also led to substantial increases in compensation. Median compensation for board members doubled between 1998 and 2004, reaching $86,000. As with Section 404 compliance costs, there has been a disproportionate impact on smaller firms. For small firms, directors' compensation per $1,000 of sales rose $1.21. For large firms, the increase was $0.10.

To some extent, Sarbanes-Oxley reduces flexibility in corporate governance decisions, which must all meet the act's requirements. There is, however, no one-size-fits-all solution to governance issues, and there is value in experimentation to identify the best approaches. Flexibility is essential to that experimentation. With less flexibility, Schumpeter would argue, there is less role for the entrepreneur in finding a better way to do things.

Flexibility can be difficult for regulators to embrace. Consider, for example, independence. Different mutual funds are organized in different ways. For some funds, the chairman of the fund is independent; in others, the chairman works for the company that sponsors the fund. The SEC believes that independence is a good thing, and has tried to require that each mutual fund have an independent chairman. There is, however, no difference in the returns for funds with independent and affiliated chairs (with a 1 basis point advantage for the affiliated funds). Costs for funds with affiliated chairs, however, are 16 basis points lower, and Morningstar ratings are higher (3.1 stars versus 2.6 stars). The rule was twice promulgated, challenged, and returned to the SEC, where it remains under consideration. It would appear, however, that different mutual fund organizations have found different but equally effective solutions for the governance issue.

D. Governance provisions in the Dodd Frank Act

Sarbanes Oxley was the first Federal law addressing corporate issues, but it was not to be the last. Calls to address the causes of the financial crisis of 2008 included numerous proposals for changes in corporate governance. Although many of these proposals were not adopted, the Dodd Frank Act included numerous provisions addressing corporate governance issues.

The so-called "say on pay" provision requires that public companies must periodically hold a non-binding advisory vote on the structure of their executive compensation plans. At least once every 6 years, companies must give shareholders the opportunity to vote on whether this advisory vote should occur every one, two, or three years. Companies must also hold an advisory vote on "golden parachutes," which provide additional compensation to managers who lose their jobs under certain circumstances.

---

[8]Steven N. Kaplan and Per Stromberg, "Leveraged Buyouts and Private Equity," NBER Working Paper 14207 (July 2008).
[9]See Roberto Romano, "The Sarbanes-Oxley Act at a Crossroads," in M. Ghertman and C. Menard, editors, *Regulation, Deregulation and Reregulation*, Edward Elgar, 2008.

Say on pay is mandatory in the United Kingdom, where there is a debate in the academic literature about its impact. Some argue that it has had positive effects on governance, but in the overwhelming majority of cases (all but eight out of thousands of votes), shareholders approve the board's proposal, and executive compensation has perhaps grown faster than in the United States. With the far larger number of companies in the United States, institutional investors are likely to focus on a relatively small number of "approved" pay plans, rather than an individualized analysis of each company's circumstances. Moreover, many institutional investors rely on a small number of proxy advisers to make recommendations about how they should vote their shares. Thus, to the extent that say on pay shifts power from boards of directors, the shift may be to the advisory firms, rather than to shareholders.[10]

Dodd Frank also expands the "clawback" provisions initially enacted in the Sarbanes Oxley Act. In the event of an earnings restatement, any bonus or equity-based compensation received in the previous three years (expanded from one year) must be repaid. The requirement also applies to a broader range of company officials, including all executive officers (instead of just the CEO and CFO). The provision is likely over inclusive; because it includes executives who may have had no responsibility for the restatement at all, but nonetheless may have to repay substantial amounts. It also risks unintended consequences. The narrower Sarbanes Oxley provision led companies to increase the amount of guaranteed salary and reduce the amount of executive compensation to both reduce the risk and compensate the top executives for the remaining risk; Dodd Frank could broaden this response well beyond the top financial executives.[11]

When Dodd Frank was enacted, the SEC was already well on its way to adopting a proxy access rule, which would require shareholder nominees for board positions to be included in the proxy materials sent to shareholders at the company's expense. The rule would likely have facilitated activism by institutional investors by reducing their costs of nominating their own candidates for the board. Congress specified that the SEC had authority to adopt such a rule, and the agency did so shortly after the statute passed. The rule would have allowed any shareholder who had owned at least 3 percent of the company's shares for the previous three years to nominate up to 25 percent of the board. These nominees would be included in the proxy statement on the same terms as the board's own nominees. The rule was reversed by the courts, however, which held that the SEC failed to give adequate consideration to the costs of the rule, including its likely effects on efficiency, competition, and capital formation. Moreover, the court noted, the agency relied on weak empirical studies and failed to respond to substantial problems identified during the rulemaking.[12]

V. SUMMARY

There are three key groups in governance issues: stockholders, the board of directors, and managers. Shareholders are the owners of the company, and their property rights are the basis of governance. They elect the board of directors, which is legally responsible for the affairs of the company. The board hires and reviews the top managers, who run the day-to-day business of the company. A frequent allegation is that it is really the managers in control. Top managers may be on the board, the board takes management's suggestions for new members, and management controls the information needed to make or evaluate decisions. Shareholders are left out.

Central to understanding governance is the agency problem: after a contract is set, the agent's incentives will differ from those of the principal. Agency problems arise whenever another person is hired to perform a task. Partial solutions to reduce agency problems include contracts that better align incentives, bonding, and monitoring. The costs of these arrangements are out-of-pocket costs; the remaining losses from agency problems are the residual loss. Corporate governance seeks to minimize total agency costs.

---

[10]Stephen M. Bainbridge, "The Corporate Governance Provisions of Dodd-Frank," (October 27, 2010). UCLA School of Law, Law-Econ Research Paper No. 10-14. Available at SSRN: http://ssrn.com/abstract=1698898
[11]Ibid.
[12]Business Roundtable v. SEC, 647 F. 3d 1144 (D.C. Cir. 2011).

Managers and shareholders may have different incentives in several different dimensions. They may differ about risk (managers are risk averse, shareholders are risk neutral), time horizons (managers are short term, shareholders are longer term), growth (managers want growth, shareholders only want profitable growth), perquisites (managers benefit, shareholders pay), and effort (managers suffer, shareholders benefit).

When managers are not good agents for the shareholders, there is an opportunity for a profitable takeover. In the 1980s, there was an extremely active market for corporate control. Many companies received takeover offers, and takeovers offered substantial premiums over previous share prices. Takeover offers were facilitated by the development of junk bond financing, which meant that far more companies and individuals could finance an acquisition, and far fewer companies were too big to take over.

The specific conflict that drove many 1980s takeovers was conflicts over free cash flows. Stockholders would like the money paid out; managers would rather retain it in the company, which reduces outside scrutiny from capital markets. Taking on more debt and giving the proceeds to shareholders in a stock repurchase is a strategy that forces managers to pay out the free cash flow over time.

Leveraged buyouts were a common solution to conflicts over free cash flow. Managers have a much larger equity stake in an LBO than in a typical publicly traded company, so incentives are better aligned. Managers' compensation is more sensitive to creating shareholder value, strengthening incentives. The board of directors is typically composed of outside capital providers, who are large shareholders. LBOs were highly successful, increasing earnings, cash flow, and productivity compared to the company's performance before the buyout. They were typically flatter organizations, with smaller headquarters staffs.

Changes in the 1990s reflected lasting effects of the takeover boom. Executive compensation increased, and shifted to become more equity based (primarily in the form of stock options). A congressional attempt to limit pay may have actually increased it. The stock options used for equity-based compensation differ from the LBO model, because they are more liquid and because they may create an incentive to manage earnings to protect the price of the executive's options in the short term. Options may create perverse incentives when a stock is overvalued.

The 1990s also saw the continued growth of institutional investors, who now own more than 60 percent of all U.S. equity. These investors are more able to monitor and attempt to exercise control over management than are individual investors. An SEC rule change made it easier for institutional investors to talk to each other to organize efforts to influence management. Activism by institutional investors, led by public employee retirement funds, increased. The evidence of the impact of that activism on corporate performance is mixed.

Boards of directors also changed in the 1990s. They made more use of nominating committees to find new members, reducing dependence on management. They became smaller, a trend that has reversed more recently. Compensation of board members became increasingly equity based.

The 21st century opened with the Enron scandal. From a governance perspective, everything looked right. The board was mostly outside directors, there was a separate audit committee of knowledgeable outsiders, and a well respected outside auditor. But everything failed at once. Mark to market accounting and the use of off-balance-sheet special purpose vehicles that were actually backed only by Enron's stock concealed the company's problems for a time, but once the problems were revealed, collapse was rapid. The company illustrates the agency problems of overvalued stock, and the perils of success. Agency problems of portfolio managers investing in an overvalued stock also contributed.

The Enron scandal led to the Sarbanes-Oxley Act of 2002. The act required the CEO and chief financial officer to personally certify financial statements. Section 404 required an audited assessment of internal controls. The act also required governance changes, including a separate audit committee that must hire the auditor directly and a requirement for the auditor to discuss with the committee any alternative treatments that were discussed with management. The law also prohibited auditors from performing certain services for audit clients, and established a Public Company Accounting Oversight Board.

Compliance costs with the Sarbanes-Oxley requirements have been significant, and disproportionately impacted small businesses. There has been some loss of access to public capital markets, with some firms going or remaining private to avoid its requirements. U.S. capital markets were put at a competitive disadvantage with markets abroad, particularly the London market. Board workloads increased, along with compensation for board members, which also disproportionately affected small firms. The act reduces flexibility in responding to governance issues.

The Dodd Frank Act also included provisions affecting corporate governance. It gave shareholders "say on pay," requiring an advisory shareholder vote on the company's executive compensation plan. Some argue that this provision is more likely to empower advisory firms that recommend to institutional investors how they should vote their shares, rather than shareholders themselves. The Act also expanded the clawback provisions originally enacted in the Sarbanes Oxley Act to cover more executives and a longer period of time. The effect may be to reduce the use of incentive compensation to executives. Dodd Frank also authorized the SEC to issue rules granting proxy access to nominations of directors from institutional shareholders. Although the SEC adopted such rules, they were rejected by the courts.

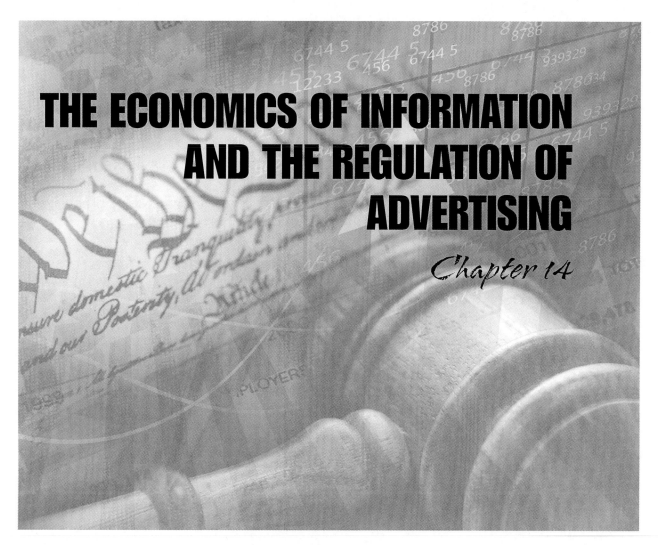

THE ECONOMICS OF INFORMATION AND THE REGULATION OF ADVERTISING

Chapter 14

As discussed in Chapter 2, the textbook model of perfect competition assumes that all participants are perfectly informed. In reality, however, information is imperfect. If consumers lack information about price, sellers will have a certain amount of power over price and can restrict output to raise the price. If consumers lack information about product characteristics, demand may not reflect the choices consumers would make with additional information. The result may be excessive consumption if consumers lack information about negative characteristics of the product, or too little consumption if consumers lack information about product benefits.

A more informative analysis, however, starts from a different premise. Like everything else in life, information is costly. There are costs of producing information, costs of disseminating information, and costs to consumers of processing, understanding, and using the information they obtain. Because information is costly, it will not be optimal for consumers, or anyone else, to become fully informed. Instead, one of the many decisions that consumers must make is how much information to obtain. Rational consumers will seek additional information until the marginal benefits of added information just equal the marginal costs of obtaining that information. The more it costs to obtain additional information, the more rational consumers will choose to remain uninformed. Reducing ignorance is simply not worth the costs.

In this chapter, we first consider markets for information, and in particular, seller incentives to provide information. We then turn to the regulation of advertising, the area of consumer protection regulation that most impacts markets for information.

I. THE MARKET FOR INFORMATION

A. Information problems

Numerous sources of information are readily available to consumers. Information is available for purchase from intermediaries such as *Consumer Reports*. Consumers can hire experts to assist them in finding the product or service that best fits their needs. They can also obtain information from press articles or product reviews. Moreover, a major source of information is consumers' own search activities: shopping.

The market for information, however, suffers from its own problems. From one perspective, information is a public good. It is, of course, costly to produce, but once it is produced, everyone can use the same information without reducing the amount available. Moreover, it is difficult to exclude others from using information. Once one person knows something, he or she can freely share that knowledge with others. Like any other public good, markets may produce too little information.

Consumer search also generates external benefits. One person's shopping for a better price encourages sellers to hold prices down to attract the shopper's business. Because sellers cannot easily charge different prices to different consumers, consumers who do not shop benefit as well. Consumers do not consider this external benefit in deciding how much to search, and therefore might not search as much as they should.

There is another side to the search externality, however, that is more important: not everyone needs to search in order to achieve competitive outcomes. As long as there are enough people searching to constitute a market worth competing for, competition for the informed minority will require sellers to charge the competitive price. Even though many, perhaps most, consumers are poorly informed, the competitive market price will prevail because informed consumers will police the marketplace.

The same process works for product characteristics as well. As long as there are enough consumers who care about the characteristic and shop for it, producers have an incentive to offer and improve that characteristic. Uninformed consumers who choose randomly will benefit as well. Again, competitive outcomes will prevail because informed consumers will police the marketplace.

B. Seller-provided information

Probably the most important source of consumer information is sellers themselves. Sellers can capture all of the benefits of information, as long as the information is specific to their product. Thus, the public good nature of information is less of a problem for the provision of information than it might be. Sellers do not care if potential buyers share the information, because all who use the information to purchase the seller's product will benefit the seller.

The seller's incentive to provide positive information about their product is obvious. That is what much of advertising seeks to do: it tells consumers about product features and characteristics they are likely to find attractive. Sellers will advertise products with different characteristics to emphasize the particular features that differentiate their product from others, to attract the consumers who find that offering most attractive. The result is competing, incomplete information. Although each product emphasizes its positive features, consumers will find it easy to find the product with the characteristics that best satisfy their preferences.

Consider, for example, the market for hot dogs. Some consumers prefer kosher hot dogs, but others do not care. Some prefer beef, some prefer turkey, and others prefer pork. Some prefer long skinny hot dogs, while others prefer shorter, plumper ones. No seller offers a checklist of the possible features of hot dogs that provides complete information. Instead, each seller emphasizes the features that it believes are most likely to attract consumers to its product. Information is incomplete, but it remains easy for consumers to find the product they prefer. We could imagine an alternative world in which non-kosher hot dogs all disclosed that fact, but it would not make it any easier for those who prefer kosher to find what they want.

Sellers also have incentives to disclose negative information about their product, as long as there are differences among the products. Less of a negative characteristic is a positive feature just like any other, and sellers have an incentive to tell consumers about their advantage. Numerous sellers, for example, advertise that their product is "fat free" or "low fat." Consumers are likely to assume the worst about a seller who says nothing, so even higher fat products also have an incentive to disclose. They will, of course, emphasize the positive, advertising that they are "reduced fat" or "less fat than Brand X." But the negative characteristic will be disclosed.

This result is known as the unfolding principle. Sellers with the least of the undesirable characteristic will disclose that fact, which sets in motion an incentive for other sellers with just a little more to disclose. Information will continue to "unfold" until all but the worst product on this characteristic disclose. Consumers will assume the worst from silence, and they will be right!

Unfolding will not work if all products share the negative characteristic. No cigarette brand, for example, can advertise that it is less harmful than another, because there are no differences among brands in the risk. Thus, unfolding never begins, and absent a requirement, no brand would have an incentive to disclose the risks of smoking. Unfolding is likely to work better when there is a standard measurement of the characteristic, because it makes it easier for sellers to communicate where they stand compared to competing brands.

C. Costs of requiring information

When there are actual or perceived problems in information markets, the most common regulatory approach is to require the provision of additional information. Disclosing an additional fact often seems like a cheap step to take, and one that regulators sometimes think cannot hurt. However, there are costs of requiring information, and too much can actually make things worse.

For consumers, additional information on a product label or in an advertisement may result in "information overload." Adding more information will increase the cost of using information, because consumers must read and understand the entire message to find the items they are interested in. If consumers decide that the information is not worth the effort, they may simply ignore the new, longer message entirely. The result may be more information on the package (or in the advertisement), but less information actually received and understood by the consumer. Over-the-counter pain relievers are a good example. Somewhere on the label is precise information about the proper dose. Rather than read the label to find the relevant information, a consumer may simply decide to take two tablets or capsules. Consumers may also misunderstand disclosed information, or draw incorrect inferences from the fact that the information is disclosed at all. An experimental test of disclosures of the yield spread premium that mortgage brokers earn, for example, found that the disclosure reduced consumers' ability to identify the lowest cost mortgage.[1]

Required information may also displace other information. Whatever is displaced has some value, even if it is only white space. White space enhances readability and can highlight other information in an ad or on a package, thereby increasing communication effectiveness. Or, the need to include specific information may lead the seller to delete or reduce the size of some other information in the communication. The value of the deleted information is part of the cost of requiring information, as is the reduced communications effectiveness of other message elements that are less likely to be noticed.

For sellers, disclosure requirements increase the cost of providing information that might trigger the requirement. Rather than face the added costs for advertising time or space, sellers may choose not to provide the triggering information. The result may be that consumers have less information than they did before the requirement. For example, an FTC requirement that advertisers disclose all material details of a warranty whenever any portion of the warranty was mentioned discouraged advertisers from promoting their warranties in advertising. Removal of the detailed disclosure requirements in 1985 offered the potential for more robust competition over warranty terms. Some further examples of this problem are discussed later in this chapter.

---

[1] J. Lacko and J. Pappalardo, *The Effect of Mortgage Broker Compensation Disclosures on Consumers and Competition: A Controlled Experiment*, Bureau of Economics Staff Report, Washington, DC: Federal Trade Commission, 2004.

A third cost of requiring information relates to warnings. Some warnings provide specific information about the hazard—that a product is flammable or poisonous, for example. Other warnings simply identify the possibility that there is a risk, without more specific identification of the risk. For years, for example, the warning on cigarettes stated that the Surgeon General had determined that smoking "may be hazardous." Such generalized warnings only convey information because they are selective. Virtually any product could truthfully be labeled as a product that "may be hazardous." The warning has value if it identifies particular risks that consumers should pay attention to, but it loses its meaning if it is used everywhere it might be true.

Finally, providing additional information can have unintended consequences. Providing measurements of certain product characteristics, for example, is likely to encourage competition on aspects that are measured, rather than other characteristics of the product. Indeed, encouraging that competition is often part of the rationale for introducing the measurement. But less attention to other attributes of the product can be the source of unintended consequences. As we noted in Chapter 10, for example, competition on gas mileage may reduce the weight of automobiles, with adverse safety consequences. Measurements of the amount of major vitamins may encourage fortification with those vitamins. The recommended daily intakes, however, are based on the assumption that the vitamins are derived from natural sources and will therefore come with adequate amounts of other trace nutrients. Fortification violates that assumption, and may result in reduced intake of other nutrients that are also important.

D. Information versus regulation

Rather than providing information, government may also decide to regulate the product directly. If the problem is lack of information, providing information is the incentive-compatible solution, and is likely to be the best way to address the problem. Sometimes, however, provision of information may not be the best solution.

Two factors favor regulation over the provision of information. First, when the costs of using information are very high, product regulation may be a better solution. Second, when consumers would all make the same choice, regulation may be a better solution.

Consider first the costs of using information. If large amounts of information are necessary to address the problem, the costs of using the information will tend to be high. Similarly, when the information is extremely complex, it may be difficult for consumers to understand, and therefore difficult for them to use. Providing information in these circumstances may not really solve the problem. The information might be available, but if it is too costly for consumers to use, it will do little to correct the market failure. There might be a disclosure-based solution to a problem like carcinogenic food additives, for example, but expecting consumers to learn about the potential risks from the wide variety of chemicals used in food production and packaging would impose tremendous information costs. Moreover, what consumers would most need to know is the relative risks of different alternatives, and providing such detailed information could be exceedingly complex.

A second factor favoring regulation is the uniformity of consumer preferences. If all consumers with complete information would make the same choice, there is little to be gained from imposing the costs of using that information on consumers. If government makes the choice, then consumers do not have to concern themselves with the issue at all. For example, given a choice between a carcinogenic food color additive and a non-carcinogenic one, presumably virtually all consumers would choose the non-carcinogenic alternative. If so, banning the carcinogenic additive is an efficient solution.

In other circumstances, however, preferences may differ. The advantage of information remedies is that they allow consumers with different preferences to choose the alternative that best satisfies their needs. Consider, for example, the saga of saccharin. In the 1970s, information began to emerge from animal studies that saccharin might cause cancer in rats. Although it was the only artificial sweetener available on the market at the time, the FDA proposed to ban the chemical. One important use was in diet soft drinks, and the proposed ban provoked an outcry among diet soft drink consumers. Many of them were willing to take the presumed cancer risk rather than have to give up soft drinks or switch to much higher-calorie beverages sweetened with various sugars. As a result, Congress created a "temporary" exemption for saccharin, allowing the sale of saccharin-containing products with a warning that the chemical had been shown to cause cancer in laboratory animals. This temporary solution continued for almost 25 years, until the government concluded that the animal studies were not relevant to human cancer risks after all. During this period, the labeling solution allowed consumers to make their own choices about whether to take the risks of cancer or calories, and many continued to consume diet soft drinks.

II. Regulating Advertising

Advertising is perhaps the regulatory arena where the connection between imperfect information and regulatory policy is most transparent. Advertising is, after all, a principal channel for the seller-provided information discussed above. Even when information is available on product labels, consumers often rely on advertising to identify which products are worthy of further consideration, and many may choose based on advertising alone.

The central tension in advertising regulation is striking an appropriate balance between the free flow of information and the need to assure that information is truthful and reliable. Because seller-provided information is so important, preserving sellers' ability to convey that information through advertising is vital as well. Moreover, since 1976 the Supreme Court has held that truthful advertising is constitutionally protected speech under the First Amendment to the Constitution. (We will explore the market impact of advertising in more detail in the next section.) At the same time, sellers often have incentives to misrepresent their products, or, more commonly, to overstate their benefits and understate their risks. Advertising is information, but it is information with a clear point of view. If consumers are to be able to rely on advertising, it needs to be truthful and reliable.

The primary agency regulating advertising is the Federal Trade Commission, although other agencies have authority over advertising for particular products. The FDA, for example, regulates advertising for prescription drugs, and the Alcohol and Tobacco Tax and Trade Bureau in the Treasury Department has authority over alcohol advertising.

Unlike many areas of government intervention, advertising regulation relies primarily on case-by-case enforcement against companies that engage in "unfair or deceptive" advertising, rather than specific rules about exactly what is permitted. Companies are generally free to say what they want, provided that it is truthful and not deceptive, subject to government enforcement if they overstep the bounds. Advertising rules are often difficult to write because context is often crucial in determining how consumers will interpret a particular claim. Case-by-case enforcement allows fuller consideration of the message a particular communication is actually likely to convey to consumers.

This section begins by considering three issues that shape advertising regulation: the effect on competition, the interpretation issue, and the problem of incomplete information. It then considers the legal standard for finding advertising or other practices deceptive or unfair, and the derivative notion that an advertiser must have substantiation for the likely truth of its claims before making them.

A. Issues in advertising regulation

1. Advertising and Competition

Advertising is an important competitive tool in markets for consumer goods and services. Much of what we know empirically about its impact on market performance stems from studies of restrictions on advertising. These studies indicate that advertising reduces consumer prices, leads to improvements in products, and reduces the disparities among different demographic groups.

Results of several key studies of the impact of advertising on price are presented in Figure 14-1. The first study examined state prohibitions on advertising of eyeglasses, and found that prices were significantly higher in states that had such prohibitions. Similarly, states that prohibited advertising of the retail prices of prescription drugs had higher prices. Such blanket prohibitions on advertising were overturned when the U. S. Supreme Court extended the First Amendment's protection of freedom of speech to "commercial speech."

Subsequent restrictions on advertising were more subtle, but still had adverse effects on market performance. Attorney advertising restrictions, for example, varied considerably, with restrictions on broadcast advertising in

Figure 14-1. Price reductions when advertising restrictions are removed.

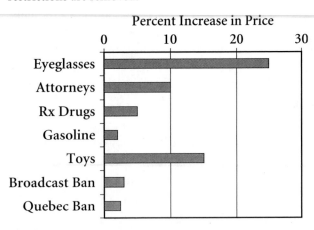

Percent Increase in Price

some states, prohibitions on the use of pictures in others, and requirements that advertising must be "dignified." States with more restrictions on advertising had higher prices for routine legal services. Restrictions on the media where advertising is permitted are associated with higher prices as well. The ban on broadcast advertising of cigarettes, for example, increased cigarette prices.

Even advertising directed to children has been found to reduce prices. The introduction of television toy advertising was associated with significant price declines, both over time as advertising was introduced and withdrawn, and across geographic markets where toys were advertised and where they were not. Similarly, Quebec's ban on television advertising to children has been found to raise the price of children's cereals in Quebec compared to other provinces. Prices for adult or family cereals, however, which could still advertise, were no higher in Quebec than elsewhere.

The price effects of advertising do not appear to depend on whether advertisements actually include price information. Price advertising has been found to lower prices in studies of retail gasoline markets, prescription drugs, and retail liquor stores. Restrictions are also associated with higher prices even where advertising rarely, if ever, includes price information, as in the studies of cereals, toys, and cigarettes discussed above. Thus, the critical factor appears to be the general competitive effects of advertising, rather than the specific effects of advertising price.

Advertising also encourages product improvements. The ability to advertise an improvement is an important part of the incentive to make such improvements in the first place. There is little incentive to develop a better product if the seller cannot tell consumers about the improvement.

Some of the best evidence of the impact of advertising on product changes comes from the introduction of health claims for foods. The FTC regulates food advertising, but the FDA regulates food labels. Until the late 1980s, the FDA regarded any claim on a food label about the relationship between diet and disease as a drug claim and therefore prohibited unless the manufacturer wanted to go through the long and elaborate drug approval process. In the 1960s, for example, the FDA had seized packages of Quaker oatmeal as a misbranded drug, because the label discussed the relationship between fiber and serum cholesterol. Although some health claims were made in advertising, they were relatively infrequent until claims were also permitted on food labels.

Regulatory change began with an act of corporate civil disobedience. For several years, the National Cancer Institute had recommended that Americans should increase the amount of fiber in their diets, because diets high in fiber could reduce the risk of some kinds of cancer. In 1984, Kellogg developed a marketing campaign for its high fiber All Bran cereal built around this recommendation. Although the campaign was in clear violation of existing FDA regulations, it was developed in conjunction with the National Cancer Institute—a different part of the same cabinet agency. Moreover, the FTC quickly endorsed the campaign, and the FDA decided not to take action against it.

The market impact of the campaign is shown in Figure 14-2. Before the campaign, there was no trend in the fiber content of cereals, despite the NCI's longstanding recommendation.[2] After the campaign began, however, there was a significant trend toward more fiber in cereals. Although some feared that fiber advertising might lead to offsetting increases in other "bad" nutrients such as sodium and fat, there was no significant trend in these

---

[2] The discussion of health claims and the figures on their impact are based on two studies by Pauline M. Ippolito and Alan D. Mathios at the Federal Trade Commission: *Health Claims in Advertising and Labeling: A Study of the Cereal Market*, August 1989; and *Information and Advertising Policy: A Study of Fat and Cholesterol Consumption in the United States, 1977–1990*, September 1996.

Figure 14-2. Findings: significant increase in market share–weighted fiber content of cereals.

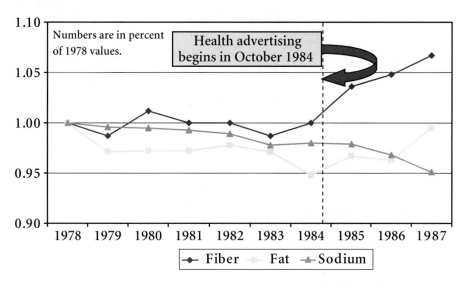

Numbers are in percent of 1978 values.

Health advertising begins in October 1984

Fiber   Fat   Sodium

nutrients either before or after the campaign. This is consistent with the unfolding principle, discussed above. If some cereals increase fiber content but increase fat or sodium as well, it is in some other seller's interest to advertise "high in fiber and less fat too."

The FDA's decision not to act against the Kellogg advertising campaign led to increases in health claim advertising in other areas as well. One prominent group of claims concerned the relationship between serum cholesterol and the risk of heart disease. Saturated fat increases serum cholesterol levels, which raises the risk of heart disease; polyunsaturated fats and monounsaturated fats can reduce serum cholesterol levels. Claims about the relationship appeared in less than 2 percent of food advertising in magazines before 1984, and rose sharply to just over 8 percent of advertising in 1989. Figure 14-3 shows that, similar to the trend with fiber, fat consumption followed the claims. Although there were some declines in fat and saturated fat consumption between 1977 and 1985, there were much sharper and more significant declines after the increase in health claim advertising.

In addition to reducing price and improving products, advertising also tends to narrow differences among demographic groups. Some people are good at finding and using information. In the absence of advertising, these people are more likely to know about, for example, the NCI's fiber recommendations or the latest

Figure 14-3. Fat and saturated fat consumption in men, 19–50 years, spring and summer.

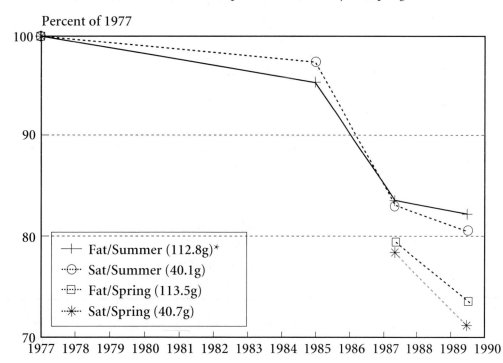

Percent of 1977

Fat/Summer (112.8g)*
Sat/Summer (40.1g)
Fat/Spring (113.5g)
Sat/Spring (40.7g)

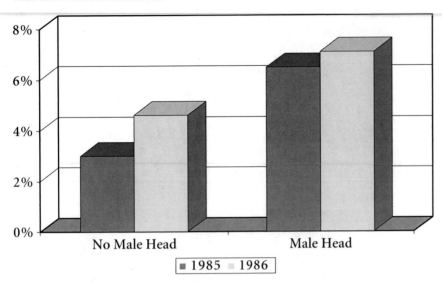

Figure 14-4. Percentage eating fiber cereals: households with and without male head.

1985 ▪ 1986

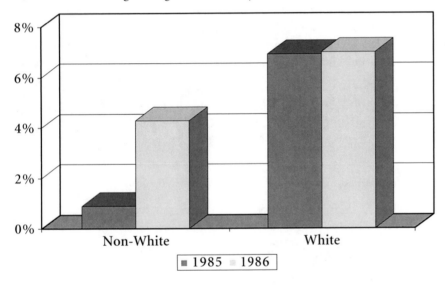

Figure 14-5. Percentage eating fiber cereals, by race.

1985 ▪ 1986

information on saturated fat and heart disease. Others are less skilled (or less interested) in using such information. When the information appears in advertising, it is likely to reach a much broader audience than it did before. As those less skilled at using information learn from advertising, differences among demographic groups tend to narrow.

Figures 14-4 and 14-5 show some of the narrowing of differences that occurred in response to health claims about fiber. Households with no male head tend to be single-parent households, which are likely to have less time for keeping up with the latest nutrition news. This group showed far larger increases in fiber consumption than the traditional two-parent family (Figure 14-4). Similarly, non-white families showed much larger increases in fiber consumption than white households (Figure 14-5). Thus, racial differences narrowed as well. Similarly, studies of the bans on eyeglasses advertising found that in states that prohibited advertising, prices were highest for the least-educated consumers.

The competitive impact of advertising highlights the importance of the free flow of information. When information can flow freely, prices are lower, products are improved, and differences among demographic groups are narrowed.

2. The Interpretation Problem

Marketing communications are almost always brief and presented in times and places where consumers may not pay full attention. Although they are carefully crafted to convey their message, any communication can go awry—the speaker intends one message, but the listener understands a message that is somewhat different. Inevitably some listeners will understand the message in a way that is not correct, and is misleading to that listener. If an advertiser shows a short message to 100 million people watching the Super Bowl, some of them are likely to get it wrong.

Misunderstanding is not confined to marketing messages. However straightforward the message might seem, some are likely to misinterpret it. In academic studies of brief communications, some aspect of both advertising and editorial content is misunderstood by 20 to 30 percent of the audience. Advertisements are slightly less likely to be misinterpreted than editorial content, but the difference is not statistically significant.

The fact that nearly any message will be misunderstood by some creates the interpretation problem. If regulators insist on communications that cannot be misunderstood, the result is likely to be communications that are also uninformative. Because every communication will likely mislead someone, it is critical to balance the accurate information provided to the majority against the potential costs to those who might misunderstand.

In the past, the Federal Trade Commission sought to insist on advertising that was clear enough that "wayfaring men, though fools" would not misunderstand. This standard, known as the "fools test," was formally abandoned in the 1980s. During its heyday, it produced some amazing cases.

In the 1940s, Clairol introduced the first hair dye that would not wash out when shampooed, and advertised it as "permanent." The FTC interpreted the message as meaning that the product would color hair that had not yet grown out. Such an approach makes it more difficult to convey a significant product advantage. The Commission challenged a one-volume desktop encyclopedia that claimed to contain "everything you ever wanted to know about every conceivable subject." In truth and in fact, the Commission said, it did not contain all of the world's knowledge. Probably the highlight of extreme interpretations to guard against any possible misinterpretation was the guides for advertising "automatic" sewing machines. With automatic washing machines, the Commission reasoned, consumers understood that all you needed to do was put in the clothes, add soap, and turn on the machine. Clean clothes will emerge when the "automatic" cycle is done. An automatic sewing machine should work the same way: put in the cloth, add thread, and out comes a freshly made garment. As recently as 1979, the Commission contended that "every body needs milk" was deceptive because it included those who were allergic to milk, a claim that was ultimately rejected by the Administrative Law Judge.

If advertising were still governed by the fools test, it would be more difficult to convey legitimate product advantages in ways that consumers would notice and remember. That, however, is an essential part of the free flow of information. As one commentator noted, "some sorts of messages must be either complex or non-informative. If complexity confuses, perhaps some confusion is acceptable."[3]

3. The Completeness Problem

Because marketing messages are short, they are inevitably incomplete. As a result, it is always possible for regulators to identify some additional information that would be useful to at least some consumers. Moreover, it is tempting to require advertisers to include that additional information. Requiring too much information, however, may effectively prevent the advertiser from providing any information at all.

One of the clearest examples is the FDA's requirements for disclosures to accompany prescription drug advertising, which were written with advertising to physicians in mind. They required the advertisement to include a so-called "brief summary" of prescribing information, amounting to roughly half a page of fine print in a medical journal advertisement. When pharmaceutical manufacturers began advertising directly to consumers, this requirement was costly but possible in print advertising, but it was impossible on television. Thus, the requirement effectively prohibited television advertising to consumers for prescription drugs. Although the FDA had relaxed its policy, it has never revised the regulation. The agency now permits direct-to-consumer television advertising to identify the major product risks and refer consumers to a print advertisement where they can see the "brief summary," although it seems unlikely that any appreciable number of consumers do so.

The response to the growth of health claims for foods provides another illustration of the effects of requiring more information. Figure 14-6 illustrates the sharp increase in claims about the relationship between diet and disease that began in 1984.[4] Congress responded with the Nutrition Labeling and Education Act of 1990, which brought significant changes to the regulatory environment for health claims. Under the statute and its implementing regulations, which became effective in 1993 (for health claims) and 1994 (for nutrient content claims), health claims were only permitted after prior FDA approval of the substance of the claim. The

---

[3]George J. Alexander, *Honesty and Competition: False Advertising Law and Policy under FTC Administration*, 1967, p. 227.

[4]The overall picture is quite similar for all health claims, regardless of the disease they concern. Focusing on heart and cholesterol claims is useful because the science supporting these claims has been clear since at least the 1960s. Figure 14-6, and the following discussion, is drawn from an FTC study that tracked the content of food advertising in magazines from 1977 to 1997. See P. M. Ippolito and J. K. Pappalardo, *Advertising Nutrition & Health: Evidence from Food Advertising, 1977–1997*, Washington, DC: Federal Trade Commission, 2002.

Figure 14-6. Heart and cholesterol claims.

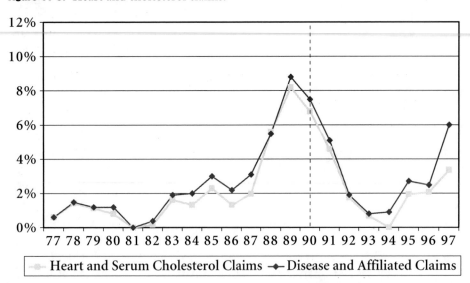

Heart and Serum Cholesterol Claims   Disease and Affiliated Claims

regulations included detailed "model claims" with large amounts of information, typically a page or so, about the relationship and which population groups were most at risk for the particular condition. Moreover, the rules prohibited claims for certain products with "bad" nutrition profiles. For example, high-fat products were no longer permitted to make claims about the relationship between fat composition and heart disease.

These changes resulted in substantial declines in the incidence of health claims, particularly those concerning heart disease and serum cholesterol. These claims fell from 8.2 percent of all advertising in 1989 to zero in 1994. A significant part of the decline was apparently due to the belief that claims must include the entire, burdensome model claims. When the FDA proposed in 1994 to clarify that the full model claim was not required (and the FTC clarified the relationship between the labeling rules and advertising), health claims again began to increase. By 1997 health claims again appeared in 6 percent of ads, and heart and serum cholesterol claims had returned to just under 4 percent.

Undoubtedly the category most heavily affected by the new rules was advertising for fats and oils. As Figure 14-7 shows, in 1988 and again in 1990, 45 percent of all advertising for fats and oils included a disease-related claim. These claims, a clear illustration of the unfolding principle, provided information about the importance of fat composition, particularly saturated fats, to the risk of heart disease. The regulations, however, prohibited health claims for products that were high in fat, as fats and oils necessarily are. Thus, by 1994, these claims had entirely disappeared from advertising for fats and oils.

Figure 14-7. Percentage of fats and oil ads with disease and affiliated claims.

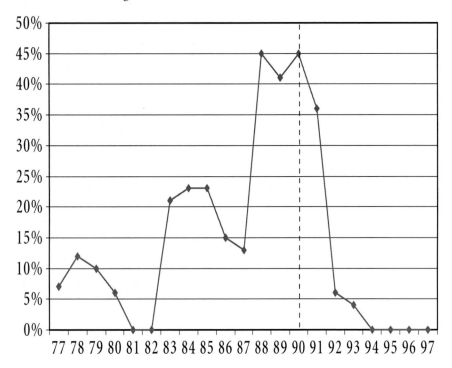

With less ability to explain to consumers why fat composition mattered, there was less incentive for fats and oils manufacturers to discuss fat composition at all. The trends are illustrated in Figure 14-8. The total number of advertisements for fats and oils

Figure 14-8. Number of fat and oil ads with saturated fat claims.

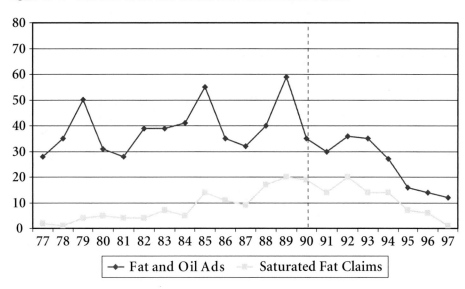

declined, as did the number of ads that included saturated fat content information. From a peak of 20 ads discussing saturated fat in 1992, the number of ads fell to only 1 in 1997. With less information about both saturated fat content and its importance to health, consumer choices shifted toward cooking oils with more saturated fat and less monounsaturated fat.[5]

Requirements for specific disclosures to accompany claims often create particularly heavy burdens for comparative advertising claims, simply because there is often more that can be disclosed: the number describing the advertised product, the competitive product, and the absolute or comparative difference in the measurement. Although always useful, and arguably necessary to prevent deception in some circumstances, it is very difficult to argue that a truthful comparison is always misleading in the absence of this full set of information. Nonetheless, the food labeling regulations generally require more information to accompany comparative claims about nutrient content, even though such claims are particularly likely to facilitate consumer choice. With the exception of comparative claims about total fat content, comparative claims generally declined in frequency after the rules took effect.

One particular example is claims about calorie content, and comparative calorie claims in particular. The trends in the incidence of such claims are illustrated in Figure 14-9. Part of the theory of the regulatory changes was that if consumers just focused on fat, calories would take care of themselves because fat is so high in calories. Thus, the regulations made claims about fat content relatively easy, and claims about total fat content increased after the rule. Calorie claims, however, decreased, and comparative calorie claims, subject to further disclosure requirements, fell even more. We succeeded in shifting the focus from calories to fat, but the increase in obesity since 1990 certainly raises questions about whether that was really an improvement.

Figure 14-9. Percentage of ads with calorie or dieting claims.

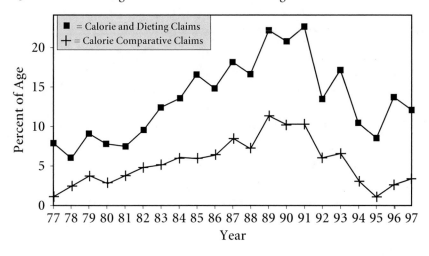

The paradoxical effect of the changes in the rules governing health claims was that an effort to fine-tune the information available to consumers resulted in the provision of less information about those product characteristics. Each individual claim that appeared may have been more

---

[5]A. Mathios. "The Importance of Nutrition Labeling and Health Claim Regulation on Product Choice: An Analysis of the Cooking Oils Market," *Agricultural and Resource Economics Review*, 27(2), 159–168 (1998).

complete and informative, but the mix of claims changed to avoid the new regulatory burdens. Advertising claims about relevant health characteristics of products generally became less common.

B. Marketing communications and the law

Under the FTC act, an advertisement or other marketing communication is prohibited if it is "unfair or deceptive." The vast majority of cases, particularly those involving advertising, are based on deception.

1. Deception

In 1983, the Commission disavowed the "fools test," which had fallen into disuse in any event, and articulated a new definition of deception. An act or practice is deceptive if it is "likely to mislead consumers, acting reasonably in the circumstances, about a material issue." We consider each element in turn.

First, a representation must be "likely to mislead." It is not necessary to establish that anyone was actually misled, because the commission is empowered to stop acts or practices before they actually cause harm.[6] In part to address the interpretation problem, however, it must be *likely* that consumers are misled, not merely possible. Maybe someone actually thought that Clairol's permanent hair dye would color hair that had not yet grown out, but that result hardly seems likely.

Second, whether a representation is misleading depends on how it is understood by "consumers acting reasonably in the circumstances." This element in particular is intended to address the interpretation problem. The issue is whether it is reasonable to think the advertiser *made* a particular claim, not whether it is reasonable to *believe* the claim is actually true. Under the deception standard, consumers are entitled to rely on what the advertiser actually said. The FTC has challenged numerous schemes promising instant riches or painless cures for every imaginable illness that arguably no reasonable consumer would actually believe. Consumers, however, are entitled to rely on the clear claims of the seller about exactly what the product will do.

Some claims are on the borderline between reasonable interpretation and reasonable belief. These claims, generally known as "puffery," claim some completely implausible feature or make some entirely subjective claim, such as "our product is the best." Such claims are not considered deceptive. A recent series of ads for Bud Light, for example, claimed such improbable properties as conveying the ability to breathe fire. After demonstrating that this might not be such an attractive feature, the ad said that the ability to breathe fire was no longer available. Surely, however, no reasonable consumer would interpret the message as claiming that they would actually breathe fire after consuming the product. Similarly, a claim that "our product is the best" is entirely subjective, and subject to numerous interpretations. It is regarded as puffery, and therefore not deceptive, because any seller would clearly say that its product was "best." Claiming that a product has the best performance, however, or even the best taste in a taste test, is not puffery. The claim is deceptive unless it is truthful.

The "reasonable consumer" standard is based on the interpretation of consumers in the intended audience of the advertisement. Physicians, for example, would likely interpret many claims differently that would ordinary consumers. If an advertisement is directed to physicians, it is their interpretation that is relevant, but if the ad is directed to ordinary consumers, how they interpret the message is the key. Other audiences, such as children, will also likely understand many advertisements differently than would the general public. The question is what interpretation a reasonable member of the intended audience would attach to the message.

Ultimately, the reasonable consumer standard is an empirical one. In close cases, copy tests or some other form of evidence is necessary to determine how real consumers actually interpret the communication. If "too many" understand the message in a way that is misleading, the Commission can require the advertiser to change the message to reduce misunderstanding. Although there is no bright line test, an advertiser is

---

[6]In one case while I was bureau director at the FTC, for example, the commission stopped claims that a home anthrax test would work. In the wake of the anthrax mailings after September 11, the company had claimed that it had a do-it-yourself anthrax test that would enable consumers to protect themselves. The product was never actually offered, and the claim was only made in a press release. According to the commission's complaint, the test failed to identify actual anthrax samples, and it falsely indicated that common, harmless bacteria were in fact anthrax. Because the product was never actually available, no one was in fact misled, but that result was likely if the company had proceeded with its claims.

generally at risk if more that 15 to 20 percent of the intended audience understands the message in a way that is deceptive.

Finally, a representation must concern a material issue. A material issue is one that is likely to affect a consumer's choice about whether to purchase the product, or their decisions about how to use the product. Claims about price or central product characteristics, such as safety or performance, are clearly material.

Sometimes, however, advertisers make clearly false claims about product characteristics that are unlikely to affect choices. Such claims are not material, and therefore not deceptive. For example, one orange juice ad emphasized that the seller picked the oranges at their peak of flavor so that the juice was as flavorful as possible. To illustrate the claim, the television ad showed a small orange, growing larger as the commercial progressed, that was plucked from the tree at the perfect moment. In the ad, the small orange was orange throughout, growing larger over time. That is a false claim: baby oranges start out green, and only turn orange when they are ripe. But no one purchases orange juice because of the color of baby oranges. The claim is simply not material.

Another example was an advertisement for Hershey's Kisses. Emphasizing that each piece was individually wrapped in foil, the ad's concluding scene was a dramatic shot in which a magnet passed over the Kisses, which all jumped up and stuck to the magnet. Try it sometime. Kisses are wrapped in aluminum foil, which magnets will not attract. However, no one buys Kisses because they want to sort their candy magnetically; the claim is not material.

An advertisement can also be deceptive because, although everything it says is true, it omits information that is critical to understanding the significance of the claim. The classic example was a product that claimed to "kill bacteria that can cause baldness." It was true; the product killed certain bacteria that could in fact cause baldness. But 95 percent of baldness is due to hereditary factors, not bacteria, a fact that the ad did not include. For the typical consumer who bought the product to treat baldness, it would be completely ineffective. The ad was therefore deceptive.

2. Unfairness

Unfairness is far less commonly used as a basis for FTC action against advertising, although it is used to attack other consumer problems such as a seller's breach of contract or lax information security practices. A practice is considered unfair if it causes or is likely to cause substantial consumer injury, without offsetting benefits to consumers or competition, which consumers cannot reasonably avoid.

The first step in the unfairness analysis is to determine whether there has been substantial consumer injury. It can be economic harm, or a threat to health or safety. Substantial injury is an objective test; emotional distress is ordinarily insufficient. Substantial injury can consist of small harm to a large number of consumers, or significant harm to each affected individual. Even in the aggregate, total injury may not be large, as in cases when the company is small or the practice is one that creates unnecessary transaction costs. But relative to the benefits, the injury may still be substantial. To qualify as substantial, an injury must be real, and it must be large compared to any offsetting benefits.

Once it is determined that there is substantial consumer injury, the next step is to determine whether the harm is outweighed by countervailing benefits to consumers or competition. High prices, for example, are not unfair in part because they provide important signals to other market participants to reallocate resources in ways that ultimately benefit consumers, such as entering the market or increasing production if they are already in the market. Generally it is important to consider both the costs of imposing a remedy (such as the cost of requiring a particular disclosure in advertising) and any benefits that consumers enjoy as a result of the practice, such as the avoided costs of more stringent authorization procedures for credit transactions or the value of consumer convenience.

Finally, a practice is only unfair if the injury is not one that a consumer can reasonably avoid. This test limits unfairness actions to those where the commission seeks "to halt some form of seller behavior that unreasonably creates or takes advantage of an obstacle to the free exercise of consumer decision-making." If consumers could have made a different choice, but did not, the Commission should respect that choice. For example, starting from certain premises, one might argue that fast food or fast cars create significant harms that are not outweighed by countervailing benefits, and should be banned. However, the concept of reasonable avoidance keeps the Commission from substituting its paternalistic choices for those of informed consumers. If any institution is to make such decisions, it should be Congress, not the Commission. Unwise consumer choices are a strong argument for consumer education, but not for law enforcement.

In the context of advertising, unfairness has most often been used to address "imitative behavior." The basic theory is that an advertiser depicts some dangerous action, which some consumers may imitate. That is the source of "substantial injury." If offsetting benefits exist at all, they are minimal. Consumers cannot reasonably avoid the injury because they are presumed unaware of the risks of the dangerous action that is depicted.

For example, the commission challenged an advertisement for Beck's beer that showed a consumer on a sailboat, leaning out over the water with one hand holding on to the railing (or a rope) and the other hand clutching a Beck's beer. Because leaning over the water and hanging on with only one hand is not a recommended safe practice in any event, let alone doing so after (or while) drinking a beer, the Commission argued that the advertisement was an unfair practice. Such cases, however, are rare.

3. Advertising Substantiation

Many FTC cases are based on the notion that an advertisement is "unsubstantiated." Under the substantiation doctrine, an advertiser must have a "reasonable basis" for believing the claim is true *before* the claim is made. In theory at least, an advertiser could be liable for a claim that was in fact true, simply because it did not have sufficient evidence to support the claim before it made it. Fortunately, however, the Commission has never brought such a case.

The basis of the substantiation theory is that any advertisement making an objective claim also implies that the advertiser has some reason to believe the claim is true. If that implied claim is false, the advertisement is deceptive. The substantiation doctrine enables the FTC to argue that the evidence is inadequate to support an advertiser's claim, even when the FTC cannot prove that the claim is false. A substantiation investigation, however, requires a careful review of the evidence the advertiser offers in support of its claim. Sometimes it is easier to simply allege that the claim is false, despite whatever evidence the advertiser might claim offers some support.[7]

Most FTC advertising cases, particularly against significant national advertisers, are based on the lack of substantiation. Moreover, although FTC orders may prohibit specific false claims, their principal provisions typically require that an advertiser have substantiation for future claims. Violations of such orders are subject to civil penalties.

What constitutes a "reasonable basis" varies with the circumstances. In substantiation cases, the key issue is generally whether the advertiser had "enough" evidence. The substantiation doctrine does not require proof with certainty, or even proof beyond a reasonable doubt. If an advertiser claims a specific level of support, such at "tests prove," then it must have that level of support. Most commonly, however, the amount of evidence required depends on the nature of the product and the claim.

The crucial factor in determining the required level of substantiation is a balancing test, between the benefits of the claim if it is in fact true and the costs of the claim if it is false. As we noted at the beginning of this chapter, the central tension in regulating information is balancing the competitive benefits of the free flow of information against the potential costs of information that is not accurate or reliable. That is what the substantiation standard seeks to accomplish in determining how much evidence is enough.

If the benefits of the claim if it is true are substantial, we do not want to risk discouraging the claim inappropriately by requiring too much evidence before it can be made. Claims about the relationship between diets high in fiber and the risk of cancer are an example. If the claims are true, the benefits are substantial; fewer people will die of cancer. On the other hand, we seek to protect consumers from the consequences of false claims. If these consequences are particularly severe, we should require more evidence supporting the claim before it is permitted. For claims about fiber and cancer, however, the consequences of false claims are relatively low. Consumers might pay a little more for a high-fiber cereal, or give up a better-tasting cereal. The more serious error, however, would be prohibiting truthful claims.

---

[7]For example, the FTC challenged claims that electronic "abs belts" would use electronic muscle stimulation to deliver the equivalent of 200 sit-ups in only 10 minutes. Rather than carefully examining the advertiser's proffered evidence, the commission simply alleged, based on substantial expert opinion, that the claims were false.

Thus, when the benefits of a true claim are large relative to the costs of a false claim, the substantiation doctrine requires less evidence to constitute a "reasonable basis." On the other hand, if the costs of a false claim are large compared to the benefits of a true claim, as they might be with many claims about prescription drugs, more evidence would be required. (The next chapter explores this concept of balancing the costs of mistakes in more detail in the context of prescription drug regulation.)

Even when the balance cautions against prohibiting truthful claims, however, the advertiser must have reasonable evidence indicating that the claim is true. The question of the amount of evidence is really about how much of the uncertainty must be removed before the claim can be made. Advertisers cannot simply make up claims that would offer great benefits if only they were true, and contend that speculative evidence is therefore enough to support the claim.

III. SUMMARY

Information can be seen as a commodity, like any other good or service. As a commodity, information is a public good. One person can consume it without reducing the amount available for others to consume, and it is difficult to prevent consumers from sharing information. The public good nature of information argues that too little information may be produced in competitive markets.

Information generation, particularly through consumer search, also generates external benefits. When one person searches, he or she gives sellers an incentive to compete by offering lower prices or better features that will attract the shopper. All consumers benefit, because those who shop end up policing the market. As long as the number of consumers who search for a particular product characteristic is large enough to be worth competing for, a minority of informed consumers can police the market and assure competitive outcomes.

Sellers have substantial incentives to provide information to consumers. Providing information about positive product features is clearly beneficial to sellers and consumers alike. The result is competing incomplete information, with consumers easily able to locate products they prefer but not fully informed about any individual product. Sellers also have significant incentives to provide information about negative product characteristics. According to the unfolding principle, all sellers except the worst on a particular attribute will disclose, because otherwise consumers will assume the worst.

Although it often seems cheap, requiring additional information has costs. These costs include information overload, displaced information, warnings that are not selective, and the potential for unintended consequences.

Providing information is often preferable to regulating products directly, because it allows consumers to satisfy their own preferences, whatever they may be. If the costs of using information are high, however, either because of the amount or the complexity of the information that consumers would need to understand, regulating the product may be a more efficient approach. Uniformity of preferences also favors regulation over disclosure, but if consumers have different preferences, disclosure is likely a more efficient solution.

The central tension in the regulation of advertising is balancing the benefits of the free flow of information against the potential costs of inaccurate or unreliable information. When information can flow freely through advertising, prices are lower, incentives for product improvement are greater, and disparities among different demographic groups are reduced. Any advertisement or other communication will inevitably be misunderstood by some; regulation must balance the risk of misunderstanding against the benefits to those who understand the message correctly. There are always benefits to additional information, but requiring too much information in each advertisement may effectively reduce the amount of information available to consumers.

An advertisement is deceptive if it is likely to mislead consumers, acting reasonably in the circumstances, about a material issue. An advertisement is unfair if it causes substantial consumer injury, without offsetting benefits to consumers or competition, that consumers cannot reasonably avoid. Advertisers are required to have a "reasonable basis" for their claims before they make them. The amount of evidence required to constitute a reasonable basis depends on balancing the benefits if the claim is true against the costs if the claim is false.

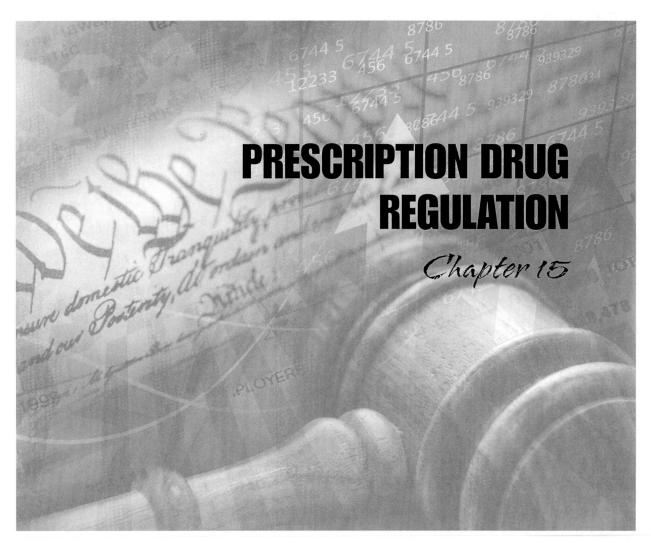

PRESCRIPTION DRUG REGULATION

Chapter 15

This chapter considers the regulation of prescription drugs, which is the responsibility of the Food and Drug Administration. We begin with a discussion of the gatekeeper approach to regulation, which is used for new drugs and certain other new products. We then consider the sources of the regulatory structure we have today, which is the result of two particular tragedies. Section III discusses the human clinical testing process that has resulted from the interplay of the economics of pharmaceutical development and the regulatory requirements. Section IV considers the trade-offs that are inherent in drug regulation. Finally, Section V discusses the changes in the drug approval process that resulted from the emergence of AIDS, and the more recent changes in response to the Vioxx recall in 2004.

I. GATEKEEPER REGULATION

The central feature of federal regulation of prescription drugs is the requirement that new products must receive government approval before they are allowed on the market. This prior approval requirement is an example of gatekeeper regulation, named because the regulatory agency controls the gateway into the marketplace. If the regulator will not open the gate, the product cannot enter. Typically the gatekeeper has considerable discretion about whether to open the gate; thus, the producer must convince the regulator that the product is "safe" and should be allowed to enter the market.

Gatekeeper regulation is used in a number of other areas as well, such as food additives. Most products, however, are not subject to gatekeeper regulation. Instead, there may be specific standards that products must meet (e.g., auto safety requirements), but the manufacturer can introduce any product that meets those standards without prior approval.

Gatekeeper regulation focuses on new risks rather than on existing risks. Its goal is to make sure that new products do not introduce new risks to the marketplace. Regulatory attention tends to focus on products in the approval process, with less oversight once they are released into the marketplace.

There are three primary reasons that gatekeeper regulation focuses on new risk. The first reason is simply practical constraints. There are too many existing risks from already marketed products to devote the same level of regulatory attention to each of them. Focusing on new products seeking to enter the market is a way to reduce the number of products that receive scrutiny to manageable levels. In fact, when new gatekeeper regulatory schemes have been adopted, they have generally "grandfathered" existing products. Even when the new standards apply to existing products, those reviews typically take place over a substantial period of time, with the product remaining on the market until the review is completed.

A second reason for the focus on new risk is a difference in perceived risk. Whatever the magnitude, consumers are more or less comfortable with the risks of existing products. If they are using the product, they have decided the risk is one they are willing to accept. New risks, however, are unknown and potentially scary. The new product may not be any more dangerous in fact, but the uncertainty about precisely what the risk might be can create a greater perceived risk for the new product. Gatekeeper regulation seeks to rule out such risks before the product is allowed on the market.

Probably the most important reason for gatekeeper regulation is that it shifts the burden of proof to the company seeking to enter. That is, the company must convince the regulator that its new product meets the regulatory standard (usually, "safe" or some variation on that notion). If the regulator has questions, that is usually enough to deny approval until those questions can be answered. There may be very good data that a product is safe when used over a one-year period, for example, but if the regulator thinks it is important to know what happens after two years of use, the company will likely have to conduct additional studies before its product can be approved and wait two more years. Similarly, if the regulator has doubts about the methodology of important studies or the adequacy of the sample sizes used, it may withhold approval until those doubts are resolved.

In contrast, when regulators seek to address existing risks, they generally must be able to demonstrate that there is a problem. The lack of data on safety after two years of use might keep a product off the market, but it is ordinarily not sufficient evidence to remove a product that is already being sold. Instead, the government must generally identify a specific risk and provide evidence that it is sufficiently large to justify removing the product.

Asking questions about someone else's evidence is obviously an easier task than developing evidence of a problem. By focusing on new risks, gatekeeper regulation shifts the burden and simplifies the task of keeping new products off the market.

Although it clearly has some advantages, there are also problems inherent in the gatekeeper regulatory approach. First, the regulatory emphasis on avoiding new risks inevitably delays the introduction of new products, whether they are risky or not. We wait longer, often much longer, to realize the benefits of the products that are eventually approved. Aspartame, for example, the artificial sweetener better known as NutraSweet, spent 15 years under regulatory review before it was approved as a food additive. Review may be fast or slow, but some amount of delay is inevitable. Moreover, the more thoroughly new products must be reviewed, the longer the delay is likely to be.

A second drawback of gatekeeper regulation is the potential for priority distortion. Existing risks may be larger, and deserving of a higher priority, than the mere possibility of new risks. Certainly more people are exposed to the existing risk; when a new product is introduced, sales almost invariably start out relatively small and grow over time if the product is successful. For the typical product, that also means that the aggregate risk starts out small. In some instances, devoting more resources to addressing existing risk may be a better use of scarce resources than an exhaustive study of a potential new product.

Third, gatekeeper regulation may prevent the introduction of a new product that poses some risk, but less risk than the products it would likely displace in the market. Regulators typically ask whether a new product is safe in some absolute sense (or at least that it poses no risks greater than some threshold). This is not a comparative analysis, balancing the risks of the new product against the risks it would replace. Even a risky product might actually reduce the overall level of risk consumers face, but gatekeeper regulation rarely addresses that question. For example, the 15 year review of Aspartame never asked whether it was a better artificial sweetner than saccharin, the only alternative then on the market.

II. SOURCES OF REGULATION

As is often the case, the regulatory structure governing new drug approvals is the outgrowth of two tragedies that generated tremendous political impetus to address the issue. In 1937, antibiotics had not yet been discovered, and the drug of choice for treating bacterial infections was a class of drugs known as sulfa drugs. Unfortunately, there was no convenient dosage form available for children. Most medicines for young children are in liquid form, because they are easier to administer. Usually the liquid used is alcohol, but sulfa drugs do not dissolve in alcohol.

One entrepreneur decided that he could make a substantial amount of money if he could develop a liquid form of sulfa drugs, so he set out to find a solvent that would work. Using trial and error, he eventually found a solvent and began marketing "Elixir Sulfanilamide." Within two months, more than 100 people, mostly children, had died.

The reason was not hard to find. The solvent that dissolved sulfa drugs was ethylene glycol—a chemical in widespread use today as antifreeze. It wasn't that the solvent's toxicity was unknown; the entrepreneur rushing to market had simply not bothered to look.

The result was the Food, Drug, and Cosmetic Act of 1938 (FDCA). Congress had been debating similar legislation for several years, but it took the Elixir Sulfanilamide tragedy to provoke legislative action. Among other things, the act required makers of new drugs to submit information about their product and its ingredients to the FDA for a safety review. If the FDA saw safety problems, it could block introduction of the drug.

In 1956, the drug thalidomide was introduced in Europe. Initially used as a mild tranquilizer, the drug was widely prescribed to treat the symptoms of morning sickness during pregnancy. Although it was never marketed in the United States, the drug was used by some physicians in their practice, which was a common research technique at the time. After the drug had been on the market for some time, doctors recognized that the frequency of a previously very rare birth defect had increased. In this birth defect, babies are born with either no long bone in an arm or leg, or with flipper-like appendages instead of hands or feet. Eventually, in 1961, after about 10,000 children were born with this defect, it was determined that thalidomide was the cause.[1]

The thalidomide tragedy was the impetus for the 1962 amendments to the FDCA. As with the original law, these amendments had been under discussion in Congress for several years, without much progress. The newly-passed amendments substantially tightened the drug approval process. First, manufacturers were required to have "substantial evidence" before a drug could be approved. In practice, this has come to mean human clinical trials of the drug, usually more than one. Second, rather than just addressing safety, substantial evidence was required to address both safety and efficacy. The substantial evidence requirement increased the amount of evidence required for approval, and the efficacy requirement added a new criterion that a drug must meet before it is marketed. Third, the amendments gave the FDA authority over the clinical testing process, since this was the only way thalidomide had been available in the United States. Thus, even experimental uses of a drug now require FDA approval as an "investigational new drug" (IND). Finally, the amendments gave the FDA exclusive jurisdiction over prescription drug advertising.

The amendments produced a substantial increase in the cost of developing a new drug. In the 1950s, the average cost of a successful new drug (including the investments in drugs that did not prove useful) was $5.4 million. In the 1960s, the average cost rose to $40.2 million. The number of new drugs introduced declined sharply as well. Over time, the FDA has continued to ask for more and more evidence before approving a drug,

---

[1]Despite the risk of birth defects, thalidomide subsequently proved to be a useful drug. It received FDA approval (in 1998) to treat a form of leprosy, and (in 2006) to treat a cancer of plasma cells.

leading to further increases in costs. In particular, sample sizes in clinical trials have tended to increase over time. In the 1970s, the average cost per successful new drug was $65.7 million; in the 1990s, it had risen to $282 million. A 2003 estimate placed the cost of a successful new drug at an astonishing $800 million.

III. Human Clinical Testing

Drug development is a complex interaction between the economics of development and the regulatory process. Because human clinical testing is enormously expensive, pharmaceutical companies have strong incentives to narrow testing to the most promising compounds. To be successful, a new drug must be safe, of course, but it must also be sufficiently effective to be economically attractive compared to other drugs that treat the same condition. Many potential drugs are abandoned along the way because the potential return is simply not sufficient to justify incurring additional costs.

The drug development process begins with the search for promising compounds that might be useful as drugs. Thousands of compounds are screened; somewhere between 2.5 and 5 percent of those screened are sufficiently promising to merit the costs of preclinical testing. Insert preclinical testing involves laboratory and animal studies that seek to identify how the compound works and its basic pharmacology and toxicology. Of compounds that enter preclinical testing, only about 2 percent are sufficiently promising to merit human clinical testing. Thus, somewhere between 1,000 and 2,000 compounds are typically screened to find one drug that is worth human clinical trials. This discovery phase of drug development ranges from one to three years, with an average of 18 months before the drug is ready for human trials.

Based on the preclinical data, the drug developer files an application to be approved as an investigational new drug (IND). This application includes all of the information from the preclinical and animal studies, along with the study plan for human testing. It is subject to FDA review for 30 days. Once trials begin, the FDA monitors their progress, and can suspend trials if it sees a problem.

Phase I studies typically involve 20 to 80 healthy subjects. Designed to assess toxicity and determine how the drug is metabolized in the human body, these studies usually use healthy volunteers to minimize the chances of serious adverse effects and maximize the chances of recovery if anything goes wrong. On average, Phase I trials take about 18 months. Seventy-one percent of investigational new drugs (IND) approved for human testing successfully complete these trials.

In Phase II clinical studies, the drug is administered for the first time to patients with the condition it is intended to treat. These studies are generally randomized controlled trials involving 100 to 300 subjects and take an average of two years to complete. Typically, studies are placebo controlled, using an inert product that looks and tastes as much like the drug as possible for comparison. Placebo controls are vital, because a significant fraction of patients given a pill that they think will make them better will in fact improve. A drug is effective only if it is significantly better than placebo. Trials are also double blind, meaning that neither the researcher nor the patients know who is getting the drug and who is getting the placebo.

Patients eligible for Phase II trials are generally carefully selected. Drug developers want to select patients they believe are most likely to benefit from the product. If the drug fails with those who are most likely to benefit, it is not likely to be worth pursuing.

Phase II trials are the real crucible of the drug testing process. Of the drugs that enter Phase II testing, 55 percent do not complete it; only 32 percent of approved INDs survive through the end of these studies. Cumulatively, the significance of Phase II studies is even more striking: 93 percent of all decisions to abandon drug development occur before the end of Phase II. Economic concerns are the single most frequent reason for abandoning research during Phase II, although safety and efficacy problems are almost as prominent. Based on these relatively small-scale and inexpensive trials, it is simply not worth pursuing drug development farther.

Phase III clinical trials are undoubtedly the single most costly and time-consuming step in the torturous journey from test tube to approval. They typically involve 1,000 to 5,000 patients, and generally take 2 to 3.5 years to complete. Decisions to abandon research during Phase III trials are relatively infrequent, amounting to 5 percent of all initially approved INDs, or 7 percent of all decisions to abandon development, or 15 percent of all products that initiate these trials. Of all drugs that enter human clinical testing, 28 percent eventually complete Phase III trials.

Phase III trials are designed to look for less frequent side effects and to confirm efficacy. Participants are less carefully selected than in Phase II trials, because the studies are seeking evidence about the likely effect of the drug in the broader patient population that will likely use it if the drug is marketed. Some trials are placebo controlled, but others compare the new drug to a "standard" treatment or are uncontrolled. Phase III trials also frequently test different dosages, to try to determine the optimal dose for the drug.

Once clinical trials are largely concluded, the manufacturer submits a New Drug Application (NDA) for FDA review. The NDA includes literally everything that is known about the drug, and may run literally millions of pages. All of the laboratory and animal studies are included, along with details of the planned manufacturing process. Of course, the results of human clinical trials are part of the application, but so are the individual patient records of everyone who participated in clinical trials. The application is assigned to an FDA reviewer (or, often, a team of reviewers with different expertise) for evaluation. Before the introduction of user fees in 1992 (discussed in the next section), FDA review averaged about two years. More recently, reviews average just over one year, although some are significantly longer.

Despite extensive testing before marketing, the possibility remains that any new drug has unacceptable side effects, but with a low enough probability that it cannot be detected in any feasible trials. A drug with a fatal side effect that killed 1 in 1,000 patients, for example, would almost certainly not make it to the market. If we test the drug on 1,000 patients, however, there is a 37 percent chance that the side effect will not happen at all. Testing on 2,000 patients will reduce the probability of not seeing the side effect to 14 percent, but even with 3,000 patients, there is still a 5 percent chance that the side effect will not be observed.

Unless it is intended to treat an extremely serious condition with no alternative treatments, a drug would be withdrawn if it killed even 1 in 20,000 patients due to side effects. Even if we test 5,000 patients, however, we would not observe a side effect with that low risk more than three-quarters of the time. As a practical matter, low probability but serious side effects can only be detected once the drug has been in use by a large population for a reasonable period of time.

Once a side effect occurs, it must be recognized as an effect of the drug. Sometimes linking the drug to the effect is straightforward, but in many instances it is quite difficult. Patients who participate in certain types of clinical trials, for example, are likely quite ill, and a number of them may die in any event. Inevitably some side effects will only be identified once the drug has been in use for some period of time.

IV. TRADE-OFFS IN DRUG REGULATION

The impossibility of detecting side effects that would be a serious concern means that some errors in approving new drugs are inevitable. Understanding the potential costs of errors and how we might keep those costs as low as possible is therefore vital.

Consider the possible outcomes of the FDA's decision about whether to approve a new drug and the (unknown) truth about whether the drug is in fact safe and effective. In reality, the drug is either safe and effective or it is not. The FDA must decide whether to approve the drug or reject it. There are four possibilities, shown in Figure 15-1.

If the FDA approves the drug, and it is in fact safe and effective (the upper left box in the figure), that is a correct decision. Similarly, deciding to reject a drug that is not safe and effective (the lower right box) is a correct decision. Accepting a drug that turns out not to be safe and effective, the upper right box, is a "type I error." In statistics, it is the significance level of the test: the probability of mistakenly accepting the alternative hypothesis when the result is really only due to chance.[2] In medical jargon, this kind of

---

[2]That is, for a statistical test at the 95 percent confidence level, there is a 5 percent probability that the result is due to chance—a 5 percent probability of a type I error.

Figure 15-1. Possible errors in the drug approval decision.

FDA Decision	True State of the World	
	Safe and Effective	Not Safe and Effective
Accept	Correct decision	Type I error; Significance level; "False positive"
Reject	Type II error; Power of the test; "False negative"	Correct decision

error is frequently referred to as a false positive: we have conducted a test, it gave us a positive result (the drug is safe and effective), but that result was false.

Rejecting a drug that is in fact safe and effective is also an error, a "type II error." In statistics, type II error corresponds to the power of the test: the likelihood that we will fail to identify a difference that is really present. The common medical terminology is a false negative. Our tests gave a negative result (the drug is not safe and effective), but that result is false.

Given the available data, there is an inherent trade-off between type I and type II error. We can only reduce the risk of one error by increasing the other. Thus, if we want to reduce the chances of making a type I error, we will inevitably increase the chances that we are making a type II error.[3] A decision should therefore consider the costs of both kinds of mistakes. We should worry most about making the error that has the most serious costs, and not quite so much about the error that will cost less if we actually make it.

The costs of mistakes depend critically on the availability of alternative treatments. Consider first a new drug where good alternatives are available; for example, another minor pain reliever to supplement aspirin, acetaminophen, sodium naproxen, and others currently on the market. If we make a type I error, and the drug is not in fact safe and effective, there may be serious consequences from side effects. If we make a type II error, however, and reject a drug that really works, patients will simply use one of the many available alternatives. There is some cost, but it is relatively minor. If there are good alternatives available, the more serious risk is making a type I error. Thus, we should try to minimize the risk of type I error when good alternative treatments are available.

The analysis is different where there are no good alternatives. Consider a drug to treat a serious and life-threatening condition with no good alternative treatments available, such as a drug to treat AIDS in the early days of the epidemic. When AIDS first emerged, a diagnosis was a death sentence, in a relatively short period of time. If we make a type I error, there may again be serious consequences from side effects. Unfortunately, however, those patients were highly likely to die anyway, from the disease itself. If we make a type II error, however, and fail to approve an effective drug, people will die from the disease who could have been saved. With no good alternative treatments available, the more serious risk is making a type II error. We should therefore try to minimize the risk of type II error when no good alternatives are available.

It is tempting to try to avoid the dilemma of choosing between type I and type II errors by seeking more information. Seeking more information, however, will take time—and in the meantime, the drug will not be available. A decision to seek more information is therefore a decision to take the risk of type II error, at least until the new information becomes available. When the risk of type II error is the more serious problem, that is precisely what we are trying to avoid.

These costs of delay can be substantial. An estimated 60 to 70 percent of new drugs are approved abroad before they are approved in the United States, delaying their availability to American patients. As discussed in the next section, changes in the approval process in the 1990s reduced this lag and provided substantial benefits to patients.

---

[3]It may be helpful to think about the extremes to see the trade-off. We could completely avoid type I errors by rejecting every new drug, but we would make a lot of type II errors. Similarly, if we approve everything, we will never make a type II error, but there will be many type I errors. As we move away from either extreme rule, we increase the chance of one error and reduce the chance of the other.

Although type II error is in some instances the most serious mistake, the drug approval process is skewed toward the avoidance of type I error. The statutory charge to the FDA is to avoid drugs that are not safe and effective; there is no corresponding statutory charge to speed important new drugs to market. Indeed, the key laws were the political response to prominent examples of type I errors, and the structure was set up to keep them from happening again.

The politics of regulatory decision making reinforce the bias to avoiding type I error. If the FDA mistakenly approves a drug that turns out to have serious side effects, there will be significant political repercussions, as the Vioxx recall in 2004 makes clear. Press reports will scrutinize the agency's decision, seeking to determine how the error occurred and seeking someone to hold accountable for the error. Congress will hold hearings about the error, asking the FDA commissioner to explain how the product could possibly have been approved, given facts that were not available at the time. No one wants to be responsible for a tragedy, and no agency or political official wants that type of scrutiny. Officials will therefore try to avoid the type I errors that might provoke scrutiny and blame.

Type II errors, on the other hand, are much less visible. Even if they have a large stake in the decision, potentially affected patients may not be aware that a decision is pending. The victims are nameless, and press scrutiny is generally minimal. From the perspective of minimizing the political consequences of mistakes, type I error is what a support-maximizing agency will seek to avoid.

V. THE EMERGENCE OF AIDS AND CHANGES IN THE APPROVAL PROCESS

The emergence of AIDS in the early 1980s changed the calculus of the drug approval process, both substantively and politically. When the AIDS epidemic began, there was no cure and no effective treatment. The drugs under development that might have been useful were intended to treat the opportunistic infections that were rare otherwise, but struck AIDS victims disproportionately. The diagnosis was a death sentence; few diagnosed with AIDS lived longer than 6 months after the diagnosis. Moreover, there were real fears that the disease would break out of the gay white male population where it was first recognized into the broader, heterosexual population.

AIDS changed the substantive balance of the costs of errors. With a fearsome, contagious disease, the costs of type II errors were substantially larger than they had been in many other contexts. It was more important to get promising drugs to market as quickly as possible because every day, AIDS patients were dying.

AIDS also changed the political calculus of the drug approval process. The gay white male population was already organized because of concerns about civil rights issues. Thus, really for the first time, there was an organized group of patients who understood that they had a large stake in the decisions that were being made in the drug approval process. Moreover, they understood that they really had no alternatives: the risk that a drug side effect would kill them was trivial compared to the consequences of the diagnosis itself.

Gay activists protested vocally. For the first time there were demonstrations outside of the FDA offices, protesting the lack of progress in making AIDS medications available. For the FDA, which has always thought of itself as a public health agency, this was a traumatic event. Demonstrators were claiming, with some justification, that rather than protecting public health, the agency was killing them.

The combination of good, substantive reasons and strong political pressures for alternative approaches produced a number of changes in the drug approval process. The first such change was the Treatment IND, adopted in 1987. Under this program, the FDA agreed to make drugs with sufficiently promising evidence of effectiveness available to patients who were not participating in clinical trials of the drug. Thus, AIDS victims could potentially receive drugs before they were approved for marketing and in consultation with their physicians, make their own decision about the balance of risks versus benefits.

The treatment IND program was intensely controversial, in part because of fears that it would deter people from participating in clinical trials. In a placebo-controlled trial, there is only a 50 percent chance that a participant will actually receive the drug; in the treatment IND program, they would receive the drug for certain.[4] In the program's first 7 years, the FDA granted treatment IND status to 29 different drugs, enabling more than 100,000 patients to receive medicines that were not yet on the market.

Treatment INDs remain an issue today because of subsequent litigation concerning the rights of patients facing terminal illness and no good alternative therapies. The FDA is continuing to explore ways to expand the availability of drugs under development for such patients.

A second change was more fundamental. In 1988 the FDA adopted an approval process that was subsequently codified and is now known as "fast track" approval. For the first time, the agency recognized that the amount of evidence needed to approve a drug depended on the circumstances. In particular, the FDA said that when a drug was intended to treat a serious or life-threatening condition for which no effective alternatives were available, the drug could be approved with less evidence than would ordinarily be required. Thus, the agency recognized the significance of type II error, and the need to avoid it.

Interestingly, the debate within the FDA was about the scope of change that was appropriate. Many recognized the political imperative to respond to the AIDS crisis with steps to accelerate drug availability, but many also thought that any response should be limited to AIDS itself. The logic of responding to type II error, however, is not unique to AIDS. There are numerous conditions, such as many cancers, that have no effective treatment, and numerous patient populations who cannot use standard therapies for serious conditions because they suffer from side effects. For these patients, like AIDS patients, avoiding type II error is the most serious concern. In the end, the broader public policy concerns prevailed. Treatment INDs and "fast track" were available for any drug treating a serious or life-threatening condition with no effective alternative, and were not limited to AIDS drugs.

A third change, user fees for reviews under the new drug approval process, was introduced in 1992 and continues today. Before 1992, the FDA was funded out of general revenues and competed with numerous other agencies for resources. The FDA always argued that approvals were slow because it lacked the resources to hire more reviewers to speed up the process. User fees, imposed on pharmaceutical manufacturers who submit a new drug application, provided the FDA with the funding for additional reviewers. Part of the political compromise that made user fees possible was a stipulation that the revenues would be devoted to improving the approval process, not other admittedly valuable functions of government. Moreover, the statute included specific goals for reducing review times.

The additional resources and new incentives that resulted from the user fee statute substantially shortened the FDA's review time, from an average of two years reviewing an NDA before the law to just over one year after its enactment. One analyst estimated that making the life-saving benefits of new drugs available one year earlier saved between 180,000 and 310,000 lives. As we noted above, the costs of delay can be substantial indeed. It appears, however, that increases in the duration of human clinical testing have largely offset the reduction in FDA review times. Whether this offsetting effect reflects changes in the types of drugs under development or changes in the regulatory requirements remains unclear.

In 1996, a fourth change in the drug approval process was introduced: accelerated approval, based on surrogate end points. For most drug therapies, particularly those for chronic or incurable conditions, the goal is to prolong the patient's life. For many cancers, for example, a common measure of treatment effectiveness is the five-year survival rate: how many patients are still alive five years after treatment begins? Although that is the ultimate goal, measuring five-year survival rates takes five years at least. If we will only approve drugs based on evidence that they actually improve the five-year survival rate, we will wait a long time indeed for new drugs to come to market.

Surrogate end points are other measures that are likely to predict improvements in long-term survival, but do not necessarily predict survival rates. The attraction of surrogate end points is that a drug's effect on these surrogates

---

[4]There was never much empirical basis for this concern. A large number of clinical trials are exploring new uses for drugs that have already been approved for some other disease. Because doctors can prescribe these legally marketed drugs for any reason, anyone who wants the drug for sure and can persuade their doctor to prescribe it can get it. There is no evidence of problems in recruiting patients to participate in clinical trials of approved drugs for additional uses, however.

can often be determined far more rapidly than its impact on long-term survival. For cancer therapies, for example, shrinkage of solid tumors is likely correlated with long-term survival, and can be observed much more rapidly than the ultimate outcome. Similarly, we can determine the effect of AIDS therapies on such proxies as virus loads or T-cell counts much more rapidly than we can determine the impact on long-term survival. Surrogate end points are a way to avoid the delays that would otherwise be necessary to determine a treatment's impact on the ultimate goal, which is survival of the patient. They are a way to reduce the costs of type II error.

There are, however, limitations on the use of surrogate endpoints that occasionally come to light, including some that have occurred quite recently. Two cholesterol-lowering drugs, Zetia and Vytorin,[5] were approved for lowering cholesterol based on clear evidence that they reduced "bad" cholesterol by 10 to 15 percent, a clinically significant reduction.[6] In 2008, however, a study was published indicating that, unlike statins, the standard cholesterol-lowering drugs, Zetia and Vytorin did not reduce the risk of heart attack. Since the reason for treating high levels of "bad" cholesterol is to reduce the risk of heart attack, this study at least calls into question the basis for their approval.

The impact of these recent examples on the drug approval process remains to be seen. There is, however, clear evidence that waiting for the "ultimate" evidence of effectiveness can be quite costly in terms of patient welfare. For example, one class of drugs used to treat hypertension is the beta blockers. Relatively short-term studies made clear in the early 1970s that they did in fact reduce blood pressure. The FDA insisted, however, that the manufacturer provide evidence that treating high blood pressure, in the absence of other symptoms, actually improved life expectancy. The result was a seven-year delay, at a cost that some have estimated at 119,000 lives lost because an effective treatment was not available. Again, the costs of type II error can be substantial.

A final change in the drug approval process occurred with the passage of the FDA Modernization Act in 1997. Apart from user fees, the changes discussed above were adopted through the regulatory process or interpretations of existing regulatory authority. Congress had not been part of the process, other than as an occasional kibitzer. In the FDA Modernization Act, however, Congress essentially codified the changes that had already occurred.

It is no accident that the major changes to accelerate the drug approval process—fast track in 1988, user fees in 1992, and surrogate end points in 1996—all occurred in presidential election years. As we noted in Chapter 6, even what appear to be technical agency decisions have a political component. Even policy changes with substantial merits on their own, such as these, often come to fruition only when good sense coincides with good politics.

The political environment of the drug approval process changed, perhaps significantly and with far broader implications, with the Vioxx recall in 2004. The drug was a pain reliever and anti-inflammatory used particularly with arthritis, although it had other uses as well. It was originally approved in 1999 under the "fast track" process for patients who could not take aspirin because they suffered from serious stomach problems if they did. These patients face a serious condition, with no effective alternatives because they could not take the drug of choice. The drug was heavily promoted in direct-to-consumer advertising, and widely used.

In 2004, a clinical trial of long-term Vioxx use to reduce the risk of colon polyps was terminated prematurely when it became clear that Vioxx increased the risk of heart attacks after 18 months of use. Once it obtained these results, Merck, the drug's manufacturer, recalled the drug on its own. Other drugs in the same category remain on the market.

The Vioxx recall provoked new attention to the risks of new drugs. It was a dramatic event, and again raised the specter of type I error in the approval process. There is, however, no reason to think that the decision to approve the drug was inappropriate. As discussed above, some type I errors are inevitable, even if we are willing to accept extremely high costs of type II errors. What happened is exactly what should happen in a

[5]Vytorin is actually a combination of Zetia and a statin drug, the standard therapy for lowering cholesterol. Zetia, however, works through a different biological mechanism.

[6]Zetia and Vytorin were not technically approved using surrogate endpoints. Rather, they were approved (as are all drugs) for a specific indication for use, reducing "bad" cholesterol. Nonetheless, there is no logical difference between narrowing the indication and approval based on surrogate endpoints. Demand for a drug to "shrink breast cancer tumors" would presumably be quite similar to demand for a drug to "treat breast cancer." In both cases, the effect is to reduce the costs of type II errors.

well-functioning process: when new information comes to light, the original decision should be revisited and changed if necessary.

The recall has generated considerable political pressure to slow down the approval process, and there is anecdotal evidence that the FDA has done so. In 2007, only 19 new drugs (new chemical entities) were approved, the lowest number in 24 years. Renewed attention to safety was also apparent. In that year, the agency issued 75 new or revised "black box" warnings, the most serious form of warning in a drug's labeling. Whether review times will again substantially lengthen or priority reviews will be used more sparingly remains to be seen. The recall has had an effect, but it may or may not prove to be a lasting effect.

VI. SUMMARY

The drug approval process is an example of the gatekeeper approach to regulation, which requires approval before a new product is allowed to enter the market. The gatekeeper approach is employed in part because of practical problems, differences in perceived risk, and because it shifts the burden of proof to the manufacturer. The gatekeeper approach, however, delays the introduction of new products, may delay or prevent the introduction of risky products that actually reduce existing risks, and may distort priorities about which risks are most important to address.

The drug regulatory process is the outgrowth of two tragedies, one involving Elixir Sulfanilamide and another involving the drug thalidomide. Today, manufacturers must have "substantial evidence" that a new drug is both safe and effective before it can be marketed. Over time, the costs of introducing a successful new drug have escalated sharply, reaching $282 million in the 1990s.

Substantial evidence is generated through human clinical trials of potential new drugs. Phase I studies involve 20 to 80 healthy volunteers, take about 18 months to complete, and seek basic safety information. Phase II trials seek to determine whether the drug works. They involve 100–300 patients and take an average of two years to complete. Most decisions to discontinue drug development are made by the end of the Phase II trials. Phase III trials are larger, involving 1,000 to 5,000 patients, and take two to 3.5 years to complete. They seek further, more representative evidence of efficacy, as well as additional information about side effects and the appropriate dosage. After clinical trials are largely complete, the manufacturer submits all of the available information as part of its New Drug Application for FDA review. Review averages just over one year.

Despite extensive clinical testing, rare side effects that would disqualify nearly any drug cannot always be detected prior to marketing. They can only be identified after a large population has used the drug for a significant period of time. Thus, some risk is unavoidable.

Regulatory decisions involve a trade-off between the costs of type I error, or mistakenly approving a drug that turns out not to be safe and effective, and type II error, or mistakenly rejecting a drug that is in fact safe and effective. If there are good alternative treatments available, the costs of type I errors are generally more significant. If there are not good alternative treatments, however, the costs of type II error are more significant, particularly if the condition is serious or life threatening. Both substantively and politically, however, the drug approval process is more geared to avoiding type I error.

The emergence of AIDS in the 1980s led to significant changes to accelerate the availability of important new drugs. With AIDS, the costs of type II errors were quite high. Moreover, for the first time, an organized patient group pressured the FDA to approve new medications more quickly, because they had no alternative. In 1988, the FDA adopted "fast track" approvals, recognizing that for serious or life-threatening conditions with no good alternative treatments, a drug could be approved based on less evidence than would otherwise be required. In 1992 Congress established user fees and used the resources to speed regulatory reviews. In 1996 the FDA adopted the accelerated approval process, allowing approval based on surrogate end points. These changes were codified in the FDA Modernization Act of 1997.

The Vioxx recall in 2004 provoked renewed attention to the risk of type I error. It generated political pressure to slow down drug approvals. Its long-term impact on the process remains uncertain.

I. THE FOOD SAFETY PROBLEM

The federal role in food safety regulation stems from Upton Sinclair's book, *The Jungle*, published in 1905. Sinclair's novel described a wide variety of truly revolting practices in the Chicago meat packing industry. Dead rats went into the sausage grinder; diseased cattle were slaughtered for meat; guts and trimmings were swept up off the floor and sold as potted ham. The public was disgusted, and, with the support of meat packers who lost substantial foreign sales, Congress responded with the Meat Inspection Act of 1906. The act established a system of federal inspectors that remains in place today.

There are actually fifteen different federal agencies with some responsibility for food safety issues, but two agencies have primary responsibility. The U.S. Department of Agriculture has responsibility for meat and poultry products. The FDA regulates virtually all other food products, including seafood and fresh produce. The two agencies share jurisdiction over eggs, the source of a major food safety incident in 2011. FDA is responsible for shell eggs and producers who use eggs as an ingredient, the Food Safety and Inspection Service in the Agriculture Department is responsible for liquid, frozen, and dried egg products, and the Agricultural Marketing Service is responsible for egg quality grading. For both agencies, the main focus of regulation is food-processing and -manufacturing operations. But each agency also has jurisdiction over labeling and label claims.

The primary food safety programs at the Department of Agriculture involve meat and poultry inspections. Developed in response to the types of problems identified in *The Jungle*, the system relies on inspectors who, in theory at least, examine each animal before it is slaughtered to make sure there is no evidence of disease. The most acute modern concern is so-called "downer" cattle that cannot walk. Inability to walk is one symptom of bovine spongiform encephalopathy, better known as mad cow disease. In addition, after slaughter each carcass is inspected, again for signs of disease or contamination.

There are at least three problems with a safety system that relies so heavily on inspectors. The first problem is resources. Over time, staffing at the Food Safety and Inspection Service has declined, while the total output of beef and poultry processing plants has increased. The result is that each inspector must examine more carcasses, and in less time. Some have claimed that the average time examining chickens on a modern processing line, for example, is a matter of seconds per bird. That kind of inspection is probably adequate to keep dead rats out of the sausage grinder, but it is too superficial to detect anything other than a fairly obvious problem.

In January 2012, the FSIS proposed changes in the poultry inspection system. Under the proposal, inspectors would be reallocated from supervising the production line to oversight of the plant's overall food safety procedures. Companies themselves would take over the quality control task of removing blemished or visibly damaged carcasses from the production line. USDA believes that the changes will allow it to both reduce the number of inspectors and improve food safety by focusing on health risks rather than cosmetic issues. It estimates that the changes will reduce the incidence of salmonella poisoning by 2.5 percent, and campylobacter infections by 0.6 percent. Some consumer groups, however, have opposed the changes, arguing that it would "privatize food safety functions." Industry generally supported the changes, which would enable them to increase the speed of processing lines by as much as 25 percent.

A second difficulty is that the system may create an incentive to rely on the inspector. Employees may, in close or ambiguous cases, let the animal go through, relying on the inspector to catch any problem. After all, that is the inspector's job. Results would be better, however, if workers used their best judgment, because they have more knowledge than the inspector can possibly acquire in a cursory examination.

By far the most serious difficulty with reliance on inspections is that even thorough "scratch and sniff" methods are clearly inadequate to detect microbial contamination. That, however, is the modern problem of food safety. How can we prevent bacterial contamination that makes consumers sick and may kill them?

Figure 16-1 provides estimates of the extent of food-borne illness from the Centers for Disease Control. There is a great deal of uncertainty in the estimates, but they indicate a significant amount of disease due to foods. In total, there are an estimated 48 million cases of food-borne illnesses per year, resulting in 128,000 hospitalizations and 3,000 deaths. Eighty percent of illnesses and 56 percent of hospitalization and deaths are due to

Figure 16-1. Food-borne illness, 2011.

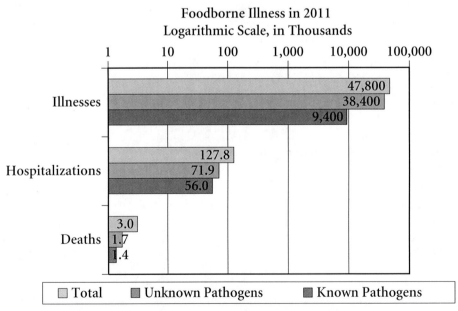

Source: CDC, Estimates of Foodborne Illness in the U.S, 2011

unknown pathogens—that is, we do not know which bug caused the disease. These estimates are significantly lower than estimates in 1996, but differences in the methodologies render comparisons difficult.

Some microbial pathogens are either newly emerging or newly recognized. *E. coli*, for example, a common bacteria found in the gut of most mammals, has long been known. Most forms of the bacteria are harmless. However, one especially virulent strain, *E. coli O157:H7*, was only discovered in 1982. It has been the cause of some of the most severe outbreaks of food-borne illness, including the spinach contamination incident in 2006. Pathogens can also spread in ways that were once though impossible. For many years, for example, it was believed that eggs were sterile as long as the shell had not been cracked. In fact, however, fresh eggs can spread salmonella, even if there are no cracks. Salmonella was first traced to eggs in 1986.

One way to control many forms of food-borne illness is proper cooking, which kills bacteria that would otherwise be harmful. In 1988, an *E. coli* outbreak in school cafeterias was apparently due to pre-cooked hamburger patties that had not been cooked to a sufficiently high temperature. The USDA promptly issued new guidelines, requiring hamburgers to be cooked to an internal temperature of 160°. That temperature, however, implied that McDonald's hamburgers were undercooked, and many believed the product was unpalatable. In 1990 the USDA reduced the temperature recommendation to 155°.

Concern about microbial pathogens reached a new peak in 1993, when several hundred people were infected with *E. coli O157:H7* after eating at Jack in the Box. The incident led the Agriculture Department to propose a new approach to meat safety regulation in 1994. This system, known as Hazard Analysis and Critical Control Points (HACCP), is considered in the next section.

II. HAZARD ANALYSIS AND CRITICAL CONTROL POINTS

The rule implementing HACCP for meat and poultry products[1] was promulgated in 1996. Implementation was phased in, with larger firms required to have programs in place by 1998, and all firms required to be in compliance by 2000.

In contrast to inspections, HACCP is a process-oriented system. It puts considerable responsibility on the food manufacturer or processor, and seeks to control problems from the beginning to the end of the production process. Inspection, in contrast, seeks to identify problems at a specific point in the process, or, as in the case of inspecting carcasses, at the end of the process.

The first step in HACCP is a hazard analysis. This analysis seeks to identify each food safety risk that might occur anywhere in the production process. These hazards, which may be physical (e.g. temperature), chemical (e.g. contamination), or biological, are likely to differ from one product to another. Thus, the hazard analysis is specific to each product that a company produces.

The second step in the analysis is to identify the critical control points. These are the points in the process where lack of control could result in introduction of a hazard. As with the hazard analysis, critical control points are product specific. For example, the slaughter process, the chilling process, the cooking process, and the packaging process might be critical control points, depending on the product. If a hazard will be eliminated at a later stage of the process, something that might otherwise be a critical control point is not. For example, a cooked product may rely on cooking to eliminate bacterial hazards, which means that bacterial contamination that might occur before cooking is not a significant risk.

For each critical control point, a plant must establish critical limits. The critical limit is the extent to which some variable must be controlled to avoid a hazard. For example, a critical limit might specify the time and temperature for chilling the product (e.g., chill to below 40 degrees within 30 minutes) to prevent bacterial growth. Critical limits may be specified in the regulations, or they may be developed and established by each plant.

---

[1]The FDA has separate HACCP rules for seafood products and juice products. The basic elements of the requirements are quite similar to the Agriculture Department rule discussed in this section.

A key part of HACCP is monitoring the critical limits. The monitoring system must assure that the critical limits are actually met—that is, that the product was actually processed within the parameters that were specified for that control point. If they are not met, the plan must identify appropriate corrective action to get the process back under control for further production, and how to deal with any product that was produced while the process was outside the critical limits (e.g., destroy the product; divert it from a fresh product to a cooked product; etc.). Finally, companies must keep detailed records to assure that the plan is being followed.

In addition to the HACCP plan, companies must have sanitation standard operating procedures (SSOPs). These procedures are written plans of the daily procedures that must be followed to assure effective sanitation in the facility. For example, SSOPs must address the steps needed to assure that surfaces and tools that will be in contact with food are clean and disinfected. Some SSOPs address steps that must taken before processing begins; others specify procedures to follow during operations.

The HACCP plan and SSOPs are backed up by regulatory performance standards that address particular hazards. Each plant must meet these standards, which use biological tests to determine whether infectious agents are present. Test results are usually not available until after the product has already been shipped, but lots can be traced and recalled if necessary. The performance standards specify zero tolerance for *E. coli O157:H7*. Any positive test result for this bacterium will lead to a recall. Zero tolerance standards for six additional strains of E. coli that produce the same toxin go into effect in 2012.

Standards for other microbes, such as salmonella, tend to be more forgiving. The performance standards are based on the baseline prevalence of the salmonella bacteria in different types of foods. Over time, the expectation is that the standards will be tightened to reduce the permissible levels of salmonella. For example, in 2011 USDA adopted significantly tighter salmonella performance standard for poultry. There is also testing for generic *E. coli*. Although this common bacterium is harmless, its presence is a useful monitor for the adequacy of controls to prevent contamination of freshly slaughtered meat. As with salmonella, the performance standards were set using the baseline incidence of *E. coli* for each type of product.

Since the HACCP rules were adopted and implemented, there have been declines in the incidence of food-borne illness from major pathogens, as shown in Figure 16-2. The one infection that shows a signficant

Figure 16-2. Relative rates of laboratory-confirmed infections with *Campylobacter, STEC* 0157, Listeria, Salmonella,* and *Vibrio* compared with 1996–1998 period, by year.

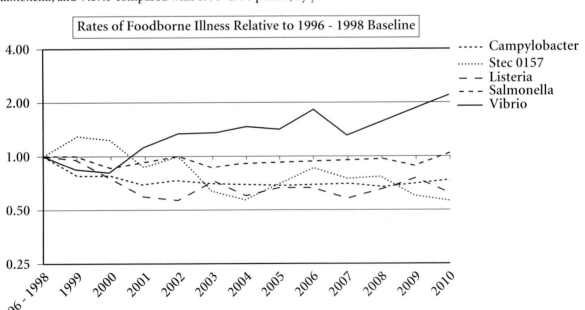

Source: CDC, Trends in Foodborne Illness in the U.S., 1996-2010

increase, vibrio, results from eating raw oysters from warmer waters. Although processing steps could reduce these risks oyster lovers (and processors) have regarded them as reducing the quality of the product. Most of the decline occurred in the early years after HACCP was implemented, however. Since 2004, illnesses from these pathogens have been essentially constant.

III. FDA Regulation of Food Manufacturing and Fresh Produce

Food recalls happen on a fairly regular basis, because some specific problem is detected either in the product or in the process. Most such recalls are relatively modest in scale, and attract relatively little public attention. When the recall is large enough, however, it may garner considerable media attention. Moreover, when a significant disease outbreak has been identified but not yet traced to its source, media attention may be intense. Several recent incidents of widespread food contamination have provoked renewed attention to the regulatory process, particularly at the Food and Drug Administration. The incidents have involved both fresh produce and manufactured food products.

Two incidents provoked particular attention to fresh produce. The first occurred in 2006, when spinach from a California processor was found to be contaminated with *E. coli O157*. The incident led to nearly 200 illnesses and five deaths. It was ultimately traced back to wild pigs defecating in a California spinach field. Then in the summer of 2008, a salmonella outbreak led to more than 1,000 illnesses and at least two deaths. The summer-long investigation first identified tomatoes as the likely source of contamination, which led to destroying large portions of the Florida tomato crop. No contaminated tomatoes were ever found, however. By the end of the summer, the source of contamination was traced back to fresh hot peppers from two Mexican farms. Salmonella was also found in a holding pond used for irrigation water at one of the farms.

Another widespread contamination incident focused attention on manufactured foods. Beginning late in 2008, more than 500 people were sickened by salmonella. More than 100 people were hospitalized and the illness may have contributed to at least eight deaths. The contamination was traced back relatively quickly to the Georgia plant of the Peanut Corporation of America, which produced peanut butter, peanut paste, and other peanut products, mostly for use as ingredients in other foods. The recall expanded in scope to include products using these ingredients. Hundreds of products were recalled because they contained PCA peanut products.

Inspections revealed a variety of unsanitary conditions at the plant. More alarming, they uncovered records indicting the company had shipped peanut products despite the fact that they had tested positive for salmonella. An unregistered plant in Texas was found to have problems as well. The recalls broadened to cover all products that PCA had shipped in 2007 and 2008. The FDA launched a criminal investigation of the company, and PCA filed for bankruptcy in February 2009.

Another incident occurred in the summer of 2010, involving salmonella contamination of shell eggs. More than 1900 cases of salmonella resulted. The source was eventually traced back to two Iowa farms, both of which initiated nationwide recalls of more than 500 million eggs in August. Inspections revealed a variety of unsanitary conditions and detected salmonella contamination in chicken feed and in water. An FDA rule regulating large egg producers had just gone into effect in July 2010. That rule, originally proposed in 2004, was a response to a series of salmonella contaminated egg incidents in the late 1990s. It requires egg producers to purchase salmonella-free chickens, and environmental and sanitation controls to prevent subsequent infection.

The food safety system relies on a series of regulations establishing "good manufacturing practices" (GMPs) for a wide variety of different product types. They govern manufacturing, packing, and storing food for human consumption, and identify good practices for personnel, buildings and facilities, equipment, and product process controls. Producing safe food is primarily the responsibility of the food manufacturer. The FDA has the authority to seize products if necessary.

Another set of FDA regulations establish food defect action levels. These levels recognize that some flaws in foods are inherent, and essentially set tolerances about how many problems can be found in each type of product. Chocolate, for example, cannot have more than 60 insect fragments in 100 grams, and cannot have more than one rodent hair in the same amount of chocolate. Canned citrus juices cannot have more than five fly eggs (or one maggot) in 250 mL of juice. Wheat flour cannot have more than 75 insect fragments per 50 grams. These contaminants are aesthetic concerns, not health threats.

The GMP regulations and food action defect levels are enforced through periodic inspections of manufacturing and processing facilities. A typical FDA inspection takes a day and a half, and can cost the government as much as $5,000. Such inspections are relatively infrequent, however. The FDA conducts about 7,000 inspections per year, but there are 150,000 domestic food-processing plants. Obviously the FDA will not inspect most plants any time soon. Moreover, around 80 percent of all inspections are delegated to state inspectors, as was the case in the Georgia peanut plant. Such inspections may be much more cursory. Georgia inspections, for example, apparently averaged around two hours.

When there is an outbreak of food-borne illness, the first step is to attempt to identify the product that is the likely source of the illness. Suspect products are identified based on commonalities in the food items that victims had eaten in the previous week. Then the process of testing begins to identify a specific contaminated product. Finding the common element can be tricky, as the pepper incident makes clear. Many victims had salsa in common, leading authorities to suspect tomatoes, but it turned out to be the peppers. Even when the food is known, finding examples of contaminated product can also be difficult.

Once a contaminated product is found, it is relatively easy to trace back a manufactured product. Producers keep records of when and where particular lot numbers were produced and where they were shipped. When the records are paper records, tracing may be more time-consuming, but the data are available to allow good tracing eventually.

Tracing back contaminated fresh produce is more difficult, because products often mix in the packing and distribution system. Packers purchase raw agricultural products from a number of different farms and mix and resort the product to send it to different markets. Some may be sold to consumers as fresh produce, some may be sold to restaurants, and some may be sold for canning, freezing, or other processing. There is no economic reason for the system to separate produce from different sources, and it does not do so.

The result is that traceback can be exceedingly complex. Figure 16-3 shows a portion of the traceback of the salmonella outbreak due to Mexican peppers. The only growers shown in the figure are those where positive samples were found; obviously there are a great many other growers supplying each of the agricultural firms and brokers shown on the diagram.

The FDA's authority over fresh produce distribution is not substantially different than its authority over manufacturers. There are, however, far more players, because every farm is potentially a source of contamination. As a practical matter, the agency relies on voluntary guidance about best practices to reduce risk.

In response to the widespread publicity surrounding various food contamination outbreaks, Congress passed the Food Safety Modernization Act (FSMA) late in 2010. The act requires all food processing facilities to register with the FDA, and renew that registration every two years. FDA can revoke or suspend the registration if there are food safety violations. Each registered facility must adopt a HAACP plan, similar to the plans used in the meat processing industry. The act requires FDA to establish science based performance standards for contaminants such as pathogens, again similar to the USDA approach. As in meat, this end-to-end focus on risk reduction is likely to facilitate more effective regulation.

Although the essence of the HAACP approach is to rely on the food processor to control risks, FSMA also mandates increased inspections. FDA must inspect all "high risk" facilities within five years, and every three years thereafter. All other facilities must be inspected within seven years, and every five years thereafter. The act, however, does not provide the funding for additional inspectors to accomplish this task. Whether Congress will provide the necessary money through the regular appropriations process remains to be seen.

Figure 16-3. *Salmonella* Saintpaul outbreak traceback and distribution.

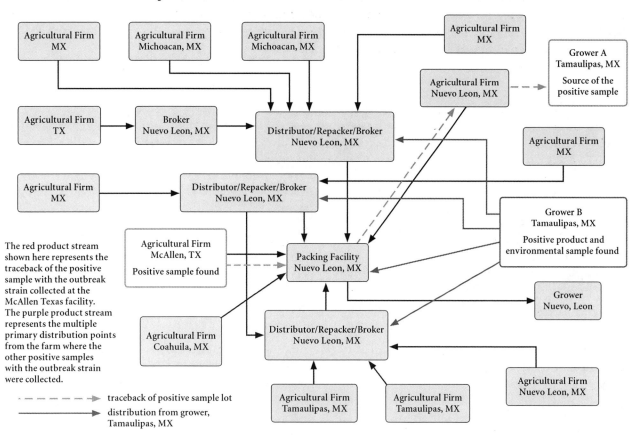

One frequent suggestion in response to incidents of produce contamination in particular has been to establish a tracing system for produce, which might help identify the source of an outbreak more quickly. The feasibility of better tracing, however, is unclear. One can imagine bar codes on grapefruits to allow an immediate determination of where they came from, for example, but it is far less clear how one might track blueberries or lettuce leaves. FSMA requires FDA to conduct pilot studies of better tracing systems and report the result to Congress, and to improve its internal abilities to trace back food products to their source. FDA must also establish recordkeeping requirements for "high risk" foods to facilitate traceback. These requirements cannot require a complete record of prior distribution history, or records of recipients other than the immediate purchaser, or require tracking at the case level. Moreover, "commingled raw agricultural commodities" are exempted from the requirement entirely—an exception that would seem to include virtually all produce.

The act also requires FDA to establish regulations for the safe production and harvesting of fruits and vegetables where it determines that regulations would minimize the risk. The regulations must address soil amendments (such as composting), hygiene, packaging, temperature control, animal encroachment, and water. They must not, however, require any steps that producers of "organic" foods cannot also take. How such regulations might keep pigs out of the spinach fields remains to be seen.

In a bow to the burgeoning local foods movement, Congress exempted farms that sell most out their output directly to consumers, retailers, or restaurants within a 275 mile radius of the farm, and that sell less than $500,000 per year. There is no reason to believe that foods from such farms are safer. For example, an outbreak of E. coli 0157 in Oregon in the summer of 2011 that killed one and sickened 15 was traced to deer encroaching on strawberry fields that sold their produce through roadside stands. Any problems will affect far fewer consumers, because of the relatively small scale of such operations.

FSMA also gave the FDA the authority to order recalls of food in appropriate cases. The practical impact of this provision, however, is unclear, because the vast majority of food manufacturers have voluntarily agreed to recalls when the FDA requested them—and the FDA has always had the authority to seize products that it thinks might be contaminated if they do not.

IV. Summary

One of the key events in establishing the federal role in food safety was the publication of *The Jungle* in 1905. The book revealed unsanitary and disgusting conditions in the meat packing industry, and it led to the Meat Inspection Act of 1906. This act established an inspection-based system of regulation for meat, poultry, and egg products, with an inspector theoretically examining each animal both before and after slaughter to prevent bad meat from entering the food supply.

An inspection-based system is dependent on sufficient resources to conduct adequate inspections. Over time, meat output has increased, but the number of inspectors has declined. The system may also create incentives to rely on the inspector to catch problems, rather than giving company employees, who likely have better information, appropriate incentives to remove suspect product from processing. Moreover, it is completely inadequate for detecting microbial contamination, which is the more current food safety problem. Food-borne pathogens cause an estimated 76 million illnesses per year, and about 5,000 deaths per year. In most cases, the specific pathogen causing the illness is not known.

The inadequacies of the inspection system led to the implementation of regulation based on the Hazard Analysis and Critical Control Points model, which was fully implemented by 2000. HACCP is a process-oriented system, seeking to control problems from the beginning to the end of the production process rather than catching possible problems at the end. Each company must develop its own HACCP plan that is specific to its products and operations. HACCP requires a hazard analysis, identifying the critical control points where hazards could affect food safety, and establishing critical limits for the operation at each of those critical control points. The plan must include monitoring to assure that critical limits are observed, and must specify corrective actions if those limits are violated. Companies must keep sufficient records to establish that they have a plan and are following it. Companies must also establish sanitation standard operating procedures, which specify the procedures they will follow on a daily basis to assure effective sanitation. The entire system is backed up with performance standards for particular microbial hazards. There is zero tolerance for contamination with *E. coli* O157. Salmonella standards are set taking into account the baseline prevalence of the organism in different products. Testing for generic *E. coli* is used to monitor the adequacy of contamination controls, with standards again based on the background incidence of the microbe.

The implementation of HACCP led initially to reductions in disease due to key pathogens, but there is some suggestion that the decline has leveled off in the last few years.

The Food and Drug Administration is the primary agency responsible for food safety in other food-processing industries. Recent incidents involving widespread outbreaks of illness from fresh produce and peanuts have prompted heightened attention to this portion of the food safety system.

The primary responsibility for assuring food safety is on the manufacturer. The FDA establishes good manufacturing practices identifying how processing should occur in various industries, and it establishes food defect action levels that are the maximum amount of various contaminants that are allowed in foods. Inspections of individual plants seek to assure that manufacturers are taking appropriate precautions to assure their products are safe. The number of inspections is limited, however, and in many instances the FDA relies on less detailed inspections conducted by state inspectors.

When outbreaks of illness occur, the first step is to locate the responsible product and trace it back to its source. Although this may be time-consuming in some instances, it is relatively straightforward for manufactured products. Traceback is much more complex when fresh produce is involved, because product from numerous different sources is frequently mixed in the distribution system. The FDA has the same authority over companies that grow and process fresh produce as it does over food manufacturing, but there are far more players. As a practical matter, the agency relies on voluntary guidance about best practices to reduce risk.

The recent outbreaks of food-borne illnesses prompted Congress to enact the Food Safety Modernization Act in 2010. The act requires all food facilities to register with the FDA, and to adopt HAACP plans. FDA must write regulations establishing performance standards to back up these plans. The act requires more frequent inspections of food processing facilities, but does not provide the funding for additional inspectors. It requires FDA to regulate the production of fruits and vegetables, and gives it the authority to order food recalls in appropriate cases.

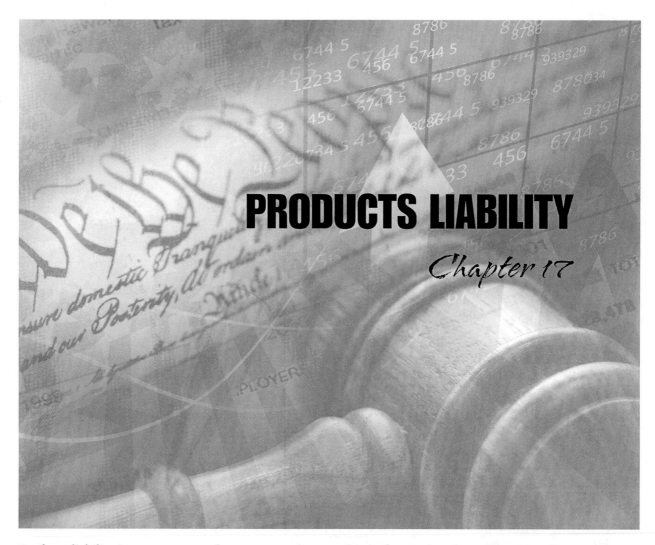

PRODUCTS LIABILITY
Chapter 17

Products liability is an ex post regulatory approach to product safety. Rather than telling manufacturers how to design their products, it lets them make their own choices, subject to liability for damages that result because they made poor choices. Nonetheless, as we consider in more detail in this chapter, the goal of the liability system is to create incentives for manufacturers to make the right choices about product safety in the first place.

Changes in legal doctrines over the last 40 years or so have led to substantial increases in product-liability litigation. In turn, the costs and uncertainties to businesses have very much put the issue on the public policy agenda. Unlike most other areas of public policy we have considered, products liability is largely a creature of state law. Although there are many commonalities across states, there are also unique characteristics of each state's requirements and restrictions.

This chapter will first consider the substantive theories for holding a manufacturer liable for problems that result from using a product. Section II considers the role of incentives in designing liability rules to highlight the goals of the system and the economic issues involved. We then turn to an analysis of each of the two major rules for determining whether the manufacturer is liable: negligence and strict liability. Section V will summarize that discussion and highlight the different functions that liability serves. Finally, we will consider some of the proposals for liability reform.

I. LIABILITY THEORIES

Product-liability cases are usually based on the branch of law known as tort law. A tort is a civil wrong that results in injury to someone else. It is a breach of some legally imposed duty or responsibility to the person who is injured. For example, if someone runs a red light and the result is a traffic accident, the case is a tort.

The driver breached a legally imposed duty to stop, and there was injury to the other person involved in the accident. There is no implication of criminal liability, although the conduct may also be criminal; that is not what the tort system addresses. Sometimes product-liability cases are based on warranty theories (the manufacturer breached an express or implied warranty about the product), but most cases are tort cases.

A manufacturer might be liable on any one of three different theories. First, liability may result from a poorly manufactured product. Under this theory, there is nothing inherently wrong with the product, but something went wrong in the manufacturing process that led to the consumer receiving a product with a flaw that causes a problem. In the days when soft drink bottles were returned to the bottler and refilled, for example, there were occasionally product-liability cases that resulted when a consumer found something disgusting in the bottle (like a bug or a mouse) along with the soft drink. There was nothing wrong with the soft drink itself, but something went awry in the in manufacturing process and led to a problem. Or perhaps a particular product misses a step in the manufacturing process and fails as a result. Again, the problem is the particular example of the product, and not the product itself.

A manufacturer may also be liable because a product is poorly designed. Something about the design of the product either creates a risk, or fails to address a risk. Under this theory, every unit of the product shares the risk, although the problem may not actually occur very often. For example, the allegation that Ford Explorer SUVs equipped with Firestone tires were especially prone to tire tread separation and vehicle rollover, which surfaced in 2000, is an allegation of a design defect. Although not every car or tire will fail, every Explorer with Firestone tires was allegedly subject to the risk.

Finally, a manufacturer may be liable because of a failure to warn consumers about a hazard. The theory here is that the injured victim would have done something differently to avoid the accident, if only he or she had known about the risk. Failure to warn theories have been a significant contributor to the increase in product-liability litigation. Attempts to avoid liability for failure to warn are behind the warnings about a wide variety of seemingly obvious hazards that accompany many products, either on labels or in owners' manuals. Hair dryers, for example, carry a warning to keep the product away from water, and not to use it in the bathtub. However implausibly, a consumer injured by using the dryer in the bathtub could otherwise argue that they were not aware of the risk and that the manufacturer could have prevented the injury with a warning.

One other aspect of liability law that is important in many product-liability cases is the doctrine of joint and several liability. Under this doctrine, anyone who contributed to the consumer's injury, however minor their role may have been, is liable for the full amount of the consumer's damages. In the Ford Explorer and Firestone tire example, for instance, an injured consumer can recover their total damages from either Ford or Firestone (assuming both contributed to the problem), but not from both. The idea behind the doctrine is that the injured consumer should not have to sort out precisely who was responsible for what; the different parties who contributed to the problem can do that separately. The consumer gets paid, and then those who contributed to the consumer's injury can squabble over how much each should pay.

Joint and several liability has another consequence, however—it encourages the search for a deep pocket. Suppose, for example, that a car's brakes fail, and that 90 percent of the cause was that the mechanic performed a repair improperly and 10 percent of the cause was the design of the brake system. Nonetheless, the manufacturer is potentially liable for the entire amount. Moreover, the mechanic may well not have sufficient money (or insurance) to cover the consumer's full damage. Thus there is an incentive to sue the manufacturer even though the problem was mostly someone else's fault. The manufacturer will almost certainly be able to pay.

II. LIABILITY AND INCENTIVES

From an economic perspective, a key goal of liability rules is to create the proper incentives for market participants to make the choices that will maximize consumer welfare. To highlight the proper rules, consider a situation that was a common source of litigation in the early days of railroads. Imagine an early steam engine, with black smoke and numerous embers streaming from its smokestack as it chugs down the track. Along the track on both sides there are fields of grain. As the harvest approaches, the grain is drying in the sun and, if a spark from the engine lands in the field, it can easily ignite a fire. To focus on the essential incentive issues, assume that the only damages from the fire are economic. Some portion of the farmer's crop burns up and is lost, but there are no personal injury issues.

Either party can take steps to reduce the losses from fires. The farmer could move his crops back farther from the railroad tracks, which would reduce the risk that a spark would land in the field. Or he might regularly clean other brush and grasses along the tracks that might spread a fire into the crop. Similarly, the railroad can take some steps to reduce the risk of damage by installing a device known as a spark arrester, which reduces the incidence of sparks (spark arresters were precisely the issue in many of the old cases).

From an economic perspective, there are two costs in this scenario. One cost is obviously the cost of fire damage. But there are also costs that would be incurred to reduce the risk of fire damage. To achieve the most efficient outcome, we want to minimize total costs, which are fire damages plus fire prevention costs. Spending more to prevent fire damage than the cost of the damage itself is not an economically sound decision. If preventing the fires is too costly, it may be more efficient to simply let the fires burn. On the other hand, failing to spend on preventive steps that would reduce fire damages by more than the steps themselves cost is not sound either. In fact, we want both the farmer and the railroad to take cost-effective steps to reduce the risk, if those steps are available.

How we assign liability for the fire damages will affect the incentives of each party. If the railroad is liable for all fire damages, then it will have an incentive to install the spark arrester as long as the avoided fire damages are greater than the cost of the spark arrester. If, however, the spark arrester costs more than the fire damage it would prevent, the railroad will simply choose to pay damages when the fire occurs. The farmer, however, now has an incentive to plant his crop as close to the tracks as possible. Because the railroad will pay for any fire damages, there is no reason for the farmer to take steps to minimize them, even if they are cost effective. Even worse, planting crops closer may increase the losses from fires, because the railroad will pay the farmer's losses.

On the other hand, if the farmer is liable for all fire damages (that is, the farmer must bear the costs of any losses that result from fires), the farmer will have an incentive to move the crop back. If doing so reduces fire damages by more than the lost grain he could have otherwise expected from planting the land, he will do so, but if the lost grain from not planting is worth more than the lost grain from fires, he will not. The railroad, however, will have no incentive to install the spark arrester. It would have to pay the costs of the spark arrester, and even if it prevents more fire damage than its cost, there is no reason to do so.

Suppose that either the spark arrester or moving the crop back will prevent all fires, at a cost that is lower than the fire damage avoided. Then we clearly want to take one precaution or the other, but there is no advantage in doing both. Taking both precautions would incur additional costs without any added benefit. The efficient outcome is to take whichever precaution is cheapest. That will avoid the fire losses and minimize the costs of prevention. Total costs of fire damage plus fire protection will be as low as possible.

We can achieve this efficient outcome if we place liability on the least cost avoider, that is, the party who can avoid the problem most cheaply. If moving the crop back is the cheapest way to solve the problem, then the farmer is the least cost avoider, and making him liable for fire losses will give him the right incentives. If the railroad is the least cost avoider, however, it is the railroad that should be liable for fire damages.[1]

Of course, the railroad fire problem is not really a product-liability issue, but it highlights precisely the same incentive issues. We want a product-liability rule that gives both manufacturers and consumers incentives to minimize the problems that might result from use of the product. Thus, asking about the effects of different liability rules on the incentives of manufacturers and consumers is a key question in evaluating alternative rules.

---

[1] If both moving the crop back and installing the spark arrester reduce the risk, then it might be efficient to take both steps. That is, the two precautions together might prevent more fires than only taking one precaution. If so, we would like to hold each party responsible for losses that result from its failure to take cost-effective steps to reduce the loss.

III. THE NEGLIGENCE RULE

The negligence rule is one of two rules for determining whether a manufacturer is liable (the other is strict liability, considered in the next section). Either rule can be used to determine liability under any of the substantive theories of liability (i.e., defective manufacture, defective design, or failure to warn). Negligence is the older rule, and is still used in cases that involve purely economic damages. It also remains widely used in other legal contexts. Automobile accident cases, for example, are decided under the negligence rule.

Under a negligence rule, the plaintiff must show that the manufacturer was negligent in some respect. In turn, the manufacturer is negligent if there were some reasonable steps that could have been taken to avoid the injury that were not taken. To prevail, the plaintiff generally needs to identify particular steps that it believes the manufacturer should have taken that were not taken. There must, in other words, be some reasonable way the manufacturer could have avoided the problem before the manufacturer is held liable.

In essence, the negligence rule is a cost-benefit test of potential steps that could have reduced the risk of harm. Consider a particular type of accident, and a device or precaution that the manufacturer could take to eliminate the risk of that accident. If the accident occurs, there is a loss to the consumer that is equal to L, and the accident occurs with probability p. Thus the expected benefits of accident avoidance are pL. The device or precaution has a cost, given by C. Under the negligence rule, the manufacturer is liable if there was a reasonable step that could have reduced losses that was not taken. A step to reduce losses, however, is only reasonable if the benefits of that step exceed the costs. Thus, the manufacturer is negligent if pL > C, and is not negligent if pL < C. This formulation is sometimes known as the Learned Hand Rule, after the judge who first formulated the test in this fashion.[2]

The incentive effects of the negligence test for the manufacturer are straightforward. If the manufacturer is negligent, it will have to pay losses of L whenever an accident occurs. On average, that will cost the manufacturer pL. On the other hand, it can avoid those losses by taking some preventive step at a cost of C per unit: installing a safety device, issuing a warning, or taking greater care in the manufacturing process. If pL > C, it will make sense to take this preventive step, but it will not make sense otherwise. Thus, the manufacturer has an incentive to take preventive steps whenever it will otherwise be held negligent.

In effect, the negligence rule places liability on the least cost avoider, at least when either party could have avoided the accident. If the manufacturer can cheaply avoid the accidents it should do so, and the negligence rule will find it liable if it does not. On the other hand, the consumer might also be negligent if he or she could have avoided a particular accident at low cost. When steps to reduce risk are available to both consumers and manufacturers, the precise incentive effects depend on the precise legal rules employed.[3] In general, however, the negligence rule creates an incentive for the manufacturer to take all available cost-effective steps to reduce the risk.

There are three difficulties with the negligence rule for determining liability. First, the rule ignores the level of activity. That is, it focuses only on whether an activity was done reasonably, not on whether it should have been done at all. In our railroad example from the previous section, the level of activity is the number of trains that run. A negligence rule asks whether the train was operated reasonably, but it does not consider whether the train should have operated at all. Perhaps shipping goods by barge is a cheaper way to reduce the fire risk than either spark arresters or moving back the crops. Similarly, in the context of automobile accidents, a negligence rule asks whether you drove reasonably, but not whether you should have made that trip at all. Because the cheapest way to reduce risk may be to reduce the level of the risky activity, the negligence rule leaves out one potential part of the solution.

---

[2]Hand actually used B for "burden of precaution" instead of C for cost of avoidance. The text uses C because it avoids possible confusion with "benefits," which in this problem are actually pL.

[3]When both parties are negligent in some regard, some jurisdictions use comparative negligence to resolve the issue—the parties share the loss in proportion to their share of causing the loss. Other jurisdictions use contributory negligence, which holds that if there is any negligence by the plaintiff, the plaintiff cannot recover. There is an extensive body of literature about the incentive effects of these and other rules for determining liability.

Second, the negligence rule is subject to marginal instability. That is, small changes in the estimates can make enormous differences to the parties involved in the lawsuit. Consider, for example, an accident that causes losses of $1 million whenever it occurs, but that only occurs one time in a million. The expected benefit (pL) is therefore $1. If the cost of avoidance is $0.99, then the manufacturer is liable and must pay $1million. If, however, the cost of avoidance is $1.01, the manufacturer is not liable, and pays nothing. A very small difference in the estimated cost of avoidance makes a huge difference in who has to bear the loss. Obviously this difference in estimates is well worth arguing about for both the victim and the manufacturer, and they are willing to expend resources on studies, experts, and the like to make sure that their estimate prevails.

The marginal instability of the negligence rule feeds the third problem as well: the system is costly to administer. Determining p, L, and C requires a great deal of information. Moreover, these values must be determined through litigation, which can be a costly and time-consuming process. Costs are likely to be particularly high for plaintiffs, who are unlikely to have a ready reservoir of knowledge about the product or different steps that could have been taken to make it safer. Thus administering a system based on negligence can be costly.

IV. Strict Liability

The shift to strict liability for product manufacturers began in the 1960s, and today strict liability is the general rule in product-liability cases involving personal injury. Under strict liability, the manufacturer is liable for damages regardless of negligence. Therefore, there is no need to inquire into what the manufacturer did, or should have done, to reduce the risk of the accident; the manufacturer is liable even if nothing could have been done to avoid the problem. Moreover, manufacturers are liable for damages that result from reasonably foreseeable misuse of the product. Thus the manufacturer may be liable even if the consumer contributed to the problem, although most states have rules to reduce the consumer's recovery in such cases.

In design defect cases, the issue is whether a product was "unreasonably dangerous." This is a negligence-like inquiry, but it is up to the jury to decide. Under negligence, whether the manufacturer failed to take reasonable steps to avoid the problem is a legal standard rather than a purely factual question. But under strict liability, the jury decides, and the jury's determinations of factual issues usually cannot be appealed. Juries are asked to conduct a risk-utility analysis, which essentially asks whether the utility of the product is great enough to justify the risk. If the jury says no, the manufacturer is liable.

The result can be some strained cases. In one case, for example, a manufacturer of above-ground swimming pools was sued because the plaintiff dove into the pool and was seriously injured. These pools are at most about four or five feet deep, which is clearly not enough water for safe diving. Nonetheless, the jury decided that the product was unreasonably dangerous—the utility of an above-ground pool was not sufficient to justify the risk that someone would dive in. The fact that the plaintiff allegedly dove in from the roof of the garage next door apparently did not matter. Apparently it also did not matter that the plaintiff was allegedly drunk at the time—a fact that may explain the entire case.

Faced with strict liability, manufacturers have to decide whether it is worthwhile to make safety improvements to their products. Although they will be liable in every case, it still may not make economic sense to change the product. If the manufacturer makes the improvement, it will incur a cost of C, the cost of avoidance, for every unit of the product. It will save pL, the expected benefit of the safety improvement, per unit. The manufacturer will choose whichever is cheaper. That is, if pL > C, the manufacturer will install the safety device. On the other hand, if pL < C, it will be cheaper to simply pay the damages that result, because the cost of avoiding those damages is too high. This, however, is exactly the same choice that a manufacturer would make under negligence. Liability may be strict, but it does not generate incentives for additional safety improvements.

It may seem counterintuitive that strict liability does not lead to safer products, but it really is not. Under negligence, if there are no reasonable steps that could have been taken to avoid the loss, a manufacturer is not liable and does not have to pay. Switching to strict liability means that the manufacturer must pay, but there are still no reasonable steps that could be taken to avoid the loss. If there are no reasonable steps to take, there is simply nothing manufacturers can reasonably do. If there are reasonable steps to avoid losses, manufacturers have the same incentive to take them under either the negligence or the strict liability rule.

What will differ under the strict liability rule is product pricing. When there are no reasonable steps to reduce risk, the manufacturer will still have to pay the losses when accidents occur. The average cost of losses per unit of the product will be pL. Manufacturers will have to cover this cost to remain in business in the long run, and in competitive markets, prices will increase by pL under strict liability. Note that the liability rule does not affect price when there are reasonable precautions. Under either rule, the price will increase (compared to no liability at all) by the cost of avoidance. Under strict liability, however, the costs of unavoidable accidents are reflected in prices as well. Thus, under strict liability, the unavoidable risk differences across products are reflected in prices, because manufacturers will have to pay to cover losses when they occur.

The fact that risk differences are reflected in product prices creates incentives that change the level of activity. The increase in price will lead consumers to purchase fewer risky products. In the above-ground swimming pool example, where there is little the seller can do to avoid the risk of someone diving in, prices will increase to cover the expected liability costs. Fewer consumers will purchase above-ground pools as a result. Thus, the level of the risky activity will change—there will be fewer above-ground pools for people to dive into.

Under strict liability, incentives for the victim are different. Because the victim can recover even if his or her own conduct contributed to the accident, there is less incentive for victims to exercise care. Some incentive remains because not all losses can be compensated financially, but incentives for victims are weaker than they are under a negligence rule.

One of the most significant problems with a strict liability rule is the risk-reducing product that is still dangerous. If a product actually reduces risk, we would like consumers to use it more extensively. But if it still has some risks, pricing liability for the risk into the product will reduce use of the product.

The classic case is vaccines. In general, vaccines reduce risk and improve public health—enough so that most jurisdictions require that children have current vaccinations against common diseases before they enter school. But many vaccines pose some risk of serious complications for a few. One common childhood vaccine is the DPT vaccine, for diphtheria, pertussis (commonly known as whooping cough), and tetanus. There is a risk, estimated at 1 in 310,000, of serious neurological reactions, including in some cases long-term mental retardation. The risk is apparently due to the pertussis component of the vaccine. When strict liability was imposed in the late 1970s, numerous manufacturers left the market and prices per dose rose sharply. The price was $0.23 per dose in 1978; by 1989 it had reached $10.84. Strict liability induced significant price increases for other vaccines as well. For example, prices of the oral polio vaccine (which uses a live virus and sometimes causes the disease) increased 325 percent, and prices for vaccines against measles, mumps, and rubella rose 40 to 56 percent.

To avoid these substantial price increases, Congress established the National Vaccine Injury Compensation Program in 1986. Funded by an excise tax on each dose of covered vaccines (without regard to risk), the program offers a no-fault way for victims to receive compensation for their injuries. Victims are required to go through this no-fault process before they sue, but they are free to reject the program's offer and file suit on their own if they are alleging the vaccine was poorly mode. Consumers cannot go to court on design defect or failure to warn theories.

A second difficulty with strict liability is that it leads to reductions in innovation. For existing products, with reasonably well-known risks, raising the price enough to cover the liability costs is straightforward. For new products, however, risks may not be completely known. Estimating how much to charge to cover liability risks is therefore more difficult. One reaction by some manufacturers is to avoid introducing new products that might pose risks that are difficult to assess. Across industries, the industries with the greatest increases in liability costs had the largest reductions in research and development expenditures and new product introductions in the 1980s.

Finally, although administrative costs of the negligence system are significant, the administrative costs of strict liability are substantial as well. Asbestos litigation costs an estimated $2.59 for every dollar that actually goes to a victim. The product liability system for DPT vaccines cost $7.54 for every dollar that went to a victim. The federal Superfund program, which imposes strict liability on companies that dumped hazardous wastes, often decades ago, has cost an estimated $8.33 for every dollar that actually goes to cleaning up abandoned sites. Using liability to compensate victims is a costly proposition.

V. LIABILITY FUNCTIONS: INSURANCE AND INCENTIVES

Products liability serves two different purposes. One is to provide the proper incentives for manufacturers to consider safety issues in product design, and for victims to exercise appropriate care in using products that may be hazardous. We have discussed the incentives involved with different liability rules in the previous sections. The incentives for manufacturers, effects on product prices, and incentives for consumers are summarized in Figure 17-1.

Products liability also serves an insurance function for victims, in addition to its effects on incentives. When someone is injured in an accident involving a manufactured product, the victim may well be completely innocent. Perhaps the classic case is vaccine liability, where the victim is an innocent child. There is no obvious reason why it is the victim who should bear the loss. One argument for strict liability is that the company is better able to bear the loss than the victim, and strict liability will transfer the loss to the company (and hence to all users of the product, rather than just the unlucky few). It will, in effect, provide insurance against product problems for all potential victims.

In effect, strict liability bundles insurance into the price of the product. Consumers must purchase insurance with the product; they cannot decide that the risk is sufficiently remote that they do not want to pay for insurance. It cannot be declined. The negligence rule offers insurance as well, but only against the manufacturer's negligence. Strict liability, in contrast, offers full insurance for any product problem.

Tort liability should seek to create proper incentives for efficient conduct. Accidents, whether involving products or not, are best avoided if the burden of their costs is placed on the least cost avoider. That is what negligence does. However, the best solution may not be the same in all instances. There is little victims can do to reduce the risk of finding some contaminant such as an insect or a mouse inside a packaged product, and strict liability on the manufacturer makes some sense. But in cases like vaccines, we want to preserve the level of the activity, and even encourage more. Negligence may be a more sensible rule from the perspective of incentives, and a separate insurance program may be a far less costly way to compensate victims who could do nothing to avoid the risk.

Figure 17-1. Negligence versus strict liability.

	Negligence	Strict Liability
Manufacturer's Incentives		
Install safety device	If pL > C	If pL > C
No safety device	If pL < C	If pL < C
Product Price		
With device	Marginal cost + C	Marginal cost + C
Without device	Marginal cost	Marginal cost + pL
Consumer Incentives Regarding:		
Care	Be careful.	No incentive.
Usage	No changes	Use less (without device)
Insurance	Negligence only	Full insurance

VI. PROPOSALS FOR REFORM

A number of different proposals have emerged to address liability reform, both for products liability and for other areas that raise essentially the same set of issues, such as medical malpractice. Since at least 1984, these issues have been on the federal agenda. Although there has been some federal legislation, there has probably been more action at the state level.

One set of proposals would shift the burden of proof to the consumer. Under this idea, the consumer plaintiff would have to show that the manufacturer knew or should have known that the product was defective. Some prominent cases of liability, such as asbestos, involve products where there seems to be general agreement that the risk was not known when the product was introduced. Under strict liability, however, that does not matter.

Another proposed reform is to employ strict liability only for poorly manufactured products. These cases are ones where there is little the victim can do to avoid injury, and where only the manufacturer has detailed information about the quality control options that might prevent problems. Design defect cases and failure-to-warn cases would be judged under the negligence standard. If there is no safer design, or no cost-effective warning, there is certainly no incentive-based reason to impose liability on the manufacturer. This approach was adopted by the American Law Institute in its *Restatement (Third)* of liability law, but it has not been widely adopted in the states.

The proposed changes that have had the most traction have been limits on non-economic damages. There are two types of non-economic damages: awards for pain and suffering, and punitive damages. The idea of pain and suffering awards is to compensate victims in some way for the pain they suffered from the accident. There is, however, no clear objective measure of how much any individual victim should get. The question is largely up to a jury, and the skill of the victim's attorney in advocating a large award. The possibility of a large pain and suffering award, however, is arguably an incentive to sue in cases that would otherwise settle.

The other form of non-economic damages is punitive damages. These damages are designed to punish the company for especially egregious conduct, above and beyond what might be needed to compensate the victims. Punitive damages can be nearly any amount, although courts have increasingly limited them over the last few years.

In one case involving an Alabama BMW dealer, the jury awarded $4,000 in economic damages for retouching the paint on new cars with damaged finishes, but $4 million in punitive damages. The U.S. Supreme Court ruled that punitive damages so far out of proportion to the actual economic losses were unconstitutional. More recently, in the 2008 Exxon Valdez case, the Supreme Court limited punitive damages to an amount equal to the actual economic damages. How widely that precedent will apply remains to be determined.

Damage limitation caps have been adopted in a number of states. Typically, total damages are limited to a multiple of the actual economic damages. In many states, total damages cannot exceed twice the economic damages. These approaches seek to take the lottery component out of liability litigation, and therefore reduce the incentive to sue. Some states have also limited joint liability for noneconomic damages.

One other noteworthy reform was enacted in 2005, allowing most class action cases to be tried in federal rather than state courts. Because products liability is largely a matter of state law, there is an incentive for plaintiff's lawyers to shop for a favorable venue in which to file suit. Particular districts in Mississippi and Illinois became widely known as "judicial hellholes" because they were so sympathetic to class action litigation. It will be interesting to see to what extent trying these cases in federal court makes a significant difference.

VII. SUMMARY

Product-liability cases are usually based on tort law. Liability may be imposed for a poorly manufactured product, for a poorly designed product, or for failure to warn consumers about a hazard. All who contributed to the injury are jointly and severally liable for the full amount of the damages to the consumer.

Liability rules seek to establish proper incentives for efficient conduct. From an economic perspective, the goal is to minimize the total costs of accidents and accident prevention costs. Placing liability for losses on the least cost avoider of the losses accomplishes this objective.

Under the negligence rule, the plaintiff must show that the manufacturer failed to take some reasonable steps that could have been taken to reduce the risk. The manufacturer is negligent if the expected losses from the accident, pL, are greater than the cost of avoidance, C. Otherwise, the manufacturer is not liable. The rule gives manufacturers an incentive to incorporate safety devices whenever $pL > C$. It gives potential victims incentives to exercise care, because they may have to bear the costs of their actions. Negligence does not address the level of activity. Negligence determinations are subject to marginal instability, and the administrative costs of a negligence system are high.

Under strict liability, the manufacturer is liable for damages caused by the product regardless of negligence. Manufacturers can also be held liable for failing to protect consumers from reasonably foreseeable misuse of the product. Under strict liability, manufacturers will compare the costs of paying damage awards and the costs of safety devices that may reduce those costs. Just as under the negligence rule, they will install safety devices if $pL > C$, and not otherwise. If there are no reasonable steps that can be taken to reduce risk, however, manufacturers will raise product prices by pL to cover the liability expenses they cannot avoid. Victims have less incentive to utilize care under strict liability, because their losses will be fully covered. Victims will reduce the level of activity, because the liability component of the price will lead them to use less of the product. Strict liability poses problems for risk-reducing products that are still dangerous, such as vaccines, because the increase in price will reduce the level of activity. It can lead to reductions in innovation. Like negligence, it is costly to administer.

Liability serves two functions. One is to create the right incentives, and the other is to provide insurance to victims of accidents. Strict liability in effect requires consumers to purchase full insurance against product problems along with the product, because the manufacturer must incorporate liability costs into the price. Consumers cannot decline or avoid this insurance.

Proposals for reform of products liability include requiring consumers to prove that the manufacturer knew or should have known about the risk. Other proposals would limit strict liability to poorly manufactured products, using the negligence rule for design defect and failure to warn cases. A number of states have enacted statutory limits on non-economic damages, and the Supreme Court has limited punitive damages. A recent reform allows class actions to be tried in federal courts, potentially reducing the problem of forum shopping.

ENVIRONMENTAL ISSUES

Chapter 18

Historically, concern for the environment in the United States was a concern about conservation, to preserve America's natural wonders unspoiled for future generations to enjoy. It was the conservation movement, for example, that led to the establishment of national parks. The beginnings of a new direction for environmental concerns came with the publication of the book *Silent Spring* in 1962. The book was about pesticides in general, and DDT in particular. Its thesis was that pesticides were killing the birds, and that we would therefore have a silent spring.

The use of DDT illustrates some of the trade-offs that are frequently involved in environmental issues, and remains controversial today. Part of the economic attraction of DDT was that it was a long-lived chemical that did not break down rapidly. For farmers, that meant fewer applications than might otherwise be needed. Unfortunately, it also meant accumulating levels of DDT in the environment. That accumulation was how DDT endangered birds: it led to weakened egg shells that were too weak to support the developing embryo, particularly for larger birds like the bald eagle.

DDT was also relatively safe for humans. It was safe enough that many southern communities sent fogging trucks through residential neighborhoods during the summer to spray for mosquitoes, with children running after the trucks to play in the fog. Modern pesticides are far more toxic to humans, as well as to insects.

The current controversy about DDT concerns its use in tropical countries for malaria control. A very effective technique is to spray the inside walls of houses with DDT. Treated houses have fewer mosquito visits (apparently they do not like DDT) and many of those that visit die. Because the application is indoors, rather than in the outdoor environment, the environmental impact is very limited. This use of DDT, which was endorsed by the World Health Organization in 2006, has split the environmental community. The Pesticide Action Network opposes any use of DDT, but the Environmental Defense Fund has supported this limited use.

Environmental regulation is the most costly set of federal regulatory requirements. Direct costs are around $260 billion annually. Costs have increased steadily over time, and are likely to continue to increase as we address new issues. In 1972, environmental regulatory costs were 0.9 percent of the GDP. By 1990 they had risen to 2.1 percent of the GDP, and to 2.6 percent of the GDP in 2000.

This chapter begins with an analysis of the roots of externalities, which is the lack of property rights. Section II considers the command and control approach to pollution issues, as it is implemented in the case of regulation to address so-called "criteria" air pollutants. Section III discusses the problems of command and control regulation. Market-based approaches to pollution control are considered in Section IV. Section V considers the global warming debate and approaches to address it that are under consideration. Section VI considers the precautionary principle, which is at the heart of many environmental debates between the United States and the European Union.

I. PROPERTY RIGHTS AND THE COASE THEOREM

When we considered externalities in Chapter 2, we saw that the root of the common property externality was the lack of property rights. We also considered better definitions of property rights as incentive-compatible ways to address external costs and external benefits. In fact, the lack of well-defined property rights is at the heart of all externality problems.

Consider a simple externality involving noise. There is a factory that makes sheet metal parts, using a large hydraulic press to stamp out parts all day long. The hydraulic press is noisy, and disturbs the neighbor. Making noise, however, reduces costs, and the factory therefore earns more than it would if it eliminated the noise. The neighbor is a cardiologist, who sees patients in his office. When he places his stethoscope against the patient's chest, the "thump thump" he hears may be the patient's heart, or it may be the hydraulic press next door. Because of interference from the noise, the doctor earns less than he otherwise would. The net gains to each party are summarized in Figure 18-1.

This externality, like any other, is reciprocal in nature. We can think of the factory creating the problem because it creates the noise, or we can think of the doctor as creating the problem by locating next door to the factory. Think, for example, of people who buy a house at the end of an airport runway and complain about the noise. The problem is the incompatible use of the resource. The factory wants to use the resource to carry away unwanted noise; the doctor wants to use it to listen to patients. With only one user, there is no externality, no matter which party it is.

The efficient outcome in this particular instance is no noise. We want to find the outcome that maximizes the total gain for both parties, and in the example total value is higher if there is no noise. One obvious way to get there is to make the factory liable for noise damages. If the factory makes noise, it will have to pay the doctor his damages: the $100 he could get with peace and quiet, minus the $40 he can get anyway. Rather than pay the doctor's damages of $60, it is better for the factory to eliminate the noise at a cost of $40.

Suppose, however, that the doctor is liable for noise damages. Thus, if there is noise, the doctor simply has to suffer the consequences. In this case, there will still be no noise. Rather than suffer $60 in damages, it is better for the doctor to pay the factory the minimum of $40 it will take to get the factory to eliminate the noise. The doctor has to pay at least $40, and if he pays anything less than $60 he is still better off without the noise. Thus, whichever party is liable, the resource is used in the same way, and the use of the resource is efficient.

This is the Coase theorem, named for the Nobel prize–winning economist who developed it. In the absence of transactions costs, externalities will not affect resource allocation. Regardless of externalities,

Figure 18-1. A noise externality.

	Payoffs for the Parties		
	Doctor	Factory	Total
Noise	40	140	180
No Noise	100	100	200

the parties will negotiate to reach the joint maximizing solution. Because the total payoff is higher if the resource is used efficiently, there are gains from trade, and the parties have an incentive to take advantage of those gains.

The central implication of the Coase theorem is that externalities stem from poorly defined property rights. When the rights are clear, however they are defined, the parties can trade to reach the efficient solution. When the rights are unclear, however, it will be much more difficult for the parties to come to an agreement, because they will first have to argue about who pays. Clear definition of property rights eliminates that question.

For the Coase theorem to work, the parties also need to be able to trade rights. If rights cannot be bought and sold, then we can only reach the efficient solution if the rights are allocated properly in the first place. When the rights can be traded, however, the initial allocation does not matter in the absence of transactions costs.

Figure 18-2. Noise externality with different control options.

	Payoffs for the Parties		
	Doctor	Factory	Total
Noise	40	140	180
No Noise	100	100	200
Factory Controls	100	120	220
Doctor Controls	82	140	222

We can complicate the situation a little more and still reach the same essential result. Consider the payoffs in Figure 18-2. Now, in addition to the option of eliminating the noise entirely, there is the possibility of either party controlling the noise. The factory might change its hours, for example, to reduce the noise problem for the doctor, or the doctor might install soundproofing to reduce the noise. Again, the figure shows each party's payoff depending on how the resource is used.

In this example, the efficient solution is for the doctor to control the noise. The total payoff of $222 is higher than with any other alternative. Clearly, if the doctor is liable, he will install soundproofing to control the noise, and we will achieve the efficient outcome.

But suppose the factory is liable. The factory could, of course, control the noise at a cost of $20 and avoid paying any damages. However, there is a better option. The factory can pay the doctor to control the noise. It will have to pay at least $18, which is what it costs the doctor to control, and it is willing to pay up to $20, which is what it will cost to control the noise on its own. Again there is a gain from trade, and again we achieve the efficient solution regardless of how the property rights are assigned.

The assumption of no transactions costs is critical to the Coase theorem result. Suppose, in the last example, there is a transaction cost of $5. This is a cost of rearranging legal rights. If a party wants to do what they are entitled to do there is no transaction cost, but if the parties want to make a deal, they must pay a lawyer $5 to write a contract. In this case, the right will stay wherever it is initially allocated. If the doctor is liable, he will control the noise. However, if the factory is liable, it will control the noise. The gain from trade with the doctor is only $2, not enough to cover the transaction cost. If transactions costs preclude trading, we will only achieve efficient resource allocation if we assign liability to the least-cost avoider.

The Coase theorem is an important insight into the nature of externalities. If transactions costs are low, the parties themselves can solve the problem. That is what happens in the market for bees and blossoms, discussed in Chapter 2. Policies that create well-defined property rights and facilitate trading can help to address externalities without the need to determine first precisely how resources should be used. This is the core idea behind market oriented approaches to pollution control, discussed in Section IV.

II. COMMAND AND CONTROL REGULATION: REGULATION OF CRITERIA AIR POLLUTANTS

Command and control approaches are at the heart of most environmental regulation in the United States. Rather than rely on markets to achieve environmental objectives, we tell people what to do. We specify maximum permissible tailpipe emissions to control automobile pollution. We require companies that discharge various hazardous pollutants to employ either the "best practicable technology" if the hazard is not too great, or the "best available technology," without regard to cost, if the hazard is more significant. If we want to make a 20 percent reduction in emissions of some pollutant, we often tell everyone over a certain size to make a 20 percent reduction. All of these are command and control approaches.

Command and control allows responsiveness to politically important groups. Congress and the regulators can set different standards for different groups if they choose. They can exempt or limit the impact on influential groups whose support is needed. An agency seeking to maximize political support has every incentive to do so. When the Clean Air Act passed in 1970, the statutory scheme carefully matched the benefits and costs of the statute in geographic terms, for example. The most polluted cities would bear the highest costs, but they would also be the primary beneficiaries of pollution reduction. As we shall see, the scheme also gave considerable discretion for state and local governments to choose which industries to regulate most intensively, enabling them to address local political concerns. Moreover, as discussed in Chapter 7, there are opportunities for rent creation in the details of creating and implementing a policy. The requirement of scrubbers on new power plants to reduce sulfur dioxide emissions was an example; it provided benefits to eastern coal producing states that produce mostly higher-sulfur coal. With scrubbers required, there was no incentive to switch to low-sulfur coal to reduce emissions, benefiting eastern producers. Moreover, the costs of restrictive policies are often well hidden with command and control approaches.

To examine command and control regulation in more detail, we will examine the air pollution regulatory structure that applies to so-called "criteria" pollutants. These pollutants were originally specified by statute, but the EPA can add additional pollutants. Criteria pollutants are sulfur dioxide, carbon monoxide, particulates, nitrogen dioxide, ground-level ozone, and lead. They were the major pollutants of concern when the Clean Air Act was originally passed in 1970, and have remained a central feature of air pollution regulation.

The first step in the regulation of criteria air pollutants is for the Environmental Protection Agency to set National Ambient Air Quality Standards (NAAQS). NAAQS are uniform, nationwide standards that specify the maximum permissible level of the pollutant in the ambient air. For example, the NAAQS for carbon monoxide is nine parts per million; the NAAQS for ozone is 0.075 parts per million (ozone is the irritating component of what is commonly known as "smog"). These standards are health based. In fact, the EPA is not allowed to consider the costs of compliance in setting the standards. NAAQS are periodically reviewed, and revised if necessary based on new scientific evidence about the health effects of a pollutant.

The NAAQS standards are based on a threshold concept. That is, the standards are based on the notion that below some level there are no adverse effects from the pollutant at all. The goal of the standard-setting process is to identify the threshold and set the standard at that level. In theory, lower levels of exposure are of no public health concern; but by definition, higher levels of pollution pose some risk to public health. The risk may be to specific populations (such as those with asthma) rather than the population as a whole, but there is a risk.

Once the NAAQS are determined, the focus shifts to state and local governments. They are required to have plans for bringing their jurisdiction into compliance with the NAAQS, subject to the EPA's review and approval. These plans typically involve emissions standards for each different source of the pollutant. Rather than specifying the allowable concentration in the atmosphere, as NAAQS do, the emissions standards specify a maximum allowable level of emissions of a particular pollutant from a particular source. Typically they are specified for each facility, and may be specified for each source of emissions within the facility. Thus, each piece of equipment within an industrial facility may be subject to its own emissions standard, separate even from other equipment that emits the same pollutant. These emissions standards are enforced through permit requirements. A "point source"[1] of pollution must have a permit authorizing it to emit a certain amount of the pollutant. Excess emissions, over and above what the permit allows, are violations of the permit, and subject to fines and other sanctions.

---

[1] A "point source" of pollution is a particular piece of equipment in a particular facility. Thus the pollution comes from a particular point. A different piece of equipment, or a different facility, or a different pollutant, is a different point source. There are also "mobile sources" of pollution such as automobiles. In the water pollution world, there are also "non-point sources." These are sources of pollution, such as storm water runoff from city streets or agricultural runoff, which does not come from a particular point.

The state and local planning process is the primary authority over existing sources of pollution. The EPA also has the authority to set new source performance standards (NSPS) for new or significantly modified sources of a particular pollutant. These standards are more generic, applying, for example, to all facilities of a particular type (e.g., a power plant) emitting a particular pollutant (e.g., sulfur dioxide). By law, a NSPS must specify a technology. It cannot allow nontechnical solutions, regardless of their effectiveness. Thus, changes such as fuel switching or changes in work practices cannot meet a NSPS, regardless of their efficacy. Moreover, a NSPS requires continuous reductions, rather than reductions only at certain times. Thus, for example, a technology that limits peak emissions, but has no effect at other times, would not suffice to comply with a NSPS.

For any given pollutant, the level of control is variable, and it depends on three factors. First, the rules typically distinguish between "major" and "minor" sources of the pollutant. On the theory that they are responsible for most of the problem, major sources are generally subject to more stringent controls. "Minor" sources, often politically influential small businesses, are subject to less stringent standards.

Second, standards differ between "old" and "new" sources of pollution. In general, it is more difficult to achieve a given level of control at an existing facility, because it may not be able to accommodate the most up-to-date technologies or processes. In a crude sense, this distinction is based on costs. The substantive idea is that it is likely to be cheaper to design in pollution controls in a new facility, compared to retrofitting an existing facility that may not be able to accommodate more modern approaches to the problem. Politically, regulating new sources more strictly may create barriers to entry that protect existing sources of pollution from competition. Moreover, firms that may want to build new sources in a particular geographic area may not know who they are at the time the regulations are adopted, and may not be part of the local political process in any event. Similarly, stricter controls on new sources of pollution are advantageous to established industrial areas, because new industrial capacity in other areas will face higher costs.

A long-running controversy, dating back to at least the Clinton administration, concerns the definition of a "new" facility. Electric utilities were the particular focus of concern. Companies have learned how to improve maintenance procedures and selectively renovate equipment or facilities to maintain, or even increase, production in "existing" facilities. The Clinton administration sought to prosecute utilities that had made "too many" repairs to be considered "existing" facilities. The Bush administration sought to clarify the rules to determine when an "existing" facility became "new." Both efforts were challenged in court. After 18 years, it is still not clear when an "existing" facility becomes "new." Such controversies are inherent in the command and control approach to regulation.

The third key factor affecting the stringency of controls is where a facility is located. "Attainment" areas are those that meet the NAAQS. That is, the air in those areas is clean enough that it does not pose a public health risk. Facilities in these areas are subject to less stringent controls. In "non-attainment" areas, however, which have not yet met the NAAQS, controls are more stringent. The idea is that where the air is clean enough that it does not pose health risks, there is little reason for costly additional controls. Where the air remains dirty, however, the benefits of stricter controls are greater.

The three criteria interact with one another. The strictest requirements apply to a major new source of pollution in a non-attainment area. As a practical matter, under the regulations on their face, it would be impossible to open such a source without some regulatory accommodation. Applied literally, that approach would have meant no significant new industrial facilities in the Los Angeles basin since approximately 1970.[2]

Rather than accept the harsh consequences of no economic growth in Los Angeles for 30 years, regulators searched for alternative approaches. One of the most-used alternatives is the policy of "offsets." Under this policy, a company that wishes to open a major new source of pollution in a non-attainment area can pay someone

---

[2]Because of its topography, Los Angeles has always been, and may always be, a non-attainment area. The basin is bordered by mountains to the east, with the predominant air flow coming from the Pacific Ocean to the west. The mountains trap polluted air, keeping it from dissipating over a broader area. The result is that pollutants accumulate in the trapped air, producing persistent violations of the NAAQS in Los Angeles.

else to "offset" its additional emissions. Usually these transactions require a net reduction in emissions. That is, the company wishing to open a new facility must *more* than offset its environmental impact, resulting in a net improvement in air quality. Each separate transaction is subject to regulatory review and approval.

Offset transactions have sometimes been quite creative. For example, Union Oil wanted to open a new marine terminal in Los Angeles in 1990, which would have been a major new pollution source. To obtain regulatory approval, it agreed to offset the emissions by purchasing (for $700) and crushing old (pre-1970) cars that have much higher emissions than newer cars.[3] The reduced emissions from some 8,400 old cars removed from the road were presumed to offset the emissions from the new marine terminal.

The regulatory approach to criteria air pollutants is command and control at its finest. There are specific requirement for each plant that must be met before the facility can operate. Often these requirements are even below the level of the individual plant. Thus, a plant may have multiple pieces of equipment that discharge a particular pollutant, but each piece of equipment may be subject to its own specific requirement. Reducing emissions from one piece of equipment will not count against the standards that apply to other equipment. Similarly, reducing a particular pollutant from one technology does not change the requirements that apply to the same pollutant from other technologies. Each point source of pollution is a world unto itself, and must meet specific regulatory standards.

III. PROBLEMS OF COMMAND AND CONTROL

A. Resource allocation

The essential problem of command and control approaches to achieving environmental goals is that they ignore efficient resource allocation. Simply put, it may be cheap to reduce pollution in some places, and vastly more expensive to reduce it elsewhere. It may be relatively cheap to incorporate the latest technology in a new plant built from the ground up, for example, but prohibitively expensive to employ that same technology in existing facilities. Market-oriented approaches take advantage of these differences to achieve the environmental objective at the lowest possible cost. Command and control approaches generally ignore them.

Consider the hypothetical electricity-generating industry depicted in Figure 18-3. The industry is emitting a total of 20 million tons of sulfur dioxide, and we would like to cut those emissions in half. Requiring each plant to eliminate half of its emissions will achieve the reduction at a cost of $3.3 billion.

Figure 18-3. Resource allocation in a hypothetical industry.

Plant	SO$_2$ Emissions, millions of tons	Cost per Ton to Control Emissions	Total Cost of 50% Emissions Reduction (millions)
A	3	$100	$150
B	4	$600	$1,200
C	2	$400	$400
D	4	$200	$400
E	1	$500	$250
F	6	$300	$900
Total	20		$3,300

---

[3]Ever worried about possible circumventions, the deal required that cars must be fully functional, not partially disassembled, and driven under their own power. In addition, they had to be registered in the Los Angeles area for the previous two years.

The least-cost solution would eliminate more pollution where pollution is cheaper to control. Plant A would eliminate all of its pollution at a cost of $100 per ton, as would plant D at a cost of $200 per ton. Together, they would eliminate 7 million tons of pollution. To achieve a 10 million-ton reduction, we need plant F to cut its emissions in half, at a cost of $300 per ton. The total cost of this solution is only $2 billion, a substantial savings.[4]

A cap and trade approach will achieve the least-cost solution. Under cap and trade, the government creates a certain number of permits to emit the pollutant, but there are not enough permits to allow existing levels of pollution to continue. This is the "cap" on total emissions. Firms must have enough permits to cover their emissions, and they can either buy or sell permits on the open market (the "trade"). (We consider the real-world cap and trade program to address sulfur oxide emissions in the next section.)

Under cap and trade, plants that can control pollution cheaply will do so. The precise details depend on how the available permits are distributed, but suppose initially that each plant gets permits for half of its total emissions, and must either eliminate the other half of emissions or purchase permits to cover them. At any price above $100, plant A will be willing to sell its permits and eliminate all of its emissions. Similarly, plant D will sell permits and eliminate all emissions if the price is above $200. Plant F will sell permits if the price is above $300 per ton, but it will buy permits if the price is lower. Plant B, however, will find it cheaper to purchase permits to cover its emissions at any price below $600.

We can trace out the supply and demand of permits in Figure 18-4. Note that each plant will either buy or sell permits depending on the price, so each plant shows up in both the supply and demand curve. The market-clearing price of permits will be $300. Plants A and D will sell their allocation of permits and make money on the deal. Plant A, for example, sells 1.5 million tons' worth of permits at a price of $300, and therefore earns $150 million even after accounting for the costs of eliminating its emissions. Plants B, C, and E will purchase permits. Plant F, the marginal supplier of permits, will use the permits it has and cut its emissions in half.

There are, of course, numerous ways we might distribute the permits. Undoubtedly the most straightforward way to do so is to auction off the 10 million tons of permits. The market-clearing price will again be $300 per ton, and each plant will make the same decision about whether to buy permits or control emissions. The government, however, will get the money. For plant A, instead of net earnings of $150 million from the sale of permits, it will have only the $300 million cost of eliminating its emissions. High cost plant B will pay $1.2 billion for permits to allow 4 million tons of emissions; it only had to pay $600 million under the scheme where it received permits for half of its emissions for free.

Figure 18-4. A hypothetical permit market.

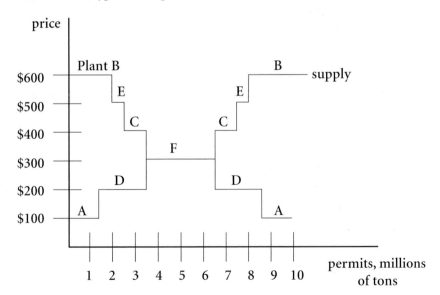

There is another market-based approach that will also achieve the least-cost solution, this one based on taxes. If the government allows firms to emit as much sulfur dioxide as they want but charges them $300 per ton of emissions, we will achieve the same outcome as the auction-based permit system. The

---

[4]Perhaps we are really willing to spend $3.3 billion to reduce emissions in this industry. If so, the least-cost solution would let us eliminate an additional 4 million tons of pollution: the remaining 3 million tons from plant F for $900 million, and half of plant C's emissions for $400 million. For the same amount of money, we achieve a 40 percent greater reduction in pollution.

low-cost plants will find it cheaper to eliminate emissions than to pay the tax; the high-cost firms will pay. Plant F will be indifferent between controlling emissions and paying the tax; either way will cost it $300 per ton.

Market-based schemes take into account efficient resource allocation. They assure the least-cost solution for any desired degree of pollution control. Because command and control schemes ignore differences in costs, they will inevitably cost more to achieve the same result.

B. Other problems of command and control

1. Information

If regulators are going to require specific technologies, they need information about the cost and feasibility of that technology, as well as comparable information about competing technological solutions. Thus, a command and control regulatory system requires fairly detailed information about the costs of controlling emissions using different technologies and approaches. Firms, however, are likely to know far more about control costs than the regulator. They have incentives to reveal that information if it helps them to achieve the policy approach they prefer, but not reveal it otherwise. Regulators are therefore at an informational disadvantage.

Consider, for example, a regulator interested in reallocating natural gas supplies. One big user of natural gas is the poultry industry, which uses gas to heat the henhouses for egg production. A warm chicken lays more eggs, thereby increasing production. Of course, poultry producers could shift to some other fuel for heat. But there is another substitute for natural gas that is obvious to chicken farmers but probably not to obvious to regulators: chicken feed. Giving chickens more to eat will also increase egg production. Thus, to the chicken farmer, but probably not to the regulator, natural gas and chicken feed are substitutes.

Market-based approaches also need information, but we need not know the technological details of how firms will choose to control emissions. We have to decide either how much pollution to allow in a permit system, or how much we are willing to spend in a tax system. Firms will have incentives to choose the least-cost solution without further prompting.

2. Incentives

Command and control approaches do not create incentives to do more than the minimum required, even if control costs are low. In our hypothetical power industry, for example, if plant A is told to cut its emissions in half, there is no reason for it to make larger reductions, even though it is relatively cheap to do so. Even worse, there may be incentives to delay making reductions that would otherwise occur. If firms anticipate the possibility that they will be required to make reductions relative to some baseline in the future, it may make sense to wait for the regulatory requirement rather than acting sooner. Acting now may mean that only more expensive control approaches are available when the new requirements take effect. Moreover, lowering emissions now may reduce the baseline, so that the firm must cut more than it otherwise would have had to cut if it makes reductions now.

Market-oriented approaches avoid these incentive problems. Firms have incentives to invest in any control that costs less than the price of a permit or the cost of the tax.

3. Innovation

Command and control approaches often do little to create incentives for innovation, to find cheaper or better ways to control emissions. If the government specifies a particular technology, there is no reason to look for an alternative (except for a technology supplier who may want the government to require firms to buy its product). There may also be positive disincentives. When the rules require the best available technology, for example, a firm that develops a new but more costly technology may find that it is required to use it. In contrast, market-oriented approaches generate incentives for innovation, because the firm will benefit if it can find a way to reduce costs.

Sometimes, command and control approaches are used that are "technology forcing." Essentially, this approach sets regulatory targets that we do not yet know how to meet, in the hopes of forcing technological progress to meet the goal. This approach was used when the government first started setting automobile emissions standards, for example. What is forcing, however, is the goal, not the approach. A requirement that cannot be achieved with current technology will generate incentives to find a solution even if it is implemented through a market-oriented system. For example, a declining number of permits over time in a cap and trade system will create strong incentives to find alternatives to the rising cost of permits. Similarly, increasing tax rates over time would generate incentives to find new solutions.

4. The Stock-Flow Problem

In many cases, command and control approaches focus on new products or new equipment and impose stringent requirements to reduce pollution. Eventually new equipment will replace old equipment, and if the standards are tighter for new equipment, the world will be cleaner when that happens.

Unfortunately, such requirements can be counterproductive in the short term because of the stock-flow problem. New equipment is the flow, into a stock of existing equipment. For example, new cars sold each year are the flow into the stock of cars on the road. Tighter requirements on new equipment raise the price of new equipment, which creates an incentive to keep using old equipment longer. Because new equipment is generally less polluting that old equipment, even without more stringent standard, the result is to slow down progress in meeting environmental goals.

Consider, for example, the stock of automobiles. Older cars are substantially more polluting than current models. A California study estimated that in 2010, cars older than the 1998 model year will account for 25 percent of the miles driven, but 75 percent of local pollution.[5] Replacing those older cars would significantly reduce pollution. But tighter standards for new cars mean that the older cars will stay on the road longer.

A similar effect occurs with industrial emissions. Tighter standards can make things worse if they lead companies to keep old equipment in use longer than they would otherwise. In fact, one study found that states with more stringent enforcement of pollution requirements have 27 percent more pollution than they would have had without the extra enforcement, because the greater enforcement efforts lead to an older capital stock.[6]

Market-based approaches are not prone to the stock-flow problem. If the cheapest way to reduce emissions is to replace older equipment, there is every incentive to do so. Moreover, the incentive is to make reductions as soon as possible.

IV. Market-Oriented Approaches

A. Cap and trade for sulfur dioxide emissions

There are alternatives to the command and control regulatory approach. By far the most prominent U.S. market-oriented pollution control system is the "cap and trade" approach to controlling sulfur dioxide emissions from electric power plants. This approach was established in the 1990 Clean Air Act Amendments.

The political impetus for this legislation was concern about the possible adverse impacts of "acid rain," particularly in the northeastern United States. When sulfur dioxide emissions, primarily from coal-burning electric utility plants, enter the atmosphere, they combine with water droplets to form dilute sulfuric acid.[7] When it rains, the rain is more acidic than it would otherwise be, and the fear was that acid rain was contributing to significant ecological damage.

---

[5]Jason E. Bordoff. Refuel Economy with Cash for Old Cars. http://www.brookings.edu/opinions/2009/0106_cash_for_clunkers_bordoff.aspx (January 2009).

[6]Michal T. Maloney and Gordon L. Brady, Capital Turnover and Marketable Pollution Rights, Journal of Law & Economics, Vol. 31 No. 1, pp. 203–226 (April, 1988).

[7]Ironically, acid rain may itself be the consequence of earlier environmental regulations. The initial sulfur dioxide regulations focused on the concentration of the pollutant near power-generating plants. To reduce the ground-level concentrations that were the initial focus of concern, utilities built taller smokestacks. The smokestacks injected sulfur dioxide higher into the atmosphere and dispersed it over a wider area. The strategy reduced the risks of ground-level exposures to high concentrations of sulfur dioxide, but it increased the risk of acid rain by giving the gas more time to combine with water vapor and form sulfuric acid.

Although a National Academy of Sciences study was under way, Congress and the administration did not want to wait for its results, and enacted the cap and trade system. When the report was eventually released, it found less environmental damage from acid rain than many had expected, but the Clean Air Act Amendments had already passed and the program was underway. The EPA believes that reduced human sulfur dioxide exposure provides health benefits that more than justify the restrictions.

Conceptually, cap and trade sets an aggregate limit on the total amount of sulfur dioxide emissions that are allowed.[8] Permits were created for each ton of sulfur dioxide emissions, and in order to emit a ton of sulfur dioxide, a firm must have a permit for that emission. Permits, however, are essentially property rights. They are owned by the firm, and marketable. A firm with permits could either use those permits to emit a ton of sulfur dioxide, or it could sell the permits to someone else. Moreover, firms can reduce emissions in any way they choose. They can install scrubbers to reduce emissions, switch to lower-sulfur coal, or use some combination of techniques. A firm that can reduce emissions more than it has to will have more permits than it needs, and can sell those permits to someone else. A firm that could not control emissions at an acceptable cost is free to buy permits from others. The only requirement is that each ton of emissions must be matched by a permit to emit that ton. Essentially, permits are a Coase theorem approach to the problem: define property rights in a way that facilitates transactions to achieve efficient resource use.

To reduce emissions, a cap and trade scheme must not issue enough permits to allow the existing level of emissions. The 1990 Clean Air Act only created enough permits for half of the existing emissions of sulfur dioxide, and required a reduction of 2 million tons of nitrogen oxide emissions as well.

For the 1990 Clean Air Act, permits were passed out to existing firms in proportion to their baseline emissions, averaged over 1985–1987. In addition, there were "bonus" allocations for utilities that used politically favored approaches to reducing sulfur oxide emissions. Firms that used scrubbers, or "clean coal" technologies, and firms in growing areas received extra permits, which they could either use or sell to others.

The success of the sulfur dioxide program has made it the model for proposed approaches to limiting carbon dioxide emissions to control global warming. Sulfur dioxide, however, is a much simpler problem. Essentially, it only comes from one source, coal-fired electricity generating plants. That made passing out permits a relatively easy process. Carbon dioxide, in contrast, comes from virtually everything that uses energy, and the problem of allocating permits is far more complex. We explore this issue in more detail later in this chapter.

The sulfur dioxide control program has clearly yielded benefits at a substantially lower cost than would have occurred with a command and control approach. At the time the program was enacted, the EPA estimated that it would cost $2.3 to $5.9 billion per year, and that the incremental cost of eliminating a ton of sulfur dioxide would be $579 to $760. Ten years later, in 2000, the actual total cost of the program was $1.1 billion, and the marginal cost of removing another ton of sulfur dioxide was only $291.

Part of the reason for lower costs than projected was that fuel prices turned out to be lower than the EPA had expected. That made it possible for some utilities to substitute lower-sulfur fuels, such as natural gas, for higher-sulfur coal. But a significant portion of the cost reduction was also because various innovations reduced the cost of emissions control.

One innovation involved railroads. With increased demand for low-sulfur coal, which often must be shipped long distances, railroads developed more efficient means to move the goods. These changes reduced the cost of the fuel-switching solution, and therefore reduced total costs. In addition, improved scrubbers were developed, reducing the cost of that compliance strategy. Electric utility generators also developed fuel blending technologies that allowed them to combine high-sulfur and low-sulfur coal to achieve any desired level of sulfur content. Before the law was enacted, this technology in particular had not been anticipated.

One of the more interesting cost reductions from the cap and trade approach to controlling emissions was that it reduced the need for excess capacity in scrubbers for firms using that technology to comply. In a command

---

[8]Nitrogen oxides can also contribute to acid rain, forming nitric acid in combination with water in the atmosphere. There are also limits on nitrogen oxide emissions, but the sulfur dioxide limits are the key element of the program.

and control system, a firm that relies on scrubbers must essentially shut down if the scrubber goes down due to scheduled maintenance or breakdown. To avoid that problem, firms can maintain excess capacity of scrubbers. Then, when one scrubber fails, another is available to take its place. That strategy, however, has obvious costs.

Cap and trade allows another alternative: if a scrubber breaks or requires maintenance, the firm can simply purchase additional permits on the market to cover the added emissions. The industry as a whole needs excess scrubber capacity to cover outages, but it needs far less excess capacity than if each individual firm must have its own reserve.

The fact that cap and trade cost less than expected is important, but far more important is the fact that it cost substantially less than the cost of command and control approaches to reducing sulfur oxide emissions. Estimates are that the cap and trade program cost only 43 to 55 percent of what command and control approaches would have cost—that is, we achieved the same benefit for roughly half the cost.

The cost reductions from market-oriented approaches to pollution control are not unique to sulfur oxides. Eleven different studies have compared incentive schemes such as cap and trade to command and control approaches. On average, these studies find that the costs of incentive-based approaches are only 16 percent of the costs of a command and control approach. Across different programs, the costs of incentive approaches range from only 4.5 percent of the costs of command and control to 93 percent of the costs. The range of cost savings is substantial, but incentive approaches are clearly a cheaper way to achieve environmental objectives.

B. Taxes versus cap and trade

Market-based approaches to pollution control are essentially ways to intervene in a market for pollution. A pollution market is shown in Figure 18-5.

The demand for pollution reflects the costs avoided by not controlling emissions; the lower the level of pollution, the higher the likely costs of additional reductions. The upward-sloping curve represents the additional damage from more pollution. As the quantity of pollution increases, the incremental damage from additional pollution is likely to increase as well. The optimal level of pollution, Q^*, is where the two curves intersect. Absent some intervention, the level of pollution will be where demand hits the horizontal axis, because the price of pollution is effectively zero.

Cap and trade systems intervene in this market by fixing the quantity of pollution. As firms buy and sell permits, the market will determine the price of a permit and hence the cost of control. The quantity, however, is known and fixed, because only so many permits are issued. If the costs of control are higher than expected (i.e., if the demand curve is shifted to the right), the price of permits will be higher, as will the costs of control, but the quantity must remain the same.

Tax-based systems intervene in this market by setting the price of pollution with the tax rate per unit of emissions. Firms choose however much pollution they want to emit at this price. Because firms will choose to control emissions to the point where the marginal cost of control is just equal to the price, we know the marginal cost of control, but we do not know for sure how much pollution will result. If costs of control are higher than expected, we will end up with more pollution than expected, because the price does not change.

Figure 18-5. The market for pollution.

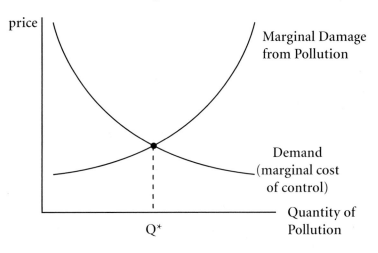

Figure 18-6. Fixing price versus fixing quantity.

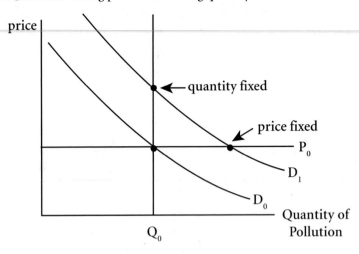

This essential difference is highlighted in Figure 18-6. Only the demand for pollution is shown, and if we think demand is D_0, the two policies are equivalent. Whether we fix the price at P_0 or the quantity at Q_0, we will achieve the same result. If demand is in fact higher, however, at D_1, fixing the quantity (the permit-based system) will result in a higher price. Fixing the price (the tax-based system), however, will result in a larger quantity of pollution than expected.

If the benefits of controlling pollution are relatively flat (i.e., they are not particularly sensitive to the level of pollution), and the costs of control are relatively steep, then the uncertainty about the quantity of pollution that results from a tax-based system is probably preferable. Because benefits are relatively flat, more pollution than we thought we would get does not have very substantial consequences. On the other hand, if the benefits of pollution control are steeply sloped and costs are relatively flat, it is more important to avoid too much pollution, and the uncertainty about the cost of control is less significant.

With price known for sure in a tax-based systems, the costs of the system are more transparent. With permits, precisely because demand is not known for certain, we are not sure how much the program will cost. The costs may be equivalent, but they are better hidden with a cap and trade approach.

The other potential difference between cap and trade and tax-based systems is where the money goes. With taxes, the money goes to the government, although the government can redistribute the money if it chooses. With cap and trade, there is more flexibility about who gets the money. Government can pass out the permits however it chooses to maximize political support or to reward influential constituencies. Government can get the money if it auctions off the permits, but it need not do so.

V. GLOBAL WARMING

For well over a decade, one of the most contentious environmental issues has been the debate over global warming. The politics of global warming have changed with remarkable rapidity. This section briefly discusses the facts about global warming and its most significant potential consequences, and then turns to the different policies to address the issue.

A. Global warming facts

1. Greenhouse Gases

Greenhouse gases trap heat in the atmosphere. Rather than allowing heat to radiate into space through the atmosphere, they retain some of that heat, causing the temperature to rise. The greenhouse gas that is usually the focus of global warming discussions is carbon dioxide, but there are numerous other greenhouse gases, some of them thousands of times more potent than CO_2 in their ability to retain heat. Usually these gases are converted to "carbon dioxide equivalents" based on their relative heat holding ability.

Carbon dioxide is emitted as a result of combustion, including the combustion of food that occurs in the human body. There are numerous sources of carbon dioxide emissions, including decaying vegetation. An estimated five percent of annual CO_2 emissions are due to humans. Carbon dioxide concentrations in the atmosphere have increased about 30 percent since the beginning of the Industrial Revolution. Projections for increased CO_2 emissions imply that the concentration of CO_2 in the atmosphere will increase 30 to 150 percent by 2100.

Another significant greenhouse gas is methane. Methane emissions are up approximately 150 percent since the beginning of the Industrial Revolution, with about two-thirds of annual emissions due to human activity. The major sources of methane are decaying vegetation in rice paddies and landfills, and the digestive processes of animals, particularly cattle. As a greenhouse gas, methane is about 20 times more potent than carbon dioxide, but it does not persist in the atmosphere for as long.

Quantitatively, the most important greenhouse gas in terms of the atmosphere's heat holding capacity is water vapor. On a planetary basis, water vapor accounts for 95 percent of the greenhouse effect. There are tremendous uncertainties about the role of water vapor in climate models, discussed in more detail below.

Life depends on the greenhouse effect. The average surface temperature of the Earth is about 55 degrees Fahrenheit. Without any greenhouse effect, it would be only 5 degrees. Cooling is also critical, however. The greenhouse effect alone implies a surface temperature of 130 degrees. Clearly, maintaining an appropriate balance is important.

Since pre-industrial times, the estimated heat holding capacity of the atmosphere has increased by 1 percent. Projections for emissions growth over the next century imply that heat holding capacity will be up 2 percent by 2100, again compared to pre-industrial times.

2. Climate Sensitivity

Given growth in emissions of greenhouse gases, a critical question is the sensitivity of climate to these changes. What we know about climate sensitivity is largely derived from climate models. These models typically divide the world into a grid and calculate climate in each square of the grid. Resolution remains rather crude; models typically cannot resolve horizontal differences smaller than about 200 km. Models focus on the bottom 15 km of the atmosphere, and divide it into roughly 20 layers.

The latest "consensus forecast" of climate sensitivity is that doubling atmospheric CO_2 concentrations would increase temperature by 2 to 4.5 degrees Celsius. The "best" estimate from the Intergovernmental Panel of Climate Changes (IPCC), an international group of scientists that studies climate issues, is that doubling CO_2 would raise temperature by 3 degrees Celsius. Temperature increases more slowly than CO_2 changes, largely because the ocean temperature changes slowly.

Since the late 1900s, the average temperature has increased an estimated 0.1 to 0.5 degrees Celsius. The current estimated rate of temperature increase is about 0.1 degree Celsius per decade. Consistent with global warming models, most of the observed warming has occurred at higher latitudes in winter. The models predict less temperature variation, with increases particularly in nighttime lows, and that is generally what has been observed.

3. Consequences

There are two major potential consequences of climate change that have attracted particular attention, although many other potential consequences have been identified. One such consequence is rising sea levels. The IPCC predicts that sea level will increase by 18 to 59 cm (7 to 22 inches) by 2100. This increase is entirely due to thermal expansion: as the oceans warm, the water expands, and sea level rises. The Pew Center on Global Climate Change estimated that this sea level increase would cost the United States $20 to $150 billion over the course of the next century.

Long term, the critical variable in determining sea level changes is the fate of two large ice sheets on land: the West Antarctic ice sheet and the Greenland ice cap. The West Antarctic ice sheet is a particular concern, because it may be unstable. If it were to slide into the ocean, (or, over a much longer time period, melt) it would raise sea level by an estimated 17 to 20 feet. At one point the EPA conducted a poll of glaciologists, who estimated there is a 1 percent to 5 percent chance of this happening. The Greenland ice cap is not subject to instabilities, but if it were all to melt, it would raise sea level by an estimated 23 feet. Presumably, however, that would happen gradually over a considerable period of time. The dynamics of ice caps are poorly understood. Recent reports suggest that both Greenland and Antarctic ice may be melting more rapidly at the edges than previously expected. However, both ice sheets also seem to be thickening in the middle.

The second major consequence of global warming is an increase in hurricanes and other weather extremes. The evidence about hurricanes actually illustrates some of the many uncertainties that surround global warming science. Until about 2003, there seemed to be a strong consensus that global warming would not affect hurricane frequency or intensity. Although ocean temperatures would increase, providing more energy for hurricanes, climate models also predicted more upper atmosphere winds. With more winds in the atmosphere, it is more difficult for a hurricane to get organized and intensify.

Then in 2005 two papers were published that suggested intensifying hurricanes, based on an observed correlation between ocean surface temperatures and the frequency and intensity of hurricanes since 1970. However, there is a long-term decadal oscillation in hurricane frequency, going back to 1900, that is very difficult to account for with only 30 years of data. Moreover, we have much better data on recent hurricanes than on ones further in the past. For many older storms, we know almost nothing about their intensity before they made landfall.

Global warming may also lead to and increased frequency of other weather extremes. Cold days and nights (below the 10th percentile in the distribution of temperatures) have become less frequent, while hot days and nights (above the 90th percentile) have become more frequent. Heat waves have also become more frequent over most land areas, and the fraction of precipitation accounted for in heavy precipitation events (above the 95th percentile) has increased.

There may also be some benefits from global warming. Fewer cold nights, for example, means less energy use for heating. A longer growing season in the northern latitudes means increased agricultural productivity. Changes in the distribution of rainfall may impact some areas favorably, and others unfavorably. Economic studies of the impact of global warming generally find that there are net benefits from warming, up to approximately 2° C.[9]

4. Uncertainties

There are two major sources of uncertainties in our understanding of global warming to date and the reliability of forecasts of the distant future. First and most important is the role of clouds and water vapor. Water vapor is critical in global warming models because it is itself a potent greenhouse gas. Significant warming depends on an added effect from more water vapor in the atmosphere, rather than CO_2 alone. This is positive feedback: CO_2 raises the temperature, which increases evaporation, which increases the amount of water vapor in the atmosphere, which increases temperature even more. Without positive feedback, the projected increases in CO_2 alone would only increase temperature by 1 degree Celsius.

When water evaporates, however, it forms clouds, which reflect more solar energy back into space. Greater reflectivity tends to reduce temperatures. However, clouds are not well accounted for in climate models, which cannot resolve horizontal features smaller than about 200 km on a side; clouds smaller than 200 km may well be important.

Related to uncertainties about clouds is uncertainty about aerosols, which are small droplets or solid particles suspended in the atmosphere. We know aerosols have a cooling effect, but again they are not fully accounted for in current climate models. Instead, models make somewhat ad hoc adjustments to try to account for their impact. Moreover, we know aerosols interact with clouds, which are themselves not well accounted for in the models.

A second major source of uncertainties is the trends in emissions of greenhouse gases. The IPCC considers six different emissions growth scenarios, with the concentration of CO_2 increasing from 75 percent to 350 percent in 2100 depending on the scenario. That is, to say the least, a considerable range. The IPCC's best estimate of the temperature changes under each scenario ranges from 1.8° C. to 4° C. One key difference among the scenarios is the assumptions about how technology will change. Will technological change favor easier discovery and/or extraction of oil and other fossil fuels, relative to other energy sources? If so, emissions will be higher because fossil fuels will be cheaper. Or will technology reduce the cost of renewable sources such

---

[9]Richard S. J. Tol, "The Economic Effects of Climate Change," Journal of Economic Perspectives, Vol. 23, No. 2, pp 29-52 (Spring 2009).

as wind energy, solar, or energy from biomass? If so, emissions will grow more slowly. Projections of population growth and economic growth are also critical factors in determining emissions levels. As discussed in Chapter 3, over century time scales, such projections are inherently unreliable.

One key fact in all of the emissions scenarios is that most of the emissions growth is in the developing world. China is now the world's largest greenhouse gas emitter, and probably the country where emissions are growing most rapidly, largely because of rapid economic growth. As a whole, the developing world between 2000 and 2004 accounted for 40 percent of total emissions, but a majority of the growth in emissions. Making significant changes in emissions trends will require participation by developing countries.

B. Global warming policy issues

The first global effort to address climate change was the Kyoto Agreement, initially signed in 1992. In this agreement, the industrialized nations agreed to a voluntary goal of stabilizing emissions of greenhouse gases at 1990 levels. At the time it looked easy. The world was in a recession, and emissions had declined in 1993. Over the long term, the goal was much easier for European nations to achieve than it was for the United States because of differences in population growth. Europe was projected to have essentially the same population in 2025 as it had in 1990. The U.S. population, in contrast, was projected to grow by 40 percent over that same period. If the Kyoto goals were achieved, the climate models predict that global temperature will be approximately 0.1 to 0.2 degrees Celsius lower than it would be otherwise.

In 1997, the Kyoto Protocol was signed. Under this agreement, which took effect in 2005, participants agreed to binding targets for a five percent reduction below 1990 levels by 2012, when the agreement expires.

In an interesting indication of how rapidly the politics of global warming have changed, before the Kyoto Protocol was signed the U.S. Senate voted 95–0 that it would not ratify any treaty unless there was no serious harm to the U.S. economy (debatable, but unlikely) and the treaty imposed binding targets on developing countries (it did not). The Clinton administration signed the agreement, but never submitted it to the Senate for ratification. When the Bush administration took office, it disavowed the agreement. As discussed below, during the 2008 presidential campaign, both major parties endorsed cap and trade approaches to address global warming, but legislation to adopt such a system collapsed in 2010. Because policy is very much in flux, this section seeks to address the issues that policy makers must confront, rather than the policies themselves.

1. Scope within a Country

Within a country, policy to address greenhouse gas emissions can be broad or narrow. A broad policy would address all greenhouse gases (except probably water vapor) from all sources; a narrow policy might address only certain gases (e.g., carbon dioxide) or only certain sources of emissions (e.g., transportation or electricity generation). A policy might take the same approach to emissions from mobile sources, or adopt different approaches to mobile sources and point sources of emissions. From an economic perspective, broader is better, because it gives more opportunities to find the least-cost solution. Because there are trade-offs between emissions from different sectors, policy should treat all greenhouse gas emissions the same, to the maximum extent possible.

2. Scope across Countries

As noted above, under all scenarios, the largest increases in emissions will occur in developing countries. As a result, it will be very difficult to address climate change without serious participation by developing countries, particularly rapidly growing economies such as China, India, and Brazil. There are, however, very good reasons why developing countries do not want to participate. Economic growth is vastly more important to countries where millions live in poverty that makes the worst conditions in the developed countries look like paradise. Like many other goods, environmental protection is a good where demand clearly increases with increases in incomes. Poorer countries are likely to consider economic growth a far higher priority than the developed countries, who value the environment more highly. From a global economic perspective, however, again, broader is better. We want to find the least-cost solution, and there are significant trade-offs between emissions in developed and developing countries. Some estimate that a uniform approach (i.e., a common world price for carbon emissions) would cost 20 to 40 percent less than if the price of emissions differs across countries.

3. Pace of Change

Rapid reduction of greenhouse gases is likely to entail sharply increasing marginal costs. For example, if we replace coal-fired electricity generating plants with alternatives as they wear out and must be replaced anyway, costs are relatively low. But if we demand rapid reductions that require abandoning existing plants, costs will be substantially higher. Benefits, on the other hand, are likely to be relatively flat. The key determinant of climate change is the concentration of greenhouse gases in the atmosphere. However rapidly we change current emissions, the atmospheric concentration will change quite slowly. Lower rates of reduction also allow more time for technological alternatives to emerge, which will likely reduce costs in the long run.

4. Flexibility

As noted above, there are considerable uncertainties in our knowledge of climate change. The facts are almost certain to change from what we know today. There are substantial uncertainties about both the benefits (e.g., what will happen to the Antarctic ice sheet) and the costs (e.g., what will alternatives to fossil fuels cost) of policies to address climate change. We need to adopt policies that can accommodate changes in what we know about both the costs and the benefits. We might need to move far more rapidly than we now expect, or we may be able to adjust over a much longer period of time. Policies that lock in fixed goals over a long period of time will make it much more difficult to take into account new information as it emerges.

5. Perspectives on Cost

To be sure, there would likely be benefits from policies to address greenhouse gas emissions. Advocates of change, however, have an incentive to minimize the costs, which are plainly substantial. Several different approaches to minimizing costs have appeared in recent debates.

One approach is to discuss costs in terms of reductions in growth rates. Policies to reduce greenhouse gas emissions may cause relatively small reductions in growth rates. Over time, however, small differences in growth rates can have a huge impact. For example, the current world GDP is approximately $43 trillion. Reducing the growth of GDP from 4 percent per year to 3 percent per year may sound relatively small, but it would mean that GDP in 50 years is $117 trillion lower than it would be otherwise. In a hundred years, GDP would be reduced by $1,345 trillion. That is a tremendous amount of wealth that our descendants will not have to address the problems they face, including climate change.

Another approach that some have used is to compare current costs to future world GDP. For example, some have argued that we can solve climate change for only 1 percent of world GDP in 2100. But at 4 percent annual growth, GDP in 100 years will be approximately $2,171 trillion. One percent of future GDP is $21 trillion. However, from another perspective, that is almost half of current world GDP.

Policies to address global warming will redirect efforts at technological change. They will unquestionably benefit some sectors of the economy, but they will also unquestionably impose significant costs on others. Investments in renewable electricity generation, for example, will be matched kilowatt for kilowatt by reduced investment or even disinvestment in coal and other fossil fuels. The necessary changes will involve significant costs to the economy. Addressing global warming is no different than addressing any other problem. If there were a "free" solution, market participants would have already adopted it without the need for government intervention.

C. Approaches to controlling greenhouse gases

By far the most straightforward policy to address global warming concerns would be a carbon tax. With a tax, it is easy to achieve broad coverage, across different fuels, different industries, and different end-users of products and services that produce greenhouse gas emissions. It is also straightforward to apply a tax across different greenhouse gases, because the relative potency of different gases is well established. One estimate is that the benefit-to-cost ratio for carbon taxes is about 5 times the ratio for the principal alternative, which is cap and trade.

A tax, however, is politically very difficult. The goal of global warming legislation introduced in 2009, for example, was a 17 percent reduction in emissions by 2020. With a carbon tax, emitters would have to pay a tax on the 83 percent of their emissions that would be permitted to continue in 2020, as well as the costs of eliminating 17 percent of their emissions. Politically this is exceedingly difficult: the government would be asking companies to pay for both the reductions in emissions and their continuing emissions—which the government agrees are acceptable! Moreover, there is little room for dispute about the costs of a tax-based system. Calculating the effect of any given carbon tax rate on the price of gasoline is completely straightforward, but politically very unpopular.

The principal alternative approach to global warming is a cap and trade system. Modeled loosely on the successful sulfur dioxide program, the proposal would set a cap on total greenhouse gas emissions, but leave it to individual companies to decide how best to comply: to reduce emissions, or to purchase permits from others. This is, however, a very different problem. For all practical purposes, there was but one source of sulfur dioxide emissions: coal-fired, electricity-generating plants. There are obviously vastly more sources of greenhouse gas emissions.

One critical question is how to allocate the permits under a cap and trade system. The approach of simply auctioning available permits to the highest bidder faces precisely the same political problem as a tax. Companies must pay for both the costs of reducing emissions, and for the costs of emissions that everyone agrees are allowed to continue. Costs to ultimate consumers may be better hidden, but costs to companies that must comply are clear. Moreover, allocating permits across different industrial sources of emissions is not a straightforward problem, particularly given that some companies have already made significant investments in reducing emissions. Passing out permits in proportion to "baseline" emissions would reward companies that have not yet taken any steps to reduce emissions.

The object lesson in the difficulties of the cap and trade approach is the initial allocation of permits in European Union's cap and trade mechanism. Each country allocated its share of permits across industries within the country to achieve its overall reduction target. Trading was allowed within countries or across countries. The result was that governments allocated more permits to industry than the allowable emissions target; the "cap" actually allowed an increase in emissions. Not surprisingly, that was exactly what occurred.

There is a further difficulty with cap and trade approaches. One attraction of cap and trade is that it may be cheaper to avoid emissions increases in developing countries than it is to achieve actual reductions in developing countries. Allowing such transactions would reduce the cost of compliance, without reducing environmental benefits. The E.U. system therefore allows credits for "clean development mechanism" projects. The idea of these credits was that companies that invested in reducing emissions (or, conceptually, emissions growth) in other countries should get credit for that effort, which, after all, reduced total worldwide emissions compared to what they would have been otherwise.

Inherent in such offsets, however, is the problem of "additionality." For any given project, it is quite possible that the project would have been undertaken anyway, even without the lure of carbon credits in the E.U. (or a future U.S.) market. If credits are awarded for projects that would have happened anyway, however, there is no actual reduction in emissions. Thus, in the E.U. system, credits are only available if there is "additionality": that is, if the project would not have occurred without the credits. Whether a project would have occurred anyway, however, is inherently speculative. Projects with obvious environmental benefits, such as capturing methane from landfills, may not depend on credits, because methane is a marketable commodity as an energy source. But many such projects have multiple revenue streams, and there is no objective basis for saying that any one revenue stream is critical to the project. Moreover, the answer to the question of whether a project would have happened anyway will become more and more speculative as the potential for carbon credits becomes ingrained in numerous projects.

The problem of "additionality" is clearest in its treatment of forests. Forests are a "carbon sink," because they absorb carbon dioxide from the atmosphere, thereby offsetting human emissions. The European Union has therefore recognized reforestation projects as legitimate sources of carbon offsets. They have not, however, recognized preserving existing forests as an offset. After all, the forest might not have been cut in any event. The result is that cutting down a forest and then replanting it is theoretically eligible for credits, but leaving it alone in the first place is not.

In any event, regardless of what criteria are actually employed, a cap and trade system that allows offsets will require a significant bureaucracy to figure out whether projects qualify for offsets. Again, this is not sulfur dioxides, where the only offset permitted is lower sulfur dioxide emissions at another facility that is also subject to the cap and trade system. Complexity and costs are likely to be much greater.

D. Regulating GHG emissions under the clean air act

During the 2008 presidential campaign, both Barak Obama and John McCain endorsed cap and trade as the appropriate policy to address global warming. Expectations were therefore high for the enactment of a cap and trade program. In 2009, the House of Representatives passed a cap and trade bill that would have required reducing carbon emissions 17 percent below 2005 levels by 2020, and 83 percent by 2050. Even in a heavily democratic House, assembling a majority proved difficult. Most of the actual carbon reductions would have come from agricultural and foreign offsets, rather than changes in US energy production or consumption. In the Senate, assembling a 60 vote majority proved impossible, and the bill died early in 2010.

In significant part, the bill faltered in the Senate because of the uneven distribution of costs and benefits that would result from a cap and trade scheme. Reliance on coal, the most carbon-intensive form of energy production, differs considerably across states. In particular, Midwestern and mountain states are much more reliant on coal for electricity generation than are the costal states, which tend to rely more on oil and natural gas (along with substantial hydroelectric power on the west coast). Costs would, of course, be higher in the more coal dependent states. Benefits of any reduction in global warming, however, would likely be greatest in the coastal states—especially because one of the most significant consequences is sea level change. No compromise was found to bridge the gap.

With cap and trade legislation dead for the indefinite future, the Obama administration shifted to reliance on the regulatory process to address global warming. The EPA issued an "endangerment finding" in 2009, concluding that greenhouse gas emissions may "reasonably be anticipated to endanger public health or welfare." This finding is the predicate for regulating greenhouse gas emissions under the 1970 Clean Air Act—the command and control regulatory scheme discussed in Section II.

EPA has not, however, attempted to develop a NAAQS for greenhouse gasses, nor is it clear how it could do so. Instead, in 2010 it adopted tailpipe emissions standards for new motor vehicles, which in effect somewhat increased the fuel economy standards that NHTSA had previously adopted. EPA calculates that this rule will reduce temperatures by 0.004° C. over 90 years, and prevent a sea level rise of 0.05 centimeters. In 2011, it also adopted fuel economy standards for heavy duty trucks and busses, the first time such standards had ever been adopted.

Under a longstanding EPA interpretation, the decision to adopt a tailpipe emissions standard automatically triggered permitting requirements for stationary pollutions sources. Under the law, this requirement would apply to any facility emitting more than 100 or 250 tons per year of pollutants, depending on the source category. For greenhouse gasses, these standards would have required individual permits for some six million facilities. To avoid this result, the EPA adopted a "tailoring" rule in 2010, which limited the permit requirement to facilities emitting more than 75,000 tons per year of greenhouse gasses. Beyond the permit itself, it is not yet clear what requirements may be imposed under these permits. Early permits essentially required facilities to do what they were already doing, but effectively made those steps legally binding.

EPA is also developing new source performance standard regulations that will address GHG emissions from power plants. At one extreme, these standards might simply require the maximum possible efficiency for electricity generation. At the other extreme, they could require the capture and sequestration of all CO2, a requirement that would likely mean the end of coal-fired electricity generation. Eventually, the requirements would extend to existing facilities as well. Early in 2012, the EPA issued a proposal that would effectively prohibit any new coal fired power plants, but would have no effect on existing plants. EPA also plans standards for refineries, which are the other large source of CO2 emissions.

All of these rules are subject to legal challenges, and will likely end up before the Supreme Court.

VI. THE PRECAUTIONARY PRINCIPLE

Many environmental issues, particular disputes between the United States and the European Union, have at their core disagreements over the application of the so-called precautionary principle. Europe believes strongly in the precautionary principle in considering environmental or consumer health and safety issues, but the

United States does not. Different approaches to issues such as global warming stem in significant part from different views of the precautionary principle. Similarly, the European Union justifies its restrictive approach to foods from genetically modified organisms based on the precautionary principle; the United States believes such restrictions are merely a modern form of protectionism.

In general, the precautionary principle addresses what we should do in the face of uncertainty, usually uncertainty about the facts or about the causal relationship between agreed facts and the possible consequences. In essence, the principle says that we should "be careful" in the face of unknowns. That, unfortunately, means very different things to different people.

This section begins by considering the spectrum of definitions of the precautionary principle, which range from the entirely reasonable to the extreme. Problems of precaution virtually always involve other risks as well; we next consider the sources of other risks. Finally, we consider the problems of precaution.

A. The spectrum of definitions[10]

There are almost as many definitions of the precautionary principle as there are authors who have written about it. We can, however, arrange the different definitions in a spectrum, ranging from weak to strong. All definitions involve some potential harm (they differ about what or how serious it might be), uncertainty about facts and causal relationships (they differ about how much uncertainty), and how strongly they urge regulation to reduce the potential risk. We will consider a weak, moderate, and strong definition of the principle.

> **Weak: If there is a potential for** *serious and irreversible* **harm, but the evidence is** *not definitive*, **we** *can* **regulate to reduce the risk.**

The weak definition focuses on serious and irreversible harms. For example, introducing a new species from another continent into the environment may lead to serious problems, and it may be virtually impossible to reverse the damage. Under the weak definition of the precautionary principle, there must be evidence for the potential harm, but the evidence need not be definitive. Finally, the weak version claims that we can regulate to reduce the risk, but presumably we can also consider the costs and decide whether the risk is large enough to justify the costs.

The weak definition is unobjectionable. It is the equivalent of advice not to go into a bad part of town alone and late at night. It is not clear that anything bad will happen, but taking along a friend is a sound, low-cost precaution.

> **Moderate: If there is a** *risk* **of harm, but** *causality is not established*, **we** *should* **regulate to reduce the risk.** *The burden of proof is on the proponent of a new technology.*

Under the moderate definition of the precautionary principle, the harm need not be serious and irreversible. Any risk is enough. Although there must be some evidence of a link between the new technology and the harm, causality need not be established. Faced with a risk, the moderate definition asserts, we should regulate, and the proponent of the allegedly risky action must prove that the risk is not present. The critical questions about the moderate definition are questions of degree. How far from established is the causal relationship between the presumed cause and the harm? And how much proof should we require to convince us that the harm will not occur? As we require less and less evidence of causality, and more and more proof of no relationship, we move to the strong definition of precaution.

> **Strong: If there is a** *possible risk* **of harm, but the evidence is** *speculative*, **we** *must* **regulate to reduce the risk** *even if the costs are high.*

The strong version of the precautionary principle is concerned with even the possibility of risk, based on even speculative evidence. Nonetheless, it is how many people understand the principle. It asserts that we must regulate, regardless of the costs of regulation, to address any risk that might be imagined. It was characterized by one analyst as a principle that says "never try anything for the first time." It is a substantially different view of

---

[10]This discussion draws on Cass R. Sunstein, "Precautions against What? The Availability Heuristic and Cross-Cultural Risk Perceptions," AEI-Brookings Joint Center for Regulatory Studies, Working Paper 04-22, October 2004.

change from the Schumpeterian notion that we should seek to facilitate change. The strong version of the precautionary principle resists any change until we have definitive evidence that nothing bad will happen. If we really followed the strong version, it is difficult to see how many of the features of modern life that we take for granted could ever have emerged.

B. Sources of other risks

The precautionary principle in all its forms urges caution against a particular risk. There are, however, almost always trade-offs among risks, and the precautionary principle offers little analytical guidance about which risk should be the focus of concern.

First, there are risks from alternatives. Different ways of addressing a particular issue, or of solving an economic problem, may each pose their own set of risks. Consider, for example, alternative methods of generating electricity. Using coal poses a set of risks from mining, various harmful emissions, and the potential for global warming. Using nuclear energy has a different set of risks, from accidents and the disposal of radioactive wastes, but it does not contribute to global warming. Which risk should we take precautions against? The precautionary principle does not help to make the choice.

Second, there are risks of benefits foregone. A new technology, or a risky technology, may produce substantial benefits that may not otherwise be attainable. Vaccines, for example, have risks, but they offer substantial public health benefits. Chlorine in drinking water may pose some environmental risks. Indeed, some environmentalists think that all uses of chlorine should be banned, on the theory that compounds resulting from chemical reactions with chlorine are harmful. But chlorine in drinking water is a cost-effective method of killing bacteria that would otherwise spread waterborne diseases. Similarly, DDT (itself a chlorine compound) poses environmental risks, but it may also be the most effective way to fight malaria in certain countries. The precautionary principle does little to help us choose which public health risk to address.

Third, there are often risks of the remedy. That is, the steps necessary to reduce one risk may increase another risk, or even the risk we were trying to avoid. A good example is asbestos, which was widely used for years as a fire-resistant insulating material, but which causes asbestosis, an often fatal lung disease. Asbestos remains in many buildings around the United States. If it is stable and behind a wall or other barrier, asbestos poses very little risk, because the danger is from inhaling small airborne asbestos particles. Removing asbestos necessarily disturbs it, creating airborne particles and the precise problem we were trying to avoid. If the asbestos is exposed or flaking, removal reduces risk, but removing asbestos just for the sake of getting rid of it creates a bigger risk. Another example is the corporate average fuel economy regulations. The remedy for the risk of excessive gasoline consumption creates the risk of additional deaths in automobile accidents. Again, the precautionary principle offers no guidance about which risk we should avoid.

Rather than the precautionary principle, a much better way to think about choices under uncertainty is the notion of type I and type II error, discussed in Chapter 15. It may make sense to be careful, but being careful surely means avoiding the more serious error, even when that increases the risk of the less serious error. That kind of caution, however, depends on an analysis of the different ways in which we might be wrong in making a particular decision. It is a systematic way to consider the risks of mistakes and decide which risk is more important.

C. Problems of precaution

The precautionary principle is more of a political principle than an analytical one. It does little to help understand which risks are important and which are not, or when we should choose one risk over another. Instead, the principle is used to argue for precautions against whatever risk is at the top of an advocate's agenda. Because it offers little analytical basis for making difficult choices, the precautionary principle risks distorting appropriate priorities. Presumably we would like to devote more time and resources to addressing more significant risks rather than less significant ones. Risks may be more worthy of attention if they affect more people, if they have more significant consequences, or if the consequences are irreversible. But the analytical principles that should guide decisions on where to spend resources to reduce risk can be distorted by the political principle of precaution.

Ignoring costs to apply the precautionary principle raises a different set of problems. As discussed in Chapter 10, costs imply a reduction in incomes for some individuals or groups. Those reductions in incomes also have health consequences. At higher incomes, people take a wide variety of different steps to reduce risk that enable them to live longer lives. Economic progress itself reduces risk, because it enables more people to make more risk-reducing choices. Thus, ignoring costs can itself create additional risks.

VIII. SUMMARY

According to the Coase theorem, in the absence of transactions costs, externalities will not affect resource allocation. Regardless of externalities, parties will negotiate to reach the joint maximizing solution. It implies that externality problems stem from poorly defined property rights. Policies that create well-defined property rights and facilitate trading can help to address externalities without the need to determine first precisely how resources should be used.

Command and control approaches are at the heart of environmental regulation. Command and control allows responsiveness to politically important groups, and makes it harder to determine the actual costs of regulation.

The regulatory structure for "criteria" air pollutants begins with the EPA setting national ambient air quality standards. These standards are uniform, national standards specifying the maximum allowable concentration of a pollutant in the air. They are health based, using the threshold concept, and periodically reviewed and revised.

State and local governments set emissions standards designed to achieve the ambient air quality standard. Emissions standards, which specify the maximum quantity of a pollutant that can be emitted for each point source of emissions, are enforced through permitting requirements. The level of control differs for major and minor pollution sources, for existing and new sources, and for sources in non-attainment and attainment areas. Controls are strictest for major new sources in non-attainment areas.

Command and control approaches do not take into account differences in the cost of controlling pollution in different facilities, and therefore do not achieve environmental goals at the lowest possible cost. Setting standards requires a great deal of information, which firms may not share with the regulator. Command and control does not create incentives to do more than the minimum required, even when doing so would be relatively inexpensive, and does not create strong incentives for innovation. It is subject to the stock-flow problem, where tighter standards on new equipment may encourage individuals and companies to use old equipment longer, thereby delaying environmental progress.

Market-based approaches can achieve environmental goals at lower cost than command and control approaches. The cap and trade program to reduce sulfur dioxide emissions is a prominent example of this approach. Firms were given permits to emit sulfur dioxide in proportion to their baseline emissions, with bonuses for clean coal technology, scrubbers, and growing areas, but there were only permits for about half of the initial level of emissions. Firms own their permits, and can buy more or sell the ones they have. Firms can reduce emissions using any method they choose, or they can purchase permits to cover their emissions. Firms that can control emissions for a cost below the price of a permit have incentives to do so, because they can then sell their permits at the market price.

The cap and trade program has been less costly than was expected when it was enacted, in part because of innovations that reduced the cost of controlling emissions. The cost was about half of what a command and control approach to solving the problem would have cost. Studies of market-based approaches have found they cost substantially less than command and control solutions.

Taxes can also be used in a market-based approach to pollution control. Firms can emit as much pollution as they want, but they must pay a tax based on the amount they emit. They can avoid the tax by controlling emissions, so they have an incentive to do so. Costs are more transparent with a tax system. With taxes, the price is certain, but the quantity of pollution that will result is uncertain. Fixing the price is a good approach when the benefits of reductions are not very sensitive to the quantity of pollution and costs rise sharply with greater reductions. With cap and trade, the quantity of pollution is fixed, but the cost of control is uncertain. Fixing the quantity is a good approach when the benefits are sharply increasing and costs of control are relatively flat.

Global warming has been a contentious environmental issue. Greenhouse gases such as carbon dioxide and methane trap heat in the atmosphere and prevent it from radiating out into space. The atmospheric concentration of carbon dioxide has increased 30 percent since the beginning of the Industrial Revolution, and is predicted to increase 30 to 150 percent by 2100. The impact on climate is estimated from climate models. The "consensus" forecast is that doubling carbon dioxide concentrations would increase the average temperature by 2 to 4.5 degrees Celsius. Most warming is at higher latitudes in the winter, particularly with higher nighttime low temperatures.

Global warming will increase sea levels due to thermal expansion of the oceans. This effect will increase sea level by 7 to 22 inches. Long term, the impact on sea level depends on what happens to the West Antarctic and Greenland ice sheets. The West Antarctic ice sheet could raise sea level 17 to 20 feet, and may be subject to instabilities. The Greenland ice cap could raise sea level by 23 feet due to gradual melting over a long period of time. Global warming may also increase the frequency and intensity of hurricanes and other extreme weather events.

Major uncertainties in climate models include the role of clouds and water vapor and the effects of aerosols. In addition, plausible scenarios for the course of emissions of greenhouse gases over the next century differ substantially, but all show most of the growth in emissions occurring in developing countries.

The Kyoto Agreement in 1992 set a voluntary goal for industrialized countries of stabilizing emissions at 1990 levels. The 1997 Kyoto Protocol set binding targets for a 5 percent reduction in emissions by 2012, when the agreement expires. The United States did not participate.

Climate change policy must address a number of policy issues. Broader policies within a country are better, because they allow more flexibility to find low-cost solutions. Uniform policies across countries would also reduce costs, but developing countries may be unwilling to participate. Determining the pace of change is an important issue, because costs are likely to increase significantly with more rapid reductions in emissions. Policy needs to be flexible, because the facts are likely to change. Even small changes in growth rates can translate into very large dollar costs for future generations.

Carbon taxes would likely be a more efficient way to address global warming concerns, but they are very difficult politically. Auctioning permits in a cap and trade system is also politically difficult. Allocating permits for greenhouse gases will be far more complex than for sulfur dioxide emissions, because there are so many more sources of greenhouse gas emissions. A cap and trade system that allows offsets will require a bureaucracy to administer and faces the problem of additionality. The EPA is moving forward to regulate greenhouse gasses under the clear Air Act, requiring tighter automobile fuel economy standards and permits for stationary sources emitting more than 75,000 tons of greenhouse gasses annually.

The precautionary principle asserts that we should be careful about new technologies. The weak version states that if there is a serious and irreversible harm, we can regulate even if the evidence is not definitive. The moderate version states that we should regulate any risk of harm even if causality is not established, and that proponents of new technology have the burden of proof. Its impact depends on how far we are from establishing causality, and on how much proof proponents must produce. The strong definition asserts that we must regulate any possible risk, even if the supporting evidence is speculative. It says we should never try anything for the first time.

The precautionary principle is a political principle, not an analytical one. A better way to think about uncertainty and risks is type I and type II error. We should seek to avoid the more serious mistake, but that depends on the particular risk. There are always other risks, from alternatives, from benefits forgone, or from the remedy. The precautionary principle can distort priorities about which risks should be addressed, and it can create risks by imposing high costs.

REGULATING INTERNATIONAL TRADE

Chapter 19

This chapter considers U.S. and international rules governing world trade. We begin with discussion of the economic effects of trade restrictions and the political economy of trade restrictions. Section II considers U.S. laws that govern dumping and foreign subsidies of trade. Section III considers the World Trade Organization and trade-related international disputes.

I. THE ECONOMICS AND POLITICS OF TRADE RESTRICTIONS

A. The economic effects of tariffs and quotas

Consider the domestic market for a good that can either be made in the United States or purchased from abroad. Such a market is shown in Figure 19-1. In the absence of trade, equilibrium will occur where demand in the United States equals the supply in the United States. Suppose, however, that we can purchase as much of the good as we want at the world price, P_w. In the absence of trade restrictions, the domestic output of the good will be Q_{US}. At a price of P_w, consumers will consume the quantity C_{US} of the good. The difference, $C_{US} - Q_{US}$, will be imports.

Now suppose we impose a tariff on imports of this good. Because importers will have to pay the tariff, the price in the United States will rise by the amount of the tariff, to Pw + tariff in Figure 19-1. Consumption in the United States will decline to C'_{US}, and production in the United States will increase to Q'_{US}. Imports, of course, will decline. Because the price in the United States is higher, consumer surplus for American consumers is reduced. There are four components of this reduction in consumer surplus, the areas labeled A, B, C, and D in Figure 19-1.

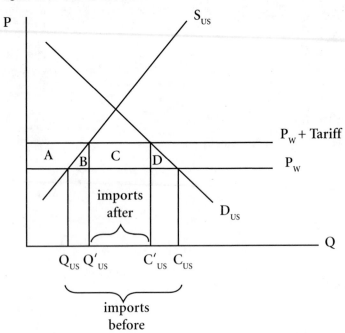

Figure 19-1. Economic effects of tariffs.

Consider first area A. This area represents higher profits for domestic producers of the good. In part, profits are higher because the quantity they were producing before the tariff now commands a higher price, and in part profits increase because the additional output sells for more than it costs to produce. Area A is a transfer payment: it is a reduction in consumer surplus, but an increase in producer surplus. Whether this is good or bad depends on which group we prefer.

Triangle B is the net cost of the extra resources used to increase domestic production of the good. The area under the supply curve between Q_{US} and Q'_{US} is the total cost of the resources used, but in the absence of the tariff, they would have been used elsewhere to produce something else. We could have had these additional goods at a cost of only P_w. The difference is triangle B, the net cost of the extra resources used. This is a deadweight loss, which reduces the total value of output in the domestic economy.

Rectangle C is the tax revenue from the tariff. The base of the rectangle is imports after the tariff, and its height is the amount of the tariff. Tax revenue represents a transfer payment, from consumers to the government. Presumably government does something useful with the money, or reduces some other tax (or its borrowing).

Triangle D is the loss of consumer surplus that results from reduced domestic consumption of the good. The value of the additional units that would have been consumed at P_w is given by the demand curve; the cost of those goods would have been the world price. Triangle D is also a deadweight loss. We could have increased total value by importing more goods, but we cannot do so because of the tariff.

Thus, the total cost of the tariff to consumers is areas A + B + C + D. The deadweight cost to the economy is areas B + D.

The economic effects of quotas, shown in Figure 19-2, are very similar. With quotas, as the price rises, we first move along the domestic supply curve, S_{US}, until we reach the world price. We then begin to import at the world price P_w, until the quota is exhausted. After that, we move along the U.S. supply curve shifted to the right by the amount of the quota, S'_{US}. The effective supply curve in the domestic market is therefore the heavily shaded curve in Figure 19-2. The figure is constructed so that the quota and the tariff are equivalent in their initial effects. Thus the increase in the price in the U.S. market is the same under either policy.

The reduction in consumer surplus again consists of four areas, A, B, C, and D, slightly rearranged but otherwise equivalent to the corresponding areas in Figure 19-1. Area A is still higher profits for domestic manufacturers. Area C is higher profits for importers, who are able to purchase goods abroad at the world

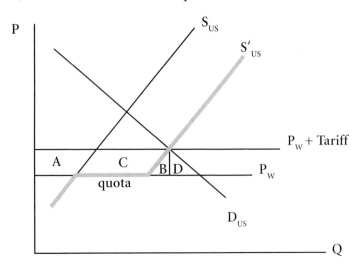

Figure 19-2. Economic effects of quotas.

price and sell them in the United States at the higher domestic price. Precisely where these profits go depends on how the quota program is structured and who has the right to bring in goods subject to the quota. They might go to foreign producers, or they might go to domestic importers. Area C is still a transfer payment, but instead of a transfer to the government, it may be a transfer out of the country.

Triangles B and D are, as they were before, the deadweight costs of the quota. B is the net cost of the extra resources used in domestic production, and D is the lost consumer surplus from the reduction in domestic consumption. Thus tariffs and quotas have the same net cost to the economy.

Tariffs and quotas differ in their effects over time as demand increases. The impact of an increase in domestic demand is shown in Figure 19-3. With tariffs, the increase in demand will simply increase imports. The effective supply in the domestic market is the line labeled P_W + tariff. Total consumption will increase to Q_T. Domestic production does not increase, and the welfare losses (triangles B and D) remain essentially the same.[1] With quotas, however, we cannot import additional goods, because the quota has already been exhausted. The increased demand can only be satisfied by increased domestic production, moving along S'_{US}. Consumption will only increase to Q_q, and the price in the United States will increase.

Figure 19-3. Effects of increasing demand.

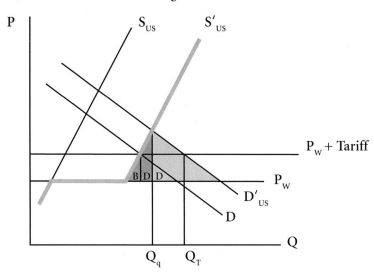

Because quotas lead to a price increase when demand increases, the costs to consumers and the welfare losses increase as well. Areas A and C will increase because of the increase in the domestic price. The welfare loss triangles increase as well. The new triangle B is the darker shaded triangle in Figure 19-3. We are using, and wasting, more resources in the United States to produce the additional output. The increase in domestic price also increases triangle D, the lost consumer surplus, which is now the lighter shaded triangle in Figure 19-3.

Thus, with quotas, an increase in demand will increase the deadweight losses due to the restriction. With tariffs, there is little or no increase in the deadweight losses; we simply increase imports. This different effect in response to changes in demand is why economists, and world trade agreements, prefer tariffs over quotas if countries decide to restrict imports.

In addition to the direct costs of trade restrictions, there can also be indirect effects as well. Restrictions on imports of certain materials may increase the costs of user industries. Restricting steel imports, for example, raises the price of domestic steel and gives a competitive advantage to foreign auto makers, who can purchase lower-cost steel on the world market. Industries protected from more efficient foreign competition may lag in taking the necessary steps to improve their competitive position. Trade restrictions also lead to the possibility of foreign retaliation against industries where the United States has a comparative advantage. Either result can simply move trade problems from one industry to another, without accomplishing anything for the economy as a whole.

The costs of trade restrictions in the aggregate are substantial. Static estimates of the welfare triangles associated with trade restrictions indicate that they are from 0.25 to 0.5 percent of US GDP, or about $36 to $73 billion in 2010. Accounting for the dynamic effects of increased competition, a study from the Institute for

---

[1] Triangle B will remain precisely the same size. If the outward shift in demand is parallel to the original demand, D remains exactly the same size as well. Otherwise, it may change slightly.

International Economics estimates that removing all trade restrictions could increase GDP by 4.1 percent, or $525 billion per year in 2010. A roughly consistent study using a model of the economy developed at the University of Michigan study estimates the gains at 3.4 percent of GDP annually.[2]

Certain types of restrictions can also change the mix of goods available in the American market. The initial competitive strategy of Japanese auto manufacturers, for example, was to sell low-priced economy cars in the United States, a market that domestic manufacturers were not serving well. As imports grew, the United States negotiated a "voluntary restraint agreement," which effectively established a quota for Japanese auto imports that applied throughout the mid-1980s. Faced with a quantitative limit on the number of automobiles they could import, Japanese manufacturers shifted their product mix toward larger, higher-priced, higher-margin vehicles—a market that had previously been owned by U.S. manufacturers. Honda launched Acura, for example, in 1986; Toyota followed with Lexus in 1989.

B. The political economy of trade

Trade is part of the dynamic process of changes in a competitive economy. Absent restrictions, there is nothing that confines creative destruction to a particular country. That change creates costs for some groups, who have every incentive to use the political process to try to avoid those costs.

The theory of public choice is a useful way to understand trade restrictions, particularly restrictions in individual industries. When restrictions are adopted, they create benefits for relatively small, compact groups. Typically a relatively small number of domestic firms benefit; they generally have a large stake in the issue and will likely find it worthwhile to participate in the political process to protect their interests. Workers are also a discrete and identifiable group with a relatively large stake in the issue. In unionized industries, the workers are also organized and can exploit the advantages of groups to protect their interest. It is no accident that trade restrictions are more common in unionized industries.

The costs of restrictions, of course, are borne by consumers. The costs are diffuse, spread across all consumers of the product. Individual consumers, however, unless they are extremely heavy users of a product subject to restrictions, will have a small stake in the issue. For most consumers rational ignorance will prevail, and they will not pay attention to or participate in the issue.

Costs of restrictions can be especially well hidden with quotas. The costs of tariffs are clear, but the costs of quotas are usually uncertain until after the fact. For example, part of the U.S. peanut price support program is a quota restricting imports to 0.1 percent of U.S. production. The equivalent tariff would be approximately 90 percent, a cost that would be more likely to provoke attention. The eventual beneficiaries of this particular restriction are those who own land suitable for peanut farming, as the rents created by the quota are bid into land prices.

Because removing individual trade restrictions is politically difficult, they have much more commonly been addressed through package deals. Package deals, addressing a number of different restrictions in a single proposal, increase the potential benefits for consumers. With more at stake, more consumers will find it worthwhile to pay attention and participate. Moreover, with package deals that are the result of international negotiations, concessions from other countries can attract domestic support from export-oriented industries that will benefit from fewer foreign restrictions.

Essential to the ability to negotiate package deals is trade promotion authority, commonly known as "fast-track" authority. This statutory authority allows the president to negotiate an agreement with foreign governments, which will then be subject to an up-or-down vote in Congress, without amendments. The no-amendment rule is critical, because if amendments are possible, individual interest groups can pick off particular provisions, and the entire deal can unravel. Under the rules, once the president submits an agreement to Congress, Congress must vote on the agreement within 90 days.

---

[2]Gary Clyde Hufbauer, "Answering the Critics: Why Large American Gains from Globalization are Plausible," Peterson Institute for International Economics, May 2008 (Available at http://www.iie.com/publications/papers/paper.cfm?ResearchID=929).

Fast-track authority and the reduction in trade restrictions it has made possible over the last 50 years are estimated to have produced $9,000 in annual benefits for the typical U.S. household. In the 1990s, it was fast-track authority that made possible North American Free Trade Agreement (NAFTA) and the World Trade Organization (WTO) agreement, which are estimated to have produced benefits of $1,300 to $2,000 for a typical household.

Fast-track authority expired in the summer of 2007, and has not been renewed. Without renewal, negotiations on important trade deals may continue, but final agreement is extremely unlikely. Even with fast-track authority, there is no guarantee that Congress will actually consider the agreement. For example, when President Bush submitted the Colombia Free Trade Agreement to Congress in April 2008, the House of Representatives suspended the rules and the 90-day window in which it was supposed to vote on the agreement. In 2012, the Obama Administration announced that it would seek renewal of fast track trade authority.

Since World War II there has been a bipartisan consensus, based on sound economics, that removing restrictions to world trade would benefit the United States. That consensus has been threatened by linkage between trade and two other issues. One set of issues revolves around labor standards. Unions in particular are concerned that lower wages in our trading partners are a threat to domestic wages and jobs, and have strongly opposed recent trade agreements. The other set of issues that has been linked to trade is environmental issues. Environmental groups are particularly concerned that several U.S. policies that were adopted in part for environmental reasons were successfully challenged as non-tariff trade barriers, in violation of various trade agreements, before the World Trade Organization. (We examine these disputes in more detail in a subsequent section of this chapter.) Moreover, environmental groups are concerned about the possibility of a "race to the bottom" in environmental standards globally. The fear is that countries with lax environmental standards will have a competitive advantage in global markets, potentially weakening environmental protections in the United States as well.

The linkage of trade to environmental and labor issues is illustrated in the fate of free trade agreements with Columbia, South Korea, and Panama. The agreements, which were substantially completed in 2007, were eventually resubmitted to Congress and approved in October 2011. From an economic perspective, the most important agreement was the one with South Korea, which was estimated to increase US national income by $17 to $43 billion per year. To secure approval, the Obama administration negotiated changes to the South Korea agreement to give US auto manufacturers greater access to the South Korean market. These changes were sufficient to secure the support of Ford Motor Company, which had strongly opposed the original agreement. It did not, however, overcome the opposition of the United Auto Workers. To secure passage of the Columbia FTA, the Administration negotiated a "labor action plan" to address concerns about labor issues in that country. In the case of the Panama agreement, that country agreed to strengthen its labor laws and enforcement.

In a recession, particularly a global recession, there is always a danger of trade restrictions to protect domestic output and employment. Indeed, there is widespread consensus among economic historians that one key factor in prolonging the Great Depression was the passage of sharply higher tariffs by the United States in 1930, followed by retaliatory tariffs in other nations. Two provisions in the Economic Stimulus Package enacted early in 2009 raised some of the same concerns.

First, the legislation contained a "buy America" provision, specifying that stimulus funds should only be used to buy from American companies. Although a caveat specified that the law did not override international agreements, those agreements only cover preferential purchases by the federal government. State and local governments, which actually spent most of the stimulus dollars, are not covered by the international agreements and are required to buy American. In June 2009, a group of Canadian cities voted to adopt "buy Canada" policies in retaliation.

Second, the legislation ended a pilot program to allow Mexican trucks to deliver goods in the United States outside of a narrowly defined border area. The U.S. government agreed to allow Mexican trucks into the United States as part of the NAFTA agreement, signed in 1992 and ratified in 1993. Faced with substantial union pressure and claims that Mexican trucks were unsafe, however, it never fully implemented the provision. Both the Clinton and Bush administrations sought to comply in various ways, but both failed. The pilot program was the latest attempt to comply, allowing Mexican trucks to enter the United States but subjecting them (and a sample of U.S. trucking firms) to more stringent inspection standards, to determine once and for all whether there was a safety difference. When Congress killed the program, Mexico imposed retaliatory tariffs on imports from the United States, as it was allowed to do under NAFTA rules. These retaliatory tariffs targeted 90 products accounting for $2.4 billion in trade.

Choosing goods for retaliation is something of an art, where the goal is to maximize the political pressure on the country that has not complied with its treaty obligations. For example, Mexico targeted fruits and vegetables from California, because the California delegation was largely opposed to Mexican trucks. It targeted frozen French fries, because the plant that exported many fries to Mexico was in the Oregon district of a key opponent of Mexican trucks. Similarly, it targeted pet food and toilet paper based on the location of facilities that sent much of their output to Mexico. In this case, the strategy worked—in 2011, the United States agreed to reestablish the pilot program beginning the next year. Mexico agreed to drop half of the retaliatory tariffs immediately, and drop the other half when trucks actually started to roll.

One potentially important round of international trade negotiations remains under way. The Doha round, launched in 2001, was intended to offer particular benefits to developing countries. These countries have sought reductions in agricultural subsidies from the United States and the European Union, which make those markets far less accessible to agricultural products from developing countries. Both resisted, and although each offered some concessions, developing countries rejected both as inadequate. The result was a significant reduction in the scope of any potential agreement, with developed countries offering relatively modest reductions in barriers to agricultural trade in exchange for modest reductions in barriers to trade in services, particularly financial services. The key to the negotiations is likely the ability of the United States. and the EU to strike an agreement with the emerging developing countries of Brazil, China, and India. The services portion of the negotiation, however, became entangled in the regulatory changes in the developed countries in the wake of the financial crisis of 2008. Developing countries saw the bailouts of financial institutions in the developed countries as an unfair subsidy, and feared that reduced barriers to trade in services would disadvantage their financial services industries in particular. Whether any agreement will eventually emerge is uncertain. Failure to reach an agreement, however, could undermine the role of multilateral organizations such as the WTO in negotiating trade agreements, and would risk undermining the WTO enforcement mechanism for existing agreements.

II. COUNTERVAILING AND ANTIDUMPING DUTY LAWS

World trade agreements allow countries to protect themselves from "unfair" trade practices by trading partners, and most countries have domestic mechanisms to do so. Two practices are most often the focus of concern: "dumping" unwanted goods on a foreign market, and subsidizing export industries. In both cases, the countries on the receiving end of the goods feel aggrieved.

A. Dumping

Under U.S. law, an exporter selling goods in the United States is guilty of dumping if the price in the United States is below either the price of the goods in their home market, or the home market cost of production, including a reasonable rate of profit. Use of antidumping provisions has grown considerably since the modern approach was initiated in 1973. In the first four years the provision was in effect, the United States issued only one order, involving one product from one country. In 2001, the peak year for orders, there were 38 orders issued involving 11 products from 21 countries.

Other countries have widely copied the U.S. approach to dumping. Worldwide, between 1987 and 1991, there were 733 antidumping investigations. In 1998–2002, the number more than doubled, to 1,581. The United States, however, uses dumping orders more heavily and more intensively than other countries. The United States accounts for approximately 15 percent of world trade, but it issues 35 percent of all worldwide antidumping orders. Compared to the European Union, U.S. orders issued between 1991 and 1995 imposed larger average duties (57 percent in the United States, compared to 30 percent in E.U. orders) and lasted longer (9 years versus 6 years).

A study of U.S. antidumping orders in effect in 1993 estimated they imposed $4 billion in costs in that year (roughly $6 billion in current dollars). Although the study has not been updated, antidumping orders today cover 75 percent more import volume.

A determination of dumping (or of subsidies) involves two U.S. government agencies. The Commerce Department determines whether goods have been subsidized or dumped, and if so, it determines the "dumping margin," which is how much below either home country price or home country cost including profit the goods were sold for in the United States. If there is dumping, the International Trade Commission (a domestic agency) investigates whether U.S. industry was "materially injured." Under the statute, material injury is a "harm which is not inconsequential, immaterial, or unimportant." In practice, the ITC finds injury if the industry is doing poorly by some objective measure, such as sales, employment, or profits, regardless of how much imports might contribute to that poor performance. For example, if the domestic industry is doing poorly largely because it uses outdated technology, but there are significant imports, the ITC will likely find injury. If the domestic industry is doing well, the ITC finds no injury, even if the industry would have been doing much better without the import competition. Thus, the test is not a "but for imports" test. The ITC finds injury in industries that face foreign competition and are doing poorly.

If both agencies make affirmative findings (i.e., there is dumping and there is material injury), then duties equal to the dumping margin or the subsidy are automatically imposed. There is no consideration of costs to the consumers, or to other industries that might rely on the imported goods.

B. Trade law problems

There are a number of problems with the way the United States administers antidumping and countervailing duty laws. These problems lead to systematically more findings of dumping, and systematically larger dumping margins, than would otherwise be the case. In practice, dumping investigations have become a way to deliver benefits to politically important groups with relatively little public scrutiny or involvement.

1. Wrong Cost Test

Because of the way the Commerce Department considers costs in assessing dumping, the U.S. approach ends up branding perfectly normal competitive market practices as "dumping" and imposing significant duties. As noted above, Commerce finds dumping if the price in the United States is below the home market cost of production, including a reasonable profit—that is, if price is below average total cost.

As we saw in Chapter 1, a competitive firm will continue to operate in the short run as long as price exceeds average *variable* costs. If there is excess capacity in the industry, either because of too much expansion in expectation of demand increases that do not materialize, or because of temporary reductions in demand (as occurs during a recession), prices will not be sufficient to cover average total cost. In the long run, some firms will exit unless demand increases, and equilibrium will be restored. But in the short run in competitive markets, all firms will lose money, because prices will not be high enough to cover average total cost.

Average total cost is the firm's total cost, including "normal" profit—the payment to shareholders for the use of their capital and the risks they are taking. When price falls below average total cost, shareholders will not receive all (or perhaps any) of this "normal" profit. But there is nothing "unfair" or suspicious about that condition, it is simply the reflection of excess capacity in competitive markets. Nonetheless, the Commerce Department test labels this perfectly normal practice as dumping.

There is an analogous concept in antitrust law, which is predatory pricing. The idea of predatory pricing is that if two firms have the same costs, the large firm can sell below cost until the smaller firm is driven out of business, and then charge the monopoly price. There is considerable reason to be skeptical of claims of predatory pricing even in the domestic context. The large firm will lose more money than the "victim," which is not likely to recommend itself as a viable business strategy. If the large firm has 90 percent of the market, for example, and sells below cost, it will lose $9 for every $1 the smaller firm loses. Moreover, even if predation

Figure 19-4. Dumping versus predatory pricing.

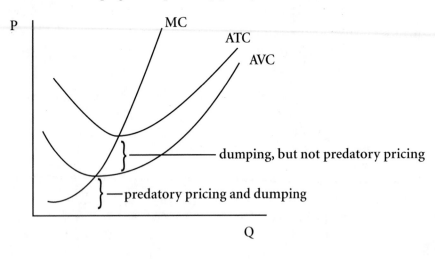

is successful, the predator cannot raise the price unless there are barriers to entry. Absent barriers to entry, when the price goes up, someone else will enter the market, and the predator will have to reduce prices again.

Concerns about predation are even less plausible in the international trade context. It is almost inconceivable that in the 2004 antidumping case against Vietnamese shrimp, for example, there was a serious prospect that Vietnam would take over the U.S. shrimp market and charge monopoly prices. Even if it did, many other countries would presumably enter the U.S. market to take advantage of high prices if the Vietnamese tried to raise the price.

To avoid penalizing normal competitive conduct, antitrust law finds predatory pricing only when price is below average *variable* cost.[3] Because no rational competitive firm would sell for less than average variable cost, something must be amiss if prices fall below that level. Antitrust law recognizes, however, that prices between average variable cost and average total cost are a normal feature of competitive markets, and not violations of the antitrust law. If charged by foreign firms, however, such prices are violations of U.S. antidumping laws. The result is a range of prices that are legal prices for U.S. firms, but that will be declared dumping if they are charged by foreign firms. This range is shown in Figure 19-4.

2. "Zeroing:" Foreign versus U.S. Price Comparisons

Countries are also dumping under U.S. law if the price charged in the United States is below the price charged in the home country. The Commerce Department, however, has a peculiar way of comparing prices that increases the likelihood of finding dumping, and increases the dumping margin if dumping is found. This practice is known as "zeroing," because it ignores certain prices entirely, and has been challenged by foreign countries in numerous complaints to the World Trade Organization.

Consider first the foreign price. The Commerce Department computes the average of prices over a six-month period, but it excludes any prices that are below average total costs. That is, it counts the "high" prices, but ignores the "low" prices in the home market in calculating the average. If there are too few prices, the price in the home market is calculated as the "constructed value" of the goods, defined as average variable costs plus 18 percent for profit and overhead.

To determine the price in the U.S. market, the Commerce Department uses actual transactions prices to calculate the average. Any price that is above the foreign price is excluded from calculation of the average. Thus, for the U.S. price, the methodology counts the "low" prices, but ignores any "high" prices.

Comparing the foreign and U.S. price calculated this way clearly overstates the extent of dumping and results in a larger antidumping duty. The estimated price in the United States is lower than the actual average price over the time period, and the estimated price in the home country is higher than the actual average. Commerce is therefore more likely to find dumping, and will find a larger dumping margin when it does. Once imposed, however, the antidumping duty applies to all transactions, not just the ones that occurred at a low price in the United States.

---

[3]Some courts define predation as a price less than marginal cost, which, again, no normal competitive firm would charge. Determining marginal cost is often difficult, however, so many courts use the average variable cost test.

Moreover, the methodology can prevent normal competitive practices such as seasonal sales. Suppose, for example, a company always sells goods at the same price in the United States and its home country, but in both places it has seasonal sales at prices below average total cost. The low sales prices in its home country will not count in calculating the average price. The high, non-sale prices will not count in the United States. The result is comparing the seasonal sale price in the United States to the regular price in the home country, and a very artificial finding of dumping.

Numerous WTO decisions have held that the practice of zeroing as applied by the U.S. in particular cases violates international trade agreements. In 2012, faced with the possibility of retaliatory sanctions from the EU and Japan, the United States agreed to change its zeroing practices, but not to eliminate them entirely. It will continue to exclude below-cost sales in the home country, but it will then compare the average home country price to the average price in the United States, rather than considering only the US transactions at a lower price than the home country. It reserved, however, the right to use zeroing "in appropriate cases," without specifying what might be an appropriate case. It remains to be seen whether the revised approach will actually resolve the issue.

3. Costs in Non-Market Economies

When dumping allegations involve a non-market economy, there is reason to doubt the reported costs in the home country. In a planned economy, prices of key inputs may be whatever the government says they are, rather than the market reflection of supply and demand. Thus, stated costs may not reflect the actual economic costs of production in that country.

To avoid this difficulty in cases involving non-market economies, the Commerce Department chooses a "comparable" market economy. To determine costs of production, it uses costs from this comparable economy, and ignores the prices in the actual home market. For example, in the shrimp dumping case against Vietnam, the department decided that too much of the Vietnamese economy is a planned economy (although the shrimp farming sector was not), and chose Bangladesh as the comparable market economy. It therefore used prices and costs from Bangladesh, sometimes based on data that were five years old, to calculate production costs, and found dumping.

The heart of the dumping allegations against Vietnam was actually competition between new and old ways of doing business. Most shrimp in the United States at the time were wild caught, using trawlers in coastal waters. In Vietnam, shrimp were farmed, often on land that had formerly been rice paddies. Farming was cheaper, and resulted in significantly lower prices for the product. There is no doubt that American shrimp fishermen were at a disadvantage, but it is difficult to see how this competition is an unfair trade practice.

4. Subsidy Determinations

Some cases involve allegations that a foreign government is subsidizing exports, thereby disadvantaging U.S. companies. Certainly subsidies can distort trade patterns, particularly when subsidies are targeted at exports rather than domestic production. Unfortunately, however, the Commerce Department's test for whether there is a subsidy is based on the benefit to the company, not whether the subsidy might distort trade.

In a case brought by U.S. steel producers against British Steel, for example, the U.S. industry alleged British Steel was subsidized. For many years, British Steel had been a nationalized company, and the British taxpayers covered its prodigious losses. By the time of the case, however, British Steel had been privatized and no longer had any connection to the government.

Commerce found that there was a subsidy, because British Steel had benefited from the fact that the government covered its losses in the past. In effect, the department argued that until the privatized company repaid past benefits from the British taxpayers, there was some residual benefit to the company, and a countervailing duty was therefore appropriate. If this refusal to demand repayment is a subsidy in any meaningful sense, however, it is one that clearly has no effect on trade flows.

5. Information

The comparisons between foreign prices, domestic prices, and production costs clearly demand a great deal of information. Because we do not want foreign companies to "game" the antidumping investigation process, it is subject to fairly tight statutory timeframes to be sure that the decision-making process moves along expeditiously. The result is that the Commerce Department makes massive requests for information from the foreign companies, which must be provided in a very short time frame. Moreover, the information provided must conform to U.S. accounting standards, regardless of how the company keeps its books.

If Commerce does not receive data in a timely fashion, or if it rejects the information it does receive for failure to meet proper accounting standards or otherwise, it can make its determination based on the "best information available." Since Commerce has no independent sources of information, the best information available tends to be what the complaining U.S. industry alleged in its complaint. As with other practices discussed above, the result is a higher likelihood of finding dumping and a systematically larger dumping margin when it is found.

6. Ties

One characteristic of the decision-making process does not have a great deal of practical significance, but it illustrates the nature of the process that has been created under U.S. law. The determination of injury is made by the International Trade Commission, which is an independent agency. Usually independent agencies have an odd number of members. Thus, if everyone participates, there are no ties, because one side or the other must win. The ITC, however, has 6 members. And because ties are therefore more likely, it also has a rule to deal with ties: ties go to the domestic complainant!

Like any other trade restriction, tariffs based on the theory that the foreign country or company was dumping raise prices for U.S. consumers. At least in the short run, they impose the same deadweight losses on the U.S. economy as any other tariff. The economic effects are the same, regardless of the reason for the tariff. The American approach to antidumping actions has made this provision a low visibility way to deliver benefits to important constituencies, with minimal risk that consumers will even notice, let alone object.

III. THE WORLD TRADE ORGANIZATION AND INTERNATIONAL DISPUTES

A. Origins

The World Trade Organization was negotiated as a part of the Uruguay round of trade negotiations, and began operations in 1995. The WTO administers trade agreements, but the basic treaty governing trade is the General Agreements on Tariffs and Trade (GATT), which, although it has frequently been amended, dates from the end of World War II.

The WTO grew out of a U.S. desire for a more effective dispute resolution process than what previously existed. Under the old process, there were no fixed time frames for resolving disputes, so they often dragged on interminably. Most important, the old process required unanimous agreement of all parties to the trade treaty in question—including the country that was the subject of the complaint. Needless to say, few disputes were resolved.

Most disputes that are brought to the WTO involve non-tariff barriers to trade. Treaties tend to be quite clear about allowable levels of tariffs, and disputes about compliance are therefore relatively infrequent. Far more common are disputes about requirements that one party believes have a permissible domestic purpose, but that another country believes operate to make foreign competition more difficult. Such cases may involve restrictions that purport to protect the health and safety of domestic consumers, labeling requirements that purport to provide consumers with valuable information, or restrictions justified as ways to protect the environment.

As tariffs have declined, nontariff barriers to trade have become increasingly important. These barriers include "technical barriers to trade," which are requirements such as health, safety or environmental standards, labeling requirements, quality standards, and the like. In 2005, the average tariff in high income countries was only 3 percent (compared to 11 percent in developing countries). Between 1984 and 1994, however, technical barriers to trade almost doubled, from 32 percent to 59 percent of affected tariff lines. Over all products, the average tariff equivalent of nontariff barriers (including technical barriers as well as quantity limits, preferential purchase requirements, and the like) is an estimated 9 percent; over products affected by these limits, the estimated tariff equivalent is about 40 percent. Thus, compared to tariffs, nontariff barriers are likely a more significant barrier to free trade.[4]

There are two key principles of trade agreements that are central in most about disputes technical barriers to trade. First, countries can adopt domestic restrictions based on measurable and observable characteristics of the product, but they cannot adopt restrictions based on how the product was produced. That is, the product must be the focus of regulation, not the production process. Consumers are affected by the characteristics of products sold in their country, and if the product poses health, safety, or environmental risks, governments are entitled to protect their consumers. The production process for traded goods, however, happens in another country. If the foreign product is produced by a different process, but is indistinguishable from products produced domestically, there is no recognized basis under international trade agreements for restricting imports.

Second, restrictions must be nondiscriminatory, both between different trading partners and between foreign and domestic companies. Trade agreements generally require all countries to give "most favored nation" status to all trading partners. Thus a country cannot make special deals with a favored partner; it must extend the same terms to all countries that wish to trade with it. There are exceptions for regional free trade agreements, but in general, all trading partners must be treated alike.

Similarly, countries cannot differentiate between domestic and foreign companies in the structure or administration of their regulations. Compliance options available to domestic companies, for example, must generally be available to importers as well. Differential treatment of domestic and foreign firms would violate the principle of nondiscrimination.

B. The dispute resolution process[5]

When one country complains that another country is violating trade rules, the WTO dispute resolution process begins with consultations. The consultation stage is an effort to encourage parties to find a solution to their dispute. On average, consultations last approximately nine months. They are successful more often than one might expect. Of the WTO's first 311 disputes, 172 were resolved in the consultation stage.

If consultation fails, the WTO appoints a panel to hear the dispute. Panels were appointed in 139 disputes through July 2004. Panel members are trade experts, not subject matter experts. In roughly half of the cases, the parties to the dispute agree on the members of the panel. If they cannot agree, the Director General of the WTO appoints them. Eighty-six percent of panel members were drawn from industrialized countries other than the United States or the European Union, or from developing countries. Only 3 percent of panel members were U.S. citizens.

Panels hold hearings, review written submissions from the parties, and hear oral arguments. Third parties can participate in the process, but only if they are governments. There is no role for non-governmental parties, although they can submit amicus briefs to inform the panel of their views. If panel members feel it necessary, they can consult with outside experts to help address difficult factual questions, or they can appoint a separate expert panel to resolve factual disputes. That approach was used, for example, to help address a U.S. challenge to European restrictions on genetically modified organisms.

When the panel reaches a tentative decision, it prepares a draft of its opinion, which circulates to the parties for comment. After taking those comments into account, the panel prepares a final decision. Unless this decision is appealed, it will become the WTO's final ruling on the dispute. The panel stage of the process takes an average of 13 months.

---

[4]John C. Beghin, "Nontariff Barriers," Working Paper 06-WP-438, Center for Agricultural and Rural Development, Iowa State University (December 2006) (available at http://www2.econ.iastate.edu/research/webpapers/paper_12703.pdf).

[5]The data in this section are drawn from an analysis of all WTO disputes from the organization's inception through July 2004.

Either party can appeal. The appeals process is completed in an average of 89 days, just under the maximum time allowed under the WTO agreement (90 days). As is the general rule in American courts, appeals are limited to legal issues only; parties cannot reargue the facts as determined by the panel. There is a permanent WTO appellate body with seven members, but individual appeals are heard by a panel of three members. The appeals panel can uphold the panel, modify its decision, or reverse its decision. Appeals decisions become final unless they are rejected by a consensus of the Dispute Settlement Body, which basically consists of all WTO members. Because the parties are also members of the Dispute Settlement Body, a consensus to overturn an appellate decision is unlikely.

The losing party in a WTO dispute is required to align its practices to the decision in a "reasonable" period of time. If it does not do so, the complaining party can seek authorization to impose trade sanctions. In these compliance proceedings, the WTO determines (through the panel process) whether the losing party has complied and what additional steps are necessary to comply. It determines the dollar amount of permitted sanctions against the trade of the losing party. Precisely which trade of the losing party is targeted is up to the party that prevailed, but sanctions are supposed to be on trade that is closely related to the trade that was at issue. Thus the approach to sanctions seeks to minimize spillovers that might lead to additional disputes in unrelated areas.

It is interesting to examine who complains to the WTO. The United States and the European Union are the complainants in 28 percent of all complaints. They are the subjects of twice as many complaints, 56 percent. Most complaints against the United States or the European Union are brought by industrialized or developing countries. Very few complaints arise from less developed countries, who are not frequent users of the process.

In WTO cases through July 2004, the United States was the complainant in 79 cases. Of those cases, 24 were resolved in the consultation stage. Of the cases where there was litigation, the United States won in 26 cases, and lost in 4 cases. An additional 24 cases were still in the process or were inactive. The United States has been the respondent in 115 complaints filed with the WTO. Of these, 17 were resolved without litigation. The United States won on 14 cases, but lost on 30; 32 cases remained in process or inactive.

D. The WTO and environmental issues

Environmentalists in the United States have been concerned in the last few years that WTO decisions are making environmental regulation more difficult. Although the WTO has an Environment and Trade Committee, it maintains that it is not an environmental agency. Thus the WTO is only concerned with environmental issues when they impact trade. Moreover, the WTO argues, environmental solutions must respect trade principles, just as solutions to other problems must respect trade principles.

Obligations undertaken in environmental treaties between nations would take precedence over trade treaty obligations, and the WTO states that if both countries involved in trade dispute were parties to the environmental treaty, the dispute should be resolved under the auspices of the environmental treaty. If only one of the countries is a party to the environmental treaty, however, the WTO may be the only forum to resolve the dispute.

To date, there do not appear to have been any such disputes. Rather, the typical dispute is a domestic environmental law with trade impacts that arguably could have been avoided. Several cases involving U.S. laws have raised particular concerns among environmental groups.

The first case to raise environmental concerns was the second case filed before the WTO after it came into existence in 1995. The United States adopted new standards for gasoline to be sold in certain parts of the country to help reduce air pollution. Refiners had to produce gasoline that improved the environmental characteristics of gasoline compared to a baseline that was computed for each refinery. Because the EPA thought that foreign refiners would not have adequate records to determine the baseline accurately, it initially proposed to require them to make reductions compared to their current product, without the option of using the historical baseline. During the rulemaking, foreign refiners convinced the EPA that they did indeed have sufficient records to establish a baseline, so the final rule allowed foreign refiners the same compliance options as it allowed for domestic refiners. Congress overruled that decision, however, and required a rule with standards that were stricter for foreign refiners than they were for U.S. refiners.

Venezuela challenged this requirement before the newly-minted WTO. In the end, the WTO ruled against the U.S. position. Although there would have been environmental benefits from a stricter standard for foreign refiners, there was also undeniably discrimination between domestic and foreign producers of the same product. Had Congress really been concerned about the environmental benefits, it could have imposed tighter standards on both domestic and foreign refiners. It was the differential requirements for foreign and domestic companies that violated trade agreements.

A second dispute involved U.S. requirements for turtle excluding devices (TEDs) on shrimp trawlers. Shrimp trawlers drag a net along the sea floor to catch shrimp. Occasionally, they also catch sea turtles. Because the turtles cannot escape from the net, they frequently drown. To avoid these turtle fatalities, the United States required domestic shrimpers to use TEDs, which prevent the turtles (but hopefully not the shrimp) from entering the net. Moreover, the United States restricted imports of shrimp from countries that did not have substantially the same requirement. However, it allowed more time for compliance and more assistance in compliance for Caribbean countries selling shrimp in the United States than it allowed for several Asian countries that also exported to the United States. The United States lost, because the WTO found the discrimination between trading partners was arbitrary and unjustified.

A third dispute involved dolphin-safe tuna. A common tuna fishing technique in the Pacific Ocean is to look for schools of dolphins, which for unknown reasons tend to swim over schools of tuna, and then circle the entire school with large nets. Almost inevitably, some dolphins get caught in the nets and drown. U.S. law requires domestic tuna fishermen to follow specific practices to reduce the risk of accidental dolphin deaths, and the United States sought to require tuna imported from Mexico to meet the same standards. U.S. law also set standards for labeling tuna as "dolphin safe," which basically required meeting the same set of standards. Mexico challenged these restrictions as a violation of trade agreements.

The WTO ruled against the United States on the substantive requirements regulating dolphin kills. Such regulations focus on the production process, not the product itself, which is completely indistinguishable from tuna caught in other ways. If such restrictions were allowed, any country could ban any import from a country where the good was produced using a different process.

The WTO panel, however, also ruled that nondiscriminatory eco-labeling is acceptable under trade rules. Controversy continues under this portion of the decision. Mexican tuna meets international dolphin conservations standards, which are supported by many, but not all, environmental groups. It does not, however, meet the more prescriptive and arguably more stringent US standard. The Clinton administration, and later the Bush administration, attempted to change the rules governing domestic labeling standards in ways that would have made it easier to import Mexican tuna into the United States. Environmental groups sued, however, and U.S. courts delayed changes. Frustrated by the absence of change in the United States, Mexico filed a new complaint focused on the labeling issue late in 2008. The heart of Mexico's argument was that the United States could achieve its basic objective with less adverse impact on trade by adopting the international standards. The WTO panel agreed with Mexico, but the United States appealed early in 2012.

A very similar case involved the US requirement for country of origin labeling on meat products adopted in 2008. Under this law, a cut of meat can only be labeled as a "product of the U.S." if the animal was born, entirely raised, and slaughtered in the United States. In a very common circumstance when the animal is born in another country (usually Canada or Mexico) but fattened and slaughtered in the United States., it must be labeled "product of U.S, Mexico [or Canada]." In 2010, meat from 2.3 million head of cattle and 5.7 million hogs would have required one of these combined labels. Canada challenged the requirement, and although the United States attempted to defend the requirement as a food safety measure that allowed consumers to avoid foreign meat if they wished, the WTO panel ruled that the requirement violated trade rules.

Another WTO decision involving environmental issues has also been controversial, although in this case it was the United States challenging environmentally motivated E.U. restrictions that impaired trade. In the United States, farmers are allowed to administer various hormones to cattle to increase productivity. The United States believes there are no adverse effects from this practice, which results in enhanced productivity and cheaper beef. Europe, however, based in significant part on the precautionary principle, believes that there may be some risk, and prohibits the sale of beef treated with hormones. The United States challenged these restrictions at the WTO and won, in part because there is a separate convention requiring a scientific basis for food safety decisions. As was its right, the European Union refused to comply with the decision, and the United States imposed retaliatory tariffs on selected imports from Europe. Because Europe still maintains the ban on beef grown with hormones, these tariffs were recently renewed.

The hormone decision has been of more concern to European environmentalists than to American groups, but all four cases raise extremely similar issues. In the cases in which the complaint was against the United States, there were clearly alternative ways to achieve the environmental objective that would have less impact on international trade. To environmental groups, however, it tends to be only the environmental effects that matter. If they can obtain more political support for restrictions drafted in a way that will also provide domestic producers with protection from foreign competition, they are more than willing to do so. That is the nature of rent creation in the policy details: the structure of the policy produces rents for particular groups, who are therefore more willing to support the policy. Long-standing trade agreements, enforced through the WTO mechanism, leave the United States free to pursue its environmental objectives. However, it must be willing to impose the same standards on domestic and foreign firms, and apply those standards uniformly across its trading partners. When the United States has lost, it has relied on an environmental excuse to violate at least one of these principles.

IV. SUMMARY

Trade restrictions imposed through tariffs or quotas have adverse effects on consumers, reducing consumer surplus. Either form of restriction raises prices for consumers and profits for domestic suppliers of the good. These additional profits are transfer payments. Tariffs increase government revenue, and quotas increase profits for those who are able to import the good. In either case, the increase is a transfer payment. Both tariffs and quotas also create deadweight losses for the economy as a whole. There is a deadweight loss because additional resources are used to expand production in the United States when those resources would have been more valuable somewhere else. There is also a deadweight loss because the higher domestic price that results from tariffs or quotas reduces the consumer surplus from consumption of goods that would have been worth more to consumers than the cost of purchasing them on the world market. The costs of existing trade restrictions in the United States are substantial.

As demand increases, the deadweight losses (and the transfers) of quotas increase. With tariffs, the primary effect of increases in demand is that imports increase. Trade restrictions may also have indirect effects, creating problems for domestic industries that use the imported good. Quotas may change the mix of imported goods available in the United States.

Trade restrictions create concentrated benefits for relatively small, compact groups with a large stake in the issue. They are more common in unionized industries, where workers are already organized. Costs are borne by consumers, who typically have a very small stake in the issue and practice rational ignorance. Costs to consumers are especially well hidden with quotas.

Package deals are a political technique to enhance the prospects for removing trade restrictions that reduce welfare. A package of changes offers more benefits for consumers, giving them a larger stake in the issue and making them more likely to participate in the process rather than remain ignorant. A package based on international negotiations can also attract support from domestic exporting industries, which may have a significant stake in trade concessions offered by other countries.

Package deals depend on the availability of "fast-track" authority, under which Congress commits to an up-or-down vote on the package, without amendments, and within a fixed period of time. Because no amendments are allowed, interest groups cannot attack particular provisions of the package, which could cause the entire deal to unravel. Fast-track negotiating authority expired in 2007, and has not been renewed.

The bipartisan consensus that freer trade is good for the United States has been threatened, because trade issues have been linked to labor (threats to U.S. wages and jobs) and environmental (WTO decisions overruling rules justified on environmental grounds) issues. The stimulus legislation included restrictions on purchasing from foreign companies, and abrogated a promise the U.S. government made in the NAFTA agreement to allow Mexican trucks to deliver goods in the United States. Mexico imposed retaliatory tariffs, and the U.S. eventually agreed to resume a pilot program allowing mexican trucks into the U.S.

Countervailing and antidumping duty laws seek to control "unfair" trade practices by imposing special tariffs to offset subsidies (countervailing duties) or dumping. Their use has grown, and countries around the world have imitated the U.S. approach, but the United States uses these restrictions more often and more intensively than other countries. Dumping is selling a good in the United States at a price lower than either the price in the home country, or the average total cost (including profit) of production in the home country. The Commerce Department determines whether there is dumping (or a subsidy), and the International Trade Commission determines whether there is "material injury" to U.S. industry. If both agencies say yes, a duty equal to the dumping margin is automatic. The effect on consumers is irrelevant.

There are significant problems in the way the antidumping and countervailing duty laws are administered. The United States uses the wrong cost test (price below average total cost, instead of average variable cost). The practice of "zeroing," which in effect compares the highest home country prices to the lowest U.S. prices, distorts price comparisons. Substituting a comparable market economy for a non-market economy allows comparisons based on arbitrary and outdated data. Subsidies are determined based on the benefit to the company, rather than on whether the subsidy has any effect on trade flows. If foreign companies cannot provide detailed information based on U.S. accounting principles in a short period of time, decisions may be based on what the U.S. complainant alleges. Moreover, ties go to the domestic company.

The World Trade Organization administers the basic trade treaties and resolves disputes between countries. It was created by the Uruguay round of negotiations, and began its work in 1995. Under trade rules, domestic policies must be based on the product, not the process of producing it. Moreover, policies must be nondiscriminatory, both between different trading partners and between foreign and domestic firms.

The dispute resolution process begins with consultations, which resolve many disputes. If the parties cannot agree, a panel is appointed to hear the dispute. Often, parties agree on the panelists; if not, the WTO appoints them. Panel members are trade experts, not subject matter experts, but can consult subject experts if needed. They hold hearings, consider written submissions, hold oral arguments, and circulate a draft of their decision. Non-governmental third parties cannot participate, but they can file amicus briefs.

Either side can appeal a panel's decision. The appellate body can uphold, modify, or overturn the panel's decision. Appeal panel decisions become final unless they are overturned by consensus.

A losing party must align its practices to the decision within a "reasonable" period of time. If it does not, the winning party can return to the WTO, which can authorize sanctions against the losing party up to a specific dollar amount.

The United States and the European Union are the subject of complaints more often than they initiate complaints. When the United States complains, it usually wins. When someone else complains about the United States, the United States usually loses.

The WTO's role in environmental regulation has become controversial with domestic environmental groups. The WTO maintains that environmental regulation must respect free trade principles. It has ruled against U.S. regulations justified on environmental grounds when they have regulated the process rather than the product, when they have imposed different standards on domestic and foreign firms, and when they have discriminated among trading partners.

CHAPTER VII

THE PROCESS OF CREATIVE DESTRUCTION

The theories of monopolistic and oligopolistic competition and their popular variants may in two ways be made to serve the view that capitalist reality is unfavorable to maximum performance in production. One may hold that it always has been so and that all along output has been expanding in spite of the secular sabotage perpetrated by the managing bourgeoisie. Advocates of this proposition would have to produce evidence to the effect that the observed rate of increase can be accounted for by a sequence of favorable circumstances unconnected with the mechanism of private enterprise and strong enough to overcome the latter's resistance. This is precisely the question which we shall discuss in Chapter IX. However, those who espouse this variant at least avoid the trouble about historical fact that the advocates of the alternative proposition have to face. This avers that capitalist reality once tended to favor maximum productive performance, or at all events productive performance so considerable as to constitute a major element in any serious appraisal of the system; but that the later spread of monopolist structures, killing competition, has by now reversed that tendency.

First, this involves the creation of an entirely imaginary golden age of perfect competition that at some time somehow metamorphosed itself into the monopolistic age, whereas it is quite clear that perfect competition has at no time been more of a reality than it is at present. Secondly, it is necessary to point out that the rate of increase in output did not decrease from the nineties from which, I suppose, the prevalence of the largest-size concerns, at least in manufacturing industry, would have to be dated; that there is nothing in the behavior of the time series of total output to suggest a "break in trend"; and, most important of all, that the modern standard of life of the masses evolved during the period of relatively unfettered "big business." If we list the items that enter the modern workman's budget and from 1899 on observe the course of their prices not in terms of money but in terms of the hours of labor that will buy them—i.e., each year's money prices divided by each year's hourly wage rates—we cannot fail to be struck by the rate of the advance which, considering the spectacular improvement in qualities, seems to have been greater and not smaller than it ever was before. If we economists were given less to wishful thinking and more to the observation of facts, doubts would immediately arise as to the realistic virtues of a theory that would have led us to expect a very different result. Nor is this all. As soon as we go into details and inquire into the individual items in which progress was most conspicuous, the trail leads not to the doors of those firms that work under conditions of comparatively free competition but precisely to the doors of the large concerns—which, as in the case of agricultural machinery, also account for much of the progress in the competitive sector—and a shocking suspicion dawns upon us that big business may have had more to do with creating that standard of life than with keeping it down.

The conclusions alluded to at the end of the preceding chapter are in fact almost completely false. Yet they follow from observations and theorems that are almost completely[1] true. Both economists and popular writers have once more run away with some fragments of reality they happened to grasp. These fragments themselves were mostly seen correctly. Their formal properties were mostly developed correctly. But no conclusions about capitalist reality as a whole follow from such fragmentary analyses. If we draw them nevertheless, we can be right only by accident. That has been done. And the lucky accident did not happen.

The essential point to grasp is that in dealing with capitalism we are dealing with an evolutionary process. It may seem strange that anyone can fail to see so obvious a fact which moreover was long ago emphasized by Karl Marx. Yet that fragmentary analysis which yields the bulk of our propositions about the functioning of modern capitalism persistently neglects it. Let us restate the point and see how it bears upon our problem.

Capitalism, then, is by nature a form or method of economic change and not only never is but never can be stationary. And this evolutionary character of the capitalist process is not merely due to the fact that economic life goes on in a social and natural environment which changes and by its change alters the data of economic action; this fact is important and these changes (wars, revolutions and so on) often condition industrial change, but they are not its prime movers. Nor is this evolutionary character due to a quasi-automatic increase in population and capital or to the vagaries of monetary systems of which exactly the same thing holds true. The fundamental impulse that sets and keeps the capitalist engine in motion comes from the new consumers' goods, the new methods of production or transportation, the new markets, the new forms of industrial organization that capitalist enterprise creates.

As we have seen in the preceding chapter, the contents of the laborer's budget, say from 1760 to 1940, did not simply grow on unchanging lines but they underwent a process of qualitative change. Similarly, the history of the productive apparatus of a typical farm, from the beginnings of the rationalization of crop rotation, plowing and fattening to the mechanized thing of today—linking up with elevators and railroads—is a history of revolutions. So is the history of the productive apparatus of the iron and steel industry from the charcoal furnace to our own type of furnace, or the history of the apparatus of power production from the overshot water wheel to the modern power plant, or the history of transportation from the mail-coach to the airplane. The opening up of new markets, foreign or domestic, and the organizational development from the craft shop and factory to such concerns as U. S. Steel illustrate the same process of industrial mutation—if I may use that biological term—that incessantly revolutionizes[2] the economic structure *from within*, incessantly destroying the old one, incessantly creating a new one. This process of Creative Destruction is the essential fact about capitalism. It is what capitalism consists in and what every capitalist concern has got to live in. This fact bears upon our problem in two ways.

First, since we are dealing with a process whose every element takes considerable time in revealing its true features and ultimate effects, there is no point in appraising the performance of that process *ex visu* of a given point of time; we must judge its performance over time, as it unfolds through decades or centuries. A system—any system, economic or other—that at *every* given point of time fully utilizes its possibilities to the best advantage may yet in the long run be inferior to a system that does so at *no* given point of time, because the latter's failure to do so may be a condition for the level or speed of long-run performance.

---

[1]As a matter of fact, those observations and theorems are not completely satisfactory. The usual expositions of the doctrine of imperfect competition fail in particular to give due attention to the many and important cases in which, even as a matter of static theory, imperfect competition approximates the results of perfect competition. There are other cases in which it does not do this, but offers compensations which, while not entering any output index, yet contribute to what the output index is in the last resort intended to measure—the cases in which a firm defends its market by establishing a name for quality and service for instance. However, in order to simplify matters, we will not take issue with that doctrine on its own ground.

[2]Those revolutions are not strictly incessant; they occur in discrete rushes which are separated from each other by spans of comparative quiet. The process as a whole works incessantly however, in the sense that there always is either revolution or absorption of the results of revolution, both together forming what are known as business cycles.

Second, since we are dealing with an organic process, analysis of what happens in any particular part of it—say, in an individual concern or industry—may indeed clarify details of mechanism but is inconclusive beyond that. Every piece of business strategy acquires its true significance only against the background of that process and within the situation created by it. It must be seen in its role in the perennial gale of creative destruction; it cannot be understood irrespective of it or, in fact, on the hypothesis that there is a perennial lull.

But economists who, *ex visu* of a point of time, look for example at the behavior of an oligopolist industry—an industry which consists of a few big firms—and observe the well-known moves and countermoves within it that seem to aim at nothing but high prices and restrictions of output are making precisely that hypothesis. They accept the data of the momentary situation as if there were no past or future to it and think that they have understood what there is to understand if they interpret the behavior of those firms by means of the principle of maximizing profits with reference to those data. The usual theorist's paper and the usual government commission's report practically never try to see that behavior, on the one hand, as a result of a piece of past history and, on the other hand, as an attempt to deal with a situation that is sure to change presently—as an attempt by those firms to keep on their feet, on ground that is slipping away from under them. In other words, the problem that is usually being visualized is how capitalism administers existing structures, whereas the relevant problem is how it creates and destroys them. As long as this is not recognized, the investigator does a meaningless job. As soon as it is recognized, his outlook on capitalist practice and its social results changes considerably.[3]

The first thing to go is the traditional conception of the *modus operandi* of competition. Economists are at long last emerging from the stage in which price competition was all they saw. As soon as quality competition and sales effort are admitted into the sacred precincts of theory, the price variable is ousted from its dominant position. However, it is still competition within a rigid pattern of invariant conditions, methods of production and forms of industrial organization in particular, that practically monopolizes attention. But in capitalist reality as distinguished from its textbook picture, it is not that kind of competition which counts but the competition from the new commodity, the new technology, the new source of supply, the new type of organization (the largest-scale unit of control for instance)—competition which commands a decisive cost or quality advantage and which strikes not at the margins of the profits and the outputs of the existing firms but at their foundations and their very lives. This kind of competition is as much more effective than the other as a bombardment is in comparison with forcing a door, and so much more important that it becomes a matter of comparative indifference whether competition in the ordinary sense functions more or less promptly; the powerful lever that in the long run expands output and brings down prices is in any case made of other stuff.

It is hardly necessary to point out that competition of the kind we now have in mind acts not only when in being but also when it is merely an ever-present threat. It disciplines before it attacks. The businessman feels himself to be in a competitive situation even if he is alone in his field or if, though not alone, he holds a position such that investigating government experts fail to see any effective competition between him and any other firms in the same or a neighboring field and in consequence conclude that his talk, under examination, about his competitive sorrows is all make-believe. In many cases, though not in all, this will in the long run enforce behavior very similar to the perfectly competitive pattern.

Many theorists take the opposite view which is best conveyed by an example. Let us assume that there is a certain number of retailers in a neighborhood who try to improve their relative position by service and "atmosphere" but avoid price competition and stick as to methods to the local tradition—a picture of stagnating routine. As others drift into the trade that quasi-equilibrium is indeed upset, but in a manner that does not benefit their customers. The economic space around each of the shops having been narrowed, their owners will no longer be able to make a living and they will try to mend the case by raising prices in tacit agreement. This will further reduce their sales and so, by successive pyramiding, a situation will evolve in

---

[3]It should be understood that it is only our appraisal of economic performance and not our moral judgment that can be so changed. Owing to its autonomy, moral approval or disapproval is entirely independent of our appraisal of social (or any other) results, unless we happen to adopt a moral system such as utilitarianism which makes moral, approval and disapproval turn on them *ex definitione*.

which increasing potential supply will be attended by increasing instead of decreasing prices and by decreasing instead of increasing sales.

Such cases do occur, and it is right and proper to work them out. But as the practical instances usually given show, they are fringe-end cases to be found mainly in the sectors furthest removed from all that is most characteristic of capitalist activity.[4] Moreover, they are transient by nature. In the case of retail trade the competition that matters arises not from additional shops of the same type, but from the department store, the chain store, the mail-order house and the supermarket which are bound to destroy those pyramids sooner or later.[5]

Now a theoretical construction which neglects this essential element of the case neglects all that is most typically capitalist about it; even if correct in logic as well as in fact, it is like *Hamlet* without the Danish prince.

---

[4]This is also shown by a theorem we frequently meet with in expositions of the theory of imperfect competition, viz., the theorem that, under conditions of imperfect competition, producing or trading businesses tend to be irrationally small. Since imperfect competition is at the same time held to be an outstanding characteristic of modern industry we are set to wondering what world these theorists live in, unless, as stated above, fringe-end cases are all they have in mind.

[5]The mere threat of their attack cannot, in the particular conditions, environmental and personal, of small-scale retail trade, have its usual disciplining influence, for the small man is too much hampered by his cost structure and, however well he may manage within his inescapable limitations, he can never adapt him self to the methods of competitors who can afford to sell at the price at which he buys.

CHAPTER VIII

MONOPOLISTIC PRACTICES

What has been said so far is really sufficient to enable the reader to deal with the large majority of the practical cases he is likely to meet and to realize the inadequacy of most of those criticisms of the profit economy which, directly or indirectly, rely on the absence of perfect competition. Since, however, the bearing of our argument on some of those criticisms may not be obvious at a glance, it will be worth our while to elaborate a little in order to make a few points more explicit.

1. We have just seen that, both as a fact and as a threat, the impact of new things—new technologies for instance—on the existing structure of an industry considerably reduces the long-run scope and importance of practices that aim, through restricting output, at conserving established positions and at maximizing the profits accruing from them. We must now recognize the further fact that restrictive practices of this kind, as far as they are effective, acquire a new significance in the perennial gale of creative destruction, a significance which they would not have in a stationary state or in a state of slow and balanced growth. In either of these cases restrictive strategy would produce no result other than an increase in profits at the expense of buyers except that, in the case of balanced advance, it might still prove to be the easiest and most effective way of collecting the means by which to finance additional investment.[1] But in the process of creative destruction, restrictive practices may do much to steady the ship and to alleviate temporary difficulties. This is in fact a very familiar argument which always turns up in times of depression and, as everyone knows, has become very popular with governments and their economic advisers—witness the NRA. While it has been so much misused and so faultily acted upon that most economists heartily despise it, those same advisers who are responsible for this[2] invariably fail to see its much more general rationale.

Practically any investment entails, as a necessary complement of entrepreneurial action, certain safeguarding activities such as insuring or hedging. Long-range investing under rapidly changing conditions, especially under conditions that change or may change at any moment under the impact of new commodities and technologies, is like shooting at a target that is not only indistinct but moving—and moving jerkily at that. Hence it becomes necessary to resort to such protecting devices as patents or temporary secrecy of processes or, in some cases, long-period contracts secured in advance. But these protecting devices which most economists accept as normal elements of rational management[3] are only special cases of a larger class comprising many others which most economists condemn although they do not differ fundamentally from the recognized ones.

If for instance a war risk is insurable, nobody objects to a firm's collecting the cost of this insurance from the buyers of its products. But that risk is no less an element in long-run costs, if there are no facilities for insuring against it, in which case a price strategy aiming at the same end will seem to involve unnecessary restriction and to be productive of excess profits. Similarly, if a patent cannot be secured or would not, if secured, effectively protect, other means may have to be used in order to justify the investment. Among them are a price policy that will make it possible to write off more quickly than would otherwise be rational, or additional investment in order to provide excess capacity to be used only for aggression or defense. Again, if long-period contracts cannot be entered into in advance, other means may have to be devised in order to tie prospective customers to the investing firm.

---

[1] Theorists are apt to look upon anyone who admits this possibility as guilty of gross error, and to prove immediately that financing by borrowing from banks or from private savers or, in the case of public enterprise, financing from the proceeds of an income tax is much more rational than is financing from surplus profits collected through a restrictive policy. For some patterns of behavior they are quite right. For others they are quite wrong. I believe that both capitalism and communism of the Russian type belong in the latter category. But the point is that theoretical considerations, especially theoretical considerations of the short-run kind, cannot solve, although they contribute to the solution of, the problem which we shall meet again in the next part.

[2] In particular, it is easy to show that there is no sense, and plenty of harm, in a policy that aims at preserving "price parities."

[3] Some economists, however, consider that even those devices are obstructions to progress which, though perhaps necessary in capitalist society, would be absent in a socialist one. There is some truth in this. But that does not affect the proposition that the protection afforded by patents and so on is, in the conditions of a profit economy, on balance a propelling and not an inhibiting factor.

In analyzing such business strategy *ex visu* of a given point of time, the investigating economist or government agent sees price policies that seem to him predatory and restrictions of output that seem to him synonymous with loss of opportunities to produce. He does not see that restrictions of this type are, in the conditions of the perennial gale, incidents, often unavoidable incidents, of a long-run process of expansion which they protect rather than impede. There is no more of paradox in this than there is in saying that motorcars are traveling faster than they otherwise would *because* they are provided with brakes.

2. This stands out most clearly in the case of those sectors of the economy which at any time happen to embody the impact of new things and methods on the existing industrial structure. The best way of getting a vivid and realistic idea of industrial strategy is indeed to visualize the behavior of new concerns or industries that introduce new commodities or processes (such as the aluminum industry) or else reorganize a part or the whole of an industry (such as, for instance, the old Standard Oil Company).

As we have seen, such concerns are aggressors by nature and wield the really effective weapon of competition. Their intrusion can only in the rarest of cases fail to improve total output in quantity or quality, both through the new method itself—even if at no time used to full advantage—and through the pressure it exerts on the preexisting firms. But these aggressors are so circumstanced as to require, for purposes of attack and defense, also pieces of armor other than price and quality of their product which, moreover, must be strategically manipulated all along so that at any point of time they seem to be doing nothing but restricting their output and keeping prices high.

On the one hand, largest-scale plans could in many cases not materialize at all if it were not known from the outset that competition will be discouraged by heavy capital requirements or lack of experience, or that means are available to discourage or checkmate it so as to gain the time and space for further developments. Even the conquest of financial control over competing concerns in otherwise unassailable positions or the securing of advantages that run counter to the public's sense of fair play—railroad rebates—move, as far as long-run effects on total output alone are envisaged, into a different light;[4] they *may* be methods for removing obstacles that the institution of private property puts in the path of progress. In a socialist society that time and space would be no less necessary. They would have to be secured by order of the central authority.

On the other hand enterprise would in most cases be impossible if it were not known from the outset that exceptionally favorable situations are likely to arise which if exploited by price, quality and quantity manipulation will produce profits adequate to tide over exceptionally unfavorable situations provided these are similarly managed. Again this requires strategy that in the short run is often restrictive. In the majority of successful cases this strategy just manages to serve its purpose. In some cases, however, it is so successful as to yield profits far above what is necessary in order to induce the corresponding investment. These cases then provide the baits that lure capital on to untried trails. Their presence explains in part how it is possible for so large a section of the capitalist world to work for nothing: in the midst of the prosperous twenties just about half of the business corporations in the United States were run at a loss, at zero profits, or at profits which, if they had been foreseen, would have been inadequate to call forth the effort and expenditure involved.

Our argument however extends beyond the cases of new concerns, methods and industries. Old concerns and established industries, whether or not directly attacked, still live in the perennial gale. Situations emerge in the process of creative destruction in which many firms may have to perish that nevertheless would be able to live on vigorously and usefully if they could weather a particular storm. Short of such general crises or depressions, sectional situations arise in which the rapid change of data that is characteristic of that process so disorganizes

---

[4]The qualification added removes, I think, any just cause for offense that the above proposition might conceivably cause. In case that qualification is not explicit enough, I beg leave to repeat that the moral aspect is in this case, as it must be in every case, entirely unaffected by an economic argument. For the rest, let the reader reflect that even in dealing with indubitably criminal actions every civilized judge and every civilized jury take account of the ulterior purpose in pursuit of which a crime has occurred and of the difference it makes whether an action that is a crime has or has not also effects they consider socially desirable.

Another objection would be more to the point. If an enterprise can succeed only by such means, does not that prove in itself that it cannot spell social gain? A very simple argument can be framed in support of this view. But it is subject to a severe *ceteris paribus* proviso. That is to say, it holds for conditions which are just about equivalent to excluding the process of creative destruction—capitalist reality. On reflection, it will be seen that the analogy of the practices under discussion with patents is sufficient to show this.

an industry for the time being as to inflict functionless losses and to create avoidable unemployment. Finally, there is certainly no point in trying to conserve obsolescent industries indefinitely; but there is point in trying to avoid their coming down with a crash and in attempting to turn a rout, which may become a center of cumulative depressive effects, into orderly retreat. Correspondingly there is, in the case of industries that have sown their wild oats but are still gaining and not losing ground, such a thing as orderly advance.[5]

All this is of course nothing but the tritest common sense. But it is being overlooked with a persistence so stubborn as sometimes to raise the question of sincerity. And it follows that, within the process of creative destruction, all the realities of which theorists are in the habit of relegating to books and courses on business cycles, there is another side to industrial self-organization than that which these theorists are contemplating. "Restraints of trade" of the cartel type as well as those which merely consist in tacit understandings about price competition may be effective remedies under conditions of depression. As far as they are, they may in the end produce not only steadier but also greater expansion of total output than could be secured by an entirely uncontrolled onward rush that cannot fail to be studded with catastrophes. Nor can it be argued that these catastrophes occur in any case. We know what has happened in each historical case. We have a very imperfect idea of what might have happened, considering the tremendous pace of the process, if such pegs had been entirely absent.

Even as now extended however, our argument does not cover all cases of restrictive or regulating strategy, many of which no doubt have that injurious effect on the long-run development of output which is uncritically attributed to all of them. And even in the cases our argument does cover, the net effect is a question of the circumstances and of the way in which and the degree to which industry regulates itself in each individual case. It is certainly as conceivable that an all-pervading cartel system might sabotage all progress as it is that it might realize, with smaller social and private costs, all that perfect competition is supposed to realize. This is why our argument does not amount to a case against state regulation. It does show that there is no general case for indiscriminate "trust-busting" or for the prosecution of everything that qualifies as a restraint of trade. Rational as distinguished from vindictive regulation by public authority turns out to be an extremely delicate problem which not every government agency, particularly when in full cry against big business, can be trusted to solve.[6] But our argument, framed to refute a prevalent *theory* and the inferences drawn therefrom about the relation between modern capitalism and the development of total output, only yields another *theory*, i.e., another outlook on facts and another principle by which to interpret them. For our purpose that is enough. For the rest, the facts themselves have the floor.

3. Next, a few words on the subject of Rigid Prices which has been receiving so much attention of late. It really is but a particular aspect of the problem we have been discussing. We shall define rigidity as follows: a price is rigid if it is less sensitive to changes in the conditions of demand and supply than it would be if perfect competition prevailed.[7]

---

[5]A good example illustrative of this point—in fact of much of our general argument—is the postwar history of the automobile and the rayon industry. The first illustrates very well the nature and value of what we might call "edited" competition. The bonanza time was over by about 1916. A host of firms nevertheless crowded into the industry afterwards, most of which were eliminated by 1925. From a fierce life and death struggle three concerns emerged that by now account for over 80 per cent of total sales. They are under competitive pressure inasmuch as, in spite of the advantages of an established position, an elaborate sales and service organization and so on, any failure to keep up and improve the quality of their products or any attempt at monopolistic combination would call in new competitors. Among themselves, the three concerns behave in a way which should be called corespective rather than competitive: they refrain from certain aggressive devices (which, by the way, would also be absent in perfect competition); they keep up with each other and in doing so play for points at the frontiers. This has now gone on for upwards of fifteen years and it is not obvious that if conditions of theoretically perfect competition had prevailed during that period, better or cheaper cars would now be offered to the public, or higher wages and more or steadier employment to the workmen. The rayon industry had its bonanza time in the twenties. It presents the features incident to introducing a commodity into fields fully occupied before and the policies that impose themselves in such conditions still more clearly than does the automobile industry. And there are a number of other differences. But fundamentally the case is similar. The expansion in quantity and quality of rayon output is common knowledge. Yet restrictive policy presided over this expansion at each individual point of time.

[6]Unfortunately, this statement is almost as effective a bar to agreement on policy as the most thoroughgoing denial of any case for government regulation could be. In fact it may embitter discussion. Politicians, public officers and economists can stand what I may politely term the whole-hog opposition of "economic royalists." Doubts about their competence, such as crowd upon us particularly when we see the legal mind at work, are much more difficult for them to stand.

[7]This definition suffices for our purposes but would not be satisfactory for others. See D. D. Humphrey's article in the *Journal of Political Economy*, October 1937, and E. S. Mason's article in the *Review of Economic Statistics*, May 1938. Professor Mason has shown, among other things, that contrary to a widespread belief price rigidity is not increasing or, at all events, that it is no greater than it was forty years ago, a result which in itself suffices to invalidate some of the implications of the current doctrine of rigidity.

Quantitatively, the extent to which prices are rigid in that sense depends on the material and the method of measurement we select and is hence a doubtful matter. But whatever the material or method, it is certain that prices are not nearly as rigid as they seem to be. There are many reasons why what in effect is a change in price should not show in the statistical picture: in other words, why there should be much spurious rigidity. I shall mention only one class of them which is closely connected with the facts stressed by our analysis.

I have adverted to the importance, for the capitalist process in general and for its competitive mechanism in particular, of the intrusion of new commodities. Now a new commodity may effectively bring down the pre-existing structure and satisfy a given want at much lower prices per unit of service (transportation service for instance), and yet not a single recorded price need change in the process; flexibility in the relevant sense may be accompanied by rigidity in a formal sense. There are other cases, not of this type, in which price reduction is the sole motive for bringing out a new brand while the old one is left at the previous quotation—again a price reduction that does not show. Moreover, the great majority of new consumers' goods—particularly all the gadgets of modern life—are at first introduced in an experimental and unsatisfactory form in which they could never conquer their potential markets. Improvement in the quality of products is hence a practically universal feature of the development of individual concerns and of industries. Whether or not this improvement involves additional costs, a constant price per unit of an improving commodity should not be called rigid without further investigation.

Of course, plenty of cases of genuine price rigidity remain—of prices which are being kept constant as a matter of business policy or which remain unchanged because it is difficult to change, say, a price set by a cartel after laborious negotiations. In order to appraise the influence of this fact on the long-run development of output, it is first of all necessary to realize that this rigidity is essentially a short-run phenomenon. There are no major instances of long-run rigidity of prices. Whichever manufacturing industry or group of manufactured articles of any importance we choose to investigate over a period of time, we practically always find that in the long run prices do not fail to adapt themselves to technological progress—frequently they fall spectacularly in response to it[8]—unless prevented from doing so by monetary events and policies or, in some cases, by autonomous changes in wage rates which of course should be taken into account by appropriate corrections exactly as should changes in quality of products.[9] And our previous analysis shows sufficiently why in the process of capitalist evolution this must be so.

What the business strategy in question really aims at—all, in any case, that it can achieve—is to avoid seasonal, random and cyclical fluctuations in prices and to move only in response to the more fundamental changes in the conditions that underlie those fluctuations. Since these more fundamental changes take time in declaring themselves, this involves moving slowly by discrete steps—keeping to a price until new relatively durable contours have emerged into view. In technical language, this strategy aims at moving along a step function that will approximate trends. And that is what genuine and voluntary price rigidity in most cases amounts to. In fact, most economists do admit this, at least by implication. For though some of their arguments about rigidity would hold true only if the phenomenon were a long-run one—for instance most of the arguments averring that price rigidity keeps the fruits of technological progress from consumers—in practice they measure and discuss primarily cyclical rigidity and especially the fact that many prices do not, or do not promptly, fall in recessions and depressions. The real question is therefore how this short-run rigidity[10] may affect the

---

[8]They do not as a rule fall as they would under conditions of perfect competition. But this is true only *ceteris paribus*, and this proviso robs the proposition of all practical importance. I have adverted to this point before and shall return to it below (§5).

[9]From a welfare standpoint, it is proper to adopt a definition different from ours, and to measure price changes in terms of the hours of labor that are currently necessary to earn the dollars which will buy given quantities of manufactured consumers' goods, taking account of changes of quality. We have already done this in the course of a previous argument. A long-run downward flexibility is then revealed that is truly impressive. Changes in price level raise another problem. So far as they reflect monetary influences they should be eliminated for most of the purposes of an investigation into rigidity. But so far as they reflect the combined effect of increasing efficiencies in all lines of production they should not.

[10]It should, however, be observed that this short run may last longer than the term "short run" usually implies—sometimes ten years and even longer. There is not one cycle, but there are many simultaneous ones of varying duration. One of the most important ones lasts on the average about nine years and a half. Structural changes requiring price adjustments do in important cases occur in periods of about that length. The full extent of the spectacular changes reveals itself only in periods much longer than this. To do justice to aluminum, rayon, or motorcar prices one must survey a period of about forty-five years.

long-run development of total output. Within this question, the only really important issue is this: prices that stay up in recession or depression no doubt influence the business situation in those phases of the cycles; if that influence is strongly injurious—making matters much worse than they would be with perfect flexibility all round—the destruction wrought each time might also affect output in the subsequent recoveries and prosperities and thus permanently reduce the rate of increase in total output below what it would be in the absence of those rigidities. Two arguments have been put forth in favor of this view.

In order to put the first into the strongest possible light, let us assume that an industry which refuses to reduce prices in recession goes on selling exactly the same quantity of product which it would sell if it had reduced them. Buyers are therefore out of pocket by the amount to which the industry profits from the rigidity. If these buyers are the kind of people who spend all they can and if the industry or those to whom its net returns go does not spend the increment it gets but either keeps it idle or repays bank loans, then total expenditure in the economy may be reduced thereby. If this happens, other industries or firms may suffer and if thereupon they restrict in turn, we may get a cumulation of depressive effects. In other words, rigidity may so influence the amount and distribution of national income as to decrease balances or to increase idle balances or, if we adopt a popular misnomer, savings. Such a case is conceivable. But the reader should have little difficulty in satisfying himself[11] that its practical importance, if any, is very small.

The second argument turns on the dislocating effects price rigidity may exert if, in the individual industry itself or elsewhere, it leads to an additional restriction of output, i.e., to a restriction greater than that which must in any case occur during depression. Since the most important conductor of those effects is the incident increase in unemployment—unstabilization of employment is in fact the indictment most commonly directed against price rigidity—and the consequent decrease in total expenditure, this argument then follows in the tracks of the first one. Its practical weight is considerably reduced, although economists greatly differ as to the extent, by the consideration that in the most conspicuous cases price rigidity is motivated precisely by the low sensitiveness of demand to short-run price changes within the practicable range. People who in depression worry about their future are not likely to buy a new car even if the price were reduced by 25 per cent, especially if the purchase is easily postponable and if the reduction induces expectations of further reductions.

Quite irrespective of this however, the argument is inconclusive because it is again vitiated by a *ceteris paribus* clause that is inadmissible in dealing with our process of creative destruction. From the fact, so far as it is a fact, that at more flexible prices greater quantities could *ceteris paribus* be sold, it does not follow that either the output of the commodities in question, or total output and hence employment, would actually be greater. For inasmuch as we may assume that the refusal to lower prices strengthens the position of the industries which adopt that policy either by increasing their revenue or simply by avoiding chaos in their markets—that is to say, so far as this policy is something more than a mistake on their part—it may make fortresses out of what otherwise might be centers of devastation. As we have seen before, from a more general standpoint, total output and employment may well keep on a higher level with the restrictions incident to that policy than they would if depression were allowed to play havoc with the price structure.[12] In other words, under the conditions created by capitalist evolution, perfect and universal flexibility of prices might in depression further unstabilize the system, instead of stabilizing it as it no doubt would under the conditions envisaged by general theory. Again this is to a large extent recognized in those cases in which the economist is in sympathy with the interests immediately concerned, for instance in the case of labor and of agriculture; in those cases he admits readily enough that what looks like rigidity may be no more than regulated adaptation.

Perhaps the reader feels some surprise that so little remains of a doctrine of which so much has been made in the last few years. The rigidity of prices has become, with some people, the outstanding defect of the capitalist

---

[11]The best method of doing this is to work out carefully *all* the assumptions involved, not only in the strong case imagined but also in the weaker cases that are less unlikely to occur in practice. Moreover, it should not be forgotten that the profit due to keeping prices up may be the means of avoiding bankruptcy or at least the necessity of discontinuing operations, both of which might be much more effective in starting a downward "vicious spiral" than is a possible reduction in total expenditure. See the comments on the second argument.

[12]The theorist's way to put the point is that in depression demand curves might shift downwards much more violently if all pegs were withdrawn from under all prices.

engine and—almost—the fundamental factor in the explanation of depressions. But there is nothing to wonder at in this. Individuals and groups snatch at anything that will qualify as a discovery lending support to the political tendencies of the hour. The doctrine of price rigidity, with a modicum of truth to its credit, is not the worst case of this kind by a long way.

4. Another doctrine has crystallized into a slogan, viz., that in the era of big business the maintenance of the value of existing investment—conservation of capital—becomes the chief aim of entrepreneurial activity and bids fair to put a stop to all cost-reducing improvement. Hence the capitalist order becomes incompatible with progress.

Progress entails, as we have seen, destruction of capital values in the strata with which the new commodity or method of production competes. In perfect competition the old investments must be adapted at a sacrifice or abandoned; but when there is no perfect competition and when each industrial field is controlled by a few big concerns, these can in various ways fight the threatening attack on their capital structure and try to avoid losses on their capital accounts; that is to say, they can and will fight progress itself.

So far as this doctrine merely formulates a particular aspect of restrictive business strategy, there is no need to add anything to the argument already sketched in this chapter. Both as to the limits of that strategy and as to its functions in the process of creative destruction, we should only be repeating what has been said before. This becomes still more obvious if we observe that conserving capital values is the same thing as conserving profits. Modern theory tends in fact to use the concept Present Net Value of Assets (= capital values) in place of the concept of Profits. Both asset values and profits are of course not being simply conserved but maximized.

But the point about the sabotage of cost-reducing improvement still calls for comment in passing. As a little reflection will show, it is sufficient to consider the case of a concern that controls a technological device—some patent, say—the use of which would involve scrapping some or all of its plant and equipment. Will it, in order to conserve its capital values, refrain from using this device when a management not fettered by capitalist interests such as a socialist management could and would use it to the advantage of all?

Again it is tempting to raise the question of fact. The first thing a modern concern does as soon as it feels that it can afford it is to establish a research department every member of which knows that his bread and butter depends on his success in devising improvements. This practice does not obviously suggest aversion to technological progress. Nor can we in reply be referred to the cases in which patents acquired by business concerns have not been used promptly or not been used at all. For there may be perfectly good reasons for this; for example, the patented process may turn out to be no good or at least not to be in shape to warrant application on a commercial basis. Neither the inventors themselves nor the investigating economists or government officials are unbiased judges of this, and from their remonstrances or reports we may easily get a very distorted picture.[13]

But we are concerned with a question of theory. Everyone agrees that private and socialist managements will introduce improvements if, with the new method of production, the total cost per unit of product is expected to be smaller than the prime cost per unit of product with the method actually in use. If this condition is not fulfilled, then it is held that private management will not adopt a cost-reducing method until the existing plant and equipment is entirely written off, whereas socialist management would, to the social advantage, replace the old by any new cost-reducing method as soon as such a method becomes available, i.e., without regard to capital values. This however is not so.[14]

---

[13]Incidentally, it should be noticed that the kind of restrictive practice under discussion, granted that it exists to a significant extent, would not be without compensatory effects on social welfare. In fact, the same critics who talk about sabotage of progress at the same time emphasize the *social* losses incident to the pace of capitalist progress, particularly the unemployment which that pace entails and which slower advance might mitigate to some extent. Well, is technological progress too quick or too slow for them? They had better make up their minds.

[14]It should be observed that even if the argument were correct, it would still be inadequate to support the thesis that capitalism is, under the conditions envisaged, "incompatible with technological progress." All that it would prove is, for some cases, the presence of a lag of ordinarily moderate length in the introduction of new methods.

Private management, if actuated by the profit motive, cannot be interested in maintaining the values of any given building or machine any more than a socialist management would be. All that private management tries to do is to maximize the present net value of total assets which is equal to the discounted value of expected net returns. This amounts to saying that it will always adopt a new method of production which it believes will yield a larger stream of future income per unit of the corresponding stream of future outlay, both discounted to the present, than does the method actually in use. The value of past investment, whether or not paralleled by a bonded debt that has to be amortized, does not enter at all except in the sense and to the extent that it would also have to enter into the calculation underlying the decisions of a socialist management. So far as the use of the old machines saves future costs as compared with the immediate introduction of the new methods, the remainder of their service value is of course an element of the decision for both the capitalist and the socialist manager; otherwise bygones are bygones for both of them and any attempt to conserve the value of past investment would conflict as much with the rules following from the profit motive as it would conflict with the rules set for the behavior of the socialist manager.

It is however not true that private firms owning equipment the value of which is endangered by a new method which they also control—if they do not control it, there is no problem and no indictment—will adopt the new method only if total unit cost with it is smaller than prime unit cost with the old one, or if the old investment has been completely written off *according to the schedule decided on before the new method presented itself*. For if the new machines when installed are expected to outlive the rest of the period previously set for the use of the old machines, their discounted remainder value as of that date is another asset to be taken account of. Nor is it true, for analogous reasons, that a socialist management, if acting rationally, would always and immediately adopt any new method which promises to produce at smaller total unit costs or that this would be to the social advantage.

There is however another element[15] which profoundly affects behavior in this matter and which is being invariably overlooked. This is what might be called *ex ante* conservation of capital in expectation of further improvement. Frequently, if not in most cases, a going concern does not simply face the question whether or not to adopt a definite new method of production that is the best thing out and, in the form immediately available, can be expected to retain that position for some length of time. A new type of machine is in general but a link in a chain of improvements and may presently become obsolete. In a case like this it would obviously not be rational to follow the chain link by link regardless of the capital loss to be suffered each time. The real question then is at which link the concern should take action. The answer must be in the nature of a compromise between considerations that rest largely on guesses. But it will as a rule involve some waiting in order to see how the chain behaves. And to the outsider this may well look like trying to stifle improvement in order to conserve *existing* capital values. Yet even the most patient of comrades would revolt if a socialist management were so foolish as to follow the advice of the theorist and to keep on scrapping plant and equipment every year.

5. I have entitled this chapter as I did because most of it deals with the facts and problems that common parlance associates with monopoly or monopolistic practice. So far I have as much as possible refrained from using those terms in order to reserve for a separate section some comments on a few topics specifically connected with them. Nothing will be said however that we have not already met in one form or another.

(a) To begin with, there is the term itself. Monopolist means Single Seller. Literally therefore anyone is a monopolist who sells anything that is not in every respect, wrapping and location and service included, exactly like what other people sell: every grocer, or every haberdasher, or every seller of "Good Humors" on a road that is not simply lined with sellers of the same brand of ice cream. This however is not what we mean when talking about monopolists. We mean only those single sellers whose markets are not open to the intrusion of would-be producers of the same commodity and of actual producers of similar ones or, speaking slightly more technically, only those single sellers who face a given demand schedule that is severely independent of their

---

[15]There are of course many other elements. The reader will please understand that in dealing with a few questions of principles it is impossible to do full justice to any of the topics touched upon.

own action as well as of any reactions to their action by other concerns. The traditional Cournot-Marshall theory of monopoly as extended and amended by later authors holds only if we define it in this way and there is, so it seems, no point in calling anything a monopoly to which that theory does not apply.

But if accordingly we do define it like this, then it becomes evident immediately that pure cases of long-run monopoly must be of the rarest occurrence and that even tolerable approximations to the requirements of the concept must be still rarer than are cases of perfect competition. The power to exploit at pleasure a given pattern of demand—or one that changes independently of the monopolist's action and of the reactions it provokes—can under the conditions of intact capitalism hardly persist for a period long enough to matter for the analysis of total output, unless buttressed by public authority, for instance, in the case of fiscal monopolies. A modern business concern not *so* protected—i.e., even if protected by import duties or import prohibitions—and yet wielding that power (except temporarily) is not easy to find or even to imagine. Even railroads and power and light concerns had first to create the demand for their services and, when they had done so, to defend their market against competition. Outside the field of public utilities, the position of a single seller can in general be conquered—and retained for decades—only on the condition that he does not behave like a monopolist. Shortrun monopoly will be touched upon presently.

Why then all this talk about monopoly? The answer is not without interest for the student of the psychology of political discussion. Of course, the concept of monopoly is being loosely used just like any other. People speak of a country's having a monopoly of something or other[16] even if the industry in question is highly competitive and so on. But this is not all. Economists, government agents, journalists and politicians in this country obviously love the word because it has come to be a term of opprobrium which is sure to rouse the public's hostility against any interest so labeled. In the Anglo-American world monopoly has been cursed and associated with functionless exploitation ever since, in the sixteenth and seventeenth centuries, it was English administrative practice to create monopoly positions in large numbers which, on the one hand, answered fairly well to the theoretical pattern of monopolist behavior and, on the other hand, fully justified the wave of indignation that impressed even the great Elizabeth.

Nothing is so retentive as a nation's memory. Our time offers other and more important instances of a nation's reaction to what happened centuries ago. That practice made the English-speaking public so monopoly-conscious that it acquired a habit of attributing to that sinister power practically everything it disliked about business. To the typical liberal bourgeois in particular, monopoly became the father of almost all abuses—in fact, it became his pet bogey. Adam Smith,[17] thinking primarily of monopolies of the Tudor and Stuart type, frowned on them in awful dignity. Sir Robert Peel—who like most conservatives occasionally knew how to borrow from the arsenal of the demagogue—in his famous epilogue to his last period of office that gave so much offense to his associates, spoke of a monopoly of bread or wheat, though English grain production was of course perfectly competitive in spite of protection.[18] And in this country monopoly is being made practically synonymous with any large-scale business.

(b) The theory of simple and discriminating monopoly teaches that, excepting a limiting case, monopoly price is higher and monopoly output smaller than competitive price and competitive output. This is true

---

[16]These so-called monopolies have of late come to the fore in connection with the proposal to withhold certain materials from aggressor nations. The lessons of this discussion have some bearing upon our problem by way of analogy. At first, much was thought of the possibilities of that weapon. Then, on looking more closely at it, people found their lists of such materials to be shrinking, because it became increasingly clear that there are very few things that cannot be either produced or substituted for in the areas in question. And finally a suspicion began to dawn to the effect that even though some pressure can be exerted on them in the short run, long-run developments might eventually destroy practically all that was left on the lists.

[17]There was more excuse for that uncritical attitude in the case of Adam Smith and the classics in general than there is in the case of their successors because big business in our sense had not then emerged. But even so they went too far. In part this was due to the fact that they had no satisfactory theory of monopoly which induced them not only to apply the term rather promiscuously (Adam Smith and even Senior interpreted for instance the rent of land as a monopoly gain) but also to look upon the monopolists' power of exploitation as practically unlimited which is of course wrong even for the most extreme cases.

[18]This instance illustrates the way in which the term keeps on creeping into illegitimate uses. Protection of agriculture and a monopoly of agrarian products are entirely different things. The struggle was over protection and not over a nonexistent cartel of either landowners or farmers. But in fighting protection it was just as well to beat up for applause. And there was evidently no simpler means of doing so than by calling protectionists monopolists.

provided that the method and organization of production—and everything else—are exactly the same in both cases. Actually however there are superior methods available to the monopolist which either are not available at all to a crowd of competitors or are not available to them so readily: for there are advantages which, though not strictly unattainable on the competitive level of enterprise, are as a matter of fact secured only on the monopoly level, for instance, because monopolization may increase the sphere of influence of the better, and decrease the sphere of influence of the inferior, brains,[19] or because the monopoly enjoys a disproportionately higher financial standing. Whenever this is so, then that proposition is no longer true. In other words, this element of the case for competition may fail completely because monopoly prices are not necessarily higher or monopoly outputs smaller than competitive prices and outputs would be at the levels of productive and organizational efficiency that are within the reach of the type of firm compatible with the competitive hypothesis.

There cannot be any reasonable doubt that under the conditions of our epoch such superiority is as a matter of fact the outstanding feature of the typical large-scale unit of control, though mere size is neither necessary nor sufficient for it. These units not only arise in the process of creative destruction and function in a way entirely different from the static schema, but in many cases of decisive importance they provide the necessary form for the achievement. They largely create what they exploit. Hence the usual conclusion about their influence on long-run output would be invalid even if they were genuine monopolies in the technical sense of the term.

Motivation is quite immaterial. Even if the opportunity to set monopolist prices were the sole object, the pressure of the improved methods or of a huge apparatus would in general tend to shift the point of the monopolist's optimum toward or beyond the competitive cost price in the above sense, thus doing the work—partly, wholly, or more than wholly—of the competitive mechanism,[20] *even if restriction is practiced and excess capacity is in evidence all along*. Of course if the methods of production, organization and so on are not improved by or in connection with monopolization as is the case with an ordinary cartel, the classical theorem about monopoly price and output comes into its own again.[21] So does another popular idea, viz., that monopolization has a soporific effect. For this, too, it is not difficult to find examples. But no general theory should be built upon it. For, especially in manufacturing industry, a monopoly position is in general no cushion to sleep on. As it can be gained, so it can be retained only by alertness and energy. What soporific influence there is in modern business is due to another cause that will be mentioned later.

(c) In the short run, genuine monopoly positions or positions approximating monopoly are much more frequent. The grocer in a village on the Ohio may be a true monopolist for hours or even days during an inundation. Every successful corner may spell monopoly for the moment. A firm specializing in paper labels for beer bottles may be so circumstanced—potential competitors realizing that what seem to be good profits would be immediately destroyed by their entering the field—that it can move at pleasure on a moderate but still finite stretch of the demand curve, at least until the metal label smashes that demand curve to pieces.

New methods of production or new commodities, especially the latter, do not *per se* confer monopoly, even if used or produced by a single firm. The product of the new method has to compete with the products of the old ones and the new commodity has to be introduced, i.e., its demand schedule has to be built up. As a rule

---

[19] The reader should observe that while, as a broad rule, that particular type of superiority is simply indisputable, the inferior brains, especially if their owners are entirely eliminated, are not likely to admit it and that the public's and the recording economists' hearts go out to them and not to the others. This may have something to do with a tendency to discount the cost or quality advantages of quasimonopolist combination that is at present as pronounced as was the exaggeration of them in the typical prospectus or announcement of sponsors of such combinations.

[20] The Aluminum Company of America is not a monopoly in the technical sense as defined above, among other reasons because it had to build up its demand schedule, which fact suffices to exclude a behavior conforming to the Cournot-Marshall schema. But most economists call it so and in the dearth of genuine cases we will for the purposes of this note do the same. From 1890 to 1929 the price of the basic product of this single seller fell to about 12 per cent or, correcting for the change in price level (B.L.S. index of wholesale prices), to about 8.8 per cent. Output rose from 30 metric tons to 103,400. Protection by patent ceased in 1909. Argument from costs and profits in criticism of this "monopoly" must take it for granted that a multitude of competing firms would have been about equally successful in cost-reducing research, in the economical development of the productive apparatus, in teaching new uses for the product and in avoiding wasteful breakdowns. This is, in fact, being assumed by criticism of this kind; i.e., the propelling factor of modern capitalism is being assumed away.

[21] See however *supra*, § 1.

neither patents nor monopolistic practices avail against that. But they may in cases of spectacular superiority of the new device, particularly if it can be leased like shoe machinery; or in cases of new commodities, the permanent demand schedule for which has been established before the patent has expired.

Thus it is true that there is or may be an element of genuine monopoly gain in those entrepreneurial profits which are the prizes offered by capitalist society to the successful innovator. But the quantitative importance of that element, its volatile nature and its function in the process in which it emerges put it in a class by itself. The main value to a concern of a single seller position that is secured by patent or monopolistic strategy does not consist so much in the opportunity to behave temporarily according to the monopolist schema, as in the protection it affords against temporary disorganization of the market and the space it secures for long-range planning. Here however the argument merges into the analysis submitted before.

6. Glancing back we realize that most of the facts and arguments touched upon in this chapter tend to dim the halo that once surrounded perfect competition as much as they suggest a more favorable view of its alternative. I will now briefly restate our argument from this angle.

Traditional theory itself, even within its chosen precincts of a stationary or steadily growing economy, has since the time of Marshall and Edgeworth been discovering an increasing number of exceptions to the old propositions about perfect competition and, incidentally, free trade, that have shaken that unqualified belief in its virtues cherished by the generation which flourished between Ricardo and Marshall—roughly, J. S. Mill's generation in England and Francesco Ferrara's on the Continent. Especially the propositions that a perfectly competitive system is ideally economical of resources and allocates them in a way that is optimal with respect to a given distribution of income—propositions very relevant to the question of the behavior of output—cannot now be held with the old confidence.[22]

Much more serious is the breach made by more recent work in the field of dynamic theory (Frisch, Tinbergen, Roos, Hicks and others). Dynamic analysis is the analysis of sequences in time. In explaining why a certain economic quantity, for instance a price, is what we find it to be at a given moment, it takes into consideration not only the state of other economic quantities at the same moment, as static theory does, but also their state at preceding points of time, and the expectations about their future values. Now the first thing we discover in working out the propositions that thus relate quantities belonging to different points of time[23] is the fact that, once equilibrium has been destroyed by some disturbance, the process of establishing a new one is not so sure and prompt and economical as the old theory of perfect competition made it out to be; and the possibility that the very struggle for adjustment might lead such a system farther away from instead of nearer to a new equilibrium. This will happen in most cases unless the disturbance is small. In many cases, lagged adjustment is sufficient to produce this result.

All I can do here is to illustrate by the oldest, simplest and most familiar example. Suppose that demand and *intended* supply are in equilibrium in a perfectly competitive market for wheat, but that bad weather reduces the crop below what farmers intended to supply. If price rises accordingly and the farmers thereupon produce that quantity of wheat which it would pay them to produce if that new price were the equilibrium price, then a slump in the wheat market will ensue in the following year. If now the farmers correspondingly restrict production, a price still higher than in the first year may result to induce a still greater expansion of production than occurred in the second year. And so on (as far as the pure logic of the process is concerned) indefinitely. The reader will readily perceive, from a survey of the assumptions involved, that no great fear need be entertained of ever higher prices' and ever greater outputs' alternating till doomsday. But even if reduced to its proper proportions, the phenomenon suffices to show up glaring weaknesses in the mechanism of perfect competition. As soon as this is realized much of the optimism that used to grace the practical implications of the theory of this mechanism passes out through the ivory gate.

---

[22]Since we cannot enter into the subject, I will refer the reader to Mr. R. F. Kahn's paper entitled "Some Notes on Ideal Output" (*Economic Journal* for March 1935), which covers much of this ground.

[23]The term dynamics is loosely used and carries many different meanings. The above definition was formulated by Ragnar Frisch.

But from our standpoint we must go further than that.[24] If we try to visualize how perfect competition works or would work in the process of creative destruction, we arrive at a still more discouraging result. This will not surprise us, considering that all the essential facts of that process are absent from the general schema of economic life that yields the traditional propositions about perfect competition. At the risk of repetition I will illustrate the point once more.

Perfect competition implies free entry into every industry. It is quite true, within that general theory, that free entry into all industries is a condition for optimal allocation of resources and hence for maximizing output. If our economic world consisted of a number of established industries producing familiar commodities by established and substantially invariant methods and if nothing happened except that additional men and additional savings combine in order to set up new firms of the existing type, then impediments to their entry into any industry they wish to enter would spell loss to the community. But perfectly free entry into a *new* field may make it impossible to enter it at all. The introduction of new methods of production and new commodities is hardly conceivable with perfect—and perfectly prompt—competition from the start. And this means that the bulk of what we call economic progress is incompatible with it. As a matter of fact, perfect competition is and always has been temporarily suspended whenever anything new is being introduced—automatically or by measures devised for the purpose—even in otherwise perfectly competitive conditions.

Similarly, within the traditional system the usual indictment of rigid prices stands all right. Rigidity is a type of resistance to adaptation that perfect and prompt competition excludes. And for the kind of adaptation and for those conditions which have been treated by traditional theory, it is again quite true that such resistance spells loss and reduced output. But we have seen that in the sports and vicissitudes of the process of creative destruction the opposite may be true: perfect and instantaneous flexibility may even produce functionless catastrophes. This of course can also be established by the general dynamic theory which, as mentioned above, shows that there are attempts at adaptation that intensify disequilibrium.

Again, under its own assumptions, traditional theory is correct in holding that profits above what is necessary in each individual case to call forth the equilibrium amount of means of production, entrepreneurial ability included, both indicate and in themselves imply net social loss and that business strategy that aims at keeping them alive is inimical to the growth of total output. Perfect competition would prevent or immediately eliminate such surplus profits and leave no room for that strategy. But since in the process of capitalist evolution these profits acquire new organic functions—I do not want to repeat what they are—that fact cannot any longer be unconditionally credited to the account of the perfectly competitive model, so far as the secular rate of increase in total output is concerned.

Finally, it can indeed be shown that, under the same assumptions which amount to excluding the most characteristic features of capitalist reality, a perfectly competitive economy is comparatively free from waste and in particular from those kinds of waste which we most readily associate with its counterpart. But this does not tell us anything about how its account looks under the conditions set by the process of creative destruction.

On the one hand, much of what without reference to those conditions would appear to be unrelieved waste ceases to qualify as such when duly related to them. The type of excess capacity for example that owes its existence to the practice of "building ahead of demand" or to the practice of providing capacity for the cyclical peaks of demand would in a regime of perfect competition be much reduced. But when *all* the facts of the case are taken into consideration, it is no longer correct to say that perfect competition wins out on that score. For though a concern that has to accept and cannot set prices would, in fact, use all of its capacity that can produce at marginal costs covered by the ruling prices, it does not follow that it would ever have the quantity and

---

[24]It should be observed that the defining feature of dynamic theory has nothing to do with the nature of the economic reality to which it is applied. It is a general method of analysis rather than a study of a particular process. We can use it in order to analyze a stationary economy, just as an evolving one can be analyzed by means of the methods of statics ("comparative statics"). Hence dynamic theory need not take, and as a matter of fact has not taken, any special cognizance of the process of creative destruction which we have taken to be the essence of capitalism. It is no doubt better equipped than is static theory to deal with many questions of mechanism that arise in the analysis of that process. But it is not an analysis of that process itself, and it treats the resulting individual disturbances of given states and structures just as it treats other disturbances. To judge the functioning of perfect competition from the standpoint of capitalist evolution is therefore not the same thing as judging it from the standpoint of dynamic theory.

quality of capacity that big business has created and was able to create precisely because it is in a position to use it "strategically." Excess capacity of this type may—it does in some and does not in other cases—constitute a reason for claiming superiority for a socialist economy. But it should not without qualification be listed as a claim to superiority of the perfectly competitive species of capitalist economy as compared with the "monopoloid" species.

On the other hand, working in the conditions of capitalist evolution, the perfectly competitive arrangement displays wastes of its own. The firm of the type that is compatible with perfect competition is in many cases inferior in internal, especially technological, efficiency. If it is, then it wastes opportunities. It may also in its endeavors to improve its methods of production waste capital because it is in a less favorable position to evolve and to judge new possibilities. And, as we have seen before, a perfectly competitive industry is much more apt to be routed—and to scatter the bacilli of depression—under the impact of progress or of external disturbance than is big business. In the last resort, American agriculture, English coal mining, the English textile industry are costing consumers much more and are affecting *total* output much more injuriously than they would if controlled, each of them, by a dozen good brains.

Thus it is not sufficient to argue that because perfect competition is impossible under modern industrial conditions—or because it always has been impossible—the large-scale establishment or unit of control must be accepted as a necessary evil inseparable from the economic progress which it is prevented from sabotaging by the forces inherent in its productive apparatus. What we have got to accept is that it has come to be the most powerful engine of that progress and in particular of the long-run expansion of total output not only in spite of, but to a considerable extent through, this strategy which looks so restrictive when viewed in the individual case and from the individual point of time. In this respect, perfect competition is not only impossible but inferior, and has no title to being set up as a model of ideal efficiency. It is hence a mistake to base the theory of government regulation of industry on the principle that big business should be made to work as the respective industry would work in perfect competition. And socialists should rely for their criticisms on the virtues of a socialist economy rather than on those of the competitive model.

THE REAL OIL PROBLEM

M. A. ADELMAN

ACCORDING TO "CONVENTIONAL wisdom," humanity's need for oil cannot be met and a gap will soon emerge between demand and supply. That gap will broaden as the economies of Europe, Japan, and several emerging nations grow and increase their energy needs. The United States is at the mercy of Middle Eastern exporters who can use the "oil weapon" to cripple the U.S. economy. Unless we increase domestic oil production radically or cut consumption, or nations like Russia quickly exploit recently discovered oil fields, the United States will find itself in an oil crisis.

But conventional wisdom "knows" many things that are not true. There is not, and never has been, an oil crisis or gap. Oil reserves are not dwindling. The Middle East does not have and has never had any "oil weapon." How fast Russian oil output grows is of minor but real interest. How much goes to the United States or Europe or Japan—or anywhere else, for that matter—is of no interest because it has no effect on prices we pay nor on the security of supply.

The real problem we face over oil dates from after 1970: a strong but clumsy monopoly of mostly Middle Eastern exporters cooperating as OPEC. The biggest exporters have acted in concert to limit supply and thus raise oil's price—possibly too high even for their own good. The output levels they establish by trial-and-error are very unstable. OPEC has damaged the world economy, not by malice, but because its members cannot help but do so.

The group's power is slowly decreasing, but I do not see it ending anytime soon. In 1979 and again in 2003, the consuming nations made a public unconditional surrender to the current cartel. They may or may not know what they are doing.

To see the harm that OPEC has done and can continue to do, we need to dispense with the myths about an oil gap and an oil weapon. Once we do that, we will begin to see that many of the problems in the world oil market are the result of this short-sighted cartel, as well as the failure of importers to seize opportunities to weaken it.

IS OIL RUNNING OUT?

Oil is not the first fossil fuel that conventional wisdom has identified as nearing exhaustion. Even before 1800, the worry in Europe was that coal—the supposed foundation of their greatness—would run out. European production actually did peak in 1913, and is nearly negligible today. Is that the result of exhaustion? Hardly—there are billions of tons in the ground in Europe. But it would cost too much for the Europeans to dig it

M. A. Adelman is professor of economics emeritus at the Massachusetts Institute of Technology. He is the author of several books, including *The Economics of Petroleum Supply: Selected Papers 1962–1993* (Cambridge, Mass.: MIT Press, 1993) and *The Genie Out of the Bottle: World Oil Since 1970* (Cambridge, Mass.: MIT Press, 1995). More recently, he published "World Oil Production and Prices 1947–2000" in the *Quarterly Review of Economics and Finance* (Vol. 42).

out. At a price that would cover cost, there is no demand. Hence, the billions of tons of European coal are worthless and untouched. The amount of a mineral that is in the ground has no meaning apart from its cost of extraction and the demand for it.

In 1875, John Strong Newberry, the chief geologist of the state of Ohio, predicted that the supply of oil would soon run out. The alarm has been sounded repeatedly in the many decades since. In 1973, State Department analyst James Akins, then the chief U.S. policymaker on oil, published "The Oil Crisis: This time the wolf is here," in which he called for more domestic production and for improved relations with oil-producing nations in the Middle East. In 1979, President Jimmy Carter, echoing a CIA assessment, said that oil wells "were drying up all over the world." Just last year, the New York Times reported that "oil reserves are expected to dwindle in the decades ahead," while the International Energy Agency forecasted that oil output will grow in the Persian Gulf between now and 2030, but it will decline elsewhere.

The doomsday predictions have all proved false. In 2003, world oil production was 4,400 times greater than it was in Newberry's day, but the price per unit was probably lower. Oil reserves and production even outside the Middle East are greater today than they were when Akins claimed the wolf was here. World output of oil is up a quarter since Carter's "drying up" pronouncement, but Middle East exports peaked in 1976–77.

Despite all those facts, the predictions of doom keep on coming.

THE REAL OIL CRISIS

The true crisis (or whatever it is) started in 1973–74 when a dozen mostly Middle Eastern nations mutually agreed to cut their output. They have been constraining production ever since. They lock away and sterilize the cheapest oil in the world to raise the price and their revenues.

The resulting effects have prompted a series of government efforts to avert an oil crisis. As a New York Times editorial observed last September, "Every president starting with Richard Nixon and the 1973 oil embargo has promised to reduce America's ravenous appetite for oil while investing heavily in new energy sources." Few members of those administrations disagreed with the Carter belief in an oil gap and an energy gap—and each administration has advocated a broad range of energy policies and government spending.

The Carter White House advanced legislation discouraging the use of natural gas for "low-end" uses like power generation, even though natural gas is plentiful and burns cleaner than oil or coal. Instead, the administration advocated tax credits and subsidies for the use of synthetic fuels and for expansion of the use of coal. The Internal Revenue Service recently confirmed that the $20 billion-a-year "spray and pray" credit, which encourages the production of a supposed synthetic fuel by spraying fuel oil on purportedly unusable coal dust to make usable lumps, is still in place. The current Energy Bill—or "Energy Barbecue"—will create all sorts of new handouts, vested interests, and jobs that will be hotly defended in later years. The more wasteful a law, the more defenders it creates.

From the Nixon White House to the present, all administrations have approached oil and energy with command-and-control policies. None of them attempted to analyze the problems using the price mechanism. "Not enough" oil was being produced, and that problem was too important to leave to a sloppy price system.

WHEN WILL THE OIL RUN OUT?

It is commonly asked, when will the world's supply of oil be exhausted? The best one-word answer: Never. Since the human race began to use minerals, there has been eternal struggle—stingy nature versus inquisitive mankind. The payoff is the price of the mineral, and mankind has won big, so far.

However, alarmists point to world oil prices and claim that what has happened "so far" will not continue much longer. They might have a point—if the world oil market featured several different, competitive suppliers. But instead, it is dominated by a monopoly supplier, so the higher prices in themselves mean nothing. To understand this, one needs a quick course in resource economics.

Minerals are produced from reserves, which are mineral deposits discovered and identified as able to be extracted profitably. Are oil reserves dwindling? Is it getting harder to find or create them? Conventional wisdom says: Of course. But once again, conventional wisdom is wrong.

Reserves are a type of warehouse inventory, the result of investment. One cannot make a decision to drill and operate an oil well without a forecast of the well's production. Moreover, as the well's output falls over time with decreasing pressure, the unit operating cost of the well's output will rise. When the operating cost rises above the price that the oil will fetch in the marketplace, the well will be shut down. Whatever oil is left underground is not worth producing, given current prices and technology. The well's proved reserves are the forecast cumulative profitable output, not the total amount of oil that is believed to be in the ground.

In the United States and a few other countries, a nation's "proved reserves" is the programmed cumulative output from existing and pending wells. In other countries, the definition of "reserves" varies, and the number is often worthless. At its best (e.g., the estimates released by the U.S. Geological Survey), the "probable reserve" is an estimate of what will eventually be produced in a given area, out of existing and new wells, with current technique and knowledge, and at prevailing prices.

ULTIMATE KNOWLEDGE?   But the size of "known reserves" is not an adequate forecast of eventual production, unless we assume that in oil, as in Kansas City, "they've gone about as far as they can go." Watching "Oklahoma!" we smile at those who actually believe this—and we should likewise smile at those who think they know how much oil will be extracted from a well or in an area. To predict ultimate reserves, we need an accurate prediction of future science and technology. To know ultimate reserves, we must first have ultimate knowledge. Nobody knows this, and nobody should pretend to know.

The dwindling of reserves is a legend firmly believed because it seems so obvious. Assume any number for the size of reserves. From it, subtract a few years' current output. The conclusion is absolutely sure: Reserves are dwindling; the wolf is getting closer. In time, production must cease. Oil in the ground becomes constantly more valuable—so much so that a gap forms between how much oil we want and how much we are able to afford because of scarcity. Civilization cannot continue without oil, so something must be done.

And indeed, in some times and places the oil does run down. Output in the Appalachian United States had peaked by 1900, and output in Texas peaked in 1972. But the "running out" vision never works globally. At the end of 1970, non-OPEC countries had about 200 billion remaining in proved reserves. In the next 33 years, those countries produced 460 billion barrels and now have 209 billion "remaining." The producers kept using up their inventory, at a rate of about seven percent per year, and then replacing it. The OPEC countries started with about 412 billion in proved reserves, produced 307 billion, and now have about 819 billion left. Their reserve numbers are shaky, but clearly they had—and have—a lot more inventory than they used up. Saudi Arabia alone has over 80 known fields and exploits only nine. Of course, there are many more fields, known and unknown. The Saudis do not invest to discover, develop, and produce more oil because more production would bring down world prices.

Growing knowledge lowers cost, unlocks new deposits in existing areas, and opens new areas for discovery. In 1950, there was no offshore oil production; it was highly "unconventional" oil. Some 25 years later, offshore wells were being drilled in water 1,000 feet deep. And 25 years after that, oilmen were drilling in water 10,000 feet deep—once technological advancement enabled them to drill without the costly steel structure that had earlier made deep-water drilling too expensive. Today, a third of all U.S. oil production comes from offshore wells. Given current knowledge and technique, the U.S. Geological Survey predicts offshore oil will ultimately comprise 50 percent of U.S. production.

The offshore reserves did not just happen to come along in time. In an old Mae West movie, an admirer of one of her rings declared, "Goodness, what a diamond!" She coldly replied, "Goodness had nothing to do with it." Likewise, offshore production did not begin and develop by providence or chance, but only when new knowledge made investment profitable. And the high potential economic rewards were a powerful inducement for the development of the new knowledge. Offshore drillers found a new way to tap oil beneath the deep ocean. Oilmen in Canada and Venezuela discovered how to extract oil from those nations' oil sand deposits. As new techniques decreased the cost of extraction, some of the oil slowly began to be booked into reserves.

NEW RESERVES   Worldwide, is it getting harder and more expensive to find new deposits and develop them into reserves? Up to about 15 years ago, the cost data clearly said no. Since then, much of the relevant data are no longer published.

To make up for that lack, Campbell Watkins and I tabulated the sales value of proved reserves sold in-ground in the United States. Our results are a window on the value of oil reserves anywhere in which entrepreneurs can freely invest. (That rules out the OPEC countries and a few more.) If the cost of finding and developing new reserves were increasing, the value per barrel of already-developed reserves would rise with it. Over the period 1982–2002, we found no sign of that.

Think of it this way: Anyone could make a bet on rising inground values—borrow money to buy and hold a barrel of oil for later sale. With ultimate reserves decreasing every year, the value of oil still in the ground should grow yearly. The investor's gain on holding the oil should be at least enough to offset the borrowing cost plus risk. In fact, we find that holding the oil would draw a negative return even before allowing for risk.

To sum up: There is no indication that non-OPEC oil is getting more expensive to find and develop. Statements about non-OPEC nations' "dwindling reserves" are meaningless or wrong.

A SINGLE WORLD MARKET

Another tenet of conventional wisdom is that the United States' energy supply is precarious because we must buy oil from Middle Eastern nations who do not like us. This tenet is no more accurate than the other "wisdoms" we have considered so far.

Most oil moves by sea, and ships can be diverted from one destination to another relatively easily. Moreover, much additional oil can be diverted from land shipment to sea. Hence, it is fairly easy to reroute shipments of oil from nations that have a sufficient supply to nations that are experiencing a shortage. It is only a minor exaggeration to say that every barrel in the world competes with every other. If one is blocked, another can replace it.

One cannot help reading a lot about how "fortunate" it is that new fields on Sakhalin Island will soon export to nearby "oil-starved Japan," or that West Africa can do the same for the "oil-hungry" U.S. East Coast. Such statements sound important but make no sense. Higher output helps consumers and lower output hurts them, no matter where the oil is from or where it goes. Exports will go to the more profitable destination. To the buyer, the distance from exporter to importer makes only a minor difference in total cost.

THE "OIL WEAPON"   Whether a supplier loves or hates a customer (or vice versa) does not matter because, in the world oil market, a seller cannot isolate any customer and a buyer cannot isolate any supplier. But conventional wisdom (there is that term again) is that Middle Eastern nations wield an "oil weapon" that they can use to punish the United States or any other nation.

In support of this belief, many people point to the 1973 "oil embargo" against the United States by Arab members of OPEC (except Iraq—Saddam Hussein profited by it). Secretary of State Henry Kissinger cruised around the Middle East many times to negotiate an "end" to it. Ten years later, he explained that the significance of the "embargo" was psychological, not economic. Recently, the London *Economist* quoted approvingly what I said in July 1973: If an embargo was declared, it would have no effect because diversion would nullify it. And so it was.

The embargo against the United States never happened, and could not happen. The miserable, mile-long lines outside of U.S. gasoline stations resulted from domestic price controls and allocations, not from any embargo. We ought not blame the Arabs for what we did to ourselves.

Presidents may declare an "urgent need" to cut imports and boost "energy independence"—no one ever lost political support by seeing evil and blaming foreigners.

The Arab and non-Arab cutbacks in output, then and later, were real though small. If we look at the amounts actually available, the United States did a little worse than Japan, a little better than Western Europe. (I think those differences are accidental results of imperfect statistics, but that is another story.)

The real moral is this: It does not matter how much oil is produced domestically and how much is imported. Presidents may declare that there is an "urgent need" to cut imports and boost "energy independence"— no one ever lost political support by seeing evil and blaming foreigners. The facts are less dramatic. Imports do not make any importer "dependent" on any particular exporter, or even all of them taken together. Therefore, direct or indirect spending to reduce imports is a waste of resources. Some public support of research into energy may bring us knowledge worth paying for, but public outlays for energy development are a waste.

So, if the ills are imaginary, what is the true problem with the world oil market?

THE WORLD MONOPOLY

The oil "crisis" started in 1971–1973 when a dozen producer nations agreed to raise oil prices by cutting their output. They continue that cooperation today. Their cost of expanding output, which is mostly the return on the needed investment, is a small fraction of the price that they charge for oil.

The price of oil should be relatively stable. Compare the basic conditions with natural gas: Oil users are much more numerous and diversified. Seasonal fluctuations are milder, and storage costs lower. In fact, for 25 years after World War II, the real (inflation-adjusted) price of oil fluctuated very little. As in many industries, there was short-run volatility—up and down. Oil prices jumped in the Middle East crises of 1956 and 1967, but then fell back quickly. Some would ascribe the price stability to the fact that most oil then being sold worldwide was controlled by a few big companies, the "Seven Sisters." However, the real price fell by about two thirds from 1945 to 1970. The Seven Sisters' control, if any, was very limited.

But in the period 1970–1980, the real price rose by about 1,300 percent. From 1980 to 1986, it dropped by about two thirds. It was fairly steady in 1986–1997, fell further in 1997–1998, and then tripled after February 1999. Why have there been such huge ups and downs in recent years, and why—unlike in the old days—did the changes not reverse quickly?

SPECULATION?   Any price is affected by the guesses of speculators. The professionals are in business to make money on price changes. But every producer, refiner, consumer, transporter, etc., who buys or sells ahead today in fear or in hope of a different price tomorrow is speculating.

Speculation affects cartel prices more than competitive prices. Oil prices fluctuate more because betting on price must include calculations about not just supply and demand, but also about OPEC's quota decisions, plus the members' fidelity to their promises. Hence, the world oil market is less predictable, more volatile, and more herky-jerky. In the huge oil price spike of late 1973, the change in supply was almost trivial yet the price effects were massive. The "crisis" was a classic case of buyer's panic.

THE CARTEL   OPEC is a forum whose members meet from time to time to reach decisions on price or on output. Fixing either one determines the other. There have in effect been several OPEC cartels since the countries first banded together more than three decades ago. The members re-constitute the cartel as needed to meet current problems.

In every oil price upheaval, there has been persistent excess capacity (which could not happen under competitive pricing). Even if we started with zero excess, every output reduction itself creates excess capacity among the OPEC countries. They refrain from expanding output in order to raise prices and profits. Recently, we have heard high prices explained by low inventories. That is true—the cartel cuts production, which lowers inventories, which raises prices. Because each member's cost is far below the price, output could expand many fold if each producer followed its own interest to expand output, which would lower prices and revenues. Only group action can restrain each one from expanding output.

The spike in oil prices since 1999 provides an excellent illustration. The Clinton and Bush administrations both applauded OPEC for setting a price target of $23–28 a barrel. But OPEC actions have kept the price persistently above even the upper limit, with the usual contemptuous indifference to arguments from U.S. cabinet secretaries. Why so?

TWO PROBLEMS   Any cartel must decide what price and output to fix for maximum profit. A higher price would cost them money because purchasers would cut consumption too far. Moreover, the price must eventually be updated, whenever supply and demand change enough to make corrective action essential. Opinions vary as to what is the right price for maximum profit, and OPEC has often had to find its right price through trial and error. The cartel made a dreadful mistake in 1980 when it pushed the price of oil to $40 a barrel (which is nearly $80 today, in inflation-adjusted terms). The member nations expected the price to go higher still, but the resulting reduction in demand forced OPEC to bring the price back down. Hence, one great problem with operating a cartel is finding—and maintaining—the right price.

The second great problem is how to allocate sales among cartelists. Each OPEC member could reap a windfall by cheating and producing over quota because the cost of production is so far below the market price. But, if some cartel members were to defect, output would climb and the prices—and windfall profits—would fall.

In 1980, Saudi Arabia (for the first and last time) unilaterally restricted its oil production. The kingdom let its cartel partners produce freely, tending to lower the world oil price. The Saudis decided only to make up the difference between the intended total cartel output and the sum of what the others produced; as other cartel members raised their production levels, the Saudis further lowered theirs.

They soon found that they could not hold the line without help. If the Saudis alone restricted output, too much oil would be produced and prices would fall. They called on the others to observe their quotas. The others preferred to keep producing and profiting at the Saudis' expense. In late 1985, Saudi exports approached zero, and they finally announced that they would match anyone else's prices. It took over eight months for the cartel ranks to re-form, and by then prices had fallen by two thirds from 1980 levels.

Since then, the Saudis have often repeated that they would never again cut output without prior assurances that the others would cut along with them. They no longer have any illusion that they can regulate the industry on their own. (So why do people in consuming countries believe that?)

As history shows, deciding on the group action is not easy. There usually is a game of chicken, until some agreement is achieved. Next comes mutual surveillance, to see who cheats how much. During the period 1986–1996, the price of oil stayed around only one-third of the 1980 highs, and was much more stable. But even then OPEC lost market share. Non-OPEC oil-exporting nations expanded their production because the current price provided a return on their investment in new capacity.

At the moment, the cartel has good reason to be pleased. Beginning in 1999 and with the half-hearted cooperation of Russia, Mexico, and Norway, OPEC was able to constrain world oil production and thus raise prices. The target at first was $17–21 per barrel, then $22–28. Since 2000, the price has rarely been below $28, and in December 2003 was over $30. There was excess capacity among OPEC members even before the output cuts, and more afterward. They have restrained the excess, observed their quotas, and faithfully colluded to maintain the price.

FUTURE PRICES AND PRODUCTION

OPEC's constant concern has been to restrict supply and resist downward price pressure. Whenever they forgot this, they were brutally reminded—as in 1980–85 and in 1997. But always, they were exhorted from inside and outside the organization to look to the bright horizon of the near future. Very soon, they were told, non-OPEC output would fail for lack of reserves and OPEC market share would rise. But non-OPEC production crept up and the share of OPEC exports fell. Once around 65 percent, OPEC exports are now 30–35 percent of the world oil market. Only as the production restriction became tighter did the cartel receive some cooperation from non-OPEC nations.

Saudi Arabia's oil minister has said that the kingdom will not cut production again without cooperation from inside and outside OPEC. Common sense supports that. Had the Saudis been the only ones to cut in 1999, they would have lost money just as in 1980, and they would have failed to make the price increase stick.

DEPENDENCE ON OIL   Price fixing by private companies on the OPEC scale would not be tolerated in any industrial country. In the United States, the officers of firms that engage in such activities go to jail. But the OPEC members are sovereign states, subject to no country's laws. Moreover, the United States and other nations want to think they have the OPEC nations' support—particularly the Saudis.

This alleged support consists in "access" to oil. But in a global market filled with buyers and sellers, everyone has access. Another myth is mutual obligation: The OPEC nations' supply oil, the United States protects them. In truth there is no choice; we must protect the OPEC nations from outsiders or neighbors. They owe us nothing for protection and will give us nothing. Of course, OPEC will supply oil. The only question is how much oil—and that determines the price. The supposed OPEC (or Saudi) obligation to supply is what lawyers call "void for vagueness." But those in government crave assurance that they are accomplishing something, and they will pay for that assurance.

After 30 years of high export earnings, the OPEC nations remain as dependent on selling oil as ever. In OPEC nations, oil exports still pay for nearly everything. Fifty years ago, Venezuela encapsulated the idea of using oil money to develop non-oil industries into a fine slogan: *Sembrar el petroleo*—"Plant the oil." In the Middle East, although some small OPEC states accumulated financial assets abroad, cartel members failed completely to develop other export industries. Those member nations now are usually broke, cannot save, and cannot plan ahead.

Where did the $3 trillion in oil revenues go? Mostly to armaments, subsidies, payoffs, population growth, and grandiose prestige projects—*far la bella figura*, as the Italians say. Showy projects look bad when neglected. The Saudis in 1980 had $180 billions in foreign assets. They are now in debt, running deficits even in the last few years.

In Iraq, history did an experiment. In 1991 when oil exports vanished because of UN action, national GDP shrank by 86 percent. Iraqi non-oil industries existed to sell to the oil industry or to locals with oil income, but suddenly there was no oil industry or income. Some Iraqi non-oil industries were state-owned Soviet-style clunkers, others were subsidized or shielded by tariffs and import quotas along with corruption. As a result, Iraq's non-oil economy—even today—is small and jobs are scarce. For thousands of years, Mesopotamia, "the land between the rivers," was a big wheat exporter, but no more. Saudi Arabia now grows and exports wheat at a cost many times the market price. To grow it, they use up underground water deposits at ever-rising cost. Of course, this builds a huge vested interest in continued spending.

OPEC nations have little but oil income, and most of them live in a rough neighborhood. Government decision-makers in those nations have a shorter time horizon than private companies. They pursue short-run gain, disregarding the long-run pain. Hence, OPEC cartels are hasty and extreme, and they push to raise prices faster and further than would private firms. OPEC members get good advice to cut their price in order to slow or stop consumers' investment in energy savings and non-OPEC oil producers' investment in new capacity. But investment takes time, and the members cannot take time.

OPEC nations will continue to "take the cash and let the credit go/Nor heed the rumble of a distant Drum." They choose higher prices now, despite lower sales later. Some 70 years ago, an oilman reported back to his company about Persian Gulf rulers: "The future leaves them cold. They want money now." They still do.

The OPEC nations' model is King Philip II of Spain, the richest king in Europe, who went broke the most often. He spent his vast mineral revenues to support bad habits, and buy glory. When a year's revenues were low, he borrowed against the following year's income. That behavior ruined Spain then, and it is ruining the OPEC nations now.

COOPERATION WITH OPEC   The International Energy Agency (IEA) and the U.S. government recently reaffirmed their cooperation with OPEC. IEA discourages importing nations from using strategic stocks, including the United States' Strategic Petroleum Reserve. The importer nations have agreed not to use those stocks unless there is a serious "real shortage." If so, they will never be used. In a market economy, the price changes to equate the amount supplied to the amount demanded, precluding a "real shortage," then or now. As ever, the IEA and the United States ignore price.

In 1974, the IEA established the rule that no strategic stocks could be used without a "gap" between demand and supply of at least 7 percent. But in 1978–80, the oil price tripled for the usual reason: not that wells were giving out but because OPEC nations, particularly Saudi Arabia, shut in production rather than let it expand to make up for Iranian fluctuations. There was no use of strategic stocks. The Carter administration had previously agreed not to use the Strategic Petroleum Reserve without Saudi permission.

OPEC has just cut production quotas for precisely the same reason: to head off lower demand later. Thus we are in the same position today as in 1979. The cartel members supposedly cooperating with us were and are committed to nothing. They will raise or lower output to increase their profits. There is and will be no shortage; they are glad to produce the amount they have themselves decided. They will never cut off output in the future, any more than in the past—it would cost them money.

Use of the Strategic Petroleum Reserve would signal that there are some limits to our patience. It would lower prices and discourage speculation.

CONCLUSION

U.S. oil policies are based on fantasies not facts: gaps, shortages, and surpluses. Those ideas are at the core of the Carter legislation, and of the current Energy Bill. The Carter White House also believed what the current Bush White House believes—that, in the face of all evidence, they are getting binding assurance of supply by OPEC, or by Saudi Arabia. That myth is part of the larger myth that the world is running out of oil.

TAKEOVERS: THEIR CAUSES AND CONSEQUENCES

MICHAEL C. JENSEN

Economic analysis and evidence indicate that the market for corporate control is benefiting shareholders, society, and the corporate form of organization. The value of transactions in this market ran at a record rate of about $180 billion per year in 1985 and 1986, 47 percent above the 1984 record of $122 billion. The gains to shareholders from these transactions have been huge. The gains to selling firm shareholders from mergers and acquisition activity in the ten-year period 1977–86 total $346 billion (in 1986 dollars).[1] The gains to buying firm shareholders are harder to estimate, and no one to my knowledge has done so as yet, but my guess is that they will add at least another $50 billion to the total. These gains to put them in perspective, equal 51 percent of the total cash dividends (valued in 1986 dollars) paid to investors by the entire corporate sector in the past decade.[2]

These corporate control transactions and the restructurings that often accompany them are frequently wrenching events in the lives of those linked to the involved organizations: the managers, employees, suppliers, customers and residents of surrounding communities. Restructurings usually involve major organizational change (such as shifts in corporate strategy) to meet new competition or market conditions, increased use of debt, and a flurry of recontracting with managers, employees, suppliers and customers. This activity sometimes results in expansion of resources devoted to certain areas and at other times in contractions involving plant closings, layoffs of top-level and middle managers, staff and production workers, and reduced compensation.

Those threatened by the changes that restructuring brings about argue that corporate restructuring is damaging the American economy, damaging the morale and productivity of organizations, and pressuring executives to manage for the short-term. Further, they hold that the value restructuring creates does not come from increased efficiency and productivity; instead, the gains comes from lower tax payments, broken contracts with managers, employees and others, and mistakes in valuation by inefficient capital markets. Since the benefits are illusory and the costs are real, they argue, takeover activity should be restricted.

The controversy has been accompanied by strong pressure on regulators and legislatures to enact restrictions that would curb activity in the market for corporate control. Dozens of congressional bills in the last several

---

[1]Estimated from data in Grimm (1986). Grimm provides total dollar values for all M & A deals for which there are publicly announced prices amounting to $500,000 or 10 percent of the firm in which at least one of the firms was a U.S. company. Grimm also counts in its numerical totals deals with no publicly announced prices that it believes satisfy this criteria. I assumed that the deals with no announced prices were on average equal to 20 percent of the size of the announced transactions.

[2]Total dividend payments by the corporate sector, unadjusted for inflation, are given in Weston (1986, p. 649) I extended these estimates to 1986.

Michael C. Jensen is Professor of Business Administration, Harvard Business School, Cambridge, Massachusetts, and LaClare Professor of Finance and Business Administration and Director of the Managerial Economics Research Center, William E. Simon Graduate School of Business Administration, University of Rochester, Rochester, New York.

---

years have proposed new restrictions on takeovers, but none have passed as of this writing. The Business Roundtable, composed of the chief executive officers of the 200 largest corporations in the country, has pushed hard for restrictive legislation. Within the past several years the legislatures of New York, New Jersey, Maryland, Pennsylvania, Connecticut, Illinois, Kentucky, Michigan, Ohio, Indiana and Minnesota have passed anti-takeover laws. The Federal Reserve Board implemented new restrictions in early 1987 on the use of debt in certain takeovers.

In all the controversy over takeover activity, it is often forgotten that only 40 (an all-time record) out of the 3,300 takeover transactions in 1986 were hostile tender offers. There were 110 voluntary or negotiated tender offers (unopposed by management) and the remaining 3,100-plus deals were also voluntary transactions agreed to by management, although this simple classification is misleading since many of the voluntary trans-actions would not occur absent the threat of hostile takeover. A major reason for the current outcry is that in recent years mere size alone has disappeared as an effective takeover deterrent, and the managers of many of our largest and least efficient corporations now find their jobs threatened by disciplinary forces in the capital markets.

Economists have accumulated considerable evidence and knowledge on the effects of the takeover market. Most of the earlier work is well summarized elsewhere (Jensen and Ruback, 1983; Jensen, 1984; Jarrell, Brickley and Netter in this symposium). Here, I focus on current aspects of the controversy. In brief, the previous work tells us the following:

1. Takeovers benefit shareholders of target companies, Premiums in hostile offers historically exceed 30 percent on average, and in recent times have averaged about 50 percent.
2. Acquiring-firm shareholders on average earn about 4 percent in hostile takeovers and roughly zero in mergers, although these returns seem to have declined from past levels.
3. Takeovers do not waste credit or resources. Instead, they generate substantial gains: historically, 8 percent of the total value of both companies. Those value gains represent gains to economic efficiency, not redistribution between various parties.
4. Actions by managers that eliminate or prevent offers or mergers are most suspect as harmful to shareholders.
5. Golden parachutes for top-level managers do not, on average, harm shareholders.
6. The activities of takeover specialists (such as Icahn, Posner, Steinberg, and Pickens) benefit shareholders on average.
7. Merger and acquisition activity has not increased industrial concentration. Indeed, over 1,200 divestitures valued at $59.9 billion occurred in 1986, also a record level (Grimm, 1986).
8. Takeover gains do not come from the creation of monopoly power.

The market for corporate control is creating large benefits for shareholders and for the economy as a whole by loosening control over vast amounts of resources and enabling them to move more quickly to their highest-valued use. This is a healthy market in operation, on both the takeover side and the divestiture side, and it is playing an important role in helping the American economy adjust to major changes in competition and reg-ulation of the past decade.

THE MARKET FOR CORPORATE CONTROL

The market for corporate control is best viewed as a major component of the managerial labor market. It is the arena in which alternative management teams compete for the rights to manage corporate resources (Jensen and Ruback, 1983). Understanding this point is crucial to understanding much of the rhetoric about the effects of hostile takeovers.

Managers often have trouble abandoning strategies they have spent years devising and implementing even when those strategies no longer contribute to the organization's survival. Such changes can require abandon-ment of major projects, relocation of facilities, changes in managerial assignments, and closure or sale of facil-ities or divisions. Takeovers generally occur because changing technology or market conditions require a major restructuring of corporate assets, and it is easier for new top-level managers with a fresh view of the business and no ties with current employees or communities to make such changes. Moreover, normal organizational resistance to change is commonly significantly lower early in the reign of new top-level managers. For example, the premium Carl Icahn was able to offer for TWA and his victory over Texas Air for the acquisition of TWA were made possible in part by the willingness of TWA unions to negotiate favorable contract concessions with Icahn—concessions that TWA management was unable to win prior to the takeover conflict. On the other hand, lack detailed knowledge about the firm poses risks for new managers and increases the likelihood of mistakes.

A variety of political and economic conditions in the 1980s have created a climate where economic efficiency requires a major restructuring of corporate assets. These factors include the relaxation of restrictions on mergers imposed by the antitrust laws, withdrawal of resources from industries that are growing more slowly or that must shrink, deregulation in the financial services, oil and gas, transportation, and broadcasting markets, and improvements in takeover technology, including a larger supply of increasingly sophisticated legal and financial advisers, and improvements in financing technology such as the strip financing commonly used in leveraged buyouts and the original issuance of high-yield non-investment-grade bonds.

Each of these factors has contributed to the increase in total takeover and reorganization activity. Moreover the first three factors (antitrust relaxation, exit, and deregulation) are generally consistent with data showing the intensity of takeover activity by industry. For example the value of merger and acquisition transactions by industry in the period of 1981–84 given in Table 1 indicates that acquisition activity was highest in oil and gas followed by banking and finance, insurance, food processing, and mining and minerals. For comparison purposes, the last column of the table presents data on industry size measured as a fraction of the total value of all firms. All but two of the industries, retail and transportation, represent a larger fraction of total takeover activity than their representation in the economy as a whole, indicating that the takeover market is concentrated in particular industries, not spread evenly throughout the corporate sector.

Many sectors of the U.S. economy have been experiencing slowing growth and, in some cases, even retrenchment. This phenomenon has many causes, including substantially increased foreign competition. This slow growth has increased takeover activity because takeovers play an important role in facilitating exit from an industry or activity. Major changes in energy markets, for example, have required a radical restructuring and retrenchment in that industry and takeovers have played an important role in accomplishing these changes; oil and gas rank first in takeover activity, with twice their proportionate share of total activity. Managers who are slow to recognize that many old practices and strategies are no longer viable are finding that takeovers are doing the job for them. Exit is cheaper to accomplish through merger and the orderly liquidation of marginal assets of the combined firms than by disorderly, expensive bankruptcy in an industry saddled with overcapacity. The end of the competitive struggle in such an industry often comes in the bankruptcy courts, with the unnecessary destruction of valuable parts of organizations that could be used productively by others.

Similarly, deregulation of the financial services market is consistent with the number 2 rank of banking/finance and the number 3 rank of insurance in Table 1. Deregulation has also been important in the transportation and broadcasting industries. Mining and minerals have been subject to many of the same forces impinging on the energy industry, including the changes in the value of the dollar.

The development of innovative financing vehicles, such as high-yield non-investment-grade bonds (junk bonds), has removed size as a significant impediment to competition in the market for corporate control. A 1987 update by the Investor Responsibility Research Center of an earlier SEC study finds that the investment grade and high yield debt issues combined were associated with 9.8 percent of all tender offer financing from January 1981 through September 1986. Even though not yet widely used in takeovers, these new financing techniques have had important effects because they permit small firms to obtain resources for acquisition of much larger firms by issuing claims on the value of the venture (that is, the target firm's assets) just as in any other corporate investment activity.

Table 1

Intensity of industry takeover activity as measured by the value of merger and acquisition transactions in the period 1981–84 (as a percent of total takeover transactions for which valuation data are publicly reported) compared to industry size (as measured by the fraction of overall corporate market value)

Industry classification of seller	Percent of total takeover activity[a]	Percent of total corporate market value[b]
Oil and gas	26.3%	13.5%
Banking and finance	8.8	6.4
Insurance	5.9	2.9
Food processing	4.6	4.4
Mining and minerals	4.4	1.5
Conglomerate	4.4	3.2
Retail	3.6	5.2
Transportation	2.4	2.7
Leisure and entertainment	2.3	.9
Broadcasting	2.3	.7
Other	39.4	58.5

[a]Grimm 1984, p. 41.

[b]As of 12/31/84. Total value is measured as the sum of the market value of common equity for 4,305 companies including 1,501 companies on the NYSE, 724 companies on the ASE plus 2,080 companies in the over-the-counter market (*The Media General Financial Weekly*, December 31, 1984, p. 17).

Managerial Myopia vs. Market Myopia

It has been argued that far from pushing managers to undertake needed structural changes, growing institutional equity holdings and the fear of takeover cause managers to behave myopically and therefore to sacrifice long-term benefits to increase short-term profits. The arguments tend to confuse two separate issues: 1) whether managers are shortsighted and make decisions that undervalue future cash flows while overvaluing current cash flows (myopic managers); and 2) whether security markets are shortsighted and undervalue future cash flows while overvaluing near-term cash flows (myopic markets).

There is little formal evidence on the myopic managers issue, but I believe this phenomenon does occur. Sometimes it occurs when managers hold little stock in their companies and are compensated in ways that motivate them to take actions to increase accounting earnings rather than the value of the firm. It also occurs when managers make mistakes because they do not understand the forces that determine stock values.

There is much evidence inconsistent with the myopic markets view and no evidence that indicates it is true.

First, the mere fact that price-earnings ratios differ widely among securities indicates the market is valuing something other than current earnings. For example, it values growth as well. Indeed, the essence of a growth stock is one that has large investment projects yielding few short-term cash flows but high future earnings and cash flows. The continuing marketability of new issues for start-up companies with little record of current earnings, the Genentechs of the world, is also inconsistent with the notion that the market does not value future earnings.

Second, McConnell and Muscarella (1985) provide evidence that (except in the oil industry) stock prices respond positively to announcements of increased investment expenditures and negatively to reduced expenditures. Their evidence is also inconsistent with the notion that the equity market is myopic, since it indicates the market values spending current resources on projects which promise returns in the future.

Third, the vast evidence on efficient markets indicating that current stock prices appropriately incorporate all currently available public information is also inconsistent with the myopic markets hypothesis. Although the evidence is not literally 100 percent in support of the efficient market hypothesis, no proposition in any of the sciences is better documented.[3]

---

[3]For an introduction to the literature and empirical evidence on the theory of efficient markets, see Elton and Gruber (1984), Chapter 15, p. 375ff. and the 167 studies referenced in the bibliography. For some anomalous evidence on market efficiency see Jensen (1978), Shiller (1981a, b). Merton (1985) provides an excellent discussion of the current state of the efficient market hypothesis.

The large positive stock price reactions to announced restructurings in the oil industry are inconsistent with the notion that the market values only short-term earnings, because the restructurings involve large write-offs that reduce accounting earnings in the year. ARCO's stock price, for example, increased by 30 percent when it announced its major restructuring in 1985. The market responded positively even though ARCO simultaneously announced a $1.2 billion write-off.

Fourth, recent versions of the myopic markets hypothesis emphasize increases in the amount of institutional holdings and the pressures they face to generate high returns on a quarter-to-quarter basis. It is argued that these pressures on institutions are a major cause of pressures on corporations to generate high current earnings on a quarter-to-quarter basis. The institutional pressures are said to lead to increased takeovers of firms (because institutions are not loyal shareholders) and to decreased research and development expenditures. It is hypothesized that because R&D expenditures reduce current earnings, firms making them are therefore more likely to be taken over, and that reductions in R&D are leading to a fundamental weakening of the corporate sector of the economy.

A study of 324 firms by the Office of the Chief Economist of the SEC (April 1985) finds substantial evidence that is inconsistent with this version of the myopic markets argument. The evidence indicates the following: increased institutional stock holdings are not associated with increased takeovers of firms; increased institutional holdings are not associated with decreases in research and development expenditures; firms with high R&D expenditures are not more vulnerable to takeovers; stock prices respond positively to announcements of such increases in R&D expenditures.

Moreover, total spending on R&D is increasing concurrent with the wave of merger and acquisition activity. Total spending on R&D in 1984, a year of record acquisition activity, increased by 14 percent according to *Business Week*'s annual survey. This represented "the biggest gain since R&D spending began a steady climb in the late 1970's." All industries in the survey increased R&D spending with the exception of steel. In addition, R&D spending increased from 2 percent of sales, where it had been for five years, to 2.9 percent. In 1985 and 1986, two more record years for acquisition activity, R&D also set new records. R&D spending increased by 10 percent (to 3.1 percent of sales) in 1985, and in 1986, R&D spending again increased by 10 percent to $51 billion (to 3.5 percent of sales), in a year when total sales decreased by 1 percent.[4]

Bronwyn Hall (1987), in a detailed study of all U.S. manufacturing firms in the years 1976–85, finds in approximately 600 acquisitions that firms which are acquired do not have higher R&D expenditures (measured by the ratio of R&D to sales) than firms in the same industry which are not acquired. Also, she finds that "firms involved in mergers showed no difference in their pre- and post-merger R&D performance over those not so involved."

I know of no evidence that supports that argument that takeovers reduce R&D expenditures, even though this is a prominent argument among many of those who favor restrictions on takeovers.

A simple alternative hypothesis explains the current facts, including the criticisms of managers, quite well. Instead of supposing that the myopic market is punishing managers for their foresightedness and for being right, suppose some managers are simply mistaken—that is, their strategies are wrong—and that the financial markets are telling them they are wrong. If they don't change, their stock prices will remain low. If the managers are indeed wrong, it is desirable for the stockholders and for the economy to remove them to make way for a change in strategy and more efficient use of the resources.

The internal control mechanisms of corporations, operating through the board of directors, should encourage reluctant managers to restructure. But when the internal processes for change in large corporations are too slow, costly, and clumsy to bring about the required restructuring or change in managers efficiently, the capital markets, through the market for corporate control, are doing so. The takeover market serves as an

---

[4]The "R&D Scoreboard" is an annual survey covering companies that account for 95 percent of total private-sector R&D expenditures. The three years referenced here can be found under "R&D Scoreboard" (1985, 1986, 1987) in the reference list. In 1984 the survey covered 820 companies; in 1985, it covered 844 companies; in 1986, it covered 859 companies.

important source of protection for investors in these situations. Other management teams that recognize an opportunity to reorganize or redeploy an organization's assets and thereby create new value can bid for the control rights in the takeover market. To be successful, such bids must be at a premium over current market value. This gives investors an opportunity to realize part of the gains from reorganization and redeployment of the assets.

FREE CASH FLOW THEORY

More than a dozen separate forces drive takeover activity, including such factors as deregulation, synergies, economies of scale and scope, taxes, the level of managerial competence, and increasing globalization of U.S. markets (Roll, forthcoming). One major cause of takeover activity, the agency costs associated with conflicts between managers and shareholders over the payout of free cash flow, has received relatively little attention. Yet it has played an important role in acquisitions over the last decade.[5]

Managers are the agents of shareholders and because both parties are self-interested, there are serious conflicts between them over the choice of the best corporate strategy. Agency costs are the total costs that arise in such arrangements. They consist of the costs of monitoring and bonding managerial behavior (such as the costs of producing audited financial statements and devising and implementing compensation plans that reward managers for actions that increase investors' wealth) and the efficiency losses that are incurred because the conflicts of interest can never be resolved perfectly. When these costs are large, the threat or actuality of takeovers can reduce them.

Free cash flow is cash flow in excess of that required to fund all of a firm's projects that have positive net present values when discounted at the relevant cost of capital. Such free cash flow must be paid out to shareholders if the firm is to be efficient and to maximize value for shareholders.

However, payment of cash to shareholders reduces the resources controlled by managers, thereby reducing the power of managers and potentially subjecting them to the monitoring by capital markets that occurs when a firm must obtain new capital. Further, managers have incentives to expand their firms beyond the size that maximizes shareholder wealth.[6] Growth increases managers' power by increasing the resources under their control, and changes in management compensation are positively related to growth.[7] Moreover, the tendency of firms to reward middle managers through promotion rather than year-to-year bonuses also creates an organizational bias toward growth to supply the new positions that such promotion-based reward systems require (Baker, 1986).

Conflicts of interest between shareholders and managers over payout policies are especially severe when the organization generates substantial free cash flow. The problem is how to motivate managers to disgorge the cash rather than invest it at below the cost of capital or waste it through organizational inefficiencies.

The theory developed here offers a seeming paradox. Increases in financial flexibility that give managers control over free cash flow may actually cause the value of the firm to decline. This result occurs because it is difficult to assure that managers will use their discretion over resources to further the interests of shareholders.

The theory explains: (1) how debt for stock exchanges reduces the organizational inefficiencies fostered by substantial free cash flow; (2) how debt can substitute for dividends; (3) why "diversification" programs are more likely to be associated with losses than are expansion programs in the same line of business; (4) why mergers

---

[5]This discussion is based on Jensen (1986).

[6]Gordon Donaldson (1984), in a detailed study of twelve large Fortune 500 firms, concludes that managers of these firms were not driven by maximization of the value of the firm, but rather by the maximization of "corporate wealth." He defines corporate wealth (p. 3, emphasis in original) as "*the aggregate purchasing power available to management for strategic purposes during any given planning period. . . . this wealth consists of the stocks and flows of cash and cash equivalents (primarily credit) that management can use at its discretion to implement decisions involving the control of goods and services.*" He continues (p. 22), "In practical terms it is cash, credit, and other corporate purchasing power by which management commands goods and services."

[7]Where growth is measured by increases in sales (Murphy, 1985). This positive relationship between compensation and sales growth need not imply, although it is consistent with, causality.

within an industry and liquidation-motivated takeovers will generally create larger gains than cross-industry mergers; (5) why the factors stimulating takeovers in such diverse businesses as broadcasting, tobacco, cable systems, and oil are essentially identical; and (6) why bidders and some targets tend to show abnormally good performance prior to takeover.

THE ROLE OF DEBT IN MOTIVATING ORGANIZATIONAL EFFICIENCY

The agency costs of debt have been widely discussed (Jensen and Meckling, 1976; Smith and Warner, 1979), but, with the exception of Grossman and Hart (1980), the benefits of debt in motivating managers and their organizations to be efficient have largely been ignored.

Debt creation, *without retention of the proceeds of the issue*, enables managers effectively to bond their promise to pay out future cash flows. Thus, debt can be an effective substitute for dividends, something not generally recognized in the corporate finance literature.[8] Debt reduces the agency cost of free cash flow by reducing the cash flow available for spending at the discretion of managers. By issuing debt in exchange for stock, managers bond their promise to pay out future cash flows in a way that simple dividend increases do not. In doing so, they give shareholder-recipients of the debt the right to take the firm into bankruptcy court if they do not keep their promise to make the interest and principal payments.

Of course managers can also promise to pay out future cash flows by announcing a "permanent" increase in the dividend.[9] But because there is no contractual obligation to make the promised dividend payments, such promises are weak.[10] The fact that capital markets punish dividend cuts with large stock price reductions (Charest, 1978; Aharony and Swary, 1980) can be interpreted as an equilibrium market response to the agency costs of free cash flow.

Issuing large amounts of debt to buy back stock sets up organizational incentives to motivate managers to pay out free cash flow. In addition, the exchange of debt for stock helps managers overcome the normal organizational resistance to retrenchment that the payout of free cash flow often requires. The threat of failure to make debt-service payments serves as a strong motivating force to make such organizations more efficient.

Increased leverage also has costs. As leverage increases, the usual agency costs of debt, including bankruptcy costs, rise. The incentives to take on projects that reduce total firm value but benefit shareholders through a transfer of wealth from bond-holders is one source of these costs. These costs put a limit on the desirable level of debt. The optimal debt/equity ratio is the point at which firm value is maximized, the point where the marginal costs of debt just offset the marginal benefits.

The debt created in a hostile takeover (or takeover defense) of a firm suffering severe agency costs of free cash flow need not be permanent. Indeed, sometimes "overleveraging" such a firm is desirable. In these situations, levering the firm so highly that it cannot continue to exist in its old form creates the crisis to motivate cuts in expansion programs and the sale of those divisions that are more valuable outside the firm. The proceeds are used to reduce debt to a more normal or permanent level. This process results in a reexamination of an

---

[8]Literally, principal and interest payments are substitutes for dividends. Dividends and debt are not perfect substitutes, however, because interest is tax-deductible at the corporate level and dividends are not.
[9]Rozeff (1982) and Easterbrook (1984a) argue that regular dividend payments can be effective in reducing agency costs with managers by assuring that managers are forced more frequently to subject themselves and their policies to the discipline of the capital markets when they acquire capital.
[10]Interestingly, Graham and Dodd (1951, Chapters 32, 34, and 36) place great importance on the dividend payout in their famous valuation formula $V = M(D + .33E)$. V is value, M is the earnings multiplier when the dividend payout rate is a "normal two-thirds of earnings," D is the expected dividend, and E is expected earnings. In their formula, dividends are valued at three times the rate of retained earnings—a proposition that has puzzled many students of modern finance (at least of my vintage). The agency cost of free cash flow that leads to over-retention and waste of shareholder resources is consistent with the deep suspicion with which Graham and Dodd viewed the lack of payout. Their discussion (chapter 34) reflects a belief in the tenuous nature of the future benefits of such retention. Although they do not couch the issues in terms of the conflict between managers and shareholders, the free cash flow theory explicated here implies that their beliefs sometimes characterized as a conviction that "a bird in the hand is worth two in the bush," were perhaps well founded.

organization's strategy and structure. When it is successful, a much leaner, more efficient, and competitive organization results.

This control hypothesis does not imply that debt issues will always have positive control effects. For example, these control effects will not be as important for rapidly growing organizations with large and highly profitable investment projects but no free cash flow. Such organizations will have to go regularly to the financial markets to obtain capital. At these times the markets have an opportunity to evaluate the company, its management, and its proposed projects. Investment bankers and analysts play an important role in this monitoring, and the market's assessment is made evident by the price investors pay for the financial claims.

The control function of debt is more important in organizations that generate large cash flows but have low growth prospects, and it is even more important in organizations that must shrink. In these organizations the pressure to waste cash flows by investing them in uneconomic projects is most serious.

Leveraged Buyouts and Free Cash Flow Theory

Many of the benefits in going-private and leveraged buyout transactions seem to be due to the control function of debt. These transactions are creating a new organizational form that competes successfully with the open corporate form because of advantages in controlling the agency costs of free cash flow. In 1985, going-private and LBO transactions totaled $37.4 billion and represented 32 percent of the value of all public acquisitions. In 1986, the total value increased to $44.3 billion representing 39 percent of all public acquisitions (Baker, 1986, Grimm, 1986). Average premiums paid for publicly held firms have exceeded 50 percent.

Desirable leveraged buyout candidates are frequently firms or divisions of larger firms that have stable business histories, low growth prospects and high potential for generating cash flows; that is, situations where agency costs of free cash flows are likely to be high.

Leveraged buyouts are frequently financed with high debt; 10:1 ratios of debt to equity are not uncommon, and they average 5.25:1 (Schipper and Smith, 1986; Kaplan, 1987; DeAngelo and DeAngelo, 1986). Moreover, the use of "strip financing" and the allocation of equity in the deals reveal a sensitivity to incentives, conflicts of interest, and bankruptcy costs. Strip financing, the practice in which risky nonequity securities are held in approximately equal proportions, limits the conflict of interest among such securityholders and therefore limits bankruptcy costs. Top managers and the sponsoring venture capitalists hold disproportionate amounts of equity.

A somewhat oversimplified example illustrates the organizational effects of strip financing. Consider two firms identical in every respect except financing. Firm A is entirely financed with equity, and Firm B is highly leveraged with senior debt, subordinated debt, convertible debt, and preferred as well as common equity. Suppose Firm B securities are sold only in strips; that is, a buyer purchasing a certain percent of any security must purchase the same percent of all securities, and the securities are "stapled" together so they cannot be separated later. Security holders of both firms have identical unlevered claims on the cash flow distribution, but organizationally the two firms are very different. If Firm B managers withhold dividends to invest in value-reducing projects or if they are incompetent, stripholders have recourse to remedial powers not available to the equityholders of Firm A. Each Firm B security specifies the rights its holder has in the event of default on its dividend or coupon payment—for example, the right to take the firm into bankruptcy or to have board representation. As each security above equity goes into default, the stripholder receives new rights to intercede in the organization. As a result, it is quicker and less expensive to replace managers in Firm B.

Moreover, because every securityholder in the highly levered Firm B has the same claim on the firm, there are no conflicts between senior and junior claimants over reorganization of the claims in the event of default; to the stripholders it is a matter of moving funds from one pocket to another. Thus, Firm B will not go into bankruptcy; a required reorganization can be accomplished voluntarily, quickly, and with less expense and disruption than through bankruptcy proceedings.

Securities commonly subject to strip practices are often called "mezzanine" financing and include securities with priority superior to common stock yet subordinate to senior debt. This arrangement seems to be sensible, because several factors ignored in our simplified example imply that strictly proportional holdings of all securities is not desirable. For example, IRS restrictions deny tax deductibility of debt interest in such situations and bank holdings of equity are restricted by regulation. Riskless senior debt need not be in the strip because there are no conflicts with other claimants in the event of reorganization when there is no probability of default on its payments.

Furthermore, it is advantageous to have top level managers and venture capitalists who promote the transactions hold a larger share of the equity. Top level managers on average receive over 30 percent of the equity, and venture capitalists and the funds they represent generally retain the major share of the remainder (Schipper and Smith, 1986; Kaplan, 1987). The venture capitalists control the board of directors (in fact, they often *are* the board) and monitor managers directly. Large equity claims by managers and venture capitalists give them a strong interest in making the venture successful because their equity interests are subordinate to other claims.

Leveraged buyouts increased dramatically in the last decade from $1.2 billion in 1979, when W. T. Grimm began collecting the data, to $44.3 billion in 1986. Less than a handful of these management buyouts have ended in bankruptcy, although more have gone through private reorganizations. A thorough test of this organizational form requires the passage of time and recessions.

Some have asserted that managers engaging in a buyout of their firm are insulating themselves from monitoring. The opposite is true in the typical leveraged buyout because the venture capitalist is generally the largest stockholder and controls the board of directors. The venture capitalist therefore has both greater ability and greater incentive to monitor managers than do directors with little or no equity who represent diffuse shareholders in the typical public corporation.

APPLYING FREE CASH FLOW THEORY TO TAKEOVERS

Free cash flow theory is consistent with a wide range of previously unexplained data. Here I sketch some empirical predictions of the free cash flow theory for takeovers and mergers and some of the facts that lend it credence.

The Oil Industry

The importance of takeovers and the relevance of free cash flow theory in motivating change and efficiency are particularly clear in the oil industry. Radical changes in the energy market from 1973 to the late 1970s meant that a major restructuring of the petroleum industry had to occur. The optimal level of refining and distribution capacity and crude reserves fell over this period; as of the late 1970s, the industry was plagued with excess capacity, although this was not generally recognized at the time. Reserves are reduced by reducing the level of exploration and development, and it pays to concentrate these reductions in high-cost areas such as the United States.

Substantial reductions in exploration and development and in refining and distribution capacity meant that some firms had to leave the industry. This is especially true because holding reserves is subject to economies of scale, while exploration and development are subject to diseconomies of scale.

At the same time price increases generated large cash flows, creating a particularly puzzling period in the oil industry because at the same time that change in the environment required a reduction of capacity, cash flows and profits were high; 1984 cash flows of the ten largest oil companies were $48.5 billion, 28 percent of the total cash flows of the top 200 firms in *Dun's Business Month* (July 1985) survey. This condition, in which high profits coincided with the necessity to shrink the industry, is somewhat unusual. It was caused by an increase in the average productivity of resources in the industry while the marginal productivity decreased.[11] However, management did not pay out the excess resources to shareholders. Instead, the industry continued to spend heavily on exploration and development even though the returns on these expenditures were below the cost of capital.

---

[11]More detailed analysis of this point is available in Jensen (1987).

Paradoxically, the profitability of oil exploration and drilling activity can decrease even though the price of oil increases, if the value of reserves in the ground falls. This decrease can occur when the price increase is associated with reductions in consumption that make marketing newly discovered oil difficult. In the late 1970s the increased holding costs associated with higher real interest rates, reductions in expected future oil price increases, increased exploration and development costs, and contrived reductions in current supply (and thus larger future potential supply) combined to make many current exploration and development projects uneconomic. The industry, however, continued to spend heavily on such projects.

The waste associated with excessive exploration and development expenditures explains why buying oil on Wall Street was considerably cheaper than obtaining it by drilling holes in the ground, even after adjustment for differential taxes and regulations on prices of old oil. Wall Street was not undervaluing the oil; it was valuing it correctly, but it was also correctly valuing the wasted expenditures on exploration and development that oil companies were making. When these managerially imposed "taxes" on the reserves were taken into account in stock prices, the net prices of oil on Wall Street was low. This low price provided incentives for firms to obtain reserves by purchasing other oil companies and reducing expenditures on non-cost-effective exploration. In this way the capital markets provided incentives for firms to make adjustments that were not effectively motivated by competition in the product markets.

The fact that oil industry managers tried to invest funds outside the industry is also evidence that they could not find enough profitable projects within the industry to use the huge inflow of resources efficiently. Unfortunately these efforts failed. The diversification programs involved purchases of companies in retailing (Marcor by Mobil), manufacturing (Reliance Electric by Exxon), office equipment (Vydec by Exxon), and mining (Kennecott by Sohio, Anaconda Minerals by ARCO, Cyprus Mines by Amoco). These acquisitions turned out to be among the least successful of the last decade, partly because of bad luck (like the collapse of the minerals industry) and partly because of a lack of managerial expertise outside the oil industry. In sum, the stage was set for retrenchment in the oil industry in the early 1980s. Yet the product and capital markets could not force management to change its strategy because the industry's high internal cash flows insulated them from these pressures.

Ultimately the capital markets through the takeover market, forced managers to respond to the new market conditions. T. Boone Pickens of Mesa Petroleum perceived early that the industry had to be restructured. Partly as a result of Mesa's efforts, firms in the industry were led to merge and in the merging process they paid out large amounts of capital to shareholders, reduced excess expenditures on exploration and development, and reduced excess capacity in refining and distribution. The result has been large gains in efficiency. Total gains to shareholders in the Gulf/Chevron, Getty/Texaco and Du Pont/Conoco mergers, for example, were over $17 billion. Much more is possible. Jacobs (1986) estimates total potential gains of approximately $200 billion from eliminating the inefficiencies in 98 petroleum firms as of December 1984.

Recent events indicate that actual takeover is not necessary to induce the required adjustments; the Phillips, Unocal and Arco restructurings all involve large stock repurchases with debt and cash, increases in dividend payments, and reductions in exploration and development. They generated increases of 20 percent to 35 percent in market value, totaling $6.6 billion.

Other Industries in Theory and Practice

Acquisitions are one way managers spend cash instead of paying it out to shareholders. Free cash flow theory implies that managers of firms with unused borrowing power and large free cash flows are more likely to undertake low-benefit or even value-destroying mergers. Diversification programs generally fit this category, and the theory predicts that they will generate lower total gains. Thus, some acquisitions are a solution to the agency problem of free cash flow while others, such as diversification programs, are symptoms of those problems.

The major benefit of diversification mergers may be that they involve less waste of resources than if the funds had been invested internally in unprofitable projects. Acquisitions made with cash or securities other than stock involve payout of resources to shareholders of the target company, and this can create net benefits even if the merger creates operating inefficiencies. To illustrate, consider an acquiring firm with substantial free cash flow that the market expects will be invested in low-return projects with a negative net present value of $100 million. If this firm uses up its free cash flow (and thereby prevents its waste) by acquiring another firm that generates zero synergies, the combined market value of the two firms will rise by $100 million. The market value increases because the acquisition eliminates the expenditures on internal investments with negative market value of $100 million.

Because the bidding firms are using funds that would otherwise have been spent on low or negative-return projects, the opportunity cost of the funds is lower than their cost of capital. As a result they will tend to over-pay for the acquisition and thereby transfer some, if not all, of the gains to the target firm's shareholders. In extreme cases they may pay so much that the bidding firm's share price falls, in effect giving the target shareholders more than 100 percent of the gains. These predictions are consistent with the evidence that shareholders of target companies reap most of the gains from a takeover.

Low-return mergers are more likely to occur in industries with large cash flows whose economics dictate retrenchment. Horizontal mergers (where cash or debt is the form of payment) within declining industries will tend to create value because they facilitate exit—the cash or debt payments to shareholders of the target firm cause resources to leave the industry directly. When Socal acquired Gulf in 1984 for $13.2 billion in cash, the oil industry shrank by $13.2 billion as soon as the checks were mailed. Mergers outside the declining industry are more likely to have low or even negative returns because managers are likely to know less about managing such firms. Oil fits this description, and so does tobacco. Tobacco firms face declining demand as a result of changing smoking habits but generate large free cash flow and have been involved in major diversifying acquisitions, as in the $5.6 billion purchase of General Foods by Philip Morris. The theory predicts that these acquisitions in non-related industries are more likely to reduce productivity, although the positive total gains to buyers and sellers indicate these negative productivity effects are outweighed by the reductions in waste from internal expansion.

Forest products is another industry with excess capacity and acquisition activity, including the acquisition of St. Regis by Champion International and Crown Zellerbach by Sir James Goldsmith. Horizontal mergers for cash or debt in such an industry generate gains by encouraging exit of resources (through payout) and by substituting existing capacity for investment in new facilities by firms that are short of capacity. Food industry mergers also appear to reflect the expenditure of free cash flow. The industry apparently generates large cash flows with few growth opportunities. It is, therefore, a good candidate for leveraged buy-outs, and these are now occurring; the $6.3 billion Beatrice LBO is the largest ever.

The broadcasting industry generates rents in the form of large cash flows on its licenses and also fits the theory. Regulation limits the overall supply of licenses and the number owned by a single entity. Thus, profitable internal investments are limited, and the industry's free cash flow has been spent on organizational inefficiencies and diversification programs, making these firms takeover targets. The CBS debt-for-stock exchange and restructuring as a defense against the hostile bid by Turner fits the theory, and so does the $3.5 billion purchase of American Broadcasting Company by Capital Cities Communications. Complete cable systems also create agency problems from free cash flows in the form of rents on their franchises and quasi rents on their installed capital and are likely to generate free cash flow problems. Drug companies with large cash flows from previous successful discoveries and few potential future prospects are also candidates for large agency costs of free cash flow.

Free cash flow theory predicts that many acquirers will tend to perform exceptionally well prior to acquisition. Empirical evidence from studies of both stock prices and accounting data indicates exceptionally good performance for acquirers prior to acquisition (Magenheim and Mueller, 1985; Bradley and Jarrell, 1985). This exceptional stock price performance is often associated with increased free cash flow which is then used for acquisition programs as observed in the oil industry. Targets will be of two kinds: firms with poor management that have done poorly before the merger and firms that have done exceptionally well and have large free cash flow that they refuse to pay out to shareholders. Both kinds of targets seem to exist.[12]

---

[12]Asquith (1983) finds evidence of below-normal stock price performance for 302 target firms in the 400 days before 20 days prior to the takeover bid. Mandelker (1974) finds negative abnormal performance for target firms in the period from 40 months before until 9 months before the outcome of the merger bid is known. Langtieg (1978) reports significant negative returns in the period from 72 months before until 19 months before the outcome date, but positive abnormal returns in the 19 months preceding the merger date.

The theory predicts that takeovers financed with cash and debt will create larger benefits than those accomplished through exchange of stock. Stock acquisitions do nothing to take up the organizations' financial slack and are therefore unlikely to motivate managers to use resources more efficiently. The recent evidence on takeover premiums is consistent with this prediction.[13]

In the best study to date of the determinants of takeover, Palepu (1986) finds strong evidence consistent with the free cash flow theory of mergers. He studied a sample of 163 firms acquired in the period 1971–79 and a random sample of 256 firms that were not acquired. Both samples were in mining and manufacturing and were listed on either the New York or American stock exchange. He finds that firms with a mismatch between growth and resources are more likely to be taken over. These are firms with high growth (measured by average sales growth), low liquidity (measured by the ratio of liquid assets to total assets) and high leverage, and firms with low growth high liquidity, and low leverage. He also finds that poor prior performance (measured by the net of market returns in the four years before the acquisition) is significantly related to the probability of takeover and, interestingly, that accounting measures of past performance such as return on equity are unrelated to the probability of takeover.

Free cash flow is only one of the many factors that go into a takeover decision. But the evidence indicates that it is an important factor and provides a useful perspective on the conflict.

CONTROVERSIAL ISSUES FROM AN AGENCY PERSPECTIVE

High-Yield, Non-Investment Grade Bonds: "Junk" Bonds

The past several years have witnessed a major innovation in the financial markets—the establishment of active markets in high-yield bonds. These bonds, rated below investment grade by the bond-rating agencies, are frequently referred to as junk bonds, a disparaging term that bears no relation to their pedigree. High-yield bonds are best viewed as commercial loans that can be resold in secondary markets. They are further evidence of the securitization that has converted formerly illiquid financial claims such as mortgages into marketable claims. Total publicly held high-yield bonds have risen from $7 billion in 1970 to $125 billion in 1986 or 23 percent of the total corporate bond market (Taggart, 1986; Drexel Burnham Lambert, 1987). By traditional standards they are more risky than investment-grade bonds and therefore carry interest rates 3 to 5 percentage points higher than the yields on government bonds of comparable maturity. In an early study, Blume and Keim (1984) find that the default rates on these bonds have been low and the realized returns have been disproportionately higher than their risk.

High-yield bonds have been attacked by those who wish to inhibit their use, particularly in the financing of takeover bids. However, companies commonly raise funds to finance ventures by selling claims to be paid from the proceeds of the venture; this is the essence of debt or stock issues used to finance new ventures. High-yield bonds used in takeovers work similarly. The bonds provide a claim on the proceeds of the venture, using the assets and cash flows of the target plus the equity contributed by the acquirer as collateral. Similarly, individuals purchase homes using the home plus their down payment as collateral for the mortgage. The structure of this contract offers nothing inherently unusual.

Some might argue that the risk of high-yield bonds used in takeover attempts is "too high." But high-yield bonds are less risky by definition than common stock claims on the same venture, since the claims of common stockholders are subordinate to those of the holders of high-yield bonds. Would these same critics argue that the stock claims are too risky and thus should be barred? The risk argument makes logical sense only as an argument that transactions costs associated with bankruptcy or recontracting are too high in these ventures or that the bonds are priced too high and that investors who purchase them will not earn returns high enough to compensate for the risk they are incurring. This overpricing argument makes little sense because there is vast evidence that investors are capable of pricing risks in all sorts of other markets.

---

[13]See Wansley, Lane and Yang (1987) who find higher returns to targets and to bidders in cash transactions, and Wansley and Fayez (1986).

In January 1986 the Federal Reserve Board issued a new interpretation of the margin rules that restricts the use of debt in takeovers to 50 percent or less of the purchase price. The rule has had little effect on takeovers because bidders otherwise subject to the constraint have instead used high-yield preferred stock rated below investment grade which is converted to debt after completion of the acquisition or bridge loans. This rule was apparently motivated by the belief that the use of corporate debt has become abnormally and dangerously high and was threatening the economy. This assessment is not consistent with the facts. Table 2 presents measures of debt use by nonfinancial corporations in the United State. The debt-equity ratio is measured relative to three bases: market value of equity, estimated current asset value of equity, and accounting book value of equity measured at historical cost.

Although debt-equity ratios were higher in 1985 than in 1961, they were not at record levels. The book value debt-equity ratio reached a high of 81.4 percent in 1984 but declined to 78 percent in 1985. Debt-equity ratios measured on a historical cost basis are relatively high because of the previous decade of inflation. Maintenance of the same inflation-adjusted debt ratios in time of inflation implies that the book value ratio must rise because the current value of assets in the denominator of the inflation-adjusted ratio is rising. The current value ratio, which takes account of inflation, fell from 50.7 percent in 1970 to 46.5 percent in 1985. The market-value ratio rose from 54.7 percent in 1970 to 80.5 percent in 1984 and plummeted to 60.8 percent in 1985. The 1985 market-value ratio was 45 percentage points below its 1974 peak of 105.2 percent. Thus, the Federal Reserve System's own data are inconsistent with the reasons given for its restrictions on the use of debt.

High-yield bonds were first used in a takeover bid in 1984 and were involved in relatively few bids in total. In 1984, only about 12 percent of the $14.3 billion of new high-yield debt was associated with mergers and

Table 2
Debt-to-equity ratios: non-financial corporations

Year	Book value	Current value	Market value
1961	57.1%	41.1%	38.5%
1962	58.2	42.5	45.6
1963	59.6	44.5	41.7
1964	59.9	45.4	39.8
1965	61.1	46.5	40.0
1966	62.7	47.4	48.4
1967	64.7	48.7	41.3
1968	67.2	50.5	40.2
1969	68.1	50.3	50.3
1970	70.5	50.7	54.7
1971	70.4	50.7	50.0
1972	70.2	50.3	48.1
1973	70.9	48.9	67.7
1974	70.2	43.9	105.2
1975	66.7	41.6	79.5
1976	65.6	41.1	74.2
1977	67.7	41.4	87.6
1978	69.1	41.1	94.8
1979	69.9	39.9	88.7
1980	68.3	37.8	70.0
1981	71.0	38.3	82.7
1982	74.3	40.0	77.7
1983	73.0	40.6	69.2
1984	81.4	46.1	80.5
1985	78.0	46.5	60.8

Source: Federal Reserve Board (1986)

acquisitions. In 1985, 26 percent of the $14.7 billion of new high-yield debt was used in acquisitions.[14] According to *Mergers & Acquisitions*, 1986 acquisition-related high-yield debt still represents less than one of every 12 dollars in acquisition value. Nevertheless, high-yield bonds are an important innovation in the takeover field because they help eliminate size as a deterrent to takeover. They have been particularly influential in helping to bring about reorganizations in the oil industry.

Historical default rates on high-yield bonds have been low, but many of the bonds are so new that the experience could prove to be different in the next downturn. Various opponents (including executives who desire protection from the takeover market and members of the financial community, such as commercial banks and insurance companies, who want to restrict competition from this new financing vehicle) have backed regulations and legislation to restrict the issuance of high-yield bonds, to penalize their tax status, and to restrict their holding by thrifts, which can now buy them as substitutes for the issuance of nonmarketable commercial loans. These proposals are premature to say the least.

Severance Contracts: "Golden Parachutes"

The increasing sophistication of takeover experts and the availability of high-yield bond financing for profitable takeover ventures means that the largest of the Fortune 500 companies are now potentially subject to takeover; mere size is no longer an effective defense. This susceptibility to takeover has created a new contracting environment for top-level managers. Roughly 50 percent of the top level managers of target firms are gone within three years of acquisition—either hostile or voluntary. Many managers are legitimately anxious, and it will take time for the system to work out an appropriate set of practices and contracts reflecting the risks and rewards of the new environment.

Unfortunately, a major component of the solution to the conflict of interest between shareholders and managers has been vastly misunderstood. I am referring to severance contracts that compensate managers for the loss of their jobs in the event of a change in control. These have been popularly labeled "golden parachutes."

These control-related contracts are beneficial when correctly implemented, because they help reduce the conflict of interest between shareholders and managers at times of takeover and therefore make it more likely that the productive gains stemming from changes in control will be realized. The evidence indicates that stock prices of firms that adopt severance-related compensation contracts for managers on average rise about 3 percent when adoption of the contracts is announced (Lambert and Larcker, 1985). There is no easy way to tell what proportion of the effect is due to the market interpreting the announcement as a signal that a takeover bid is more likely and what proportion is due to the reduction in conflict between managers and shareholders.

At times of takeover, shareholders are implicitly asking the top-level managers of their firm to negotiate a deal for them that frequently involves the imposition of large personal costs on the managers and their families. These involve moving costs, the loss of position, power and prestige, and even the loss of their jobs. Shareholders are asking the very people who are most likely to have invested considerable time and energy (in some cases a life's work) in building a successful organization to negotiate its sale and the possible redirection of its resources.

It is important to confront these conflicts and to structure contracts with managers to reduce them. It would make no sense to hire a realtor to sell your house and then penalize him for doing so. Yet that is the implication of many of the emotional reactions to control-related severance contracts. The restrictions and tax penalties imposed on these severance payments by the Deficit Reduction Act of 1984 are unwise interferences in the contracting freedoms of shareholders and managers and should be eliminated.

---

[14]Source: Drexel Burnham Lambert, private correspondence.

Golden parachutes can be used to restrict takeovers and to entrench managers at the expense of shareholders. The key to deciding whether a contract is well-designed is whether it helps solve the conflict-of-interest problem between shareholders and managers. Solving this problem requires extending control-related severance contracts beyond the chief executive to those members of the top-level management team who must play an important role in negotiating and implementing any transfer of control. Contracts that award severance contracts to substantial numbers of managers beyond this group are unlikely to be in the shareholders' interest. Beneficial Corp. awarded such contracts to over 200 of its managers (Morrison, 1982). These are likely to be difficult to justify as in the shareholders' interests.

Severance-related compensation contracts are particularly important in situations where it is optimal for managers to invest in organization-specific human capital; that is, in skills and knowledge that have little or no value in other organizations. Managers will not so invest where the likelihood is high that their investment will be eliminated by an unexpected transfer of control and the loss of their jobs. In such situations, the firm will have to pay for all costs associated with the creation of such organization-specific human capital, and it will be more costly for the firm to attract and retain highly talented managers when they have better opportunities elsewhere. In addition, contracts that award excessive severance compensation to the appropriate group of managers will tend to motivate managers to sell the firm at too low a price.

No simple rules can be specified that will easily prevent the misuse of golden parachutes because the appropriate solution will depend on many factors that are specific to each situation (like the amount of stock held by the managers and the optimal amount of investment in organization-specific human capital). In general, contracts that award inappropriately high payments to an excessively large group will reduce efficiency and harm shareholders by raising the cost of acquisition and by transferring wealth from shareholders to managers. The generally appropriate solution is to make the control-related severance contracts pay off in a way that is tied to the premium earned by the stockholders. Stock options or restricted stock appreciation rights that pay off only in the event of a change in control are two options that have some of the appropriate properties. In general, policies that encourage increased stock ownership by managers and the board of directors will provide incentives that will tend to reduce the conflicts of interests with managers.

Targeted Repurchases: "Greenmail"

Most proposals to restrict or prohibit targeted repurchases (transactions pejoratively labeled "greenmail") are nothing more than antitakeover proposals in disguise. Greenmail is actually a targeted repurchase, an offer by management to repurchase the shares of a subset of shareholders at a premium, an offer not made to other shareholders. Greenmail is an appellation that suggests blackmail; yet the only effective threat possessed by a greenmailer is the right to offer to purchase stock from shareholders at a substantial premium. The "damage" to shareholders caused by this action is difficult to find. Those who propose to "protect" shareholders by paying greenmail hide this fact behind emotional language designed to mislead. But management can easily prohibit greenmail without legislation: it need only announce a policy that prohibits the board or management from making such payments.

The ease with which managers can prevent targeted repurchases makes it clear that the problem lies with managers who use such payments to protect themselves from competition in the market for corporate control. Three careful studies of these transactions indicate that, when measured from the initial toehold purchase to the final repurchase of the shares, the stock price of target firms rises (Holderness and Sheehan, 1985; Mikkelson and Ruback 1985, 1986). Therefore, shareholders are benefited, not harmed, by the whole sequence of events. However, when greenmail is used to buy off an acquirer who has made an offer for the firm, shareholders are harmed by the loss of the takeover premium. There is some indication that the stock price increases represent the expectation of future takeover premiums in firms in which the targeted repurchase was not sufficient to prevent ultimate takeover of the firm (see Mikkelson and Ruback, 1986). If so, then, as in the final defeat of tender offers found by Bradley, Desai and Kim (1983), all premiums are lost to shareholders in firms for which the repurchase and associated standstill agreements successfully lock up the firm, preventing any voluntary reorganization.

Problems in the Delaware Court: "Poison Pills"

Delaware courts have created over the years a highly productive fabric of corporate law that has benefited the nation. The court is having difficulty, however, sorting out the complex issues it faces in the takeover area. The result has been a confusing set of decisions that, in contrast to much of the court's previous history, appears to make little economic sense.[15]

One key case involved a unilateral decision from the board of directors of Household International to change the nature of the contractual relationship with Household's shareholders in a fundamental way. Effectively, the board restricted the alienability of the common stock by prohibiting shareholders from selling their shares, without permission of the board, into a control transaction leading to merger at a premium over market value lower than about $6 billion. Since Household had a market value of about $2 billion at the time, this step prevented its shareholders from accepting any premium less than 200 percent—more than four times the average takeover premium of 50 percent common in recent times. This decision is difficult to justify as in the shareholders' interests, but the Delaware Supreme Court upheld in November 1985 the right of the board to take such action.

The Delaware court's model of the corporation is founded in the business judgment rule—the legal doctrine that holds that unless explicit evidence of fraud or self-dealing exists the board of directors is presumed to be acting in the interests of the shareholders. In particular, the board is presumed to act altruistically and never out of incentives to preserve the interests of managers or their own positions as board members.

The altruistic model of the board that is the implicit foundation of the business judgment rule is obviously incorrect as a description of human behavior. But in spite of its falsity, the altruistic model has been sufficiently robust to yield good law for a wide range of cases for many years. Alternative agency models of the corporation that incorporate conflicts of interest between board members and shareholders are much more complicated.[16] The court is now being forced to deal with these complexities, but it is doing so with an inadequate analytic foundation.

To illustrate the problem the Delaware court is facing, consider the simple situation in which a principal (stockholder) hires an agent (managers and board of directors) to take some actions on his or her behalf. To effect this arrangement, the principal delegates to the agent a set of decision rights. On entering the relationship, the principal wants the courts to enforce the contract that delegates decision rights to the agent. One of the primary purposes of the business judgment rule is to keep the courts out of the business of second-guessing the agent's decisions and holding the agent liable for damages. Doing so would make it difficult or impossible for principals to hire agents in the first place, which would eliminate the benefit of specialization. Under this rule, the court refused to second-guess the decision of the Household board of directors.

The principal may want to delegate a wide range of decision rights to the agent. In no event, however, will it be sensible for the principal to delegate the ultimate control rights to the agent: the rights to hire, fire, and set the compensation of the agent (Fama and Jensen, 1985). If the principal were to delegate the control rights to the agent, the agent could not be fired and would have the right to set his own compensation. In this circumstance the agent would become the effective owner of the decision rights (although he probably could not alienate them) and could be expected to use them in his own interests.

If the business judgment rule is applied to conflicts over control rights between principals and agents, the courts are effectively giving the agent the right to change the control rights unilaterally. In the long run, this interpretation of the contract will destroy the possibility of such cooperative arrangements, because it will leave principals with few effective rights.

---

[15]See, for example, *Moran v. Household Intl., Inc.*, 490 A.2d 1059 (Del. Ch. 1985) aff'd 500 A.2d 1346 (Del. 1985) (upholding poison pill rights issue), *Smith v. Van Gorkom*, 488 A.2d 858, (holding board liable for damages in sale of firm at substantial premium over market price), *Unocal v. Mesa*, 493 A.2d 946, 954 (Del. 1985) (allowing discriminatory targeted repurchase that confiscates wealth of largest shareholder), *Revlon Inc. v. MacAndrews & Forbes Holdings Inc.* 506 A.2d 173, (Del. 1986) (invalidation of Revlon's lockup sale of a prime division to Forstmann Little at a below-market price).

[16]Easterbrook (1984b) and Jensen and Smith (1985) provide summaries of much of the work in the area.

The courts have applied the business judgment rule to conflicts between management and shareholders over the issuance of poison pill preferred stock, poison pill rights, and discriminatory targeted repurchases, and have given managers and boards the rights to use these devices.[17] Poison pill securities change fundamental aspects of the corporate rules that govern the relationship between shareholders, managers and the board of directors when a control-related event occurs. They are called "poison pills" because they alter the company to make it indigestible to an acquirer. In doing so, the courts are essentially giving the agents (managers and the board) the right to change unilaterally critical control aspects of the contract, in particular, the right to prevent the firing of the agents.

The Delaware court decision upholding the decision of the board of Household International has unleashed a flood of poison pill adoptions by American corporations. Ryngaert (forthcoming) and Malatesta and Walkling (forthcoming) study the effects of over 300 of these plans adopted primarily in the period since the *Household* and *Unocal* decisions. They find statistically significant negative stock price effects on the announcement of the adoption of the plans; they find also that the plans tend to be implemented in firms in which managers own relatively little of their firm's stock. Malatesta and Walkling also find that firms adopting such plans are significantly less profitable than other firms in their industries in the year prior to adoption.

The court has erred in allowing the Household board, under the business judgment rule, to make the fundamental change in the structure of the organization implied by the rights issue without vote of its shareholders. Several other poison pill cases have been heard by the courts with similar outcomes, but one New Jersey and two New York courts have recently ruled against poison pills that substantially interfere with the voting rights of large-block shareholders.[18] An Illinois district court recently voided a poison pill (affirmed by the Seventh Circuit Court of Appeals) and two weeks later approved a new pill issued by the same company.[19]

The problem with these special securities and the provision they contain is not with their appropriateness (some might well be desirable), but with the manner in which they are being adopted; that is, without approval by shareholders. Boards of directors show little inclination to refer such issues to shareholders.

The continued application of the business judgment rule to conflicts over control has far-reaching consequences. If the current trend continues, this process will erode the limits to judicial interference in the management of corporations historically provided by the business judgment rule and severely cripple the corporation in the competition for survival. Indeed, the protection afforded managers by the business judgment rule is already eroding.[20] The court seems to be imposing a higher standard on corporations that adopt a poison pill. This erosion of the business judgment rule appears to be motivated by the court's understanding that the pill gives management and the board great power. So the court is brought into the business of second-guessing managers' business decisions. The court currently seems to be inclined to give this scrutiny only to control transactions.

I believe that this erosion of the business judgment rule will be checked because the court will recognize the problems with its current approach. The easiest solution to the problem is for the court to deny protection under the business judgment rule to managerial decisions on control issues unless those decisions have been ratified by shareholder vote.[21]

---

[17]*Moran v. Household Intl.*, and *Unocal v. Mesa.* Full citations provided in note 15.

[18]*Ministar Acquiring corp. v. AMF Inc.*, 621 Fed Sup 1252. Dis NY, 1985 *Unilever Acquisition Corp. v. Richardson-Vicks, Inc.*, 618 Fed Supp 407. So Dist. NY 1985, *Asarco Inc. v. M. R. H. Holmes a Court*, 611 Fed Sup 468. Dist. Ct. of NJ, 1985, and *Dynamics Corp. of America v. CTS Corporation.*

[19]*Dynamics Corp. of America v. CTS Corp., et al.* U.S. District Court, Northern District of Illinois, Eastern Division, No. 86 C 1624, (April 17, 1986), affirmed Seventh Circuit Court of Appeals Nos. 86–1601, 86–1608, and *Dynamics Corp. of America v. CTS Corp., et al.* (May 3, 1986).

[20]See *Revlon Inc. v. MacAndrews & Forbes Holdings Inc.*, 506 A.2nd 173, 180 (Del. 1986), in which the court seems to be reviewing very detailed aspects of the board's decision leading to the invalidation of Revlon's lockup sale of a prime division to Forstmann Little at a below-market price. The Court of Appeals for the Second Circuit in *Hanson Trust v. SCM Corp.*, (Nos. 85–7951, 85–7953, 2d Cir. Jan. 6, 1986) (written opinion filed Jan. 6, 1986), enjoined lockups given by SCM defending itself from takeover by Hanson Trust. See also Herzel, Colling, and Carlson (1986) for detailed analysis of these cases and lockups in general.

[21]See Koleman (1985) and Investor Responsibility Research Center (1985).

SEC 13d Disclosure Rules and the Creation of Externalities

It has become popular to argue there is too much takeover activity. Yet the opposite is most likely true because of free-riding problems caused by the current regulations that require disclosure of holdings and intentions of the purchaser in SEC 13d reports.[22] These reports must be filed within 10 days of acquisition of 5 percent or more of a company's shares and must disclose the number of shares owned, the identity of the owner, and the purpose of the acquisition. Current rules allow the acquiring firm to buy as many additional shares as it can in the 10-day window between the time the 5 percent filing barrier is reached and the time of filing. This rule allows buyers to acquire shares that average 13.9 percent of the target firm.[23]

Since market prices adjust to the expected value of the takeover bid immediately after the 13d announcement, most of the acquirer's profits are made almost entirely on the difference between the price paid for the shares purchased prior to the filing of the 13d and their value after the acquisition. This drives a wedge, however, between the private benefits earned by the acquirer and the total social benefits of the acquisition; the acquirer pays 100 percent of the acquisition costs and, on average, captures less than 14 percent of the benefits. The remaining benefits go to the other shareholders. The activities of Mesa Petroleum, for example, have yielded benefits to the shareholders of companies involved in its transactions that exceed $13 billion. Mesa itself has paid hundreds of millions of dollars in financing, legal, and investment banking fees and borne all the risks of loss. Yet it has earned only about $750 million on these transactions.

Consider an acquisition that promises total expected gains of $100 million. If the acquirer expects to capture only $14 million of this amount if the bid is successful, the bid will occur only if the legal, investment banking, and other costs (including the required risk premium) are less than $14 million. All such acquisitions that are expected to cost more than this will not be made, and shareholders and society are thus denied the benefits of those reorganizations. If the costs, for example, are expected to be $15 million, the bid will not occur and the $85 million benefit will not be realized.

The solution to this problem is to abolish the SEC 13d reporting requirement or to increase significantly the trigger point from the current 5 percent level. Unfortunately, current proposals in Congress to reduce the 10-day window to one or two days and to reduce the trigger point to 1 percent or 2 percent are moves in exactly the wrong direction. It is clear why antitakeover forces want such restrictive legislation. But the effect of this proposal is equivalent to that of an anti-patent law which requires public disclosure of all inventions and denies the inventor all but a one or two percent property right in the proceeds of his or her invention. Shareholders will clearly be harmed by such regulation.

CONCLUSION

Although economic analysis and the evidence indicate that the market for corporate control is benefiting shareholders, society, and the corporation as an organizational form, it is also making life more uncomfortable for top level executives. This discomfort is creating strong pressures at both the state and federal levels for restrictions that will seriously cripple the working of this market. In 1985, 1986 and 1987 there were dozens of bills in the congressional hopper proposing various restrictions on the market for corporate control. Others proposed major new restrictions on share ownership and financial instruments. Within the past several years the legislatures of numerous states have passed antitakeover laws and the Supreme Court has recently upheld the Indiana law that prohibits someone who purchases 20 percent or more of a firm's shares without permission of the board of directors from voting those shares unless such approval is granted by a majority vote of disinterested shareholders. The New York state law bars the purchaser of even 100 percent of a firm's shares from doing anything with the assets for five years unless permission of the incumbent board is obtained.

---

[22]Grossman and Hart (1980) present an extensive discussion of the free-riding problem in corporate takeovers.

[23]Mikkelson and Ruback (1985) show that average holdings for 397 initial 13d filings in 1928–80 is 20.9 percent. However, 120 of these 13ds (with average holdings of 37 percent) were filed simultaneously with announcement of a takeover. Eliminating these yields estimated average holdings for non-takeover filings of 13.9 percent.

This political activity is another example of special interests using the democratic political system to change the rules of the game to benefit themselves at the expense of society as a whole. In this case, the special interests are top level corporate managers and other groups who stand to lose from competition in the market for corporate control. If these special interests are successful, the results will be a reduction in efficiency and a significant weakening of the corporation as an organizational form.

■ *This research is supported by the Division of Research, Harvard Business School, and the Managerial Economics Research Center, University of Rochester. I am grateful for the research assistance of Michael Stevenson and the helpful comments of Sidney Davidson, Harry DeAngelo, Jay Light, Robert Kaplan, Nancy Macmillan, David Mullins, Susan Rose-Ackerman, Richard Ruback, Carl Shapiro, Timothy Taylor, Wolf Weinhold, Toni Wolcott, and, especially, Armen Alchian. The analysis here draws heavily on that in Jensen (forthcoming).*

REFERENCES

Aharony, Joseph, and Itzhak Swary, "Quarterly Dividend and Earnings Announcements and Stockholder's Returns: An Empirical Analysis," *Journal of Finance*, 1980, *35*, 1–12.

Asquith, Paul R., "Merger Bids, Uncertainty, and Stockholders Returns," *Journal of Financial Economics*, 1983, *11*, 51–83.

Asquith, Paul R., Robert F. Bruner, and David Mullins, "Merger Returns and the Form of Financing," unpublished working paper, Harvard Business School, June 1987.

Baker, George, "Compensation and Hierarchies," Harvard Business School, January, 1986.

Blume, Marshall E., and Donald B. Keim, "Risk and Return Characteristics of Lower-Grade Bonds," The Wharton School of Finance, December 1984.

Bradley, Michael, Anand Desai, and E. Han Kim, "The Rationale Behind Interfirm Tender Offers: Information or Synergy? *Journal of Financial Economics*, April 1983, *11*, 183–206.

Bradley, Michael, and Gregg Jarrell, "Evidence on Gains from Mergers and Takeovers," presented at the Conference on Takeovers and Contests for Corporate Control, Columbia University, November 1985.

Bruner, Robert F., "The Use of Excess Cash and Debt Capacity as a Motive for Merger," Colgate Darden Graduate School of Business, December 1985.

"Cash Flow: The Top 200," *Dun's Business Month*, July 1985, 44–50.

Charest, Guy, "Dividend Information, Stock Returns, and Market Efficiency—II," *Journal of Financial Economics*, 1978, *6*, 297–330.

DeAngelo, Harry, and Linda DeAngelo, "Management Buyouts of Publicly Traded Corporations," In Copeland, Thomas E., ed., *Modern Finance and Industrial Economics: Papers in Honor of J. Fred Weston*. Oxford, England: Basil Blackwell, 1986.

Donaldson, Gordon, *Managing Corporate Wealth*. New York: Praeger, 1984.

Drexel Burnham Lambert, "The Case for High Yield Bonds," company report, 1987, 4–5.

Easterbrook, F. H., "Two Agency-Cost Explanations of Dividends," *American Economic Review*, 1984a, *74*, 650–59.

Easterbrook, F. H., "Managers' Discretion and Investors' Welfare: Theories and Evidence," *Delaware Journal of Corporate Law*, 1984b, *9*, No. 3, 540–571.

Elton, E., and M. Gruber, *Modern Portfolio Theory and Investment Analysis*. New York: Wiley, 1984.

Fama, Eugene F., and Michael C. Jensen, "Organizational Forms and Investment Decisions," *Journal of Law and Economics*, 1985, *14*, 101–119.

Federal Reserve Board, "Balance Sheets, Flow of Funds." Washington, D.C.: GPO, October 1986.

Graham, Benjamin, and David L. Dodd, *Security Analysis: Principles and Technique*. New York: McGraw-Hill, 1951.

Grimm, W. T., *Mergerstat Review*. Annual editions 1984, 1985, 1986.

Grossman, S., and Oliver Hart, "Takeover Bids, the Free-Rider Problem, and the Theory of the Corporation," *Bell Journal of Economics*, Spring 1980, 42–64.

Herzel, Leo, Dale E. Colling, and James, B. Carlson, "Misunderstanding Lockups," *Securities Regulation*, September 1986, 150–180.

Hall, Bronwyn, "The Effect of Takeover Activity on Corporate Research and Development," presented at NBER Conference on the Effects of Mergers & Acquisitions, February 1987.

Holderness, Clifford G., and Dennis P. Sheehan, "Raiders or Saviors? The Evidence of Six Controversial Investors," *Journal of Financial Economics*, December 1985, *14*, 555–579.

Investor Responsibility Research Center, Inc., "Voting by Institutional Investors on Corporate Governance Questions," 1985 Proxy Season, Corporate Governance Service, 19–25.

Jacobs, E. Allen, "The Agency Cost of Corporate Control: The Petroleum Industry," Massachusetts Institute of Technology, March 1986.

Jensen, Michael C., ed., "Symposium on Some Anomalous Evidence on Market Efficiency," *Journal of Financial Economics*, June/September 1978, *6*, 95–101.

Jensen, Michael C., "Takeovers: Folklore and Science," *Harvard Business Review*, Nov.–Dec. 1984, 109–121.

Jensen, Michael C., "Agency Costs of Free Cash Flow, Corporate Finance and Takeovers," *American Economic Review*, May 1986, *76*, 323–29.

Jensen, Michael C., "The Takeover Controversy: Analysis and Evidence." In Coffee, John, Louis Lowenstein, and Susan Rose-Ackerman, eds., *Takeovers and Contests for Corporate Control.* New York: Oxford University Press, forthcoming. Also published in slightly abridged form in the *Midland Corporate Finance Journal,* Summer 1986.

Jensen, Michael C., and William H. Meckling, "Theory of the Firm: Managerial Behavior, Agency Costs and Ownership Structure," *Journal of Financial Economics,* 1976, *3,* 305–360.

Jensen, Michael C., and R. Ruback, "The Market for Corporate Control: The Scientific Evidence," *Journal of Financial Economics,* April 1983, *11,* 5–50.

Jensen, Michael C., and Clifford Smith, Jr., "Stockholder, Manager, and Creditor Interests: Applications of Agency Theory." In Altman, Edward I., and Marti G. Subrahmanyam, eds. *Recent Advances in Corporate Finance.* Homewood, Illinois: Irwin, 1985, pp. 93–131.

Kaplan, Steven, "Management Buyouts: Efficiency Gains or Value Transfers," manuscript, Harvard Business School, November 1987.

Koleman, Joe, "The Proxy Pressure on Pension Fund Managers," *Institutional Investor,* July 1985, 145–147.

Lambert, R., and D. Larcker, "Golden Parachutes, Executive Decision-Making, and Shareholder Wealth," *Journal of Accounting and Economics,* April 1985, *7,* 179–204.

Langtieg, T. C., "An Application of a Three-Factor Performance Index to Measure Stockholder Gains from Merger," *Journal of Financial Economics,* December 1978, *6,* 365–384.

Magenheim, Ellen B., and Dennis Mueller, "On Measuring the Effect of Acquisitions on Acquiring Firm Shareholders or Are Acquiring Firm Shareholders Better Off After an Acquisition Than They Were Before?" Presented at the Conference on Takeovers and Contests for Corporate Control, Columbia University, November, 1985.

Malatesta, Paul H., and Ralph A. Walkling, "The Impact of Poison Pill Securities on Stockholder Wealth," *Journal of Financial Economics,* forthcoming.

Mandelker, Gershon, "Risk and Return": The Case of Merging Firms," *Journal of Financial Economics,* December 1974, *1,* 303–336.

Mergers and Acquisitions, May—June 1987, *21,* 16.

Merton, Robert C., "On the Current State of the Stock Market Rationality Hypothesis," Working Paper No. 1717-85, Sloan School of Management, MIT, October 1985.

Mikkelson, Wayne H., and Richard S. Ruback, "An Empirical Analysis of the Interfirm Equity Investment Process," *Journal of Financial Economics,* December 1985, *14,* 523–553.

Mikkelson, Wayne H., and Richard S. Ruback, "Targeted Repurchases and Common Stock Returns," manuscript, June 1986.

Morrison, Ann, "Those Executive Bailout Deals," *Fortune,* December 13, 1982, 82–87.

Murphy, Kevin J., "Corporate Performance and Managerial Remuneration: An Empirical Analysis," *Journal of Accounting and Economics,* April 1985, *7,* 11–42.

Palepu, Krishna G., "Predicting Takeover Targets: A Methodological and Empirical Analysis," *Journal of Accounting and Economics,* 1986, *8,* 3–35.

"R&D Scoreboard: Now, R&D is Corporate America's Answer to Japan Inc.," *Business Week,* June 23, 1986.

"R&D Scoreboard: Reagan & Foreign Rivalry Light a Fire Under Spending," *Business Week,* July 8, 1985, 86–87.

"R&D Scoreboard: Research Spending is Building Up to a Letdown," *Business Week,* June 23, 1987, 139–140.

Roll, Richard, "Empirical Evidence on Takeover Activity and Shareholder Wealth." In Coffee, John, Louis Lowenstein, and Susan Rose-Ackerman, eds., *Takeovers and Contests for Corporate Control,* New York: Oxford University Press, forthcoming.

Rozeff, M., "Growth, Beta and Agency Costs as Determinants of Dividend Payout Ratios," *Journal of Financial Research,* 1982, *5,* 249–59.

Ryngaert, Michael, "The Effect of Poison Pill Securities on Shareholder Wealth," *Journal of Financial Economics,* forthcoming.

Schipper, Katherine, and Abbie Smith, "Corporate Income Tax Effects of Management Buyouts," unpublished manuscript, University of Chicago, July 1986.

Shiller, Robert J., "Do Stock Prices Move Too Much to be Justified By Subsequent Changes in Dividends?" *American Economic Review,* 1981, 421–36.

Smith, Clifford W., Jr., and Jerold B. Warner, "On Financial Contracting: An Analysis of Bond Covenants," *Journal of Financial Economics,* 1979, *7,* 117–161.

Taggart, Robert A., "The Growth of the 'Junk' Bond Market and Its Role in Financing Takeovers," manuscript, Boston University, September 1986.

Wansley, James W. and A. Fayez, "Determinants of Return to Security Holders from Mergers," manuscript, Louisiana State University, 1986.

Wansley, James W., William R. Lane, and Ho C. Yang, "Abnormal Returns to Acquired Firms by Type of Acquisition and Method of Payment," *Financial Management,* Autumn 1983, *12,* No. 3, 16–22.

Wansley, James W., William R. Lane, and Ho C. Yang, "Gains to Acquiring Firms in Cash and Securities Transactions," *Financial Review,* forthcoming.

Weston, J. Fred., and Thomas E. Copeland, *Managerial Finance.* Chicago: Dryden Press, 1986, p. 649.

THE STATE OF U.S. CORPORATE GOVERNANCE: WHAT'S RIGHT AND WHAT'S WRONG?

Bengt Holmstrom
Steven N. Kaplan

ABSTRACT

The U.S. corporate governance system has recently been heavily criticized, largely as a result of failures at Enron, WorldCom, Tyco and some other prominent companies. Those failures and criticisms, in turn, have served as catalysts for legislative change (Sarbanes-Oxley Act of 2002) and regulatory change (new governance guidelines from the NYSE and NASDAQ). In this paper, we consider two questions. First, is it clear that the U.S. system has performed that poorly; is it really that bad? Second, will the changes lead to an improved U.S. corporate governance system? We first note that the broad evidence is not consistent with a failed U.S. system. The U.S. economy and stock market have performed well both on an absolute basis and relative to other countries over the past two decades. And the U.S. stock market has continued to outperform other broad indices since the scandals broke. Our interpretation of the evidence is that while parts of the U.S. corporate governance system failed under the exceptional strain of the 1990s, the overall system, which includes oversight by the public and the government, reacted quickly to address the problems. We then consider the effects that the legislative, regulatory, and market responses are likely to have in the near future. Our assessment is that they are likely to make a good system better, though there is a danger of overreacting to extreme events.

Bengt Holmstrom
Department of Economics
MIT
E52-271d
Cambridge, MA 02139
and NBER
bengt@mit.edu

Steven N. Kaplan
Graduate School of Business
The University of Chicago
1101 East 58th Street
Chicago, IL 60637
and NBER
steven.kaplan@gsb.uchicago.edu

To a casual observer, the United States corporate governance system must seem **to be** in terrible shape. The business press has focused relentlessly on the corporate board and governance failures at Enron, WorldCom, Tyco, Adelphia, Global Crossing, and others. Top executive compensation is also routinely criticized as excessive by the press, academics, and even top Federal Reserve officials.[1] These failures and concerns, in turn, have served as catalysts for legislative change—in the form of the Sarbanes-Oxley Act of 2002—and regulatory change, including new governance guidelines from the NYSE and NASDAQ.

---

[1]For example, see Marco Becht, Patrick Bolton, and Ailsa Roell, "Corporate Governance and Control," in *Handbook of Economics and Finance* (G. Constantinides, M. Harris, and R. Stulz, eds.). North Holland (2002), "CEOs Are Overpaid, Says Fed Banker," *The Washington Post*, September 11, 2002, and "After 10 Years, Corporate Oversight Is Still Dismal," by Claudia Deutsch, *The New York Times*, January 26, 2003.

The turmoil and the responses to it suggest two important questions that we attempt to answer in this article. First, has the U.S. corporate governance system performed that poorly—is it really that bad? Second, will the proposed changes lead to a more effective system?

In addressing the first question, we begin by examining two broad measures of economic performance for evidence of failure of the U.S. system. Despite the alleged flaws in its governance system, the U.S. economy has performed very well, both on an absolute basis and particularly relative to other countries. U.S. productivity gains in the past decade have been exceptional, and the U.S. stock market has consistently outperformed other world indices over the last two decades, including the period since the scandals broke. In other words, the broad evidence is not consistent with a failed U.S. system. If anything, it suggests a system that is well above average.

Next, we discuss how important aspects of the U.S. corporate governance system have evolved over the last two decades and the implications of those changes. Again, contrary to the popular impression, the major changes in U.S. corporate governance in the past 20 years—notably, the dramatic increase in equity-based pay and the institutionalization of U.S. shareholders—appear to have been positive overall. As we discuss below, such changes played a central role in the highly productive restructuring of U.S. corporations that took place during the 1980s and 1990s. But the changes did have an unfortunate side effect. Besides spurring productivity improvements, the rise of equity-based pay—particularly the explosion of stock options—and the run-up in stock prices in the late '90s created incentives for the shortsighted and at times illegal managerial behavior that has attracted so much criticism. Our view, however, is that the costs associated with such incentives and behavior have been far outweighed by the benefits.

Having addressed where the U.S. system is today and how it got there, we finally consider the probable near-term effects of the legislative, regulatory, and market responses to the perceived governance "problem." We conclude that the current changes are likely to make a good U.S. system a better one, although not without imposing some unnecessary costs. In fact, the greatest risk now facing the U.S. corporate governance system is the possibility of overregulation.

How Bad is U.S. Corporate Governance?

Given the volume and intensity of criticism of U.S. corporate governance, one would think that the U.S. stock market must have performed quite badly, particularly since the scandals broke in 2001. But, the data summarized in Table 1 indicate otherwise. Table 1 reports the total returns (measured in dollars) to the Morgan Stanley Capital International indices for the aggregate U.S., European, and Pacific stock markets over five different time periods through the end of 2002. Although the U.S. stock market has had negative returns over the last several years, it has performed well relative to other stock markets, both recently and over the longer term. In fact, the U.S. market has generated returns at least as high as those of the European and Pacific markets during each of the five time periods considered—since 2001, since 1997, since 1992, since 1987, and since 1982. The returns to the U.S. stock market also compare favorably to the returns of the stock markets of the larger individual countries (including France, Germany, Great Britain, and Japan) that make up the indices.

Because many factors affect stock returns, it would be inappropriate to claim that superior U.S. corporate governance explains the differences in returns. We can conclude, however, that whatever the shortcomings of the U.S. system, they have not been sufficiently great to prevent the stock returns of U.S. companies from outperforming those of the rest of the world.

It is worth pointing out two additional implications of the stock performance results. First, the returns to U.S. stocks have been at least as large as the returns to European and Pacific stocks since 2001, the period in which the U.S. corporate governance scandals first emerged. One possible explanation is that the effects of the governance scandals on U.S. stock values have not been particularly large relative to other factors that have weighed on most national economies. Another possibility is that while there may be some problems with the U.S. corporate governance system, the problems confronting the governance systems of other nations are even worse. But in our view, the most plausible explanation is that while parts of the U.S. system failed under the exceptional strain of the 1990s' boom market, the damage was limited because the overall system reacted quickly to address the problems.

The second important point to keep in mind about stock returns is that they reflect publicly available information about executive compensation. Returns, therefore, are measured *net* of executive compensation payments. The fact that the shareholders of U.S. companies earned higher returns *even after* payments to management does not support the claim that the U.S. executive pay system is designed inefficiently; if anything, shareholders appear better off with the U.S. system of executive pay than with the systems that prevail in other countries. As we discuss later, however, the higher U.S. returns do not rule out the possibility that some top U.S. executives are paid more than is necessary for incentive purposes and that our incentive pay system can be improved.

Overall country productivity provides another broad measure of performance. Again, one might expect a less effective corporate governance system to lead to lower productivity growth. Table 2 presents calculations of the percentage change in GDP per capita for developed countries since 1982. The results do not suggest the presence of an ineffective U.S. governance system. From the beginning of 1992 to the end of 2000,[2] growth in GDP per capita was greater in the U.S. than in France, Germany, Great Britain, or Japan. And given the strong U.S. productivity numbers through the recent downturn, this gap has probably widened since then.

Again, these results do not necessarily demonstrate that the U.S. corporate governance system is the principal cause of the larger productivity improvements. Many other forces operate at the same time. The results do suggest, however, that any deficiencies in the U.S. corporate governance system have not prevented the U.S. economy from outperforming its global competitors.

CHANGES IN U.S. CORPORATE GOVERNANCE OVER THE LAST 20 YEARS[3]

Corporate governance in the U.S. has changed dramatically since 1980. As a number of business and finance scholars have pointed out, the corporate governance structures in place before the 1980s gave the managers of large public U.S. corporations little reason to make shareholder interests their primary focus. Before 1980, corporate managements tended to think of themselves as representing not the shareholders, but rather "the corporation." In this view, the goal of the firm was not to maximize shareholder wealth, but to ensure the growth (or at least the stability) of the enterprise by "balancing" the claims of all important corporate "stakeholders"—employees, suppliers, and local communities, as well as shareholders.[4]

The external governance mechanisms available to dissatisfied shareholders were seldom used. Raiders and hostile takeovers were relatively uncommon. Proxy fights were rare and didn't have much chance of succeeding. And corporate boards tended to be cozy with and dominated by management, making board oversight weak.

Internal incentives from management ownership of stock and options were also modest. For example, in 1980 only 20% of the compensation of U.S. CEOs was tied to stock market performance.[5] Long-term performance plans were widely used, but they were typically based on accounting measures like sales growth and earnings per share that tied managerial incentives less directly, and sometimes not at all, to shareholder value.

Partly in response to the neglect of shareholders, the 1980s ushered in a large wave of takeover and restructuring activity. This activity was distinguished by its use of hostility and aggressive leverage. The 1980s saw the emergence of the corporate raider and hostile takeovers.

---

[2]This is the most recent period for which data are available.

[3]This section summarizes some of the arguments in Bengt Holmstrom and Steven Kaplan, "Corporate Governance and Takeovers in the U.S.: Making Sense of the '80s and '90s," *Journal of Economic Perspectives*, pp. 121–144 (Spring 2001) and Steven Kaplan, "The Evolution of U.S. Corporate Governance: We Are All Henry Kravis Now," *Journal of Private Equity*, pp. 7–14 (1997).

[4]See Gordon Donaldson and Jay Lorsch, *Decision Making at the Top* (Basic Books, New York, 1983), and Michael Jensen, "The Modern Industrial Revolution," *Journal of Finance*, pp. 831–880 (1993).

[5]See Brian Hall and Jeffrey Liebman, "Are CEOs Really Paid like Bureaucrats?" *Quarterly Journal of Economics*, 112, pp. 653–691 (1998).

Raiders like Carl Icahn and T. Boone Pickens became household names. Nearly half of all major U.S. corporations received a takeover offer in the 1980s—and many companies that were not taken over responded to hostile pressure with internal restructurings that made themselves less attractive targets.[6]

The use of debt financing by U.S. companies was so extensive that, from 1984 to 1990, more than $500 billion of equity was retired (net of new equity issuances), as many firms repurchased their own shares, borrowed to finance takeovers, or were taken private in leveraged buyouts (LBOs). As a result, corporate leverage ratios increased substantially. Leveraged buyouts were extreme in this respect, with debt levels typically exceeding 80% of total capital.

In the 1990s, the pattern of corporate governance activity changed again. After a steep but brief drop in merger activity around 1990, takeovers rebounded to the levels of the 1980s. Hostility and leverage, however, declined substantially. At the same time, other corporate governance mechanisms began to play a larger role, particularly executive stock options and the greater involvement of boards of directors and shareholders.

The preponderance of the evidence is consistent with an overall explanation as follows: In the early 1980s, the wedge between actual and potential corporate performance became increasingly apparent. In some cases, changes in markets, technology, or regulation led to a large amount of excess capacity—for example, in the oil and tire industries. In others, it became apparent that diversification strategies carried out in the late '60s and '70s were underperforming.[7] The top managers of such companies, however, were slow to respond to opportunities to increase value. As mentioned above, limited ownership of stock and options gave managers little monetary incentive to make major changes that might weaken their "partnership" with other corporate stakeholders. But perhaps equally important, some corporate leaders persisted in their conviction that growth and stability were the "right" corporate goals and they simply refused to believe what the capital markets were telling them. This appears to have been true, for example, of the U.S. oil industry in the early 1980s, when oil companies traded below the value of their oil holdings because of industry-wide overinvestment in exploration.

At the same time many U.S. companies were failing to maximize value, the U.S. capital markets were becoming more powerful because of increased stock ownership by large institutions. It was the potential for improved corporate performance combined with the increased ownership of institutional investors that gave birth to the takeovers, junk bonds, and LBOs of the 1980s. In some cases, the capital markets reversed ill-advised diversification through "bust-up" transactions (such as KKR's acquisition of Beatrice Foods in 1986). In other cases, the financial markets effectively forced managers to eliminate excess capacity (as in Chevron's leveraged acquisition of Gulf Oil in 1984). More generally, the capital markets disciplined managers who had ignored shareholders for the benefit of themselves and other stakeholders. As we discuss below, the incentive and governance features of LBOs are particularly representative of the discipline that the capital markets imposed.

The initial response of U.S. executives was to fight takeovers with legal maneuvers and to attempt to enlist political and popular support against corporate raiders. Over time, these efforts met with some legislative, regulatory, and judicial success. As a result, hostile takeovers became far more costly in the 1990s than in the previous decade.

But the accomplishments of the 1980s were by no means forgotten. By the 1990s U.S. managers, boards, and institutional shareholders had seen what LBOs and other market-driven restructurings could do. With the implicit assent of institutional investors, boards substantially increased the use of stock option plans that allowed managers to share in the value created by restructuring their own companies. Shareholder value thus became an ally rather than a threat.

This general embrace of shareholder value helps to explain why restructurings continued at a high rate in the 1990s, but for the most part on amicable terms. There was also less of a need for high leverage because deals could now be paid for with stock without raising investors' concerns that managers would pursue their own objectives at the expense of shareholders.

---

[6]See Mark Mitchell and Harold Mulherin, "The Impact of Industry Shocks on Takeover and Restructuring Activity," *Journal of Financial Economics*, pp. 193–229 (1996).

[7]See Jensen (1993), cited earlier, and Andrei Shleifer and Robert Vishny, "The Takeover Wave of the 1980s," *Science*, 249, August 17, pp. 745–749 (1990).

The merger wave of the 1990s also appears to have had a somewhat different purpose than the wave of the 1980s, representing a different stage in the overall restructuring process. The deals of the 1980s were more of a bust-up wave whose main effect was to force corporate assets out of the hands of managers who could not or would not use them efficiently. The transactions of the 1990s, by contrast, had more of a "build-up" effect in which assets were reconfigured to take advantage of growth opportunities in new technologies and markets. This logic also fits with the increased use of equity rather than debt in funding the deals of the 1990s.

The move toward shareholder value and increased capital market influence has also been apparent in the way corporations have reorganized themselves. For example, there has been a broad trend toward decentralization. Large companies have been working hard to become more nimble and to find ways to offer employees higher-powered incentives. At the same time, external capital markets have taken on a larger role in capital reallocation, as evidenced by the large volume of mergers and divestitures throughout the '90s. During the same period, the amounts of funds raised and invested by U.S. venture capitalists—who help perform the key economic function of transferring funds from mature to new high-growth industries—also increased by an order of magnitude over the 1990s.[8]

In sum, while corporate managers still reallocate vast amounts of resources in the economy through internal capital and labor markets, the boundary between markets and managers appears to have shifted. As managers have ceded authority to the markets, the scope and independence of their decision-making have narrowed.

We now focus more specifically on changes in three key elements of the U.S. (and indeed any) corporate governance system: executive compensation, shareholders, and boards of directors.

Changes in executive compensation

The total pay of top U.S. executives, particularly option-based compensation, has increased substantially over the last two decades. For example, a study published in the late '90s reported that during the 15-year period from 1980 to 1994, the average compensation of CEOs of large U.S. companies tripled in real terms. The study also concluded that the average annual CEO option grant (valued at issuance) increased roughly sevenfold and, as a result, equity-based compensation in 1994 made up almost 50% of total CEO compensation (up from less than 20% in 1980).[9] Moreover, as reported in a more recent study, this trend continued from 1994 to 2001, with CEO pay more than doubling and option-based compensation increasing at an even faster rate.[10]

Overall, then, CEO compensation appears to have increased by a factor of six over the last two decades, with a disproportionate increase in equity-based compensation. The effect of the increase in equity-based compensation has been to increase CEO pay-to-performance sensitivities by a factor of more than ten times from 1980 to 1999.[11]

These increases in executive compensation, particularly options, have generated enormous controversy. The recent scandals and stock market declines have led some observers to argue that such increases represent unmerited transfers of shareholder wealth to top executives with limited if any beneficial incentive effects. For example, one recent survey of corporate governance concludes: "It is widely recognized . . . that these options are at best an inefficient financial incentive and at worst create new incentive or conflict-of-interest problems of their own."[12]

---

[8] See Raghu Rajan and Julie Wulf, "The Flattening Firm," working paper, University of Chicago (2002), and Paul Gompers and Josh Lerner, "The Venture Capital Revolution," *Journal of Economic Perspectives*, pp. 145–168 (2001).

[9] Hall and Liebman (1998), cited earlier.

[10] See Brian Hall and Kevin Murphy, "Stock Options for Undiversified Executives," *Journal of Accounting and Economics*, pp. 3–42 (2002) and Brian Hall, "Six Challenges in Designing Equity-Based Pay," in this issue of the *JACF*.

[11] The levels of executive compensation and managerial equity ownership appear to be high not only relative to 1980, but also relative to earlier periods. Holderness, Kroszner, and Sheehan compare equity ownership by officers and directors in 1935 and 1995 and find that equity ownership was substantially greater in 1995 than in 1935. See Cliff Holderness, Randall Kroszner, and Dennis Sheehan, "Were the Good Old That Good? Changes in Managerial Stock Ownership Since the Great Depression," *Journal of Finance*, pp. 435–470 (1999).

[12] See Marco Becht, Patrick Bolton, and Ailsa Roell, (2002), *ibid*. See also, Lucian Bebchuk, Jesse Fried, and David Walker, "Managerial Power and Rent Extraction in the Design of Executive Compensation," University of Chicago *Law Review*, pp. 751–846 (2002).

There are several reasons to be skeptical of these conclusions. First, as we have already pointed out, the performance of the U.S. stock market and the strong growth in U.S. productivity provide no support for such arguments.

Second, the primary effect of the large shift to equity-based compensation has been to align the interests of CEOs and their management teams with shareholders' interests to a much greater extent than in the past. Large stock option grants fundamentally changed the mind-set of CEOs and made them much more receptive to value-increasing transactions. The tenfold increase in pay-for-performance sensitivities implies that a one dollar increase in a company's stock price was ten times more valuable to a CEO at the end of the 1990s than at the beginning of the 1980s. As we noted earlier, this shift played a significant role in the continued restructuring of corporations in the 1990s.[13] It also helps explain the 1997 decision of the Business Roundtable—a group of 200 CEOs of the largest American companies—to change its position on business objectives (after years of opposition and ambivalence to shareholder value) to read "the paramount duty of management and the board is to the shareholder and not to . . . other stakeholders."

A third reason to be skeptical of the criticism of U.S. top executive pay practices is that both buyout investors and venture capital investors have made, and continue to make, substantial use of equity-based and option compensation in the firms they invest in. A 1989 study by one of the authors reported that the CEOs of companies taken private in LBOs increased their ownership stake by more than a factor of four, from an average of 1.4% before the LBO to 6.4% after. The study also found that management teams as a whole typically obtained 10% to 20% of the post-buyout equity.[14] More recent research and anecdotal evidence suggest that such levels of managerial equity ownership are still typical in today's buyout transactions.[15]

This feature of LBOs is particularly notable. LBO sponsor firms such as KKR, Texas Pacific Group, and Thomas Lee typically buy majority control of the companies they invest in through the partnerships that the sponsors manage. The individual partners of the LBO sponsors have strong incentives to make profitable investments since the sponsors typically receive 20% of the profits of a particular buyout partnership, and the sponsors' ability to raise other funds is strongly related to the performance of their existing investments.[16] And the fact that such sponsors also insist on providing the managers of their companies with high-powered incentives suggests that incentives have been a critical ingredient in the success of LBOs.

Two other aspects of compensation contracts designed by LBO sponsors for the top executives of their portfolio companies are worth mentioning. First, the equity and options held by those top executives are typically illiquid—usually by necessity because most of the companies are private—unless and until the company has clearly succeeded through an IPO or a sale to another company. This means that top management cannot trade in and out of the stock (nor can it easily hedge its positions). Second, neither LBO sponsors nor venture capitalists typically index the executive compensation contracts they employ to industry performance or market performance. If nonindexed options and equity grants were so inefficient, as critics of executive compensation have argued, we would expect to see more indexing of private equity contracts.

Unfortunately, while the greater use of stock-based compensation has likely been a positive development overall, critics of the U.S. governance system are correct in pointing out that higher-powered incentives have not come without costs.[17]

---

[13]For additional evidence consistent with this conclusion, see John Core and David Larcker, "Performance Consequences of Mandatory Increases in Executive Stock Ownership," *Journal of Financial Economics* (2002), who find that option grants or increases in equity ownership are related to improvements in stock and accounting performance.

[14]See Steven Kaplan, "The Effects of Management Buyouts on Operations and Value," *Journal of Financial Economics*, pp. 217–254 (1989).

[15]P. Rogers, T. Holland, and D. Haas, "Value Acceleration: Lessons from Private-Equity Masters," *Harvard Business Review*, June (2002).

[16]See Steven Kaplan and Antoinette Schoar, "Private Equity Returns: Persistence and Capital Flows," working paper, University of Chicago, December (2002).

[17]Other critiques are offered in Lucien Bebchuk, Jesse Fried, and David Walker, "Managerial Power and Rent Extraction in the Design of Executive Compensation," *University of Chicago Law Review* 69 (2002), pp. 751–846, Becht, Bolton, and Roell, (2002) *ibid.*, Brian Hall "Equity-Pay Design for Executives," working paper, Harvard Business School (2002), and Tod Perry and Marc Zenner "CEO Compensation In The 1990s: Shareholder Alignment Or Shareholder Expropriation?" *Wake Forest Law Review* (2001).

First, as executive stock and option ownership have increased, so has the incentive to manage and manipulate accounting numbers in order to inflate stock market values and sell shares at those inflated values.[18] This arguably was important in the cases of Global Crossing and WorldCom, among others.

Second, and related to the first, much of the compensation of top U.S. executives is fairly liquid—and, as we argue below, considerably more liquid than shareholders would like it to be. Unlike LBO sponsors, boards do not put strong restrictions on the ability of top executives to unwind their equity-based compensation by exercising options, selling shares, or using derivatives to hedge their positions. And finding a workable solution to the problem of optimal liquidity for top executive compensation is an important challenge faced by today's boards.

Third, most options are issued at the money because accounting rules do not require the cost of such options to be expensed. It is plausible that because the cost of the options does not appear as an expense, some boards of directors underestimate the options' cost. It is undeniable that the size of some of the option grants has been far greater than what is necessary to retain and motivate the CEOs. In 2001, for example, ten most highly rewarded CEOs in the S&P 500 were granted option packages with an estimated average value (at time of grant) of $170 million per person. Even if some of these grants represent multiyear awards, the amounts are still staggering. It is particularly disconcerting that among the executives receiving the largest grants in the past three years, several already owned large amounts of stock, including Larry Ellison of Oracle, Tom Siebel of Siebel Systems, and Steve Jobs of Apple. It is hard to argue that these people need stronger shareholder incentives. An obvious explanation is that they have been able to use their positions of power to command excessive awards.

Even so, it would be a mistake to condemn the entire system based on a few cases. That such cases are far from representative can be seen from the pronounced skew in the distribution of CEO incomes. In 2001, for example, the same year the top ten U.S. CEOs received average option grants of $170 million, the median value of total compensation for CEOs of S&P 500 companies was about $7 million. Thus, U.S. executive pay may not be quite the runaway train that has been portrayed in the press.[19]

Changes in shareholders

As mentioned above, the composition of U.S. shareholders also has changed significantly over the past two decades. Large institutional investors own an increasingly large share of the overall stock market. For example, from 1980 to 1996, large institutional investors nearly doubled their share of ownership of U.S. corporations from less than 30% to more than 50%. (Conversely, individual ownership declined from 70% in 1970 to 60% in 1980 and to 48% in 1994.[20])

There are at least two reasons public company shareholders are likely to monitor management more effectively today than in the 1980s. First, the large increase in the shareholdings of institutional investors means that professional investors—who have strong incentives to generate greater stock returns and are presumably more sophisticated—own an increasingly large fraction of U.S. corporations.

Second, in 1992 the SEC substantially reduced the costs to shareholders of challenging management teams. Under the old rules, a shareholder had to file a detailed proxy statement with the SEC before talking to more than ten other shareholders. Under the new rules, shareholders can essentially communicate at any time and in any way as long as they send a copy of the substance of the communication to the SEC afterward. The rule change has lowered the cost of coordinating shareholder actions and blocking management proposals. (Not surprisingly, the Business Roundtable and other management organizations were extremely hostile to this rule change when it was proposed.)

---

[18]See Jeremy Stein "Efficient Capital Markets, Inefficient Firms: A Model of Myopic Corporate Behavior," *Quarterly Journal of Economics*, Vol. 104, pp. 655–669 (1989) for a model explaining this behavior. See also Joseph Fuller and Michael Jensen, "Just Say No to Wall Street," *Journal of Applied Corporate Finance*, Vol. 14 No. 4 (2002).

[19]A part of the problem is that the press has traditionally reported the value of exercised options instead of the value of options at the time they have been granted. This is changing, too.

[20]See Paul Gompers and Andrew Metrick, "Institutional Investors and Equity Prices," *Quarterly Journal of Economics* (2001), and James Poterba and Andrew Samwick, "Stock Ownership Patterns, Stock Market Fluctuations, and Consumption," Brookings Papers on Economic Activity, pp. 295–357 (1995).

Consistent with these two changes, shareholder activism has increased in the U.S. since the late 1980s. The evidence on the impact of such activism, however, is mixed. For example, a 1998 summary of the results of 20 empirical studies of the effects of formal shareholder proposals and private negotiations with managements reported evidence of small or no effects on shareholder value.[21] When interpreting such evidence, however, it is important to keep in mind the difficulty of measuring the extent and effects of shareholder activity, in part because so much of this activity takes place behind the scenes and is not reported. And the fact that a recent study reported that stock returns over the period 1980–1996 were higher for companies with greater institutional ownership suggests that our large institutions may indeed be playing a valuable monitoring role—one that translates into higher stock prices.[22]

Changes in boards of directors

In an influential study of U.S. corporate boards in the second half of the 1980s, Jay Lorsch and Elizabeth MacIver pointed out a number of deficiencies and offered several recommendations. Chief among them were the following: (1) board selection by a nominating committee rather than the CEO; (2) more equity compensation for directors; and (3) more director control of board meetings through appointment of a lead director or outside chairman, annual CEO reviews, and regular sessions with outside directors only ("executive sessions").[23]

Since the publication of that study in 1989, the boards of U.S. companies have made progress in implementing all three of these recommendations. U.S. companies have significantly expanded the use of nominating committees and lead directors. Executive sessions are increasingly common (although, as suggested below, not as common as directors would like). Boards of U.S. companies now include a larger percentage of independent and outside directors, and have become somewhat smaller over time (smaller boards are thought to be more effective in disciplining CEOs and tend to be associated with higher valuations).[24] Also encouraging, directors today receive a significantly larger amount of their total compensation in the form of stock or options. For example, one study reported that stock-based directors' compensation increased from 25% in 1992 to 39% in 1995, and that trend has since continued.[25]

The CEO turnover process—one of the most widely used measures of the effectiveness of a governance system—suggests that the CEO labor market has become broader and, arguably, more efficient. One recent study of CEO turnover for large companies from 1971 to 1994 found a marked increase in both forced CEO departures and the hiring of new CEOs from outside the company. Within the study, the incidence of forced turnovers and outside succession was highest from 1989 to 1994,[26] a trend that also appears to have continued. The same study reported that CEO turnover was more sensitive to poor performance—as measured by reductions in operating income—during the 1989–1994 period than in earlier years.[27, 28]

On the negative side, however, antitakeover measures such as poison pills and staggered boards have increased substantially in the past two decades. And recent research finds that over the 1990s, companies with

---

[21]Jonathan Karpoff, "The Impact of Shareholder Activism on Target Companies: A Survey of Empirical Findings," Working paper, University of Washington (1998).

[22]Paul Gompers and Andrew Metrick, "Institutional Investors and Equity Prices," *Quarterly Journal of Economics*, Vol. 116 (1), 2001, pp. 229–260.

[23]Jay Lorsch and Elizabeth MacIver, *Pawns or Potentates*. Harvard Business School Press (1989).

[24]See David Yermack, "Higher Market Valuation of Companies with a Small Board of Directors," *Journal of Financial Economics*, Vol. 40, 1996, pp. 185–202.

[25]For a summary of these changes, see Ben Hermalin and Michael Weisbach, "Boards of Directors as an Endogenously Determined Institution: A Survey of the Economic Literature," *Economic Policy Review* (2003).

[26]See M. Huson, Robert Parrino, and Laura Starks, "Internal Monitoring Mechanisms and CEO Turnover: A Long-Term Perspective," *Journal of Finance*, pp. 2,265–2,297 (2001).

[27]On the other hand, Murphy (1999) finds that CEO turnover is less sensitive to industry-adjusted stock performance from 1990 to 1995 than in earlier years. Kevin J. Murphy, "Executive Compensation." In O. Ashenfelter and D. Card (eds.), *Handbook of Labor Economics*. North Holland, pp. 2,485–2, 525 (1999).

[28]Rakesh Khurana in *Searching for a Corporate Savior: The Irrational Quest for Charismatic CEOs*, Princeton University Press (2002) has argued that the CEO labor market is flawed because it is overly focused on outsider, charismatic CEOs. The operating performance evidence in Rakesh Khurana and Nitin Nohria, "The Effects of CEO Turnover in Large Industrial Corporations: A Study of the *Fortune* 200 from 1978–1993," Harvard Business School (1997), however, is not consistent with such a conclusion.

a high level of anti-shareholder provisions experienced substantially lower returns than firms with a low level of such provisions.[29]

Despite the improvements noted above, the recent events at companies like Enron, Tyco, and WorldCom suggest that the boards of U.S. companies continue to exhibit less than the optimal amount of independence and oversight. The Senate report on Enron's board is particularly critical in this respect. When a company is not doing well, everyone pays close attention—lenders and investors as well as board members. But when a company appears to be doing well, as was the case with both Enron and Tyco, investors and the board are likely to be less critical.

A recent survey of more than 2,000 directors by Korn Ferry in early 2002 (and thus before the passage of Sarbanes-Oxley and the issuance of the new NYSE and NASDAQ regulations) is very interesting in this regard. The directors who responded to the survey consistently favored more monitoring than was the practice on the boards on which they served. For example, although 71% of the directors said they believed boards should hold executive sessions without the CEO, only 45% said their boards actually did so. And whereas almost 60% felt their boards should have a lead director, only 37% reported that their boards had one.

Our bottom line on boards, then, is that the structure and operating procedures of U.S. corporate boards have improved since the 1980s, but they are still far from perfect.

International developments

Indirect evidence of the effectiveness of the U.S. governance system is provided by changes in corporate governance in other countries. In recent years, as the forces of deregulation, globalization, and information technology have continued to sweep across the world economy, other countries have begun to move toward the U.S. model. Traditionally, European and Japanese firms have reallocated capital from sunset industries to sunrise industries mainly through internal diversification. External market interventions of the sort seen in the U.S. were almost unheard of. In the late 1990s, however, Europe experienced a sudden rise in hostile takeovers. In 1999 alone, 34 listed companies in Continental Europe received hostile bids, representing a total value of $406 billion (as compared to 52 bids for just $69 billion over the entire period 1990–1998).[30] These transactions included Vodafone's bid for Mannesmann, TotalFina's bid for Elf Aquitaine, and Olivetti's bid for Telecom Italia.

Shareholder activism has also been on the rise, with strong support from American institutional investors. For example, Telecom Italia's attempt to split off its wireless unit (at an unacceptable price) was blocked when TIAA-CREF put pressure on the Italian government. In France, shareholder activists managed to defeat a poison-pill proposal by Rhone-Poulenc. European universal banks also have begun to pay more attention to the value of their financial stakes than to their positions of power. These actions appear to have been very much influenced by the U.S. model of market intervention and by the fact that more than $1 trillion of U.S. funds have been invested in Western Europe in the 1980s and 1990s.

Another way in which companies can make use of the market to reallocate capital more effectively is to repurchase their own shares. In the last several years, Japan, France, Germany, and several other European countries have relaxed prohibitions or restrictions on share repurchases, and companies in those countries have responded by buying back increasing numbers of shares. Finally, the use of stock options for executives and boards is increasing around the world. Japan recently eliminated a substantial tax penalty on executive stock options, and a 2002 study based on Towers Perrin's yearly surveys reported that the rate of adoption of stock options in Europe has matched that of the U.S. in the 1990s.[31]

In sum, the conventional wisdom on corporate governance has changed dramatically since the 1970s and early 1980s, when the U.S. market-based system was subjected to heavy criticism and the bank-centered systems of

---

[29]Paul Gompers, Joy Ishi, and Andrew Metrick, "Corporate Governance and Equity Prices," Working Paper 8,449, NBER, 2001.
[30]Rick Escherich and Paul Gibbs, Global Mergers and Acquisitions Review, JP Morgan (2002 April).
[31]Brian Hall, "Incentive Strategy II: Executive Compensation and Ownership Structure," Harvard Business School, Teaching Note N9-902-134 (2002).

Japan and Germany were held up as models.[32] Since the mid-1980s, the American style of corporate governance has reinvented itself, and the rest of the world seems to be following the U.S. lead.

RECENT REGULATORY CHANGES

The Sarbanes-Oxley Act (SOX), which was enacted in the summer of 2002, mandated a number of changes in corporate governance for publicly traded companies. The NYSE and NASDAQ also mandated corporate governance changes for firms listed on their respective exchanges. In this section, we discuss the likely effect of these changes on U.S. corporate governance.

Sarbanes-Oxley

SOX mandated changes that will affect executive compensation, shareholder monitoring, and, particularly, board monitoring.

One provision requires the CEO and CFO to disgorge any profits from bonuses and stock sales during the 12-month period that follows a financial report that is subsequently restated because of "misconduct." (We assume this provision also covers any hedging transactions the CEO or CFO undertakes.) Until "misconduct" is clearly defined, this provision increases the risk to a CEO or CFO of selling a large amount of stock or options in any one year while still in office. Some CEOs and CFOs will choose to wait until they are no longer in those positions before selling equity or exercising options. To the extent CEOs and CFOs behave this way, their equity holdings become less liquid and they will care less about short-term stock price movements. This would be a positive change. In addition, the rule will act as a deterrent to negligent or deliberate misreporting.[33]

Shareholder-related provisions include changes in restrictions on insider trading regulation and enhanced financial disclosure. Executives will now have to report sales or purchases of company stock within two days rather than the current ten days, which will have the effect of making executive shares somewhat less liquid. SOX also requires more detailed disclosure of off-balance-sheet financings and special purpose entities, which should make it more difficult for companies to manipulate their financial statements in a way that boosts the current stock price.

SOX also includes a number of provisions meant to improve board monitoring. These focus largely on increasing the power, responsibility, and independence of the audit committee. SOX requires that the audit committee hire the outside auditor and that the committee consist entirely of directors with no other financial relationship with the company.

Finally, SOX increases management's and the board's responsibility for financial reporting and the criminal penalties for misreporting. The increased responsibility and penalties have clearly increased the amount of time that executives of all companies must spend on accounting matters. For companies that are already well-governed, that extra time is unnecessary and therefore costly. At least initially, some of the extra time meeting SOX's requirements will be time that could have been devoted to discussing strategy or managing the business. SOX has also caused companies to increase their use of outside accountants and lawyers. But part of the resulting increase in costs is likely to be recouped in the form of valuable new information not previously available to some CEOs, CFOs, and boards. Furthermore, the additional time and costs should decline as companies become more efficient at complying with SOX.

So, what has the new legislation really accomplished? The provisions of SOX deal both directly and indirectly with some of the deficiencies of U.S. corporate governance. But many U.S. companies would have instituted some of these changes anyway. The law already punished fraudulent reporting, including the misreporting

---

[32]See for example Michael Porter, "Capital Disadvantage: America's Failing Capital Investment System," *Harvard Business Review*, September-October (1992), pp. 65–83.

[33]This provision could lead to a modest substitution of cash compensation for equity-based compensation. However, this would have to be accomplished entirely through salary increases because cash bonuses are also subject to the same disgorgement provisions.

uncovered in Enron, Tyco and WorldCom. Furthermore, the Enron scandal brought the costs of such misreporting into sharp focus before the passage of SOX. No CEO wants to be the CEO of the next Enron. And no board member wants to be on the board of the next Enron.

There are two potentially significant dangers associated with SOX. First, the ambiguity in some of the provisions, particularly those that overlap with and even contradict aspects of state corporate law, will almost certainly invite aggressive litigation. The fear of such litigation will lead CEOs and CFOs to direct corporate resources to protect themselves against potential lawsuits. Fear of litigation is also making it harder to attract qualified board members—certainly an unintended consequence of all the effort to improve board effectiveness. The second, broader concern is that SOX represents a shift to more rigid Federal regulation and legislation of corporate governance as distinguished from the more flexible corporate governance that has evolved from state law, particularly Delaware law.[34]

At this point, SOX has probably helped to restore confidence in the U.S. corporate governance system. Apart from that, the Act's expected overall effect is as yet unclear. Our guess is that the effects will be positive for companies with poor governance practices and negative for companies with good governance practices. Because some of the additional costs of complying with SOX are fixed rather than variable, the effects will be more negative for smaller companies than for larger ones. At the margin, this may lead some public companies to go private and deter some private companies from going public. And because of companies' initial uncertainty about how to comply with the Act, we expect the effects of SOX to be somewhat negative in the short term with compliance costs declining over time.

NYSE and NASDAQ corporate governance proposals

In 2002, both the New York Stock Exchange and NASDAQ submitted proposals designed to strengthen the corporate governance of their listed firms. Both exchanges will require the following:

(1) shareholder approval of most equity compensation plans;
(2) a majority of independent directors with no material relationships with the company;
(3) a larger role for independent directors in the compensation and nominating committees; and
(4) regular meetings of only nonmanagement directors.

Compared to SOX, these proposals address U.S. corporate governance deficiencies both more directly and with lower costs. The three provisions relating to board monitoring are particularly noteworthy in that they directly address some of the concerns mentioned by Lorsch and MacIver in 1989 and by outside directors in the Korn Ferry survey.

The closest historical parallel to these proposals is the Code of Best Practices (based upon the recommendations of the Cadbury Committee) that was adopted by the London Stock Exchange (LSE) in 1992. The Code included recommendations that boards have at least three outside directors and a nonexecutive chairperson. Although the Code is voluntary, the LSE requires companies to state whether they are in compliance.

There is evidence that the Code can make a difference. A recent study of all LSE companies reported that both CEO turnover and the sensitivity of CEO turnover to performance increased following the adoption of the Code—and that such increases were concentrated among those firms that had adopted the recommendations. Furthermore, the changes in turnover appear to have been driven by the increase in the fraction of outsiders on the board rather than the separation of the chairperson and CEO.[35]

Overall, then, the NYSE and NASDAQ changes should prove to be unambiguously positive.

---

[34]We thank Andrew Nussbaum for suggesting this possibility.

[35] J. Dahya, J. McConnell, and Nickolaos Travlos, "The Cadbury Committee, Corporate Performance, and Top Management Turnover," *Journal of Finance*, Vol. 57 (2002), pp. 461–483.

The conference board recommendations

In response to the recent scandals, the Conference Board—an association of prominent U.S. companies—put together a Commission on Public Trust and Private Enterprise with the aim of advising companies on best practices in corporate governance.

The first report by the Commission, released in September 2002, provides a set of principles to guide boards in designing top executive compensation. The report begins by noting the exceptional circumstances that led to the abuse of stock options—the equivalent of a "Perfect Storm"—and then makes the following recommendations:

(1) compensation committees should be independent and should avoid benchmarking;
(2) performance-based compensation should correspond to the corporation's long-term goals—"cost of capital, return on equity, economic value added, market share, environment goals etc."—and should avoid windfalls related to stock market volatility;
(3) equity-based compensation should be "reasonable and cost effective";
(4) key executives and directors should "acquire and hold" a meaningful amount of company stock; and
(5) compensation disclosure should be transparent and accounting-neutral—*i.e.*, stock options should be expensed.[36]

Overall, we have a mixed reaction to these recommendations. Several are clearly beneficial. In particular, greater transparency and appropriate expensing of options will make the costs of options more clear not only to shareholders but also to boards. It also will "level the playing field" for options versus other forms of equity-based compensation.

Requiring key executives to hold a meaningful amount of company stock will reduce the temptation to manipulate earnings and stock prices in the short term by making executive stock holdings less liquid. Typically, stock options vest in one to four years, which is short given that most options are exercised and sold fairly soon after vesting. Economic logic suggests that boards should encourage longer-term holdings and a build-up of sizable executive stakes.

The Commission also endorses indexation of some kind to eliminate windfall gains. Indexation has been recommended by economists for a long time, yet practitioners have not adopted it. It is true that there has been an important accounting disadvantage to indexation in that indexed options must be expensed. But the fact that indexed options are rarely used by LBO investors and venture capitalists also suggests that there are hidden costs to indexation or that the benefits are low.

While it may be useful to experiment with some forms of indexation, we think it would probably be just as effective and more transparent to index implicitly by granting stock-based incentives more frequently and in smaller amounts. Mega-grants covering several years at a fixed price have proved too unstable; the options may go underwater and then need to be bailed out (to maintain incentives), making it hard initially to determine the true expected cost of the incentive plans. In general, the incentives from stock options are more fragile than those provided by restricted stock, a problem that more frequent, smaller awards would help alleviate.[37]

We are also skeptical of the recommendation to use performance-based compensation tied to a long list of potential long-term goals, including cost of capital, return on equity, market share, revenue growth, and compliance and environmental protection goals. Such performance plans would appear to take us back to the 1970s, an era that few incentive experts remember fondly. If the problem is windfall gains, then indexed stock options

---

[36]Andy Grove, Chairman of Intel, disagreed with the majority in not recommending expensing of stock options, while Paul Volcker, former Chairman of the Board of Governors of the Federal Reserve System, argued that fixed-price stock options should not be used at all. Both filed dissenting opinions.

[37]See Brian Hall and Thomas Knox, "Managing Option Fragility," Harvard NOM Research Paper 02-19, Harvard Business School (2002). It is interesting that fairness arguments often lead people to advocate options with exercise prices set well above current market price (for instance, Michael Jensen argues that the exercise price should rise with the cost of capital). Given the problems of fragility, this takes us in exactly the wrong direction. Restricted stock (an option with a zero exercise price) is more appealing, because its incentive effect is robust to variations in the stock price.

or, more simply, frequent (quarterly) issues of stock options are much preferred. If the problem is manipulation of the market, it should be evident that accounting measures of the kind endorsed by the Conference Board are very problematic. It was in large part because of their vulnerability to manipulation that standard performance plans were replaced by stock-based incentives in the 1980s. This is not to say that accounting-based incentives should never be used, just that they should not form the core of a CEO's incentive plan.

We are also somewhat skeptical of the recommendation that the compensation committee "act independently of management . . . and avoid benchmarking that keeps continually raising the compensation levels for executives." First, dictating terms without consulting with the executives about their preferences goes against efficient contracting principles; contracting is a two-sided affair. Second, the intent seems to be to give individual compensation committees the responsibility for the overall level of executive compensation. But it is hard to see how pay levels can be set in a fair and efficient way without benchmarking. Prices, including wages, are ultimately set by supply and demand, and benchmarking is nothing more than looking at market prices. The main problem with executive pay levels is not the overall level, but the extreme skew in the awards, as we noted earlier. To deal with this problem, we need more effective benchmarking, not less of it.

Despite good intentions, then, we see potentially serious flaws in the recommendations of the Conference Board. It is also important to keep in mind that good incentive designs are sensitive to economic circumstances and to the desired performance. One size does not fit all. And because each situation requires its own compensation plan, the need to customize that plan will often conflict with the goals of benchmarking and transparency.

WHAT WILL THE FUTURE BRING?

Working together with normal market forces, the Sarbanes-Oxley Act, the new NYSE and NASDAQ regulations, and the guidelines offered by groups like the Conference Board will significantly influence U.S. corporate governance.

Board behavior will be most strongly affected by these measures. External pressure will lead most boards to monitor top management more aggressively. Yet the relationship between boards and directors need not become more adversarial. The new regulatory requirements provide cover for a more independent and inquisitive board. Actions that in the past might have been construed as hostile will now be interpreted as following best practice. The mandated changes may in fact help reduce the tension inherent in the dual role boards play as monitors of management, on the one hand, and as advisors and sounding boards, on the other.

In addition to the changes in oversight and monitoring, boards also are likely to change their approaches to executive compensation (even though SOX and the exchanges did not address executive compensation directly). In particular, boards will increasingly restrict top executives from exercising options, selling stock, and hedging their positions. As noted earlier, some of the incentives for the executives at Global Crossing, Tyco, and WorldCom to manage earnings came from their ability to sell shares when their stock prices were overvalued. Restrictions on such selling reduce the incentive to manage short-term earnings. While such restrictions have costs, particularly in the form of lack of diversification, the benefits in terms of improved incentives arguably outweigh them. Private equity firms routinely impose such restrictions on the management of their portfolio companies. Furthermore, CEOs typically are wealthy enough that the benefits of diversification may not be so great.

Many corporate boards will decide to expense options and equity compensation even if they are not required to do so. We suspect that boards will discover that investors and the stock market have neutral or even positive reactions to such expensing (in contrast to the predictions of many executives). Sophisticated investors already know the extent of option issuance from their disclosure in footnotes. Expensing will provide the additional signal to sophisticated investors that the board and the company are serious about compensation and corporate governance.[38]

---

[38]The argument that options cannot be expensed because no one knows their true value is wrong. On that basis, one could argue that we should not depreciate assets because it is impossible to measure the assets' true rate of depreciation. Nevertheless, it remains to be seen how fluctuations in the value of stock options will influenc the information content of reported earnings. The never-ending debate over the best way to handle depreciation suggests that expensing options is going to be discussed for years to come.

Boards of directors and compensation committees also will begin to change their behavior in issuing options and equity-based compensation. This will be particularly true of boards that decide to expense options. Expensing the options will make their costs more clear and will reduce the size of option grants, particularly large, onetime grants. Moreover, some companies that do expense equity compensation will choose to issue restricted stock rather than options. Restricted stock grants have the advantages of being easier to value, providing the incentives that do not vary with stock price movements, and thus being less vulnerable to repricing.[39]

CONCLUDING REMARKS

Despite its alleged flaws, the U.S. corporate governance system has performed very well, both on an absolute basis and relative to other countries. It is important to recognize that there is no perfect system and that we should try to avoid the pendulum-like movement so typical of politically inspired system redesigns. The current problems arose in an exceptional period that is not likely to happen again soon. After all, it was almost 70 years ago that the corporate governance system last attracted such intervention.

The fact that the American public and political system became outraged and involved in corporate governance does not mean the system was broken. The U.S. public and the political system are part of the broader system of corporate governance. At the same time, an effort to regulate the system so that such outrage will never again occur

Table 1
Stock Market Performance
Stock returns reported by Ibbotson Associates for total return on Morgan Stanley Capital International (MSCI) Indices for the United States, Europe, Pacific, Great Britain, France, Germany, and Japan from January 1 of the given year through end of December 2002.

	U.S.	Europe	Pacific		
From 1982 (January)	1222%	1145%	276%		
From 1987	436%	266%	3%		
From 1992	164%	113%	−27%		
From 1997	28%	13%	−39%		
From 2001	−32%	−34%	−32%		

	U.S.	Great Britain	France	Germany	Japan
From 1982	1222%	1223%	1567%	595%	90%
From 1987	436%	290%	236%	93%	−37%
From 1992	164%	121%	147%	84%	−42%
From 1997	28%	11%	47%	5%	−39%
From 2001	−32%	−32%	−45%	−53%	−34%

Table 2
Changes in Real GDP per Capita
Changes in real GDP per capita for the U.S., the U.K., France, Germany and Japan. Calculated using the Penn World Tables.

	U.S.	Great Britain	France	Germany	Japan
From 1982 (beginning) to 2000	54%	58%	37%	44%	55%
From 1987 to 2000	38%	36%	28%	29%	36%
From 1992 to 2000	29%	24%	12%	12%	8%
From 1997 to 2000	14%	11%	11%	8%	3%

---

[39]See Hall (2002), *ibid*, for a detailed discussion.

would be overly costly and counterproductive. It would lead to inflexibility and fear of experimentation. In today's uncertain climate, we probably need more organizational experimentation than ever. The New Economy is moving forward and, in order to exploit the potential efficiencies inherent in the new information technologies, new business models and new organizational structures are likely to be desirable and valuable. Enron was an experiment that failed. We should take advantage of its lessons not by withdrawing into a shell, but rather by improving control structures and corporate governance so that other promising experiments can be undertaken.

REFERENCES

Becht, Marco, Patrick Bolton, and Ailsa Roell, 2002, "Corporate Governance and Control," Handbook of Economics and Finance, Constantinides, Harris and Stulz, eds. North Holland.

Bebchuk, Lucian, Jesse Fried and David Walker, 2002, "Managerial Power and Rent Extraction in the Design of Executive Compensation," University of Chicago Law Review 69, 751–846.

Core, J. and D. Larcker, 2002, "Performance consequences of mandatory increases in executive stock ownership," Journal of Financial Economics.

Dahya, J., J. McConnell, and N. G. Travlos, 2002, "The Cadbury Committee, Corporate Performance, and Top Management Turnover," Journal of Finance, 57, pp. 461–483.

Donaldson, G. and J. Lorsch. 1983. Decision Making at the Top. Basic Books, New York, New York.

Donaldson, G. 1994. Corporate Restructuring. Harvard Business School Press, Boston, MA.

Escherich, R. and P. Gibbs, 2002, Global Mergers and Acquisitions Review. JP Morgan, April.

Felton, B., A. Hudnut, and J. Von Heeckeren. 1997. "The Dollar Value of Board Governance." Mckinsey Quarterly.

Fried J. and D. Walker, 2002, "Managerial Power and Rent Extraction in the Design of Executive Compensation," University of Chicago Law Review, 751–846.

Gertner, R., and S. Kaplan. 1996. "The Value-Maximizing Board." Working Paper, University of Chicago.

Gillan, S., and L. Starks. 2000. "Corporate Governance Proposals and Relationship Shareholder Activism: The Role of Institutional Investors." Journal of Financial Economics. 57, No. 2, pp. 275–305.

Gompers, Paul and Andrew Metrick. 2001. "Institutional Investors and Equity Prices." Quarterly Journal of Economics, Vol 116(1), 2001, 229–260.

Gompers, Paul, Joy Ishi, and Andrew Metrick. 2001. "Corporate Governance and Equity Prices", Working Paper 8449, NBER, 2001.

Hall, B. 2002, "Equity-Pay Design for Executives," working paper, Harvard Business School (2002)

Hall, B. and T. Knox, "Managing Option Fragility," Harvard NOM Research Paper 02–19, Harvard Business School. (2002)

Hall, B., and J. Liebman. 1998. "Are CEOs Really Paid like Bureaucrats?" Quarterly Journal of Economics. 112, No. 3, pp. 653–691.

Hall, B., and J. Liebman. 2000. "The Taxation of Executive Compensation." Working Paper, National Bureau of Economic Research.

Hall, B. and K. Murphy, 2002, "Stock options for undiversified executives," Journal of Accounting and Economics, 3–42.

Hermalin, B. and M. Weisbach. 2001. Boards of Directors as an Endogenously Determined Institution: A Survey of the Economic Literature.

Holderness, C., R. Kroszner, and D. Sheehan. 1999. Were the Good Old That Good? Changes in Managerial Stock Ownership Since the Great Depression. Journal of Finance. 54:2, pp. 435–470.

Holmstom, B. and S. Kaplan, 2001, "Corporate Governance and Takeovers in the U.S.: Making sense of the '80s and '90s," Journal of Economic Perspectives, Spring, 121–144.

Huson, M., Parrino, R., and Starks, L., 2001, "Internal Monitoring Mechanisms and CEO Turnover: A Long Term Perspective." Journal of Finance 56, 2265–2297.

Jensen, M. 1988. "Takeovers: Their Causes and Consequences." Journal of Economic Perspectives. 2, pp. 21–48.

Jensen, M. 1989. "The Eclipse of the Public Corporation." Harvard Business Review. No. 5, pp. 61–74.

Jensen, M. 1993. "The Modern Industrial Revolution." Journal of Finance, 48:3, 831–80.

Jensen, M. and M. Fuller, 2002, "Just Say No to Wall Street," Working paper, Harvard Business School.

Karpoff J., 1998, "The Impact of Shareholder Activism on Target Companies: A Survey of Empirical Findings," Working paper, University of Washington.

Kaplan, S. 1989. "The Effects of Management Buyouts on Operations and Value." Journal of Financial Economics. 24, pp. 217–254.

Kaplan, S. 1997. "The Evolution of U.S. Corporate Governance: We Are All Henry Kravis Now." Journal of Private Equity, 7–14.

Kaplan, S. and A. Schoar, 2002, "Private Equity Returns: Persistence and Capital Flows," working paper, University of Chicago, December.

Khurana, R. 2002, Searching for a corporate savior: The Irrational Quest for Charismatic CEOs. Princeton University Press.

Khurana, R. and N. Nohria, 1997, "Substance and symbol: The Effects of CEO Turnover in Large Industrial Organizations," working paper, Harvard Business School.

Lorsch, J. and E. MacIver. 1989. Pawns or Potentates. Harvard Business School Press.

Mitchell, M. and H. Mulherin. 1996. "The Impact of Industry Shocks on Takeover and Restructuring Activity." Journal of Financial Economics. pp. 193–229.

Murphy, Kevin J. 1999. "Executive Compensation." In O. Ashenfelter and D. Card (eds.), Handbook of Labor Economics. Volume 3, North Holland, pp. 2485–2525.

Perry, T. 2000. "Incentive compensation for outside directors and CEO turnover." Working paper, Arizona State University.

Perry, T., and M. Zenner. 2000. "CEO Compensation In The 1990s: Shareholder Alignment Or Shareholder Expropriation?" Wake Forest Law Review.

Porter, M. 1992, "Capital Disadvantage: America's Failing Capital Investment System," Harvard Business Review, September-October, 65–83.

Poterba, J. and A. Samwick, 1995, "Stock Ownership Patterns, Stock Market Fluctuations, and Consumption." Brookings Papers on Economic Activity. 2, 295–357.

Rajan, R. and J. Wulf, 2002, "The Flattening Firm," working paper, University of Chicago.

Rogers, P., T. Holland and D. Haas, 2002, "Value Acceleration: Lessons from Private-Equity Masters," Harvard Business Review, June.

Stein, J., 1989, "Efficient Capital Markets, Inefficient Firms: A Model of Myopic Corporate Behavior," The Quarterly Journal of Economics, Vol. 104, 655–669.

Yermack, David. 1996. "Higher market valuation of companies a small board of directors." Journal of Financial Economics. 40, pp. 185–202.

ADVERTISING AND THE MARKET PROCESS

A Modern Economic View

ROBERT B. EKELUND, JR. AND DAVID S. SAURMAN

ADVERTISING, PRICES, AND QUALITY

A difficult concept for some is how advertising can have the effect of actually lowering, and not raising the money prices charged by firms for products and services. While the effect of lowered full prices may appear plausible, it seems reasonable to argue that the resources that go into advertising are not without cost and that they must be paid for. If advertising is an input into the production and distribution of goods and services, it will also enter as a factor in determining the costs of producing these goods and services. Thus, if products are marketed or advertised, costs are incurred that would not exist if there were no advertising at all. The use of advertising by firms must also increase the money prices of goods and services sold by firms. The argument, in one sense, is partially correct. But costs of production are not the *only* factor that determine what prices in fact emerge in markets.

An even more difficult notion to accept and understand is that advertising, or the lack thereof, may influence the *quality* of a product or service. A hamburger is a hamburger is a hamburger, and no amount of advertising can change the freshness of the bun or the sensation of taste to the consumer. However, as we will show, for some products and services quality is not an absolute, fixed characteristic determined either solely by the subjective valuations of consumers or fixed by producers in a vacuum. It is a characteristic that is both supplied and demanded in varying degrees. As such, product or service quality in some markets is closely intertwined with advertising activity. The amount of information consumers have about prices, qualities, availability, and characteristics of competing products plays a major role in determining prices charged and quality supplied by firms. Since information is transferred with advertising, consider some evidence concerning advertising, prices, qualities, and markets.

An interesting study in the statistical economic literature, written by Robert Steiner (1973), highlights the above point in research on the market for children's toys and television advertising.[1] Steiner points out that toy manufacturers advertised little on television until the Mattel Toy Company began purchasing time on The Mickey Mouse Club TV show in the mid-1950s. Since the audience of the Mickey Mouse Club was primarily composed of children, and since the ads proclaimed the merits of the advertised toys, giving little if any information on prices, allegations of devious advertising resulted. Critics charged that the minds of children were swayed to induce parental expenditure, all in the name of profit. (The charge remains popular as the discussion of "kiddie-video" shows; see Chapter 7.) Steiner points out that prior to the mid-1950s, a toy whose suggested retail price was $5 generally sold at around $4.95. After the Mattel ad campaign, along with increased advertising expenditures of other toy makers in cities where television advertising was relatively frequent, the

[1]Robert L.Steiner. "Does Advertising Lower Consumer Prices?" *Journal of Marketing* 37 (1973): 19–26.

price of the $5 toy charged by retailers had *fallen* to an average of about $3.50, with occasional sale prices of $3.00. In cities where there was little or no advertising, prices continued to average roughly $4.95.

This episode indicates that advertising (even in the face of a mild inflationary period during which prices could be expected to rise) may be viewed as an agent whose effect can be the substantial lowering of market prices. Price increases attributable to increased advertising costs have been minimal in many cases. Through its informational content, advertising produced a greater turnover in toys. Greater turnover permitted smaller profit margins and increased the number of known substitutes for consumers. This permitted greater price comparison shopping and limited or reduced the maximum price a retailer was able to charge *and still expect consumers to buy.*

Other cases are similar, but not identical, to the toy case. But instead of looking for something that occurred due to advertising, such as a drop in toy prices, one can look for things that have *not* happened. Recall that certain contemporary positive economists view advertising not as a barrier to entry into markets, not as an anticompetitive tool of monopolies and oligopolies, but as a device that makes markets more competitive. Evidence strongly supports this view. It is then a short step to reason through the following argument: If advertising is a means of competitive entry and lower prices, it would be in the economic interest of incumbent firms to somehow prevent advertising so as to eliminate or minimize competitive effects. After all, businesses are seeking to maximize profits, among other things.

The crucial question concerns the manner in which advertising is restricted. For one, all the firms in an industry could come to a gentleman's agreement not to advertise. But when profits are at stake, such agreements tend to break down quickly. The problem with the gentleman's agreement (apart from being illegal) is enforcement, and in most free societies one firm does not have the legal right to prevent another firm from advertising. The answer then lies in finding a method of preventing or discouraging advertising in such a way so as to guarantee that no or very little advertising will occur. The method must also make sure that if anyone does advertise, he will be caught, severely punished, and perhaps legally expelled from the industry.

The solution is to *pass a law*, and this is exactly what has been done in a number of industries. Laws, allegedly in the consumer's interest and strictly enforced by various levels of government, have been passed prohibiting advertising in certain industries. If advertising helps produce competitive results in markets, then it seems likely that a ban or prevention of advertising will likely produce anticompetitive or monopolistic outcomes. Specifically, new neoclassical economics leads one to expect prices to be higher than would otherwise be the case in industries where there is some degree of legal advertising prevention.

One of the most famous studies of this hypothesis analyzes the market for eyeglasses. This particular market provides a fertile area of analysis for several reasons. First, some states in the U.S. (over the period of study) did not ban advertising of eyeglasses and eye examination prices, but enough banned or inhibited advertising so that scientific comparisons could be made. Secondly, the states that did ban price advertising did so expressly in the public interest. Lee Benham (1972) examined the prices of eyeglasses and eye examinations charged in states that allowed or had few restrictions on advertising, and in states that did not allow advertising of these products and services in 1963.[2] Benham first subjected data to regression analysis to discern whether or not the effect of a prohibition on advertising would be a statistically significant factor causing prices to be higher in states where there existed effective prohibitions on advertising. After accounting for the effect other variables may have had on the price of glasses and exams (such as family income, age of customer, family size, and sex), Benham's results showed that advertising prohibitions were a statistically significant variable in causing prices to be higher in states prohibiting advertisements.

Consider Table 5–1, which reproduces some of Benham's results concerning price differentials. The upper half of Table 5–1 shows average prices in the two types of states when forty-eight states plus Washington, D.C. are included in the sample. Prices for glasses were 25 percent higher on average in states that restricted or banned advertising. The lower half of Table 5–1 is even more interesting. It compares the "worst" and the "best." That

---

[2]Lee Benham. "The Effect of Advertising on the Price of Eyeglasses," *Journal of Law and Economics* 15 (1972): 337–52.

Table 5–1. Effect of Advertising on Price of Eyeglasses and Eye Examinations (1963 Prices).

All States with Complete Restrictions on Advertising Price	All States with No Restrictions on Advertising Price	Difference in Price in Price	Percentage Difference
Eyeglasses			
$33.04	$26.34	$6.70	25%
Eyeglasses + Examination			
$40.96	$37.10	3.86	10%
North Carolina	Washington, D.C. & Texas		
Eyeglasses			
$37.48	$17.98	$19.50	108%
Eyeglasses + Examination			
$50.73	$29.97	20.76	69%

SOURCE: Lee Benham, "The Effect of Advertising on the Price of Eyeglasses." *Journal of Law and Economics* 15 (1972): 342.

is, Washington, D.C. and Texas had virtually no advertising impediments on glasses or exams in 1963 but North Carolina had wide-ranging advertising restrictions that had been in force for a number of years. The numbers speak for themselves. Benham's statistical results indicate that the *prohibition* of advertising had caused prices to be higher. These price differentials may seem small, but remember that they are all expressed in terms of 1963 dollars. When adjusted for general price inflation so that the price differentials are expressed in terms of 1988 purchasing power dollars, the numbers grow. For example, the price differential on the examination plus eyeglasses between North Carolina and Texas/Washington, D.C. in terms of current prices is roughly $80.00. The study also indicates that the price differentials tend to be dramatically larger the greater the degree of difference in advertising laws.

In certain circumstances it may be difficult (costly) for groups of sellers to induce lawmakers to provide them with the competition-restricting legislation. Legislation is not the only method available to collusive groups of sellers that restricts the flow of information to consumers and reduces competition in the market. It may be the best method, but there are substitutes.

In later research, Lee and Alexandra Benham (1975) return to the market for eyeglasses and analyze the notion of what they termed "regulating through the profession."[3] Many professions have codes of ethics and conduct to which members of the profession must adhere or risk being officially excluded from membership. Sanctions may effectively prevent a supplier from transacting with consumers (local medical boards) or merely stigmatize the miscreant.

Professional associations probably have diverse objectives. The Benhams focus their attention on the American Optometric Association (AOA) and its state affiliates and suggest that one function of the AOA is to inhibit the flow of information available to consumers through the advertising of eyeglasses and eyecare by member optometrists. If advertising can be inhibited through private organizations, the same qualitative effect on prices (presumably to the benefit of association members) that legal advertising restrictions have could be obtained.

The Benhams observed that the AOA codes had declared such practices as advertising professional superiority, wider range of services, and lower fees to be unethical and unprofessional conduct. Use of a brand name for a company or clinic was also taboo to the AOA. The state affiliate ethical codes reinforced the theme. For example, the Michigan Optometric Association rules in 1969 imposed a point system for membership. Table 5–2, a condensed form of the Michigan code, details how members achieved and maintained good standing. A

---

[3]Lee Benham and Alexandra Benham, "Regulating Through the Professions: A Perspective on Information Control," *Journal of Law and Economics* 18 (1975): 421–47.

Table 5–2. Michigan Optometric Association Membership Point Scale.

Activity by Association Members	Total Points
Not advertising (media, telephone books, window displays)	30
Not locating practice in an establishment whose primary public image is one of reduced prices and discount optical outlet	25
Limiting office identification sign to approved size and content	15
Participation in education activities (professional meetings)	14
Sufficient physical (laboratory and examining room) and functional (equipment) facilities	16

SOURCE: Lee Benham and Alexandra Benham, "Regulating Through the Professions: A Perspective on Information Control." *Journal of Law and Economics* 18 (1975): 425.

minimum of eighty-five points out of one hundred was required yearly to maintain membership, with fully seventy points constituting information/advertising constraints. Twenty-twenty vision is not required to appreciate the intent of the Michigan code.

Given that the AOA and various state codes had the effect of severely limiting advertising activity on the part of members, the Benhams measured the effects of these information restrictions on the prices paid for eyewear. They argued that a good measure of the degree by which consumer information is suppressed can be had by calculating the percentage of optometrists in a state that are members of the AOA through the state affiliate organizations. In their data sample, taken in 1969, this fraction ranged from 43 percent to 93 percent. After adjusting for such factors as the purchaser's family size, age, sex, race (males tend toward better unaided vision than females, and blacks better than whites), city versus rural locations, and consumer income, results on price effects of AOA affiliation were obtained. The Benhams found that eyewear prices would rise by a statistically significant $36.40 (1988 purchasing power dollars) as the AOA membership rate rose from 43 percent to 91 percent. These results were not as dramatic as Benham's previous study and Benham did not adjust for "quality" in either study, an issue we address below. However, the smaller magnitude of the more recent study's effects may reflect the possibility that the AOA advertising restriction mechanism is less efficient than legislation.

The Benhams' research also addressed two other issues closely related to markets and advertising. Their study indicated that individuals buy eyeglasses with greater frequency in areas where professional control (AOA membership) is lower. With lower prices in these areas, this is a reasonable conclusion. But *given the effects of price*, will "commercialism" in the provision of this facet of health care lead suppliers to fleece unsuspecting consumers with advertising-induced "unneeded" eyewear? An answer to this question was given by separating individuals in the sample into two groups. One group purchased eyewear from optometrists or physicians (professional sources) while the other bought from "commercial" sources. The statistical results indicated that, *given the effects of other factors, especially price*, consumers who shopped and lived in "commercial" environments did not purchase eyewear any more or less frequently than those who purchased in the "professional" advertising-restricted markets.

Carrying this line of reasoning one step further, advertising's critics argue that advertising preys on those least able to cope with it. That is, the credulous and ignorant purchase "unneeded" glasses. Professional control, such as the AOA's code of ethics, are needed to protect the less competent from commercialism, at least in health care.

The Benhams faced this argument directly and assumed that those less able to cope with the impact of advertising messages are individuals with a low level of education, as indicated by years of schooling. They again divided the sample data into two groups: those with more than thirteen and those with less than eight years of schooling. After adjusting for all other factors, they found that advertising/informational restrictions associated with the AOA codes *increased price by more to the less educated group* than the more educated group.

While data limitations restrict the ability to make broad generalizations from such studies, as the Benhams readily admit, it appears that professional codes of "ethics" show no signs of improving consumer welfare. From a number of vantage points, at least given the limited data sample of eyewear consumers, such restrictions tend to impair consumer well-being.

Advertising and quality

The natural response of most people when confronted with the price-increasing effects of advertising prohibitions is to voice concern for the quality of goods or services. It is often argued that advertising restrictions really attempt to guarantee consumers a certain level of product or service quality. Advertising restraints are intended, in this view, to prevent charlatans and quacks from foisting inferior grade services and commodities on unsuspecting consumers. Such concerns are legitimate, especially when related to the professional services we buy. Eyesight, for example, is probably the most valuable of all human senses. Most of us who have less than perfect vision would probably find it difficult to distinguish subtle quality differences among the providers of vision care. Moreover, in the case of eyecare the quality of service would be difficult to judge *before* purchase with the distinct possibility that poor quality care could lead to permanent and costly damage to eyesight. A bad pizza may be cheaply thrown away. Low-quality eye care can damage vision forever. It would be informative then to measure the effect on the quality of such services that advertising restrictions have had. If restrictions actually produce a generally better quality of care along with higher prices, then there *might* be some positive social benefit associated with having such restrictions. If, on the other hand, legal advertising impediments do not improve quality, or if they reduce quality and increase prices, then laws of this kind work to the detriment of consumers. Higher prices *and* an inferior product are certainly not in the best interest of consumers.

One might imagine that measuring a slippery concept as the quality of eyecare services for the purpose of statistical analysis would be nearly impossible. However, the Federal Trade Commission's Bureau of Economics was able to do just that and to produce a study that contains surprising results.[4] With the cooperation of representatives of the American Academy of Ophthalmology, the American Optometric Association, and the Opticians Association of America, the FTC was able to devise a method of measuring how well eyecare practitioners had "fit" contact lenses to patients. Thus, an index of the quality of a services was devised. Each of the three organizations provided qualified, professional practitioners to measure and grade certain characteristics of contact lens fit for a sample of contact lens wearers. Such characteristics as accuracy of prescription, incidence of corneal abrasion, and pathological corneal conditions, all of which indicate the quality of the fitting service, were measured in a manner designed to minimize inconsistency and subjective evaluations.

Subjects were asked to identify the fitter of his or her contact lenses. From this information, the FTC staff were able to identify lens wearers who were fit for their contact lenses by either "commercial" or by "noncommercial" optometric practices. Commercial practices were defined as those that advertised and/or employed a trade (or brand) name (a form of advertising). Noncommercial practices engaged in neither of these activities. Such activity is prohibited or inhibited in some states by statutes and licensing board regulations. In this manner the stage was set for a comparison of the quality of service provided by advertisers versus non-advertisers.

The results of the FTC's statistical analysis are interesting. The FTC found statistically significant differences (though at the 10-percent level) in the quality of hard contact lens fitting service among commercial and noncommercial optometrists. However, it was not the fitters who were restricted in their advertising abilities that had the higher quality-of-fit scores as advertising critics would suggest. Commercial optometrists, the ones who advertise in the yellow pages and in newspapers or television, the ones who operate practices under trade names or in mercantile locations (such as shopping malls), were the group that produced the greatest quality of hard contact lenses fitting. In the soft lens market, commercial fitters again scored higher on the quality scale than noncommercial fitters, though the difference was not statistically significant.

The FTC could find *no evidence whatsoever* for the notion that commercial practices such as advertising and the use of trade or brand names, even in a market where quality is extremely important yet difficult for consumers to judge, reduces the quality of the service provided to consumers. If anything, the FTC discovered the

---

[4]Gary D. Hailey, Jonathan R. Bromberg, and Joseph B. Mulholland, "A Comparative Analysis of Cosmetic Contact Lens Fitting by Ophthalmologists, Optometrists, and Opticians," Report of the Staff of the Federal Trade Commission (Washington, D.C.: Bureau of Consumer Protection and Bureau of Economics, 1983).

opposite to be the case. This, of course, makes sense when we recall the results of market advertising predicted by the modern analytical approach. Advertising, by whatever method, lowers consumer search costs. Since at least some consumers have quality information (even though it may not be very good), the cost of finding or trying to find a relatively high (or higher) quality practitioner in a market where advertising activity exists to a relatively large degree is lower than in a market where advertising activity is not widespread. Suppliers know that reputations of poor service quality will, sooner or later, spread to consumers and in the process deplete the value of their advertising expenditures. In this type of market, buyers have relatively lower costs of switching suppliers (or avoiding low-quality suppliers) and finding higher quality care than they do in a market where a dearth of advertising information exists. Suppliers likewise face the prospect of losing more customers and losing them more rapidly if they try to sell low-quality care as well as depreciating the customer-attracting value of their advertising dollars. The FTC evidence seems to suggest that a higher quality of eyecare exists in markets where advertising activity is allowed. At worst, the evidence suggests that a lower quality of service is not prevalent in these markets. This conclusion is compatible with the modern view of the economics of advertising.

Two other items of interest surface in the FTC's contact lens study, both of which contradict the traditional view of the effects of advertising in markets and the effect on prices. The FTC staff designed a "standard package" that contact lens wearers normally purchase (the lenses, an eye exam, follow-up care, etc.), calculated the prices paid by study subjects for this given set of items and services, and then adjusted these prices for general cost-of-living differences of subjects residing in different parts of the United States. Statistical analysis of this data yields additional results worthy of attention.

Table 5–3 shows the average prices charged by commercial and noncommercial optometrists as well as ophthalmologists for both hard and soft lenses. Commercial optometrists charged the lowest prices of the groups for both kinds of contact lenses. This conclusion, coupled with the FTC's findings on quality, provides fairly persuasive evidence in support of the point that advertising and other associated commercial information-transferral activities work to the advantage of consumers.[5]

The FTC conducted one additional test. By examining contact lens price data taken from cities where commercial optometrists were the dominant practitioners, the FTC was able to compare the average prices charged by eyecare practitioners in two ways. Prices charged by different types of practitioners within these relatively high intensity advertising areas could be compared to one another as well as merely comparing prices across these areas. Results indicate the power of competitive markets where the degree of competition is proxied by the (relative) ability to disseminate information through advertising. Ophthalmologists and noncommercial

Table 5–3. Comparison of Prices Charged by Commercial and Noncommercial Optometrists and by Ophthalmologists (1988 Prices).

	Hard Lenses		Soft Lenses	
Type of Fitter	Average Price Charged	Percent Above Commercial Optometrist Price	Average Price Charged	Percent Above Commercial Optometrist Price
Ophthalmologists	$312.99	54%	$399.28	56%
Noncommercial Optometrists	$262.17	29%	$332.87	30%
Commercial Optometrists	$202.94	—	$255.48	—

SOURCE: Gary D. Hailey. Jonathan R. Bromberg, and Joseph B. Mulholland, "A Comparative Analysis of Cosmetic Contact Lens Fitting by Ophthalmologists, Optometrists, and Opticians," *Report of the Staff of the Federal Trade Commission* (Washington, D.C.: Bureau of Consumer Protection and Bureau of Economics, 1983), pp. C—F.

Note: Original source prices were measured over the period 1977–1979 and converted to 1988 prices by the authors through the use of the Consumer Price Index: All items, as measured in 1978 and 1988.

---

[5]Ibid., p. 35.

optometrists had a smaller upward influence on average price in areas that were relatively heavily commercialized. In the commercialized areas, lens prices charged by commercial and noncommercial optometrists were *not* significantly different. This contrasts sharply with Table 5–3, which shows that the noncommercial charge was about 30 percent higher than commercial optometrists' fees overall. The inference is clear. Sellers who do not advertise but operate in market areas where the extent of advertising and other commercial activities are fairly widespread are forced by competitive pressures to more closely match prices of other sellers who do advertise. Competitive advertising affects what the non-advertiser is able to do in the market.

It appears that the traditional view of advertising, in whatever form chosen to interpret it, is an empty box. Eyecare market studies strongly indicate that statutory impediments, be they laws, licensing requirements, or professional codes of conduct, that restrict information do not benefit consumers. At best, they produce higher consumer costs with no evidence of offsetting quality improvement or, worse, both higher costs and inferior quality.

Other price effects of advertising

Another interesting study, one that examines advertising and retail drug prices, was conducted along the same lines as the Benham study but provides additional insight as to who benefits, consumers or suppliers, from advertising prevention. Like Benham, John Cady (1976) divides states into those that allow retail drug advertising and those that have laws prohibiting advertising.[6] While most people think of these laws as part and parcel of some code of ethics instituted to protect consumers or to guarantee some level of professional quality, the laws tend to be economic in nature. If the code of conduct and "points table" of the Michigan Optometric Association was not convincing enough, consider the following excerpt from the Maryland law regarding drug advertising: "The Board of Pharmacy is hereby granted power and authority . . . to suspend or revoke [a pharmacist's] license for advertising to the public by any means . . . the prices for prescriptions . . . or fees or services relating thereto or any reference to the price of said drugs or prescriptions whether specifically or as a percentile of prevailing prices, or by the terms 'cut-rate,' 'discount,' 'bargain,' or terms of similar connotation."[7]

There is not much said about consumer benefit in the statute, and its intent is clear—to prevent price advertising of prescription drugs. Cady found that prescription drug prices are higher by 5 percent in states that inhibit price advertising. If that does not seem like a large difference, consider what it implies in terms of consumer expenditure on prescription drugs in the states that prohibit advertising.

Cady estimates that in 1975, the additional cost to consumers of these advertising regulations in terms of higher drug prices was about $380 million (about $820 million in 1988 dollars). Additionally, given the size of the pharmacy, measures of service levels (emergency deliveries, regular deliveries, recordkeeping, waiting areas, credit, and so on), which can be taken as examples of the quality of service, are generally no different in the two types of states. The actual evidence again suggests that advertising prohibitions do *not* benefit consumers by lowering prices. They increase prices above what they would have been in the absence of the advertising impediments. The quality and level of service are not significantly increased by such laws either, and may be decreased. It appears from the available evidence that consumers are made worse off by paying more than they would have for smaller amounts of (at best) equal quality than in the absence of such laws.

As a final example of the effect of advertising on prices, consider the posting of prices at a business establishment in plain view for customers. Since price posting supplies information to consumers prior to purchase in a relatively low cost fashion, it clearly falls within the definition of advertising. Thom Kelly and Alex Maurizi (1978) examined the phenomenon of service stations posting gasoline prices on billboards in plain view of customers and potential customers and the effects this form of advertising had on market prices of

---

[6]John F. Cady, *Restricted Advertising and Competition: The Case of Retail Drugs* (Washington, D.C.: American Enterprise Institute, 1976). The reader should not confuse the type of drug advertising being discussed here with the drug advertising and promotion that Leffler (1981) analyzed. Leffler considered advertising and promotion expenditures by pharmaceutical companies aimed at physicians, not at pharmacy advertising aimed at the ultimate consumers, patients.

[7]Ibid., p. l.

gasoline.[8] They obtained data from fourteen geographical areas of the country for two weeks in November of 1970. They surmised that the billboard posting of price would affect the average market price charged by tending to lower it, and that the higher the percentage of stations in a given area using billboards to post prices (the higher the posting or advertising intensity) the lower would be the average market price charged. Not only would the viewing of one sign (advertisement) alone give the consumer information about price, but also the viewing of one station's billboard and *being able to compare it to others cheaply* would limit somewhat the amount stations are able to charge consumers. Reading a price posted of $1.00 per gallon is useful, but it is even more useful to see a price of $1.00 posted at one corner and prices of $0.90 and $1.10 on billboards across the street.

After adjusting for such factors as family income in the area, gasoline taxes, whether or not trading stamps were offered, and whether the station was a major brand or an independent, Kelly and Maurizi found that the act of billboard advertising of prices significantly reduced the average price of gasoline charged, and that the intensity of posting prices in areas also tended to significantly reduce gas prices. For leaded regular gasoline, the combined effects of posting prices and of "billboard" intensity were to reduce gas prices on an average of 5.5 percent, while the combined effect on leaded premium gas was a price about 7.7 percent lower than it would have been in the absence of this type of advertising and advertising intensity.[9] Thus, billboard advertising appears to lower prices and to increase consumer welfare in certain markets. Though billboards are often singled out as eyesores by social critics, the information they contain yields net economic value to society. Completely ignored is the additional time saved by consumers in price-searching activities that billboard price advertising makes possible. Pro-competitive effects, moreover, have most likely had a far greater affect in lowering prices than any increase in costs brought about by advertising.

ADVERTISING AND DERIVED CONSUMER DEMAND

Before turning to an analysis of contemporary issues related to advertising (Chapter 7 and 8), we present some evidence concerning one last area. At the close of Chapter 4 we discussed the theory of advertising as developed by Ehrlich and Fisher (1982), which had its roots in the works of Nelson (1970, 1974). One basic inference we can draw from the Ehrlich-Fisher study is that advertising is consistent with, and can be expected to be an important characteristic of, competition and competitive markets. Recall that these economists argue that business advertising messages represent a derived demand. That is, the origin of advertising is the consumer's desire for information, which is the desire to reduce the full price of purchases. Competition, in the new neoclassical and Austrian views, generally provides advertising information in a form that will be efficient for the average consumer. Efficient information depends on market characteristics, especially the characteristics of consumers. These characteristics include the product or service being transacted, how frequently it is purchased, search or experience attributes, information consumers already possess, and so on.

David Laband (1986) examines the question of whether suppliers will in fact provide consumers information in the fashion outlined above—whether the market outcome, as far as the kinds of advertising that occur in the market are concerned, actually reflect the kind of information consumers desire.[10] Laband examines these issues with the aid of a rather unusual source of data—the Yellow Pages.

Laband argues, along the lines of Nelson and Ehrlich-Fisher, that one avenue of firm competition within industries is competition through supplying consumers with the most useful type of advertising. In particular he argues that consumers will, in varying degrees and depending on the circumstances, want information on product or service quality. And the greater the amount of quality information consumers want, the greater will be the incentive of firms to provide it. Thus, goods and services for which quality information would be of most benefit will be those goods and services whose advertisements emphasize quality characteristics relatively more than others.

---

[8]Thom Kelly and Alex Maurizi, *Prices and Consumer Information: The Benefits from Posting Retail Gasoline Prices* (Washington, D.C.: American Enterprise Institute, 1978).
[9]Ibid., p. 35.
[10]David N. Laband, "Advertising as Information: An Empirical Note," *Review of Economics and Statistics* 68 (1986): 517–21.

The circumstances and market characteristics that identify goods for which we would expect to see ads of this type are not difficult to pinpoint. Consumers tend to rely on quality information provided by advertisements in buying relatively high priced and infrequently purchased items. For frequently purchased items, consumers already have a large stock of information that has been garnered through the act of purchase and consumption. Hence, additional quality information is of little additional value. Also, inexpensive goods entail a very low cost to the consumer of making a purchase "mistake" and buying something of unexpected low quality. We would then expect that advertisements of goods and services that are purchased infrequently and are comparatively high priced to contain the larger amount of quality information. Nelson's search good category seems to fit these kinds of purchases. Additionally, the stock of information on search goods that consumers already have will, in part, be a factor. Quality information provision, or "signalling" in Laband's terminology, will be more prevalent in areas or markets where consumers have smaller existing stocks of information.

For purposes of his study, Laband measures quality-signalling by references in the Yellow Pages to licensure, certification, and professional membership association on the part of the vendor, as well as to ads listing the experience of the vendor.[11] Laband compared the Washington, D.C. and Baltimore Yellow Pages for ads of both low price-repeat purchase (corresponding to experience goods) and high price-infrequently purchased goods and services (search goods). In both localities, Laband finds the percentage of ads containing quality signalling to be significantly greater in his search goods, as opposed to experience goods, category. The differences run from four times greater to twelve times greater.

Comparison of the Yellow Pages ads of the two cities reveals even more. Laband contends that the average consumer in Baltimore has resided in that city more years than has the average Washingtonian. Consumers in Washington should then benefit *more* at the margin from Yellow Pages quality signalling than would the average consumer living in Baltimore. The Baltimore resident has a larger stock of existing quality information developed through actual past sampling of vendors, among other obvious means. In a competitive market setting, the benefits to Washingtonians of vendor quality signalling in the Yellow Pages provide the incentive for businesses in Washington to quality signal relatively more heavily than in Baltimore. Comparing search goods and services categories across the Yellow Pages lends evidence in support of the new neoclassical approach. A statistically significant larger fraction of ads in the Washington Yellow Pages convey seller quality information. Laband's evidence suggests that advertising, more particularly its form, character, and quantity, is heavily influenced by consumers. Further, his study is consistent with the view that market competition induces suppliers to provide the information to consumers that *consumers* deem most beneficial.

CONCLUSION

Evidence on a wide-ranging number of issues regarding the economic effects of advertising has been covered in this and the previous chapter. A large quantity of evidence indicates that advertising, however measured and in whatever form, does not appear to be a tool used by monopolists or oligopolists in an attempt to raise prices or to increase profits.[12] Rather, accumulating evidence reveals that advertising is a characteristic of competition—a means of entry into markets, a vehicle for price reduction, and a benefit to consumers. In this role it is part and parcel of a rivalrous competitive process with profound implications for the functioning of a market economy. In Chapter 7 we evaluate, in light of the new neoclassical view, a number of recent cases before the Federal Trade Commission relating to advertising regulation.

---

[11]While we showed earlier in the chapter that quality of service was certainly not guaranteed by professional membership associations in the contact lens market, vendor associations may impart some minimum quality characteristics to consumers for the goods Laband studies.

[12]We do not, of course, mean to imply that many other regulated commercial restrictions do not increase the price of goods and services. A recent empirical study of employment, location, branch office and trade name restrictions in optometry, for example, concludes that such commerical practices raised consumer costs by $4.7 million for eye examinations and eyeglasses in 1977: see Deborah Haas-Wilson, "The Effect of Commercial Practice Restrictions: The Case of Optometry," *Journal of Law and Economics* 29 (1986): 165–186. Methods of vertical coordination, such as exclusive distributorships, are also often cited as sources of monopoly in markets, but recent research casts doubt upon this proposition. In a study of exclusive distributorships and advertising restrictions in the beer industry Ekelund, *et al* find that higher beer prices are the result of the intensity of state advertising restrictions and other artificial constraints upon the competitive process and are not the result of exclusive arrangements between beer manufacturers and their distributors: see Robert B. Ekelund, Jr., *et al*, Exclusive Territories and Advertising Restrictions in the Malt Beverage Industry," (manuscript, 1988).

THE REGULATION OF PHARMACEUTICALS

Balancing the Benefits and Risks

HENRY G. GRABOWSKI
JOHN M. VERNON

INTRODUCTION

Regulation of the pharmaceutical industry dates back to the early part of this century. The system of government controls that has evolved is among the most extensive and stringent for any product class. The regulatory process is centered on the premarket screening of new pharmaceutical agents. All new drug therapies must be approved as safe and effective by the Food and Drug Administration (FDA) before they can be marketed. In addition, there are significant regulatory controls over the clinical research process, over the labeling and promotion of drug therapies, and over laboratory and manufacturing practices.

Many of these controls stem from the passage of the 1962 Kefauver-Harris amendments to the Food, Drug, and Cosmetic Act and the regulations issued by the FDA in implementing those amendments. Since 1962 there have been a number of adverse trends in pharmaceutical innovation. The annual rate of new chemical entities (NCEs) introduced has fallen, research and development (R and D) costs have risen, and the United States has lagged significantly behind other countries in making new drug therapies available. These trends have led to a great deal of interest in and controversy about regulatory reform at the FDA.

In this introductory chapter we examine the origins and development of the regulatory process in pharmaceuticals. Next we discuss "market failure" as a rationale for government regulation. We then analyze the problems of "nonmarket failure" arising from the FDA's regulatory intervention in a research-intensive innovative industry such as pharmaceuticals.

Historical background of food and drug regulation

The first law regulating pharmaceuticals was the Pure Food and Drug Act of 1906, which prohibited adulteration and mislabeling of food and drugs sold in interstate commerce.[1] The law was passed in the progressive era of President Theodore Roosevelt's administration and was largely a response to publicity generated by Upton Sinclair's *The Jungle* and the works of other muckrakers of that era. At the time of passage, there were no constraints on the sale of pharmaceuticals to consumers (such as the need to obtain a physician's prescription), and prescription drugs constituted less than a third of all drugs consumed. Many patent medicines with extensive medical claims but of doubtful value were being sold.

The 1906 law and a subsequent amendment in 1912 were designed to correct such patent medicine abuses by prohibiting false or misleading claims. The law was generally ineffective in accomplishing this objective because initially only a very small staff of chemists was available for enforcement and, more significantly, because a series of court decisions put the burden on the government to demonstrate fraud in prosecuting

---

[1] For a recent account of the history of drug regulation, see Peter Temin, *Taking Your Medicine: Drug Regulation in the United States* (Cambridge, Mass: Harvard University Press, 1981). See also William M. Wardell and Louis Lasagna, *Regulation and Drug Development* (Washington, D.C.: American Enterprise Institute, 1975), chap. 1.

---

producers making unproven claims for their products. The law did allow the FDA to remove from the market some products whose contents were incorrectly represented as well as some products involving obvious fraud.

During the first term of President Franklin Roosevelt, legislation was introduced to strengthen the powers of the FDA. It was not until 1938, however, after a major drug disaster involving the drug sulfanilamide, that new legislation was passed by Congress. In attempting to formulate a liquid form of sulfanilamide, a major sulfa drug, the Massengill Company created an elixir that used diethylene glycol as a solvent without testing it for toxicity. More than a hundred children died from this liquid combination because diethylene glycol turned out to be a poisonous chemical.

After this drug disaster, Congress passed the Food, Drug, and Cosmetic Act of 1938, which required firms to submit a new drug application (NDA) to the FDA before introducing any new pharmaceutical into interstate commerce. The application had to enumerate the uses of the drug and demonstrate that it was safe under the recommended conditions. The application was automatically approved in sixty days unless the secretary of agriculture (under whose jurisdiction the FDA rested at the time) determined that it did not contain sufficient tests of drug safety. The law also provided the basis for subsequent FDA regulations that separated pharmaceuticals into ethical drugs, which may be purchased only with a physician's prescription, and proprietary drugs, which may be sold over the counter to all consumers.[2]

Despite these new regulatory controls, innovation in ethical drugs flourished over the next two decades. Many major advances were achieved, including the introduction of antibiotics (penicillin, tetracyclines), tranquilizers, antihypertensives, diuretics, and antidiabetic agents. Competition in the drug industry increasingly focused on the discovery and development of new chemical entities. Total industry R and D expenditures increased dramatically along with the volume of NCEs.

Although the premarket safety reviews of the FDA obviously caused time lags in introducing NCEs and kept some drugs out of the marketplace, regulatory review times were still quite short (seven months on average), and the annual volume of NCEs introduced was at record levels (over fifty per year) at the end of the 1950s. Indeed, the focus of congressional oversight committees in this period turned to the high profits earned by some prescription drugs and to company patents and trademarks as the source of above-average profits. Senator Estes Kefauver held a number of hearings on this issue and attempted to get Congress to pass legislation designed to curb these perceived competitive abuses through compulsory licensing of drug patents and prohibition of separate brand names for prescription drugs.

Senator Kefauver was unsuccessful in gaining legislative support for these economic-oriented policy changes. A major regulatory bill was passed in 1962 under his sponsorship, however: the Kefauver-Harris amendments to the Food, Drug, and Cosmetic Act. This law passed after the well-known and tragic events associated with thalidomide. This drug, which produced fetal deformities in pregnant women, had been introduced in several European countries but not in the United States, where its introduction had been delayed by an FDA investigation. The large-scale media publicity about thalidomide's toxic properties caused the Kefauver Committee to shift its focus from economic to safety concerns. The 1962 amendments were then quickly drafted and passed with little opposition by Congress.

Two basic provisions of the amendments directly affected the process of drug innovation—a proof-of-efficacy requirement for approval of new drugs and establishment of FDA regulatory controls over the clinical (human) testing of new drug candidates.

The amendments required firms to provide substantial evidence of a new drug's efficacy based on "adequate and well controlled trials." Subsequent FDA regulations interpreted this provision to mean the use of experimental and control groups to demonstrate a drug's efficacy as statistically significant. The preferred mode of study was "double blind" control, where neither patient nor physician knew whether the patient was receiving

---

[2]The prescription-only or ethical drug classification developed out of a relatively minor legislative provision in the 1938 law allowing labeling exemptions. This provides an excellent historical example of how FDA discretion in interpreting the law has been successfully employed by the agency to expand its regulatory controls and authority. See Temin, *Taking Your Medicine*, pp. 46–51.

the experimental drug or a standard therapy or placebo. According to industry sources, the FDA's regulations concerning substantial evidence of safety and efficacy led to large increases in the resources necessary to obtain approval of a new drug application (NDA), especially in therapeutic areas where analyses of patients' responses are necessarily subjective (such as analgesics and antidepressants).

The second major change in the 1962 amendments influencing drug innovation was the institution of investigational new drug (IND) requirements for clinical testing. Before any tests on human subjects, firms were required to submit a new drug investigational plan giving the results of animal tests and research protocols for human tests. After evaluating the IND and subsequent reports of research findings, the FDA may prohibit, delay, or halt clinical research that poses excessive risks to volunteer subjects or that does not follow sound scientific procedures. As a result of the IND procedures, the FDA shifted after 1962 from essentially an evaluator of evidence and research findings at the end of the R and D process to an active participant in the process itself. This shift contributed to the higher development costs and longer times for pharmaceutical R and D.

The amendments also repealed the automatic approval of an NDA within 60 days if the FDA did not take action to prevent the drug from reaching the market. The FDA now had to take affirmative action on an NDA for the drug to enter the marketplace. It was supposed to make a decision within 180 days, but no sanctions were provided for longer deliberation times. The law also set into motion the Drug Efficacy Study Implementation (DESI) program to review the effectiveness of drugs on the market under the 1938 statute. Drugs that could not meet the new standards of evidence of efficacy were to be removed from the market by the FDA.

In addition to these regulations regarding proof of safety and efficacy, the law regulated various other aspects of firms' behavior. First, the amendments imposed controls on the advertising and promotion of prescription drugs. They required firms to include generic names on drug labels in addition to brand names and to restrict all advertised claims to those approved by the FDA in labeling and packaging inserts. Second, they required drug firms to adhere to standards of good manufacturing practice, which would be set out in detailed FDA regulations.

The 1962 amendments were thus a culmination of the shift of primary decision-making authority in pharmaceuticals from market mechanisms to a centralized regulatory authority. The early regulatory laws in this area had essentially sought to make the market work better through government provision of information and the elimination of false claims and misinformation. The 1938 and 1962 legislative actions, which followed highly publicized adverse drug incidents, had a very different objective. They sought to protect consumers by barring undesirable products from the market. The judgment about what was desirable or undesirable was to be made by a central regulatory authority rather than by market forces and the voluntary choices of suppliers, physicians, and patients.

After the 1962 legislation, the external environment surrounding FDA decisions on new drug approvals also changed significantly. The thalidomide disaster, widely reported in the popular press, focused the attention of Congress and the media on the potential risks of new drugs.

Former FDA Commissioner Alexander Schmidt has emphasized the problems these external pressures create for the maintenance of balanced and rational decision making at the FDA. As he observed in a speech while commissioner during the mid-1970s:

> For example, in all of FDA's history, I am unable to find a single instance where a Congressional committee investigated the failure of FDA to approve a new drug. But, the times when hearings have been held to criticize our approval of new drugs have been so frequent that we aren't able to count them. . . . The message to FDA staff could not be clearer. Whenever a controversy over a new drug is resolved by its approval, the Agency and the individuals involved likely will be investigated. Whenever such a drug is disapproved, no inquiry will be made. The Congressional pressure for our negative action on new drug applications is, therefore, intense. And it seems to be increasing, as everyone is becoming a self-acclaimed expert on carcinogenesis and drug testing.[3]

---

[3] Alexander Schmidt, "The FDA Today: Critics, Congress, and Consumerism," speech delivered before the National Press Club, Washington, D.C., October 29, 1974.

In the two decades that have elapsed since more stringent regulation of pharmaceuticals took effect in the early 1960s, pharmaceutical innovation has exhibited a number of adverse trends. These include sharp increases in the R and D costs and the gestation times for NCEs, large declines in the annual rate of NCE introduction for the industry, and a well-publicized lag in the introduction of significant new drug therapies when compared with other developed countries such as the United Kingdom and West Germany. These phenomena are discussed in detail in chapter 3. By the end of the 1960s these adverse trends were becoming readily apparent. A number of research studies linking the more stringent regulatory climate with the higher costs and lower levels of pharmaceutical innovation were published. One particularly well-known study, by Sam Peltzman, also reported that the benefits of the 1962 amendments were small.[4]

These studies sparked considerable debate and controversy among policy makers. Successive FDA administrations attempted to show that other factors besides regulation (such as a depletion of research opportunities) accounted for the slowdown in innovation. They also attempted to minimize or even completely deny the loss of significant therapeutic benefits associated with the lag in NCE introductions.

By the end of the 1970s, however, Congress focused increased attention on the drug lag question and the adverse effects on innovation of the regulatory process. A comprehensive drug reform act initiated by the Carter administration in 1978 had some features designed to reduce drug lag (but also several features that arguably would have operated to slow the process further). This bill failed to receive sufficient support to be enacted.

The concern with drug lag and the adverse incentives to innovation of FDA regulation has continued to intensify. In 1980 the General Accounting Office (GAO) issued a report documenting significant lags in introducing therapies that the FDA itself ranked as important medical advances and pointing out a number of deficiencies in regulatory procedures and in the NCE approval process.[5] Two congressmen, Representatives Fred Scheuer and Albert Gore, initiated a series of hearings on FDA regulatory procedures. Also in 1981 a task force of academic experts, FDA officials, and congressional White House staff representatives was assembled to recommend ways of improving the regulatory process and reducing its adverse effects on innovation.

Although the relation of regulation to innovation in pharmaceuticals remains a complex issue subject to continuing research, there appears to be a growing political consensus that regulation has had significant negative effects on innovation and that some changes in current procedures are desirable. The new administration has given its initial attention to possible changes in FDA regulations rather than legislative changes in the Food, Drug, and Cosmetic Act. Several changes now being proposed are considered in chapter 5.

Market failure as a rationale for drug regulation

Pharmaceutical agents have frequently been described as two-edged swords. They can be the source of great therapeutic benefits as well as very great risks. Even established drugs of therapeutic choice are not free of risk. Taken in a dosage too low or too high, they can have serious or even fatal consequences. Moreover, the combination of therapeutically beneficial drugs can produce toxic side effects not associated with them individually. And possible idiosyncratic response to pharmaceutical agents—though relatively infrequent or rare—may pose very serious dangers to a small group of patients.

The therapeutic benefits and risks of potential new drug entities in very early stages of development are to a high degree uncertain. The uncertainty can be reduced by various tests on animals and people. In an unregulated free-market institution, decisions about how much testing to undertake and when and whether to market a new product would be based on profit incentives. Private profit incentives would be influenced and shaped by various societal institutions, including medical training and the medical delivery system (given the central role of physicians in decisions on drug use), the tort and medical malpractice laws (which set the penalties for product defects and misuse), and patent and product substitution laws (which influence the terms of permissible imitation for new products).

---

[4] Sam Peltzman, *Regulation of Pharmaceutical Innovation: The 1962 Amendments* (Washington, D.C.: American Enterprise Institute, 1974).
[5] U.S. General Accounting Office, *FDA Drug Approval—A Lengthy Process That Delays the Availability of Important New Drugs*, HRD-80–64, May 28, 1980.

The justification for replacing the forces of the market and its attendant institutions with regulatory authority is generally framed in terms of a "market failure" analysis. The presumed failure is that free-market forces would lead to the introduction and consumption of drug products with excessive risks compared with benefits. This could occur because a supplying firm, to gain the advantages of first introduction or simply to avoid high costs, performed insufficient premarket testing. Firms might also overstate good points and understate negative points in promoting and labeling drugs. Of course, any such tendencies would be constrained to some extent by tort laws as well as by the long-term damage to good repute caused by negative experiences with new drugs.

The source of market failure in this situation is generally called by economists "information imperfection." It is the problem that the customer has in obtaining information about the benefits and risks of new drugs. There are reasons to doubt the completeness of firm-supplied information. Furthermore, because of the "public good" nature of information, it is unlikely that third parties would find it profitable to supply the needed information in sufficient quantity. While such information problems surround many consumer products, the potential threats to human health from the consumption of drugs, which can be severe and irreversible, make them particularly strong candidates for government intervention.

Two alternative strategies for remedying information imperfection are generally available to government policy makers. The first is to try to make the market work better through such measures as government subsidy and provision of information and by altering private incentives to behave in a socially undesirable way (through tort law sanctions and other such penalties). The second is to replace decentralized market decisions with a centralized regulatory control structure so that decisions about premarket tests and market introduction are placed directly in the hands of government officials.

The history of U.S. pharmaceutical regulation is one of steady evolution away from the first strategy—making the market work better—toward the second approach of strong centralized regulatory control over firms' decisions about pharmaceutical testing and marketing. The current system offers a particularly stringent form of product quality regulation, which few other industries, if any, have experienced.

Some have viewed the history of drug regulation as providing convincing evidence of the inadequacies of the first approach and demonstrating the need for strong, centralized regulatory controls. The period from the passage of the 1906 Pure Food and Drug Act to 1938 was characterized by a market-oriented approach—government policing of adulteration and mislabeling of drugs and prosecution of violators through the court system. This approach was insufficient to prevent many market abuses, including the sulfanilamide tragedy, which led directly to the premarket safety reviews of the 1938 legislation.

It can be argued, however, that the ineffectiveness of the early regulatory structure in remedying market imperfections and performance has very limited relevance to the current situation. Early regulation was exclusively directed to sins of commission and had severe constraints placed on it by the congressional mandate and subsequent judicial decisions. Furthermore, there was no government provision of information about new pharmaceuticals and only limited policing of misinformation after the product had been introduced. The market environment for pharmaceuticals was also very different. The vast majority of pharmaceuticals were not dispensed through physicians prescriptions but were proprietary patent medicines. Furthermore, the tort laws of that period can best be categorized as caveat emptor rather than the extensive and elaborate system of laws dealing with product defects and faults that exists today.

The FDA regulatory program between 1938 and 1962 can be viewed as a blend of the two approaches. The law required premarket application and submission of proof of safety, but approval was automatic after sixty days if the FDA did not raise specific objections. The thrust of regulation during this period seemed oriented to preventing outlier or extreme situations (a few "bad actors"). Most drugs were cleared without major objections by the FDA, and the clearance process seldom took more than several months to complete. The FDA essentially performed a certification role concerning the NDA submission and stood ready to block deficient new drug applications that posed significant safety risks.

The 1962 amendments ushered in a period of strong, centralized regulatory controls over introductions of new drugs and drug product quality. All new drug applications were subject to significantly greater evidentiary standards, requiring proof of safety and efficacy. The approval process became an exhaustive case-by-case review taking two to three years to complete rather than several months. Furthermore, regulatory jurisdiction was extended to the clinical research process, to manufacturing practices, and to the labeling and promotion of drugs. The applicable model for drug regulation therefore apparently shifted from one of dealing with occasional market failure associated with outlier situations or a few "bad actors" to the presumption of a more pervasive and health-threatening market failure that required extensive codification and enforcement of very stringent standards for all new drugs introduced.

Regulatory failure versus market failure

The benefits of government regulation in this and other areas are not costless. The most significant cost of more stringent regulatory controls over introduction of new pharmaceuticals is a slower rate of pharmaceutical innovation.

Ideally, a system of government intervention would give comparable weight to the costs and benefits of regulatory decisions. In practice this is difficult to accomplish. The legislative mandate and regulatory procedures of the FDA evolved as a response to the perceived problems of unsafe or ineffective drugs. Little initial attention was given by Congress or regulators to the potential adverse effects of increased regulation on drug innovation. This asymmetric focus of regulatory officials on the benefits of regulation and relative insensitivity to its costs, a more general phenomenon that has frequently been observed in health and safety regulatory situations, can be a major source of "government failure."

To illustrate the relevance of this point, it is useful to analyze the FDA's regulatory function in terms of a standard statistical decision-making framework (see figure 1). We assume that a new drug application is submitted to the FDA and that some uncertainty exists about whether the drug is safe or effective. The FDA must use the information submitted in the application to make a subjective probability assessment of safety and efficacy and either accept or reject the application. No pharmaceutical is absolutely safe in the sense that it is completely free of adverse side effects. Effectiveness can also vary among patients and clinical situations. Determination that a drug is safe and effective is therefore a relative decision involving an informed judgment that therapeutic benefits exceed risks.

In this decision-making situation there are two correct types of decisions and two types of errors. The correct decisions are FDA acceptance of drugs that are safe and effective and rejection of those that are not. Type 1 error is FDA rejection of a "good" drug or one whose benefits would exceed risks in clinical practice. Type 2 error is acceptance of a drug when the reverse is true. Both types of error influence patients' health and well-being since consuming a "bad" drug or not having access to a "good" drug can have deleterious effects on health.

It can be plausibly argued, however, that our regulatory structure does not have a neutral stance between type 1 and type 2 errors. The mandate to the FDA is drawn in very narrow terms—to protect consumers against

FIGURE 1. FDA Decision Making on New Ddrug Applications

State of the world

		New drug is safe and effective	New drug is not safe and effective
FDA decision	Accept	Correct decision	Type 2 error
	Reject	Type 1 error	Correct decision

unsafe or ineffective drugs (that is, to avoid type 2 errors). There is no corresponding mandate to avoid type 1 errors or to compel equal concern with new drug innovation and improved medical therapy. In point of fact, the institutional incentives confronting FDA officials strongly reinforce the tendency to avoid type 2 errors at the expense of type 1 errors. An FDA official who approves a drug subsequently shown to be not safe or effective stands to bear heavy personal costs. Such an outcome, even if it occurs very infrequently, tends to be highly visible and is one for which both the FDA and the regulatory official are held politically accountable. The costs of rejecting a good drug are borne largely by outside parties (drug manufacturers and sick patients who might benefit from it). They are also much less visible. The signals emanating from Congress and the media have tended to reinforce risk avoidance at the FDA. As the earlier quotation from Commissioner Schmidt emphasizes, there have been scores of congressional hearings on controversies over approvals of new drugs, but little attention has been given, at least until very recently, to the FDA's failure to approve new drugs.

One may argue that this analysis is somewhat misleading in that the main effect of the FDA's regulatory behavior is not to prevent useful new therapies from entering the marketplace but rather to delay their introduction. The FDA official may elect to avoid type 2 error not by rejecting a new drug application outright but by opting for more tests before a final decision can be made. By requiring more tests and longer delays, regulators can presumably lower the objective and subjective probability of both type 1 and type 2 errors by obtaining further information from premarket domestic trials and from foreign marketing experience. There are thus strong incentives inherent in the present structure to delay and to increase the number of tests performed before a final decision is reached. At some point, however, one would expect useful new therapies to be approved by the regulatory officials if their domestic and foreign experience is favorable.

The general trade-offs arising from this risk avoidance are depicted further in figure 2. As the required premarket testing increases, the expected R and D costs that must be undertaken for a new drug approval increase in rough proportion. Insofar as the greater testing increases the drug development period, we would also observe delay in the availability of some useful therapies, or "drug lag" costs. At the same time, the expected information about a drug's safety and efficacy also increases with increased testing, so that the expected health costs from the introduction of an unsafe or ineffective drug decline. Because any information so obtained will eventually be subject to sharply diminishing returns, the last curve will tend to flatten out with increased testing while R and D and drug lag costs rise steadily.

Hence, if regulators try to be cautious and avoid type 2 error by ordering more and more resources devoted to premarket testing, they will push firms to the point on these curves where large increments of R and D investments tend to buy very little additional information about safety and efficacy. In short, the FDA might be viewed as being primarily concerned with minimizing expected health costs rather than total costs, thereby setting the level of testing too far to the right in figure 2.

It has also been argued by some critics that inefficiencies in interactions between the FDA and firms in the testing process have caused R and D costs to be considerably higher than the minimum feasible level. To the extent that this is true, R and D costs would shift upward as shown by the dashed curve in figure 2.

The long-run consequences of the regulatory behavior depicted in figure 2 will be to increase R and D costs and times above what is socially desirable. This in turn will result in a decline in new drug introductions (or drug loss) because, with higher R and D costs, some potentially beneficial new drugs are no longer profitable or feasible innovations. While it is very difficult to measure the extent of this drug loss since these drugs are never introduced, the loss will tend to be concentrated among drugs with potentially small markets or above-average riskiness to develop. There will thus be forgone health benefits to consumers from the loss of these undeveloped drugs.

We may now summarize the main points of the discussion of market failure and regulatory failure in terms of the analysis presented in figures 1 and 2. Because of the presence of insufficient information incentives and related market imperfections, the unregulated market is seen as prone to insufficient premarket testing (that is, a point too far to the left in figure 2) and consequently to the consumption of too many drugs that are not safe and effective (that is, a type 2 error in figure 1). The incentives and biases associated with our current regulatory regime, however, tend to result in more testing and delay than are socially desirable (that is, a point too

FIGURE 2. Cost Trade-offs in Premarket Testing

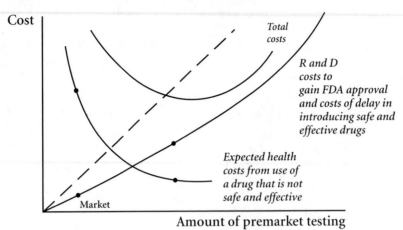

Cost

Total costs

R and D costs to gain FDA approval and costs of delay in introducing safe and effective drugs

Expected health costs from use of a drug that is not safe and effective

Market

Amount of premarket testing

SOURCE: Authors.

far to the right in figure 2). This tends to produce type 1 errors, in which useful drugs are delayed or fail to be introduced at all because of the adverse economic effects of government regulatory decisions and the general insensitivity of the regulatory process to such costs.

In the chapters that follow, we review the empirical evidence concerning the positive and negative effects of FDA pharmaceutical regulation. The final chapter is devoted to a discussion of various proposals that have been advanced in the literature to improve regulatory performance.

ENVIRONMENTAL PROGRESS AND ITS DISCONTENTS

STEVEN F. HAYWARD

A RETROSPECTIVE ON A CENTURY OF ENVIRONMENTAL PROGRESS: ANOTHER "GREATEST STORY NEVER TOLD"

Quick: What's the largest public-policy success story in American society over the last generation? The dramatic reduction in the crime rate, which has helped make major American cities livable again? Or welfare reform, which saw the nation's welfare rolls fall by more than half since the early 1990s? Both of these accomplishments have received wide media attention. Yet the right answer might well be the environment.

As Figure 1 displays, the reduction in air pollution is comparable in magnitude to the reduction in the welfare rolls, and greater than the reduction in the crime rate—both celebrated as major public-policy success stories of the last two decades. Aggregate emissions of the six "criteria" pollutants[1] regulated under the Clean Air Act have fallen by 53 percent since 1970, while the proportion of the population receiving welfare assistance is down 48 percent from 1970, and the crime rate is only 6.4 percent below its 1970 level. (And as we shall see, this aggregate nationwide reduction in emissions greatly understates the actual improvement in ambient air quality in the areas with the worst levels of air pollution.) Measures for water quality, toxic-chemical exposure, soil erosion, forest growth, wetlands, and several other areas of environmental concern show similar positive trends, as this *Almanac* reports. To paraphrase Mark Twain, reports of the demise of the environment have been greatly exaggerated. Moreover, there is good reason to believe that these kinds of improvements will be experienced in the rest of the world over the course of this century. We'll examine some of the early evidence that this is already starting to occur.

The chief drivers of environmental improvement are economic growth, constantly increasing resource efficiency, technological innovation in pollution control, and the deepening of environmental values among the American public that have translated to changed behavior and consumer preferences. Government regulation has played a vital role, to be sure, but in the grand scheme of things regulation can be understood as a lagging indicator, often achieving results at needlessly high cost, and sometimes failing completely. Were it not for rising affluence and technological innovation, regulation would have much the same effect as King Canute commanding the tides.

The American public remains largely unaware of these trends. For most of the last 40 years, public opinion about the environment has been pessimistic, with large majorities—sometimes as high as 70 percent—telling pollsters that they think environmental quality in the United States is getting worse instead of better, and will continue to get worse in the future. One reason for this state of opinion is media coverage, which emphasizes bad news and crisis; another reason is environmental advocacy groups, for whom good news is bad news. As the cliché goes, you can't sell many newspapers with headlines about airplanes landing safely, or about an oil tanker docking without a spill. Similarly, slow, long-term trends don't make for good headline copy.

IMPROVING TRENDS: CAUSES AND CONSEQUENCES

Most environmental commentary dwells on the laws and regulations we have adopted to achieve our goals, but it is essential to understand the more important role of technology and economic growth in bringing

Figure 1. A comparison of crime rate, welfare, and air pollution, 1970–2007

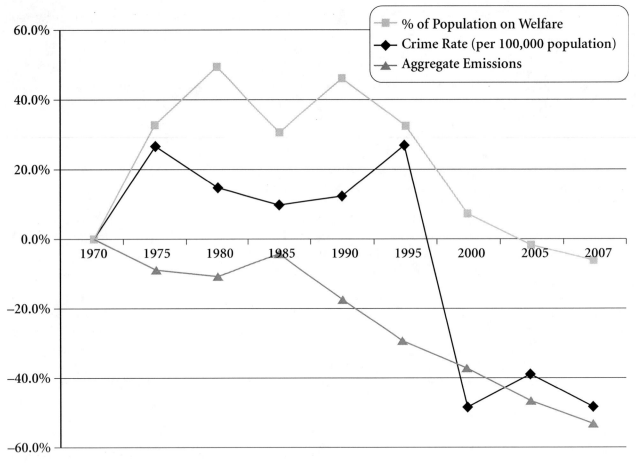

SOURCE: FBI Uniform Crime Reports, U.S. Department of Health and Human Services, EPA.

about favorable environmental trends. The best way to see this is to look at some long-term trends in environmental quality that predate modern environmental legislation.

To be sure, the earliest phases of the Industrial Revolution led to severe environmental degradation. But the inexorable process of technological innovation and the drive for efficiency began to remedy much of this damage far earlier than is commonly perceived. In addition, new technologies that we commonly regard as environmentally destructive often replaced older modes of human activity that were far worse by comparison. A good example is the introduction of coal for heating and energy in Britain.

In their quest for firewood, Britons had nearly denuded the country of forests by the mid-17th century. Wood for any purpose in Britain had become scarce and expensive. "This period in British history," economist William Hausman wrote, "has been identified as containing the first 'energy crisis' of the modern era."[2] Coal emissions are certainly harmful, but the adoption of coal reversed the severe deforestation that had taken place. The environmental tradeoff of air pollution for forest and habitat preservation was probably favorable in the short run.

In the fullness of time the environmental harm from coal smoke intensified as urban areas grew more densely populated and modern industry emerged. In the United States, the most infamous air-pollution event occurred in Donora, Pennsylvania, where a smog siege in October 1948 killed 20 people and sickened thousands.[3]

Figure 2. Air pollution and bronchitis deaths, Manchester, England

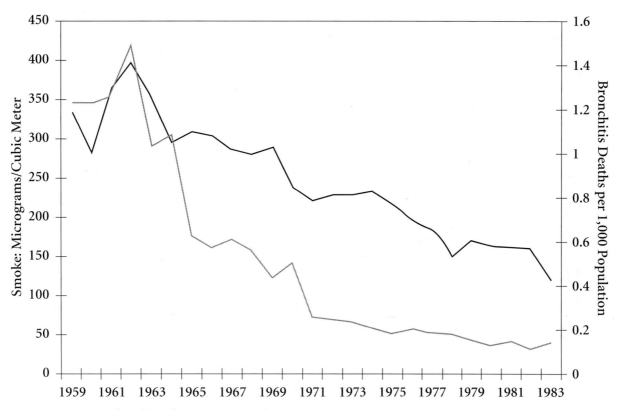

SOURCE: Environmental Health and Consumer Protection Department, City of Manchester.

This era culminated in the great London "fog" of 1952, in which nearly 5,000 people, and uncounted hundreds of farm animals, died from coal smoke in a severe winter inversion. It was this episode that led to the term "smog" to describe urban air pollution. Britain moved swiftly to restrict the use of coal and wood for urban fuel purposes; this step was possible only because efficient substitutes such as electricity and natural gas had become available. The kind of severe urban air crisis that used to plague British cities no longer occurs anywhere in modern industrialized nations. The health benefits from reducing high levels of urban air pollution were immediate and dramatic. Figure 2 shows the decline in wintertime bronchitis deaths in Manchester, England, following the decline of smog in that industrial city. Bronchitis deaths fell by two-thirds as ambient smoke concentrations fell by more than 80 percent.

Similar improvements in urban air quality in American cities can be observed long before the first clean air acts were enacted at the federal and state levels. Although comprehensive data gathering about urban air quality did not begin until about 1970, there are a few datasets available that provide a good look at the long-term picture. Sulfur dioxide levels fell by a third in the decade before the first federal Clean Air Act. Figure 3 shows the trend for settleable dust in the industrial city of Pittsburgh between 1925 and 1965.[4] The rapid decline in the early years between 1925 and 1940 is attributable to the simple efficiency gains from industry's upgrading its technology. The industrial drive for cost-saving efficiency typically leads to cleaner technology.

An equally vivid example of the long-term role of economic growth and technological progress can be seen in the trend of wood used for heating and fuel in the United States in the 20th century. At the turn of the century, nearly one-third of America's heating was obtained by burning wood. As fuel oil, natural gas, and electricity became widely adopted starting in the early decades of the century, the use of wood for fuel began declining rapidly, as seen in Figure 4: from approximately five billion cubic feet in 1900 to less than 500 million cubic feet in 1970.

Figure 3. Settleable dust in Pittsburgh

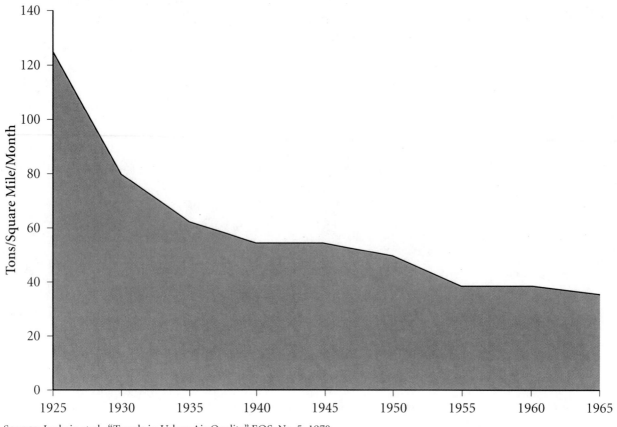

SOURCE: Ludwig et al., "Trends in Urban Air Quality" EOS, No. 5, 1970.

Figure 4. The decline in wood used for fuel in the United States

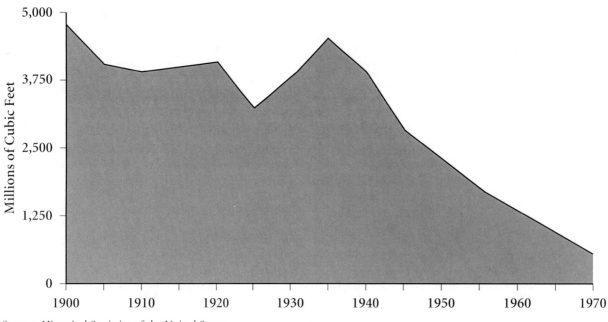

SOURCE: Historical Statistics of the United States.

Although there was no national "spot market" for fuel wood as there were for other commodities in 1900, the price for construction lumber can be taken as a reasonable proxy. The inflation-adjusted price of lumber in 1900 was five times the price of lumber in 1970. It is worth noting in Figure 4 when wood use ceases to decline and heads back up again—during the Great Depression, when fewer people could afford new gas and oil furnaces, and when businesses reduced spending for capital equipment.[5] Here is a clear example of the effect of economic growth—or the lack of it—on resource use and environmental quality. It is ironic to recall that during the "energy crisis" of the 1970s one of the favored popular remedies was a return to woodstoves, which would have represented a step backward for both air quality and forest habitat.

Coal and wood smoke were not the only air quality hazards faced by our forebears in urban locations. At the turn of the century a primary mode of intra-city transport was still the horse-drawn cart or truck. There were about 1.4 million horse-drawn transportation vehicles in the U.S. in 1900; New York City alone had more than 200,000 transport horses in 1900. The transport capacity of horses was three-quarters as great as the transport capacity of the railroads in 1900; as late as 1911 the value of horse-drawn transportation equipment produced was greater than the value of railroad equipment produced.[6] The air and water quality hazards from horse dung are obvious; a single horse might produce 12,000 pounds of manure and 400 gallons of urine a year, much of which fell on city streets. According to one estimate, three billion flies *a day* hatched in horse-manure piles in American cities in 1900. In 1894 the *Times of* London predicted that by 1950 every street in London would be buried under nine feet of manure. In New York it was estimated that manure would reach a depth of three stories by 1930.[7] The pollution control technology of that time was a broom.

Less obvious is the huge amount of cropland necessary to grow feed for the thousands of draft animals needed for this mode of transportation and freight hauling. The average horse consumed about 30 pounds of feed a day, or five tons a year. The amount of land used for growing feed for horses and mules peaked at 93 million acres in 1915, an area nearly a third larger than the area of all U.S. cities today. (See Figure 5.) Almost no land

Figure 5. Amount of Land Used to Grow Feed for Horses and Mules

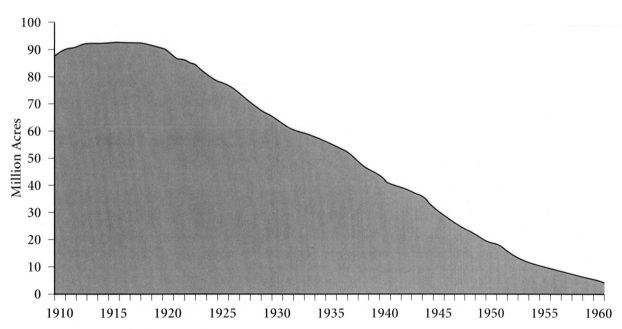

SOURCE: Historical Statistics of the United States.

is used to grow feed for horses now (the U.S. government discontinued this data series in 1961, because the acreage had shrunk almost to zero), and this decline in land use to produce feed for draft animals has doubtless contributed to the reforestation that has taken place in the United States.[8]

So serious was the urban pollution problem of the day that the famous inscription on the Statue of Liberty—"huddled masses yearning to breathe free"—might be regarded as the first (unintentional) environmental manifesto for urban air quality in America. The substitution of the internal combustion engine for horse-drawn urban transport represented an environmental *improvement*, with lower amounts of urban particulate air pollution and water pollution from animal waste, as *Scientific American* foresaw in an article that appeared in August 1900: "The streets of our great cities can not be kept scrupulously clean until automobiles have entirely replaced horse-drawn vehicles. At the present time women sweep through the streets with their skirts and bring with them, wherever they go, the abominable filth which is by courtesy called 'dust.' The management of a long gown is a difficult matter. Fortunately, the short skirt is coming into fashion, and the medical journals especially commend the sensible walking gown." Transportation researcher Eric Morris concluded, "Per vehicle and per mile, it seems highly likely that the environmental problems caused by the horse were far greater than those of the modern car."[9]

The rise of widespread fossil-fuel use in the early 20th century contributed significantly to improvement in human health. Respiratory disease rates in the United States, for example, fell eightfold during the 20th century; this improvement is owing to many factors, of course, but lower pollution is certainly prominent among them.

ENVIRONMENTAL PERFORMANCE AND ECONOMIC FREEDOM

Most environmentalists now concede that we aren't in imminent danger of running out of natural resources, a shift in thinking from the *Limits to Growth* days of the 1970s. But pollution and the degrading of ecosystems remain a pre-eminent concern.

The overuse of an ecosystem is relatively easy to observe on the local level. Good examples of unsustainable ecosystems in the U.S. might include Pittsburgh in the heyday of the coal and steel industry in the first half of the 20th century, Los Angeles as the smog worsened in the 1950s and 1960s, and the fouled waters of Lake Erie prior to the first Earth Day in 1970. The dramatic reversal of the environmental degradation of these local ecosystems shows the resiliency of nature and provides the basis for optimism that we can meet our environmental challenges. In advanced industrialized nations, many forms of pollution have been falling for decades, and although pollution is increasing in many developing nations, research and experience suggest that nations with growing economies can look forward to falling pollution rates over time.

Yet the question remains whether the progress to date is sufficient in the aggregate, or whether the degradation of ecosystems in the developing world will overwhelm the progress being made in the developed world. Is the earth's ecosystem as a whole being sustained? We currently lack systematic data and reliable metrics to answer this question definitively.

The most useful effort at assessing environmental conditions on the global scale is the Environmental Performance Index (EPI), a joint effort of the World Economic Forum, the Yale University Center for Environmental Law & Policy, and the Columbia University Center for International Earth Science Information Network. The Environmental Performance Index, first produced in 2000 and updated at two-year intervals, offers a performance score from 0 to 100 (with 100 being optimal performance) for 163 nations based on 25 indicators and 68 related variables. This methodology enables cross-national comparison of environmental progress.[10] The EPI notes the limitations of its data and methodology: "The EPI uses the best available global data sets on environmental performance. However, the overall data quality and availability is alarmingly poor. The lack of time-series data for most countries and the absence of broadly-collected and methodologically-consistent indicators for basic concerns, such as water quality, still hamper efforts to shift pollution control and natural resource management onto more empirical grounds." Hence the EPI no longer purports to be a measure of "sustainability."

That had been its initial goal. In fact, the first version of the EPI was called the "Environmental Sustainability Index." But the aforementioned difficulties of defining sustainability in a consistent and rigorous way led the Yale team to change the framework to "performance" rather than "sustainability." The EPI does not attempt to make aggregate judgments about the sustainability of the entire planet, noting in its 2008 edition that "While we accept the premise that politics, economics, and social values are important factors worthy of being sustained, we do not think that there is a sufficient scientific, empirical or political basis for constructing metrics that combine all of them along with the environment. . . . Scientific knowledge does not permit us to specify precisely what levels of performance are high enough to be truly sustainable, especially at a worldwide scale."

On the EPI scale for the year 2010, Finland came in first, with a score of 73.9, and Kuwait came in last, with a score of 23.9. One of the most notable findings of the 2010 EPI is the poor ranking of the United States: The U.S. ranked 46th, with a score of 53.2. The EPI notes that extensive changes in methodology prevent a comparison of rankings with previous iterations of the report, meaning that changes in the rankings cannot be used to judge progress or regress from recent years. However, it is worth noting in passing that the ranking of the United States has fallen consistently with each iteration of the EPI, even though by many individual measures (such as air and water quality and forest cover) environmental conditions in the U.S. have steadily improved over the last decade.

The U.S. ranked 11th in the first EPI, in 2000, with a raw score of 66. In the 2006 EPI the U.S. ranked 28th, but it fell to 39th place in the 2008 EPI. This steady decline in the United States' EPI ranking is a reflection chiefly of increased weights given to per capita greenhouse gas emissions. (Greenhouse gas emissions are assigned the second-largest weighting in the calculation of the latest EPI score.)

Yale professor Daniel Esty, one of the lead designers of the EPI, notes an interesting irony on this point. When he presented the findings of earlier editions of the EPI that ranked the U.S. more highly, some American audiences asked how it was that the U.S. scored so *poorly* on the rankings (Americans being used to appearing near the very top of all international rankings of good things). In Europe, professor Esty says, audiences wondered how it was possible that the U.S. scored so *well*. Surely there must be some dreadful mistake in the methodology that gave the United States the unjustified high rank of 28th place in 2006! Sure enough, when the United States fell to 39th place in 2008, the *New York Times* celebrated with the headline, U.S. GIVEN POOR MARKS ON THE ENVIRONMENT. In both 2008 and 2010, the U.S. ranked last among the G-8 nations.

Global indices of this kind are always vulnerable to methodological critiques, but this should not detract from their ability to illuminate important issues and trends—the kind of general conclusions that methodological changes would not significantly affect. In the case of the EPI, the data make clear two critical aspects of environmental improvement: the correlation of wealth or prosperity (and hence economic growth) with environmental quality, and the centrality of property rights and the rule of law to environmental protection. The EPI makes this point in its own analysis of the data: "Wealth correlates highly with EPI scores. In particular, wealth has a strong association with environmental health results." Figure 6 displays the correlation between per capita income and EPI scores. This is a graphic depiction of what economists call the "Environmental Kuznets Curve" (named for Simon Kuznets), according to which environmental quality degrades during the early stages of economic growth, but begins to improve after a certain level of income is reached.[11] (See sidebar "The Environmental Kuznets Curve.")

There is considerable variance in the data points (the correlation has an R^2 value of 0.37). The EPI notes and explains a crucial second-order factor: "But at every level of development, some countries fail to keep up with

Figure 6. Relationship between income and environmental performance

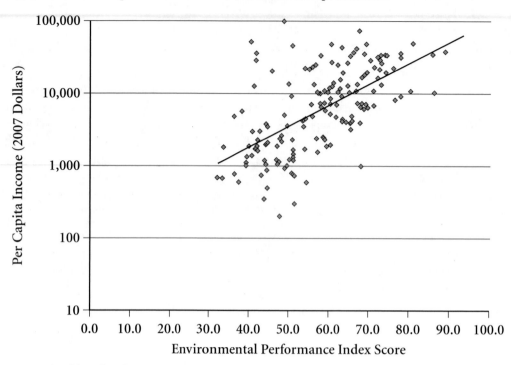

SOURCE: World Bank and EPI.

their income-group peers while others achieve outstanding results. *Statistical analysis suggests that in many cases good governance contributes to better environmental outcomes*" (emphasis added). While the EPI approaches "good governance" through particular measures of the effectiveness of government administration, it is useful to examine a key subset of "good governance," namely, the status of property rights and the rule of law.

Two different cross-indices can be used to make this analysis. The first is the Fraser Institute's *Economic Freedom of the World (EFW)* study, which ranks nations according to 42 metrics organized into five major categories (size of government, property rights and the rule of law, soundness of the monetary system, freedom of international trade, and regulation).[12] The *EFW* study (2009 is the most recent year available) rates each country in each category on a scale of 1 to 10 and generates a composite score. Figure 7 displays the correlation between *EFW* scores and EPI scores, offering evidence that increased economic freedom is associated with better environmental performance.

A comparison of the *EFW*'s property rights and rule of law scores and the EPI yields a stronger relationship, as shown in Figure 8. Figure 9 breaks out the data by quartiles, showing a 20-point gap in EPI scores between nations in the lowest quartile of property rights protection and nations in the highest quartile of property rights protection.

The *Economic Freedom of the World* metric for property rights protection and the rule of law employs seven variables that focus mostly on whether a nation's legal system is independent and impartially enforces contracts and property law; these variables are drawn from several sources, including the World Bank's comprehensive Worldwide Governance Indicators project. This project surveys 45 variables for its metric of the rule of law, which includes property rights protection. The difference in EPI scores by quartile is even more stark in the World Bank's ratings than in the *EFW* ratings, as shown in Figure 10.

These comparisons bolster the case that the best strategy for sustainability is not something new but something old: free markets and liberal democracy. Yet both points are matters of serious contention or confusion

Figure 7. Relationship between economic freedom and environmental performance

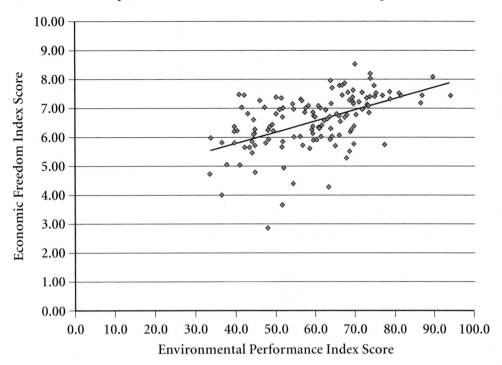

SOURCE: EFW and EPI.

Figure 8. Relationship between property rights protection and environmental performance

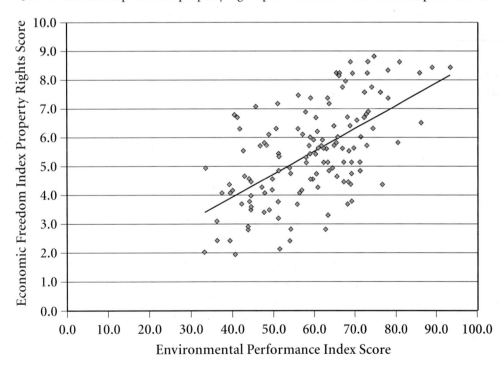

SOURCE: EFW and EPI

Figure 9. Relationship between EFW property rights protection scores by quartiles and EPI scores

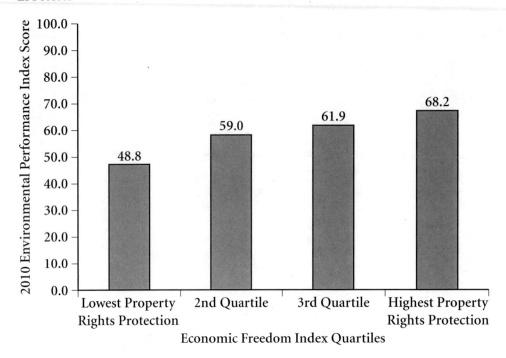

SOURCE: EFW and EPI

Figure 10. Relationship between world bank rule of law scores by quartiles and EPI scores

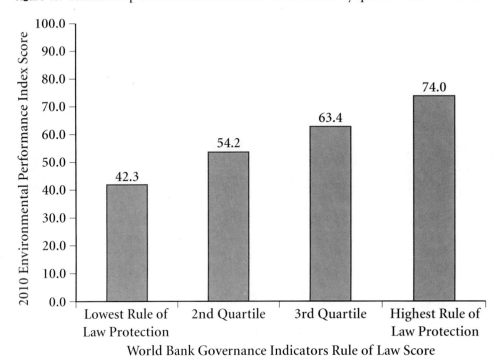

SOURCE: World Bank and EPI.

among many leading environmentalists. In the 1970s, during the "limits to growth" phase of popular environmentalism, many leading environmentalists were openly opposed to economic growth. The late David Brower once took out a full-page advertisement in the *New York Times* with the headline "Economics Is a Form of Brain Damage." While this kind of crude anti-intellectualism has given way to a broader appreciation of economic perspectives among most environmentalists, there is still a strong current of environmentalist sentiment for "steady-state economics" (a term used by Herman Daly and others), which explicitly rejects the idea of economic growth or substitutes a vague concept of "sustainable" growth that fails any real-world test of applicable rigor. At the very least, the idea of "sustainable" growth would require highly authoritarian government control of resources and individual economic decisions—a point some environmentalists, such as Paul Ehrlich, openly admit.

Emphasis on property rights is also anathema to many environmentalists. For example, one of the leading legal theorists of environmentalism, law professor Joseph Sax (pre-eminently associated with expanding the "public trust" doctrine), has written, "a quarter century of development in environmental protection is jeopardized by ill-conceived legislative proposals that purport to protect property rights."[13] Hostility to property rights is a popular theme among environmental bloggers, such as Planetsave.com's Shirley Siluk Gregory: "Has it ever occurred to you that the whole concept of private property might be innately harmful to the natural environment?"[14] (Gregory's blogpost is headlined, "Is Private Property Anti-Environment?") Australian legal scholar Paul Babie asks on BraveNewClimate.com whether "private property is the solution or part of the problem."

> Or might it be more appropriate, as Mike Hulme suggests, to ". . . *see how we can use the idea of climate change—the matrix of ecological functions, power relationships, cultural discourses and material flows that climate change reveals—to rethink how we take forward our political, social, economic and personal projects over the decades to come*." Before we pin our hopes on it as a cure-all, we might ask first whether the liberal concept of private property is ripe for just such a reappraisal.[15] (Emphasis in the original.)

This represents an extraordinary myopia as regards one of the most powerful means of enhancing environmental values. Nor is respect for property rights just a means for wealthy nations and individuals. One good example of how property rights have played a positive role in a developing economy comes from Niger. In contrast to many other African nations, which are experiencing high rates of deforestation, Niger has experienced reforestation, and is now greener than it was 30 years ago. The *New York Times* reported on this story in 2006. "Millions of trees are flourishing," the *Times*' Lydia Polgreen wrote; more than seven million acres of land have been reforested, "without relying on the large-scale planting of trees and other expensive methods often advocated by African politicians and aid groups for halting desertification."

What explains this turnaround? Polgreen explains:

> Another change was the way trees were regarded by law. From colonial times, all trees in Niger had been regarded as the property of the state, which gave farmers little incentive to protect them. Trees were chopped for firewood or construction without regard to the environmental costs. Government foresters were supposed to make sure the trees were properly managed, but there were not enough of them to police a country nearly twice the size of Texas.

> But over time, farmers began to regard the trees in their fields as their property, and in recent years the government has recognized the benefits of that outlook by allowing individuals to own trees. Farmers make money from the trees by selling branches, pods, fruit and bark. Because those sales are more lucrative over time than simply chopping down the tree for firewood, the farmers preserve them.[16]

There is academic literature showing that the example of Niger's forests applies generally in the developing world. Economist Seth Norton conducted a cross-national study of property rights and various measures of human well-being, and found statistical evidence that deforestation rates decline with increased property rights, while access to sanitation and clean water increases. Norton concluded: "Environmental quality and economic growth rates are greater in regimes where property rights are well defined than in regimes where property rights are poorly defined."[17]

Another example comes from the greatest global commons of all—the oceans. It is not news that oceanographers are concerned that overfishing has already caused the collapse of several regional fisheries, such as North Atlantic cod, with some specialists warning of a total global collapse as soon as the year 2048. (Remarkably, there is no systematic database of global fish biomass, and yet this seems not to deter sweeping apocalyptic predictions.) But in a stunning example of the insularity of environmental orthodoxy, *Science* magazine breathlessly reported in the fall of 2008 what market-oriented environmentalists have known and proclaimed for twenty years: that applying property rights to fisheries was an effective way of protecting and enhancing fish stocks. "Privatization Prevents Collapse of Fish Stocks, Global Analysis Shows," *Science*'s September 19, 2008, headline proclaimed. The magazine's news summary of the actual journal article reported that "scientists have . . . taken a broad look at how fisheries are managed and come up with a more hopeful view," as if the idea of applying property rights to fisheries were an intellectual and empirical breakthrough. In fact, Donald R. Leal of the Property and Environment Research Center (PERC), among others, has been writing and publishing data and case studies on this idea for years.[18]

To be sure, the actual *Science* article, "Can Catch Shares Prevent Fisheries Collapse?" is an important contribution to the literature on this subject. It offers a meta-analysis of global fish catch data going back to 1950, and it also, as a thought experiment, takes what is known about fishery conditions in the few places—chiefly Alaska, New Zealand, Iceland, and Australia—that have employed property-rights-based approaches to fisheries and extrapolates from that to generate an estimate of how all fisheries would have performed if they all had rights-based systems.[19] The result is dramatic: global adoption of rights-based fisheries could have reduced fishery collapse by nearly two-thirds, from the roughly 26 percent we have experienced to about 9 percent. The results of this thought experiment are shown in Figure 11.

The authors were careful to control for selection bias and other statistical errors, generating a cautious result that "probably underestimates ITQ benefits." The authors duly conclude that "Institutional change has the potential for greatly altering the future of global fisheries . . . as catch shares are increasingly implemented globally, fish stocks, and the profits from harvesting them, have the potential to recover substantially."

WHAT ARE THE WORLD'S MOST SERIOUS ENVIRONMENTAL PROBLEMS?

In the midst of the out-of-control *Deepwater Horizon* oil spill in the Gulf of Mexico in the spring and early summer of 2010, it became common hyperbole to describe the spill as the "worst environmental disaster in American history." While the spill was undeniably significant, environmental experts chimed in to say that there is no objective way of determining what is the "worst" environmental disaster; ranking environmental problems is a partly subjective exercise. For example, a number of experts assign high rank to the 1979 Three Mile Island nuclear accident, for opposite reasons: nuclear power opponents point to it as a prime example of the hazards of nuclear power, while supporters of nuclear power point to it as the cause of shutting down further nuclear power development, which has increased America's dependence on coal-fired electricity—a net loss for the environment. To their credit, a number of media outlets have offered useful perspective on this

Figure 11. Simulation of trends in fisheries with global ITQs

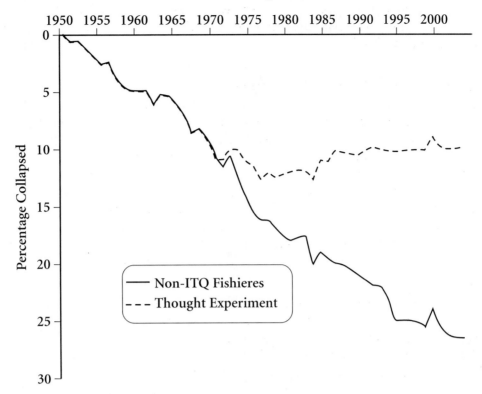

SOURCE: Costello et al., "Can Catch Shares Prevent Fisheries Collapse?"

problem, including *Newsweek, Foreign Policy*, and the *New York Times*.[20] The *Washington Post*'s Joel Achenbach captured the flavor of many of the skeptical views thus:

> Doesn't necessarily look to me as though it's in the same category as the Dust Bowl, the destruction of the Everglades, or the many and various slow-motion environmental disasters involving habitat destruction, monocultural agriculture, toxic wastes, uglification of pastoral landscapes, etc. Some of this stuff has just become the baseline, and so we don't pay much attention to it. It's our wallpaper, our soundtrack.[21]

With this caveat in mind, it is useful to highlight a 2008 report from the New York–based Blacksmith Institute and Green Cross Switzerland on The World's Worst Pollution Problems.[22] The top 10, listed alphabetically (or so the report says—doesn't "Groundwater" come before "Indoor" and "Industrial"?) rather than by a qualitative rank, are:

1. Artisanal Gold Mining
2. Contaminated Surface Water
3. Indoor Air Pollution
4. Industrial Mining Activities
5. Groundwater Contamination
6. Metals Smelting and Processing
7. Radioactive Waste and Uranium Mining
8. Untreated Sewage
9. Urban Air Quality
10. Used Lead Acid Battery Recycling

Two observations leap from this list and the text of the full report. First, greenhouse gas emissions and climate change are conspicuously missing from the list. From the sheer amount of media coverage, a casual reader would suppose that climate change is easily the most important global environmental problem. This leads to the second observation: these environmental problems are seldom seen in any significant way in the United States or any other wealthy nation; they are overwhelmingly problems of poor and developing nations, once again reinforcing the central point that economic growth and development is the essential pathway to environmental improvement.

Blacksmith and Green Cross recently updated their 2008 report with a sequel focusing on "solutions and success stories with 12 notable examples that have been effective in reducing pollution and improving health." The authors acknowledge that their selections are partly subjective. That said, the list offered is congruent with the previous list in concentrating on the problems of developing nations:

Phasing Out Leaded Gasoline—Global
Disarming and Destroying Chemical Weapons—Global
Reducing Indoor Air Pollution—Accra, Ghana
Managing Mine Tailings to Protect Scarce Water Supply—Candelaria, Chile
Mitigating Nuclear Contamination—Chernobyl Affected Zone, Eastern Europe
Improving Urban Air Quality—Delhi, India
Removing Lead Waste—Haina, Dominican Republic
Preventing Mercury Exposure—Kalimantan, Indonesia
Mitigating Lead Exposures—Rudnaya River Valley, Russia
Disposing of DDT—Old Korogwe, Tanzania
Transforming an Urban Waterway—Shanghai, China
Removing Arsenic—West Bengal, India

The Blacksmith/Green Cross report commented in a manner that reinforces the main point of this *Almanac*:

In the past 40 years in the United States, Western Europe and similarly industrialized countries, the field of environmental remediation, combined with a renewed focus on environmental health, has nearly ended many of the daily life-threatening issues that many in developing countries face. All across developing countries, environmental legislation, enforcement and even trained engineers in hazardous waste removal are just beginning to emerge.

CONCLUSION

"A global transition from poverty to affluence"

If the observations in the previous section about economic growth and property rights are combined with the notice taken here of the most serious environmental problems of poor nations, a clear conclusion emerges: the most serious environmental problem is not a particular phenomenon such as air pollution, oil spills, or even global warming, but the general lack of freedom and prosperity. It is worth noting the emphasis of UC Berkeley physicist Jack Hollander, author of the 2003 book *The Real Environmental Crisis: Why Poverty, Not Affluence, Is the Environment's Number One Enemy*. As professor Hollander explains, "*[T]he essential prerequisites for a sustainable environmental future are a global transition from poverty to affluence, coupled with a transition to freedom and democracy.*"[23] (emphasis in the original) This should be the mission statement of every 21st-century environmental organization.

The burgeoning economic literature about the EKC covers the usual controversy over econometric methodology and the robustness of the model. Most of the empirical and econometric research on the EKC examines air and water pollution, as those offer the best datasets for cross-national analysis. Critics argue that the EKC is not statistically robust, that it does not apply to the full range of environmental impacts, and that it does not

The environmental Kuznets curve

The relationship between economic growth and environmental conditions in developing nations such as China, India, Mexico, and Brazil is the focus of a controversial concept known as the "Environmental Kuznets Curve" (EKC). The EKC holds that the relationship between economic growth and environmental quality is an inverted U-shaped curve, according to which environmental conditions deteriorate during the early stages of economic growth, but begin to improve after a certain threshold of wealth is achieved. (See Figure 12.)

The original Kuznets Curve was named for Nobel laureate Simon Kuznets, who postulated in the 1950s that income inequality first increases and then declines with economic growth. In 1991, economists Gene M. Grossman and Alan B. Krueger suggested that the Kuznets Curve applied to the environment as well.[1] It was a powerful counterargument to the once-conventional view, popular during the Limits to Growth enthusiasm of the 1970s, that economic growth was the enemy of the environment. The EKC gained wide acceptance as a key development concept in the 1990s, including at the World Bank.[2]

account for displacement effects, i.e., the "race to the bottom" whereby richer nations outsource their environmentally harmful production functions to poorer nations with lower environmental controls, resulting in net increases in global pollution.[3]

Defenders of the EKC argue optimistically that the EKC is actually dropping and shifting to the left, meaning that the environmental turning point will be reached sooner in the present-day developing world than it was in today's wealthy nations. Developing nations, it is thought, will skip over some of the stages of growth and pollution by adopting cleaner technologies earlier in their development path and developing regulatory institutions to control pollution.

While further empirical research will no doubt advance our understanding of the strengths and weaknesses of the EKC, China has emerged as a real-world test case. Several EKC studies conclude that sulfur dioxide pollution begins to decline at a per capita income level in the range of $5,000 to $9,000, and particulates begin to decline at a per capita income range from $5,000 to $15,000. China is still far away from the bottom of these ranges, with a current per capita income of about $3,500. However, by some measures, China's SO_2, ozone, and particulate levels may have already peaked and begun declining, offering preliminary evidence that the EKC is dropping and shifting to the left. Another example that should be encouraging for China and India is Mexico City, whose severe air pollution has been declining for more than a decade.[4]

Figure 12. Stylized Environmental Kuznets Curve

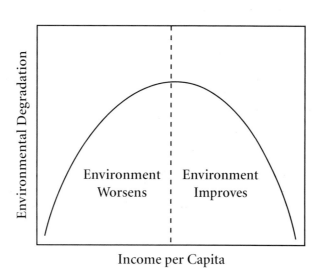

CLIMATE CHANGE RISKS AND POLICIES: AN OVERVIEW

MICHAEL TOMAN

INTRODUCTION AND SUMMARY

A great deal of controversy surrounds the issue of climate change. Some participants in the debate say that climate change is one of the greatest threats facing humankind, one that calls for immediate and strong controls on greenhouse gases, particularly carbon dioxide emissions from fossil fuel burning and releases of other gases such as methane. Others say that the risks are weakly documented scientifically, that adaptation to a changing climate will substantially reduce human vulnerability, and that consequently little action is warranted other than further study and development of future technological options. The same kinds of divides arise in discussing policy options to reduce greenhouse gas emissions, with some predicting net benefits to the economy and others fearing the loss of several percentage points of national income.

These disagreements surface in the ongoing efforts of the international community to negotiate goals and actions under the 1992 Framework Convention on Climate Change. They reflect not only different interpretations of the evidence but different interests as well. Article 2 of the Framework Convention requires signatories to take actions to "prevent dangerous anthropogenic interference with the climate system" from greenhouse gas emissions (and other actions such as deforestation). However, the term "dangerous" in Article 2 does not have an unambiguous, purely scientific definition; it is inherently a question of human values.

To help sort through the tangle, in this paper I attempt to summarize some ways to think about climate change risks and policies that can be useful for considering both international agreements and actions by the United States. The paper starts with some background on the current state of the knowledge and then presents a six-step decision framework. The steps include the following:

- Think comprehensively about risks and costs.
- Think long term.
- Address adaptation.
- Think internationally.
- Keep distributional issues in mind.
- Estimate control costs realistically.

Using this framework, I also suggest some points for enhancing the effectiveness of climate policies:

- Allow flexibility in the timing of cumulative emissions reductions to reduce overall costs.
- Incorporate economic incentives into emissions-reduction policy.
- Provide opportunities for emissions reductions wherever possible.
- Encourage development of the climate change knowledge base and improved technology for emissions reduction.
- Increase the emphasis on adaptation.

Each of these points is elaborated on in this paper. However, as an overview, the discussion necessarily is somewhat abridged. Other Issues Briefs to be produced for RFF's Climate Economics and Policy Program will explore in greater detail the issues raised here. I conclude with some brief comments on the draft protocol promulgated by the Clinton Administration in January 1997.

BACKGROUND

In its recent Second Assessment, Working Group I of the Intergovernmental Panel on Climate Change (IPCC)—a body of several hundred distinguished scientists established by the United Nations—concluded that a human cause for the climate change now observed is likely, not just possible. This is a much stronger conclusion than the one the IPCC reached in its First Assessment several years ago, although it is dogged by skepticism from some who feel that dissenting views were not adequately represented in the process. In its First Assessment, the IPCC stated that although all signs pointed to human-induced climate change, crucial evidence for cause and effect was not yet available. The evidence at the time indicated that atmospheric greenhouse gas concentrations had increased in the previous 130 years and that the global climate had warmed; however, when applied retrospectively, complex computer simulations of climate change predicted a larger warming than had actually occurred and did not adequately represent climate changes in different regions and at different altitudes.

The latest generation of models can now replicate the past with greater realism. In particular, new models include analysis of the cooling effect of aerosols—tiny particles—in the air formed during the burning of fossil fuels. By including in their analyses the cooling effects of aerosols and stratospheric ozone depletion, most of the latest studies have detected a significant climate change. The Summary for Policymakers of the Working Group I report states that "the observed warming trend is unlikely to be entirely natural in origin.... The balance of evidence suggests a discernible human influence on global climate."

While the improved capacity of climate models to track past events increases confidence in their capacity to explain observed changes, future changes in climate could depart from the models' predictions. In particular, the change may be neither gradual nor continuous, but abrupt and surprising. Despite recent improvements, however, climate models are still unable to project the details of climate change on a regional scale, complicating assessment of potential impacts and response options.

In the latest assessment, Working Group II of the IPCC addresses many potential impacts of climate change, including the effects on agriculture, forestry, terrestrial and marine ecosystems, hydrology and water resource management, human health, human infrastructure, and financial services. While the potential impacts of climate change are broad, some aspects of human society are more sensitive than others. In particular, more highly managed systems like agriculture, where skills and resources for investing in adaptation are available, may be less sensitive than less managed systems like wilderness areas. By the same token, some of the adverse effects of climate change may fall disproportionately on poorer parts of the world where adaptation capacity is more limited. Particularly if climate change were very rapid, damage could be severe and long-lived, perhaps irreversible. However, such rapid change may be unlikely and is difficult to predict.

In any event, the ability to quantify future damage and adaptation potential varies greatly across sectors. The physical consequences of a given magnitude of sea level rise, or the impacts of climate change on agricultural yields and forest conditions, can be projected with higher confidence than, say, impacts on wetlands and fisheries. Yet even when confidence is high that a certain effect will occur if climate changes, its magnitude cannot be predicted precisely. In addition, already significant damage to ecosystems and human structures arising from population growth, industrial expansion, and changes in land use may be of more immediate concern than how best to respond to climate change risk. Over the longer term, however, these forces could combine with the effects of climate change to push already stressed systems "over the edge."

In evaluating the context for climate change policies, several points need to be kept in mind.

Some degree of climate change appears inevitable. Given current emissions trends and the inertia of the climate system, even if emissions were stabilized or substantially reduced, the scientific models suggest that climatic changes and their consequences would continue. To stabilize atmospheric concentrations of greenhouse gases and thus their effects would eventually require very large cuts in emissions from current levels (let alone future levels implied by continued economic growth under a "business as usual" scenario). For example, to stabilize carbon dioxide concentrations at something over twice pre-industrial levels would require emissions ultimately to fall by over 70 percent from their *current* level.

The problem is global.   Rich and poor countries argue over how the burden of greenhouse gas emissions reductions should be allocated. However, no solution can be effective in the long term unless it ultimately leads to reductions in total *global* emissions, not just emissions in selected countries.

It is the human consequences of climate change that will animate public support for policies.   The findings of climate scientists or studies of physical impacts from climate change cannot drive policy alone. This simple but important point often seems to be overlooked in debates about "what the science says," and it leads to our next major topic—what kind of framework is useful for evaluating climate risks and policies?

DECISION FRAMEWORK

Although substantial scientific and socioeconomic uncertainties exist about the risks that climate change poses, these uncertainties do not justify taking no action. At the same time, priorities must be set in how the public's scarce resources will be used. At the broadest level, there must be some weighing and balancing of the benefits and costs of different actions in response to climate change risks. The values served by reducing the risks from climate change can only be appreciated in comparison with other values to which society devotes its scarce resources.

The need for such balancing casts doubt on the usefulness of a strict "safety first" framework that puts a high premium on any and all forms of risk reduction. We cannot devote disproportionately huge amounts of resources to reducing climate change risks while, for example, utterly ignoring health care needs. Moreover, not all the effects of climate change are likely to be equally serious, so it is not helpful simply to argue that the risks of climate change should be minimized.

Some analysts argue that we can enjoy the benefits of reduced climate change risks without significant economic costs or even with net benefits from economic and environmental improvements arising from greenhouse gas control. They suggest that pervasive but latent markets exist whose failure to operate, once fixed, will yield substantial economic and environmental benefits. Many people who have examined this argument—including participants in IPCC Working Groups II and III—seem to agree that some low-cost reductions in greenhouse gases are feasible through revitalized markets for new product development. However, for reasons discussed below, I believe that some skepticism is warranted regarding sweeping claims about the potential for low-cost emissions reductions.

If a strict "precautionary principle" of the type sketched above is of limited practical use for evaluating the risks of climate change, there are also limits to what can be gleaned from conventional benefit-cost analysis. Climate change risks and policies inherently have substantial distributional effects that may operate both within generations (who bears what share of response costs) and across generations (how much the future benefits from our actions to reduce climate change risks). In addition, uncertainty surrounding the risks and costs of climate change is especially large, and there is at least the possibility of very large-scale impacts that human responses will have a hard time mitigating. These issues are not easily handled through normal benefit-cost calculations that calculate expected net benefits over time.

While there is no easy cookbook answer to what should go into a climate change decision framework, and no approach that commands universal agreement, several elements seem useful.

Think comprehensively about risks and costs.   Given the number of risks associated with climate change, efforts to gauge the benefits of reducing them should be as broad as possible. Elements to consider include the impacts on market goods like agriculture; effects on human health; effects on nonmarket resources like wilderness areas and wetlands that provide both recreational values and ecological functions; and the ancillary benefits of greenhouse gas reduction such as improved air quality.

Given the current state of knowledge, it will be difficult to attach monetary values to many of these risk reductions. This uncertainty is likely to persist for many risk categories (especially those related to ecological impacts) even if uncertainty about the physical manifestations of climate change declines. Nevertheless, these risks are important to consider, lack of information about a risk should not be confused with that risk being negligible. Where economic assessments are problematic, information about the likelihood, potential magnitude, and timing of impacts still is useful for decisionmakers. In this connection, an assessment of climate change risks should go beyond a sequence of "best guess" estimates of atmospheric changes, biophysical impacts, and socioeconomic impacts. It is necessary to consider the variability of possible consequences as well. At the same time, the assessment should not be limited only to severe but unlikely effects in "worst case" scenarios.

Assessments of the costs of response options should similarly be broad and sensitive to uncertainties. For example, the overall economic costs of abatement policies that distort existing patterns of employment, investment, and innovation may be a multiple of direct out-of-pocket compliance costs. By the same token, technical progress over time in reducing greenhouse gases can lower abatement costs. Cost assessment should also address ancillary effects of policy responses—some positive, like reduction of conventional air pollutants with reduced energy use, and some negative, like increased indoor air pollution from tighter insulation, or increased pressures to develop hydroelectric capacity on scenic rivers. Finally, a comprehensive approach must be concerned with other greenhouse gases besides carbon dioxide (such as methane from pipeline leaks and landfills), and with changes in carbon sequestration in forests due to shifting land use patterns.

Think long term. The risks posed by climate change depend on the path of changes in the atmospheric concentration of greenhouse gases over many decades and centuries, not just on the emissions of these gases over a relatively short period of time. The long-term aspect of climate change means that we are dealing with the cumulative effect of many smaller influences on the biosphere, a process with a great deal of natural inertia. Having to deal with the distant future greatly complicates risk assessment and the development of consensus for policy actions. To be effective, at least some actions must be taken in anticipation of long-term impacts, before all of the scientific evidence is clear. Our political system arguably is less effective at responding to such issues than to a single large and immediate concern. On the other hand, the long-term nature of climate change risks means we also have time to hone our scientific understanding and policy responses over time; we need not do everything right away.

Address adaptation. In a number of areas such as agriculture, managed forestry, and human settlements, intuition and experience in other contexts suggest a medium-to-high degree of potential adaptability to natural changes, given enough lead time and investment. Adaptation possibilities include development of new plant varieties and crop patterns, changes in irrigation technology, relocation of coastal infrastructure, and expanded protection of wetlands to compensate for their potential future damage. Failure to account for adaptation as a viable response to climate change will cause climate change risks to be overstated.

Adaptation may be difficult in other cases, for example in response to potential damage to natural ecosystems whose functions are not well understood. Even where adaptation seems problematic, it should not automatically be treated as negligible. Improving the capacity to adapt where it is weak—as in many poor developing countries—may be the one of the most effective ways to respond to some climate change risks, at least until the cost of stabilizing atmospheric concentrations of greenhouse gases falls.

Think internationally. Long-term global climate change risks will not diminish to any significant degree until total *global* emissions are reduced. This will require global cooperation, not just action by today's rich countries. This point deserves to be underscored in light of the likely future decline in the share of total emissions from advanced industrial countries (currently about 50 percent) as economic growth proceeds in other areas. The efficacy of any policies the United States pursues to reduce climate change risks thus will depend on the actions taken by others.

No simple rules of thumb exist as to how the international burden of emissions control should ultimately be allocated. Developing countries note that rich countries are responsible for the vast bulk of emissions to date. They assert that allowing developed countries to maintain high emissions levels while constraining the growth of emissions in developing countries to reduce climate change risks would impose unacceptable burdens on the latter countries' economic development. Developed countries note that most emissions growth will occur in developing countries, that past economic progress has had at least some global benefits, and that simply treating all countries as having equal rights to carbon emissions (after adjusting for population differences) would impose unacceptably high control costs on developed countries. The ongoing tension over the responsibilities of different parties to the Framework Convention can only be resolved by negotiation among the parties themselves.

Keep distributional issues in mind.   Climate change risks and response capacities vary with income level. There is also a fundamental asymmetry between the timing of response costs—which will be borne to a significant extent by the current generation—and the benefits of reduced climate change—which will largely accrue to future generations. This asymmetry complicates a comparison of benefits and costs, since we cannot simply compare the costs of reducing the risk with the value of enjoying the ultimate benefits. Instead, we must assess both the costs members of the current generation would bear and the strength of our concerns for the well-being of future generations—not just our own descendants, but all those who would be vulnerable in the future. These are economically and ethically complex questions about which we know little and which require a very mature political debate.

Some analysts have argued that intergenerational equity concerns should be incorporated into climate risk assessments by applying a lower "philosophical" discount rate to the evaluation of benefits received by future generations, so as to not trivialize these benefits relative to current costs. A weakness of this approach is that it attempts to reduce a very complex ethical debate to the value of a single parameter. A more general approach is to carry out the best possible assessment of the costs to be borne in the short to medium term (taking into account various effects on productivity and economic growth as well as such benefits as reduced air pollution), combined with the best possible enumeration of the potential advantages (physical and economic) of our actions for future generations. Such an approach would give policymakers the information they need to make more explicit, well-informed judgments about the desired level of risk reduction.

Estimate control costs realistically.   As already noted, some people argue that market inefficiencies are so rife, and opportunities for innovation so plentiful, that emissions abatement is actually a low-cost proposition that might even benefit the economy. This point of view is in sharp contrast to the outputs of economic models indicating that stabilizing emissions may cost as much as several percent of a country's gross domestic product (implying that deeper cuts in emissions to reduce greenhouse gas concentrations in the atmosphere would be even more expensive). This divergence of opinion reflects in part a long-standing disagreement about the cost of improving energy efficiency. Energy analysts have argued that opportunities for large and low-cost improvements in technical efficiency have been missed because of market failures that require government action, while economists have generally assumed that most of the supposed failures to act were actually rational responses to factors such as the likelihood that a new technology was not going to perform as expected.

Most people who have looked at the debate seem to agree that some low-cost improvements in energy efficiency exist. Reducing subsidies and other distortions in energy markets that encourage excess energy use can reduce greenhouse gas emissions while improving economic and environmental well-being. However, it is open to question whether these opportunities are substantial compared to, say, the amount of abatement needed to stabilize greenhouse gas emissions. Against the backdrop of future increases in global energy demand, the cost of longer-term reductions in greenhouse gas emissions cannot help but rise unless further progress occurs in the development of nonfossil energy alternatives. In assessing medium-to-long-term costs, it is a mistake to treat technical progress as a panacea for reducing abatement costs, or to assume no technical progress.

Another argument offered in the debate over the cost of greenhouse gas emissions reductions is that our tax system is so distorted that we can use energy taxes to reduce greenhouse gas emissions and use the proceeds to lower other taxes that hamper economic growth. However, recent analysis calls into question this "double dividend. While the technical details can be complicated, the basic point is that broader-based taxes like the income tax tend to cause less overall economic distortion than narrow-based taxes like energy taxes. Adjusting other taxes might soften the economic bite of an added carbon tax, but not to negligible levels. Moreover, any tinkering with the tax system is possible only if politicians take the difficult step of imposing higher energy taxes in the first place.

Most studies of greenhouse gas abatement costs assume the application of idealized least-cost policy measures like a comprehensive "emissions trading" program or a comprehensive carbon tax. The costs of meeting any particular emissions reduction goals likely will be significantly higher if less well-designed measures are followed. The debate about which greenhouse gas reduction targets are appropriate cannot be conducted independently of discussions about what concrete measures can and should be used to actually restrict emissions.

POLICY LESSONS

In assessing climate change policies, we must consider complex "portfolios" of actions that include abating emissions, investing in technical innovations to reduce emissions sources and increase adaptation capacity, and improving risk assessment. In putting together a portfolio of policies, it is important to consider the synergies among them, such as the effects of economic incentives to reduce greenhouse gas emissions on the rate of innovation for new energy sources and other types of emissions reduction options. Because of the long-term nature of the climate change problem, the ultimate goals for responding to it also must be long-term. Such a perspective offers increased opportunities for implementing low-cost strategies to reduce emissions and promote adaptation opportunities through new investment.

Beyond these general observations, the decision framework developed above has several implications for how to formulate policy.

Allow flexibility in the timing of cumulative emissions reductions to reduce overall costs.   This approach takes into account the inertia in the economic system that makes rapid adjustments more costly; for example, it may be cheaper to replace long-lived electricity generating capacity more slowly while also achieving improved energy efficiency when the capital is replaced. It also provides increased scope over time for investments in knowledge to enhance technological change. The cost savings from intertemporal flexibility in meeting long-term emissions reductions goals depend on the assumptions made, but it appears that savings of at least 20 percent or more are possible.

Taking this approach does not mean that all or even most policy actions are deferred to the future. It simply means that the emphasis is placed on sequential decisions that add up to avoiding unacceptable damage from anthropogenic greenhouse gas emissions. Some actions will be appropriate in the short term as first steps down the policy path, or to enhance the domestic or international credibility of policy agreements. Other actions may be more useful later. Unless we start with a longer-term perspective, it is impossible to consider these tradeoffs.

Incorporate economic incentives into emissions-reduction policy.   Such incentives are crucial to both short- and long-term policy successes because they make emissions limitations less expensive. Both a large body of analysis and a small but growing body of evidence in areas other than greenhouse gas control show that incentive-based policies help bring about the lowest-cost options and stimulate innovative new methods for abatement. (Both Articles 3 and 4 of the Framework Convention support the concept of such cost-effective policies.)

The main alternatives for incentive-based policies (beyond "no regrets" actions like reductions in energy subsidies) are carbon taxes on energy sources, and various forms of "tradable permits" systems. The latter approach would effectively establish quotas on emissions but allow trade in emissions, so that sources with higher control costs could (in effect) pay emitters with lower control costs to assume more of the reduction burden. A full discussion of the pros and cons of different tax and tradable permit schemes is beyond the scope of the paper. It should be noted, however, that both types of policies have advantages, and neither should be written off. Moreover, there are many policy combinations that might be relevant in future policy debates (such as a mixture of emissions trading with command and control for different sectors) whose performance is largely unknown.

Provide opportunities for emissions reductions wherever possible. Given the international nature of the problem and the need for international action to solve it, policies should seek to provide abatement opportunities everywhere, not just in the industrialized countries that constitute the "Annex I" group under the Framework Convention—the group that already is committed to emissions reductions targets. One example of such opportunities is "joint implementation" (JI) programs, whereby emitters in, say, the United States, can satisfy any emissions reductions requirements they face through actions that reduce emissions in non-Annex I countries. The emissions reductions are achieved through the transfer of technology and investment to a host country in order to reduce emissions below some established baseline level. Formal emissions trading programs among sources in countries with quantified emissions reduction targets also are possible.

A number of analyses indicate that the cost savings from using JI and other forms of international emissions trading to meet emissions reduction goals could be very large. As with intertemporal flexibility, the savings depend on the assumptions made, but savings of 50 percent or more seem possible. At the same time, properly designed JI projects should convey considerable economic development and environmental benefits to host countries.

A number of practical problems need to be addressed in pursuing JI. There must be international agreement that such actions count toward meeting emissions reduction requirements, or else incentives to generate the reductions will remain weak. Procedures must also be established to ensure that large-scale JI trading volumes could occur without excessive red tape, while also ensuring that credible emissions reductions occur relative to some well-defined baseline. Last but not least, the credibility and appeal of JI to potential host countries in the developing world must be increased.

Encourage development of the climate change knowledge base and improved technology for emissions reduction. The flow of technology transfer and new investment occurring as a matter of course in world markets presents plenty of opportunities for greenhouse gas limitations. Particularly in a number of developing countries and economies in transition to market systems, many opportunities exist to improve energy and economic efficiency at the same time. Even where there are some costs to upgrading capital stock and improving energy efficiency, they may be more than offset by the gains from improved environmental quality. To realize these gains requires policymakers worldwide to come to grips with broader handicaps that thwart economically sound and environmentally sustainable development.

Even if we do all the best things possible to reduce emissions given the current state of knowledge, economic growth—especially in developing countries—will continue to push up greenhouse gas emissions and atmospheric concentrations. Unlike limiting pollutant gases such as sulfur dioxide, for which a variety of technical control options is available, limiting carbon dioxide emissions requires either reduced energy use (greater energy efficiency) or substitution of energy sources with lower carbon content. To avoid unacceptable climate change risks ultimately will require a fundamental change in our energy systems toward much greater reliance on other energy sources—solar, biomass, and possibly nuclear. Such a transition would be too costly now, given the current state of knowledge. To make the transition economically manageable will require continued or enhanced investments in basic and applied knowledge.

The government has an inescapable role to play, not just in creating the incentives for private parties to seek better technologies but also in funding the development of basic knowledge about technology as well as climate change impacts. At the same time, we must recognize that our understanding of what policy can actually do to induce climate-friendly innovation is weak at best. We must also recognize that diverting resources from other areas to research on low-carbon energy systems may well reduce innovation elsewhere in the economy—technical progress is not a free good.

Increase the emphasis on adaptation. Adaptation is part of an optimal response strategy in any event. Indeed, it is the means of transcending the narrow concern about our vulnerability to climate change from greenhouse gas emissions to a broader concern with global-scale changes that place stress on natural systems and pose threats to human well-being. Furthering human capacity to adapt to climate change entails investment in improved understanding of the options and their international diffusion. It also entails adjusting economic and other distortions that limit adaptation potential (such as assistance programs that subsidize coastal development or water use). In many cases, the best climate policy may have little to do with greenhouse gases or climate per se, and much more to do with developing better basic social infrastructure for natural resource conservation and use and public health protection.

CONCLUDING REMARKS: THE U.S. DRAFT PROTOCOL

The "U.S. Draft Protocol Framework" which the Clinton Administration issued on January 17, 1997 embraces a number of policy ideas that, if implemented, could significantly enhance the cost-effectiveness with which any emissions reduction targets are achieved. To comply, countries agreeing to emissions limits would be allowed to average emissions over a number of years (though a precise number is not proposed in the framework). They would be able to trade emissions internally and internationally (not just within specified groups, like European Union), and they would be able to bank emissions for future use. To smooth out the cost of emissions reductions over time, they could borrow from the future to meet current obligations. (Both unspecified limits on volumes borrowed and a significant (20 percent) "repayment premium" on borrowed emissions allowances are included to help ensure that the achievement of long-term emissions reductions goals would not be undermined. However, the use of both tools for this purpose is redundant, and the high repayment premium will cause uneconomically early emissions reductions.)

Developing countries would be encouraged to participate in several ways. Joint implementation with countries not yet accepting national emissions targets would be fully sanctioned, including fully usable and transferable credits for emissions reductions. In addition, developing countries would be required to identify and adopt "no regrets" measures for greenhouse gas reductions, and all countries would be required to "facilitate investment in climate-friendly technologies," although these important action areas are not spelled out in any detail. Emissions reporting procedures and practices also would be strengthened. Finally, while no future emissions targets for developing countries are specified, the proposal does call (in Article 16) for all countries to accept some quantified emissions limitation targets (which could be different from the targets accepted by developed countries) by a particular future date (2005 is suggested in the draft). This proposal is consistent with the idea that comprehensive participation ultimately is required for success in avoiding unacceptable impacts of climate change, though it is bound to be controversial among developing countries who do not currently have any emissions limitation targets.

In establishing international emissions targets among industrialized countries (a new "Annex A" group that includes the current Annex I countries), the U.S. proposal calls for all such countries to reduce their emissions over time by common (not yet specified) percentages of their respective baseline levels. Other countries that either have achieved substantially greater energy efficiency improvements earlier or believe that such reductions may simply be too costly in light of their fossil fuel use hotly contest this approach. It remains to be seen whether the United States can secure agreement for its approach or will be forced to modify it.

The U.S. Administration has stated that it will accept and support legally binding emissions reductions. The draft protocol does not specify any concrete emissions targets (although it does call for periodic review of whatever targets are established). The actual targets remain to be negotiated, and the proposal does not indicate what criteria should be used to determine acceptable targets from the U.S. perspective.

Last but not least, the draft protocol does little to address adaptation. This neglect reflects not a weakness in the proposal so much as a broader weakness in the Framework Convention, which has viewed adaptation as an individual country concern. Adaptation must gain greater prominence in the debate over climate policies.

The U.S. draft protocol is an important contribution to the negotiating process and to domestic debate over U.S. climate policies. However, further discussion of the issues identified above—and of the analyses the Administration and others are performing to determine what it will cost to meet different emissions reductions targets—is a prerequisite to building broader understanding of climate change risks and policies, and political support for a new climate agreement.

# # #

FURTHER READING

For a broad overview of all climate change issues, some perusal of the three volumes of the IPCC Second Assessment Report is essential. All three have the main heading "Climate Change 1995" and the following subtitles: "The Science of Climate Change" (Working Group I), "Impacts, Adaptations and Mitigation of Climate Change: Scientific-Technical Analysis" (Working Group II), and "Economic and Social Dimensions of Climate Change" (Working Group III). Each volume contains a Summary for Policymakers that is quite informative (though not a perfect guide to the contents of the volume), and the first two volumes contain Technical Summaries as well. The main body of each report contains a wealth of information and analysis, though some of it is quite technical and, in some cases, a little dated. The reports are published by Cambridge University Press (fax: 212-691-3239). Find out more about the IPCC at http://www.unep.ch/ipcc/ipcc-0.html.

High-Tech Protectionism: The Irrationality of Antidumping Laws

Claude E. Barfield

Introduction

The explosion of high-technology products onto the world market, in addition to making many aspects of our lives easier, is one of the principal engines driving economic growth.[1] In computers, pharmaceuticals, telecommunications, the Internet, and countless other areas, advances in high-technology sectors are redefining the way we live. High-technology sectors cover a range of industries, of course, but they share one defining trait—they require intensive research and development (R&D) for inputs, either directly at the final manufacturing stage or through the intermediate goods used in their production. The capital outlays, while varying by industry, are often quite large and well beyond the capacity of single individuals or firms.

In an era of globalization, it should not come as a surprise that the competitive environment is much more intense. Contrary to what some misguided politicians and antiglobal activists have argued, however, foreign competition has served both American companies and consumers, competition (both domestic and forcing most U.S. companies to become more efficient.

A prerequisite for reaping the benefits of foreign competition, of course, is an international trading system that fosters the free flow of goods, services, and investment among nations. Broadly speaking, such a system exists. From the signing of the General Agreement on Tariffs and Trade (GATT) in 1947, to the formation in 1995 of its successor, the World Trade Organization (WTO), the multilateral trading system has become increasingly open, with trade and investment barriers steadily coming down. The result is that global economic welfare has increased, and millions have been lifted out of grinding poverty.

Unfortunately, no institutional system is perfect, and the multilateral trade regime is no exception. WTO rules allow countries to arbitrarily define "unfair" trading practices of other countries and to restrict the free flow of goods by invoking trade remedy laws designed to protect domestic industries. Unable to compete effectively on their merits, companies can ask government to restrict foreign competition, rather than becoming more efficient. The weapon of choice for many of these companies is antidumping law. The law targets allegedly "unfair" trading practices of foreign competitors accused of exporting (or "dumping") products into a foreign market at prices below the cost of production, or below the prices charged in domestic or third markets (price discrimination). If a foreign competitor is found guilty of dumping, the WTO Antidumping Agreement of 1994 allows countries to impose antidumping duties on those imports (Boltuck and Litan 1991; Lindsey 1999).

Antidumping laws are fundamentally at odds with the free trade policies that have dramatically increased global economic welfare over the past half-century. They are tantamount to "WTO-legalized protectionism" and a "major loophole in the free-trade disciplines of the world trading system," in the words of Brink Lindsey of the Cato Institute (Lindsey 1999, 5). Further, the procedures by which antidumping laws are applied are arbitrary and do not properly identify allegedly "unfair" trading practices. Antidumping laws also do little to offer effective remedies for companies that claim to have been "materially injured" by "unfair" foreign competitors and their pricing practices.

Two facts about the recent history of antidumping actions should be underscored: First, there has been a great proliferation in the use of antidumping cases among WTO members (particularly by developing countries), combined with a rising number of cases targeting the United States. Second, the current Doha Round of WTO negotiations is being jeopardized by a backlash against the antidumping rules and by threats to block trade liberalization in other areas unless the antidumping rules are reformed.

Figure 1 shows the trend in new antidumping measures for both developed and developing countries from 1979 to 2002. For the past decade (1990–2002), developed country new antidumping measures have fluctuated from a low of 33 to a high of 105. But the striking change has come in the numbers for developing countries, which have risen almost steadily each year from 3 in 1990 to a high of 146 in 2002. By mid-2002, India (150 measures in place), South Africa (98), Mexico (61), and Argentina (58) were moving up the ranks to join the United States (264), the European Union (219), Canada (90), and Australia (56) as the most frequent antidumping users (WTO 2002a). Both developed and developing countries have been targeting more users. At the end of 2002, the United States led the brigade, with actions in place against 48 countries; but developing countries were also expanding their antidumping targets: between 1995 and 2002, India jumped from 7 to 39 countries; Brazil from 12 to 24; and Mexico from 13 to 17 targeted countries. The European Union maintained measures in place against 34 countries at the end of 2002 (WTO 2003a).

And finally, the United States stood third behind China and South Korea as the most popular target of antidumping investigations. From January 1995 through December 2002, the United States was the subject of 115 investigations initiated by 18 different countries. During the same time interval, 67 definitive measures were imposed against U.S. exports (WTO 2003f).

Antidumping: A threat to future WTO negotiations

Though developing countries, defensively, have become keen students of the protectionist antidumping game, they are still novices, far behind the United States and the European Union in the exploitation of antidumping actions to stifle international competition. The United States, with over 250 measures in place, and the EU, with more than 200, still far outdistanced even the most eager learners among the developing countries.

It should come as no surprise, then, that reform of the WTO antidumping rules has become a hotly debated topic in the new Doha Round of multilateral trade negotiations. Leading developing countries such as Brazil, Korea, China, Mexico, Argentina, Egypt, South Africa, and others have threatened to hold all other negotiating issues hostage to changes in this protectionist vestige from the past. Japan has also been a leading advocate of reform as a result of its long history as the chief target of antidumping actions by the United States and European countries (*International Trade Reporter* [*ITR*] November 1, 2001; May 2, 2002).

FIGURE 1. Antidumping Measures by Importing Countries: Developing vs. Developed Countries, 1979–2002

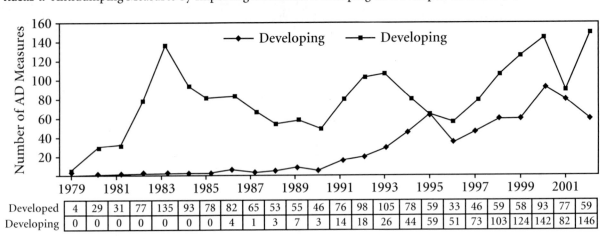

	1979		1981		1983		1985		1987		1989		1991		1993		1995		1997		1999		2001	
Developed	4	29	31	77	135	93	78	82	65	53	55	46	76	98	105	78	59	33	46	59	58	93	77	59
Developing	0	0	0	0	0	0	0	4	1	3	7	3	14	18	26	44	59	51	73	103	124	142	82	146

Source: WOT 2002a.

Note: All of the high-income OECD members (23 countries in total) are counted as "developing" countries.

Demands for fundamental changes in WTO trade remedy rules will present the Bush administration with its most difficult challenge in the Doha Round negotiations. In the run-up to the launching of the round in November 2001, while the administration beat back attempts in Congress to tie its hands completely, both houses of Congress passed strongly worded resolutions advising the president not to agree to major revisions in the current regime. the House of Representatives resolution passed 410 to 4 just one week before the Doha meeting (*ITR* November 15, 2001). Defenders of U.S. trade laws wanted the administration to veto *any* discussion of these issues in the upcoming negotiations.

In order to break a deadlock that would have prevented the launch of the new round, however, U.S. Trade Representative Robert Zoellick agreed to language that placed trade remedies laws on the table—but, at least in the American view, under tightly restricted conditions and terms. The Doha Declaration allows negotiations "aimed at clarifying and improving disciplines" under the WTO's existing antidumping and subsidies agreements, but the mandate also states that such negotiations will preserve the "basic concepts, principles and effectiveness of these Agreements, their objectives and instruments" (*ITR* November 15, 2001; February 14, 2002).

In preliminary negotiations since November 2001, proponents of major reform in the existing WTO trade remedy regimes have put forward increasingly bold proposals for technical reforms of current antidumping rules, calculations, and procedures. The United States has firmly resisted all of these proposals, arguing that they violate the Doha Declaration's mandate that negotiations preserve the "basic concepts, principles, and effectiveness" of existing antidumping national regimes (*ITR* May 2, 2002; May 9, 2002; July 7, 2002; October 17, 2002; October 24, 2002).

Clearly, the Bush administration's strategy is to wait until the very end of the Doha Round negotiations before dealing with proposed antidumping reforms. What defenders of the current system fear—and opponents hope for—is that in order to seal a "grand bargain" in the closing hours of negotiations, U.S. Trade Representative Zoellick will be forced (or will claim to be forced) to accept at least some of the major demands that have been put forward by developing countries. The problem with this approach is that developing countries thus far have been adamant in opposing any interim agreements absent movement on antidumping issues. Thus, the outcome of antidumping negotiations—and of the Doha Round itself—remains doubtful.[2]

The folly of antidumping actions in high-tech sectors

While the application of antidumping laws is problematic in any sector, it is particularly troublesome in high-technology sectors for three primary reasons. First, given the inherently dynamic nature of high-technology sectors, the specific products which have duties imposed upon them are often obsolete by the time the inevitably contentious antidumping case is resolved. The famous Moore's Law (Gordon Moore was a cofounder and later chairman of Intel) that capacity of semiconductor chips doubles every eighteen months still holds. Under such conditions, the petitioner in the domestic market rarely achieves meaningful relief. Second, identifying so-called strategic industries is usually a fool's errand; in many cases what is labeled "strategic" in one year quickly becomes merely a commodity over the next few years (for example, dynamic random access memory [DRAM] semiconductors). Third, the high degree of multisourcing from different countries in the chain of production results in situations where antidumping duties are sometimes actually imposed on domestic competitors (Hindley and Messerlin 1996).

Over the past two decades, the United States has compiled a dismal record in its attempts to use antidumping actions as an industrial policy tool to create, foster, or protect important high-tech sectors. The goal of this study is to set forth the history of these actions for policymakers and the interested public in a nontechnical manner, and to draw public policy conclusions and recommendations from this analysis. Specifically, the study will analyze how American antidumping laws have been applied in three high-technology industries: supercomputers, flat-panel displays (FPDs), and DRAM computer chips. In addition, the study will examine the U.S. steel industry. Today, steel is considered the quintessential "basic" industry, one which naturally gravitated to less developed economies that enjoy a comparative advantage from the abundance of cheap, unskilled labor and production techniques that prize brawn over brains. This study's conclusions regarding steel, however, are twofold: First, traditional industries such as steel can survive in advanced industrial economies if they become "high-tech" industries by moving rapidly up the technological ladder through the introduction of advanced industrial processes and techniques. Second, government intervention to protect increasingly obsolete domestic steel technologies, symbolized by Big Steel (the integrated U.S. steel companies), has only hindered the emergence of a truly competitive, technologically advanced steel sector, symbolized (and actualized) by the so-called minimills (which use advanced technologies to transform scrap steel into semifinished and finished products).

The most important policy conclusion of this analysis is that protectionist antidumping actions had the following general results: (1) negative consequences for other industries U.S. consumers, and workers that far outweighed the purported protectionist benefits (DRAMs, FPDs, and steel); (2)political interventions that traduced the integrity of administrative and legal processes (supercomputers and FPDs); (3) dumping actions that were based upon the historically erroneous prediction that U.S. competitiveness was inextricably wrapped up in the protection of a particular "strategic" industry (DRAMs, supercomputers, FPDs, and steel); and (4) the serendipitous appearance of new technologies that rendered irrelevant the original antidumping actions (DRAMs and supercomputers).

Regarding individual industries, antidumping actions had the following results: Antidumping actions in DRAMs transferred at least $4–5 billion dollars from U.S. computer manufacturers and consumers to Japanese semiconductor companies. Antidumping actions on flat-panel displays ultimately drove U.S. and foreign computer manufacturers offshore, displacing thousands of American workers. Despite the predictions of hand-wringing industrial policy advocates, the U.S. economy has not only survived but thrived without an FPD industry. The naked political intervention of the Commerce Department in the supercomputer case resembled the actions of a third world government. Finally, in the case of the longest and most costly government intervention—steel—the cost to American taxpayers has been estimated at between $46 billion and $74 billion.

RECOMMENDATIONS

Through case studies of the semiconductor, supercomputer, flat-panel-display, and steel industries, this study has attempted to demonstrate both the damage antidumping actions do to market competition and their futility as weapons to save uncompetitive companies and sectors. This is especially the case in high-technology sectors where short product cycles, global strategies and pricing, multiple sourcing of parts, and multinational production facilities render impossible precise targeting of allegedly unfair trade practices. As former Deputy Secretary of the Treasury Ken Dam has warned:

> Potentially even more serious is the impact of antidumping proceedings on the industry structure in many high-tech industries. Modern manufacturing involves use of components. Hence administrative protection through antidumping cases threatens final product manufacturing in the United States (say, in computers as opposed to memory chips). Yet under the applicable law, one cannot take into account the impact on U.S. industries other than the component-making industry. (Dam 2001, 160)

Antidumping actions were problematic in the old economy; they are ludicrous in the new economy.

Further, as some of the most successful U.S. global companies such as IBM, General Motors, and Caterpillar have begun to point out, antidumping actions are two-edged swords that can be wielded against U.S. exporters. Until recently, the United States and the European Union were the leading practitioners of this form of protection. During the 1990s, however, developing countries showed a remarkable learning ability: in 1990, the United States had 193 antidumping orders in place, the EU had 95, and all other countries had 118. By mid-2002, the United States had 264, the EU had 219; and all other countries had 706 (WTO 2002a). In particular, India, South Africa, Mexico, Brazil, and Argentina had become star pupils. As of 2000, more than seventy nations had antidumping laws on their statute books, and each year the number grows (Barfield 1999; Miranda, Torres, and Ruiz 1998; WTO 2002a).

What follows is a series of recommendations for changes in the U.S. antidumping regime and subsequently in WTO trade remedy rules. In recent years, governments, public and private interest groups, and academics have advanced a plethora of reform proposals. Also, as described above, the issue of antidumping reform has emerged as a major point of conflict in the current WTO Doha Round of trade negotiations.

A word about the priorities given to the recommendations: Clearly, the more sweeping the proposed reform, the more difficult it will be to accomplish. Given the overwhelming political power domestic producers have demonstrated over the years, a number of policymakers and policy analysts have drawn back and concentrated on highly technical changes to redress the bias against importers in the extraordinarily complex national and WTO antidumping regimes. This study endorses a number of these proposals, but there are two reasons priority must first be assigned to pressing for more fundamental changes: one, it is important to iterate and reiterate for politicians and the voting public the basic truth that current antidumping regimes are intellectually without foundation and that *even on their own terms* they cannot accomplish intended goals; and two, while many of the technical proposals have real merit, the history of antidumping rules since 1945 demonstrates the ability of domestic producers and their legislative allies quickly to revise and twist proposed technical legislative changes back in a protectionist direction (Finger 1993). Proponents of reform are thus likely to be playing "catch-up" continually.

Repeal antidumping laws and substitute antitrust actions

Clearly, if political considerations were not present, the most economically sensible (and equitable) course would be to treat allegations of price discrimination and below-cost pricing as potential infractions against a country's competition policy regime. Under this scenario, domestic antidumping laws would be repealed, and countries would substitute actions against alleged abuses of competition policy or law. Such a course would entail smashing through the rhetorical interpretations of certain historical developments and focusing relentlessly on the underlying economic fundamentals. It would directly challenge arguments made in recent years by both the Clinton and the Bush administrations, which aligned themselves with the flawed and deceptive arguments of academic and legal defenders of antidumping actions.

A prime argument advanced by both the Clinton and Bush administrations is historically accurate but masks an underlying economic falsity: antidumping laws cannot be judged by the same standards as competition policy laws and regulations because they have evolved with different goals in mind and serve different constituencies. As a statement of historical fact, this political divergence is accurate. Taking note of the original common antimonopoly rhetoric of both antitrust and antidumping adherents, Alan Sykes of the University of Chicago has described the evolved and different attributes of the two systems, as follows:

> Antitrust and antidumping law come from the same family tree, but the two branches have diverged widely.... [I]n the modern era, antitrust concentrated on the pursuit of economic efficiency... address[ing] problems associated with concentrated economic power, primarily through a common law process that left to the courts much of the task of delineating the practices that violate antitrust law. . . . By contrast, antidumping law was intended to create a politically popular form of contingent protection that bears little, if any connection to the prevention of monopoly.... Likewise, the political constituency for antidumping law is not an antimonopoly constituency, but one for the protection of industries facing weak markets or long-term decline. (Sykes 1998, 1–2)

Seizing upon this historical divergence, both the Clinton and the Bush administrations have argued that competition policy laws cannot substitute for antidumping laws. As the Clinton administration stated in a brief to a WTO trade and competition policy working group, "If the antidumping laws were eliminated in favor of competition laws or modified to be consistent with competition policy principles, the problems which the antidumping rules seek to remedy would go unaddressed" (WTO 1998, 1).

The fallacy behind this assertion is that all of the antidumping "problems" identified as distinct from competition policy concerns are based upon rationales that cannot stand scrutiny on grounds of either efficiency or equity. Regarding efficiency, Sykes has accurately stated, "Although economic theory identifies a few plausible scenarios in which antidumping measures might enhance economic efficiency, the law remains altogether untailored to identifying them or limiting the use of antidumping measures to plausible cases of efficiency gain" (Sykes 1998, 2). On equity grounds, antidumping actions repeatedly flout a fundamental principle of "fairness" in the multilateral trading system—that is, the principle of national treatment, or that corporations and citizens of foreign countries will receive the same treatment under law that is accorded domestic citizens and corporations. Under antidumping rules, many actions that are clearly legal under U.S. domestic law are deemed "unfair" competition when taken by foreign corporations.

The underlying efficiency principles

As described at the outset of the study, economists have identified a number of circumstances in which dumping, as defined by U.S. and WTO rules (sales below the fully allocated cost of production or international price discrimination) is likely to have no adverse economic consequences. These include "market expansion" dumping, in which a company exports goods at a lower price than it charges in the home market in order to increase worldwide market share; "cyclical dumping," or exporting during periods of low demand and excess production capacity in the home market; "state-trading dumping," in which state-owned entities export at low prices, usually in order to gain hard currency; and "life cycle pricing" in high-tech industries, in which prices are initially set below fully allocated costs in order to generate sales, and over the short life-cycle of the product, "learning by doing" will drastically reduce production costs. As economist Robert Willig has argued, all of these forms of "nonmonopolizing dumping" are "entirely consistent with robustly competitive conditions in the importing nation's market" (Willig 1998, 66).

Predatory ("monopolizing") dumping, however, could very well hurt consumers and producers of the importing nation. Predatory dumping occurs when an exporter has the ability to lower prices for an extended period of time in order to drive companies in the importing country out of business and achieve a monopoly. As we have noted earlier, for predation to be successful, certain market characteristics must apply: a large home market for the exporter; substantial entry and reentry barriers in the exporter's home market and market of the importing nation; relative concentration in the importing market so that monopoly power is readily achieved when a few companies leave the industry; and, if there are several predators, the ability to collude in keeping prices excessively low.

Antitrust authorities, in evaluating anticompetitive effects from alleged predation, could readily contrive a series of rather straightforward questions, such as:

- Is the alleged dumping likely to reduce the number of rivals (both domestic and foreign) in the importing country's market?
- What share of the market would the dumpers have if the complainants left the market?
- Is the market share of the dumpers growing rapidly?
- If there are two or more alleged dumpers, could they plausibly be colluding?
- Are there significant entry and reentry barriers, and concomitantly, does entry require significant capital requirements and sunk costs? (Shin 1998; Willig 1998)

Antitrust authorities in many countries have substantial experience in dealing with just these questions, and there is no reason that such analysis could not be applied in cases of alleged dumping.

Response to "sanctuary market" and "strategic dumping" allegations: Target offending policies directly, after proving that they exist

If for political reasons, it proves impossible to do away with national antidumping laws entirely, fundamental reforms should be introduced into national antidumping regimes, the aim of which would be to force those systems to address directly and systematically allegations that government policies or market characteristics of the exporting country result in "injurious" dumping into the importing country. (For an analysis with conclusions similar to those set forth here, see Finger and Zlate 2003.)

In recent years, proponents of antidumping actions have advanced a much more sweeping rationale based upon the supposed advantages of firms exporting from so-called "sanctuary markets," or markets that as a result of government policies or private sector practice are closed to outside competitors. This situation need not involve a goal of predation, but it theoretically allows exporters to earn high profits at home and sell abroad at "artificially" low prices. In October 2002, the Bush administration, in a document submitted to the WTO defending current antidumping rules, framed the potential danger this way:

> A government's industrial policies or key aspects of the economic system supported by government inaction can enable injurious dumping to take place. . . . For instance, these policies may allow producers to earn high profits in a home "sanctuary market," which may in turn allow them to sell abroad at an artificially low price. Such practices can result in injury in the importing country since domestic firms may not be able to match the artificially low prices from producers in the sanctuary market. (WTO 2002b, 4)

The Bush administration's submission is quite brief and a bit sheepish ("antidumping measures should be seen not as an ultimate solution to trade-distorting practices abroad. . ."). In 1998, however, the Clinton administration had presented a much longer, unabashed defense of the system and a comprehensive review of domestic policies and practices that might trigger antidumping actions. For its candor, *chutzpah*, and the sweeping expansion of the sources of "injurious" dumping, the document deserves careful scrutiny—and rebuttal.

The Clinton administration began by describing a pristine world of "fair" competition based upon "natural" comparative advantage: "In other words, 'fair' trade envisions that producers will use only natural comparative advantages, such as natural resources, a favorable climate, advanced technology, skilled workers, greater efficiency or lower labor costs, and not any artificial advantage." "Injurious" dumping, according to the Clinton submission, results from artificial advantages stemming from two situations: "market-distorting industrial policies and/or differences in national economic systems" (WTO 1998, 7). Antidumping policies, then, constitute a means of achieving a "level playing field."

For the balance of the document, the Clinton administration assembled a veritable farrago of government policies and "differences in national economic systems" that, in its view, lead to injurious dumping. Included in this list is an extraordinarily diverse set of examples, including: high tariffs; government subsidies; price controls; government limitations on investment; limitations on the number of producers in a particular sector; anticompetitive sanitary and phytosanitary standards; a range of services barriers, including restrictions of provision of financial services, regulation of international data flows and data processing; misuse of standards, testing and certification procedures; permissive policies toward vertical and horizontal restraints of competition; cross-subsidization in multiproduct firms; employment and social policies that result in "artificial" advantages for domestic firms; and contrasting business practices that give rise to differing debt/equity structures between domestic and foreign firms.

The above list is not complete, but the inescapable conclusion is that virtually every area of domestic public policy can be a cause of antidumping action under this expansive interpretation of artificial advantages. This study will comment on only a selected few of the examples advanced in the submission.

Market-Distorting Industrial Policies. It should be noted that the line between public policies and differences in economic systems is blurred, and so the following designations are somewhat arbitrary. High tariffs and subsidies are two of the simplest government (industrial) policies to describe and rebut as necessitating the use of antidumping actions. The tariff rates have been set as a result of negotiations by individual nations in the Uruguay Trade Round. If a nation has negotiated high tariffs, so be it; if it breaks the agreement and raises its rates, it must renegotiate rates with all other members of the WTO or face retaliation. Industrial subsidies lead to a similar situation: the WTO has set rules for illegal and legal subsidies, and if a nation believes these rules have been violated, it will bring a case to the WTO—thus obviating (indeed precluding) the use of national trade remedy systems.

The submission also mentions government policies to limit the number of producers in a sector or limitations on foreign equity participation or ownership in a sector. Two points are relevant in this case: First, like other nations, the United States has long limited investment in certain quite important sectors, such as airlines and telecommunications. It thus comes with ill grace for the U.S. government to take unilateral action against other governments for the same practice. Second, GATT and WTO rules, except in unusual circumstances generally in the services area, do not cover investment issues; thus, there are no legal impediments to governments' applying certain restrictions (as the United States has done).

The examples cited relating to rules for competition are also of questionable validity, particularly with regard to cross-subsidization and relaxed limitations on vertical restraints.

In the United States and numerous other countries, many firms have multiple product lines, and there is no restriction on cross-subsidization *per se*, absent some other anticompetitive practice by the firms. Thus, companies such as IBM and Texas Instruments for many years produced computers and computer components such as chips, with chips being priced to increase the competitiveness of the final product. In no case did the U.S. government object—nor should it have. Similarly, while U.S. competition policy has changed greatly over the past half-century, current thinking holds that under most conditions vertical restraints of trade are not anticompetitive. To lump these industry practices as evidence of an "artificial" advantage is hypocritical and deceptive.

Differences in National Economics. Several of the above citations could also be counted as the result of "differences in national economies." But the most significant example given by the Clinton administration is the potential for "injurious dumping . . . when social and legal arrangements for employment and under-employment differ between countries. . . ." The Clinton submission (odd for an administration with at least vaguely social democratic aspirations) in effect charges that industries in nations with greater protection of labor and employment will unfairly reduce prices while forced to hold onto existing employees during economic downturns. Under this proposed reading of antidumping laws, most nations of the European Union, whose domestic laws contain many such protections for labor organizations and employment, would seem to face the prospect of endless antidumping actions.

With the introduction of potential injurious dumping from national labor practices or social welfare systems, the questions raised by the current rationale for dumping actions have moved far from border prices and deep into the social and economic fabric of individual nations. Under current antidumping regimes in any country, judgments cannot be established about whether a nation's labor practices, allegedly lax rules on vertical integration, subsidies to key industries, or health and safety regulations create artificial advantages or are merely evidence of "robustly competitive" conditions in importing markets.

Reform of U.S. (and WTO) antidumping rules

By broadening the alleged goals of antidumping laws to include a defense against all "artificial" or "unnatural" advantages, defenders of the current system have opened a Pandora's box for themselves. Even the most ardent proponents admit that the mere existence of price discrimination or below-cost sales does not "prove" market distortions in the exporting economy are the causal factor. Many perfectly natural competitive conditions can cause variations in price. To be credible and fair, therefore, U.S. rules and the WTO Antidumping Agreement should mandate that the petitioning industry and the domestic antidumping authority identify the purported market distortion and establish a causal connection between this alleged distortion and injurious dumping, as evidence by either below-cost sales or price discrimination. If, for instance, government limitation on the number of producers in a sector results in a closed sanctuary market that allows below-cost pricing in foreign markets, that competitive impediment should be identified and the injurious connection established. Similarly, if cross-subsidization in multiproduct companies results in component prices that have no relation to costs of production, this subsidization should be pointed out and made part of any antidumping allegation. The respondents should be given the opportunity to rebut, with evidence to the contrary, all allegations regarding market-distorting government policies or "differences in economic systems" that result in "unnatural" advantages.

As envisioned here, the presentations of the petitioner and the respondent would largely establish the facts and economic evidence in a case, though the government agency should be allowed limited investigatory power to clear up conflicting claims by the two private parties. This compromise—regarding the roles of the private parties and the government agency in the importing country—attempts to balance a concern that national antidumping authorities will create huge new factual burdens on the foreign respondents against the reality that, given the expanded causal connections that must be established, these antidumping authorities may need some independent analysis and counsel.

Competition Policy Analysis. In addition, certain elements of the antitrust economic analysis should be introduced into antidumping proceedings. First, a clear distinction should be drawn between industries with a large number of producers worldwide and those with relatively few producers. By and large, the presumption would be that dumping cannot occur when many firms are competing against one another in numerous markets. (An exception would be if the importing country could demonstrate the existence of a cartel fixing domestic prices in the exporting country, or the existence of an international cartel.) Under this scenario, a high legal threshold would exist for proof of dumping in the steel industry as it has evolved worldwide.

In industries where there are only a few producers and the possibility of sanctuary markets exists, the priority of the WTO should be opening the sanctuary market of the exporting country, not creating another sanctuary market in the importing country. Antidumping authorities that claim sustained differential-price dumping should be required to produce an explanation of how a higher price is maintained in the home market, either through private action or with some government support. Once they satisfactorily provide this explanation, negotiations would first be conducted between the exporting-country and importing-country governments, aimed at dismantling the barriers to entry into the sanctuary market. Should these fail, antidumping penalties could be imposed immediately. Evidence from these negotiations could also be grounds for antidumping actions by other WTO members (Hindley and Messerlin 1996).

The National Interest. A third reform is the expansion of antidumping economic analysis to include an assessment of the costs and benefits of individual actions across the entire economy. Presently, only the costs to the petitioning industry are examined by the USITC. A broader analysis, as suggested here, would include the costs and benefits to corporate users of the dumped products, as well as the overall costs to final consumers of the product. As noted above, consumer groups and downstream corporate industries should have standing to appear before antidumping authorities to present evidence and their viewpoints into the proceedings. In the current Doha Round, the European Union, as well as a group of nations pushing for substantial reforms in the WTO antidumping regime, have endorsed the idea of a "public interest test" to measure the effects of antidumping orders on the whole national economy, not just on the fortunes of the petitioning industry (*ITR* May 2, 2002; July 11, 2002).

In the longer term, policymakers should give serious consideration to a more fundamental structural change in the U.S. antidumping regime: providing that in certain circumstances, the president can intervene at the end of the process, invoke a national interest clause, and craft a solution that is based upon economic considerations in combination with other U.S. national political goals and imperatives. The original reason behind granting authority to an independent commission (USITC) on antidumping cases was to ensure a nonpolitical, "scientific" decision. However, the history of the current process for deciding antidumping cases renders laughable the idea that science or fundamental economic theory plays any significant part in the final antidumping determinations. There are two reasons for this: one, over the past four decades. Congress has continuously legislated rules and instructions to the USITC which overwhelmingly tilt the criteria for "injurious" dumping in favor of the domestic petitioners; two, with some outstanding exceptions, members of the commission have been political hacks, with neither interest in nor competence for economic analysis. More often than not, they are congressional staffers who use the position as a stepping stone to lucrative private sector jobs or more prestigious executive branch appointments.

More broadly, a body of literature and analysis now exists that questions independent commissions in general (see Wallison 2003). Those who argue against allowing the president or his direct appointees to have a say in the final determination claim the process would be subject to great political influence and lobbying. The argument on the other side—particularly given the evolution of the antidumping regime—is that capture of an independent commission by the regulated industry, either through legislative fiat or control of appointments, means that the public interest has already been subverted, and in this circumstance would be better served by a direct and transparent judgment by a political officer. Also, in the trade remedy area, safeguard actions end with a final political decision by the president, as discussed below. With all the political pressures that have come to bear on this process over the years, the outcomes on safeguards dictated by the White House have generally served the national interest well.

Substitute safeguard actions for antidumping

The final broad, longer-range recommendation is to shift national trade remedy actions away from antidumping toward the greater use of safeguard actions. Under U.S. law (Section 201 of the basic trade law), as sanctioned by WTO rules, the government may intervene to ameliorate the negative effect of import surges on industries and workers. As Section 201 operates—upon petition by an industry or union, the House and Senate trade committees, or the president—the USITC may determine an industry is threatened by "serious" injury caused by a sudden increase in imports and recommend remedies to the president, who then makes the final decision. Under current WTO rules, the relief can be granted for up to four years, with the possibility of an extension for another four years. (If the relief is granted for less than three years, other countries cannot demand compensation for tariff increases or quantitative restrictions that are part of the remedy.)

There are four strong advantages for substituting safeguard actions for antidumping actions (Barfield 1999). First, safeguard actions are much more flexible in both substance and duration; the president, who has final authority to put the trade remedy package together, can tailor such a package to match individual situations. As we have seen, antidumping duties, once levied, remain in place for at least five years—and thus can continue long after the alleged dumping has ended.

Second, in determining a safeguard action, the president can take into account the overall national welfare (including consumer and corporate user's interests) and other political and diplomatic factors—which cannot be done with antidumping. For example, in the semiconductor and flat-panel displays situations of the late 1980s, use of safeguards would have allowed the Reagan and Bush administrations to assess the overall impact of trade actions on the U.S. computer industry.

Third, safeguard actions require that the petitioning industry, as a condition of receiving temporary protection, put together a plan to increase its competitiveness. Thus, unlike antidumping actions, safeguards introduce pressure for action-forcing results and do not allow industries to drift supinely for years under the cover of government protection (though in many cases a successful recovery strategy may not be possible).

Finally, increased use of safeguard actions would reduce the inflammatory and often-spurious comparisons made between "fair" and "unfair" trade practices. With more naked honesty, the government would temporarily decrease imports in order to allow a U.S. industry to put together and execute a plan for recovery. Certainly there would be pressure to extend these bailouts to the fullest allowable time, but at least consumers and U.S. industries whose interests would be damaged by the protective package could have their voices heard in opposition up front and on a continuing basis.[5]

Important technical changes to antidumping rules

During 2002, a group of WTO members opposed to current WTO rules governing antidumping actions put forward several sets of proposals for major technical changes relating to procedures, methods of calculation for antidumping duties, and the means of determining injury to a domestic industry. Among the nations who have signed on to these proposals (the group is loosely called the "Friends of Antidumping") are: Brazil, Chile, Colombia, Costa Rica, Hong Kong, Israel, Japan, Mexico, Norway, Singapore, South Korea, Switzerland, Thailand, and Turkey (*ITR* May 2, 2002; July 11, 2002; November 28, 2002). Scholars at the Cato Institute have published several excellent studies detailing the flaws in the current rules and offering analytically strong analysis and twenty-one recommendations for reform (Lindsey and lkenson 2002a, 2002b). In December 2002, the United States signaled its strong opposition to many of the proposals of the "Friends of Antidumping." The EU, in typical fashion, is trying to have it both ways—on the one hand courting proponents of reform by backing a few of their recommendations, while on the other hand opposing key elements of the reform package, which would force substantial changes in the current EU antidumping regime.

Full details of all the proposed technical reforms are available in the Lindsey and lkenson trade policy papers and on the WTO website. For this study, only the most important recommendations will be described and endorsed.

Revise Existing Rules for Cost Comparisons Between Home and Foreign Market Sales. Under current WTO rules (Article 2.2.1 of the Antidumping Agreement), dumping margins are determined by a comparison of export prices to "normal" prices in the exporter's home market. The problem lies in the determination of which prices are "normal" and stem from the "ordinary course of trade." Under the cost test now allowed, antidumping authorities may exclude home market prices that are found to be below the cost of production. This produces comparisons of all export prices with prices in the home market that are above the cost of production (that is, with the highest prices). Such an asymmetric method of calculation and comparison inevitably skews the result toward a finding of dumping, and Lindsey and Ikenson call it the "most egregious methodological distortion in contemporary antidumping practice." They go on to point out, "The existence of below-cost sales in the home market is actually affirmative evidence of the *absence* of a sanctuary market. A sanctuary market, after all, is supposed to be an island of artificially high prices and profits. If home-market sales at a loss are found in significant quantities, isn't that a fairly compelling indication that there is no sanctuary market?" (Lindsey and Ikenson 2002b, 15).

Reformers call for Article 2.2.1 to be rewritten to clarify that under most circumstances, sales below the cost of production should not be excluded automatically. Only under specific circumstances—for example, sales of damaged goods—should these exclusions be allowed.

Zeroing. Under this practice, in determining dumping margins, national authorities use different methodologies to compare export producer prices with the "normal value" of prices in the importing country (usually determined by the average price of like products in the home market). When the export price is lower than the normal value in the importing market, the difference becomes the basis for the amount of dumping for that sale. However, when the export price is higher than the normal value in the importing market, the dumping amount is calculated as zero. The results are then averaged to arrive at a dumping margin, which is then assessed as the final dumping duty. Obviously, zeroing out lower-than-average prices for exporters skews the result toward a conclusion that dumping has occurred, even when it clearly has not.

In March 2001, the WTO's Appellate Body ruled that the EU's application of "zeroing" violated WTO rules, concluding that it did not meet the standards of articles 2.4 and 2.4.2 of the Antidumping Agreement, which required a "fair comparison" between export price and normal values. Without taking into account the prices of *all* comparable export transactions, the EU's application could not provide a "fair comparison" (WTO 2001a). However, the extent to which this ruling will force widespread changes in price comparisons remains uncertain. On technical grounds not dealt with here, the EU has only partially complied, and the U.S. Department of Commerce has not changed its zeroing practices, even though they would seem clearly to go against the Appellate Body's decision.

In order to give full force to the sensible and equitable conclusion of the Appellate Body, current Doha Round antidumping negotiations should amend Article 2 of the WTO Antidumping Agreement to prohibit zeroing at any point in antidumping proceedings. Thus, in the determination of antidumping margins, when export prices are higher than normal value they should be given their exact value when averaged in with other export prices.

"Lesser Duty" Application. Article 9.1 of the Antidumping Agreement encourages WTO members to establish dumping duties only to the level that will remove the injury to the domestic industry: specifically, it states it is "desirable" that antidumping duties "be less than the [dumping] margin if such lesser duty would be adequate to remove the injury to the domestic industry." The EU and some other WTO members follow this practice and apply a "lesser duty rule" when determining dumping duties. Research has shown a substantial difference in some cases between the final dumping margins and the actual rate that would be noninjurious. Since the avowed aim of the antidumping action is to remove injury, the Article 9.1 provision should be amended to require that antidumping duties be less than the dumping margin, if the lesser duty is sufficient to remove the injury.

Causation of Injury. The current system of rules for determining whether foreign dumping has injured a domestic industry is flawed and unworkable. In addition to establishing that dumping has occurred, the WTO

Antidumping Agreement requires a finding that dumped imports are causing or threatening to cause "material injury" to the affected industry, before dumping remedies can be applied. Unfortunately, the agreement does not provide standards or a methodology for determining a casual connection between dumping and material injury of the domestic industry.

In the United States and a number of other WTO member countries, the standard used by the antidumping authorities merely seeks to establish dumping as "a cause" of the injury. This allows the U.S. Department of Commerce to ignore the impact of overall economic conditions, the competitive condition of the industry, and a host of other factors that could be the real cause of lower export prices and increased imports.

The Uruguay Round made an attempt to tighten up the criteria for finding "material injury" as a result of dumping. Specifically, Article 3.5 of the Antidumping Agreement provides that dumping authorities are required "to examine any known factors other than dumped imports which at the same time are injuring the domestic industry, and the injuries caused by these other factors must not be attributed to the dumped imports" (WTO 1995). In a 2001 case, the Appellate Body of the WTO, in interpreting the new mandate, muddied the water by introducing what even opponents of antidumping regimes admit is probably an impossible standard for determining injury. The Appellate Body ruled that antidumping authorities identify all the factors that could be causing injury, disentangle them from the effects of alleged dumping, and calculate the injurious impacts separately, though it admitted that, as a practical matter, it might not be easy to distinguish the specific effects of different causal factors (WTO 2001b). Defenders of antidumping regimes argue that if this ruling becomes the new standard, demonstrating injury will be virtually impossible. Even opponents of most antidumping practices and rules fear a backlash that could result in much laxer injury standards.

In order to avoid this result, the Doha Round antidumping negotiations should take up the issue and reach agreement on a new standard. The focus should be to isolate the effects of alleged dumping and draw back from the enormously complicated and analytically difficult goal of evaluating and putting a number on all possible causes of injury to the domestic industry. If dumping alone is found to be a substantial cause, or even a threat, of material injury, then injury is established and duties can be levied.